# Communication and Lonergan: Common Ground for Forging the New Age

*Bernard Lonergan, SJ*

# Communication and Lonergan: Common Ground for Forging the New Age

*Edited by*

*Thomas J. Farrell*
*and*
*Paul A. Soukup*

**Sheed & Ward**

Sheed & Ward™ is a service of The National Catholic Reporter Publishing Company.

**Library of Congress Cataloguing-in-Publication Data**

Communication and Lonergan : common ground for forging the New Age /
    edited by Thomas J. Farrell, Paul A. Soukup ; with a foreword by
    Robert M. Doran
        p.    cm. -- (Communication, culture & theology)
    Includes bibliographical references and index.
    ISBN 1-55612-623-9  (alk. paper)
    1. Communication--Religious aspects--Christianity.  2. Lonergan,
Bernard J. F.--Contributions in Christian aspects of communication.
I. Farrell, Thomas J.  II. Soukup, Paul A.  III. Series.
BV4319.M538   1993
254'.3--dc20                                 93-37360
                                                      CIP

Published by:    Sheed & Ward
                    115 E. Armour Blvd.
                    P.O. Box 419492
                    Kansas City, MO 64141

To order, call: (800) 333-7373

*To*

*Walter J. Ong, SJ*

*a pioneer of communication studies*

# Table of Contents

# Foreword: Common Ground

I am honored to have been asked to write the foreword to this important volume. It is my belief that the essays presented here not only signal what are emerging as the central themes in a new period of Lonergan studies—community, dialogue, otherness, mediation, plurality—but also will significantly advance the discussion of these issues.

I have been asked by the editors to limit my comments to the question, How does Bernard Lonergan's work provide a common ground? With my first complete reading in 1967 of Lonergan's *Insight* (1957/1992), I was convinced that he had gone a long way toward meeting one of the aims he expressed in the preface to that book, namely, to seek a common ground on which people "of intelligence" might meet. What I did not know then, of course, was how much more desperate the exigence for such an open space for dialogue would become in the latter third of the 20th century. The fragmentation of knowledge that Lonergan describes so eloquently at the end of chapter 16 of *Insight* has, it would seem, grown only more acute, and with it the potential for ideological stalemates, mutual recriminations of all sorts, and the denial through silence of the very existence of those with views other than our own. Nor are such crises limited to the rarefied atmosphere of the academy. As Lonergan argues persuasively in chapter 7 of *Insight*, wherever the possibility of independent inquiry and open communication has been stifled, the seeds of totalitarianism have already been sown.

It may be, though, as some of Lonergan's musings on our age encourage us to hope, that the intensity of the crisis of meaning that affects us is also in part a function of the fact that something very new, something with enormous positive potential, is occurring in history. I regard the essay "Natural Right and Historical Mindedness" (1985, pp. 169-183) as presenting Lonergan's most developed presentation of the issue of the dialectic of history, a topic that he kept coming back to for over 40 years preceding this late statement of its contours. In this essay historical process is understood radically in terms of the advance and dissemination of meaning; and we stand at the very beginning of a new stage or plateau in that process. Earlier plateaus involved, first, the development of practical intelligence and ideas, and second, the differentiation of consciousness that occurs when people acquire habits of mathematics, science, and philosophy. But today concern has shifted from meanings to acts of meaning, from products to source. And the Babel of our day may be a function of more or less complete success in moving onto this new plateau—and of course of the strident survival in our midst of minds and hearts that will not make this move at all. From this perspective, Lonergan's search for a common ground can be clarified as a progressive and cumulative effort to articulate a normative source of meaning, and so to express the horizon that those who have entered onto the new plateau might share if that horizon could be adequately thematized. From this perspective, too, the major moments in the development of Lonergan's own thinking can be viewed as successive increments in the clearing of the common ground. For, it turns out, the book that I first read in 1967 was only the beginning of Lonergan's articulation of the new plateau's horizon.

What I propose to do, ever so briefly, in this foreword, then, is to highlight these major moments, in the hope that this developmental overview might provide some context, immanent to Lonergan's own writings, for the encounters in the space Lonergan has cleared that are the topic or at least the objective of most of the essays assembled in this volume.

*Insight* is, of course, the basic breakthrough, for it is there that the common ground emerges, not as a set of contents of cognitive acts, but as a basic group of operations that constitute all human beings as knowers. The central operation emphasized is insight itself, the act of understanding. Its structure, Lonergan tells us, is always and everywhere the same. He is convinced (and elsewhere argues persuasively) that Aristotle and Aquinas grasped basic features of insight that their late medieval and modern interpreters overlooked. But even if these interpreters had not neglected insight, their articulation, like Aquinas's, would have been for the most part metaphysical, not psychological, and that is not the kind of radical recovery of insight that Lonergan advances in this book.

Rather, he begins by appropriating the modes of modern scientific understanding and by offering a generalized heuristic discussion of what is common to the myriad instances of common sense and common nonsense. From these he moves us step by step closer to his goal of a common ground. In the course of the book, we are presented with and asked to appropriate at least the following kinds of insight:

- the direct insight that grasps intelligibility in the presentations of sense and imagination, whether in science or in common sense;
- the inverse insight that grasps that, in a sense, there is no intelligibility to be grasped;
- the identifying insight that discovers a unity-identity-whole in data;

- the reflective insight that ascertains that the conditions for a prospective judgment have (or have not) been fulfilled;
- the introspective insight that grasps intelligibility in the data of consciousness;
- the basic philosophic insights that articulate the structure of knowing, the meaning of "being," and the elements of objectivity;
- the metaphysical insights that work out the implications of a basic isomorphism between knowing and known, that acknowledge that the truly known is being, and so that greet being as intrinsically intelligible;
- the genetic insights that specify the operators of development;
- the dialectical insights that press for coherence between performance and content and so reverse what is incoherent with the basic positions on knowing, being, and objectivity;
- the practical insights that size up situations and, when moral, grasp what possibly it would be good for one to do;
- the limit insights that grasp one's own incapacity for sustained development on the basis of one's own resources;
- the religious insights that discern the gift of a higher integration;
- the theological insights that employ analogies to ground a few stuttering words about transcendent mystery.

But with all of this, the point is missed entirely if one concentrates exclusively on the content of these insights. The only common ground of all of these insights is that they are insights, acts of understanding. And this is a common ground whether they all occur in one human subject or in many. In the one subject, it is a common ground whence there can be derived, through a metaphysics, the integration of the known. In many subjects, it is a common ground for communication and collaboration. The fact that we all understand, and so share the common dynamic that the early chapters of the book unfold, is, when affirmed, the basic and radical move onto the common ground. And the fact that we are asked not only to acknowledge that common ground, but also to appropriate it by relating insight to its antecedent conditions and its results in human knowing and living marks that new and common ground as also a new plateau. The beginning of Lonergan's articulation of what in *Insight* is called the common ground, which he later would call the normative source of meaning, has begun with insight into insight.

But this insight is also an owning, an appropriation, a claim upon a natural right, and the acknowledgment of a task, a responsibility, an imperative. All of these different types of insights occur in a common field named consciousness or self-presence—the subject as subject. This field can never be fully objectified, since the human subject doing the objectifying is al-

ways and inescapably beyond the subject being objectified. This is important. Lonergan's variety of a "turn to the subject" is not a turn to the subject as object of some controlling "inner look." The field in which the turn
occurs, consciousness, is not perception, representation, or knowledge (except in the limited sense that *experience* is knowledge as presentation of
data). It is rather the field of the awareness of self, the self-taste (Hopkins),
that accompanies all conscious acts and states. The objectification of it that
is possible can occur only through a humbling and purifying heightening of
awareness itself, a heightening that enables not only an attending to, and
insight into the relations of, the successive operations and states that occur
in the unfolding of conscious dynamism, but also a personal judgment that
this is what I am and a decision to be faithful to it.

Moreover, *Insight* discloses other operations besides those of experience of data of sense and of consciousness and insight into those data. The
link between these two levels of consciousness is the question for intelligence: What? Why? How often? etc. And the insight itself is productive
of the "inner word" or set of concepts that, when formulated in language,
prompts a further question, this time for critical reflection: Is it so? This question is satisfied by the reflective insight that (1) grasps that the conditions for a
judgment are or are not fulfilled, (2) grounds the inner word of yes or no, and
so (3) results in judgment. Holding the entire process together is the desire to
know, which is spontaneous and unrestricted but not automatic. While it is
never satisfied on any issue until the yes or no of reasonable judgment is
reached, and while it then resumes the process by turning to other questions, its
governance of conscious performance can be blocked by bias. And so Lonergan's uncovering of the various forms of bias is a further disclosure of the
common ground, but this time of its darker elements.

Furthermore, in *Insight* Lonergan made an initial move toward clarifying what he would only later acknowledge as a distinct level of consciousness, that of decision, so that the language that *Insight* will use for the clearing of the common ground is "the self-appropriation of one's rational self-
consciousness." And before he turns to decision and ethics, Lonergan draws
out the implications of the self-affirmation of the empirically, intelligently,
and rationally conscious knowing subject by outlining an integral heuristic
structure of the *known*, a metaphysics, that constitutes a brilliant beginning
upon overcoming the fragmentation of knowledge.

With the eventual recognition that decision names a fourth level of
activity beyond those constituting us as knowers, Lonergan gradually shifts
the language for the common ground from "rational self-consciousness" to
"intentionality." The normative source of meaning consists of more than the
acts of meaning that in *Insight* are called formal (conceptualization) and full
(judgment). Meaning is effective and constitutive, and grounding its constitutive function is the world constitution and self-constitution, the making of
being, that occurs in the existential moments in which we realize that it is

up to ourselves to decide individually and communally what we are going to make of ourselves. Lonergan's later reflections on these moments, for example in *Method in Theology* (1972), go far beyond the limited and somewhat limiting analysis of decision in *Insight*, even as they preserve the latter's essential grasp of the utter contingency of decision and action in relation to the knowledge that precedes it.

One of the new emphases, which will become increasingly important as we move toward Lonergan's most complete statement on the normative source of meaning in "Natural Right and Historical Mindedness," is the role now accorded to feelings. Potential values are apprehended in intentional feelings, that is, in those feelings that respond to an apprehended object or course of action. The process of deliberation that follows is one in which a person ascertains whether the possible value thus apprehended is truly or only apparently good. The truly good, while it may also be immediately satisfying, is not discerned on the basis of that criterion, for what is satisfying may also not be a genuine value. The truly good, rather, carries us to transcend ourselves, and on that basis Lonergan suggests a normative scale of values that, I believe, is of utmost importance for historical understanding and action: Values are vital, social, cultural, personal, and religious, in an ascending order of self-transcendence, and the levels of value are related in a complex fashion. Thus, to focus only on the areas most important in the present volume, the collaborative and communicative process of open and honest conversation about what is most significant for human living is itself a cultural value, perhaps the central cultural value. But it arises upon and is conditioned by the infrastructural foundation of the social institutions that either encourage its occurrence or, in Habermas's terms, more or less systematically distort communication; it depends upon the authenticity of the persons who engage in it and so on the extent and solidity of the processes of conversion they have undergone; and to the extent that it is effective it changes both these persons in their capacity as originating personal value and the social institutions that constitute part of its infrastructural base.

With the acknowledgment of decision as a distinct level of what he came to call intentional consciousness, Lonergan moved to the articulation of a far richer notion of the human good than the purely cognitional foundations of *Insight* permitted. I cannot here go into its elaborate structure, but will simply indicate that the grounds for its unfolding lie at least in part in the integration that deliberation effects of the knowing that *Insight* differentiated and of the feeling that is acknowledged in the later works as a distinct element in the normative source of meaning or common ground of communication and collaboration.

To this point, then, the common ground, when appropriated, is a distinct plateau consisting of four levels of intentional consciousness—in shorthand, experience, understanding, judgment, and decision—and of the feelings that are the mass and momentum of intentional consciousness and that must be submitted to a self-appropriation analogous to that which Loner-gan's analysis of intentionality enables with respect to operations.

The next step in the clearing of the common ground or the ascent to a new plateau is the revelation and appropriation of love as the supreme instance of personal value and the highest confluence of intentional operation with feeling. This theme emerges with particular poignancy in the late essays published in *A Third Collection* (1985). Love is total commitment, whether in intimacy, in the family, in interpersonal relations, in the civic community, or in relationship with Transcendent Mystery. It can be so powerful as to dismantle previous horizons, reveal new values that one could not previously have apprehended, and start one on a whole new course of living, transform one into a new creation. Its working, then, is often strangely independent of the upwardly moving creative dynamism that proceeds through knowledge to decision. However much it is sometimes preceded by knowledge of the beloved, it is always something that happens to us. We fall in love. And it need not always be preceded by knowledge, especially when our falling in love is initiated by, and has as its term, a Transcendent Mystery that we do not and cannot apprehend.

Love's movement through the common ground, the field of consciousness, is inverse to the movement that has preoccupied us to this point. It first reveals values in their splendor and efficacy, and transvalues our values as it shapes a new horizon. It then discloses, among values, the value of truth, and so strengthens us in the pursuit of intelligibility and truth through our cognitive operations. And usually ever so slowly, it transforms our very sensitive, dramatic, and intersubjective spontaneity, so that body joins psyche and spirit in one total loving commitment, one complete yes to existence in the cosmos and to our negotiated and discerned place within it.

It is my view, though, that the most important moment or step in Lonergan's clearing of a common ground on which all men and women could, if they so wish, meet was formulated only after all of the above elements had been worked out in his major writings. In some of the essays that he wrote in the last 10 years of his life, many of which, again, are contained in *A Third Collection* (1985), he portrays this four-tiered structure of intentional consciousness and concomitant feeling as *open on both ends*, open to what he variously calls (1) a tidal movement that precedes waking experience on one end and that goes beyond responsible decision on the other end, or (2) the passionateness of being that is the very upwardly and indeterminately directed universal dynamism that in *Insight* he called finality. Most significant of all is the assertion that the normative source of meaning consists of more than intentional operations. It lies in an entire ongoing process of self-transcendence that embraces the levels of intentional operations in a more inclusive whole. Underpinning the subject as experientially, intelligently, rationally, morally conscious is a symbolic operator that through image and affect coordinates neural processes with the goals of intentionality.

Accompanying that same subject, as we have seen, is the mass and momentum of feeling. And going beyond that subject is an operator of interpersonal relations, total commitment, and religious love. The latter elements are now located, not on the fourth level of intentional consciousness, but on a level or even levels beyond what intentionality analysis alone can disclose. And the former ingredients introduce a most elemental level of consciousness that can be called, at least tentatively, primordial psychic process.

My own way of articulating this development is as follows: If intentional consciousness, at least in its dramatic pattern of operations, can be called the search for direction in the movement of life, then this tidal wave or passionateness of being that underpins, accompanies, and overarches intentional operations is the very movement of life itself. It too calls for negotiation, as did the intentional operations whose working and interrelations Lonergan discloses. But negotiating the operations is distinct from negotiating the movement, however much each negotiation has to Be Attentive, Be Intelligent, Be Reasonable, and Be Responsible. The normative source of meaning is, in the last analysis, more than intelligence and more than intentional operations. It is the dialectical interplay of these with an autonomous but related movement of life that begins before intentional operations, in neural processes and psychic imagery and affect, and that reaches beyond intentional operations in a total being-in-love in families, in communities, and with God. The entire ongoing process of self-transcendence that is the normative source of meaning is more than intentional operations, and this "more" is what Lonergan pointed to and began to articulate towards the end of his life. It is also what I have attempted to articulate in the notion of psychic conversion (Doran, 1981, 1990), a notion which Lonergan assured me in personal correspondence is a "necessary complement" to his own work.

And so we end, not with a fully cleared field for common ground, but with a further task to which Lonergan pointed but did not complete. His own achievement, from this perspective, can be viewed as fulfilling his modest claim of providing an operational analysis that is not subject to radical revision, however much it may be further refined. That in itself is the secure movement onto a new plateau. It remains for us who have been brought to ourselves in a most intimate way by his writings now to make our home on this new plateau. Being at home on the plateau to which Lonergan brought us will happen to us as we negotiate the tidal movement of life by employing the very operations that he taught us to acknowledge, discriminate, claim as our own, and relate to one another. Eventually, while we may still limit intentional operations to four levels of consciousness, we will have to acknowledge in all at least six levels on which we are present to ourselves. For we will have to add an underpinning in elemental psychic process and an overarching context of a total commitment of being-in-love. We will also need to disengage distinct operators for these further levels.

And we will need to be far more attentive to the feelings that accompany our intentional operations and function as a kind of moral criterion of their dramatic integrity or authenticity. In building a home, as in constructing a ship (to borrow another image from the preface to *Insight*), one has to go all the way. It is to Lonergan's undying credit that he never claimed, at any step in the process that I have outlined here, that he had gone the whole way. Always there was, and, I hope, always there will be, a next step. If I have called attention to Lonergan's own pointing to the present next step, it is not to imply that taking it will finally bring us the whole way. For one thing, there is no possible mediation of totality—this is the very meaning of the move to the new plateau; for another thing, there can be a totality of mediation only asymptotically; and for a third thing, even on that mediation we have only begun. May this volume not only analyze but also encourage and release the communication that will enable many hands together to build a common home on the new plateau.

—Robert M. Doran, SJ
Regis College and
Lonergan Research Institute
University of Toronto

# Preface: Transforming the Wasteland

Dog sleds once carried the mail and other goods over the snow in Canada and the northern United States, a bit of life commemorated by American artist Howard Sivertson in his oil painting *Mail from Nipigon—1790*. In recent years, the Duluth area has also commemorated the practice with a dog sled race up the north shore of Lake Superior and back. In the 1993 race, one musher's team quit before the race was over. There was nothing wrong with the dogs in his team, he explained, but since he did not have a lead dog, the other dogs just refused to go on with the race and quit. Ironically, about the same time, the Disney movie *Iron Will* was being filmed in the Duluth area. It is about a dog sled race in which the favored musher loses his lead dog and the race.

These stories suggest an analogy to the human race: We work together well when we have a leader. Leaders are always in short supply, but the late Canadian Jesuit philosopher and theologian Bernard Lonergan (1904-1984) surely ranks as one of the seminal leaders of thought in our time. As Robert M. Doran has explained in the foreword, Lonergan's work provides the common ground for a unified philosophical approach to knowledge and, some claim, for forging "a new age" (Crowe, 1992, p. 138). At first blush, that might strike some people as an overly optimistic claim. Given the scope of Lonergan's enterprise, it is not. Lonergan sought common ground in the structures and operations of human consciousness. These form not only the basis of understanding, but also the ground of communication.

Indeed, Lonergan's critical realism is an instrument for forging the new age envisioned in the Christian scriptures. For with it people can come to recapitulate what Eric Voegelin calls the classic experience (1990a, pp. 265-291). Not surprisingly, Lonergan (1985, pp. 188-192) in commenting on this idea in Voegelin's work sees the classic experience as desirable for people to recapitulate. The experience is characterized by what Lonergan refers to as conversion, his term for Plato's term *periagoge*.[1]

Lonergan's insights relate to our own situation of blocked communication and methodological impasses. But the challenge for us today—whether in communication studies, literary studies, theology, philosophy, sociology, writing, or any academic area—runs far beyond any disciplinary concern. The very world in which we live lies under threat of war, of environmental collapse, of the interpersonal and structural violence that leads to abominations such as the Holocaust or "ethnic cleansing." How can we transform the wasteland of limited vision and distorted communication?

Lonergan's philosophical and methodological work invites us to see with different eyes and to reflect with transformed understanding on what we do. He urges all human beings to "authenticity"—a word that in his writings summarizes honesty, integrity, attentiveness to experience, and overcoming distorted communication through faithfulness to his five "transcendental" or "self-affirming" precepts: Be Attentive, Be Intelligent, Be Reasonable, Be Responsible, and Be in Love—precepts whose meanings will emerge as we consider his writings.

However, Lonergan's work is not well known outside of philosophical and theological circles, though as the essays in this volume argue, it has wide applications. The card index of the Lonergan Research Institute at the University of Toronto shows that doctoral dissertations devoted to his thought around the world number in the hundreds; and in 1988, the University of Toronto Press began publishing the anticipated 22-volume *Collected Works of Bernard Lonergan*.[2] Many have begun to apply Lonergan's

---

[1] Since Lonergan (1974, pp. 1-9) regularly inveighs against what he calls classicism in Roman Catholic philosophy and theology, it is important to distinguish such classicism from the classic experience. The classicist mentality decried by Lonergan involves an over-valuation of propositional truth. It usually is characterized by closed-systems thinking, which often leads to a smug, self-satisfied, fascination with allegedly universal truths without taking historical considerations into account sufficiently (Farrell, 1992a, pp. liii-liv). Consequently, Lonergan often contrasts the classicist mentality with historical-mindedness, which "means that to understand men and their institutions we have to study their history" (1985, p. 171).

[2] Bernard Lonergan was born on 17 December 1904 in Buckingham, Quebec, Canada. In 1922 he entered the Society of Jesus. After a two-year novitiate and two years of classics at Guelph, Ontario, he proceeded to England for philosophical studies at Heythrop College (1926-1929) and a "general degree" from the University of London (1930). For the next three years (1930-1933), he taught at Loyola College, Montreal. He then went to Rome, where he studied theology at the Gregorian University and was ordained a priest in 1936. Entering the doctoral program at the Gregorian University, he received an S.T.D. in 1940 after he completed his dissertation on St. Thomas Aquinas's thought on operative grace, which was published as a series of articles in *Theological Studies* in 1941 and 1942. He taught at Loyola College, Montreal, from 1940 to 1946. From 1947 to 1953, he was professor of theology at Regis College, Toronto; from 1953 to 1965, professor

thought to various realms of scholarship. The collection, *Lonergan's Hermeneutics*, edited by Sean E. McEvenue and Ben F. Meyer (1989), explores some implications of Lonergan's critical realism for biblical and literary interpretation, and Geoffrey B. Williams (1991) uses Lonergan's critical realism to provide a vantage point from which to study the use of ambiguity in the poetry of T. S. Eliot. John C. Kelly (1981) outlined a philosophy of communication based on Lonergan's work and that of the Austrian phenomenologist Alfred Schutz, and John Angus Campbell (1985) has begun the task of exploring the implications of Lonergan's writings for the study and use of rhetoric. But these efforts remain little known by other scholars interested in studying rhetoric and communication. For example, the collection *Rhetoric and Philosophy* (Cherwitz, 1990) examines eight philosophical positions, but Lonergan's critical realism is not mentioned anywhere in the volume, despite Campbell's 1985 review essay about Lonergan in the *Quarterly Journal of Speech*. (A revised and expanded for of his essay appears as chapter 1 in the present collection.) Similarly, the collection *Rhetoric in the Human Sciences* (Simons, 1989) does not treat Lonergan, although he is mentioned once in passing by Campbell in a subsequent collection edited by Herbert W. Simons, *The Rhetorical Turn: Invention and Persuasion in the Conduct of Inquiry* (1990). Despite Steve Fuller's obvious desire in *Philosophy, Rhetoric, and the End of Knowledge* (1993b) to figure out how some fields of study can surmount disciplinary boundaries, he too apparently knows nothing about Lonergan's work and the common ground Lonergan has identified that could enable disciplines across academia to see the cognitive ground they share in common.[3] This neglect is all the more striking in the light of Wayne C. Booth's judgment that Lonergan's thought is "first class" (1974, p. 95).

---

of theology, Gregorian University. A series of studies he did about the concept of *Verbum* in the writings of St. Thomas Aquinas appeared in *Theological Studies* from 1946 to 1949. In 1957 *Insight: A Study of Human Understanding* was published; in 1972, *Method in Theology*. He died 26 November 1984. (For other details about Lonergan's early life, see Crowe, 1992, pp. 1-38; for a highly circumstantial account of Jesuit life in the 20th century, see McDonough, 1992; for a detailed account of Lonergan's own experience of "intellectual conversion" while he was studying in Rome in the mid-1930s, see Liddy, 1993.)

[3] Likewise, other recent books such as *The Rhetoric of Science* by Alan G. Gross (1990) and *Contending Rhetorics: Writing in Academic Disciplines* by George L. Dillon (1991) contain no mention of Lonergan, nor do any of the 17 volumes published thus far in the Rhetoric of the Human Sciences Series put out by the University of Wisconsin Press (Ball, 1985; McCloskey, 1985; White, 1985; Maranhão, 1986; Connolly, 1987; Dumm, 1987; Garver, 1987; Nelson, Megill, & McCloskey, 1987; Tyler, 1987; Bazerman, 1988; Shapiro, 1988; Kellner, 1989; Simons & Melia, 1989; Bazerman & Paradis, 1991; Rubenstein, 1991; Selzer, 1993; and Fuller, 1993b, which was just discussed above; also see Jones, 1982; Chalmers, 1990; Dear, 1991; Brown, 1992; Roberts & Good, 1993).

Scholars in rhetoric and communication can learn from other scholarly circles, where Lonergan's work has been shown to stand up well. For example, Michael H. McCarthy (1990) champions Lonergan's critical realism over the programs of Frege, Husserl, Wittgenstein, Carnap, Sellers, Dewey, Quine, and Rorty; and Hugo Meynell (1991b) shows how Lonergan's philosophy answers issues raised in analytic philosophy. Frederick E. Crowe (1980) has suggested that Lonergan's work is an organon for our time, and Doran (1981a) has indicated how Lonergan's work could lead toward a reorientation of the human sciences.[4]  But up to this time Lonergan's work has been examined largely in terms of issues raised in the fields of philosophy or theology, before the recent interest in the rhetorical dimension of all academic disciplines emerged. *Communication and Lonergan* aims to explore some of the issues raised by those various scholarly studies of rhetoric and suggest how Lonergan's thought can address them. This collection, then, begins the larger task of relating Lonergan's thought to rhetorical and

---

[4] The scrutiny of Lonergan in essays published in periodicals has resulted in a vast body of literature, far too massive to enumerate here.  A hefty collection of impressive essays pertinent to the issues treated in the present collection could be published, perhaps under the title *Lonergan's Critical Realism Under Scrutiny* (see Lamb, 1965; Barden, 1970; Johann, 1971; Flanagan, 1972; Ryan, 1973; Marsh, 1975; Conn, 1976a, 1976b, 1977; Sala, 1976; Kroger, 1977; Meynell, 1978; Fitzpatrick, 1982; Lawrence, 1980; McKinney, 1982, 1983, 1987; Riley, 1983; Kidder, 1986; Cooley, 1988; Meyer, 1991; Shea, 1991).  Where should readers of the present collection go for further reading?  If they are new to Lonergan's thought, the best introductions to Lonergan's *Insight* are *The Achievement of Bernard Lonergan* by David Tracy (1970) and *An Introduction to the Philosophy of Bernard Lonergan* by Meynell (1991b). Tracy situates *Insight* in the context of perspectives suggested by theology, while Meynell locates it with respect to issues raised in analytic philosophy.  *The Lonergan Enterprise* by Crowe (1980) is an accessible discussion of the potential of the project initiated by Lonergan.  The essays by Crowe gathered together in the first part of the collection *Appropriating the Lonergan Idea* (1989, pp. 3-160) are also accessible, as is Crowe's *Lonergan* (1992).  For more advanced studies of Lonergan's thought, readers may wish to consult the essays gathered together in the collections *Creativity and Method* (Lamb, 1981a), *Religion and Culture* (Fallon & Riley, 1987), *The Desires of the Human Heart* (Gregson, 1988), and *Lonergan's Hermeneutics: Its Development and Application* (McEvenue & Meyer, 1989). Papers presented at the annual conference about Lonergan's work at Boston College are published periodically in the (now nine) volumes entitled *The Lonergan Workshop* (Lawrence, 1978- ), and more specialized studies of his work can be found in *Method: Journal of Lonergan Studies* (Morelli, 1983- ), which has come out in two issues annually for better than 10 years now.  Listings of publications about Lonergan's work can be found in the 14 volumes of the *Lonergan Studies Newsletter* (1980- ); back issues of it may be obtained from the Lonergan Research Institute; 10 St. Mary Street, Suite 500; Toronto, Ontario; Canada M4Y 1P9.  Readers who are interested in feminist perspectives might want to look for the collection Cynthia Crysdale has recently edited about Lonergan and feminism, which is scheduled to be published soon by the University of Toronto Press.  John Angus Campbell's annotations in the references at the end of this volume also guide readers to some further reading.

communication studies. For this undertaking to be fruitful, however, others will have to follow up the efforts begun here.

In this preface we will first consider some aspects of Lonergan's thought relevant to rhetoric and communication, particularly those developed in his major works, *Insight: A Study of Human Understanding* (1957/1992) and *Method in Theology* (1972). Second, we sketch in more detail how Lonergan's work relates to the role of rhetoric in contemporary academia. After then briefly introducing the contributors and their topics, we conclude the preface with acknowledgments and the dedication.

## 1. Lonergan and the Levels of Consciousness

Doran notes (paraphrasing Lonergan himself) that Lonergan's work provides a common ground on which people of intelligence might meet (1991, p. 2). Doran's explication of that common ground is worth quoting at length:

> That common ground is the very act of human understanding or insight. "To grasp [insight] in its conditions, its working, and its results is to confer a basic yet startling unity on the whole field of human inquiry and human opinion" [Lonergan, 1957/1992, p. 3]. The book *Insight* is a prolonged effort at enabling the reader to appropriate the structure and dynamics of his or her own activities of inquiry, insight, reflection, and judgment, and to derive from that appropriation the basic structure of a dynamic and evolutionary worldview. The program of the book is summarized in its introduction as follows: "Thoroughly understand what it is to understand, and not only will you understand the broad lines of all there is to be understood, but also you will possess a fixed base, an invariant pattern, opening upon all further developments of understanding" [Lonergan, 1957/1992, p. 22]. (Doran, 1991, p. 2)

Lonergan refers to this analysis of understanding or analysis of the levels of consciousness as "intentionality analysis" or "cognitive theory." In a nutshell, he claims that all forms of human inquiry involve the use of certain identifiable cognitive operations. Those operations provide common ground for looking at all forms of inquiry across academia and beyond. As noted in passing, Lonergan's philosophic position is referred to as "critical realism," to distinguish it from what he calls "naïve realism" and from other philosophic positions. (See the glossary at the end of the volume for definitions of the technical terms in the preceding paragraphs.)

Lonergan identified the "invariant structure" of human cognition, by which he means the basic cognitive operations employed in the levels of consciousness. The structure is invariant in the sense that if we do not follow certain steps, then we will fall into predictable errors. But his analysis of cognitive structures goes beyond the mere analysis of logic; therefore, the steps he has called attention to are referred to together as "generalized empirical method." The precepts he formulated are designed to direct people to follow the basic steps needed for generalized empirical method to work well.

Briefly, generalized empirical method proceeds through what Lonergan refers to as three levels of consciousness: empirical consciousness, intelligent consciousness, and rational consciousness. All learning begins in empirical consciousness when people pay attention to sensory data and the data of feelings and imagination. Lonergan sums up the proper orientation of empirical consciousness in the precept Be Attentive (rather than inattentive). Failure to attend to the processes of empirical consciousness can lead to oversights, which in turn require subsequent corrective action.

Intelligent consciousness is oriented toward conceptualization and interpretation of the data of empirical consciousness. Lonergan's precept for intelligent consciousness is Be Intelligent (instead of stupid) by carefully considering alternative explanations of data/situations. Failure to consider alternative interpretations or conceptualizations can lead to ill-conceived or incomplete interpretations, which will call for later correction, or worse, leave the individual immersed in his or her biases.

Rational consciousness is oriented toward predication (the expression of a reasonable judgment) about what is the best explanation/interpretation. It posits judgments about what is or is not the case or what is the case to a certain degree after careful consideration and weighing of the factors or conditions involved. Up to the point where a carefully considered judgment is posited, one's concept or idea is considered simply a hunch or an hypothesis about what is the case. Lonergan's precept for rational consciousness is Be Reasonable (instead of silly) in the claims we make. Rational consciousness emerges through careful and thorough pro and con debating about what is the case. Failure to be reasonable in our predications leads to over- or under-stating things, which calls for objection and correction later on. Note that the processes Lonergan describes as constituting cognition and leading to understanding are inherently rhetorical: They involve asking pertinent questions and weighing relevant evidence to "persuade" oneself about what is the case. Although we do not normally think of engaging in these processes as "persuasion" or rhetoric, they involve persuasion of the most basic kind, and when we subsequently move to communicate our insights and judgments to others, we more obviously employ persuasion or rhetoric as we proceed to elicit their agreement or questions or responses.

Before going on, it is important to stress that, for Lonergan, knowledge involves more than just taking a good look. Any epistemology that equates knowing with just taking a good look, he terms "naïve realism" because taking a good look is an exercise only of empirical consciousness. But the data of empirical consciousness must then be processed at the levels of consciousness that Lonergan refers to as intelligent consciousness and rational consciousness. "Naïve realism" fails to advert to and explicitly acknowledge these steps in the process of knowing. Brian Davies's remarks about St. Thomas Aquinas's account of knowledge can elucidate why knowledge involves more than just taking a good look:

For Aquinas, therefore, the model for knowing is not so much *seeing* as *talking*. Though he often uses the image of intellectual vision in speaking about knowledge, his argument is that to know or understand is to be able to deploy meanings or concepts. Knowledge, he affirms, is not of *individuals* [i.e., the data of the empirical level of consciousness] but of *forms* [i.e., the data of the intelligent level of consciousness]....[O]n the basis of acquaintance with particulars, we gain ideas or concepts in terms of which particulars can be classed, understood, or talked about. When we do this, he says, the forms of things come to be in a different sense from the way they exist as exemplified by the individuals whose forms they are. When knowledge or understanding occurs, forms come into being that are not the forms of individual material things, but the forms of these things as considered as objects of knowledge. Such forms are the "intelligible species," as Aquinas calls them. And they come to be in us. They are the result in us of our minds getting to work on the data of sense experience [i.e., the data of the empirical level of consciousness] and transforming them from a "big, booming, buzzing confusion" to a world of meaning and understanding [i.e., at the intelligent level of consciousness]. (1992, p. 127)[5]

However, at the intelligent level of consciousness, there are various ways in which data from the empirical level of consciousness can be examined. Generally speaking, the descriptive sciences employ ways of processing empirical data that accentuate efficient causality and instrumental reason. But these commonly used ways of examining empirical data surely do not exhaust the ways in which empirical data may be examined, as Lonergan has shown in the latter chapters of *Insight* (1957/1992) and in his later works:

Lonergan's later work would add to the exploration of insight and judgment a quite distinct analysis of the structure and dynamics of deliberation and decision, a positive account of feelings especially as they figure in deliberation, and a pronounced emphasis on love as the power that renders sustained authenticity or self-transcendence possible. (Doran, 1991, p. 2)

---

[5] While Aquinas undoubtedly influenced Lonergan's thought, that influence came later in his life (roughly from 1938 onward), when he started to work on his doctoral dissertation about operative grace in the thought of Aquinas (which was later published in 1971). Earlier he had been deeply influenced by John Henry Cardinal Newman's *Grammar of Assent*. According to Crowe, "*An Essay in Aid of a Grammar of Assent* had a profound influence on Lonergan's developing epistemology" (1989, p. 4). Newman's focus on what it means to live with faith leads him to set forth implicitly a rhetorical theory, as Walter Jost (1989) has shown. As James L. Kinneavy (1987a) has suggested, the Christian term "faith," which replaced the earlier Hebrew way of speaking of trusting in God, was most likely appropriated from ancient Greek rhetoric. There the term *pistis* referred to believing in what was probably true but not absolutely certain. Since Lonergan apparently was not aware of Aristotle's treatment of probabilities in connection with rhetoric, the rhetorical cast of Lonergan's thought seems to derive in part from the influence of Newman's *Grammar* on him and in part from his attempt to take into account modern science's orientation toward probabilities.

In the classical tradition of rhetoric, deliberation and decision have long oc-
cupied the central place in deliberative rhetoric, which involves debating in
a legislative context the pros and cons of various possible courses of action,
and in forensic rhetoric, which involves establishing facts for legal deliberation. But the intellectual processes involved in the traditional concept of
rhetoric also occur not only in decision-making in various organizational
and even personal contexts, but also in all contexts involving establishing
facts and interpreting them (Farrell, 1992b, p. 163). Lonergan's precept for
properly orienting and directing decision-making is Be Responsible, and his
fifth precept, Be in Love, aims at properly orienting one's basic, all-inclusive approach to personal and social life.

Attention to the operations of one's consciousness may lead to authentic human living. "Authenticity," a key concept for Lonergan—and one he
has refined beyond other 20th-century thought—characterizes the lives of
those who continually and assiduously follow the precepts he has formulated, which he refers to both as "transcendental" and as "self-affirming":

> For authenticity results from a long-sustained exercise of attentiveness, intel-
> ligence, reasonableness, responsibility. Long-sustained attentiveness notes
> just what is going on. Intelligence repeatedly grasps how things can be bet-
> ter. Reasonableness is open to change. Responsibility weighs in the balance
> short- and long-term advantages and disadvantages, benefits and de-
> fects....Moreover, authenticity in man or woman is ever precarious: [O]ur
> attentiveness is ever apt to be a withdrawal from inattention; our acts of un-
> derstanding, a correction of our oversights; our reasonableness, a victory over
> silliness; our responsibility, a repentance for our sins. (1985, pp. 9, 8)

Lonergan has observed that "self-transcendence reaches its term not in right-
eousness but in love and, when we fall in love, then life begins anew"
(1985, p. 175). In consequence, the fifth and final precept formulated by
Lonergan is Be in Love, which may be the key to actuating human growth
and overcoming blocked communication.

This whole process contributes to what Lonergan calls "conversion," a
term akin to Plato's *periagoge*, a term which for him describes more than
just a philosophical transformation. In *Method in Theology* (1972), Lonergan wrote about conversion as religious, moral, and intellectual. Later, he
further described how the aspects or dimensions of conversion actually
change the person:

> Conversion involves a new understanding of oneself because, more funda-
> mentally, it brings about a new self to be understood....It is intellectual inas-
> much as it regards our orientation to the intelligible and the true. It is moral
> inasmuch as it regards our orientation to the good. It is religious inasmuch
> as it regards our orientation to God....By intellectual conversion a person
> frees himself from confusing the criteria for knowledge of the world of im-
> mediacy with the criteria for knowledge of the world mediated by meaning.
> By moral conversion he becomes motivated primarily not by satisfactions but
> by values. By religious conversion he comes to love God with his whole

heart and his whole soul and all his mind and all his strength; and in consequence he will love his neighbor as himself. (Lonergan, 1985, pp. 247-248)

Conversion effectively puts an end to what Lonergan refers to as drifting
(1967/1988, pp. 222-231; 1985, p. 208). Since the idea of drifting is a key
point of contrast used by Lonergan to clarify his notion of authenticity, it may
be worthwhile to look at a lengthy statement of the contrast as he sees it:

> This process [of gradually enlarging the field in which a person does things
> for oneself, decides for oneself, finds out for oneself] reaches its climax, its
> critical and decisive phase, when one finds out for oneself what one is to be,
> when one lives in fidelity to one's self-discovery and decision. It is the exis-
> tential moment that the drifter never confronts. The drifter thinks as every-
> body thinks, says what everybody says, does what everybody does, and so do
> they. The mass of unauthentic humanity lacks the courage to take the risk of
> thinking things out for themselves. It lacks the resoluteness that decides and
> the fidelity that stands by its decisions. The development that reaches its
> goal in the existential decision and in fidelity to that decision is the emer-
> gence of the autonomous subject. (Lonergan, 1984, p. 10)

Lonergan's method, then, has as its goal a transformation of the individual,
which leads in turn to a transformation of society. But Lonergan does not
see the transformation of the individual as a strictly solitary venture, as it
were. For example, Lonergan (1984) writes about mutual self-mediation, a
topic Francisco Sierra-Gutiérrez explores in chapter 13.

To sum up this part, Lonergan formulated the five precepts—(1) Be
Attentive, (2) Be Intelligent, (3) Be Reasonable, (4) Be Responsible, and (5)
Be in Love—to help people direct their energies in ways that could lead to
that transformation. They grew out of his detailed analysis of the levels of
consciousness—(1) empirical, (2) intelligent, (3) rational, and (4) existential,
which as we have seen involve respectively the operations of (1) experiencing, (2) understanding, (3) judging, and (4) deciding. Each of the first four
precepts listed above is aimed at properly orienting and directing the functioning of the respectively numbered level of consciousness and its corresponding cognitive operations. The fifth comprehends the totality of the
human person. Lonergan's five precepts and general empirical method can
apply more directly to communication, particularly if we see them against
the background of contemporary rhetoric.

## 2. Lonergan and the Scope of Rhetoric

Northrop Frye provides a helpful introduction to the scope of rhetoric. Borrowing an expression from St. Augustine, Frye asserts that "rhetoric belongs
to a moral, *quid agas* or 'What should we do?' mode" (1990, p. 77; also cf.
p. 16). Following Frye further, we can distinguish (1) the rhetorical verbal
mode from what he calls (2) the descriptive mode of verbal expression, (3)

the imaginative or poetic mode of verbal expression, and (4) the dialectic or conceptual mode of verbal expression. These distinctions help to establish that biblical texts, for example, should not be read as though they were examples of the modern descriptive mode of verbal expression, which is the point Frye wishes to make.

However, all the modes do have rhetorical dimensions. The 400 instances of forms of the Greek word for "persuasion" (*peitho*) in Plato's writings indicate a persuasive or rhetorical dimension in philosophy and dialectic (Mode 4) as well as in action-oriented deliberative rhetoric (Mode 1). Philosophy and dialectic *moves* us to agree with the argument being presented or does not *move* us.[6] Similarly, the imaginative or poetic mode (Mode 3) *moves* or does not *move* us by its words, images, and portrayed actions to have appropriate imaginative, emotional, and aesthetic responses. But at first blush the descriptive mode of verbal expression (Mode 2) seems different. We have often heard it said that the facts speak for themselves. But people select facts and interpret them and then arrange them in a manner that either contributes to or detracts from their persuasiveness, and so even arguments constructed with empirical facts are indeed *constructed* and do thereby have a rhetorical dimension. As a matter of fact, Frye's modern descriptive mode of verbal expression can be seen as an extension of forensic rhetoric beyond courtroom concerns. Forensic rhetoric involves arguing about propositions of fact, and the modern descriptive mode implicitly involves arguing about propositions of fact, even when it mutes the argumentative aspect or when the facts are not disputed.

When we recognize the rhetorical or persuasive dimension of the four broad modes of verbal expression, then we can see that Lonergan's analysis of human consciousness provides a support for a philosophical theory of communication. His intentionality analysis or cognitional theory could contribute to the development of an understanding of the psychodynamics involved in the four modes of verbal expression more adequate than what Frye or anybody else has developed to date.

---

[6] For all practical purposes, though, rhetoric in antiquity was generally understood to refer primarily to civic discourse, as in government assemblies and courts (cf. Kinneavy, 1987b; Gabin, 1987). In the 20th century, rhetoric has usually been considered as encompassing a far broader range of discourse, as can be seen in the work of Morris W. Croll (1966), Kenneth Burke (1945, 1950, 1966), Richard Weaver (1953, 1970), Richard McKeon (1987), Stephen Toulmin (1958), Chaim Perelman and L. Olbrechts-Tyteca (1958/1969), Wayne C. Booth (1961), I. A. Richards (1965, 1991), Edwin Black (1965), Martin Steinmann (1967), James L. Kinneavy (1971), Paolo Valesio (1980), and others. Theresa Enos and Stuart C. Brown (1993) have pulled together a useful collection of essays that survey various 20th-century approaches to the study of rhetoric. For bibliographic essays concerning historical and contemporary rhetoric, see Winifred Bryan Horner (1990).

## 3. Rhetoric in Academia: Present, Past, and Future

*3.1  A View of the Present*

In the marketplace of ideas in academia, few academics outside the fields of speech communication and written composition place much stock in instruction in speech or writing. Ironically, in recent years it has become fashionable in certain circles in literary studies and in philosophy to talk a lot about rhetoric, yet all the recent attention to rhetoric has not enhanced the prestige of the fields long concerned with rhetoric. Why not? As one wag in philosophy likes to say, the subject matter of speech and writing instruction are processes, not content. Because these two fields do not have a content similar to the definable content of other fields of study across academia, they are defined more by their attention to processes, although surely neither ignores content. One could look at the overall situation in academia as simply involving a division of labor among various fields of study with most fields devoted to content (the equivalent of cumulative commonplaces in the old oral/rhetorical tradition) and the fields of speech communication and written composition devoted more to processes (the equivalent of analytic commonplaces).

Since Lonergan accentuates process (i.e., cognitive operations) to an unprecedented degree, an examination of how academia historically arrived at its present situation wherein the process-oriented fields suffer low prestige will be worthwhile. If Lonergan's thought were to prevail in the future, then all disciplines across academia would join rhetoric and content as process-oriented. All fields of inquiry, including philosophy, would attend more carefully and reflectively to the cognitive operations involved in thinking and communicating—in other words, to their own rhetorical thought.

*3.2  A View of the Past*

Bruce A. Kimball (1986) provides us with a useful history of the idea of liberal education in Western culture, by describing it in terms of the tension between orators and philosophers. The low status accorded speech communication and written composition probably arises in part from the dominance of what Kimball calls the philosophers' position in education and in part from the lack of a modern reformulation of what he calls the orators' position. Briefly, he sees a tension in the aim of Western education between the practical orientation of the orators and the theoretical orientation of the philosophers.

In antiquity Isocrates, Cicero, and Quintilian represented the orators' position in Kimball's estimate, while Socrates, Plato, and Aristotle represented the philosophers' position.[7] In the high Middle Ages, the philoso-

---

[7] No doubt there is a point to the contrast Kimball has set up. However, Cicero's and Quintilian's ideal of the orator may have closely approximated the *daimonios*

phers' position dominated education.  With the Renaissance humanists came
a rebirth of the orators' orientation toward education, and even in colonial
America, rhetoric enjoyed a rebirth in the schools.  The two orientations
co-existed for several centuries in Western education, until the rise of the
liberal-free ideal, as Kimball characterizes it.  Kimball sees the 18th-century
*philosophes* as the forerunners of an ideal that came to be embodied in the
19th-century research university and that dominates 20th-century thinking
about education.  He considers the liberal-free ideal the modern reformulation of the older position of the philosophers.  According to him, there is no
modern counterpart of the older position of the orators.  What, then, characterize the orators' and the philosophers' positions?

Kimball refers to the orators' position as the *artes liberales* ideal, and
in each of its several historical formulations he sees it as embodying seven
characteristics (1986, pp. 37-38, 53-54, and 111-112):  (1) The goal was to
train good citizens to lead and be decision-makers in society; (2) prescribed
values and standards for character and conduct were necessary to produce
good citizens; (3) the students were expected to be committed to the prescribed values and standards for personality formation and civic responsibility; (4) authoritative texts provided moral and literary instruction simultaneously; (5) those people who adopted the personal and civic virtues expressed
in the texts became an identifiable elite group within the larger population;
(6) the orators were pragmatic, rather than analytic and speculative, in in-
structing the students about the personal and civic virtues; and (7) the *artes
liberales* ideal was an end in itself.  A modern reformulation of the orators'
position needs to begin with the resurrection of the first point mentioned by
Kimball—a rededication of education to helping students become good decision-makers, which involves learning to use pro and con debating in the
effort to follow Lonergan's precept to Be Reasonable and then following the
precept to Be Responsible.  In the long run the students as private individuals, as workers in some capacity, and as citizens will be well served by their
education if they have learned to think in this manner.

Kimball also sees the modern liberal-free ideal, as he calls it, as having seven characteristics:  (1) It emphasized freedom, especially freedom
from a priori strictures and standards; (2) the desire for freedom led to an
emphasis on intellect and rationality; (3) the liberal-free ideal built on critical skepticism; (4) the liberal-free ideal espoused tolerance because certainty
was believed to foster intolerance; (5) the relativizing of standards and
norms tended to favor egalitarianism; (6) tolerance and egalitarianism led to
an emphasis on individual volition rather than on the obligations of citizenship; and (7) the liberal-free ideal stood as an end in itself (Kimball, 1986,
pp. 119-122).

---

*aner* envisioned by Plato and the *spoudaios* envisioned by Aristotle, which are
discussed by Thomas J. Farrell in chapter 6 (concerning Cicero, see Voegelin,
1990a, pp. 275-276).

Adherents of the liberal-free ideal understood the modern scientific method to consider all truths as in principle tentative hypotheses to be tested further. In regard to this point, it is instructive to compare Kimball's account of the orators' position and the philosophers' position with Richard A. Lanham's account of *homo rhetoricus* and *homo seriosus* (1976, pp. 1-9). Lanham notes that "the Western self has from the beginning been composed of a shifting and perpetually uneasy combination of *homo rhetoricus* and *homo seriosus*, of a social self and a central self" (1976, p. 6). Most of the orators in ancient Athens described by Josiah Ober (1989) exemplify *homo rhetoricus*, while Socrates, Plato, and Aristotle exemplify *homo seriosus*. In antiquity these two selves could also be found, respectively, in the orators' position and the philosophers' position concerning liberal education. Moreover, just as Kimball finds a perennial tension between those two positions, so too Lanham finds that it is the business of the two selves to "contend for supremacy" (1976, p. 6):

> The rhetorical view of life threatens the serious view at every point [p. 6]. Rhetoric's real crime, one is often led to suspect, is its candid acknowledgment of the rhetorical aspects of "serious" life [p. 7]. We find here the explanation for rhetorical training's paradoxical durability. To leave it out cuts man in half [p. 6]. The study of rhetoric does not free us from rhetoric. It teaches, rather, that we *cannot* be freed from it, that it represents half of man. If truly free of rhetoric, we would be pure essence. We would retain no social dimension [p. 8].

While Lanham identifies the social dimension with role-playing, Kimball's work reminds us that the orators' position of old was primarily concerned with developing leaders involved in decision-making. This explicit concern for practical decision-making, missing in the liberal-free ideal, emerges in Lonergan's precept to Be Responsible.

The freedom, tolerance, and egalitarianism of the liberal-free ideal no doubt sound more appealing to many in academia than anything smacking of elitism. But when it comes to research and writing, only professional researchers and creative writers of the first order—an elite group, to say the least—try to embody the liberal-free ideal of originality in their written work. Conversely, college-educated people in the workplace are involved in practical decision-making at various levels, and usually their work contributes to decision-making processes. Moreover, college-educated people, like other people, are engaged in personal decision-making all the time. But there is no modern reformulation of the orators' position emphasizing decision-making. Even textbooks that claim to be drawing on classical rhetoric do not emphasize decision-making (e.g., Corbett, 1990; Horner, 1988; Lunsford & Connors, 1992). Recently Thomas O. Sloane (1989) has called attention to the potential for invention of pro and con debating as advocated by Cicero—without calling attention to the obvious usefulness of pro and con debating for informed decision-making. While Lonergan's precept to

Be Responsible is most obviously directed toward decision-making, his prior precept to Be Reasonable reminds us of the inherent value of genuine pro and con debating in reaching reasonable judgments.

## 3.3 A View of the Future

The orators' orientation to Kimball's liberal arts education grows out of the oral life-world described by Walter J. Ong (1982), while the philosophers' view of liberal education emerges from the literate mentality as described by Ong. In Ong's terminology, the liberal-free ideal arose from the same deep interiorization of literacy that gave rise to Romanticism (1971, pp. 255-283). Although we have seen that Kimball finds no modern reformulation of the orators' position, Ong argues that Western culture today has entered what he calls a secondary oral culture, an oral culture dependent in some ways on reading and writing. Consequently, perhaps the time has come to move toward reformulating the orators' position.

A modern reformulation of the orators' position might well include Linda Brodkey's (1987) points about seeing the "scene" of writing (and, more broadly, of all expression) as re-populated rather than solitary and as more pragmatic than Romantic. Brodkey uses Kenneth Burke's visual metaphor of "scene" to call attention to the pervasive Romanticism involved in our thinking about writing. For example, the Romantic scene stands opposed the pragmatic scene as does the solitary scene to the populated scene. However, the visual metaphor of "scene" apparently leads her away from thinking in more personalistic or vocal terms: the old oral/rhetorical image of the orator as a person of many voices in the agora of a community, even a textual community. But Ong notes the vocal image and has recently pointed out how the concerns of contemporary literary critics with intertextuality and with reader response also hearken back to concerns of the oral/rhetorical tradition, while the now old New Criticism and continental Formalism accentuated the visual aspect of texts and considered them to be "quiescently reified" (1988, p. 263).

A reformulation of the orators' position would need to include more points than just those. Since a re-populated, pragmatic orientation for writing hearkens back to the pre-Romantic image of the orator in the agora, Ong's treatment of the cumulative and analytic commonplaces used by the orators of old can help us formulate a more realistic approach to what most of us actually do most of the time when we express ourselves: We use the stock ideas of a textually-defined community—the content taught in so-called content courses is used by informed people as the cumulative commonplaces of old were used by orators and poets alike. And we employ commonly used ways of organizing and developing ideas, which we have learned by studying examples of other people's writing and speaking—the counterparts of the old analytic commonplaces. In addition, the old oral/rhetorical tradition can serve to remind us that deliberative rhetoric involved decision-making. Lonergan's cognitional analysis and his precept, Be Reasonable, fit well with this tradition. Furthermore, Lonergan's first four precepts can be seen as analytic commonplaces writ large, in the sense of providing a basic set of directions to follow in various contexts.

To be modern, however, a reformulation of the orators' position needs to take the human subject, the person, into account, for modernity is characterized by the inward turn to the subject, as Ong reminds us (1982, pp. 178-179; 1986, pp. 127-159). Lonergan's analysis of the levels of consciousness grows out of his attention to the human person as subject. We can take the subject into account by expanding a point Brodkey makes in passing and seeing all expression as an autobiography of the speaker or writer in the act of speaking or writing (1987, p. 407). Liberal education should help students be more aware of the intersubjective dimension of thinking by teaching them to use pro and con debating in expression and decision-making because it calls attention to their own processes of thinking and accentuates the self-other dimension of intersubjectivity.

Finally, liberal education can help students to follow the Lonergan's precept to Be in Love, at least in the sense of learning out of a love for learning. Following this precept, they presumably would be motivated by the pure, disinterested, detached desire to know that Lonergan writes about in *Insight* (see the Index under "desire to know" for page references). But as the essays in the collection make clear, this is not the only dimension of communication that Lonergan's work can help us better understand.

## 4. Overview of the Collection

Broadly speaking, the essays represent an interdisciplinary attempt to examine how Lonergan's thought might apply to communication. As such, they invite the reader to consider both Lonergan and communication from unaccustomed perspectives. Consequently, the editors hope that readers will venture beyond a single discipline in reading the essays and savor all that they offer. This volume will have succeeded if it manages to catalyze the thinking of people about the potential applications and extension of Lonergan's thought.

In general, the authors of the four introductory studies in the collection have assumed that readers know relatively little about Lonergan's thought. While the other essays in the collection are more specialized in focus, they, too, are designed to be accessible to the educated reader as well as to specialists. Chapters 1 to 3 stake out the familiar ground of rhetoric in approaching Lonergan. Chapter 4 ranges more widely through communication topics and thus prepares the reader for Part II, whose studies examine intercultural communication, interpretation, interpersonal communication, scientific rhetoric, various postmodernist questions, and the ways in which communication interacts with culture.

In chapter 1 John Angus Campbell of the University of Washington in Seattle, who has distinguished himself in the scholarly study of the rhetoric of science, situates Lonergan's thought in the context of rhetorical theory. While Plato and Aristotle wrote notable works about rhetoric, few other philosophers have made distinguished contributions to the study of rhetoric and communication. Lonergan may be an exception, Campbell suggests, because his attention to cognitional analysis goes to the heart of what is involved in rhetoric and communication. Consequently, Campbell is able to place Lonergan in the broad panoply of modern rhetorical thinkers. For readers who are used to seeing Lonergan primarily in the context of modern philosophers or theologians, Campbell's essay should provide a fresh view of him. Other readers may be used to seeing only philosophers like Habermas or Austin, Searle, and Grice as having something to say that is pertinent for the study of rhetoric and communication; they may be pleasantly surprised by Campbell's account of Lonergan's work. Originally published in 1985, Campbell's review essay has been revised and expanded for this collection.

In chapter 2 Thomas J. Farrell of the University of Minnesota at Duluth explores how Lonergan's work can help writers attain a rounder view of the intellectual processes involved in writing. As a foil for developing his ideas, he uses the Romantic image of the writer as a solitary figure striving for unique expression. He delineates how each person develops his or her own subjectivity through interacting with and learning from others. So each writer's subjectivity is formed intersubjectively. Writing from sources, then, further extends the writer's subjectivity, thus calling attention to how subjectivity is formed intersubjectively. But the writer who self-consciously follows Lonergan's transcendental precepts—Be Attentive, Be Intelligent, Be Reasonable, Be Responsible, and Be in Love—will reflect carefully on the intellectual processes involved in writing. Such reflection should enhance the writer's sense of intersubjectivity, move the writer toward the self-appropriation described by Lonergan, and enable the writer to experience authenticity as Lonergan defines it.

In chapter 3 Sister Carla Mae Streeter, OP, of the Aquinas Institute of Theology at Saint Louis University examines how Lonergan's work can be applied to preaching to make it more efficacious. Having completed her doctoral dissertation about Lonergan at the University of Toronto, she is presently working on a book-length glossary of Lonergan's terminology, parts of which she has contributed as the glossary at the end of the present collection. In her essay she examines preaching as one particular kind of communication. Treating it as an instance of "evaluative hermeneutic," she argues that Lonergan's generalized empirical method and cognitional theory provide a check against bias and therefore balance Gadamer's acceptance of "prejudice" as a part of interpretation. Her argument can be extended, of course, beyond preaching to any communicative or interpretive situation.

In chapter 4 Frederick E. Crowe of the Lonergan Research Institute at the University of Toronto, whose works have been mentioned above, surveys the corpus of Lonergan's work to identify those texts where he wrote about one or another aspect of communication. While Crowe's survey is not exhaustive, it is comprehensive in that it provides the interested reader with ample information about places where Lonergan treats topics related to communication. A student of trinitarian theology, Crowe begins his survey with a handy delineation of trinitarian theology. Readers who are unaccustomed to the rigors of Christian theology may be surprised to learn that communication is actually central to the Christian concept of the triune God. But Crowe quickly moves beyond the heady concepts of trinitarian theology to more familiar considerations of communication. He covers the aspect of communication interior to each of us. Then he takes up the aspect of human communication that involves moving out of oneself to communicate with others. In the longest section of his article, he considers the cross-cultural context that communication with others has for Lonergan's own discipline of theology. He concludes with a shorter section on communication between God and humankind.

As noted above, the essays in the second section have a more specialized focus. In chapter 5 Crowe applies Lonergan's thinking in a more specific way to the general problem of cross-cultural communication. The first part of Crowe's title, "Neither Jew nor Greek, but One Human Nature and Operation in All," could be paraphrased by inserting various terms used by different authors to characterize contrasting thought patterns: Hebrew and Greek (Boman, 1954/1960), Hopi and Standard Average European (Whorf, 1956), primary oral and literate (Ong, 1967; Havelock, 1978, 1982), or "black" and "white" (Kochman, 1974, 1981). The second part of Crowe's title would be applicable to all of them: There is one human nature—we all share humanity in common—and the cognitive operations employed by all human beings are essentially the same, even when our particular cultural thought patterns may vary—as they do in significant ways (cf. Farrell, 1983). As Crowe notes, that is the essential point of Lonergan's work. He calls attention to how comprehensive and inclusive the cognitive operations identified by Lonergan are: Everybody today uses them, and historically everybody used them. Thus, Lonergan would found the possibility of cross-cultural communication on understanding the operations of consciousness.

In chapter 6 Farrell returns to describe Voegelin's exegesis of Plato's thought about philosophers and sophists. He connects the maturity that Voegelin attributes to Plato with Lonergan's thought about self-appropriation. Further, Farrell aligns Lonergan's remarks about drifting and drifters with Plato's negative assessment of the sophists. Drifters are still living in the state of mystification (Bradshaw, 1992), that is, in the cave described by Plato. The people who have left the cave and entered into the sunlight outside it have experienced "conversion," to use Lonergan's term. To experience conversion in its fullness, they need to be healed of the aftereffects of childhood traumas (cf. Bradshaw, 1988). Toward the end of the chapter, Farrell suggests a fresh view of why Plato chose to commemorate the memory of Socrates by writing dialogues: The communication involved in the dialogues of the historical Socrates may have engendered and advanced Plato's own personal healing and growth toward the maturity Voegelin attributes to him.

In chapter 7 Hugo A. Meynell of the University of Calgary in Canada shows how Lonergan's thought can address a quandary of philosophy first posed by Kant: "On what foundation rests the relation of that in us we call 'representation' to the object?" Put less abstractly, the problem touches on how we can establish what is meant in oral or written communication. In his analysis, Meynell situates Lonergan's generalized empirical method in the context of contemporary philosophy; he argues that both reasonable judgment and "cognitive self-transcendence" are possible. On the basis of these, communication itself becomes meaningful.

In chapter 8 William Rehg of Saint Louis University, author of a new book on Habermas and communicative ethics (1993), suggests that rhetoric forms an essential aspect of an account of rational or scientific inquiry based on Lonergan's method. To arrive at this conclusion, he places Lonergan in dialogue with Habermas. Habermas' social theory of rationality, he claims, supplies a necessary intersubjective amplification of Lonergan's cognitional theory. Rehg's overall effort situates Lonergan's thought in the heart of contemporary thinking on the nature of scientific method and on the nature of communicative competence.

In chapter 9 Frederick G. Lawrence of Boston College examines how Lonergan's thought can address concerns raised by postmodernist critiques, particularly their wholehearted hermeneutics of suspicion. Lawrence, like many others who follow Lonergan's thought, writes out of the context of theology and its attempts at interpretation of a tradition. His discussions of the postmodern "turn to the subject" and concern for otherness will certainly interest those in communication studies and literary studies, who also wrestle with the same undeniably important themes.

In chapter 10 Meynell returns to present a critique of Gadamer's *Truth and Method*, a work that, as we have seen, relates to Lonergan's work in several respects, not the least being its treatment of culture. Meynell argues that Gadamer's hermeneutics leaves one with an unacceptable degree of relativism and skepticism. As a corrective, he proposes Lonergan's method of rational inquiry and judgment.

In chapter 11 Geoffrey B. Williams of Campion College at the University of Regina in Canada, whose 1991 book on Eliot was mentioned above, shows how the functional specialties of theology described by Lonergan in *Method in Theology* (1972) can be applied to literary history. He chooses to study the "narrative by which people 'read' and reveal themselves" as his point of entry to the world of discourse. Sensitive to the postmodernist situation of subjectivity within the realm of language, Williams argues that any act of communication is a manifestation of literary history. His insight involves connecting this state of affairs with Lonergan's method of appropriation of human consciousness.

In chapter 12 Lawrence raises the question of language in a different way: Using the metaphors of learning a new language and of conversation, he examines Lonergan's account of the structure of the human good against the backdrop of alternative ancient and modern theories of the human good. The shifting definition of the good brings with it issues of interpretation and translation—and ultimately of "conversion." Once again, the encounter with Lonergan's thought leads to fundamental questions for communication studies as well as for theology and political theory.

In chapter 13 Francisco Sierra-Gutiérrez of the Pontificia Universidad Javeriana in Bogotá, Columbia, describes how Lonergan's thought can ground a philosophy of communication, opening up fresh approaches that go beyond semiotics, sociolinguistics, and pragmatics. He takes epistemology as his starting point and proposes that we understand communication "as a relevant case of mutual self-mediation of human beings," borrowing the analysis of mediation from Lonergan. The major part of his essay suggests a "communicative reading" of Lonergan's structure of human good—the same material Lawrence examines in the previous chapter. Sierra-Gutiérrez provides an interesting perspective on that material because he writes against the background of Latin American communication theory and research.

In chapter 14 Jesuit theologian J. J. Mueller of Saint Louis University takes up the cultural context of communication and analyzes the role of theological symbols in mediating culture. Noting that the Christian vision is expressed in symbols, especially the resurrection symbol, he undertakes a critical examination of the meaning of the resurrection symbol and of the possibilities it contains to help form a vision of a world-culture.[8] Indirectly, he argues that theology is "the process, language, and act of communication" between religion and culture.

---

[8] Mortimer J. Adler (1991) has long argued that a system for world government needs to be developed, as have others. A growing body of literature in the social sciences treats the actually emerging global culture and globalization (see, for example, Featherstone, 1990; Robertson, 1992; Carnoy, Castells, Cohen, & Cardoso, 1993). Thomas Langan (1992) has explored the kind of respectful discourse that will be needed as the emerging world system brings different cultures into contact with one another.

## 5. Acknowledgments and Dedication

The editors gratefully acknowledge the assistance of many individuals and institutions, particularly the University of Minnesota at Duluth (UMD), Santa Clara University, and the Centre for the Study of Communication and Culture (CSCC) in London, England, where Paul Soukup spent the better part of his sabbatical in 1992-1993. (It has since been relocated at Saint Louis University.) Kenneth C. Risdon and William A. Gibson of UMD generously contributed their computer expertise when they were asked for advice or assistance, and Roger W. Petry and Joel R. Ness of UMD graciously assisted us with "translations" of computer files when they were needed. JoAnne Johnson of UMD helped with the many secretarial tasks needed to carry out the project, as did Maria Way at CSCC. Elwood Mills at Santa Clara provided the graphic art work for the book.

The editors also acknowledge the cooperation of publishers and authors in granting permission to reprint marterial in this volume. John Angus Campbell's "Insight and Understanding: The 'Common Sense' Rhetoric of Bernard Lonergan" originally appeared in the *Quarterly Journal of Speech*, *71*, 476-488; copyright by the Speech Communication Association, 1985; it is reprinted here with the permission of the publisher and of the author, who adapted and expanded it for this collection. We also thank Frederick E. Crowe and the Provincial Superior of the Philippine Jesuits for permission to reprint "Neither Jew nor Greek, but One Human Nature and Operation in All," which originally appeared in 1965 in *Philippine Studies*, *13*, 546-571, and was reprinted in a recent collection of Crowe's essays (1989, pp. 31-50). In addition, for permission to reprint "The Fragility of Consciousness: Lonergan and the Postmodern Concern for the Other," which originally appeared in 1993 in *Theological Studies*, *54*, 55-94, we thank the editor of *Theological Studies* and Frederick G. Lawrence, who expanded it for this collection. We are also grateful to Professor Lawrence for granting us permission to reprint "The Human Good and Christian Conversation" from *Searching for Cultural Foundations*, edited by Philip McShane (Lanham, MD: University Press of America, 1984, pp. 86-112). Next, we thank the editor of *Theology Digest* for permission to reprint a diagram by Carla Mae Streeter, which was published originally in 1985 in *Theology Digest*, *32*, 326. For permission to quote copyrighted material, we thank the following copyright holders: (1) the Bernard Lonergan Estate, for permission to quote from *Insight, Method in Theology*, and *A Third Collection*; (2) the Crossroad Publishing Company (USA) and Sheed & Ward (UK), for permission to quote from the English translation of Hans-Georg Gadamer's *Truth and Method*; and (3) Louisiana State University Press, for permission to quote from Eric Voegelin's *Published Essays, 1966-1985*, edited by Ellis Sandoz, Vol. 12 of *The Collected Works of Eric Voegelin* (1990a). Additionally, we thank the *Globe and Mail* of

Toronto for permission to reprint the frontispiece photograph of Bernard Lonergan taken on 26 March 1970 by Erik Christensen.

This project would not have started without the generous encouragement of Frederick E. Crowe of the Lonergan Research Institute at the University of Toronto, who also kept the readers of the *Lonergan Studies Newsletter* posted as it advanced steadily through its stages of development. We are grateful for his steadfast interest and encouragement. Similarly, we are grateful to Robert A. White of the Gregorian University in Rome for his strong words of encouragement in the early stages of planning this volume. Naturally, we want to thank our own publisher, Sheed & Ward of Kansas City, and especially managing editor Andrew Apathy.

Next, the editors wish to acknowledge their indebtedness to Shirley MacLaine for making talk about the so-called "New Age" popular in the United States today. While responses to such talk vary, Father Mark Makowski, recent pastor of St. Benedict's Church in Duluth, likes to say, "We Christians are supposed to be the New Age." His observation reminds us of the unfulfilled promise of Christianity. Lonergan's work could be integral to the actuation of that promise, because the experiences of conversion and authenticity that he writes about are integral to the experience of new life described in Christian scriptures (see esp. 1985, p. 192; for a fuller discussion of this correspondence, see Farrell's chapter 6).

Finally, the editors dedicate the collection to Walter J. Ong, SJ, teacher and friend. Both editors studied under him at Saint Louis University. His wide-ranging approach to communication studies provided us with the broad orientation that encouraged us to attempt the present explorations of Lonergan's thought and communication.

—Thomas J. Farrell
University of Minnesota, Duluth

—Paul A. Soukup, SJ
Santa Clara University

# Part I

# Introductory Studies

# Insight and Understanding: The "Common Sense" Rhetoric of Bernard Lonergan

## John Angus Campbell

The work of the late Bernard Lonergan constitutes an ongoing revolution in Catholic thought and is a multifaceted, encyclopedic achievement rich with implications for scholars across disciplines. Unfortunately, many readers who begin *Insight* in the hope of realizing its wealth will soon feel like the pioneers confronting the Great Plains or the Rockies. The forbidding scientific examples of *Insight*'s first five chapters are not in the least engaging and demand of the reader either technical facility or a dogged "Oregon or bust" mentality. My purpose in this chapter is to persuade the reader to brave the journey. To this end, I will provide a brief topographical map featuring four landmarks: Lonergan's implicit perspective on the role of rhetoric in human self-understanding, his cognitional theory, his epistemology, and his metaphysics. I will also relate Lonergan's enterprise to the current hermeneutic turn in communication scholarship.

In *Beyond Objectivism and Relativism,* Richard Bernstein spoke for many humanists when he underscored the need to reclaim as knowledge, practices and understandings larger than the sphere of science (1983, pp. 48-49). A major advantage of the turn toward interpretation, or hermeneutics, according to Bernstein, is that it lends to the object of communication studies—human beings—an ontological and epistemological importance unknown since before the rise of positive science in the 17th century and the spread of scientism in the 18th, 19th, and 20th centuries. Bernstein also noted and attempted to answer the chief objection to the hermeneutic turn, which is the prospect of endless interpretations and the abyss of relativism (for example, pp. 8-16, 223-231). Bernstein's book may be understood as

Originally published in 1985 in the *Quarterly Journal of Speech, 71*, 476-488. Revised and expanded by the author.

an attempt to move beyond the narrow space between the foundationalist rock and the relativist hard place. This is familiar territory to communication scholars, since finding the middle ground has been a preoccupation of philosophically-minded rhetoricians since antiquity.

Lonergan's enterprise complements both Bernstein's project and that of Hans-Georg Gadamer (1990), whose thought Bernstein productively extends. All three scholars are at pains to recover distinctions among fields of knowledge drawn clearly by Aristotle in the *Nicomachean Ethics,* but to avoid Aristotle's commitment to any one science (for example, mathematics) as a model of the truly apodictic or absolute. Like Bernstein and Gadamer, Lonergan also wishes to show that behind the positivist intimidation of the humanities is a failure to apprehend the field-dependent character of rationality. Lonergan's approach to this common aim, however, differs from Bernstein's in one important particular. While Lonergan opposes what Bernstein calls "objectivism," that is, the epistemological assumption that in knowing, a subject mirrors or correctly represents objective reality, Lonergan offers an alternative epistemology that gives the term "objectivity" a meaning immune from the usual critiques directed against objectivism. Lonergan, in effect, addresses what Bernstein calls "Cartesian anxiety" by revealing the cognitive intention behind Cartesianism and thereby showing how the anxiety can be changed to wonder. The key to Lonergan's approach to objectivity is his cognitional theory. But as Lonergan's rhetoric is a field-dependent extension of his cognitive theory, an examination of his rhetoric offers a natural beginning vantage point for surveying his project as a whole.

## 1. The Role of Rhetoric in Human Self-Understanding

Though Lonergan does not speak directly of rhetoric, it is not difficult to discover the implicit role of rhetoric in his works. Three themes will provide orientation to Lonergan's implied rhetoric: (1) his placing of the human person in the scene of action, (2) the relation of his theory of cognition to practical life, and (3) his understanding of the constitutive role of common sense and language in the lives of individuals and communities.

With Aristotle (1991), Vico (1968), Edmund Burke (1909), John Henry Newman (1903) and with Kenneth Burke (1945, 1950), Perelman (1969, 1982), Garver, (1987), Jonsen and Toulmin (1988), and Toulmin (1990)—indeed with what Ernesto Grassi (1980) has identified as the "humanist" tradition of rhetoric—Lonergan understands rhetoric as the science of human action. Rhetoric for Lonergan is not primarily a theory of persuasion but a specialization of human intelligence. In its ordinary practice and in most of its positive teachings, rhetoric is the cognitive capacity Aristotle described as finding in the individual case the available means of persuasion. While the proximate aim of rhetoric for Lonergan, as for Aristotle, is persuasion, Lonergan would, with Aristotle, place rhetoric within the larger scene of the quest for right order. We may appropriately describe Lonergan's rhetoric as a rhetoric of "common sense."

Lonergan's notion of common sense corresponds to that distinct type of intellection championed by Bernstein and Gadamer, to which Aristotle gave the name *"phronesis,"* which Newman called "the illative sense," and which Vico and Grassi celebrate under the term *"ingenium"* (Grassi, 1980, pp. 13-14). In keeping with the spirit of Italian humanism, as exemplified in the works of Petrarch, Salutati, Bruni, Valla, and Machiavelli (Seigel, 1968; Struever, 1970, 1992), the cognitional theory that informs Lonergan's notion of common sense understands human consciousness as spontaneously intelligent and rational. That is, presented with data, human consciousness does not merely respond with an involuntary twitch, nor does it merely recapitulate conventional associations; to the contrary, it takes the initiative and spontaneously asks questions: "what is it?" "how often?" "of what kind?" "from what cause?" and so on. When a person has an insight, consciousness shows itself to be rational as well as intelligent by spontaneously questioning its own productions as it asks further questions: "but is it so?" "always ?" "probably?" "am I just imagining it?" "is this really true, or would I just like to believe it?" and so on. Consonant with both the humanist rhetorical tradition and the anti-rhetorical Enlightenment tradition, Lonergan clearly distinguishes common sense from scientific or "theoretical" knowing. But just where Lonergan seems to recapitulate a conventional dichotomy, his thought takes a distinct turn, which underscores the unique vantage point his cognitional theory provides for understanding the epistemic root shared by rhetoric and science.

For Lonergan, theoretical or scientific knowing and common sense are alike in that both are concerned with the world mediated by meaning, as opposed to the world of sensory immediacy known to infants. Theoretical and common sense knowing are different not because one is intelligent and rational while the other is not, but because of the distinct field-dependent intentions that guide their equally intelligent and rational treatment of data. Lonergan affirms with Italian humanism that the peculiar task of common sense is to relate "things to ourselves," where the "thing" is not the object of scientific knowledge, either in the Aristotelian sense of universal and necessary truths, or even in the modern scientific sense of statistical probabilities, but the object of a human good as revealed through a practical task. Theoretical knowing, by contrast, relates "things to one another," where the "thing" is not an image known to sense and imagination, but a verified concept that, while it might have been generated from an image, moves beyond images and sense to discover—the "point" of classical geometry (a position without magnitude) or the "anti-matter" of modern physics. Parallel with theoretical knowing, whether Aristotelian or modern, common sense requires insight to solve its task. This involves intelligence and thus transcends the infant's world of immediacy to the world mediated by meaning known to every normal adult. The crucial distinction between theoretical and common sense knowing for Lonergan is not that one is certain while the other is merely probable (for modern science is not true but on the way to truth), not that one will yield eternal verities while the other yields shadows, but that common sense knowing does not systematically deduce premises from its insights, nor does it ground its conclusions in clear implicative structures. In Newman's terms, living thought "determines what science can not determine, the limit of converging probabilities and the reasons sufficient for a proof" (Newman, 1903, p. 360). In Grassi's terms:

> Ingenium grasps the relationship between things in a concrete situation in order to determine their meaning. This capacity has an "inventive" character, since it attains an insight without merely bringing out what is present in the premises as reason does in a logical derivation. (Grassi, 1980, p. 86)

Or, as Lonergan says of common sense:

> Such a procedure, clearly, is logical, if by "logical" you mean "intelligent and reasonable." With equal clearness, such a procedure is not logical, if by "logical" you mean conformity to a set of general rules valid in every instance of a defined range; for no set of general rules can keep pace with the resourcefulness of intelligence in its adaptations to the possibilities and exigencies of concrete tasks of self-communication. (1957/1992, p. 201)

Newman's "illative sense," Vico's "*ingenium*," and Lonergan's "common sense" are further alike in being anti-dualistic. Since both situate intelligence in the context of human action, what *ingenium* reveals is at once fact and value. As a solution to determining an appropriate course of action in a contingent situation, the fruit of *ingenium is* fact. As the revelation of a human good, the fruit of *ingenium is* value.

Of special relevance for contemporary rhetorical theory, Lonergan extends the same praxis-centered perspective to theoretical knowing. In place of Descartes' confrontational view of truth, whose root dichotomy between the "looker" and the "looked at" has historically led to idealism, materialism, and skepticism, Lonergan affirms the unity of consciousness in the diversity of its acts. The one mind is involved equally in a scene of action, whether it is mediating the exigences of theory (as in the periodical table of the elements), or of common sense (as in the rhetorical topics). Neither as a theorist nor as a person of common sense is a normal human adult ever called upon to address a world "already out there now real" in the truly unmediated sense of an infant's world of "blooming buzzing confusion." In common with Aristotle, Vico, Edmund Burke, John Henry Newman, Kenneth Burke, Perelman, Garver, and Jonsen and Toulmin, Lonergan's rhetoric of common sense is thus constitutive rather than persuasive, and epistemic rather than emotive. In contrast, Whately's rhetoric is persuasive rather than epistemic; Blair's, de Quincey's, and Nietzsche's are primarily aesthetic; and Campbell's is primarily psychological or emotive rather than epistemic.

In yet further contrast, postmodern rhetoric is unlike even earlier stylistic rhetorics for, lacking commitment to literary tradition, political or religious community, it is "sophistic" in the conventionally pejorative as opposed to the historical sense (Vickers, 1988; Toulmin, 1990; Olmsted, 1991; Jarratt, 1991; deRomilly, 1992). In common with Aristotle's teaching on the evidentiary value of "artistic" modes of proof, Lonergan's rhetoric aims at putting the audience in a frame of mind where they may intelligently grasp a potential good and reasonably affirm it as prudent or just in the particular case.

## 2. Cognitional Theory

The congruence between Lonergan's rhetoric and contemporary rhetorical theory can be underscored further by contrasting his cognitional theory with the "modern" rhetorical tradition and its cognitional theory. Modern rhetorical theory from Adam Smith (1983) through George Campbell (1988) built its theory of cognition (and hence of invention) upon the model of the natural sciences. For Smith, Campbell, and Reid (Grave, 1960; Olson, 1975), the model for the human sciences is the achievement of Newton. At the heart of this model is the human being as an instance of matter in motion, objectivity as thinking substance passively mirroring nature or extended substance, and knowing as looking. The position that knowing is a matter of a subject "in here" passively gazing at, or reflecting on an object "out there," Lonergan calls the "perceptualist" theory of cognition or "picture thinking." Starting ultimately with John Locke and proximately with Hume, modern rhetorical theory wedded itself to picture thinking and in contrast to both classical and contemporary rhetorical theory understood the human person not as an actor but as acted upon, not as a mover but as moved. In placing itself in what Lloyd F. Bitzer (1985) has recently called "a scene of truth," modern rhetoric has understood its task as involving two basic steps. First, the rhetor gets his or her facts straight (mirrors nature); second, he or she sets out to motivate the audience to believe the facts. The distinctly rhetorical aspect of this process is to make one's case so vivid that one's arguments will rival the force of sense perceptions and thus motivate belief. Argument, in the modern rhetorical tradition, is thus not understood as a matter of intellectual apprehension, but as a psychological process in which feeling is transferred from "sensation" to "ideas" through association. Lonergan refers to this perceptualist standpoint on human cognition as "the principle of the empty head" (1972, p. 204) and finds it common to behaviorism, positivism, and modern scientistic reductionism in general. The root error of perceptualism is not only the primacy it gives to the infant's world of sensory immediacy, but also its consequent inattention to both the adult world mediated by meaning and the active role of human consciousness in constituting that world. The epistemological consequences of perceptualism are readily apparent in the low cognitive status assigned to argument in modern rhetorical theory; argument for modern rhetorical theory, with the partial exception of Richard Whately (1963), does not involve "insight" or a distinctly intellectual "seeing." Argument is merely a means for generating vivacity.

In tying itself to a single unified and universal logic, which it shared with science and philosophy, but to which it contributed nothing of its own, modern rhetoric cut itself off from concern with the personal and social good that were characteristic of classical rhetorical theory. Plato's and Aristotle's concern for the individual and the public good, Cicero's concern for discussing the subjects that ought to be discussed, Vico's concern for rhetoric as constitutive of the common sense of the community, and Edmund Burke's concern that the politician be a philosopher in action have no place in modern rhetorical theory as found in Smith, Reid, Blair (1965), Campbell (1988), Whately (1963), and de Quincey (1967). Similarly, the topics have no place. Instead of the human world where men and women must ask and resolve dialectical questions, questions of definition, and questions of value, modern rhetoric starts from an astro-physical universe where a human "lively and glowing idea" is just another illustration of one billiard ball striking another. Finally, in modern rhetoric, style, like argument, is a psychological inducement to persuasion devoid of cognitive import. For Smith, Blair, and Campbell, a trope is more on the order of what 19th-century biology called a "tropism," rather than that peculiarly human and intellectual turning Paul Ricoeur (1977) discusses as "meta-phora," Vico as *"ingenium,"* and Lonergan as "insight." Modern rhetoric, in refusing to discriminate between the world of sensory immediacy and the world mediated by meaning and motivated by value, between a Newtonian science of motion and a properly human science of action, only comes to its "common sense" at the brink of a radical skepticism that knows neither the universe nor the human world. The failure of modern rhetoric to move beyond a phenomenalist cognitional base to an epistemology adequate to a genuine human science and its failure to measure up to the classical achievement in its theory of invention, arrangement, topics, and style give contemporary rhetoric its starting point and Lonergan a special relevance to contemporary rhetorical theory.

Lonergan and the humanist rhetorical tradition as exemplified by Petrarch, Salutati, Bruni, Valla, Machiavelli, and Vico ground their epistemological alternative to the anti-rhetorical rationalism of the Enlightenment in the heuristic precept that a human science must begin with human beings themselves and not sacrifice humans to some apodictic first truth. Modern rhetoric, as exemplified in Reid, Campbell, Blair, and Whately begins from the world of motion and ends by doubting even that. By contrast, Lonergan and the Italian humanists take as their starting point the actual world of practical human questions and limited specific concerns. The radically non-apodictic and praxis-centered epistemology implicit in Italian humanism is aptly summarized by the question posed by Lonergan's cognitional theory: "What is one doing when one is knowing?" When one reflects upon this question, one discovers the root motive of the topical system.

The topics (topoi) were literally "places" or "haunts" where material for argument could be found. Topical reason is well manifest in the "stasis" logic of forensic oratory that—far from dealing with "mere" form—posed the substantive questions necessary for a legal case to proceed (Dieter, 1959). What is the fact? Did the defendant steal the property of the plaintiff? What is the proper definition? Was the removal of the property theft? What is the value at issue? Was it a good thing that the item was removed? Who is to judge? Does this court have jurisdiction? The indeterminacy of a topic is its peculiar cognitive and heuristic virtue making it the humanistic counterpart in Walter Jost's words "of the exact concept, algorithm, or mathematical proof" (1989, p. 18). Because the topic can be adjusted to its object, topical reason can encompass ambiguity without being overwhelmed by it and can organize inquiry without prejudging the outcome (Jost, 1989, pp. 17-18; Olmsted, 1991). In Lonergan's account, when we set aside all apodictic certitudes and trust the dynamism of our own intelligent action, we discover a three-tiered cognitive structure that assembles itself through nine distinct operations. In his later work Lonergan expands "judgment" to include "deliberation"—thus indicating not only that we reflect on matters of fact, but that we deliberate on matters of value (Lonergan, 1980, p. 32).

The first level of cognition is experience, the second is intellect, and the third is judgment (see Figure 1.1, p. 10). On the first level, one finds the three operations of sensing, attending, and imagining. On level two, one finds the three operations of inquiry, insight, and formulation. On level three, one finds the three operations of reflection, determining the sufficiency of evidence, and judging. Beyond mere knowing, Lonergan posits a fourth level, of "will," which may or may not carry forward what intelligence has grasped and affirmed. The independence of will from knowing lends Lonergan's key notion of "self-appropriation" a double relevance for rhetorical theory: first, for the bridge it provides between theory and praxis; and second, for the implications it holds for an ethics of rhetoric. Parenthetically, despite Lonergan's anti-dualism, his notion of self-appropriation reveals his debt to the pioneering cognitional theory of Descartes. "Self-appropriation" is the Lonerganian correlate of the Cartesian "cogito."

Self-appropriation is a matter of first adverting to, then understanding, and finally affirming oneself as the performer of the nine operations of cognition listed above. To borrow a Marxist term, one might say self-appropriation is a matter of demystifying knowing, thereby revealing the active creativity of the knower. While knowing would consist in the correct performance of the operations of cognition, whether one adverted to them or

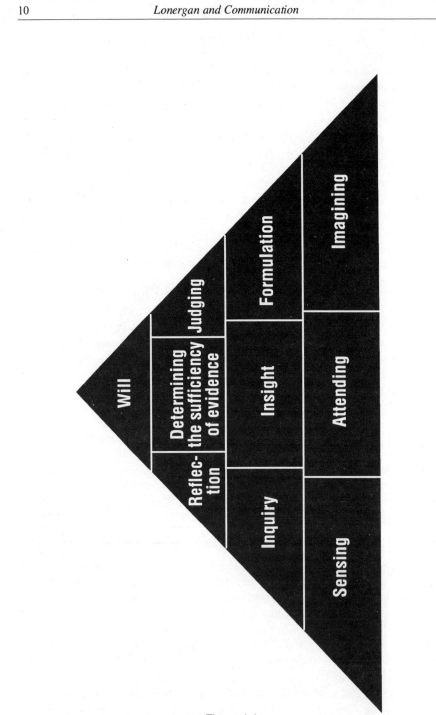

*Figure 1.1*

not, by adverting to them one may become aware of oneself as active, conscious, intelligent, reasonable, and responsible.

Self-appropriation challenges several assumptions about knowing. By encouraging one to note the immanent dynamism of one's efforts to understand and of how new questions and insights change one's understanding, self-appropriation challenges conceptualism's assumption that knowing is a matter of abstracting unchanging concepts from experience and placing them in eternally correct logical relations. By making one aware that inquiry, insight, conceiving, and judging are not simply more sophisticated sense perceptions, self-appropriation challenges the assumption that transcendence is a matter of getting outside a self "in here" to an independently existing world of things "out there." By making one aware of how one's self-understanding changes as one moves from an earlier horizon of questions to a later, larger horizon of still further questions, self-appropriation challenges the subjectivist tenet that one is or already has a "self." Through inquiry and through reflection on one's own practice as an inquirer, one realizes the "self" as an intelligent center of dynamic operations open to "being"—the fuller range of questions proportionate to one's capacity to ask, inquire, and proximately resolve. By making one aware of the immanent norms that propel inquiry from one question to another and at last constrain one to entertain only a critically determined range of answers, self-appropriation challenges epistemological subjectivism or anarchy—that in knowing "anything goes." Finally, for Lonergan, the self—at least the self responsive to the desire to know—is not merely a completed "thing" but a dynamic activity of consciousness yet in process. Lonergan's sense of the "self" as the site of a perpetual epiphany of knowing and repentance—of movement toward a more adequate horizon and renunciation of an inadequate one—gives him significant community with his contemporary philosopher of consciousness, Eric Voegelin. One of the most perceptive readers of both these thinkers, Eugene Webb, fruitfully explores the tension in Lonergan between his view of the self as the site where proportionate being is illuminated—and his concern to prove that the self "exists" as a "thing" in a world of things (Webb, 1988, pp. 84-90).

Self-appropriation establishes a non-arbitrary foundation for that union of ethics and aesthetics Alfred North Whitehead regarded as the gift of specialization to culture and named "the ultimate morality of mind" (1929, p. 24). Such a cognitionally based ethics is universal, for, as Aristotle observed, "All men by nature desire to know" *(Metaphysics,* Book A. (1), 980a). Cognitional ethics is also non-elitist for every normal person specializes in some type of "common sense" and hence asks the questions the topics systematize and makes the kinds of judgments the topics anticipate. Thus, parallel to the *Nicomachean Ethics,* where Aristotle sketches the difficult road toward becoming an ethically responsible person, and parallel to Kenneth Burke's dramatism, where no person can escape the drama of his or her own living, the point of Lonergan's self-appropriation is to make one aware of how one is constantly involved in a movement toward, or a flight from, a fuller self. By urging individuals to notice, understand, and affirm themselves as the unity that endures throughout the operations of knowing and in response to whose intelligent will the operations of cognition are called forth and executed, Lonergan's self-appropriation provides a contemporary and democratic expression of Aristotle's ideal of the *spoudaios* or mature person.

Highlighting the importance of self-appropriation, Lonergan observes that "the ultimate basis of our knowing is not necessity but contingent fact, and the fact is established not prior to our engagement in knowing, but simultaneously with it" (1957/1992, p. 356). This succinct statement contains the germ of a humanist epistemology that is an alternative not only to Descartes, Locke, and Hume, but also to a thinker whose perceptualist epistemology made "objectivism" and "relativism" our dominant philosophic options—Immanuel Kant.

As Lonergan's cognitional theory resonates with the topics in its praxis-centered question, "What is one doing when one is knowing?" so his epistemology accents the union of theory and praxis in its further question, "Why is doing that knowing?" Though I cannot here give a full rendering of the rhetorical epistemology Lonergan thematizes, the following summation, based on Giovanni Sala's meticulous contrast between Kant and Lonergan (reported in Robert M. Doran, 1979b, pp. 193-210), should provide rhetoricians with an indication of the formal alternative to materialism and idealism latent in their own tradition.

For Kant, knowledge of reality—of what truly is—comes only through sense experience. The notions of cause and effect, space and time, the universal and the necessary (the latter being ideals of classical though not of modern science) are modes of the mind's operation and tell us nothing about the *Ding an sich*—the thing in itself. For Kant, the operations of cognition add no independently real dimension to the final and complete object of knowledge. Thus in Kant's understanding, the mind may know something when it reaches a judgment, but its knowledge is merely sensual, phenomenal: The "thing itself" is never directly known.

For Lonergan, by contrast, Kant's sensory experience is pure presentation and yields neither knowledge of the "what" nor of the "is." If one is to find "what" is represented and then resolve whether this "what" truly "is," one must add to sense the non-sensory contributions of intelligence and judgment. Thus, the short answer to Lonergan's epistemological question, "Why is doing that knowing?" is that knowing is not exclusively sensory, but is a three-part process in which experience is the first part and provides data; intelligence is the second part and adds intelligibility to data; and judgment is the third part and affirms or denies reality to the intelligibility that insight (intelligence) discovered. For Lonergan, "one must consider the entire structure of knowledge in order to grasp how a process that is clearly also empirical can have contents and qualifications that are not empirical" (Sala quoted in Doran, 1979b, p. 195). In place of Kant's various *a priori* categories, Lonergan has the pure *a priori* intention of consciousness itself that is not any particular category, but is the ground of every category.

Lonergan's action-centered epistemology offers a cogent answer to the rhetorical problem of "objectivity." Aristotle, of course, offered the simplest criterion in his insistence that the mark of the educated person was not to ask for greater proof than a thing admitted of. Hence, one should not settle for probabilities in a demonstrative science (mathematics), and one should not ask for more than probabilities from a non-demonstrative science (rhetoric). While Lonergan was apparently not aware of Aristotle's treatment of probabilities in connection with rhetoric, he builds upon Aristotle's foundation, but without the Aristotelian assumption (mistaken in light of contemporary science) that there truly is an apodictic science. (Contemporary science examines the probable. Thus, while science is not civic discourse, its concern for the probable relates it to rhetoric in a way not possible for Aristotle.) Objectivity for Lonergan is not a simple notion as in Kant's perceptualist assumption that sense is the only portal to the real and that the operations of cognition never get "outside" the mind. For Lonergan, "objectivity" is a compound notion involving three distinct kinds of objectivity: (1) the objectivity of experience in attending to sensory data, (2) the objectivity of intelligence in providing an intelligible explanation of the data, and (3) the objectivity of judgment in neither offering judgment on the basis of insufficient reasons, nor refusing it when the particular relevant criteria for sufficiency are satisfied.

One may characterize Lonergan's theory of knowing as an epistemological radicalization of hermeneutics. Like the humanist tradition of rhetoric, Lonergan starts by affirming knowledge as a fact and finding the root of knowledge in the dynamic cognitional operations of the knower. Lonergan has exchanged Descartes', Locke's, and Kant's unanswerable ontological-epistemological question of how one gets outside the self to the world, for Gadamer's answerable hermeneutical question of how one transcends from one horizon of interpretation to another: Lonergan's answer, made profound by his cognitional counter to perceptualism, is the hermeneutical commonplace that one gets from one horizon to another (including from the horizons of experience to intelligence and from intelligence to judgment) by asking further questions. Asking and answering questions in a rigorous way (within the relevant field constraints of theory or common sense) is what both Lonergan and Gadamer mean by objectivity. (For further consideration of Lonergan and Gadamer, see chapter 10 by Hugo A. Meynell.)

While Lonergan's thought is markedly congruent with the humanist tradition and much contemporary rhetorical theory in many ways, it is also different. First, unlike the humanist tradition of Valla, Nizolio, and Melanchthon (Vickers, 1988, pp. 178-196) and unlike some contemporary rhetorical humanists such as Fisher (1987, pp. 47-49, 62-78) or in a different vein such as Gross (1990, pp. 48-53), Lonergan has no desire to subordinate theoretical knowing to narrative (Fisher) or science to rhetoric (Gross); and second, while he shares the prevalent contemporary suspicion of traditional metaphysics, he also provides an alternative metaphysics of his own.

The reasons why Lonergan has no polemic against theoretical knowing we have already rehearsed. For Lonergan, common sense and theoretical knowing each has a cognitive domain, and each is sovereign within it. In Lonergan's view, the wise person will pursue and value both, for one needs theoretical knowing to grasp the universal and common sense to master the particular (1957/1992, pp. 202-203). As in Books III and IV of Aristotle's *Nicomachean Ethics,* science and common sense, rhetoric and philosophy, in Lonergan's view, are understood as both complementary and distinct. No cognitional pride of place is given to either, and no "transcendence" of the rhetorical is envisaged for humanity in some mythical positivist stage when science will remove all need for concrete particular insights into concrete particular situations.

The reason Lonergan does not share the contemporary animus against metaphysics is his conviction that humanity has no innate capacity for sustained development. The problem is not with humanity's essential nature, which is both free and intelligent, but with its effective freedom, which is historically constrained and empirically characterized by a mixture of intelligence and stupidity. The point of Lonergan's metaphysics is to give essential human nature a workable lever against history's effective constraints. Lonergan's metaphysics takes its immediate justification from the inherent blindness in each kind of human knowing. Whenever common sense or theory pretends to omnicompetence—which each is prone to do—we have a compound case of what Whitehead called "the Fallacy of Misplaced Concreteness" (1926, pp. 52, 53). If the original fallacy results from the presumptuousness of the theorist in insisting that reality beyond his or her specialty must conform to the theoretical objects known within it, the same fallacy is committed by common sense in presuming to dispense with theoretical reflection altogether. If we call the one the "Philosopher's Fallacy" and the other the "People's Fallacy," we have "the fallacies of misplaced concreteness," and we may say that together they are two sides of the same counterfeit cognitional coin. As Whitehead has already exposed the Philosopher's Fallacy, a brief comment on the People's Fallacy will underscore the resources Lonergan's metaphysics would deploy to extend essential human freedom against history's effective limits.

Wherever reflection has no adequate public forum, as today in the former Yugoslavia and in Somalia, we have what Lonergan calls "the social surd." Though reflection would show that each new round of blood letting serves only to deepen the irrationality of the situation, the bias of common sense discourages reflection: Pure common sense—just like pure theoretical knowing—carries no innate disposition to acknowledge its limits. As Lonergan observes, "Besides the progressive accumulation of related insights, there is the cumulative effect of refusing insights" (1957/1992, p. 242). Unless informed by reflection, a rhetoric grounded only on common sense will invite on different grounds the familiar epithet "mere."

Mediating the dialectical tension between theoretical and common sense knowing is the permanent function of metaphysics in Lonergan's thought. The specific resources at the disposal of metaphysics for the pursuit of its task are the "transcendental precepts" Lonergan finds implicit in the immanent dynamism of human cognition as it spontaneously goes from sensory attentiveness to insight, from insight to judgment, and from judgment to action: "Be Attentive, Be Intelligent, Be Reasonable, Be Responsible, Be Loving, develop and, if necessary, change" (Tracy, 1970, p. 4). By using these transcendental precepts as root topoi, a rhetoric based on Lonergan's thought would generate strategies for commending intelligence and reasonableness as normative guides for men and women as they struggle in uncertainty to make sense of themselves and their world.

The mission of metaphysics to expand humankind's essential freedom and thus sustain human development is rendered problematic by what Lonergan calls the "polymorphism" of the human mind (1957/1992, pp. 410-412). By "polymorphism" Lonergan means that the mind has many "patterns of experience." Among these patterns are the aesthetic, where beauty or delight are enjoyed for their own sakes; the egoistic, where reality is settled by autobiography; the dramatic, which corresponds exactly to what Kenneth Burke understands by dramatism; and the intellectual, which is governed—to the extent one is in it—by the desire to know (Lonergan, 1957/1992, pp. 415-421). Lonergan's notion of human experience as a unity in a plurality of patterns underscores the importance of the task he assigns to a metaphysically informed rhetoric. As our examination of self-appropriation illustrated, beyond knowledge, whether of theory or of common sense, is will. While theoretical knowing takes one beyond images to concepts, sensitive living continually demands images to guide the life of practical action and wisdom. Thus, Lonergan observes that even if strict scientific knowledge were obtained in all domains where it is possible, "dynamic images [would still be needed to] make sensible to human sensitivity, what human intelligence reaches for or grasps" (1957/1992, p. 571).

Lonergan formally defines metaphysics as "the integral heuristic structure of proportionate being" (1957/1992, pp. 415-421). While this definition requires some unpacking, it can be said at once that "metaphysics," in Lonergan's sense, is the heuristic praxis of work-a-day science, or common sense thematized and affirmed. Lonergan styles metaphysics as an "integral heuristic structure" because what one knows at the outset of an investigation is not what one discovers at the end of it. The first thing to be known about knowing is that it is an open process. What one starts with is a question, an "x," a "known unknown." To advance investigation, one then works out the properties of the unknown. Whether one's concern is with natural or human science, if one is to know, one must always raise further questions if one is to reach further resolutions. As even this brief account illustrates, Lonergan's notion of metaphysics as "integral" to knowing makes it the very opposite of something imposed upon knowing from the outside. To repeat, the rationale for Lonergan's metaphysics is the practical task of extending essential human freedom by combating the biases of theory and common sense that effectively limit it. We may say that metaphysics is to Lonergan what "perspective by incongruity" is to Kenneth Burke: The function of both is to keep open the possible further questions that the "trained incapacity" of theory and common sense would refuse to ask unless *ingenium* were somehow allowed to defeat mere reasoning.

Second, metaphysics is "heuristic" because its primary aim is to make explicit what is known about the process, as opposed to the results of discovery—a reversal of the usual order of *an sit* first, then knowledge (Lonergan, 1957/1992, pp. 421-427). For Lonergan, the term "proportionate being" refers to the intended range of an act of judgment: what Lonergan calls "grasping the unconditioned" (1957/1992, pp. 296-303, 305-312). To make a secure judgment, in Lonergan's theory, does not require certainty about everything, as it does for Kant, but only that one grasp the limiting conditions surrounding the particular in question. Thus, a judgment for Lonergan is a limited and specific commitment, as it is for modern science and as it always has been for rhetoric. To judge, "The defendant is guilty as charged," requires "a conditioned" notion of the defendant, who, not necessarily, but merely in fact, happens to have fulfilled the conditions prescribed by the charge. Another way of putting it is to say that what is intended by an act of judgment is "the real," or "being." If "the real" or "being" were not intended by judgment, cognition would end with insight or conception. But we commonly observe of insights and their formulation in concepts that "bright ideas are a dime a dozen." The inherent dynamism of human cognition, when not blocked by violence, indifference, or desire (other than the desire to know), drives past plausible explanations to resolve whether the explanations offered by insight and conception are true. Presumably the reader is engaged in this very activity in reading this essay. "But," one might object, "'being' is all there is to be known about everything, and acts of understanding in principle are limited and particular; hence we cannot know 'being.'" Lonergan would agree with the first part of this response in that the intention behind our questions is an unrestricted desire to know everything about everything, but he would urge that the conclusion is overly broad. Since knowledge is a fact and is limited, it is appropriate to characterize knowledge as knowledge of "proportionate being" (Lonergan, 1957/1992, pp. 470-476).

Four additional comments are in order concerning Lonergan's metaphysics. First, Lonergan's metaphysics is neither idealistic nor materialistic. It is not idealistic because it has no prior commitment to affirming that ultimate reality is an "idea." By the same token, neither has Lonergan any prior commitment to affirming that everything is "matter." All Lonergan is committed to affirming is that the real is established in particular by the relevant specialized sciences and by common sense and that each specialization of knowledge presents an object whose claim to being real can only be verified through the cognitional acts through which the object is rendered. If ultimate reality turned out to be Hegel's "absolute," no adjustment would be required in Lonergan's standpoint, nor would any be required if reality turned out to be "matter." Any conclusion that was correctly drawn would employ the cognitive operations Lonergan has outlined, so Lonergan has no prior commitment for or against any particular result. Even as cognitional process is open toward the "known unknown" to be given in correct judgment, so Lonergan's view of ultimate reality is equally open; the real is whatever is intelligently grasped and rationally affirmed in correct judgment. Lonergan has described his position as "an intelligent and reasonable realism between which and materialism the half-way house is idealism" (1957/1992, p. 22).

Second, unlike metaphysics as conventionally understood, Lonergan's metaphysics allows no appeal to authority, save the authority of the cognitional process as manifest in its successful operation (hence the rationale for his tireless use of scientific examples), and no deductions from first principles claimed to be self-evident.

Third, and surely unique among approaches to metaphysics, Lonergan's metaphysics is verifiable. This claim is neither surprising nor outrageous if one bears in mind what metaphysics is for Lonergan. Metaphysics responds to the question "What is known when one is doing that?" by correctly performing the nine operations listed above. If one asks, "But what are the criteria of 'correctness'?" one would be referred to the state of the art procedures in the field in which one is interested in conducting an inquiry. If one objected, "But these procedures themselves need correction," Lonergan would probably make two further suggestions: First, one would be invited to formulate more adequate procedures, and, second, one would be invited to heed, understand, and affirm what one was doing in the course of doing that. If one countered, "But occasionally I am mistaken myself," Lonergan would again recommend attention to the immanent norms of correctness manifest in one's own recognition of being mistaken. He would probably further point out that dispensing with the notion of correctness would be dispensing with the notion of rational inquiry and that if one denied the notion of correctness on principle, one would effectively defeat the desire to know implicit in one's own questions.

In brief, according to Lonergan, what one intends in asking a question and what one knows in reaching a correct judgment—a judgment that satisfies the relevant questions—is "being," apart from which there is nothing. The warrant for regarding what is known in a correct judgment as real is human intentionality; what we intend in our questions and by our correct judgments is not a fiction but reality, not a story but a true story. Since for Lonergan reality is intelligible, either through the correct judgments we can make now, or through the anticipated correct judgments that we could make at some future date if the horizon of inquiry remains open, metaphysics, as "the integral heuristic structure of proportionate being," is an anti-obscurantist principle. Lonergan's metaphysics thus performs two functions: On the one hand, by affirming that what we know when we are knowing correctly is reality or being, Lonergan's metaphysics provides ontological grounding for a dynamic culture committed to nurturing the desire to know in politics, the natural sciences, art, religion, and the human sciences; on the other, by insisting that metaphysics be verifiable, he transforms metaphysics from something sterile and unworldly to an imperative for rapproachment between theory and praxis—between our interpretations of knowing and the norms immanent in our cognitional acts (1957/1992, pp. 549, 569, 661).

Fourth, while Lonergan does not discuss satire or humor in connection with metaphysics, it is appropriate to do so because if metaphysics is "the integral heuristic structure of proportionate being," satire and humor function in his project as the corrective therapies that keep this heuristic structure open.

A deep problem with the desire to know, as Lonergan has sketched it, is that this desire in the first place is merely a human potential and in the second, its operation in most of us is, at best, episodic. If, following Lonergan, we may conceive our distinctly human capacity for understanding as the apex of a cognitive pyramid, the base of which is matter or chemistry, followed by biology, sensitive psychology and then intellection, reflective judgment, and will (see Figure 1.1, p. 10), the pyramid is "ruled" neither from the top down nor from the bottom up. Lonergan underscores that to be human is to live in a sensitive manifold in which diverse and competing cognitive desires succeed one another and intermingle in consciousness. As human consciousness is "polymorphic" and is sensitive, practical, aesthetic, ethical, and intellectual in various degrees, or in succession, the desire to know is but one desire among many.

The peculiar task of satire and humor in Lonergan's view of cognition is to save consciousness for intelligence. Lonergan develops his discussion of satire and humor by reference to Kierkegaard (1957/1992, pp. 647-649). Kierkegaard distinguished an aesthetic, an ethical, and a religious mode of consciousness. According to Kierkegaard, one moves from one of these modes of life and understanding to the next less by argument than by acts of recognition that strike one in the way one is struck by a joke. Satire, by forcing one to acknowledge the self-centeredness of merely aesthetic consciousness, opens one to the life of ethical seriousness. Humor, in which one is made sensible of the sanctimoniousness inherent in one's own ethical striving, leads to a recognition of one's limits and thus, as if by grace, to religion (see Figure 1.2).

One way of depicting this process is to think of cognition as a parliamentary democracy. The parliamentary image recommends itself for it portrays accurately both the hierarchical character of consciousness and the way all the "constituencies" of cognition are represented in deliberation. The psychic "government" of an individual in this schema is a coalition with a perpetually unstable majority. The coalition may be shakier in some persons than in others, but in almost everyone reflective action is easily derailed by the urgencies of the moment, by a possession of power, or by idiosyncratic preferences hardened into patterns of unreflective routine. Our earlier discussion of "the fallacies of misplaced concreteness" underscores two different temptations by which the coalition government of consciousness may go wrong. By capitulating to the demands of common sense a person's psychic "government" could refuse to recognize the legitimate demands of theory and the same could happen if the individual were to disregard the just demands of prudence in deference to a pet theoretic abstraction. Satire and humor perform their function as Members of Parliament representing "the integral heuristic structure of proportionate being" by bursting in upon thought like hecklers in parliamentary debate. Though they may be back benchers and out of power (and even under the best of circumstances are too politically unreliable for any government right, left, or center to want in a cabinet)—they draw attention to what has been omitted, overlooked, or suppressed. By putting policy in a different and unwanted light, they may provide either mere interruption or may bring the house to its senses. In the parliament of consciousness, their services may force a change in policy, a shuffling of the cabinet, or, in cases of conversion or nervous breakdown, a dissolution of the old government and a new election.

As our illustration suggests, Lonergan sees satire and humor as having a profound significance in the daily politics of the examined life, for both are tacit allies of the desire to know. If the claims of the desire to know are ignored by the routines of life, the caustic opinions of workmates, the car-

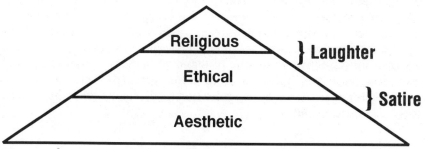

*Figure 1.2*

toons on the editorial pages, the caricatures in popular films, and even the sitcoms on evening television allow satire to push the claims of reason right back on to the agenda of consciousness. Where discretion fears to tread, satire rushes in—or where reflection has been too thoroughly intimidated to show its face, it will wear the mask of the wise fool. Through laughter, reason bursts upon human consciousness not enthymematically, through a shared premise, but empathically, through a shared humanity. As Lonergan puts it, "[humor] occurs with apparent purposelessness, and that too is highly important for, if men are afraid to think, they may not be afraid to laugh" (1957/1992, p. 649). Or again, "Yet proofless, purposeless laughter can dissolve honored pretense; it can disrupt conventional humbug; it can disillusion man of his most cherished illusions, for it is in league with the detached, disinterested, unrestricted desire to know" (1957/1992, p. 649).

Satire and humor keep the integral heuristic structure of proportionate being open to reality by addressing respectively the "objective" and the "subjective" poles of consciousness. Satire with "cool objectivity" laughs at and breaks in upon consciousness from without. By depicting the contemporary face of the flight from understanding, satire sets the stage for an about face—within the individual, within society, or within both. Humor breaks forth within consciousness as a kind of moral insight for it laughs with rather than at and enables an individual to accept inevitable limitations without surrendering principle. Or, one might say, humor enables us to have principles without the principles having us. As Lonergan puts it:

> humor keeps [principle] in contact with human limitations and human infirmity. It listens with sincere respect to the Stoic description of the Wise Man, and then requests an introduction....It questions neither aspirations nor ideals nor high seriousness...but it refuses to calculate without men as they are, without me as I am. For if satire becomes red with indignation, humor blushes with humility. (1957/1992, p. 649)

Satire, in short, forces reason on us by ambush—as in a surprise party—where we may be surprised by joy and where laughter may provoke thought as well as tears. Humor nudges or awakens reason from within—the way an old friend or prudent advisor may counsel us to persevere or to recognize when enough is enough.

In a project in which the gates of cognition—indeed of metaphysics—are guarded by hecklers, and, as it were, where every court appointed philosopher cannot set forth in public without an accompanying court appointed fool, we are entering a realm of thought where the legitimate epistemic claims of rhetoric are more than secure. What we have in Lonergan is a perspective on the life of the mind that is full rounded as well as robust and in which rhetoric, even in the seemingly "merest" forms of satire and humor, is the precondition for intellectual rigor, true seriousness, and reason itself.

## 3. Conclusion

I began by observing that *Insight* is a demanding work by a major Catholic thinker. These two points are connected. One way of characterizing *Insight* is to say that it is a fundamental rethinking of the interrelated projects Aquinas set for himself in the *Summa theologiae* and *Summa contra Gentiles*. In an occasional address, Lonergan noted that the flight from modern culture characteristic of the Church since the 17th century has put it out of touch with its own essential genius—its ability to penetrate the surrounding culture with its own forms of thought (1974a, p. 44). If the legacy of Aquinas is manifest in the tone and exposition of *Insight*, the spirit of that eminently rhetorical and humanistic thinker, John Henry Newman, provided Lonergan his specific inspiration. Newman's legacy can be seen in Lonergan's starting point—the actual operations of the human mind as manifest in the achievements of theory as well as of common sense—the centrality for both thinkers of judgment and the character of knowledge for both as a personal achievement of the whole individual (Lonergan, 1980, pp. 34-35; Worgul, 1977, pp. 317-332). If I understand the subtext of *Insight,* it is an attempt to revolutionize Catholic thought and at the same time make it a dynamic cultural force. Lonergan's radical endeavor to use the epistemological insights of Newman to restate Aquinas, purged of essentialism, and Descartes, purged of perceptualism, has implications beyond Catholic philosophy; for his project fundamentally alters the terms of the dialogue between the rhetorical tradition and the modern world.

From the standpoint of Lonergan's analysis, the ill repute of rhetoric in the modern epoch is only partially a function of foundationalism as described by Bernstein. More radically, it is a function of the perceptualist paradigm that equated knowing with looking. Once mathematics secured cognitional pride of place via the triumph of Newton and the enduring prestige of Descartes, scientism became a dominant motif, and rhetoric and religion together began their decline to the low estate from which Vico and Newman commenced the restoration of the one and Pascal, Kierkegaard, and Newman, the restoration of the other. If we survey the history of rhetorical theory from Peter Ramus to Kenneth Burke, Vico and Newman stand virtually alone as a magnificent exceptions to the prevailing perceptualist epistemology (concerning Ramus, see chapter 2 by Thomas J. Farrell). Vico's *verum factum* principle marks the first modern attempt to make rhetoric a constitutive human science rather than a theory of style, a branch of information theory, or strictly a study of persuasion. Newman's extension of Aristotle's *phronesis* to the specific rationality of faith at once broke the hold of scientism on apologetics—particularly in England—and reclaimed practical life in all its breadth and depth for intelligence. Indeed, Vico and Newman alike provide a natural bridge to Lonergan whose project may be arguably stated as an extension of Vico and Newman's affirmation of the constitutive power of the mind to the object of scientific thought itself. Lonergan's congruence with Vico and Newman and the hermeneutic cast of his cognitional theory place him in dialogue with the most exciting developments in contemporary rhetorical theory. If Lonergan has achieved what he has claimed—to have freed objectivity from the perceptualist theory of knowledge—he has accomplished what Bernstein holds no foundationalist philosophy can do. He has provided a radical alternative to the horizon in which relativism and objectivism have dominated our philosophic options.

# 2

## Writing, the Writer, and Lonergan: Authenticity and Intersubjectivity

### *Thomas J. Farrell*

In a recent publication I lamented the lack of reflection on the intellectual processes involved in writing, and I suggested that not only writing teachers, but also writers of all kinds need to see the importance of those intellectual processes (Farrell, 1992b). The work of Bernard Lonergan can help us reflect on the intellectual processes involved in writing and thereby enable us to become more self-conscious as writers.

In chapter 1 John Angus Campbell has used the image of a parliament to characterize how a person's consciousness can function. This is a strikingly apt image for how a writer's consciousness should function because it is an image that builds in a respect for the processes of debate and deliberation, at least if we imagine a parliament at its functional best. When a person is writing from sources and the writing involves interpreting material and taking a stand that is genuinely debatable, then the writer should go through intellectual processes of pro and con debating, just as a parliament does. Pro and con debating at its best can keep a legislative body from taking actions that are not thought through carefully. Similarly, such debating can enable writers to think through carefully the matters they are writing about. In short, it can help them form reasonable judgments, as Lonergan would put it. Indeed, once we recognize that each person's subjectivity is best understood as his or her intersubjectivity, then we can see that the image of a parliament is a more appropriate image of the writer and the writing process than the still prevalent Romantic image of the writer and writing as a solitary and oppositionless process.

Unfortunately, the Romantic image decried by Linda Brodkey (1987) still survives today, even among mature writers. In the United States people begin to assimilate the Romantic image in high school literature classes. When they are then assigned to write papers from sources, whether in high school or in college or at work, they are not presented with an adequate alternative image. Writers who have assimilated the Romantic image un-self-consciously tend to see themselves as solitary figures expressing them-selves as though they were simply broadcasting their views for others to hear, not as though they were debating with someone and were expected to actually engage the issues. They do not see themselves as debaters who are expected to know not only what they wish to express, but also what the opposition might say so that the issue between them might adequately be joined.

Lonergan's work suggests considerations that are needed to round out and complete the deficient Romantic image, and the image of a parliament at its best, albeit a parliament within the writer, calls to mind structures and procedures that are central to Lonergan's concerns. In this chapter, I exam-ine the cognitive processes discussed by Lonergan that are involved in dif-ferent kinds of writing, the nature of authenticity according to Lonergan, and the role of intersubjectivity in writing from sources. The argument de-veloped in this chapter begins with a brief overview of Lonergan's thought, followed by a more detailed discussion of how writing from sources is inter-subjective. The subsequent sections cover the different aspects of the per-son involved in different kinds of writing, Lonergan's account of how authenticity emerges, a lengthy discussion of his self-affirming precept to Be Reasonable in light of the practice in classical rhetoric of refutation, and a brief conclusion. I show that Lonergan's work provides new grounds for a positive reappraisal of the classical tradition of rhetoric, suggesting how it can be useful for contemporary writers to learn. Thus this essay offers a needed corrective to C. H. Knoblauch and Lillian Bannon's (1984) cavalier denigration of the classical tradition of rhetoric.

## 1. Overview of Lonergan's Thought

Lonergan maintains that the processes involved in following the transcendental precepts with respect to the empirical, the intelligent, and the rational levels of consciousness are essential to all human inquiry. If he is correct, then these same intellectual processes are involved in various forms of writing. In short, writing involves the processes essential to all human inquiry. Moreover, the steps in the generalized empirical method formulated by Lonergan can be aligned with the steps prescribed in the classical tradition for an oration in de-liberative rhetoric. Even though Lonergan himself did not explicitly advert to this correspondence, his work enables us to see greater potential in the standard steps of classical rhetoric than Knoblauch and Bannon have seen, and calls attention to a needed corrective to the actual practice of rhetoric in classical Athens, where objectivity was rarely achieved (Ober, 1989, p. 151). Objectiv-ity is certainly a valid aim according to Lonergan, and his work indicates that some of the elements that were standard features of classical rhetoric can con-tribute to the development of objectivity.

Lonergan's work is admittedly abstract, and people need to learn to be extremely reflective to follow the transcendental or self-affirming precepts he has formulated. But if writers are willing to develop the reflectiveness involved in following those precepts, then they will begin to experience the kind of self-appropriation that enabled Plato to leave the cave he described in the *Republic*. Following Lonergan's precepts is designed to engender such reflectiveness, which involves a certain amount of abstractness. If writers are not willing to develop the requisite abstractness, then they will remain "in the cave" and use their intellectual processes only unreflectively.

Intersubjectivity is a topic that Lonergan mentions repeatedly in his most seminal works, *Insight: A Study of Human Understanding* (1957/1992, see the Index) and *Method in Theology* (1972, see the Index). As he sees the situation, human subjectivity is intersubjective. Taking hints from Lonergan and Campbell, I suggest that advanced writing is intersubjective, because writers draw on meanings and values they have received from others. I focus on mature or experienced writers in this essay to avoid the objection that basic writers and writers in freshman composition are just being initiated into the processes discussed here. The points developed in this chapter are applicable *mutatis mutandis* to writers in freshman composition and basic writing. But I wish to focus on writers who have already been initiated to academic and professional writing and who are looking for ways to adjust themselves to the processes involved in writing from sources, as distinct from engaging in writing that is simply personal expression or creative writing. The things I say in this chapter should be pertinent to all writing from sources.

My claim is that writing from sources is intersubjective, because the writers draw on the thought of other authors in constructing their arguments. They thereby develop their own subjectivity as they proceed to deepen their understanding of the issues they are investigating. As a parliamentary debate might proceed to a greater and more complex treatment of the issues at hand before a resolution of the debate is reached, so too their understanding of the issues grows, and their intersubjectivity grows proportionately.[1]

---

[1] Somebody might respond, "Who would have thought otherwise?" The answer is, "To the degree that my claims are true, they should be obvious." The point of articulating the obvious is to make us more aware of the processes involved. The people in the cave described by Plato are not reflectively aware of what is going on. Reflective awareness is essential to what Lonergan refers to as self- appropriation, which is tantamount to leaving the cave described by Plato and seeing clearly in the light of day. So greater awareness of the intellectual processes involved in writing from sources is what this chapter aims to promote. Greater awareness should enable us to see the potential importance of well-informed writing instruction.

## 2. Writing as Intersubjective

The image of intersubjectivity needs to be appropriated and adapted to the context of writing from sources, because sociological and literary uses of intersubjectivity are not attuned to the situation of the expository writer. George Herbert Mead (1934) pioneered the study of the social construction of the self, which Peter L. Berger and Thomas Luckmann (1966) later popularized. But the sociological study of symbolic interaction largely ignores what Lev S. Vygotsky and A. N. Sokolov call "inner speech," the conversation, so to speak, that people carry on within themselves after they have learned speech from others. In literary criticism Mikhail Bakhtin has called attention to the multi-voiced dimension of each literary writer's consciousness. Wayne C. Booth has handily summarized the points of Bakhtin's *The Dialogic Imagination* (1981) that are pertinent for our present treatment of intersubjectivity:

> We come into consciousness speaking a language already permeated with many voices—a social, not a private language. From the beginning, we are "polyglot," already in process of mastering a variety of social dialects derived from parents, clan, class, religion, country. We grow in consciousness by taking in more voices as "authoritatively persuasive" and then by learning which to accept as "internally persuasive." Finally we achieve, if we are lucky, a kind of individuality, but it is never a private or autonomous individuality [but one that] respects the fact that each of us is a "we." (1984, p. xxi)

Bakhtin's view of the literary writer as multi-voiced echoes the Homeric view of the poet as a person of many voices.

While this has now become an accepted view of literary writers, it needs to be adapted to apply to expository writers who are writing from sources. Since the literary view implicitly calls attention to human intersubjectivity, it can be extended to writing from sources to help expository writers see their use of different resources in constructing arguments as orchestrating a polyphony of voices/sources. Mary J. Carruthers' (1990) detailed study of the composition or mental construction of thought in ancient and medieval times shows that "voices" (*voces*) of established authors were used extensively. In consequence, all forms of composition prior to Peter Ramus (1515-1572) were radically dialogic and debate-oriented, as Carruthers has shown, compared to the oppositionless, solitary scene of writing introduced by Ramism and later heightened by Romanticism.

As Carruthers' study indicates, the image of writing as intersubjectivity is a rhetorical image because it captures some features long associated with the practice of rhetoric in the Western world, features that Lonergan apparently knew nothing about. Furthermore, the image of writing as intersubjective opens the way for writers to develop authentic subjectivity as Lonergan sees it, which goes beyond the personal expression fostered by concerns with "authentic voice" in student writing (cf. Faigley, 1989). But Lonergan's treatment of authenticity involves a different aspect of the human person than what is involved in the personal expression of so-called "authentic voice," and so I draw on other authors to develop a vocabulary for discussing the different dimensions of the human person, the *I*, the *me*, and the *self*.

In his later writings Lonergan identified the fourth and fifth *self*-affirming precepts, Be Responsible and Be in Love, and he regularly referred to two worlds that people live in, the world of immediacy and the world mediated by meaning and motivated by values. In explaining the latter he also implicitly called attention to how it is formed intersubjectively:

> From infancy onward they live in a world of immediacy, a world revealed by sense and alive with feelings. Gradually they move into a world mediated by meanings and motivated by values. In this adult world the raw materials are indeed the world of immediacy. But by speech one asks when and where, what and why, what for and how often. Answers cumulatively extrapolate from what is near to what is ever further away, from the present to one's own and to others' memories of the past and anticipations of the future, from what is or was actual to the possible, the probable, the fictitious, the ideal, the normative. (1985, p. 6)

Mead (1934) has made us aware of how social reality shapes the world of immediacy, which is to say that even the world of immediacy is a social construction to a certain degree. When people move from the world of immediacy of the *I* and the *me* to the world mediated by meaning and motivated by values, they reflect on that very construction. In a sense they learn how to deconstruct their own socially influenced constructions to discover the world of meaning and value. Inasmuch as they follow the *self*-affirming precepts, they achieve authenticity, for "authenticity is reached only by long and sustained fidelity to the transcendental [i.e., *self*-affirming] precepts" (1985, p. 8):

> Such meanings and values may be authentic or unauthentic. They are authentic in the measure that cumulatively they are the result of the transcendental precepts, Be Attentive, Be Intelligent, Be Reasonable, Be Responsible. They are unauthentic in the measure that they are the product of cumulative inattention, obtuseness, unreasonableness, irresponsibility. (1985, p. 7)

Lonergan sees authentic meanings and values as emerging in the context of a community, although he is well aware that communities can be seriously inauthentic in certain respects. Individual people appropriate the authentic meanings and values of the community inasmuch as they are members of the community, and their appropriation of the community's authentic meanings and values forms their subjectivity, which thereby constitutes their intersubjectivity:

> By a community is not meant a number of people within a frontier. Community means people with a common field of experience, with a common or at least complementary way of understanding people and things, with common judgments and aims. Without a common field of experience, people are out

of touch. Without a common way of understanding, they will misunderstand
one another, grow suspicious, distrustful, hostile, violent. Without common
judgments they will live in different worlds, and without common aims they
will work at cross-purposes. Such, then, is community, and as it is community that hands on the discoveries and inventions of the past and, as well,
cooperates in the present, so it is community that is the carrier of power.
(1985, pp. 5-6)

While individual people obviously may live within more than one community thus defined, the fields of study within academia can be seen as communities: "There are many differentiations of consciousness....With each
differentiation there is a shift of horizon, a transformation of available
meanings, a transvaluation of values" (1985, p. 7). Studying within a field
amounts to an induction within that community. The induction affects and
expands the intersubjectivity of the inductee. Thus when the inductee is
able to pass muster, as it were, by expressing the authentic meanings and
values of the field in his or her writing, that writing is an expression of the
intersubjectivity of the inductee. Clearly a more detailed account of the intersubjectivity of writing is called for.

Because everyone's subjectivity develops through interactions with
others, it is from one standpoint more accurate to speak of intersubjectivity
than of subjectivity, which no doubt is why Lonergan regularly writes about
intersubjectivity. A passage that Brodkey (1987, p. 406) quotes from Virginia Woolf's *A Room of One's Own* in effect calls attention to another
aspect of intersubjectivity:

> For I am by no means confining you to fiction. If you would please me—
> and there are thousands like me—you would write books of travel and adven-
> ture, and research and scholarship, and history and biography, and criticism
> and philosophy and science. By so doing you will certainly profit the art of
> fiction. For books have a way of influencing each other. (1929, p. 113)

As Woolf's last statement implies, written texts have intertextuality because
each writer's subjectivity is conditioned by intersubjectivity. For the
writer's intersubjectivity expands and is enriched through reading good writing. However, when writers are writing primarily out of the *me*, their writing will involve personal expression. Then they are not as likely to be
aware of their own intersubjectivity as when they are writing out of the *self*.
Writing out of the *self* makes writers more aware of how they have been
influenced by others.

Intersubjectivity is the other side of the coin of intertextuality. For
intertextuality is one outward manifestation of our manifold intersubjectivity. Walter J. Ong's discussion of intertextuality will help me make the
point I wish to make about intersubjectivity:

> Intertextualist critics look for the most unexpected "traces" of other texts in a
> given text, "a set of relations with other texts" (Leitch 1983, p. 59) cued in
> by various methods....

> Intertextuality has upset many persons by countering the more or less re-
> ceived Romantic doctrine that the successful writer was marked by "original-
> ity," an ability to produce quite fresh verbiage, something new and pre-
> viously unrealized. This most often unarticulated but strong presumption has
> produced the state of mind that Harold Bloom treats in *The Anxiety of Influ-
> ence*—the nervous fear that, after all, one may be inevitably more bound to
> one's textual predecessors than it is comfortable to admit....Although every-
> one is aware that everyone's verbal expression is somewhat derivative, to
> think of writing as essentially self-expression is in some ways to encourage
> the most anti-intertextualist mindset possible. (1988, pp. 262-263)

Ong has for a long time been calling attention to the personalistic orientation of the old oral/rhetorical tradition, and he no doubt found 20th-century
personalism so attractive because it hearkened back to this long-standing
orientation of Western culture (1962, pp. 233-259). Ong has recently
pointed out how the concerns of contemporary literary critics with intertextuality and with reader response also hearken back to concerns of the old
oral/rhetorical tradition, while the now old New Criticism and continental
Formalism accentuated the visual aspect of texts and considered them to be
"quiescently reified" (1988, p. 263).[2]

The old oral/rhetorical orientation calls attention to the fact that human
subjects generate speech. Moreover, the subjects learn speech from other
subjects. Likewise, subjects generate written texts. But written texts are
characterized by intertextuality, just as subjects are characterized by intersubjectivity. Not only do we learn language that we can use in speech from
other people (i.e., subjects). We also learn a stock of ideas (like the old

---

[2] In chapter 11 Geoffrey Williams treats intertextuality in greater detail than it is
treated in this essay. While apparently not familiar with Ong's work, he suggests a
view of the literary historian that is compatible with the view of the writer and
writing explored in the present essay, although far more complex. All writers could
be viewed as literary historians in a large sense inasmuch as their subjectivity and
therefore their writing have been conditioned by the textual communities in which
they have been formed. In other words, their cultural identity has been shaped by
their appropriation of a textual tradition. While "texts" and "textual communities"
occur only in places where writing exists to help make "texts," the cultural identity
of people in a primary oral culture (cf. Ong, 1982) has been influenced in an
analogous manner by oral tradition. But it is not entirely satisfactory to refer to oral
tradition as though it were a form of textuality because "text" is something produced
by writing. However that may be, even the cultural identity of people with a written
tradition has been influenced to a certain degree by oral tradition. On the one hand,
everybody in effect experiences primary orality before they learn to read and write.
On the other hand, even people who know how to read and write very well are still
influenced to some degree by oral communication and still engage in oral
communication. Indeed, it is hard to imagine a textual community coming into and
continuing in existence without the aid of oral communication. But if oral
communication is seen as a form of narrative, as Williams sees it, then each person
could be thought of as a kind of literary historian, even though the word "literary"
etymologically refers to "letters" used in writing.

cumulative commonplaces) and a stock of ways to organize and develop ideas (like the old analytic commonplaces) from other people as we grow up and are educated (concerning the cumulative and analytic commonplaces of old, see Ong, 1967, pp. 80-81, 85). As Ong elsewhere notes, "all our think-ing...is learned and developed only through communication with others" (1962, p. 56). The formation of our subjectivity through our learning both in our informal and our formal education results in our intersubjectivity, which is to say that our private and public selves are socially constructed.

In *Writing for Social Scientists*, Howard S. Becker suggests that writ-ers should think of the process of making arguments out of ideas appropri-ated from other authors as like the process of a carpenter making a table out of wood acquired from a lumber yard (1986, pp. 141-142). In the old oral/rhetorical tradition, that is how orators in effect were trained to think of themselves as they composed their arguments. As Becker notes, we do use thoughts culled from other authors to construct our own arguments. C. Wright Mills seems to have understood this aspect of the writing process very well, because he urges scholars to build files of "ideas, personal notes, excerpts from books, bibliographical items, and outlines of projects" (1959, p. 198). As a matter of fact, we use the thoughts of others in a manner strikingly akin to the way Cicero, Augustine, Dante, Chaucer, Shakespeare, Lyly, Nashe, Milton, Sterne, Pope, and other writers educated in the old rhetorical tradition used cumulative commonplaces, except that we usually try to acknowledge our sources more than they did. Moreover, acknow-ledging the sources of the ideas one is using through attribution and docu-mentation is the opposite of having anxiety over influence. Furthermore, we use stock analytic commonplaces such as comparison and contrast, defini-tion, classification, and the like to organize and develop our thought.

To use T. S. Eliot's classic terms (1919/1975), academic and profes-sional writers who are writing from sources stand as individuals in relation to a tradition, a body of materials passed on to them by other people living and dead. At the risk of over-simplifying, the education of an academic writer involves learning and storing up materials to write about and a stock of ways to organize and develop material. Even the self-affirming precepts formulated by Lonergan can be seen as analytic commonplaces of a macro order, as distinct from the micro order of stock ways to organize thought, for those precepts are ways to direct our cognitive behavior. When Loner-gan's precepts taken together are referred to as constituting a generalized empirical method, the word "method" accentuates the point I am making here in saying that the precepts are in effect analytic commonplaces.

But Lonergan suggests that there is more to achieving authority than balancing the "sincere" self and the "social" self, as Richard A. Lanham has suggested (1987, pp. 101-104), and Lonergan's remarks about authority call attention implicitly to intersubjectivity once again. While he does not refer explicitly to authority in writing, his comments about authority are nevertheless worth considering in relationship to writing. For surely when Lonergan refers to "the word of authority" (1985, p. 6), he could be referring to the written expression of the word of authority:

> ...authority belongs to the community that has a common field of experience, common and complementary ways of understanding, common judgments, and common aims. It is the community that is the carrier of a common world mediated by meaning and motivated by values. It is the validity of those meanings and values that gives authority its aura and prestige. (1985, p. 7)

Thus on Lonergan's view, authority in writing comes not so much from balancing our private and public selves as from the validity of the meanings and values expressed in the writing, which validity is recognized by the community because the meanings and values have been formulated, shared, and established and verified intersubjectively.

The disciplinary nature of academic writing implicitly suggests that academic writers need to understand themselves to be writing in and for specific textual communities. Academic writers as textbook writers presumably write to introduce and welcome students into the specific textual community of their fields with its many voices, while academic writers as scholars presumably write to voice their thoughts and further the discussion in one way or another in the specific textual community of their field. The textual field is the agora. The meanings and values proffered by various voices in the field are assessed by the textual community to determine their validity, as Lonergan reminds us. Writers in the workplace write for analogous communities.

The student as academic writer is learning to become informed enough to write in the specific textual community of a given field, by appropriating and applying the meanings and values that are considered to have validity within the field. To develop sufficient mastery to be able to write, the student needs to be open to and listen to the ideas already involved in the dialogue going on in the specific textual community. To the degree that the dialogue of the field is taken in and appropriated by the student, the agora of the textual community becomes part of his or her intersubjectivity. The outer agora becomes inner. The various academic writers the student reads are presumably writing to communicate with each other in the textual community. Inasmuch as the authors are knowledgeable within the textual community in which they write, their writing is intersubjective. For their personal understanding of the field has come to them from others.

But some people might resist acknowledging this not only because of a Romantic valorization of unique expression, but also because of Aristotle's valuing artistic proofs over inartistic proofs (*Rhetoric* 1355b, 1375a-1377b; 1991, pp. 37, 108-118). Arguments appropriated from others are presumably inartistic proofs. While parts of an extended argument using sources may indeed be what Aristotle considered inartistic proofs, the arrangement and building of the overall argument are the dimensions where the writer's artistry most obviously comes into play, even though Aristotle did not comment on this dimension of building arguments from sources. To use Becker's analogy with carpentry, not everyone can build a beautiful cabinet from the necessary materials as well as a master cabinet maker can. Similarly, not everyone can prepare as fine a meal from the necessary ingredients as a gourmet chef can. Likewise, not everyone can build an effective argument from sources. At the minimum, people need guidance about effective arrangement, but then they also need to try different combinations of ideas and receive feedback from thoughtful readers about what works well and what does not. Reflecting on well thought out feedback and the strengths of the arguments being made are necessary steps in developing what Lonergan means by authenticity.

## 3. Authenticity and Lonergan's Self-Affirming Precepts

The theory of the human person developed by Thomas Patrick Malone and Patrick Thomas Malone (1987), an Atlanta-based father-son team of psychiatrists, enables us to speak more clearly about what dimension of the person is involved in personal expression and what dimension is involved in following Lonergan's self-affirming precepts. The Malones claim that the human person is constituted of an *I*, a *me*, and a *self*, which they distinguish from Freud's well-known constructs about the structure of the human psyche:

> *Me, myself*, and *I* are not the same as superego, id, and ego. Ego, superego, and id are *structural* components of the individual's psyche. *I, me*, and *self* are *functional* components of relationship. There are *I, me*, and *self* aspects in all structural components of the psyche. (1987, p. 32)

The *I* is outer-directed, the *me* inner-directed, and the *self* other-directed in the best sense of the term (not in the sense of being a people-pleaser). What Ken Macrorie (1970) calls "Engfish," what Walker Gibson (1966) calls "stuffy talk," and what Lanham (1987) calls the "bureaucratic style" arise from writing too exclusively from the *I*. What Brodkey calls the Romantic image of the writer as a solitary, oppositionless figure can involve writing from either the standpoint of the *I* or the *me*. Psychologists assure us that people need to develop the *me* dimension of themselves to become fully functioning persons affectively (see, for example, Horney, 1945; Rogers, 1961; A. Miller, 1979/1981, 1980/1983, 1981/1984, 1988/1990a, 1988/1990b, 1990/1991; Bradshaw, 1988, 1990, 1992). But on Lonergan's account of human authenticity, more than the expression of the *me* is needed to develop genuine authenticity. Since allegedly "authentic voice" in student writing often involves little more than the expression of the *me* (cf. Faigley, 1989), it is important to understand what more Lonergan sees as involved in the development of genuine authenticity.

Perhaps some readers will find the following explication of the *I* and the *me* by the Malones helpful:

> This expression "Me, myself, and I" implies that there are significant differ-
> ences between the three. We suggest that the differences are indeed signifi-
> cant. The priest and poet Gerard Manley Hopkins saw these differences
> clearly: "...my self-being, my consciousness and feeling of myself, that taste
> of myself, of I and *me* above and in all things...." If you say or think "*I*," it
> feels very different from when you say or think "me." Just as words do,
> grammar teaches; it carries natural patterns in it. *I* am the subject and *me* is
> the object....*I* am initiating, *I* am intrusive, *I* am the actor, *I* am always relat-
> ing to the world around me in one way or another. *I* am the exerciser of
> control, decision, denial, clarification, manipulation, closure, and countless
> other behaviors aimed at my being in the surrounding world accommodating
> to it, dealing with its effects on me....
>
> In contrast, things happen to *me*. Others "let me have it," "appreciate
> me," "do a number on me," or "make love to me." It would really be more
> accurate to say things happen within *me*. *I* acts. *Me* feels the hurt or happi-
> ness. *Me* is both historically conscious and forward-looking; *me*, as summa-
> tion of past and projection into future, is the foundation on which *I* stand to
> look out. *Me* is psychologically planning, deciding, arranging *inner* values,
> experiencing my self-esteem, and dealing with my motivations with respect
> to the world around me. *I* looks out; *me* looks in. *Me* decides what should
> or has to be done; *I* decides how to do it. *Me* is my character; *I* is my
> personality. (1987, p. 32; their emphases)

The *I* lives in shared space; the *me*, according to the Malones, lives in personal space.[3]

---

[3] While the terminology concerning the *I* and the *me* appears to have been coined by
the Malones, the realities named by these terms have also been identified by John
Weir Perry, who named them "the Logos way" and "the Eros way," respectively
(1974; see the Index under Logos and Eros for specific page references). The
child's early relationship with the mother is extremely important for the
development of the Eros way, the *me*. If the mother is overly controlling, then the
child will not develop the Eros way. Instead, the child will in turn become overly
controlling. That is, the child's Logos way, the *I*, will become skewed toward a
power orientation. In such cases, the archetypal self-image, from the aspect of the
person the Malones refer to as the *self*, will be compensatorily inflated so that such
people will seem at times to have grandiose views of themselves, while at other
times they will have unduly deflated views of themselves because the Eros way, the
*me*, in them is deflated (i.e., not properly functioning). However, it might be more
apt to speak of "the Agape way," instead of "the Eros way," to avoid the genital
connotations of "eros." Freud to the contrary notwithstanding, it just seems out of
place to speak of genital sexuality in a pre-pubertal child, as Alice Miller has argued
(1988/1990a, pp. 42-43). As a matter of fact, Anthony Stevens reports that Greek
nurses who cared for infant orphans at the Matera Babies Center just outside Athens
used the Greek word *agape* to characterize the special attachment they had formed
with infants (1982, p. 11). Moreover, it would be a serious mistake to see the
Agape way as in play only between the mother-figure and the child; even though
that relationship usually develops first and is usually stronger initially than the

Since the *I* lives in shared space, it is the aspect of the person that is involved in seeking "honor" in honor-shame societies (cf. Peristiany, 1966). Because the *me* lives in personal space, it is the aspect of the person that experiences shame-based syndromes (cf. Bradshaw, 1988; Kaufman, 1985, 1989). Lanham's (1976, pp. 1-9) *homo rhetoricus* involves the *I*; *homo seriosus* as exemplified in Socrates, Plato, and Aristotle involves the *self*. When Lanham in a later publication (1987, pp. 101-104) refers to the "social" self and the "sincere" self, he appears to be referring to the *I* and the *me*, respectively, not to the *homo seriosus* exemplified in Socrates, Plato, and Aristotle. Happily, though, his advice about balancing them coincides with the Malones' contention that the experience of the *self* comes from experience of the *I* and the *me* at the same time (1987, p. 48). While Lanham suggests that authority in writing comes from balancing the "social" and the "sincere" selves, Lonergan suggests that attaining authority involves more than simply experiencing the *self*.[4]

The conditions for human authenticity of concern to Lonergan involve the *self*. Writers of non-fiction need to develop a *self*-oriented way of writing, as Lonergan and some others already have. Non-fiction writers need to learn how to attain objectivity inasmuch as that is possible in their writing.

---

child's relationship with the father-figure, the relationship with the father-figure also involves the Agape way. By the same token, the relationship with the father should not be seen as the only source of the Logos way, for the mother undoubtedly plays a key role in the development also. Leaders of thought such as Lonergan and Ong tend to excel in the Logos way. If we look at public figures, we can see that President Ronald Reagan, the Reverend Jesse Jackson, President Bill Clinton, and Robert Moore, a leading spirit in the men's movement, have well developed the Agape way. While public figures who have fallen into the skewed controlling behavior described by Perry abound (e.g., Margaret Thatcher, Ross Perot), it is hard to think of any public figures who have well developed both the Agape way and the Logos way.

[4] When St. Paul says "it is no longer I who lives, but Christ who lives in me" (Gal. 2:20 NRSV), he in effect is saying that he now is living out of the *self*. The new life referred to in Christian writings involves the *self*. When people learn how to experience the *self*, they are in a position to learn how to access properly the archetypes of maturity described by Robert Moore and Douglas Gillette (1990, 1992a, 1992b, 1993a, 1993b). As they learn to do that, they will experience "new" life, which will be qualitatively different from living exclusively out of the *I* and the *me* as they did before, when the *me* was still crippled by the aftereffects of childhood traumas (cf. A. Miller, 1979/1981, 1980/1983, 1981/1984, 1988/1990a, 1988/1990b, 1990/1991). As long as the *me* is still suffering the aftereffects of childhood traumas, there will be a limit on the person's capacity to experience the *self*. The *me* needs to be freed of such aftereffects. For this to happen, the person needs to experience the pain associated with the original traumas. Only by experiencing the pain later in life can the person be freed of the aftereffects of childhood traumas and thereby enabled to learn how to access the archetypes of maturity properly. (See chapter 6 for further discussion of the archetypes of maturity.)

It may be possible to the degree to which they have attained reflective awareness of their intersubjectivity. For "genuine objectivity is the fruit of authentic subjectivity," Lonergan claims (1972, p. 292). Following Lonergan's self-affirming precepts would most likely help writers learn how to attain both genuine objectivity and authentic subjectivity. His treatment of human authenticity provides the groundwork for writers to develop a *self*-oriented approach to writing. Lonergan believes that people must follow the *self*-affirming precepts he has formulated for human authenticity to emerge:

> It is quite true that objective knowing is not yet authentic living; but without objective knowing there is no authentic living; for one knows objectively just insofar as one is neither unperceptive, nor stupid, nor silly; and one does not live authentically inasmuch as one is unperceptive or stupid or silly. (1967/1988, p. 220)

Since we often tend to state judgments without considering alternative explanations, Lonergan's step-by-step approach to reaching judgments aims to hold that tendency in check and requires us to be more circumspect in our affirmations.

In a paper presented in 1973, Lonergan recounts how he came to work on *Insight*, outlines the scope of *Insight* as he sees it, and goes on to say that his aim is "to help people experience themselves understanding, distinguish it from other experiences, name and identify it, and recognize when it recurs" (1974a, p. 269). He sees his aim as "parallel to Carl Rogers' aim of inducing his clients to advert to the feelings that they experience but do not advert to, distinguish, name, identify, recognize" (p. 269). But while Rogers' aim is primarily concerned with the *me*, Lonergan's project is primarily oriented to the *self*. "My *self* comes out of my experiencing *I* and *me* simultaneously," the Malones claim (1987, p. 48), and so Rogers surely is to be commended for his efforts in helping people to experience the *me* more fully and self-consciously because without recovering the *me* from the after-effects of inadequate parenting they would not be in a position to experience the *I* and the *me* simultaneously. In effect, he was teaching people what adequate parenting would have taught them if they had received appropriate mirroring from their parents at the right times in their lives. But the *I* and the *me* live more in the world of immediacy than the *self* does. The *self* lives more in the world mediated by meaning and motivated by values than in the world of immediacy. Following the *self*-affirming precepts formulated by Lonergan would enable writers to weigh their thoughts and words appropriately, thereby opening themselves to human authenticity. Lonergan claims that "genuine objectivity is the fruit of authentic subjectivity" (1972, p. 292), and non-fiction writers should usually aim for objectivity in their writing.

Lonergan was delighted when Abraham Maslow (1968) wrote a book about the psychology of being, because Lonergan had already published his most seminal book about being-values, *Insight*. To accentuate the "being" dimension of his precepts, Lonergan at times capitalizes only the "Be" in each precept. Indeed, people learn to be all that they can be and experience authentic subjectivity through long and sustained fidelity to the five self-affirming precepts. While the present essay is primarily concerned with showing how the first three of the five self-affirming precepts formulated by Lonergan—and especially the third—are pertinent to advanced writing, the fourth and fifth precepts, Be Responsible and Be in Love, need to be discussed briefly.

Perhaps some remarks Lonergan makes in *Insight* can help us bring the precept to Be in Love down to earth. There Lonergan refers to the pure, detached, disinterested desire to know (1957/1992, see the Index under "desire to know" for page references). The pure desire to know is the key to experiencing authentic subjectivity. Moreover, the experience of the pure desire to know is an expression of what Lonergan later comes to refer to as Being in Love. In other words, the pure desire to know is an actuation of love. In more familiar terms, learning for the sake of learning is an expression of the pure desire to know. But writers can be motivated by other motives. For example, they can desire to prove themselves lovable in the eyes of others by virtue of their achievements, which is often a carryover from childhood conditioning wherein children learned to do things to win the approval of their caregivers. Or they can desire to establish their superiority over others, which is the underlying motive of racism and other forms of social discrimination. No doubt the desire to establish superiority over others has motivated the achievements of many people, so the pure desire to know is not easy to come by. But surely writers should be able to tell whether they are motivated by learning for the sake of learning or some other motive. If they are not motivated by the pure desire to know, then they are not likely to experience authentic subjectivity, according to Lonergan.[5]

If it strikes some readers as overly ambitious to urge advanced writing students today to follow the *self*-affirming precepts formulated by Lonergan, then they need to remember that for centuries teenage boys

---

[5] Even though the idea of acting out of love is etymologically suggested by the "philo-" in "philosophy," it would be impossible to assess whether or not people trained in classical rhetoric attempted to follow the precept to Be in Love. But in their own way they surely were attempting to follow the precept to Be Responsible, because deliberative and judicial rhetoric invariably occurred in an existential decision-making context. In other words, the most common forms of rhetoric occurred in the very context in which Lonergan sees the precept to Be Responsible coming into play. In addition, the standard but adaptable parts of a speech involved following the precepts to Be Attentive, Be Intelligent, and Be Reasonable, as I indicate in the following discussion of classical rhetoric. However, it is impossible to say how many people trained in classical rhetoric were motivated by the pure desire to know, which Lonergan sees as essential to experiencing authentic subjectivity.

who were trained in classical rhetoric (only rarely did girls receive such training) learned to follow the prescribed parts of a speech that in effect required them to follow the *self*-affirming precepts. Winifred Bryan Horner handily summarizes the standard parts of a classical oration in *Rhetoric in the Classical Tradition* (1988, all of the following quotes are from p. 233). The *exordium* is the opening. The *narratio* "provides the [background] facts or history of the situation." To do this one would need to employ empirical consciousness and Be Attentive to the data involved in the situation. The *explicatio* "defines terms and explains issues." To do this would bring intelligent consciousness into play and require one to Be Intelligent in interpreting and analyzing the situation. The next three steps together would require the use of rational consciousness and would require one to carefully consider alternative explanations of the situation. The *partitio* or thesis statement "states the proposition or particular issue that is to be proved." The *confirmatio* or proof "supports and develops the thesis." The *refutatio* or refutation "answers the opposing arguments." And the *peroratio* or conclusion "summarizes the arguments and sometimes urges the audience to action." Action would involve the fourth level of consciousness identified by Lonergan: existential consciousness. Lonergan's precept for directing the orientation of existential consciousness is Be Responsible (instead of irresponsible) in our actions, to the degree that that is possible in given situations.

The so-called I-shaped essay is just a highly truncated version of the standard format of an oration.[6] Richard M. Coe (1987) has defended teaching students to use the I-shaped essay on the grounds that writers need to have a ready-made form at hand to help them organize their thought, which is to say that the I-shaped essay serves as an analytic commonplace for organizing thought. The standard parts of an oration taken together also constitute an analytic commonplace or form for organizing one's thought, and advanced writing students today need such a structure as much as orators in the past did. Since pro and con debating is essential to following the precept to Be Reasonable, the standard form of classical rhetoric with its built-in requirement of refutation is a more adequate form of thought for writers to learn to work through than is the form of the I-shaped essay, which actually encourages the image introduced by Ramism and decried by Brodkey of the writer as a solitary, oppositionless figure because it does not require the self-other dialogue involved in refutation.

---

[6] The term "I-shaped essay" is a bit of jargon used to refer to an essay with an introduction, body, and conclusion, where the introduction and conclusion presumably present qualified generalizations that are broader in scope than the more specific supporting material in the body; thus the shape of the letter "I" is supposed to suggest an easy-to-remember image for the overall shape of the essay.

## 4. Considering Alternatives

In writing an explanation and defense of a key consideration in Lonergan's generalized empirical method, Frederick E. Crowe, the founding director of the Lonergan Research Institute at the University of Toronto, uses an example reminiscent of Aristotle's discussion of judicial rhetoric to illustrate one aspect of Lonergan's account of judgment:

> The lawyer *needs* the testimony of the witnesses to make out a case [which testimony becomes in this context the empirical data to be explained by the lawyers]; the jury *needs* the lawyer's explanation, needs differing explanations, in fact, to form a judgment... (1985, p. 11; his emphasis)

In fact, we all *need* differing explanations of situations in order to make balanced and sound judgments, according to Lonergan and Crowe. In this respect, Crowe could have made the same points he makes in this quoted passage about any parliamentary debate and about the debate that each person should engage in in deliberating significant matters—in the parliament of his or her own intersubjectivity. All of us need to learn how to engage in pro and con debating so that we can make reasonable judgments. Pro and con debating involves articulating reasons both for and against a position and then being able to answer the reasons against. In the Western tradition, refutation was a standard part of educated discourse for centuries. When refutation is done honestly and carefully, it usually alerts one to grandiose tendencies in one's argument and thereby enables one to curb unreasonable statements, and in the end it also builds one's confidence in the reasonableness of one's position.

The refutation could involve what Robert M. Doran refers to as either a dialectic of contradictories or a dialectic of contraries:

> There are opposites that are contraries. Such are matter and spirit, consciousness and the unconscious, the masculine and feminine dimensions of the psyche, the ego and the personal shadow [technical terms in Jungian psychology] as victim of social and personal history. Between such opposites there can be established a dialectal integration, a creative tension that constitutes personal integrity. (1990, p. 349)

Apart from personal applications, contraries almost invariably constitute the "opposites" found in Ramist dichotomies; Ong has reported only one instance of a contradictory in a Ramist dichotomy, life and death—where the second term was not subdivided into further dichotomies. To use terms mentioned in the preface, Hebrew and Greek thought (Boman, 1954/1960), Hopi and Standard Average European thought (Whorf, 1956), primary oral and literate thought (Ong, 1982; Havelock, 1982), and "black" and "white" styles (Kochman, 1974, 1981) are in each instance contraries. That is why Ong (1982) speaks of orality-literacy "contrasts"; using the terms "orality" and "literacy" as though they were contradictories will most likely result in "good guy" vs. "bad guy" thinking. However that may be, Doran also provides some remarks about contradictories:

> But there are also opposites that are contradictories. Western epistemology has for centuries formulated the opposition of the true and the false in the principle of contradiction. An analogous opposition of contradictories is that of good and evil. A dialectic of contradictories cannot be resolved by integration, only by choice. And the choice bears precisely on the negotiation of the various dialectics of contraries: either their dialectical and creative tension, or their dissociation and the consequent distortion of their relation with one another. (1990, p. 349)

Once again, he situates his discussion in the person and draws out the significance of decision-making within the person (although his observation can also be extended to virtually any kind of group decision-making). Since Ramism set aside debate with the contradictory position, our primary focus here is to establish once again that people need to learn how to identify and consider the contradictory position when they are engaged in deliberation and argumentation, in argumentation involving a proposition of fact and in argumentation involving a proposition of policy.

In the context of a trial, for example, the issue is whether or not the defendant is guilty as charged. That is one example of a contradictory: guilty or not guilty. The argumentation here involves a proposition of fact; that is, argumentation that involves establishing facts and interpreting them. Each side will present arguments about the evidence involved and about how to interpret the situation. Their arguments could involve contradictory positions ("This-is-so" vs. "It-is-not-so"). But very often the arguments involve different interpretations of certain matters, and those positions usually involve contraries, not contradictories.[7]

In the context of a debate in any situation where parliamentary procedure is followed, the basic issue is to argue for and against the motion-as-worded, and so the basic issue involves contradictory positions ("Yes, the motion should be passed" vs. "No, the motion should not be passed"). The basic argumentation, once a motion has been made, involves a proposition of policy, which answers the question, "What should we do?" Apart from

---

[7] For example, in the first trial concerning the beating of Rodney King by police officers, the case hinged on how his actions were interpreted. The videotape of the beating was played over and over again. His various movements were open to different interpretations. While the initial rejection of one posited interpretation may begin with a statement that is truly a contradictory ("No, that is not the case"), the counter-interpretation that follows will most likely be a contrary to the one that it is intended to replace. Nobody argued that he did *not* move, because that would have contradicted what the videotape showed. If there had been no videotape and if Rodney King had claimed that he had *not* moved after he was on the ground, then that claim would have contradicted the police officers' claim about his movements. But the argument did not proceed that way.

the basic issue, though, the arguments presented may be contraries, rather than contradictories.

To work out the refutation of the contradictory position, one first negates one's thesis by asserting the antithesis (usually by inserting "not" in the thesis statement). One then formulates reasonable arguments supporting the antithesis. Next, one responds to those arguments with counter-arguments. While identifying the contrary position does not involve negating one's own position, the procedures of formulating arguments for the contrary position and then arguing against them would still be applicable. In short, both kinds of refutation eventually involve pro and con debating, but the polarities needed to begin the debating are set up differently. While debating with both the contradictory and the contrary positions can build one's confidence in the reasonableness of one's own position, debating with the contradictory position is usually more fruitful in this regard.

In the 16th century Ramus dropped the previously obligatory refutation as a standard part of an oration and thereby changed the history of rhetoric so that today many people do not recognize that the Western tradition of refutation involved pro and con debating. Ong's (1958) account of the history of logic and rhetoric enables us to see that Lonergan and Crowe are in effect calling attention to a standard feature of educated discourse in the West, before Ramus changed the course of that history by dispensing with the refutation. Although neither Lonergan nor Crowe explicitly mentions it, the tradition of refutation in Western rhetoric and philosophy before Ramism shows that the refutation was connected with explaining and thereby further supporting a judgment.[8] However, as Lonergan and Crowe well know, St. Thomas Aquinas exemplified the tradition of refutation spectacularly in the *Summa theologiae*, where he regularly arrayed objections and then responded to each in turn. But there was a longstanding tradition behind his practice, and we will turn now to look at it.

---

[8]This is an aspect of the rhetorical tradition that is different from the aspect studied by Thomas O. Sloane (1989)—namely, invention (pro and con debating can indeed also be used as a means of invention). Moreover, writing textbooks that draw on the classical tradition of rhetoric do not stress the importance of the refutation for sound judgment (cf. Corbett, 1990; Horner, 1988; Lunsford & Connors, 1992). For example, Andrea Lunsford and Robert Connors merely list the refutation as a part of classical oration without any explanation of why it might be a desirable part of one's thinking processes (1992, p. 91). In the sample student essay that they then reprint to illustrate how the parts of an oration can be used to construct an effective argument (pp. 92-98), they do note with a sidebar comment where the refutation occurs in the essay (p. 97). But nowhere in their 800-page book do they recommend that writers systematically engage in pro and con debating.

### 4.1 The Refutation in Classical Rhetoric

A brief review of the Western tradition of rhetoric will show the centrality of the feature to which Lonergan and Crowe call attention. Early in the *Rhetoric* Aristotle makes the following statement about the value of rhetoric:

> Further, one should be able to argue persuasively on either side of a question, just as in the use of syllogisms, not that we may actually do both (for one should not persuade what is debased) but in order that it may not escape our notice what the real state of the case is and that we ourselves may be able to refute if another person uses speech unjustly. (1355a; 1991, p. 34)

Furthermore, Aristotle in effect aligns the domain of rhetoric with all issues needing pro and con debating:

> And we debate about things that seem to be capable of admitting two possibilities; for no one debates things incapable of being different either in past or future or present, at least not if they suppose that to be the case; for there is nothing more [to say]. (1357a; 1991, p. 41; the bracketed material is Kennedy's.)

In this passage "debate" in effect means to engage in pro and con debating.

Aristotle also underlines the importance of pro and con debating when he advises orators to anticipate counter-arguments and refute them. In discussing arrangement in Book III, he says the following: "Replies to the opponent belong to the proofs; and reply by comparison is amplification of the same, so it is a part of the proofs" (1414b; 1991, p. 259). Later in Book III, he elaborates this point:

> Refutations of the opponent are not a separate species but belong to proofs. Some [refutations] disprove by objection [to a premise], some by [a counter] syllogism. In both deliberation and in court, the opening speaker should [usually] state his own premises first, then should meet those [expected] of his opponent by disproving and tearing them to pieces before he can make them. (1418b; 1991, p. 276; the bracketed material is Kennedy's.)

So not only would the judges/audience consider competing arguments by listening to the opposing speakers; even the opposing speakers themselves would consider competing arguments as they developed their refutations. However, Josiah Ober concludes that "objectivity was not considered possible or even particularly desirable" in Athens either at the level of state policy formation or legal judgment (1989, p. 151). Thus the refutation did not automatically foster the kind of objectivity that Lonergan and Crowe wish to see engendered in people today, even though it may have fostered a certain kind of intersubjectivity. William M. A. Grimaldi's (1990) account of *ethos* in Aristotle's *Rhetoric* calls attention to how keenly aware Aristotle was of the intersubjective dimension of public speaking: He expected orators to be well aware of the role of the judges/auditors in the making of meaning and to tailor the presentation of self and substance accordingly. Ober's descriptions of various Athenian orators confirms that they were indeed usually well aware of the role of the judges/auditors.

Brian Vickers provides a convenient overview of the Western rhetorical tradition concerning debating when he notes that refutation was considered to be a standard part of a speech in the *Rhetorica ad Herennium*, Cicero's *De Inventione*, and Quintilian's *Institutio Oratoriae*:

> While various systems emerged, a popular division [of speeches] was into six parts: *exordium, narratio, partitio, confirmatio, refutatio* (or *reprehensio*), and *conclusio*....The author [of *Rhetorica ad Herennium*] discusses each part in some detail (1. 3. 4-2. 31. 50), in terms similar to Cicero's in *De Inventione* (1. 4. 19-1. 56. 109)....Quintilian discusses the whole sequence, as one might expect, fully, with much mature and sensible advice. (1988, pp. 68-69, 71)

Thus the practice of pro and con debating was explicitly institutionalized in the orators' position by the requirement of the refutation.

## 4.2 *Debating as Self-Other Dialogue*

Pro and con debating involves a self-other dialogue within oneself, which was undoubtedly a central feature of the dialogic quality of the oral/rhetorical tradition as Ong treats it in *Ramus, Method, and the Decay of Dialogue: From the Art of Discourse to the Art of Reason* (1958). He aligns the art of discourse in effect with pro and con debating, and the art of reason with print and the new mentality fostered by print. Ramist method was pivotal in the larger movement from conceptualizing thought in terms of pro and con debating to conceptualizing thought as the activity of one person working inside himself or herself, with no dialogue with the contradictory position, not even interior dialogue. Consequently, in the preface to the 1983 paperback edition of *Ramus, Method, and the Decay of Dialogue*, Ong sums up the effect of print on Ramism this way: "Print gave to visualist organization and to textuality (both initiated much earlier by writing) a force unknown before, and in doing so...dissociated knowledge from discourse and gave it a quasi-monologic setting" (p. vii). More often than not the refutation in classical rhetoric involved arguing with the adversarial position that was the contradictory of one's own position. But almost invariably the Ramist dichotomies involved what Doran calls contraries, not contradictories.

Because Ramism dispensed with pro and con debating as an integral part of the "art" of discourse, Ramism in principle was irenic in orientation in the sense that it eliminated from the exposition of any "art" the standard refutation of possible adversarial positions, as I have explained elsewhere (Farrell, 1991, pp. 27-28). Adversaries were fended off or demolished by Ramus in separate published lectures apart from the "art" itself. Ramism as an "art" favored oppositionless, quasi-monologic exposition, in which the method of following dichotomies to invent and organize arguments supplanted arguing with actual or hypothetical adversarial positions. The solitary scene of writing of concern to Brodkey is a later descendant of the shift in conceptualization ushered in by Ramism.

As mentioned above, Crowe (1985) has called our attention to the need to consider alternative explanations of data and situations in order to form what Lonergan would call a reasonable judgment. In the writing process, sooner or later all of the pertinent considerations will have been identified. That is when pro and con debating is most useful and should come in to play. At that point, the writer is moving toward forming a judgment, as Lonergan would call it. A well formed judgment should be supported and the alternative judgment(s) should be refuted in the sense of being explained. When writers can explain the reasons for their judgments and against the counter-judgments, they usually feel confident about their positions. When they cannot articulate sound reasons against counter-judgments, then they truly are not ready to affirm their own judgments.[9]

When writers fail to use pro and con debating in forming their judgments about the positions they are espousing, they run the risk of producing Engfish, stuffy talk, and bureaucratic prose, because they will be operating out of the image decried by Brodkey of the writer as a solitary, oppositionless figure. In such cases, the writers are operating almost exclusively out of what the Malones call the *I*, or *homo rhetoricus* (Lanham, 1976, pp. 1-9); Rogerian rhetoric encourages writers to operate more out of the *me*. But using pro and con debating can move writers toward operating more out of the *self*, or *homo seriosus* as exemplified in Socrates, Plato, and Aristotle, if they are motivated by the pure, detached, disinterested desire to know that Lonergan writes about.

The *self*-other dialogue involved in the refutation is a paradigm of intersubjectivity within one's subjectivity, because to carry on such debating within ourselves involves dividing our subjectivity and role-playing the pro

---

[9] Even so, some people might argue that Rogerian rhetoric is better suited for writing today than pro and con debating is. Rogerian rhetoric is named after Carl Rogers, and as we saw above, Lonergan praised his efforts to help people learn how to name their feelings. Clearly Rogers was a gifted therapist who helped many people learn how to recognize and express their feelings. In terms I have used above, he was primarily concerned with the *me*, while Lonergan is more centrally concerned with the *self*. By Lonergan's account, genuine authenticity involves more than the expression of feelings. But Lonergan applauded Rogers's efforts to help people name and recognize their feelings, because Lonergan wants to help people go beyond that step and learn how to name and recognize their own cognitive operations. While nothing in so-called Rogerian rhetoric precludes using pro and con debating to form a judgment, it does not prescribe that kind of systematic and rigorous sic et non examination of the alternatives. That is its weakness. It does not build in a systematic way to check against the grandiosity that Bradshaw writes about (1988, pp. 21, 136). Pro and con debating needs to be conducted to hold grandiosity in check. (For defenses of Rogerian rhetoric, see Young, Becker, & Pike, 1970, pp. 7-8, 274-290; Hairston, 1976; Teich, 1990; and Brent, 1991.)

and con roles in the debate. Thus we call attention to the built-in capacity to give voice to different positions that usually bespeak different subjectivities. The capacity to hold different subjectivities in tension and dialogue is a microcosm of the larger macrocosm of intersubjectivity that constitutes one's subjectivity. The writer who actively employs pro and con debating is like an orchestra conductor signalling different voices when to come into play and harmonizing them with one another.

But Ober's assessment of the Athenian situation, quoted above, is instructive: In debate people can get carried away with the spirit of contentiousness and not even consider objectivity to be a desirable goal. Plato presumably was calling attention to how rhetoric can be skewed toward adversativeness when he used three pairs of contrasting terms in the *Republic*: (1) justice (*dikaiosyne*) and injustice, which Plato sees as characterized by *polypragmosyne* (an untranslatable term); (2) *philosophos* (the philosopher as conceived of by Plato) and *philodoxos* (another untranslatable term); and (3) *aletheia* (truth) and *pseudos* (falsehood or lie) (Voegelin, 1957b, pp. 63-70; see also chapter 6 of this volume). For Plato, the participant in debate or dialogue must be motivated by the desire to discover justice, wisdom, and truth. For Lonergan, the person engaged in inquiry must be motivated by the pure, detached, disinterested desire to know. Simply put, the inquirer needs to be devoted to learning for the sake of learning and not get skewed toward a win-lose orientation in debate. For debate to lead to objectivity, whether in a public forum or in the interior parliament of one's own consciousness, the desire to learn the truth inasmuch as possible must motivate the debate, and the debate must be informed by an honest knowledge of both the arguments and the counterarguments. As Lonergan indicates, such an orientation requires a person to be detached and disinterested.[10]

---

[10] St. Thomas Aquinas is an example of somebody who was schooled presumably in the skewed adversativeness of classical rhetoric but who overcame the limitations of that orientation by his devotion to what Plato refers to as justice, wisdom, and truth and what Lonergan refers to as the pure, detached, disinterested desire to know. In the Summa theologiae he (1) poses questions that have come up in the Judaeo-Christian-Islamic tradition of thought over the centuries, (2) arrays "objections" that could be raised against the position he plans to take by citing answers to the question given by various Jewish, Christian, and Islamic thinkers over the centuries, (3) states his own position, and (4) responds to each "objection" in turn. That is surely an adversative structure, and yet it does not appear that Aquinas was usually engaging in the spurious contention that Plato objected to. Despite the adversativeness expressed in the label "objections," Aquinas is in effect providing a "review of literature" about the question at hand, and then in the reply to each objection he presents his carefully reasoned response to it, which would be hard to categorize as spurious contention because he obviously considers each objection to be worthy of serious enough consideration as to warrant mention and a reply. So he used an obvious debate format. Did the debate format catalyze his own thinking, prompt him to consider matters he might not have considered otherwise, and enable him to form more reasonable judgments about the matters he treated? It would appear that it did, even though it occasionally led him to construct

In a recent work Paul Ricoeur (1990/1992) explores a sense of "self" that is *not* personal. What he describes as the "self" corresponds essentially to what the Malones (1987) mean by the *self.* The *self* is not personal in the sense that it is beyond or above or at least different from personalized ego-consciousness as expressed in the *I* and the *me.* In this regard the *self* can be considered a universal subject, as Ricoeur suggests. The *self* as universal subject presumably constitutes the universal audience discussed by Chaim Perelman and Lucie Olbrechts-Tyteca (1958/1969; see Index under "audience, universal"). And the *self* as universal subject may also elucidate Eliot's remark that poetry "is not the expression of personality [of the *I* and the *me*], but an escape from personality [into the *self*]" (1919/1975, p. 43). However, it might be more apt to refer to the transpersonal self, instead of the universal subject. Edward F. Edinger offers some observations that are pertinent to the distinctions being made here:

> To put it concisely, we might say that the ego [i.e., personalized ego-consciousness] is windowless, but the *Self* is a window on other worlds of being. The ego is the center of subjective identity; the *Self*, the center of objective identity. (1972, pp. 170, 166)

For Lonergan, authentic subjectivity refers to the *self* and is equivalent of Ricoeur's universal subject and of Edinger's objective identity. Authenticity, then, is the expression of the *self*—not of the *I* nor the *me* that constitute personalized ego-consciousness and what Eliot calls personality. And Lonergan suggests that genuine objectivity arises from the authentic subjectivity of the *self.*[11]

---

spurious arguments (see Kinneavy, 1990, pp. 91-93). We might conclude then that debating can strengthen one's thinking if it is properly motivated by the pure, detached, disinterested desire to know that Lonergan writes about. But it can be motivated by baser motives and lead to the spurious contention that Plato objected to.

[11] When two people mutually experience the *self* in relationship with one another, they thereby experience not only what Martin Buber (1923/1970) refers to as an I-Thou relationship, but also what Victor Turner (1969) refers to as liminality and communitas. Now, in the Christian tradition liturgical gatherings should aim to engender the experience of liminality and communitas among those gathered. This means that leaders of such gatherings must be able to open themselves up to experiencing the *self* in relationship to those gathered together for the service. That needs to be the case during all parts of the service, not just in the part in which preaching occurs. Since Carla Mae Streeter discusses preaching in chapter 3, perhaps some further remarks about it are in order here. In the sub-title of his major work on ritual, Turner (1969) uses the terms "structure and anti-structure." While he happens to have used the term "structure" with reference to social structures (i.e., in which the *I* is defined) and the so-called "anti-structures" to experiences that call people's attention to their common humanity (i.e., the domain of the *self*), they are suggestive terms when applied to forms of rhetoric. Elsewhere I have used the terms "male mode of rhetoric" and "female mode of rhetoric" to distinguish approaches to forms of persuasive speech and writing that are, respectively, highly

## 5. Conclusion

I have argued that we need to move beyond the Romantic image of writing to a rounder image of writing as intersubjectivity, since one's personal subjectivity is like a parliament of views one has acquired. The Romantic image of writing provides no rationale for learning the ideas of others either through reading or listening. But the aim of formal education is to help people to expand their intersubjectivities by learning the meanings and values of the different academic disciplines. The image of writing as intersubjectivity clearly suggests that the writer needs to appropriate commonly known ideas from within the various textual communities, to use Brian Stock's (1983) term, in order to be able to write effectively within each textual community or discipline. It is axiomatic that one cannot write well about a topic without a certain mastery of the material. An advanced writing student in literary studies, for example, must master the nomenclature or cumulative commonplaces of literary studies, for his or her work to be considered seriously by an audience of professionals. The same is true for advanced writing students in other fields. Thus there is a rationale for listening to lectures and reading. For these are the means by which the writer becomes conversant with the ideas of a particular textual community. Writing in turn becomes a means by which writers demonstrate that they are

---

structured versus approaches that are more field-oriented and methectic (Farrell, 1979). For preaching to contribute to the aim of enabling the people present to experience liminality and communitas, preachers would be well advised to eschew the more structured approaches of the so-called male mode of rhetoric and employ the more indirect ways of the so-called female mode. Since the aim of preaching is not only for the preacher to experience the *self*, but also for the members of the congregation to experience the *self*, the so-called female mode of rhetoric is more suitable for engendering such an experience in the congregation than the male mode. Since the present essay is about writing, it should be noted that the male mode of rhetoric is usually more effective in writing and in teaching than the female mode of rhetoric is. The female mode of rhetoric would appear to be most effective in live interactions, especially at times when it would be appropriate to try to get people to move beyond their ordinary "structured" approaches to thinking to a broader way of seeing things. Now, Streeter may have put her finger on a key move preachers need to make to move themselves toward using the female mode of rhetoric. In her extended example about Ed, she suggests that he needs to relate what is being expressed in the selected passage to something in his own experience. In terms Lonergan uses, this step involves relating the passage to one's empirical level of consciousness. In the Malones' terminology, it involves the *me* in responding to what is being expressed in the passage. According to them, the experience of the *self* occurs when we simultaneously experience the *I* and the *me*. So Streeter's advice for preachers seems to be sound. Moreover, it would seem to follow that preachers should share with the congregation how they are able to relate what is being expressed in the passage to their own experience as a way to help the congregation relate it to something in their own experience.

conversant with the meanings and values of the particular textual community.

According to Lonergan, meanings and values "are authentic in the measure that cumulatively they are the result of the transcendental precepts, Be Attentive, Be Intelligent, Be Reasonable, Be Responsible" (1985, p. 7). Lonergan sums up his own position by saying, "I have placed the legitimacy of authority in its authenticity" (p. 11). For Lonergan, authenticity results from following the transcendental precepts. He claims that "authenticity legitimates authorities, and unauthenticity destroys their authority" (p. 8).

Inasmuch as advanced writing students have been inducted into the textual communities of the academic disciplines, they should be able to express the meanings and values of the disciplines in their writing, which involves the *self* in orchestrating and harmonizing various voices in the field. When they do, their writing is intersubjective, because their personal subjectivities have been expanded to include the meanings and values that have been voiced and developed in the disciplines in question. Moreover, inasmuch as they have followed the *self*-affirming precepts formulated by Lonergan, their writing will also be authentic, especially if they have used pro and con debating honestly to consider alternative positions and made reasonable affirmations as a result. Engaging in such pro and con debating involves cultivating what Bakhtin refers to as the dialogic imagination in literary works, but in the context of writing expository prose from sources.

Lonergan's thought has shown that certain features of classical rhetoric deserve a more positive evaluation than the classical tradition received from Knoblauch and Bannon (1984). Beyond that, his thought has indicated that the intellectual processes involved in writing are also involved in virtually all forms of intellectual inquiry. While this chapter has deliberately focused on advanced writers, the points developed here are also applicable *mutatis mutandis* to freshman composition when forms of writing other than the personal essay or creative writing are involved.[12]

---

[12]I wish to thank Thomas D. Bacig of the University of Minnesota at Duluth for many stimulating conversations about topics treated in this chapter. I also wish to thank Noël M. Valis of Johns Hopkins University and Paul A. Soukup of Santa Clara University for their helpful comments and suggestions for revisions.

# 3

# Preaching as a Form of Theological Communication:
# An Instance of Lonergan's Evaluative Hermeneutics

*Carla Mae Streeter, OP*

Many people today desperately seek meaning in life. The Enlightenment opposition of science and religion, assumed by many to be an emancipation, may be giving way to a new interest in the relationship between science and mysticism as manifested in some recent trends in popular culture.[1] At the same time there is a lingering tendency in our times to keep religious love domesticated and fenced neatly within the confines of religion. This mentality allows many people to carry on human existence out of a horizon that keeps religion in its place while the rest of life struggles for meaning in some vacuous sphere labeled "secular." The result is alienation, a divorce that has left life on the personal, interpersonal, and societal levels like an embodiment trying desperately to recover its soul.

But the contemporary emphasis on a faith that does justice is a summons to integration. The call is to move away from the schizoid perspective that perpetuates our double vision and double standard. While we are aware of the world of religious concerns, we live more in the world of secular demands. To cope, we set up rules for each world and survive by keeping them separate. The bubble bursts when we realize that the perspective itself is an illusion. There is only one world. It has a religious and a secular dimension, and a culture rises or falls on the mutual collaboration of the two.

---

[1] This interest is evident in the popularity of such past writings as Marilyn Ferguson's *The Aquarian Conspiracy* (1980), John Naisbitt's *Megatrends* (1982), Michael Talbot's *Mysticism and the New Physics* (1980), and Fritjof Capra's *The Tao of Physics* (1975). More recently we have Capra joining David Steindl-Rast in *Belonging to the Universe: Explorations on the Frontiers of Science and Spirituality* (1991) and John Hitchcock's *The Web of the Universe: Jung, the 'New Physics' and Human Spirituality* (1991).

This essay explores an alternative to the schizoid perspective. For the Christian who does theology, religious love is a constitutive part of interpreting religious literature accurately and communicating its full meaning. Religious love, used here as a reference for Divine Mystery grasping the human person, needs to be accounted for in a credible way whether or not one has had such an experience, because religious literature is unintelligible without an adequate understanding of religious love.

Preaching is a form of religious communication. This essay will explore the possibility that preaching as a distinct form of theological communication is an instance of what Bernard Lonergan calls an evaluative hermeneutic. It is a publicly proclaimed religious interpretation that calls forth choices based on value judgments as well as understanding. A theology functioning critically and given voice through sound preaching could be a powerful means of healing for a culture in search of authentic religion.

Religion as a human reality cannot be dismissed as insignificant in American life. For philosophy to omit the question of Religious Mystery is for it to deal incomprehensively with the human situation. The longing for the sacred may lead to integrity or mislead into cultic extremism, but it will not go away.

With this in mind, theology in the Christian tradition is restructuring itself, a task which in history has always meant an enfleshment of the word of revelation in language relevant to the times, a communication that connects the revelatory literature with contemporary life and concerns. Linguistic relevance is an emphasis of our times, as is epistemological ambiguity. The infrastructural challenge demands that theology address the renewed interest in epistemology. But the restructuring of theology will succeed only to the extent that it is aware of the importance of authentic human communication.

How one comes to know religious data is central to theology's restructuring task. Some theologians identify theology as the mediating discipline between religion and the cultural matrix in which religion finds itself. Such is Lonergan's approach (1972, p. xi). In *Method in Theology*, Lonergan proposes an entire restructuring of theology grounded in the empirical observation of the recurrent process of human consciousness itself.

## 1. Definition of Key Terms

To begin this task, Lonergan invites theologians to clarify three terms. First, by "culture" he understands the meanings and values of a group of people in any place. In this way culture is understood empirically in contrast to the past when one culture was considered normative of others.

Second, the term "religion" needs to be distinguished from the term "theology." Religion has to do with a human encounter with Religious Mystery. In this encounter, the human being is first addressed *by* Mystery.

Religion is "the prior word God speaks to us by flooding our hearts with his Love" (Lonergan, 1972, p. 112). The human being is grasped by religious love. Lonergan is convinced that religious love must give an account of itself *functionally* as it operates in human consciousness. Being grasped by love is sometimes referred to as direct or "unmediated" religious experience. Such experience is still mediated, however, in the sense that the experience takes place in human consciousness and is thus mediated by that consciousness.

Divine Mystery addresses us ordinarily in a realm Lonergan calls "common sense." This realm is the shared experiential understanding of a particular group. In common sense mode, Transcendent Reality is mediated existentially, dramatically, and practically in and through the way we live. Entering this more common context, Mystery then creates a world of distinctly *religious* experience. Common worship is one fitting response. Religion becomes visible in the beliefs, rituals, and behaviors of a specific religious tradition in a culture.

*Theology* is another fitting response. Theology moves the responder into the realm of theory. Here another mediation takes place. Experience is now mediated by *explanations* making use of specific theological distinctions. The experience is not merely being *described*; it is being *explained*. Theology is theoretical explanation that takes revealed data into account along with the reflection of human minds on that data within specific historical and cultural contexts. In contrast to religious studies, which can limit itself to the observable phenomena of religious traditions, theology as understood by Lonergan takes into account the conversion wrought by religious love in the consciousness of the believer and gives conversion explanatory categories.

The inclusion of religious love in theology, and an account of the change it brings about in the human person, brings a new dimension to the task of restructuring theology. Because theology mediates between religion and culture, this mediating function is actually an interpretive function. As it functions, then, theology is hermeneutical. The inclusion of religious love as a factor suggests that theology as hermeneutic uncovers choices that reveal religious *value*, or what is of ultimate worth to the believer, as well as religious *meaning*. Lonergan's insights would move theology in its restructuring task to address more than a hermeneutic of *understanding*. Lonergan calls for an *evaluative* hermeneutic—interpretation that also discloses the value judgments that lead to choices.

## 2. Theology's Anthropological and Religious Base

Theology calls religion to account for conversion in the realm of theory. It presses religious experience for explanatory categories. To mediate authentically between religion and culture, theology must operate out of a common base with elements from *both* the realms of common sense and theory.

What occurs must then be explained. Being grasped by religious love occurs, and so it must be explained. The blueprint for such a base for explanation exists in Lonergan's philosophical methodology.

The blueprint that Lonergan offers is not a fad, a new theory of knowing in exchange for one that has grown stale. Lonergan invites the critical mind to what he refers to as "interiority analysis." This is a call for the thinker to attend to how he or she processes data. It is a summons to be attentive to the recurring pattern of one's own mental operations, an empirical observation of how consciousness functions.

The pattern of conscious operation needs to be charted. The recurring pattern of the operations is the basis for a theory of cognition. Such a cognitive theory would be unique, for it is drawn from the empirical observance of the *functioning* of consciousness in the realm of common sense and then theoretically *explained*. The explanation is not drawn merely from theoretic possibility, but from empirical observation by any number of persons.

An accurate account of the functioning human intelligence is what Lonergan calls the *anthropological* dimension of the base needed for interiority analysis. It is knowing how one's own mind works. A theory of cognition needs to be critiqued not only in terms of the soundness of the theory itself, but in terms of the empirical accuracy of its *functioning*.

In addition to an adequate account of intellectual processing (the anthropological dimension), Lonergan's blueprint calls for an account of the religious dimension. Interiority analysis requires attentive functional observation and sound theoretical explanation. Part of that functional observation includes the clear impact religious love has on the thinker. That impact is observable and can no longer be dismissed as mere piety. A consciousness grasped by religious love is different from one not so grasped, and that change cannot be left to mere description. It must be *explained*. Explanation moves religious love into the realm of theory to give a coherent account of itself.

Because it is attentive to functional data, interiority analysis will not be content with a phenomenological or merely historical account of religious traditions and practices. It seeks a thematized or explanatory account of how religious love enters and transforms the human consciousness. It is concerned with how being grasped by *ultimate* meaning and value effects a change or "conversion."

Lonergan prefers the title "methodologist" for himself to designate the real intent of his work: making explicit what is implicitly going on in the recurring pattern of human intelligence. His primary concern is with *this* method, the method of the mind operating in any field whatever. This concern directs his readers to a clear focus. Lonergan's primary concern is not with "the objects theologians expound but with the operations that theologians perform" (1972, p. xii).

To understand the intent of such a statement, we must take note of what Lonergan means by "method." As indicated above, he is not using the word to mean a set of principles and rules, a procedure. He is referring to method *concretely* as a human "normative pattern of recurrent and related operations yielding cumulative and progressive results" (1972, p. 5). The normative pattern of which Lonergan speaks can be further nuanced, but as a basic pattern it is non-revisable as he has charted its actual operations. It is what human beings "do" as they come to understand anything.

This *functional* approach frees Lonergan from the static categories of a decadent Scholasticism and enables him to move behind them empirically to the operations from which categories arise. It is understanding how one understands that enables the process to come under critical assessment by oneself and by others. This "empirical method" produces a sharp and accurate cognitional theory that accounts for the operations of the subject and identifies among those operations the point of arriving at (objective) judgment of what is true or real. Lonergan's charting of cognitional process provides a cognitional theory that gives substance to and provides criteria for the recovery of a sound interpretation not only of meaning, but also of the values held by the writer of a text.

Interiority analysis, which requires knowledge of how consciousness functions, holds promise for critical issues facing hermeneutics itself. To these we now turn.

## 3. Three Hermeneutical Problem Areas

Keeping Lonergan's distinct approach in mind and remaining aware that theology is being restructured with its hermeneutical function coming to the fore, we will now consider some of the problems in present hermeneutical discussion.[2] These problems can be grouped under three headings:

- The problem of method and language
- The problem of ideology
- The problem of hermeneutical consciousness (McKinney, 1983, pp. 281-282)

In the first problem area, that of method and language, the writings of Emilio Betti, Hans-Georg Gadamer, and Paul Ricoeur focus the main concerns. Chief among these is the Betti-Gadamer debate.

---

[2] It may be puzzling that the theological hermeneutics of the "Word" represented by Bultmann, Barth, Fuchs, Ebeling, etc. is not treated here. The approach of these writers is important and presupposes a faith stance. I have chosen to begin instead in this consideration from the position that does *not* take faith as a presupposition. The authors I will be referring to represent those whose understanding is seeking faith in contrast to those whose faith is seeking understanding. The reflections of the important writers named above can be found in Robinson and Cobb (1963).

Emilio Betti (1980) is concerned with hermeneutical objectivity and insists that the writings of Hans-Georg Gadamer propose a relativist hermeneutical philosophy. Gadamer is accused of overlooking matters Betti considers vital to a sound hermeneutic: original meaning, objective recovery, and methodology. Gadamer chooses instead to remain with his phenomenological starting place, with what is really occurring empirically in the lived human experience of *Verstehen*. Gadamer is also suspicious of the Cartesian overtones of what Betti demands (Lawrence, 1972, p. 201).

The context of the debate is the familiar subject-object dichotomy: Either the human subject is of prime importance, the objective content of meaning being but a product of a properly functioning subjectivity; or the objective content, what is meant, is of prime importance and must be determined apart from any subjective influence. The argument remains fixed in either/or terms, when what is needed is an inclusive framework accounting for both the operating subject and objective truth content.

Diverse theories of language relate to both sides of this controversy. Outstanding among these language theories is that of Paul Ricoeur. Ricoeur holds that initial philosophical reflection and conceptual analysis of language have led to two distinct hermeneutical positions: One presupposes distortion in language and is based on the *destruction* of such distortion; the other presupposes that language is revelatory and in need of historical *recovery* (1970, pp. 9-32). Each position has theological implications that influence how theology functions and communicates with its public.

The second problem area is that of ideology. It is focused in the Gadamer-Habermas/Apel dialectic, or the controversy between Gadamer and the Critical School. This school, led by K.-O. Apel and Jürgen Habermas, finds Hans-Georg Gadamer's hermeneutical work insufficiently critical in two areas: First, his view of language overlooks the possibility of language to be a medium of domination; second, his naiveté assumes that the healthy "prejudice" of tradition always has something to teach us and overlooks the fact that tradition itself may be biased and in need of critique. The Critical School insists that Gadamer's philosophical hermeneutics is in need of social analysis to be adequate. Gadamer's reply to his Critical School opponents brings the controversy into sharp relief: What is to guarantee that *your* critique is not simply another ideology? (McKinney, p. 283). The unstated nub of the problem is what Lonergan exposes as "bias." The dilemma is how to explain its presence and how to deal with it in seeking an adequate understanding.

The third problem area is concerned with the hermeneutical consciousness itself. Once again, as in the first two problem areas, Gadamer is prominent in the discussion. He points to consciousness itself as the critical factor. The two former problem areas were concerned with the subject/object dichotomy and with bias foiling the workings of a sound hermeneutical process. What has not been addressed at all is exactly *what is going on* in consciousness. Although convinced that consciousness is the key, Gadamer falls silent in the face of the critical question of what takes place there. He has no clear cognitional theory.

## 4. The Lonergan Contribution

Lonergan's distinctively empirical methodology has much in common with the thought of Hans-Georg Gadamer.[3] Both thinkers refer to the data of consciousness as key to the hermeneutical task. Both affirm that not all consciousness is *objectifying* consciousness. Consciousness is structured as horizon, and one is not always aware directly or *objectively*. If explicit direct awareness of objects is not the whole reality of consciousness for these two thinkers, what is missing?

While honoring the entire spectrum of objectifications, consciousness is also capable of simply experiencing itself. This consciousness capability Gadamer refers to as "hermeneutic." It is a consciousness that simply does not overlook *itself*. Gadamer maintains *that* this is so, but does not explain *how*.

But *how* this subject-as-subject operates is crucial. The question still remains: What is going on in consciousness? Lonergan will explain that the subject's primitive self-presence is utterly non-reflexive. He distinguishes between awareness as "intentional" (objectifying) and awareness as simply "conscious" (non-objectifying). Non-objectifying consciousness is a *conscientia experientia* in contrast to objectifying consciousness, which is a *conscientia perceptio*.[4] Non-objectifying consciousness is completely nonreflexive, a simple *attending* rather than *intending*.

By this distinction Lonergan intends to make room once again in consciousness for that contemplative moment of wonder that simply attends to reality. It is akin to Heidegger's "hearing" and is distinct from directly intending any reality as object of intellectual consideration.

This fine distinction identifies two moments in consciousness. It opens the possibility of "objective" consideration of any reality, the operations of the thinker included. The fact that reflexive consciousness reaches truth in the act of judgment in Lonergan's analysis frees him from subjectivism, an entrapment in the subject itself. At the same time it fleshes out

---

[3] See the references for the works of Frederick G. Lawrence which I found most valuable. Lawrence's doctoral work on Gadamer was followed by several publications that were concerned with a valuable Gadamer-Lonergan comparison. I am also indebted to both Robert M. Doran and Michael Vertin for clarifying Lonergan's position on reflexive knowing. For Lonergan's own distinction in this matter see 1967, pp. 226-227, 175-192, and 248-249.

[4] For a fuller treatment of Lonergan's position on this, see his *De constitutione Christi ontologica et psychologica* (1956, p. 131). See also "Christ as Subject: A Reply" (1967/1988, p. 175). For Lawrence's comments on Gadamer in this regard, see 1972, pp. 198-199.

Gadamer's philosophical hermeneutics with an explanation of how consciousness moves from "attending" to the "intending" operations that eventually arrive at an objective judgment. Arriving at truth is part of the intelligent process of the human subject functioning authentically. The subject/object dichotomy dissolves.

In tandem with Gadamer, who calls for beginning phenomenologically as does his mentor Heidegger, Lonergan begins phenomenologically and traces the functioning consciousness *empirically through observation.* He fills in Gadamer's silence as to "what is happening" in consciousness by distinguishing and charting its recurrent pattern of operations and by making distinctions based on empirical observation.

Gadamer is a leading exponent of the ontological turn-to-the-subject in a context until recently dominated by positivism and neo-Kantianism. Gadamer's "prejudice-as-corrective" is not credible because he offers no real distinctions in the operating consciousness to show how one perspective might be a corrective of another. No distinct cognitional theory is addressed by Gadamer. This clarification is Lonergan's unique contribution.

Lonergan distinguishes cognitional theory (what is actually going on) *from* epistemology (why only the *whole* of what is going on can be called "knowing"). This distinction, noted empirically, is necessary to free the epistemological question from any Cartesian overtones. What I *think* knowing is may not be what knowing actually is. Cognitional theory explains what I am actually *doing* when I am knowing. It answers a concrete *functional* question, offering an empirical charting of the operations of human consciousness. Epistemology, in contrast, wants to know why *these operations*, all of them, not any others, are an accurate account of human knowing.

For Lonergan, cognitional theory is an empirical explanation of what is going on when a human being comes to know. Drawing from this cognitional data judged as accurate, epistemology then deals with the broader question of why that cognitional theory is an adequate account of what human knowing actually is. A charting of the pattern sequence itself is cognitional theory based on empirical analysis of functioning operations.

The relationship of one operation to the others, the precise recurring sequence of operations, how truth is reached at the point of judgment, and why *all* of this, not only part, is what true "knowing" is—this is epistemology for Lonergan. Cognitional theory is simply an explanation of what is going on. Epistemology deals with the further question of why that total account is what human knowing is—and why nothing else qualifies. Knowing is not merely imaging. It is not experiencing. It is not sensing or feeling. It is not "picture thinking" or creating a mental concept. It is not even understanding something, for the understanding may be inadequate. Knowing is reaching a judgment that what I understand is accurate—it is truly so; it is real. In judgment, the questioning consciousness comes to rest as to the truth of a matter. The mind may rest in sociological or economic reality. It may also rest in truth that is religious.

Theology as a hermeneutical discipline mediates between religion and culture. To communicate its truth adequately, theology needs a base drawing from both religion and the culture in which it finds itself. Interiority analysis insists upon drawing from both theory and common sense. Theory presses for explanation. Common sense deals with simple description of how things go on culturally. A common base in interiority is established by integrating attentiveness to common sense realities with critical explanation of how and why things are the way they are, based on a knowledge of how human consciousness functions. In the discipline known as theology, the common sense realm includes being grasped by Ultimate Concern. Interiority analysis, for Lonergan, is using one's knowledge of how the mind functions to critique any intellectual search for truth in any area, including the conversion implied in one's personal theology.

The shift to this realm of interiority is a conversion Lonergan names "intellectual." It is attentiveness to one's own operations of consciousness. It "identifies in personal experience one's conscious and intentional acts and the dynamic relation that links them to one another" (1972, p. 284).

It is distinctions like these and the precise explanation of cognition made possible from interiority analysis that Lonergan brings to the hermeneutical debate. Any attempt to understand Lonergan's hermeneutical methodology must take his explicit cognitional theory and its grounding in interiority analysis as its base.

This base in interiority, drawing from common sense, theory, and self-knowledge regarding consciousness is important to the hermeneutical impasse sketched earlier. No amount of emphasis on historical consciousness (Dilthey), objectivity (Betti), or social consciousness (Habermas, Apel) alone is adequate. Cognition is going on. It is going on well or poorly. An accurate theory of what exactly is going on cognitionally is key to any critique of any system. An epistemology based on sound cognitional theory enables a critique of various theories of language (Ricoeur). It turns a critical spotlight on approaches that overlook the insidious infiltration of bias (Gadamer).

This cluster of problems calls for an adequate and universal "hermeneutic consciousness." To be adequate, such a consciousness must be free from binding Cartesian certitude that presupposes the illusion of a subject-object split in human knowing. The solution needs to be deeper than, but inclusive of, partial concerns such as "aesthetic" or "historical" consciousness (Lonergan, 1967, pp. 226-227).

But truth alone is not enough. In his later writings Lonergan included an account not only of cognition in human consciousness, but also of decision and the role of feelings in coming to decision. His work with the operations of consciousness reveals an *evaluative* function in coming to decisions. The question of value becomes significant for the hermeneutical problem concerning ideology. Lonergan's evaluative hermeneutic emerges here.

Introducing the element of *evaluative* meaning in addition to the element of *cognitive* meaning addresses the ideological dilemma. Value involves ranking, prioritizing. Human societal criteria exist. A position must be critiqued not only in its meaning, but also in the value it presents. When the field is theology, Ultimate Value with a view to commitment is being proposed.

It follows that the framework we seek for theological communication must be comprehensive enough to account for the ultimate value of being grasped by a Love that is religious. This reality is not to be ignored if it has hermeneutical significance when religious literature is before us for critique. Meaning as *intentional* can be noted through interiority analysis. But what if that analysis reveals judgments of value as well as judgments of truth?

Cognitional operation is but a higher integration of a sensitive psyche, and this psyche is an energy field of the ongoing flow of perceptions, images, and feelings that move in human consciousness. What explicitly influences this sensitive flow most is the *value or worth* of what is being considered. Religious experience can exert such a value influence, and when it does so, the imaginal and emotional base out of which cognition arises is affected.

Being grasped by Ultimate Value, by religious love, effects a change in the interpreter, and this affects not mere procedure and technique, but the human agent from which all procedure and technique proceed. Any significant transformation in the interpreter's consciousness has hermeneutical significance if we are seeking what identifies an adequate hermeneutical consciousness. Religion or its neglect is a part of existential living. The transformation wrought by encounter with Religious Mystery cannot be swept aside to some irrational dust bin. Full accountability is urgent especially at this time when hermeneutics is becoming more identified with the theological task itself (Lawrence, 1981, 1983; van Beeck, 1987, p. 327; Mahaney, 1988, pp. 55ff.).

The word *conversion* has more than pious connotation. It has anthropological significance. Conversion must be given clear explanatory categories. Mere description is not enough. The influence of Ultimate Value on the human being needs to be thematized.

We resist change in our lives because we are blinded by different forms of bias. Lonergan differentiates bias as that element in Gadamer's "prejudice" that is not just to be accepted as inevitable. It is to be detected, named, dealt with critically, and if necessary, overcome. In this way Lonergan pushes Gadamer where the concerns of Habermas and Apel regarding social analysis must be taken seriously.

Lonergan maintains that being grasped by religious love alters the *interpreter*. There is a converted *new self* doing the interpretive task, one who not only takes a position based on truth, but on the urgency that arises out of a value judgment.

The strength of Lonergan's interiority analysis is the explicit recognition and account of *insight*, the act of organizing intelligence itself. So familiar, so obvious and simple is the pivotal act of insight that it is not part of the explicit consideration of the work of any other major philosophical thinker. Its function in cognitional activity is so central, Lonergan explains, "that to grasp it in its conditions, its working, and its results is to confer a basic yet startling unity on the whole field of human inquiry and human opinion" (1957, p. xi). Insight is a pivot, a lever, that fuses elements of an image or phantasm into the "I get it!" known as understanding.

We need to ask what relation this understanding has to the urgency brought about by encounter with Ultimate Value.


## 5. Preaching as a Form of Theological Communication

Communication that blends both truth and religious urgency is the proclamatory theological communication called preaching. This distinct form of communication is conviction clothed in feeling, in urgency, in motivational power that generates commitment to effect change.

Preaching is not synonymous with teaching (Hill, 1976-1977; Motl, 1990). Teaching intends ordered information. Preaching pushes on to the behavioral transformation we identify as conversion. Although distinct in intent from teaching, preaching incorporates sound teaching, and a good teacher often moves students toward behavioral change.

As a form of theological communication, preaching flows from theological substance. While theological balance identifies it as having solid content, this form of communication succeeds when it moves hearers to act. Committed members of religious traditions operate from intense feelings that bespeak the values of a group. Values have to do with priorities, just as meaning has to do with understanding. If theology is to mediate between religion and culture, it must do so by addressing the feeling that motivates a group as well as its beliefs. Value comes through *feeling*, as Lonergan has noted: "...feeling gives intentional consciousness its mass, momentum, drive, power. Without these feelings our knowing and deciding would be paper thin" (1972, pp. 30-31). No form of theological communication manifests this evaluative function as explicitly as the preaching act.

Preaching is the culmination of the theological process. The process begins with sources, proceeds with pertinent questions, and reaches persuasive conclusions. Feelings register the value of these conclusions. This value prompts action. Conversely, what is acted upon reveals what is valued, not just what is held as true. Preaching addresses both meaning and value.

Lonergan's explanation of the theological process is sketched in the accompanying diagram (see Figure 3.1). Human consciousness moves from

# THE HUMAN CONSCIOUSNESS FUNCTIONING THEOLOGICALLY

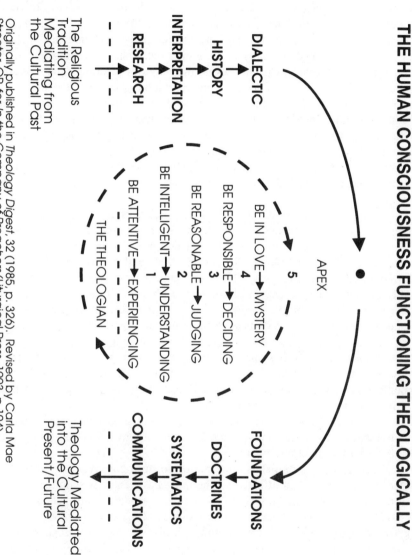

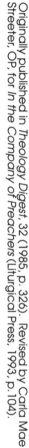

Figure 3.1

Originally published in *Theology Digest*, 32 (1985, p. 326). Revised by Carla Mae Streeter, OP, for *In the Company of Preachers* (Liturgical Press, 1993, p. 104).

sources to convictions, and from convictions to commitment. But theology's mediating role has two phases: the phase mediating religious meaning *from* the culture by means of the texts and traditions already there, and the phase mediating religious truth, interpreted anew in light of contemporary questions and concerns, *back into* the culture. In the first phase, theology mediating from the culture, the mind attends to the writings, art, and symbols the culture has provided, seeking the religious truth intended. Theology's first functional specialty is therefore "research," a seeking out of the sources, texts, artifacts, etc. that reveal the religious meanings and values of a people. The functional specialty "interpretation" follows. It is the search in the sources for the intention of the mind that authored or created them. "Interpretation" includes exegesis and hermeneutics proper. A third step emerges as threads of meaning are uncovered, meaning that moves forward and develops. This is Lonergan's understanding of "history" as a functional specialty. A final step is "dialectic," attending to the direct opposition of various meanings and the need to rank the value of each as held in that culture.

These first four functions provide a sketch of the empirical analysis done in any science. They are done by believer and non-believer alike.

Not so with phase two. The information provided in the first four functions springs from the culture. Scholarship deals with it. To enter phase two, however, one deals directly with the commitment or stance of the theologian. This position reveals a distinct perspective or horizon. If the scholar continues into phase two, he or she begins functions proper to a theologian, one who reflects upon and seeks to articulate the religious experience of a community from the position of a commitment within that community.

Figure 3.1 indicates that the movement in phase two is from above downwards. The last three functions, "doctrines," "systematics," and "communications," will flow from "foundations," which objectifies the distinct religious conversion of the theologian.

Addressing conversion objectively as a function of theology is unique to Lonergan. He calls for the thematization of conversion and thus its examination by critical intelligence.

Lonergan distinguishes four major forms of conversion: religious, moral, intellectual, and affective. The most basic form is religious conversion, which Lonergan describes as "being grasped by ultimate concern" (1972, p. 240). This "being-in-love" with God "is not the product of our knowledge and choice. On the contrary, it dismantles and abolishes the horizon in which our knowing and choosing went on and sets up a new horizon in which the love of God will transvalue our values and the eyes of that love will transform our knowing" (1972, p. 106).

When notions are formed in light of all that is known of the past tradition uncovered in phase one, the theologian shapes the language to speak that ancient truth in doctrinal language suited to the times. "Doctrines" is the function of forming propositional statements of belief out of a faith perspective. Lonergan carefully distinguishes faith from belief. Faith is a knowing born of loving, while beliefs are propositions to express faith convictions. These doctrinal propositions are then interrelated, becoming a coherent "systematics." Areas of belief must have meaning in themselves and in relation to one another. An integral systematics speaks meaning to this age as well as remaining in continuity with the past.

Finally, theological "communications" emerges as a specific function. All that has been clarified, distinguished, and explained in the realm of theory must now be translated from the theoretic mode to the realm of common sense where men and women live, struggle, rejoice, and die. The theologian writes, enters the classroom to teach, or stands before a congregation to preach. If this return is not done well, people might hear only the precise, specific, but cold language of theology. They may understand little or nothing of this language. The specific function called theological "communications" focuses on transposing theological meaning into the common sense language of the women and men on the streets and in our families. These hearers have little or no access to theological jargon. Its distinctions and clarifications, essential for the precision of the theological discipline, are a foreign language for the butcher, the baker, or the Buick sales manager.

Theological "communications" is concerned with theology in its external relations. It is concerned with theology's relations to its "public" (Lonergan, 1972, p. 132). To be effective, theological "communications" must be concerned with three types of external relations: those relations that are interdisciplinary, those that call for general transposition from the realm of theory to the realm of common sense, and those that need to be ready to adapt to the various media used in the culture. It is the second type of relations, the transposition from the realm of theory to the realm of common sense, that is the focus of our considerations.

When this transposition has intellectual information as its goal, we are dealing with teaching. The ethical or moral transformation of the learner may occur as a result of teaching, but these outcomes will not be listed as one of the objectives of a course. When theological communication does have the ethical and moral transformation of the hearer as direct and primary objective, conversion is the goal, and preaching emerges as a distinct form of theological communication. As with teaching, the preacher must communicate truth to *this* culture to challenge it to the transformation that makes it more distinctly human.

Neither culture nor religion itself is exempt from this transformation. The preacher too, as attentive hearer, is often the first to be converted in the struggle to communicate.

For Christians, the double dynamic of an inner experience of being grasped by religious love moving toward an outer historicized manifestation suggests an incarnational pattern. The Spirit, encountering human willingness in the Jewish woman Mary, brings forth the Word in the historical, Jewish Jesus. This incarnational paradigm is reflected in every authentic theological effort: Through the Spirit, a new word is again enfleshed in and through the historical human language of a particular time and place.

## 6. Preaching as an Evaluative Hermeneutical Transposition

Preaching is theological understanding transposed to challenge not only the understandings but also the lives of the common man and woman on the street. This means the skillful development of transpositional language—expressions rich with imagery, metaphor, and analogy—that carry theological meaning without bogging the hearer down in theological jargon. As hermeneutics proper is a transposition *from* the common sense language of a text into the realm of the theoretical understanding of its meaning, so preaching as a form of evaluative hermeneutics transposes not only meaning, but also the value horizon established by religious conversion, *back to* those listening.

When done well, preaching is the communication of one who is in love. It declares not only what one understands, but what one must *do* as a result. As a result, preaching mediates between the word of God and the word the culture seeks to instill in us. It may directly challenge the values of the culture. It may reinterpret the religious tradition itself in light of contemporary questions and needs.

Preaching is the primary act of the self-constituting process that Christians identify as "church." The community called church is actually formed by the word preached in its midst. It is brought more and more into being every time that word is preached. The community actually enters into its own formation by its willingness to let the word transform it. The word is God's word. But the word is also human. It is kneaded with our surrender, watered with human tears, baked in the oven of human grief, and served at the table of our gathering together. Because preaching is informational, formational, and transformational, it presses for an interpretation and expression of priorities. By means of the truth, the skilled preacher arouses feeling, the feeling shapes motivation, and the motivated person makes choices. But inviting informed and free human response is a far cry from cultic manipulation. Authentic human response constitutes what people in a culture recognize as progress. If so, then sound preaching midwives the human in its search for what is of true value.

As a form of theological communication, preaching mediates through several types of transposition. The preacher mediates between the word of God and the congregation by transposing theological understanding back into the language of common struggle. These transpositions modulate theological distinctions into the power that effects change. One is reminded of the power in the words of a Gandhi or Martin Luther King, Jr.

The first transposition takes place when the scriptural text enters the preacher's awareness. The preacher's first task is to hear the word in the language of its time and writing. Sound biblical theology is critical at this stage. Unless the preacher is trained to respect the scriptural word in its historical meaning through an accurate communal interpretation (exegesis and sound cognitive hermeneutic), the proclamatory task is crippled from the start. A merely pietistic or fundamentalist hearing imprisons the word in the preacher, or worse, becomes an eisogesis—an imposition of the preacher's agenda onto the word.

A second subtle transposition takes place when the preacher is evaluated by the scriptural word. The text challenges the preacher's imagery and concepts. In this transposition the emphasis is no longer on the scriptural word, but on the preacher's experience. The preacher has a personal theology, a way of interpreting possible religious meaning in events. Whether implicit and undefined or explicit and finely nuanced, the theology of the preacher will be challenged by the text. If there is little or no biblical or theological depth in the preacher, or more harmful, if the theological formation that is there arises from a fundamentalist mindset, then the word will be limited by this personal factor. In silence before the word, it is often the preacher's former images and favorite concepts that must undergo change. This is experienced as healthy unrest, as a questioning, as a humble search for understanding. The personal distorted beliefs of the preacher need to be purged in light of the scriptural word. But it is here also that the preacher becomes aware that he or she is part of a community drawing on a common faith tradition. The rich but ambiguous depths of scriptural language pass into a focused interpretation in continuity with the meaning and value that the community recognizes as its own. The faith of the community provides a dark light in which *meaning* for the preacher shows itself. In the context of the religious love that grasps the preacher, a sense of the meaning and value of the text emerges for human life.

It is in this second transposition that we can detect a movement from mere cognitive hermeneutics (meaning) to the full evaluative hermeneutic (value) that manifests the priorities of not only the preacher but of the *community*. The evaluative hermeneutic that is Lonergan's contribution to the hermeneutical discussion now finds an explicit oral articulation.

From the mutual encounter of the preacher with the word and the word with the struggling humanness of the preacher, the third transposition becomes possible. Using all the skills of the preaching art, the word understood through theological reflection must now once again be clothed in the rich language of imagery and analogy, metaphor and story, to impact a congregation today where it lives here and now.

*How* the message will actually transform the listeners is not the preacher's concern. Good preaching is clear, direct, and persuasive. It is utterly concrete and practical. A concrete example may serve to illustrate how this three-fold transposition actually occurs.


## 7. An Example of Preaching

It is Advent. The setting is a small church in northern Wisconsin. The minister, Ed, who pastors this little church with his wife, Marilyn, sits down to be with the word of God for a while in preparation for the service he will conduct on Sunday. The text is Luke's annunciation narrative.

If he is wise, Ed will temporarily put aside "preparing a sermon." Instead, he will simply bring himself before the word of God and listen, letting it first prepare him. Ed has been educated in biblical theology at a Lutheran seminary, and what he has learned about biblical interpretation will form a context for his encounter with the text. Often because of degrees and preparation, this first transposition is a vulnerable moment for the preacher. It invites one into a terrifying silence, and time pressure will often be the excuse for skipping this first transposition. Allowing oneself to stand silent before the word of God is claiming a distinct posture. The stillness bespeaks radical need and identifies the preacher with the poverty of the people who will be gathering. The need creates a hunger in the preacher, a hunger for meaning and insight. It is here that the preacher becomes a beggar in search of the bread of the word that nourishes. The cry of the poor (here the preacher) will not go unheard. Like a reed hollowed out, the preacher is readied by this first transposition for the piper's breath. There is room for what God wants said because of the emptiness this first transposition creates. Without it, the word given may be merely the preacher's. Ed knows the scholarship and the commentaries. He knows that a fundamentalist, literalist exegesis of this text is not tenable. But his silence is another kind of school. The love that has driven him into ministry fills him with awe and reverence. This positioning takes him beyond his historical-critical work, beyond literary analysis. It postures the human mind before the incomprehensible.

The second transposition begins as the text becomes a mirror to the preacher. Was this woman Mary like this, Ed wonders? Was she so empty of egoism that there was room for the breath to move? The messenger tells her that being like this is blessed; being empty, needy; being creature. God is looking for welcome space, like a bird seeking a nesting place. A woman's womb? Tissue? Blood and bone? Hands, feet, and hair? This is too much. God should know better than to get mixed up in all this. This can *hurt*.

Ed and Marilyn have two children, with a third on the way. The memory of the joy and mutual surrender of their lovemaking intrudes itself into Ed's thoughts, and he is almost embarrassed. Yet it fits—he can't deny it: their "yes" with this woman Mary's yes, their fruitfulness and hers. Is that how it is with us, he wonders? Is that how close God wants to come? Ed thinks of the old ones in his congregation, of the widows, of the single, and of the divorced. He remembers the children and the teens. What of them? What of their hungers? Will this holy One find welcome? What will these incarnations look like?

This time the word itself has provided him with a structure. It is familiar to all his hearers. There is a lot of space in northern Wisconsin. He decides to go with the image. Much space, but some hearts may not have any. Can we be needy before God? Can we admit that we don't have it all together, that we long for many things, some of them selfishly? Can we empty ourselves enough of some of the rubble at least to let God breathe love in us?

If we say yes, then the incarnation can start, the space can come alive. Things may need to change. The rubble has to go. The space must be filled with words to be said or left unsaid; the walking in someone else's skin; the telephone call; noticing the look on someone's face. Why doesn't God just leave us alone? To come to meet us in skin, in hair, in blood and bone and tissue and tears is just a little too much. Or is that just what is being "announced" to us today—something not just for Mary, but for all of us? Is God asking us to give our little worlds a good word, a word-made-flesh? In *our* flesh—yours and mine?

This second transposition moves the preacher's reflection from what the text simply *means* to what the text *means for the preacher's life*, or what *value* it has for the human struggle. The meaning of the text is interiorized. It finds a home in the heart of the preacher's own reality. In Lonergan's terms, the religious love that grasps the preacher recognizes the word as its own, but needs expression to bring it to completion (Lonergan, 1972, p. 113).

That expression will take the form of Ed's preaching. His actual delivery, not the writing of the sermon, will effect the third transposition. The meaning of the word and its value for our lives will be shared with others through the images Ed uses, through the way he links one insight to another, through the way he uses his voice, through the way his own face and body enter into what he is trying to say.

## 8. Conclusion

The human community struggles with double vision. We are in need of a good word that fuses the sacred with the secular in every facet of human living, each with its own contribution, but inseparable in life as it is actually lived.

Communications is the culmination of Bernard Lonergan's theological method. Preaching is a distinct form of theological communication. It is an articulation not only of the meaning to be conveyed, but of the value of that meaning for changing both the preacher and those who might hear the preaching.

By insisting that an account of conversion be included in theological processing, Lonergan is calling attention to what is there and needs to be accounted for. In his account of how theology moves from researching data to communicating conviction, Bernard Lonergan moves religious love from the limbo of pietism to a reality causing a state or condition that alters the horizon of the interpreter. The mental horizon of the person religiously in love includes Ultimate Concern and differs from the mental horizon of one not so in love.

When a person religiously in love engages in the distinct form of communication known as preaching, we have an example of an oral evaluative hermeneutic in action. A text is being interpreted not only as to its meaning, but also as to its value to transform human life.

An evaluative hermeneutic is Lonergan's distinct contribution to the hermeneutic discussion. It is a distinction that rests on the empirical analysis of the pattern of consciousness itself, the missing piece in the discussion of philosophical hermeneutics. Without an understanding of how the human mind processes data in order to understand, judge, and finally decide, the theological task of interpreting religious texts written in the context of religious love has no critical compass. What is going on needs to be accounted for, and that account must be made in relation to all else that is going on.

Theology as a cognitive and evaluative hermeneutic can enrich both the religion and the culture it seeks to serve. As an oral evaluative hermeneutic, preaching can be a key to bringing about human transformation.

Preaching can be the key to the unveiling of the actual fusion between the sacred and secular dimension of human life. Struggling people deserve a good word, a word about what is real, and a word about what is ultimately real. Cultures long for justice. As a form of theological communication, preaching can bring a good word that not only calls for compassion but for justice. In hope, the religions and cultures of our world wait.

# 4

# The Spectrum of "Communication" in Lonergan

## Frederick E. Crowe, SJ

The spectrum of Bernard Lonergan's ideas on communication as well as on other topics runs through philosophy and theology and, by extension, through all the sciences and disciplines with which philosophy and theology are in reciprocal relationship. His own work was directly theological, but his theological categories were either general, regarding "objects that come within the purview of other disciplines as well as theology," or special, regarding "objects proper to theology" (Lonergan, 1972, p. 282). But even on the level of categories there is a close connection of theology with other disciplines, especially philosophy and the human sciences. On the existential level the connection is closer still, for there we are dealing with our human race in its concrete reality, and it makes a difference from end to end of the spectrum whether we live in a universe designed for our partnership with God or in one where we are left on our own, perhaps even in a universe without any design at all.

It will therefore be important in this volume in which Lonergan's ideas on communication are to be studied from many particular viewpoints, to keep in mind the broad spectrum of theology, philosophy, and the natural and human sciences and studies, over which his mind ranges. Accordingly, this essay aims to do something to meet this need. It is an omnium-gatherum of ideas in Lonergan that relate, either centrally or tangentially, to the topic of communication. It has therefore to be sketchy on those ideas singly, but may provide an overall framework in which more detailed studies can be located and related to one another.

That does not mean that this chapter attempts a synthesis of Lonergan's views: It remains simply a collection, from end to end of the spectrum, of points that seem to be relevant. Still, even an omnium-gatherum should show some order, based on an external principle if not on the intrinsic analysis of communication itself. So I have structured this chapter in five parts on the basis of two simple divisions: the division between divine and human reality; and the division between what is interior and what moves out to others.

Part 1, then, treats communication in divine interiority. Of the two aspects of human communication, Part 2 covers the one interior to each of us. The other aspect of human communication involves moving out of oneself to communicate with others. This latter aspect, as most directly related to communication in its normal sense, requires more elaboration, so I preface it by some philosophic points in Part 3, and then in the longest section, Part 4, I discuss communication with others in the context it has for Lonergan's own discipline of theology, namely, the cross-cultural. I conclude with a shorter section, Part 5, which as a complement to Part 1 treats communication between God and humankind.

## 1. Communication Within God

Lonergan's views on communication within God suppose the common Catholic doctrine on the Trinity, gradually developed in the early centuries, and magisterially set forth for the Christian West in the fifth-century creed, *Quicumque (Whoever)*. Further, on the ontological aspect of communication, his views are the commonly held theology of his church: The Father communicates being, power, all the divine attributes, to the Son; and Father and Son communicate them to the Spirit. What is not communicable is personal identity: The Father's fatherhood cannot be communicated to the Son, and so too with the other distinctive personal notions; but this incommunicability is so little opposed to the communication of the divine attributes that it is in fact required for their communication (Lonergan, 1964a, pp. 171-173).

What is more characteristic of Lonergan's trinitarian theology (and more controversial) is the addition of the conscious factor. The study of consciousness, an accepted part of philosophy in modern times, has inevitably been extended to theology as well; in particular, questions have been raised about the self-consciousness of Jesus, focusing in Protestant theology first on his consciousness of being Messiah, and in Catholic theology more on his consciousness of his divinity. Lonergan's interest in such questions can be traced through the theory of human consciousness that he developed in *Insight* (1957/1992, chapter 11: "Self-Affirmation of the Knower," pp. 343-371) and applied to the consciousness of Christ (Lonergan, 1964b, thesis 12a: *De scientia Christi*, pp. 332-416).

But it is in his trinitarian theology that the question becomes relevant in a quite specific way to the topic of communication. The three in God are not only persons in an ontological sense, but also conscious subjects in a psychological sense: conscious not as we are conscious, only on the higher levels of our being, but in every aspect of their being (Lonergan, 1964a, pp. 186-193).

Now this bears directly on communication within God. The ontological incommunicability of the person does not preclude conscious communication in the fullest sense among the persons. For within God there are intersubjective relations among the three, and their intersubjectivity is as much a part of their conscious life as their being and knowledge and willing and other aspects of their divinity. That is, each of the three is conscious of the divine being and of the divine self that that person is, and also conscious of, and consciously related to, each of the other two. Lonergan adds that, in so far as "I" and "Thou" signify the most perfect possible interpersonal relations, we can understand those terms as applicable also to the divine three (1964a, p. 196).[1]

In summary: Communication among the three divine persons is full and complete in what are called the absolute perfections of God (being, knowledge, power, and so on), but the relative properties that maintain personal distinctions (fatherhood, sonship) are not communicated. To this standard doctrine Lonergan adds his special focus on consciousness: Communication among the three is fully conscious, conscious in the community of the divine being, conscious in the community of interpersonal relations.

To those who fear that three Gods would result from this, Lonergan's answer is simple: As one essence and one divinity is possessed by all three, and thus there is but one God yet so as to leave the three distinct in their possession of the one essence and one divinity, so there is one divine consciousness possessed by all three, and thus there is but one conscious God yet so as to leave each person distinct in the possession of the one consciousness (see 1964a, pp. 192-193).

My presentation in this part is necessarily brief, but I think it important to note this aspect of Lonergan's views on communication, partly because his trinitarian theology is tied in with the whole range of his thinking, partly because the example brings out at once a main feature and orientation of his thought, and the direction of his progress beyond traditional Scholasticism: in a phrase he himself has used, the progress from substance to subject, illustrated in the religious sphere when "being in Christ Jesus" advances from "the being of substance" to the being "of subject" (Lonergan, 1967/1988, pp. 230-231).[2]

---

[1] Lonergan speaks here of what he will say "infra"—which I take to mean the section on *perichoresis*, pp. 205-208. Note, however, that when one is thinking in terms of the psychological analogy of *Dicens, Verbum, Amor*, it is only the Father who utters a Word; that Word, of course, expresses all that is, the divine being and the three in God; it is an *affirmatio infinita* (p. 204).

[2] There is a more humdrum daily advance with the "emergence of consciousness in the...dream, where human substance yields place to the human subject" (Lonergan, 1985, p. 208).

## 2. Communication Within the Human Being

Communication within God, in both its ontological and conscious aspects, is essentially interpersonal communication within one being. But on the human scene, however much we strive for and achieve unity with others, interpersonal communication essentially relates one being to another being. That external relationship must be central in our study, but I would draw attention first to a communication that is internal to the individual human being, one that is less commonly associated with communication in the modern sense, one that relates level to level in the multiform constitution of a human person, and one in which Lonergan may make a distinctive contribution.

A human being is a unity constituted by many levels: physical, chemical, biological, sensitive, intelligent, rational, affective. Each successive level is viewed as a higher integration of activities that would be merely a coincidental manifold on the lower. Thus, the wonder that is observed in a child falls outside the system of laws that govern its sensitive life, and recurring acts of wonder would be only a coincidental manifold in the context of sensitive life, but they become systematic in the higher integration of intelligent life. Further, there is interaction between levels, and a principle of correspondence that merits the name of communication, when what is merely coincidental on a lower level (say, the child's recurring wonder) is brought under law through a systematizing form on the next higher level (Lonergan, 1957/1992, p. 555).

Thus, we are material beings, so the laws of physics apply to us, and we fall from a height as stones do. There is a chemistry in the human body, so oxygen burns in our lungs as it does in the laboratory. There is a biological level on which, like other living things, we obey the laws of cellular formation. But in Lonergan's view of emergent probability, lower levels have a finality toward the higher, and the higher take over and subsume the lower within their own finality (1957/1992, Index: under Emergent probability). Maybe we would be justified in speaking of an ontological communication here on these lower levels, but it is in the conscious realm with its several sublevels—sensitive, intelligent, reasonable, affective—that the question of communication especially and properly arises.

In this conscious realm correspondence goes far beyond that of, say, chemistry and biology in the human body. There is operative now the factor of *intentionality*, a conscious interior dynamism that works spontaneously to lift us from level to level. This factor is seen most vividly in the questions that continually arise to propel us beyond the slow torpor of ontological finality. Data of the sensitive and imaginative life are met by this dynamic intentionality with the question, What? or, Why? or, How often? The result is an idea, or more often a number of alternative ideas, or when the idea is pursued, by a coalescing cluster of ideas. These in turn are met by our dynamic intentionality with the question, Is it so? Are our ideas all wrong? Or is perhaps one of them right? The result is a judgment on the fact of the matter, and our judgments grow incrementally to give us a view of a situation, only to be met again by our dynamic intentionality with the requirement that we act: What is to be done? More specifically, what am *I* to do? And, most comprehensively, what are my values? To whom do I commit myself in love?

We should not think of this higher integration, correspondence, and communication as simply an upward progress from level to higher level. It is equally a communication from higher to lower. Indeed, it is fundamentally that, for we begin life and develop consciously in the ambience of loving trust rather than on the basis of data examined and understood. In virtue of that loving trust, we adopt almost unconsciously a view of life and our world, a set of beliefs and judgments, understanding of which follows much later to make our experience mature and perceptive. In the mature person, then, there can be various communications of level with level, in either the upward or the downward process, or a mixture of the two. There is a continual two-way traffic, all along the route, or between two points on the way, or between a point as reached in the upward progress and the same point as reached in the downward movement.

All this is familiar enough in itself, but I am not aware that it has been examined in relation to communication studies, and I believe it would add to them a dimension not generally appreciated. Let me therefore illustrate some of its latent richness in a more specific point that Lonergan makes about communication between sensitive and intelligent levels.

The levels are quite distinct; their distinction is seen in the difference between human and animal activity: "When an animal has nothing to do, it goes to sleep. When a man has nothing to do, he may ask questions" (Lonergan, 1957/1992, p. 34).[3] Now these two distinct levels are found in human beings, in psychic and intellectual activity. The intellectual level is quite distinct, with its own dynamic factor (the "operator," in Lonergan's terms): "[O]n the intellectual level the operator is concretely the detached and disinterested desire to know. It is this desire, not in contemplation of the already known, but headed towards further knowledge, orientated into the known unknown." This occurs on a higher level than the psyche. Nevertheless, the "principle of dynamic correspondence calls for a harmonious orientation on the psychic level, and from the nature of the case such an orientation would have to consist in some cosmic dimension, in some intimation of unplumbed depths, that accrued to man's feelings, emotions, sentiments" (Lonergan, 1957/1992, p. 555).[4]

---

[3] See also Lonergan, 1957/1992, pp. 208-209: "Animals, safely sheathed in biological routines, are not questions to themselves. But man's artistry testifies to his freedom. As he can do, so he can be what he pleases. What is he to be? Why?"

[4] Lonergan relates this to the nonrational element in Rudolph Otto's *Idea of the Holy* (1923/1958); his own work is not so much a study of that element as a framework in

In a later work Lonergan speaks of this correspondence in terms of "internal communication." The context is the role of the symbol in linking organic and psychic levels with the higher. There is a need, he says:

> for internal communication. Organic and psychic vitality have to reveal themselves to intentional consciousness and, inversely, intentional consciousness has to secure the collaboration of organism and psyche. Again, our apprehensions of values occur in intentional responses, in feelings: Here too it is necessary for feelings to reveal their objects and, inversely, for objects to awaken feelings. It is through symbols that mind and body, mind and heart, heart and body communicate. (1972, pp. 66-67)

I leave this part of the chapter reluctantly, having room only to mention the array of omitted questions: the relation of understanding to the image, the function of reflection in relation to concepts and to the whole range of experience, the role of symbol as affect-laden image, and so on. Further, these notions on "internal communication" seem especially pertinent to the problem to be seen later (section 4.1) of the unity of consciousness in Jesus. Further still, it may be that they will not only widen the categories of communication theory, but will also be analogous to, or even a paradigm for, our communication with one another, and thus more directly affect what we may call the "external communication" to which we now turn.

## 3. Human Interpersonal Communication: Philosophic Points

Far the most important area of study in Lonergan and communication regards the transmission of divine revelation from one cultural group to another, and this will get the lion's share of my attention (Part 4 below), but as background for it I need some philosophic points on communication: the ontological unity of the human race, the priority of intelligence over language, the dynamics of expression, a view on intersubjectivity.

### 3.1 The Ontological Unity of the Human Race

I mention, to begin with, a curious view Lonergan expressed in an early essay to the effect that what is first is a kind of universal human being, and what comes second is the individuation of this into subsistent persons. The essay, written when he was a student and never published in his lifetime, developed at length the theme of human solidarity, and in this context we find such statements as these.

> [Man] is not simply an individual....Philosophically, man is one universal nature *in regard to what he is,* and man is many merely in virtue of the modality of his being, *in regard to the way he is.* Man is one in virtue of his form, and he is many merely in virtue of matter....Man as these many par-

---

which to locate it and relate it to total human activity.

ticulars is contingence and materiality; man as a universal nature is an intelligible essence and a limited aspect of the divine essence....[T]he difference between men is less real than the unity of men. (Lonergan, 1991, p. 151)

Lonergan does not seem to have pursued this line in later life, but neither, as far as I know, did he repudiate it. In fact, it may be echoed in his remark in *Insight* on "the concrete universal that is mankind in the concrete and cumulative consequences of the acceptance or rejection of the message of the Gospel" (Lonergan, 1957/1992, p. 764). And there is a quite remarkable counterpart to this ontological solidarity in the psychological and intersubjective solidarity, which we will presently notice (section 3.4 below).

## 3.2 The Priority of Intelligence.

The priority of intelligence over language is a qualified position taken in response to the view "that the meaningfulness of language is essentially public and only derivatively private." In two ways Lonergan is prepared to acknowledge the role, and even admit the priority in a restricted sense, of expression. "First, I do not believe that mental acts occur without a sustaining flow of expression. The expression may not be linguistic. It may not be adequate. It may not be presented to the attention of others. But it occurs." He will go further. "Secondly, I have no doubt that the ordinary meaningfulness of ordinary language is essentially public and only derivatively private. For language is ordinary if it is in common use. It is in common use...because all the individuals of the relevant group understand what it means." Thus "children and foreigners come to learn a language...by learning how it ordinarily is used, so that their private knowledge of ordinary usage is derived from the common usage that essentially is public" (Lonergan, 1972, pp. 254-255).

Originally, however, and in the unqualified sense, that is not the case.

> Thirdly, what is true of the ordinary meaningfulness of ordinary language is not true of the original meaningfulness of any language, ordinary, literary, or technical. For all language develops...developments consist in discovering new uses for existing words, inventing new words, and in diffusing the discoveries and inventions. All three are a matter of expressed mental acts.... Unlike ordinary meaningfulness, then, unqualified meaningfulness originates in expressed mental acts, is communicated and perfected through expressed mental acts, and attains ordinariness when the perfected communication is extended to a large enough number of individuals. (Lonergan, 1972, pp. 255-256)

To understand this view we must go back, I believe, to the "insight into phantasm" that was one of Lonergan's earliest and most original contributions but is still so widely ignored. The basic question seems to be whether mental acts exist or are just occult entities. But their existence can be discovered only through appropriation of one's own interiority, and the mental act that is most likely to claim our attention, and to be "discovered" in interiority, is the act of insight that Lonergan describes so vividly at the beginning of chapter 1 of *Insight*, illustrating it with the "Eureka!" of Archimedes (1957/1992, pp. 27-31).

### 3.3  The Dynamics of Expression

Against this background I can be brief on my next heading, the dynamics of expression, set forth in chapter 17 of *Insight*. The context is interpretation, the presupposition of interpretation is the occurrence of expression, and so Lonergan has a section on "Levels and Sequences of Expression" (1957/1992, pp. 592-595). He would classify modes of expression in terms of meaning, and so discusses "distinctions...between (1) sources, (2) acts, and (3) terms of meaning" (1957/1992, p. 592). Next, levels of expression depend on "the sources of meaning both in the speaker or writer and in the hearer or reader" (Lonergan, 1957/1992, p. 592). But with his strong sense of the historical, Lonergan cannot leave the matter in this somewhat static aspect.

> Besides levels of expression, there also are sequences. Development in general is a process from the undifferentiated to the differentiated, from the generic to the specific, from the global and awkward to the expert and precise. It would simplify enormously the task of the interpreter if, from the beginning of human speech and writing, there existed and were recognized the full range of specialized modes of expression. But the fact is that the specializations had to be invented, and the use of the inventions presupposes a corresponding development or education of prospective audiences or readers. (1957/1992, p. 594)

Perhaps I may leave here a topic that is likely to be studied more thoroughly in other contributions to this volume, but a word of caution is in order. It would be easy to take an impoverished view of expression as coldly instrumental, forgetting poetry, song, laughter, and other everyday modes of expression. One has to watch, therefore, in this chapter 17 of *Insight*, for references to literary modes, to the incidental and even the accidental factor, to elementary patterns of experience, to the aesthetic, dramatic, and practical, to the mystical, to non-explanatory meaning, to the application of the canon of residues in this field, to "dynamic constellations of the writer's psyche" (Lonergan, 1957/1992, p. 613), and to such statements as the following:

> Expression not only is an instrument of the principal acts of meaning that reside in conception and judgment, but also a prolongation of the psychic flow from percepts, memories, images, and feelings into the shaping of the countenance, the movement of the hands, and the utterance of words. (Lonergan, 1957/1992, p. 615)

Again, to quote from *Method in Theology*:

> With Giambattista Vico, then, we hold for the priority of poetry. Literal meaning literally expressed is a later ideal and only with enormous effort and

care can it be realized, as the tireless labors of linguistic analysts seem to show. (Lonergan, 1972, p. 73).[5]

## 3.4 Views on Intersubjectivity

All this touches directly on intersubjectivity. That topic is surely vital to a theory of communication, but for my purpose a few simple points will suffice.

Chapter 17 of *Insight* supposes, of course, the basic possibility of intersubjective communication for its theory of expression and interpretation, but Lonergan goes much further than that. Parallel to our first point on the ontological unity of the human race, he has views on a primordial psychological unity of persons.

> Prior to the "we" that results from the mutual love of an "I" and a "thou," there is the earlier "we" that precedes the distinction of subjects and survives its oblivion. This prior "we" is vital and functional. Just as one spontaneously raises one's arm to ward off a blow against one's head, so with the same spontaneity one reaches out to save another from falling. Perception, feeling, and bodily movement are involved, but the help given another is not deliberate but spontaneous. One adverts to it not before it occurs but while it is occurring. It is as if "we" were members of one another prior to our distinctions of each from the others. (Lonergan, 1972, p. 57)

Further, there is communication on this level. Lonergan, drawing on the work of philosophers and phenomenologists, lists some of the ways in which feelings are communicated: "community of feeling, fellow-feeling, psychic contagion, and emotional identification" (1972, pp. 57-59), and goes on to speak of intersubjective communication of meaning, comparing the meaning of a smile with linguistic meaning (1972, pp. 59-61). The sociologists too make their input with their stress on the social origin of one's awareness of self, along with personalists who "have urged that the notions of 'I' and 'you' emerge as differentiations of a prior 'we' or 'us'" (Lonergan, 1985, p. 56).

Lonergan, however, separates himself from those phenomenologists who maintain, on the basis of their cognitional theory, that we know other persons only intersubjectively. His own cognitional theory allows him to escape this limitation.

> I would point out that, just as we pass from consciousness of the self as subject to an objectification of the self in conception and judging, so too we pass from intersubjectivity to the objectification of intersubjectivity. Not only do we (two subjects in a subject-to-subject relation) speak and act. We speak about ourselves; we act on one another; and inasmuch as we are spo-

---

[5]The most extensive presentation of Lonergan's ideas on poetry, drama, and other forms of art, is in the ninth of his lectures on education, given at Xavier University, Cincinnati, 1959 (to appear as *Topics in Education*, volume 10 of the *Collected Works*, 1993).

ken of or acted on, we are not just subjects, not subjects as subjects, but
subjects as objects. (Lonergan, 1974a, p. 131)

One very important point in the philosophy of communication has
been omitted: interpretation, the counterpart of expression. But that enters
deeply into Lonergan's theology, and so I transfer discussion of it to the
fourth part of this chapter.


## 4. Communication in the Theological Context

To turn to communication in Lonergan's special field of endeavor is to shift
attention from individual relationships to the relationship of generations distant in time from one another, or to the relationship of groups distant in
cultural ways from one another. If this seems to some a very abrupt change
of direction, the reason may be that they think of Lonergan as focused on
the individual rather than on the community. The truth is that from beginning to end of his career it was the community that was central; his seeming
concentration on the individual was more a withdrawal in a grand strategy
of withdrawal and return. Obviously the present volume is not the place to
debate that question, but this prefatory paragraph may help eliminate much
misunderstanding.

Of quite central interest to this volume, however, is the last chapter (14)
of Lonergan's *Method in Theology*, called simply "Communications" (1972, pp.
355-368). The views expressed there have a clear and very pointed reference to
our present topic, but they are the result of a long development and clarification, and my present task is to see how he arrived at them.

### 4.1  From Jesus to Gospel

We have to go back, then, to what is to be communicated. This, for Lonergan the theologian, was the revelation given by God and, for Christians, the
revelation given by God in the Son: "Long ago God spoke to our ancestors
in many and various ways by the prophets, but in these last days he has
spoken to us by a Son" (Hebrews 1:1-2, here and elsewhere as in the
*NRSV*). "...no one knows the Son except the Father, and no one knows the
Father except the Son and anyone to whom the Son chooses to reveal him"
(Mt. 11:27). Our study of communication in Lonergan the theologian must
begin therefore with the message of Jesus.

The Christian position on this question is dominated by the doctrine of
the human knowledge Jesus had, the Catholic position adds the doctrine of
what is called the beatific vision, and Lonergan's position adds his cognitional theory (1964b, Thesis 12a: *De scientia Christi*, pp. 332-416). In this
theory, "vision" is considered an unhappy word choice, for it suggests ocular experience and a view of human knowledge analogous to ocular vision.
Lonergan spoke rather of the ineffable knowledge Jesus had and of the

struggle it was to make the ineffable "effable" (I take some liberty with English here, in order to have two words that correspond to Lonergan's Latin pair, *ineffabilis* and *effabilis*).

To understand the ineffable knowledge of Jesus, we must go to analogy, for by hypothesis this knowledge is beyond properly human understanding. Lonergan finds an analogy in the Thomist agent intellect, or in the notion of being we all have, a notion that encompasses everything in anticipation but nothing in determinate categories (1964b, pp. 337-338, 405-406). Analogy is partly the same and partly different. In this case there is difference in that we operate in pursuit of the goal, with a desire to "see" God, where Christ operated from the attained goal, struggling to communicate to others what he had received. But there is a similarity in that his knowledge and mine, each in its own way, is all-encompassing. Similarity too in that the vision of God gave Jesus no actual knowledge that was expressible. He had to win this slowly; he labored to express what was first given him in an inexpressible form (Lonergan, 1964b, pp. 405-412). I suggest, for an idea of this labor, the struggle that mystics like St. Teresa of Avila had in expressing what is not communicable in human terms except by metaphor for the mystic or by analogy for the theologian.

Jesus then was faced with the first great problem in Christian communication. How much he was aware of it and what the terms are in which he might be able to describe it are good questions, but from my viewpoint the problem is located, as a special case, within the area of internal communication dealt with earlier (Part 2). At any rate, Jesus did achieve the needed measure of internal communication and did go on to communicate divine revelation to his followers, in terms he and they could understand, in "effable" language; they in turn communicated it to their world in teaching and preaching, in writing and worship, in a "way," as the Acts of the Apostles several times puts it (v.g., 9:2, 19:9, 19:23). And so the revelation given Jesus by God the Father passed on to the church of Palestine.

That church, however, was to embrace all nations: "Go into all the world and proclaim the good news to the whole creation" (Mk. 16:15). And there the problem of communication emerged in a new form, for those nations were an extremely heterogeneous multitude. The new problem existed from the time the "message" left Palestine and was preached to the Greco-Roman world, but it became formulated in a precise manner, and so became consciously a problem, only with the rise of historical consciousness in our time, roughly in the last two centuries. The church fathers and the medieval scholastics could dip into the scriptures and transfer a text across the centuries without a clear sense of the vast chasm that separated their culture and manner of thinking from that of the earliest church. Today that is no longer possible.

Lonergan came to grips with the problem in two steps: the problem of moving from the early church to the doctrines of the later church and the problem of moving from these doctrines to our contemporary world in its irreducible plurality. His early theology is concerned with the first step, and one could say that his later work, *Method in Theology*, is focused on the second, since he makes it the topic of his final chapter and the crowning phase of theology: Communications, he says, "is a major concern, for it is in this final stage that theological reflection bears fruit" (1972, p. 355).

Logically, both steps were contained in a discovery he made in the early 1930s.

> In the summer of 1930 I was assigned to teach at Loyola College, Montreal, and despite the variety of my duties was able to do some reading. Christopher Dawson's *The Age of the Gods* [1928] introduced me to the anthropological notion of culture and so began the correction of my hitherto normative or classicist notion. (Lonergan, 1974a, p. 264)

But it is quite unlikely that Lonergan saw at once the full implications of this discovery; the German Historical School seems to have been a factor here, and that influence came later, when he was teaching in Rome: "The new challenge came from the *Geisteswissenschaften...*" (Lonergan, 1974a, p. 277).

## 4.2  From Gospel to Doctrine

The correction of his "hitherto...classicist notion" was introduced first into the transition from the sources to conciliar and Catholic doctrines. There is no simple path from one to the other. The sources are not like Euclid's elements of geometry, which may offer a problem to understanding, but present no special problem of interpretation: "[W]hile there is a task of coming to understand Euclid, there is no task of interpreting Euclid....While there have been endless commentators on the clear and simple Gospels, there exists little or no exegetical literature on Euclid" (Lonergan, 1972, pp. 153-154). With the scriptures then there is a problem of interpretation, and it exists in principle, for they are written not in the systematic order that puts axioms and theorems first and their consequences and applications later, but in the common sense order that puts immediate applications and relevance first and is little concerned with going back to axioms and theorems.

There is a parallel in the origin of the sciences. Thus chemistry (to take an example Lonergan used over and over) began in daily life with the infinite variety of materials encountered there by everyone, with what is first for us; in the course of history, it arrived at the systematic presentation of the periodic table, which, however remote from experience, can be made basic, a first in itself, in teaching the science. For Lonergan, the history of Catholic thinking from scripture to church doctrines was analogous to the history of chemistry from everyday materials to the periodic table (Lonergan, 1967, pp. 61-62). And the problem of interpretation (that is, of communication between the centuries, of the early church speaking to us, and of our hearing the early church) is focused on that history and its justification.

Lonergan struggled with this first problem for some 20 years or more and especially during his 12 years teaching in Rome, when he was confronted more directly with the problem of the *Geisteswissenschaften* (Lonergan, 1974a, p. 277). We may take as basis for discussion his course of 1958-1959 at the Gregorian University there, *De intellectu et methodo* (Lonergan, 1959). There is a transition from one manner of thinking in the sources of church doctrines to another quite different manner of thinking in the doctrines themselves; a gap has opened: in Lonergan's Latin-Greek term, a *chasma*. We leap across the gap, and the question is how to justify the leap.

Through 10 pages, single-spaced and legal-size, Lonergan struggles with the answer (1959, pp. 16-25 of the MS). We do not reach our foundations and justify the leap by the external form of the words we use; here one may surely think of the "fundamentalists," for whom words do serve as foundations. And not through manipulation of concepts and judgments—one thinks now of the "conceptualists," adversaries in the *verbum* articles Lonergan had written some years earlier (1946b)—for that works only with a given system. Lonergan had already rejected deduction as a means of transition and returns to it again to declare it helpless when questions arise that the system cannot account for—precisely the situation when there is a leap from one way of thinking to another.

His own solution does not surprise us. It is to go behind the words, behind the concepts and judgments, and appeal to intelligence itself and its threefold formation through understanding, science, and wisdom (Lonergan, 1959, p. 16). A long discussion follows of wisdom and the way it lies deeper than words and concepts. Wisdom was a key concept in Lonergan's early writings. Later, individual wisdom yielded to a collective wisdom gained through dialectic and foundations. But in both the individual and collective approaches the goal is true judgment, the truth of the transposition of doctrines from one culture to another.

We can round off discussion of communication in this first step with a point Lonergan makes in his 1962 lecture on "Hermeneutics" (1962) and repeats in chapter 7 of his *Method in Theology* (1972). About half the lecture is devoted to the first two of the basic questions for dealing with a text that requires interpretation: (1) understanding the text and (2) judging how correct one's understanding of the text is. Given Lonergan's cognitional theory, there is no special problem here. It is the role of "scholars"—we anticipate here his later distinction between scholarship, a matter of learning and erudition, and science, a matter of principles and laws (Lonergan, 1972, pp. 233-234)—to become familiar with the common sense expressions of another age and culture. As we gradually come to understand our own language by years of experience of its use, so scholars gradually come to understand the language of another time by years of experience with its monuments, artifacts, language, relics.

The real problem emerges in the third of the basic exegetical tasks, when scholars try to state the meaning of the text and communicate their findings to us; Lonergan devotes the second half of his lecture to this (1962, pp. 9-16 of the MS). On the face of it the problem may seem fabricated: If the scholars know the meaning of a text and want to tell the rest of us what it is, why don't they just go ahead and tell us? But a moment's reflection reveals the problem. What language are they going to use? Not the language of the documents they study, for that is the language needing interpretation in the first place; if they use that, we are no further ahead than if we read the documents ourselves. But they cannot simply turn to our modern language either, for by hypothesis there is a gap between the text and ourselves, between the language of the text and our language; our initial problem was how to make and justify the leap over that gap, and simply to turn from the language of the documents to our own leaves us no better off than patristic and medieval exegesis was.

We may turn to chapter 7 of *Method in Theology* (Lonergan, 1972) for a definitive treatment of the question. Here, in the context of this third problem, three cases are distinguished. "The exegete qua exegete expresses his interpretations to his colleagues technically in notes, articles, monographs, commentaries." In this case, exegetes will use all the instruments provided by research: grammars, lexicons, and so on. They will also relate their work functionally to previous work in the field. Secondly, the "exegete also speaks to his pupils, and he must speak to them in a different manner. For notes, articles, monographs, commentaries fail to reveal the kind of work and the amount of work that went into writing them. That revelation only comes in the seminar" (Lonergan, 1972, p. 170).

Neither of these first two cases presents the real problem, which is how to speak to those who are neither scholars (at least in the relevant field) nor in training to be scholars: the problem, in other words, of how to speak to the rest of us. Lonergan brings his categories of description and explanation to bear on this (1972, pp. 171-173). Following the practice of reliable scholars at the descriptive stage, he would have the biblical theologian respect the originality of each of the inspired authors.

> He [the biblical theologian] will appear to be happy to proceed slowly, and often he will follow the ways of beginners. His descriptions will convey a feeling for things long past; they will give the reader an impression of the foreign, the strange, the archaic; his care for genuineness will appear in the choice of a vocabulary as biblical as possible; and he will be careful to avoid any premature transposition to later language, even though that language is approved by a theological tradition. (1972, p. 171)

Finally, he will be wary of general presentations of the divine plan running through history.

To this basic procedure Lonergan would add his own specific contribution.

> What is needed is not mere description but explanation. If people were shown how to find in their own experience elements of meaning, how these

elements can be assembled into ancient modes of meaning, why in antiquity the elements were assembled in that manner, then they would find themselves in possession of a very precise tool, they would know it in all its suppositions and implications, they could form for themselves an exact notion, and they could check just how well it accounted for the foreign, strange, archaic things presented by the exegetes. (1972, pp. 172-173)

## 4.3 From Doctrine to the Living Word

So much for the first step, the theological problem of hearing an ancient word in our time. But perhaps before leaving this step I may recall the point made in section 3.3 above—that it is "easy to take an impoverished view of expression as coldly instrumental, forgetting poetry, song, laughter, and other everyday modes of expression." For it is likewise easy to take an impoverished view of interpretation, forgetting that in everyday life we are continually interpreting one another; as a smile, a frown, a gesture is someone else's expression, so it calls for my understanding, that is, interpretation. And what is true of everyday life for all of us is true also in the special case of the media: The newspaper headline, the television program, and other communications of this kind are expression calling for interpretation.

That same wide application of general principles is likewise to be kept in mind as we turn to the second step in our theological problem, the handing on of what we have received; though the concern of this chapter is more with the technical side of theology, the points made apply also to the mother teaching her child to pray, to the catechist explaining the Mass in a primary school, and so on.

For hearing the ancient word in our time is only half the battle, as we discover when Lonergan lines up the two phases of theology: "If one is to harken to the word, one must also bear witness to it. If one engages in *lectio divina*, there come to mind *quaestiones*. If one assimilates tradition, one learns that one should pass it on. If one encounters the past, one also has to take one's stand toward the future" (1972, p. 133). And that presents new problems that Lonergan dealt with rather late in life.

I have said that, in logic, the problem of a further transmission of the message we have ourselves received should have surfaced simultaneously with the problem of receiving the message. If interpretation of the faith of the early church is a problem precisely because the early church expressed its faith in a way of thinking that is foreign to us, then presumably there will be a similar problem when we go on to express Catholic doctrine in the equally foreign categories of the various particular cultures of the world.

Lonergan, however, came to that second problem later; even in 1954, two decades and more after reading Dawson (1928), when he had been teaching theology 14 years, it hardly bothered him; that year he could write the following about systematic theology:

> It bestows upon one's teaching the enviable combination of sureness of doc-
> trine with versatility of expression. Finally...it is fixed upon one's intellec-
> tual memory. So we find that non-Catholic clergymen, often more learned in
> scripture and the fathers, preach from their pulpits the ideas put forward in
> the latest stimulating book or article, while the Catholic priest, often bur-
> dened with sacerdotal duties and administrative tasks, spontaneously ex-
> pounds the epistle or gospel of the Sunday in the light of an understanding
> that is common to the ages. (1967/1988, p. 125)

It was only later that Lonergan came to appreciate the problems presented in this second step of communication, and then he realized that there
was a parallel here with the scholarship needed to understand the documents
of antiquity; just as the exegete must become familiar with the artifacts, the
monuments, the writings, of the culture being investigated, so the missionary must become familiar with the culture of the people being evangelized.
As the theological community must labor to overcome the gap between antiquity and the doctrines of the church today, so the pastor or missionary
must labor in the reverse order to overcome the gap between church doctrines and the culture or subculture of the pastoral or mission area.

That is the focal point in Lonergan's final chapter in *Method in Theology*, "Communications" (1972, pp. 355-368). The chapter may seem to lack
direction, and we may wonder why he rambles on about ontology, society,
state, church, Christianity today, redemption, social science, and the rest.
But all this is integral to his position and reveals what his fundamental view
of communication is. In that view, the solidarity of the human race across
space and time, the very idea with which he began to write some 40 years
earlier, the ontological solidarity that finds a psychological counterpart in
spontaneous intersubjectivity—this is a basic supposition. If we go on to
think of society constituted by meaning, of meaning having many different
expressions in the many nations that make up the church, then we have the
framework for his more specific views on communication.

These he expresses as follows.

> The Christian message is to be communicated to all nations. Such communi-
> cation presupposes that preachers and teachers enlarge their horizons to in-
> clude an accurate and intimate understanding of the culture and the language
> of the people they address. They must grasp the virtual resources of that
> culture and that language, and they must use those virtual resources crea-
> tively so that the Christian message becomes, not disruptive of the culture,
> not an alien patch superimposed upon it, but a line of development within the
> culture. (Lonergan, 1972, p. 362)

But we are not out of the woods yet. As the route from Gospel to
doctrines had its specific problem, so also does the route from doctrines to
their communication in a particular culture. Doctrines are necessary; they
have "the function of explaining and defending the authenticity of the
church's witness to the revelation in Christ Jesus" (Lonergan, 1985, p. 245).

But they are not the primary thing. That privilege belongs to the Gospel, and how to relate Gospel, doctrines, and preaching the Gospel to all nations is the present question.

Several times in his post-*Method* period, Lonergan took his lead in this matter from the views on a pastoral council expressed at the time of the Second Vatican Council by M.-D. Chenu (1964); we may refer to an unpublished lecture, "A New Pastoral Theology," given in Toronto in 1973 and a year later in New Haven (Lonergan, 1974b), and to a published one, "Pope John's Intention," given in Boston in 1981 (Lonergan, 1985, pp. 224-238). Negatively, we should not reduce "pastoral" to the application of doctrine and reduce that application to the tactics of classical oratory (Lonergan, 1974b, p. 7 of the MS). It is quite inadequate to begin from doctrines, abstracted in the first place from the living word, and attempt to flesh them out again into living speech (Lonergan, 1974b, pp. 8-9). If pastoral "means no more than the logical application of universal norms to particular cases, there is no need for a pastoral council or...pastoral theology" (Lonergan, 1974b, p. 17).

Positively, something more is needed, and "that something has to be found in what escapes the universal, in the individual and the personal, in the concrete community and the ongoing process of history" (Lonergan, 1974b, p. 17). As philosophy has now to "take its stand on the inner experience of the individual and from that basis proceed to an understanding of human process, human community, human history" (Lonergan, 1974b, p. 18), so theology must become existential, taking its stand on the human subject who lives the reality that is expressed in doctrines. It must be worked out in relation to authentic Christian experience that is alive, that as shared is intersubjective, as shared by many is community, as transmitted is historic, and so on (Lonergan, 1974b, pp. 15-16). In this way the leap forward that Pope John (1963, pp. 791-792; 1964, p. 44) desired his pastoral council to take would lie in "the enrichment of the technical formulation by the vital, the personal, the existential" (Lonergan, 1985, p. 227).

Lonergan is complex, but his various statements hang together. Especially worth noting is the grounding in the same way of the two major steps we are studying in this fourth part. We saw that exegetes, to communicate what they have learned through scholarly research, must turn to their interior: "If people were shown how to find in their own experience elements of meaning, how these elements can be assembled into ancient modes of meaning, why in antiquity the elements were assembled in that manner, then they would find themselves in possession of a very precise tool..." (Lonergan, 1972, p. 172). With slight changes this could be said of our preaching the Gospel today: "If we could find in our own experience elements of meaning in our faith, see how these elements could be assembled in the language of the people we wish to evangelize, knowing their culture well enough to understand why what we preach in their language is faithful to the Gospel, then we would possess a very precise tool...."

This long part has focused on the theological problem of communication between cultures. The basic supposition is the solidarity of the human race; solidarity across space but especially across time, for ours is a historic, communitarian religion. Something was given us once for all, and it was given long ago and far away; its transmission and reception is a classic problem of communication.

## 5. The Two-way Communication of God and Humankind

I have talked of the divine interior communication of the three in God, of the communication internal to the many-leveled entity that a human being is, of the external communication of human being with human being and especially of culture with culture, of the theological problems presented in the move from Jesus to Gospel, from Gospel to doctrines, and from doctrines to preaching the Gospel. There remains the important question (all-important to each of us) of the mutual communication of God and humankind.

It is customary to speak of God's self-communication. "Self" may be understood here to denote a person, and then we think of each of the three, not communicating the selfhood which that person is (for that is incommunicable, both within God and externally), but entering into the intimate and loving relationship that in human affairs makes the other the *dimidium animae meae* (half of my soul) and in divine-human communication constitutes a union and a sharing that is incomparably greater. But "self" may be used impersonally, as when we speak of the thing itself. In this sense one may think of the divine nature itself as being communicated to the human race, always remembering that the divine nature is not a lifeless, unconscious thing, but the fullness of understanding, truth, love, peace, the consciousness that is internal "experience."

This second sense is found in Lonergan's theology of grace, most succinctly in the little work, *De ente supernaturali* (1946a). Here the first thesis states that there is a created communication of the divine nature, or a created principle of those operations in which the creature may attain to God as God is in the divine being. The second thesis states that this created communication of the divine nature exceeds the grade of being of any creature whatever and is simply supernatural. All this, of course, is a fairly straightforward Scholastic rendition of 2 Peter 1:4, where we are said to share in the divine nature.

The first usage of "self" also is found in Lonergan's theology, along with the term "self-communication," but with the caution of the theologian, he states that it is the divinity (not the selfhood) that the divine self communicates. Thus, "there is a threefold personal self-communication of divinity to humanity...in Christ the Word becomes flesh...through Christ men become temples of the Spirit...in a final consummation the blessed know the Father" (Lonergan, 1985, p. 26). Again, "the self-communication of divinity in love...resides in the sending of the Son, in the gift of the Spirit, in the hope of being united with the Father" (Lonergan, 1985, p. 31).

Much more personal to Lonergan (and possibly unique, for I have not noticed it in other authors) is the way he integrates this doctrinal position into his theology of the trinitarian relations. In standard Catholic theology there are four real relations within God; Lonergan finds in the economy of salvation four divine graces par excellence, and he correlates the four graces with the four trinitarian relations in a one-to-one correspondence.

Thus sanctifying grace is a created participation in the relation we call active spiration of the Spirit, and so has a special link with the Holy Spirit within us; likewise, the great virtue of charity is a created imitation of the relation we call passive spiration, and so it links us to Father and Son as principle of the Spirit. The grace of the incarnation is a created participation of fatherhood, and so is found in the Son, while the light of glory is a created participation of sonship, and so is found in the vision the blessed have of the Father (Lonergan, 1964a, pp. 234-235). This seems to me an extraordinary suggestion, with manifold implications. Lonergan offers it rather tentatively; I am not aware that he pursued it at any time in later life; but again there is no evidence that he dropped it.

One final point. Communication between God and humankind is mutual. One may speculate that St. Ignatius Loyola's *Spiritual Exercises* influenced Lonergan here as it has influenced countless Jesuits. For the crowning contemplation of the *Exercises* has the purpose of attaining love, and Ignatius prefaces the exercise with the remark that "Love consists in a mutual communication between the two persons" (Loyola, 1991, p. 176, no. 231). So if God communicates with us from the divine side, we must ask what kind of communication there is from our side with God.

It is a matter of adoration and prayer, beginning with that "orientation to transcendent mystery" that is "the primary and fundamental meaning of the name, God" (Lonergan, 1972, p. 341), moving to a "response to transcendent mystery [in] adoration" (Lonergan, 1972, p. 344), and culminating in a "withdrawing from the world mediated by meaning into a silent and all-absorbing self-surrender in response to God's gift of his love" (Lonergan, 1972, p. 273).

Whether or not theologians experience this withdrawal and to what extent they should speak of such personal experience are questions on the border between religion and theology. What is clearly a theological question is the relation of religion and theology, and this Lonergan indicates with laconic brevity:

> Man's response to transcendent mystery is adoration. But adoration does not exclude words....[W]ords, in turn, have their meaning within some cultural context.... Accordingly...the worship of God and...the religions of mankind

stand within a...context and...generate the problems with which theologians attempt to deal. (1972, p. 344)

Keeping to my purpose of showing the spectrum of passages in Lonergan relevant to communication, I can do no more than indicate his position on the intersubjectivity of God and the human race. It is an area that would surely repay study, but would require a piecing together of many scattered observations. Still, theologians are believers before they are theologians, and so was Lonergan. It was not his style to speak of such matters, but it is known how important to him his prayer life was, how in early years he had to struggle with prayer, how in later years it became a joyful experience.

But he knew that the duality of believer and theologian can give rise to conflict. The prayer of Thomas Aquinas at the end of his life "became so intense that it interfered with his theological activity. But earlier there could have been an alternation between religious and theological differentiation, while later still further differentiation might have enabled him to combine prayer and theology as Teresa of Avila combined prayer and business" (Lonergan, 1985, p. 242). In such a way the limited communication of mind with Mind that the theologian enjoys becomes the believer's full communication of heart with Heart, when *cor ad cor loquitur* (heart speaks to heart).

# Part II

# Specialized Studies

# 5

# Neither Jew nor Greek, but One Human Nature and Operation in All

*Frederick E. Crowe, SJ*

## 1. Introduction: Cultural Diversity and Underlying Unity

The differences between Hebrew and Greek thought-patterns are a common-place today in the academic world and are rapidly becoming such in popular journalism. One sees the dynamic opposed to the static, the existential to the essentialist, the concrete view to the abstract, the active surrender of faith to the cold speculation of reason. The temporal and historical are contrasted with the timeless and unchanging and permanent, and the total view, in which knowing includes loving, to the analytic tendency that distinguishes faculties, habits, and acts, categorizing the latter according to their specifically differing objects.

It is no argument against the core of truth in these contrasts to say that they have begun to be used as mere clichés, without effort to define and be precise, without sense of limits, nuances, exceptions, without urge to investigate accurately the truth of the matter. It is not even relevant in this context to remark that the clichés are sometimes uttered in the same breath with a rather haughty condemnation of the Scholastic clichés they would replace, nor is it any refutation of their fundamental truth that they can be and are made to serve personal interests as well as scientific objectives. For clearly at their origin was a moment of creative insight, which responsible scholar-

**Author's note:** This essay was first published in 1965 in *Philippine Studies*, *13*, 546-571. Though the opening paragraphs reflect an immediate context that is no longer relevant, the focal point of the essay seems unaffected by the passing of the years (how Lonergan's ideas escape the limits of a given time is, in fact, close to being the focal point), and since the theme is clearly linked to the topic of the present collection, I have agreed to let it be reprinted here without change except in the stylistic points that bring it into conformity with the rest of the volume. I am grateful to the Reverend Provincial Superior of the Philippine Jesuits for granting permission for the reprint. I may note here that it has been reprinted also in the collection of my essays edited by Michael Vertin, *Appropriating the Lonergan Idea* (Crowe, 1989, pp. 31-50).

ship has been concerned to formulate with care, elaborate in detail, and verify by patient research. Whatever the exaggerations, therefore, in their further use and whatever the unauthenticity of the user, the differences between Hebrew and Greek are now part of our patrimony of learning, and only the most uninstructed of theologians would dispute the need of taking the distinctive character of Hebrew ways into account when interpreting the Bible.

This particular set of differences—more familiar, of course, to those who ply the trade of theologian—is nevertheless just an instance of the widespread phenomenon of differentiation that can be observed in mentalities, mores, institutions, civilizations, and cultures, between successive ages of history, between peoples living in isolation from one another in a given age, and even between groups and social castes within a given tribe or people. Hebrew and Greek, opposing one another across the great divide between East and West, may already forecast the full possibilities of differentiation inherent in human ways, but their differences are after all minor compared to those that exist between the extremes of Oriental and Occidental cultures—differences so radical that missionaries sometimes feel forced to question the validity of our most basic philosophical principles, to ask whether it is not simply more of European imperialism when we try to impose them on the peoples of the Far East, whether we must not learn a quite different philosophy from Chinese or Indian thought, and learn to express our Christian faith in terms that bear little or no relation to the Judaeo-Hellenic terms in which the early Church formulated it. Further, this difference between Far East and European-New World West is itself, perhaps, by no means the most radical phenomenon of its kind: The study of the pre-logical mentality of primitive peoples that has produced such interesting results in this century provides indications of still more fundamental differences among those we nevertheless recognize as belonging to the human community.

Finally, there is the fact, with its own relevance to the present problems of theology, that within a given culture and among those who greet one another from day to day, there are comparable differentiations. A few years ago C. P. Snow, in the Rede Lecture at Cambridge University, gave what has become almost classic expression to the alienation of scientific and literary scholars from each other. Working in the daytime with scientists and spending evening hours with literary colleagues, he felt he "was moving among two groups—comparable in intelligence, identical in race, not grossly different in social origin, earning about the same incomes, who had almost ceased to communicate at all" (1959, p. 2; also see Snow, 1964). Most readers will have some acquaintance with the storm of conflict the lecture caused.[1] But whatever the flaws in Snow's argument and however

---

[1] One indication: The article of F. R. Leavis and the consequent flood of letters in *The Spectator*: See 9 March 1962, pp. 297-303, and 16 March 1962, pp. 329-333. German interest in the question can be gauged from P. K. Kurz (1965).

real the victory claimed by his opponents, the situation remained problematical enough for *Daedalus* (Winter 1965) to devote a special issue to the theme "Science and Culture" in order "to study some of the connections that exist" between the activities represented by those two headings and "to gauge the accuracy of popular views that emphasize the supposed isolation of humanists, scientists, and artists" (Graubard, 1965, p. iii).

Such phenomena as I have been sampling have not failed to excite the interest of philosopher and theologian, and to enter largely into theories of history, development, cross-cultural communication, and the like. In this field Vico (1668-1744) is credited with founding the philosophy of history with his *Principii di una scienza nuova...*, setting forth the development of nations in the three stages of the age of the gods, the heroic age, the human age. We know the tremendous advances achieved by this science in the centuries since Vico's time and the relevance of those achievements to the task of theologians, whether they be engaged in the cross-cultural task of transition from biblical categories to theological, or the task, likewise cross-cultural, of passing from theological terms to a kerygma that is differentiated, adapted, contemporaneous, immediate, relevant to their hearers in their present concrete situation.

But the purpose of this article is not to talk about differentiations of culture—it presupposes them—but to ask about the community that is prior to the differentiations, to sketch one view of its structure and list some of its manifestations, and to suggest lines for investigating its relevance to the diversity of Jew and Greek. Is there a community that lies behind their differences and makes communication between the cultures possible, allows transition from one to another as well as integration of their goods and achievements in the realm of spirit? A rather consistent and, in my opinion, inevitable concern of students of culture has been to find something like a universal base from which to attempt a general critique of the various cultures. It is that underlying unity that is the theme here, rather than the more obvious diversity. Though positivists despair of finding such a unity and resist what they would regard as philosophical imperialism in this field, the philosopher and theologian should be open to its discovery. For if it is found, it should greatly promote the solution of the cross-cultural problems that beset us today in the sacred sciences. No doubt the problem of communication generally admits an ad hoc solution; as Robert Oppenheimer said of the tensions that develop in modern society between scholars in diverse academic pursuits, there is a remedy open to us in this, that "we can have each other to dinner" (quoted by Holton, 1965, p. xii)—an ambiguous suggestion, perhaps, should we happen to be dealing with a cannibalistic culture, but even then means of communicating could surely be worked out at some elemental human level of understanding and sympathy. But our concern is for a basic theory that might systematize the various ad hoc proposals and be fertile in the creation of better ones.

## 2. The Basic Community of Human Nature

To speak of differentiations is already to suppose an original unity from which the differences developed. Moreover, that usage is justified in some fundamental sense by the fact that our problem concerns members of one human race, for there is surely some obscurely glimpsed reason for the unanimity with which we set the creature we call "human" apart from other beings in the visible world. Even those who are most vocal in their rejection of a philosophical a priori, in their denial of anything like an "essence" in humans, take this stand for the paradoxical reason that humans are such as to be clearly distinguished from the world of animals, plants, minerals, etc. Very well, that "suchness" that is the basis of their discrimination, I will refer to as "nature," for even though that nature is simply "possibility," it is a possibility that animals do not share; and then we can say that the community of human nature that lies behind differentiation supplies also the underlying possibility of communication and integration. One might add a further a priori unity from a religious side, in the will of God that all humans be saved, in the universal application of redemption and the Gospel, but in this article I limit discussion to more secular factors. Hence my title. Though my title will seem deliberately provocative to the enemy of the secular in religious questions, it indicates quite accurately the scope of my article.

Let us begin not with the basic community itself, but with a rather simple clue to the way we might profitably investigate our question. The clue consists in the stability of the descriptive categories used in the natural sciences, as contrasted with the extreme variety and change of the categories that pertain to the cultural side of human life (see Lonergan, 1964a, pp. 42-47). Thus, colors, sounds, the feel of things, hot and cold, hard and soft, light and heavy—all these categories remain relatively constant for humans across time and space. We observe other people reacting in the same way as we do to external stimuli, and though we have no access to their internal experience, we presume reasonably enough that they see the same colors in the spectrum and hear the same range of musical notes; if some people are obviously color-blind or tone-deaf, we put it down to a defect in their organic or nervous system. Similarly, we are accustomed within limits to common modes of operation, seeing people everywhere using their legs for locomotion, their hands for guiding tools in doing and making, their vocal apparatus for speaking. On the other hand, whatever pertains to the cultural exists in the widest variety, beginning with the very words we use to describe our common experiences: "hot," "*chaud*," etc. The music and dance of India are so different from those of Europe as barely to be included within the same category; one does not readily pass from knives and forks to chopsticks; a hockey fan can be extremely bored at a cricket game; and so forth.

What accounts for this contrast? Clearly, the sensing and performing structures of the human body are the constant factor that make the same colors distinguishable by all, that make "hot" and "cold" categories that apply everywhere, that make all people walk about in an upright posture. But the structures are merely formal as regards the materials to be "processed," and with regard to these materials and their combinations, the greatest variety is possible. All people use their eyes to see, but they see different things; they look for different things to see, and—most important of all— they can use their free imaginations to construct different objects for observation or contemplation. Similarly, all people use their legs to move about, but they go different places. All use their hands for performing delicate operations on materials—*organum organorum* (instrument of instruments), Aristotle and medieval thinkers called the hands—but they make different artifacts. Thus, human ingenuity plus the variety of materials result in the differences of "hot" and "*chaud*," of Indian dance and European, of hockey and cricket, and so likewise of boomerang and rifle, of guild and labor union, of cave dwelling and skyscraper, of *Arabian Nights' Entertainment* and *Hamlet* or *King Lear*.

I have called the foregoing merely a clue, for our concern is not with hockey and cricket, obviously, but with more basic activities. The very fact that one person uses his or her eyes on a wheat field and finds interest there, while another is completely absorbed in looking at a set of black ink marks on paper, suggests that there is an "internal" activity that is more properly human than merely seeing or hearing, using hands or feet, one that determines the choice of objects at which to look and the use of the body's members. But there is a clue in these more "external" activities, in that we can discern in them something like a formal structure that remains relatively constant and distinguish from it the materials that continually change, enter into different combinations, issue in extremely diversified products. And the question now is whether there is in this more properly human activity some counterpart of that distinction—and some analogous structure that remains as a permanent way of operation in all the changes of the *operata* (products of the operation). We may even ask in anticipation whether that internal structure will not be so much the more stable as it belongs to "spirit" rather than to "body" and so is removed from even the chance variations that have their possibility in the material substrate and, occasionally, issue in malformed human beings.

The purpose here is to go beyond generalities. Everyone who talks about "humans" must concede, grudgingly perhaps, some basic community that makes us one and offers the possibility of communication. Almost any Thomist would go further and assign the basis of differentiation in a subjective element of potentiality, corresponding to an objective element. Objectively, there is the infinite potentiality of matter that admits of such a bewildering variety of forms in the physical, chemical, biological, zoological realms, matter that is open to development, not merely through chance variation and emergent probability, but also through the intervention of the artificer, that may be molded into tools, buildings, artifacts and institutions of boundless variety. Corresponding subjectively, there is the infinite resourcefulness of intelligence, *potens omnia facere* (able to create all things), capable in its wide-ranging fertility of conceiving mentally and directing the creation in reality of all of the forms that the material universe offers in potency. Now I certainly do not contemn such generalities as these; in the long run they are more significant than the notion of structure to be exposed in this article. But they are even less likely to interest specialists and, as I shall explain, it is the specialists who must eventually take up the challenge if we are to see more of a community between Hebrew and Greek than we have done in the recent past. We have to be more specific therefore, and so we speak of common structures.

### 3. Structures Common to Humanity

The notion of structure received a 748-page introduction in Bernard Lonergan's *Insight*, the aim of which was "to assist the reader in effecting a personal appropriation of the concrete, dynamic structure immanent and recurrently operative in his own cognitional activities" (1957/1992, p. 11; also see Lonergan, 1967). His exposition, which I follow here, may be briefly outlined as follows. In the beginning is experience: I hear and taste and feel and smell and, most of all, I see. So, of course, does my dog; but there is the difference between me and my dog that I get ideas about my experience; more basically, there is in me a wonder, a capacity to inquire and seek the intelligibility of experience; it is this wonder that gives rise to ideas. Sooner or later, however, in the self-correcting process of learning, I discover that my ideas are not always right, that error abounds when I accept my ideas uncritically, that ideas in general are just *possible* explanations of the data, and if I am to be rational, I must institute a further inquiry—I must reflect on the correctness of my ideas; it is this reflection that gives rise to rational truth and knowledge of the real. So there are three levels: (1) experience (data, presentations of sense, representations of imagination); (2) understanding (ideas, thoughts, suppositions that are possible explanations); (3) reflection (grasp of evidence grounding judgment and knowledge). And the dynamism that operates the transition from level to level is manifested in a twofold question: (a) the question for understanding that turns experience into something to be understood and (b) the question for reflection that turns the idea into something to be investigated for its truth. Furthermore, within each of the two higher levels there is the extremely important element of formulation, the Thomist twofold *verbum* (word): On the level of understanding, ideas are formulated in concepts (transition from engagement with the particular to release from the particular in universalization); on the level of reflection, grasp of evidence is formulated in judgment (transition from subjective grounds for affirmation to objective judgment and the "public" character of knowledge and the possibility of communication).

The foregoing account was limited to the three levels of cognitional activity. If we add now the very essential further element of the affective and voluntary, we have four levels of human consciousness and activity: (1) the empirical (experience), (2) the intellectual (understanding), (3) the rational (reflection), (4) the moral (voluntary). To quote a summary account that Lonergan himself gives in a recent article:

> If one wakes, one becomes present to oneself, not as moved but as moving, not as felt but as feeling, not as seen but as seeing. If one is puzzled and wonders and inquires, the empirical subject becomes an intellectual subject as well. If one reflects and considers the evidence, the empirical and intellectual subject becomes a rational subject, an incarnate reasonableness. If one deliberates and chooses, one has moved to the level of the rationally conscious, free, responsible subject that by his choices makes himself what he is to be and his world what it is to be.
>
> Does this many-leveled subject exist? Each man has to answer that question for himself. But I do not think that the answers are in doubt. Not even behaviorists claim that they are unaware whether or not they see or hear, taste or touch. Not even positivists preface their lectures and their books with the frank avowal that never in their lives did they have the experience of understanding anything whatever. Not even relativists claim that never in their lives did they have the experience of making a rational judgment. Not even determinists claim that never in their lives did they have the experience of making a responsible choice. There exist [human] subjects that are empirically, intellectually, rationally, morally conscious. (1967/1988, p. 210)

Notice that the special interest in our quotation is the human subject as subject, as conscious and present to him- or herself; however, the four levels of consciousness are the same as the four levels of operation.

## 4. Common Structures Verified in Two Key Examples

The question now is of the verification of this structure in different activities of different cultural groups, for the universality of the structure remains just an idea until rational reflection on the evidence grounds its assertion. That is, just as the intrinsic dynamism of the structure, if it exists objectively, calls for verification of every idea conceived in the human mind, so it calls for verification of our ideas about the structure itself. We have to adduce some evidence that scientist, artist, philosopher, theologian, believer—types at first sight so alien to one another—nevertheless, operate in patterns that are similar in form, isomorphic. So I propose to indicate that isomorphism here in two paradigm comparisons: (1) that of Thomist procedures with those of empirical science and (2) that of the latter with everyday intersubjective procedures. Then in the following part, I shall go on to suggest that biblical procedures themselves follow a similar pattern. For simplicity's sake, I will limit my brief considerations to cognitional structures, there being less doubt, I should think, about the fact of a moral conscience operating in all people in some manner that is relevant to their particular activities.

The first point, the isomorphism of Thomism and science in their cognitional structures, has been the object of a special study by Lonergan himself (1967/1988, pp. 133-141), and I simply summarize his findings here. Briefly, the relation of hypothesis to verification in science is similar to the relation of definition to judgment in Thomism, the empirical character of science rendering verification necessary just as the freedom of divine providence determines the need of Thomist judgment in addition to definition. Further, with regard to origins, "just as the scientific problem leads to a scrutiny of sensible data that ultimately results in a hypothesis, so the Thomist question leads to a scrutiny of sensible data that ultimately results in a definition" (1967/1988, p. 135). Again, Thomist abstraction corresponds to scientific invariance, both claiming independence "of the spatio-temporal conditions of their origins on the level of sense" (1967/1988, p. 136). And as scientific scrutiny leads only to approximate laws, so too Thomist effort to define is marked by a parallel modesty that recognizes very few essential definitions and struggles towards its goal by a reasoning process rather than by a leap of intuition. Then scientific anticipations form a heuristic structure similar to the metaphysics that results from Thomist operations:

> It is remarkable that the scientist conceives as his ideal goal knowledge of theories verified in any number of different instances and that the Thomist will add that by verification the scientist knows contingent existence, by theories he knows essences and forms, and by appealing to instances he acknowledges matter as well as form and existence....Because every revision is simply a repetition of the same general process of experience, of hypothesis, and of verification, the structure of scientific knowledge is a constant, and that methodical constant squares with the Thomist metaphysical constant of potency, form, and act. (1967/1988, pp. 137, 140)

Finally, besides the moving object of understanding (quiddity or form emergent in sensible or imagined objects), there is the end or goal that is being in its full sweep, and this, besides being explicit in Thomism, continually challenges the scientist to proceed beyond the narrow limits of his or her specialty, and so "contemporary science finds itself compelled to relinquish its traditional naïve realism and to come to grips with philosophic issues" (1967/1988, p. 140).

It should be repeated that the structural isomorphism allows full scope to differences arising from different materials, different "formal objects" of the various sciences, different sources of truth (1967/1988, p. 133).[2] The

---

[2] "Isomorphism, then, supposes different sets of terms; it neither affirms nor denies

significant point here is that the scientist deals with data, hypotheses, and verification, where the Thomist cognitional structure deals with *sensibilia*, *intelligibilia*, and *vera* (objects of sense, objects of understanding, and objects of truth), relating them to the corresponding elements of the ontological counterpart, potency, form, and act.[3] If the materials are so different, that very fact makes the similarity of pattern in the operations all the more remarkable, suggesting already a more universal occurrence of the pattern.

That suggestion receives strong and perhaps unexpected confirmation in the entirely different situation of everyday life and its cognitional activity. For there is little trouble in showing that cognitional activities occur here in the very same general relationship and pattern as they do in science.[4] Both scientists and the ordinary persons begin with experience. Scientists observe data: the paths of the planets, the lid of the tea kettle puffing up and down, the more controlled experiments of the laboratory. Ordinary persons observe data: the rattle in the car, the look of anger from an employer, the strange silence in the house when they go home. Both the scientist and the ordinary person are concerned to understand. "Why" is as familiar a word to one as to the other; each in his or her own way ponders, turns over the data in imagination, puzzles, worries, finally gets an idea. Both the scientist and the ordinary person are concerned with the truth. Ordinary persons do not rest content with an idea, at least not when something they value is at stake; if, for example, there is question of investing money, the mere possibility that things may be as represented by the salesperson does not move them; they want to check and make sure, to get at the truth of the matter. Further, they can be quite adept in conversation at exposing the defects in their neighbor's view, pointing triumphantly to contradictions there, marshalling evidence for their own position. They might be repelled by such words as "verification," "crucial experiment," and the like, but the procedures those terms name are not totally unknown to them. It has even to be said that ordinary persons, like scientists, are concerned in due measure to formulate their understanding, to find words to communicate it. Undoubtedly, this exigence is less demanding in everyday life where understanding so often remains in the pre-conceptual state, where the death of a child brings father and mother together in wordless sorrow. But even then they feel the need to talk, to put their sorrow into words; and the other children,

---

similarity between the terms of one set and those of other sets; but it does assert that the network of relations in one set of terms is similar to the network of relations in other sets" (Lonergan, 1967/1988, p. 133).

[3] The reader will ask for documentation of this point (the relation of cognitional and ontological structures in Thomism), but here I can only refer to my article, "St. Thomas and the Isomorphism of Human Knowing and Its Proper Object" (Crowe, 1961).

[4] For the relation of our cognitional theory and structures to "common sense" and "mythic consciousness," see *Insight* (Index under those words).

too young for speeches, find a solace in hearing their parents give voice to the common grief of all.

Again, of course, the differences are great. The lacunae in the procedures of ordinary persons are more obvious than the structural elements that are present. They do not pursue understanding as a career; they easily give up the attempt to formulate their thoughts; except in certain restricted areas, their efforts at verification are half-hearted; they do not consciously set the universe of being as their goal, but recognizes mind's exigence mostly in the field of the practical and so when the family's needs are provided for, are quite content to sit with slippers on and rest without caring to dominate the universe by knowledge. But the fact that they *sometimes* follow the same pattern as the scientist and philosopher, that they *can* inquire into the meaning of data, formulate an idea, and investigate its truth, makes it legitimate to ask whether the more noticeable lacunae, instead of indicating a quite different procedural structure, are not rather signs of a failure to respond to the native exigence of human spirit, a failure that is perfectly understandable in the context of practical life and the pressing need of earning a living for their dependents.

There is a connected area that seems to me extremely important for this question; I add a word on it here by way of appendix to this section. We find, in modern literature, almost an obsession with the problem of meaning in interpersonal relationships. A novelist is not content, for example, to have his characters join in love as brute animals do; the relationship must be suffused with meaning, and invested with a ceremonial, and lifted to the level of the artistic. Just as eating and drinking are an artistic performance in men and women and their execution in a merely animal way revolting, so also the marital relationships of man and woman. This is so much the case that it provides a clear and generally applicable distinction between pornography and art, the one merely unreeling a succession of images to arouse animal passions, while the other is concerned to give meaning and dignity to those same passions and their consequents by raising the biological to the artistic (Lonergan, 1957/1992, p. 210).

Now that concern seems relevant to our exposition of cognitional structure and even to scientific procedures. True enough, since Dilthey a whole school of thought has diligently distinguished "understanding" in the human area from "explanation" in the natural sciences: I *understand* my friend's need, but I *explain* the eclipse of the moon. However, it seems to me that both examples are concerned with the exigence for understanding in some more fundamental sense, with the need, let us call it, for *intelligibility* in the world, be it the human world or the world of nature. To be accurate here, we should notice that the artist also *creates* meaning and intelligibility, endowing otherwise brute materials and actions with form and dignity and meaning, and so the analogy is not so much with pure science as with technology. If this evokes a still keener protest from the artist, who certainly does not want the characters of his novel compared to mousetraps and detergents, I can only reply again that this is to attend to the differences of materials, which may be enormous, but is to overlook the common structure that is my only concern in this article.

One can press the isomorphism further still and insist that even the exigence for formulation and abstract conceptual expression appears in the field of art. Not necessarily in the artist himself, who will sometimes decline to formulate the meaning of his work, but in the work of critics. What are the critics doing if not attempting to detach the meaning of the artistic creation from the particular image or form in which it is embodied or incarnate and to universalize it, make it public intellectual property through words and concepts? However much artists may condemn the critics as parasites on their creativity, it seems clear that the human race is not going to dispense with them; they answer to a basic need of the human cognitional structure. Finally, the exigence for truth is implicit in the moral judgment of artists, when they ask, not whether their work has value as art, but what the morality is of their executing the work and presenting it to the public, *this* public in a particular state of development, education, etc. I think that despite all their rebellion against the less intelligent elements in law and censorship, responsible artists do experience and submit to this exigence.

## 5. Isomorphism of Hebrew and Greek Structures

We come now to the chief interest of this article: the isomorphism of Hebrew and Greek cognitional structures, to put the theme in the most unprepossessing terms. In entering this important field of debate and proposing to say something on this vexed question, I would respect the norm that always guides me as a responsible writer but presses on me here with a special urgency, of not pronouncing on matters that lie beyond my competence and of informing my readers as well as possible what I am trying to do. First, then, my purpose here is merely to suggest possible lines of approach. We very much need a *thorough* study of the type that is only hinted at here, even if it should come to conclusions opposed to those I anticipate—especially so, in that case. But it would have to be done by a specialist in biblical thought. As a theologian, I cannot very well undertake the detailed investigation, though I believe that a theologian has to conceive the question, set the terms of the inquiry, and propose the general procedures consonant with the question that is being investigated—I shall return to that point presently. Secondly, the biblical data that I will study in a tentative way are the question for understanding, the question for reflection, and the objective of truth. But the study will not consist in writing dictionary articles on the biblical words for question, understanding, reflection, truth; it will consist in studying the activities denoted by those words. The search is not for these ideas *in actu signato* (in the act as thematized) as themes, but *in actu exer-*

*cito* (in the act as performed), as lived and practiced. Thirdly, I make no concession to the view that creates a mystique of the Hebrew mind. I assume that the word "why" manifests similar mental operations whether it occurs in the mother of Jesus or in Aristotle. If my assumption is wrong, my error can be demonstrated, but the demonstrator will be asked to give me his or her views on the general community and differences of cultures, the relationship of nature and grace, the potentiality of intellect with regard to natural science and divine mysteries, and other matters that pertain to the presuppositions of such a demonstration.

My first question regards the biblical interest in questions for understanding. As stated, we will not pursue a linguistic study of the word "question" (see H. Greeven's article on *erotao* and its cognates in Kittel's *Theologisches Worterbuch zum Neuen Testament*) or write a commentary on the "useless questions" that are a theme in the Pastoral Epistles (1 Tim. 6:4; 2 Tim. 2:23; Tit. 3:9), necessary as those lines of investigation may be in the thorough study that is desired. Our few and hasty soundings have to do with the *performance* of questioning; they cannot be independent of words that are after all the immediate object of study on the *sacra pagina* (page of scripture), but they will regard words that denote the activity in its occurrence, and not as thematized. The relevant words are "what," "why," "how," and the like, rather than "question," "inquiry," "heuristic," etc. Here innumerable instances leap to mind. The occurrence of "what?" on finding food in the desert: "When the Israelites saw it, they said to one another, 'What is it?' For they did not know what it was" (Ex. 16:15, here and elsewhere as in the *NRSV*); or in the wonder created by Jesus's first miracle as recorded by Mark: "They were all amazed, and they kept on asking one another, 'What is this?'" (Mk. 1:27). The occurrence of "why?" in Mary's "Child, why have you treated us like this?" (Lk. 2:48), or in Jesus's "But if I have spoken rightly, why do you strike me?" (Jn. 18:23). The occurrence of such words as "how?" in Mary's "How (*pos*) can this be, since I am a virgin?" (Lk. 1:34), or Nathanael's "Where (*pothen*) did you get to know me?" (Jn. 1:48).

A more reflective attitude, though still occurring without thematization of the questioning nature of humans, is found in statements indicating the inner tension of inquiry, the dynamism of the search for understanding. Luke tells us that "But Mary treasured all these words and pondered them in her heart" (Lk. 2:19), where the word "pondered" is the same one he uses for the "discussion" of the Jewish rulers on how to handle Peter and John (Acts 4:15), and for the "debate" in which the Athenian philosophers engaged Paul (Acts 17:18). Linked with this is the occurrence of wonder in its milder forms. Generally *thaumazo* refers to the amazement of those witnessing signs and prodigies, but it can also refer to sentiments of simpler curiosity, more akin to our English *wonder*, as when outside the sanctuary "the people were waiting for Zechariah, and wondered (*ethaumazon*) at his delay in the sanctuary" (Lk. 1:21). And in general there seems to be a wealth of relevant data in the references to the teaching process, the lack of understanding charged as a failure (see, e.g., Mk. 6:52; Lk. 2:50; Acts 7:25), the request for explanation indicating an existential need (see, e.g., Mt. 13:36), the apparent satisfaction that explanation gave (see, e.g., Mt. 13:51; 16:12; 17:13; Lk. 24:45).

There is a second type of question: the reflection that requires evidence enough to justify a judgment on the matter. This question regards truth; it asks which side of a contradiction is right or, in the absence of contradiction, whether my idea is the right one. Again, we do not demand a thematization of the terms "reflection," "grasp of sufficient evidence," "verification," and so on, in the biblical record; we simply look for the performances that correspond, at least in a rudimentary way, to the elaborate procedures that we now denote by those terms. A paradigm will be helpful here, and a famous one exists historically in Abelard's *Sic et non*. The reader will remember that that book, so characteristic of the Middle Ages, so influential in promoting the dialectical spirit of those times, drew up with regard to some 158 propositions, the reasons for and against acceptance. It is a classic formula for the dialectical way to truth.

Now the Bible seems to give many instances, in its own way, of that sort of thing. A story of the legendary wisdom of Solomon supplies one perfect instance, when the two prostitutes stood before the king and argued: "'Then this woman's son died in the night....She got up in the middle of the night and took my son...' But the other woman said, 'No, the living son is mine, and the dead son is yours'" (1 Kings 3:19ff.); an open contradiction, if ever there was one—no more to be admitted by the Hebrew mind than by the Greek, as Solomon's judgment brought out in dramatic fashion. Or one could take an instance of a pattern that is recurrent in John: "And there was considerable complaining about him among the crowds. While some were saying, 'He is a good man,' others were saying, 'No, he is deceiving the crowd'" (Jn. 7:12). Later, we have the significant statement: "So there was a division (*schisma*) in the crowd because of him" (Jn. 7:43).

In the light of this practically explicit admission of the principle of non-contradiction, one might examine more closely other episodes in the Bible. There is the test to which the Pharisees put Jesus on the marriage law: "They said to him, 'Why then did Moses command us to give a certificate of dismissal and to divorce her?'" (Mt. 19:7). The objection, it seems to me, has as implicit presupposition the principle of non-contradiction: "You are saying one thing; Moses said the opposite—how do you get out of that?" Likewise, there is the question of Jesus's own disciples later in the chapter: "'Then who can be saved?'" (Mt. 19:25). God was certainly savior, and their Bible seemed to make prosperity a sign of his favor; but against that is a statement that seems to make salvation impossible to the wealthy—explain the contradiction. Clearer still is Jesus's own cross-questioning of the Pharisees on the Messiah: "'Whose son is he?' They said to him, 'The son of David.'...'If David thus calls him Lord, how can he be his son?'" (Mt. 22:42-45).[5]

Questions for reflection lead naturally to their complement of truth, the judgment that answers "yes" or "no" and gives us knowledge. For the third time I insist on my procedure here: My appeal will not be to the biblical use of the word "truth"[6] but to the performance of asserting the truth. In that context, a very significant word is the simple copula "is." When John wrote that the signs in his book "are written so that you may come to believe that Jesus *is* the Messiah, the Son of God..." (Jn. 20:31), he is a witness for my case that the biblical writers are concerned with truth in the Scholastic sense of the word. Of course, the special interest of those writers appears in the very next line: "and that through believing you may have life in his name." But no amount of insistence on this aspect ought to dilute the force of that "is." Such instances are legion, as when the centurion in Mark said, "Truly this man *was* God's son!" (Mk. 15:39), or when the high priest challenged Jesus: "I put you under oath before the living God, tell us if you *are* the Messiah, the Son of God" (Mt. 26:63).[7]

---

[5]The questions that, following *Insight* (cf. Index), I divide into types may be introduced by the same interrogative and show the same grammatical form; so it is the *intention* of the questioners that determines the type of question. Do they intend to put an objection as one contradicting a statement regarded as false, that is, as one concerned with the truth? Or do they intend to ask for explanation, as one puzzled and desiring understanding? I would assign Mary's question in Luke 1:34 to the latter type, Jesus's in Matthew 22:45 to the former, but this is a point for exegesis to decide. Generally, I should think, questions put in sarcasm (Jn. 1:46) or hostility (Jn. 6:42, 52) intend to contradict and hence regard the level of truth, whereas a more neutral attitude such as that shown by the Jerusalem delegation to the Baptist (Jn. 1:25) could pertain to either level. In fact, the average person freely mingles both levels in confusion, and there is no reason for insisting that a given question must be a pure case of one or the other type. Add one final note: Many questions are implicitly statements, and then they pertain to our next paragraph.

[6]The stock specialist account has been that the Hebrew meant by truth, not the "Greek" *adaequatio intellectus ad rem* (correspondence of mind with reality), but something like fidelity. But that great debunker, James Barr, an Old Testament specialist himself, has recently produced a mass of evidence to show a common usage of the word in Greek and Hebrew writers (1961, see esp. pp. 187-200). Our procedure avoids this controversy.

[7]It is remarkable that little two-letter words should have such a profound philosophical and theological significance. "Is" is a prime example, but "yes" is equally pregnant; and so is "no" corresponding to "is not." Not only that, but a language may dispense with the copula, as Hebrew sometimes does, and then the same effect is gained without words, by the juxtaposition of subject and predicate or by other means. The answer of Jesus to the high priest was clearly an assertion, but may have been in an Aramaic form that would hardly be recognized as an assertion by a Westerner; so Mark translates very simply, "I am" (Mk. 14:62).

What I have been trying to point out is an isomorphism of structure, a similarity in relation between cognitional acts, a formal likeness of biblical performance in this field to Greek and modern. If readers wish to judge the truth of my idea, they should attend rather exactly to the data I have presented, and not to some other data illustrating the more familiar differences between Hebrew and Greek. It is quite easy to be misled here by the vast difference in materials, or by the subtler difference between performance and thematization of the performance. Certainly, the Hebrew "What is it?" is exercised on other materials than Aristotle's "Let us state what...substance should be said to be" (*Metaphysics*, VII, 17), and is much farther from thematization of performance; but is the performance itself similar in the two cases? Does each question manifest the same need of understanding, the same dynamism of intellect seeking explanation? Certainly the Hebrew "No, the living son is mine, and the dead son is yours" is very different from the Aristotelian "They do not all agree as to the number and the nature of these principles [of things]. Thales...says the principle is water....Anaximenes and Diogenes make air prior to water....Anaxagoras...says the principles are infinite in number" (*Metaphysics*, I, 3), but is there a similarity in the dialectical form in which the argument is carried out and the truth pursued? Certainly, the Hebrew way of thinking in the question, "If David thus calls him Lord, how can he be his son?" is a long way from the explicit and thematic formulation "The most certain principle of all is...that the same attribute cannot at the same time belong and not belong to the same subject and in the same respect..." (*Metaphysics*, IV, 3), but would Jesus's point be valid without his implicit recognition of the principle Aristotle formulated, or would his case be cogent against the Pharisees unless they too recognized implicitly the principle involved? I believe that if one gets hold of my point and achieves personal openness to the possibility of isomorphic structure in cognitional activity, he or she will have little trouble in discovering what seems so obvious to me, a basic community of mentality that underlies all the more superficial differences between Jew and Greek.

## 6. Thematizing the Structures: Some Reflections

I have said that the thorough investigation of the topic I have merely introduced would have to be undertaken by a biblical specialist, but that the determination of the topic and of the general procedures consonant with its nature, the procedures that should be followed if *that* question is to be investigated and not some other, belongs to the more systematic tasks of the theologian. After all, one who reads the modern exegete will really not expect him to undertake an enthusiastic study of Aristotle's *Posterior Analytics*! Yet we can hardly have an expert knowledge of what a question in general is if we ignore that kind of book; and not to have an expert knowledge of what a question is would be a very bad beginning for the investigation of the questioning nature of the Hebrew and the structure of his cognitional activity. It seems then that there must be place for more philosophical and theological considerations at the very outset of the study, and I should like to enlarge on that point before concluding.

It is a striking fact that almost every page of the New Testament is crowded with questions, and yet the *theme* of the question hardly occurs at all in the biblical dictionaries, commentaries, and manuals. But perhaps the oddity of that will disappear if we look at a few parallel cases in the history of theology. It is probable that the first treatise we know to have been called *De trinitate* was written by Novatian around 250 C.E., but afterwards treatises under this title slowly became the fashion. And similarly other treatises begin at a point in time, to become later a regular occurrence: *De incarnatione* in the early fourth century, *De spiritu sancto* in the late fourth century, and so on. Not as if no one had worshipped the Father, Son, and Holy Spirit before 250 C.E., but the holy three as such were not a theme; they *could* not be a theme, for by all evidence, no one had even *counted* them before the last decades of the second century. The point is that thematization supposes a moment of creative insight; one must have the idea at least obscurely in mind first, and then one attends more diligently to the data, either for conceptual formulation or for judgment on the fact. The Messiahship was a theme in the early Church, and the Christian community ransacked the Old Testament for prophecies and elaborated on their fulfillment in the New. The destiny of the Jewish people became a theme for Paul in the Epistle to the Romans, and he wrestled with the data to discover and explain to himself God's mysterious dealings with the chosen people.

Now the idea of human spirit as marked by its questioning character, as almost constituted by inquiry, though it has a kind of charter in Greek philosophy, became an explicit theme of philosophy only in relatively recent times—the human mind is so ponderously slow. The idea therefore could not possibly be a theme of investigation in New Testament studies before our times. This is not to claim that the idea must first occur to philosophers before it can enter biblical studies; as Gilson has long and eloquently insisted, many fundamental ideas of "Christian" philosophy were conceived under the influence of the word of God. My point is that the idea must occur somewhere and be at least obscurely formulated in someone's mind before it becomes a theme; it is most likely to occur to those who make a career of ideas; but even if it occurs in study of the New Testament itself, thematization will involve a return to the New Testament data for a thorough and proper investigation.

I have been talking of the priority of certain ideas in investigating the isomorphism of Hebrew and Greek mentalities, the need of a prior *Begriflichkeit* (conceptuality), and I illustrated the need with the example of the question. This kind of program is not at all alien to the spirit of modern biblical research or of scientific investigation in general. It is another commonplace today that the interpreter brings suppositions in every case to the task at hand, that the ideal of presuppositionless inquiry, which prevailed when history was an emerging science, is really nonsense. The favorite example here is Bultmann, who has very definitely formulated presuppositions, uses them openly in his exegesis of the New Testament, and so far from repenting of his misdeeds, states that all other interpreters do what he does, only without acknowledging the fact. There can hardly be any doubt that Bultmann's program contains a valid point, for the only one who lives without presuppositions is the newborn babe: The infant is not much of a scholar, and neither would adults be competent interpreters if they tried to leave all ideas behind as they came to their task.

Nevertheless, we have to be accurate here to avoid relativism. An obvious objection might run like this: As your presuppositions, so your interpretation; modern science has taught us to be obedient to the facts, but the approach through presuppositions seems to determine beforehand what the facts are going to be allowed to be. The objector will supply instances of the corrupting influence of presuppositions on judgment: Decadent Scholastics insist on finding their notions of eternal procession, logical truth, substantial form, etc., in biblical terms that have a verbal resemblance, and similarly the uninstructed exegete cannot bear to find anything in the biblical record that savors of Scholastic procedures of defining terms, stating and proving a thesis, etc.

The answer to the objection consists in subjecting the cliché about presuppositions (for it too is a cliché) to precise analysis. What it seems to mean is that one's presuppositions yield a range of *possible* interpretations; they limit interpretation to a field, but within that field they do not determine which interpretation we must accept. It now becomes clear that the way to escape relativism is to adopt the universal viewpoint, to be open to all explanations and interpretations, excluding none a priori, admitting none a posteriori till rational evidence is forthcoming. The analogy here is the creative mind of God. It is filled with ideas of possible worlds; and the greater the number and variety of ideas, the greater God's freedom in creating, the less the necessity imposed on God's actual choice of a world. That is, God's ideas are an a priori on the level of possibility that eliminates any imposed a priori on the level of actuality. Similarly, the wider the viewpoint of the interpreters, the greater the number of possible interpretations open to them, and the greater their freedom in discovering an acceptable one.

But the universal viewpoint is not enough either, if we do not take possession of the operational structures that are ours. The world of objective being and the openness of subjective spirit can be completely universal, and our conversion to the universality of object and subject can be as genuine as you please; but if we have no grasp of the structure we necessarily use in guiding spirit to being, we can hardly avoid the most serious blunders.  We need then a critical awareness, an appropriation and evaluation of our own powers of intelligent grasp and reasonable affirmation of the universe of being; we need also an awareness and appropriation of our power for harmonious accord with the universe, but the emphasis of this chapter has been on the cognitional side rather than on the affective.  It was this taking possession of our operational structures that was treated in the third and fourth parts above.

Finally, there is knowledge of the particular differentiations that result when the structure is used on different materials and with different interests and with different degrees of correspondence to the dynamism that the human person is.  Here the role of the specialist is to the fore.  Every differentiated culture requires its own specialists, the Hebrew culture likewise requires its own, and my modest efforts in the fifth part of this chapter should not be taken as a specimen of what a specialist might be able to do with the same material.  But it seemed important to attempt a sketch myself, for otherwise the point of the preceding paragraphs was less likely to come through, or they might seem to be mere a priori reasoning without application to the biblical documents.

There is indeed an a priori element in them, not an a priori that requires us to find, for example, the principle of non-contradiction in biblical writers, but the kind that enables us to see it if it is there.  I think that the implicit admission of the principle is there and that the apparent neglect of it on some occasions is explained here as it would be if found elsewhere, even among logicians—by the contradiction not being brought sharply to their attention, by the matter lying outside their present field of interest, etc.  If then I were told by exegetes that ancient Hebrews cared nothing for my principle, I should listen, I hope, with respect; I should not label the exegetes incompetent in their own specialty.  But I should want to examine their presuppositions; I should regard it as within my competence to judge those presuppositions, and if I found them faulty, I should continue to look for specialists who are open to the universe of being, who have a view of the human condition that does not a priori exclude Hebrew openness to the universe of being, and then I should put my question to them:  Do you find an isomorphism in the cognitional structures of Hebrew and Greek?

The same general attitude should be taken towards specialists in every culture, for, despite all the protests of the specialists and due regard being paid to the real dangers of imperialism on the part of general science, it can hardly be denied any longer that certain very general presuppositions guide all investigators who are worth their salt, and it is the business of general science to examine those presuppositions.  This remark is made in relation to a short note of E. Brehier (1949).  Brehier's thesis is that whereas study of primitive mentalities had formerly been dominated by the idea of genesis (that is to say, early myths are but an imperfect form of the true explanation science will discover), Lévy-Bruhl on the contrary discovered in the primitive mind irreducible structures not to be supplanted by "better" ideas; we are dealing with thinking of another nature, quite content with its achievements. But everything here depends on how deeply one penetrates. The example given in the article is that of "causality": Primitive myths are not to be reduced to a primitive idea of causality. Our notion of structure goes deeper than such comparisons, just as our notion of intelligibility goes deeper than causality; and so there is room for putting the question again: Is there an isomorphism between the primitive mentality and ours?

# 6

# Eric Voegelin on Plato
# and the Sophists

## *Thomas J. Farrell*

Socrates and Plato and Aristotle professed to believe that the sophists of their day generally were dishonest rhetoricians, using their intellectual and verbal skill to trick their audiences and teaching their disciples to do the same....If the charge is true, the sophists were rhetorical deceivers; if it is not, their accusers were guilty of the rhetorical deception of which they accused the sophists.

—Walter J. Ong (1990, p. 2)

Eric Voegelin (1901-1985) and Bernard Lonergan (1904-1984) both recognized the affinity between their works, but neither explored in detail how their respective insights could be aligned with one another. Here I propose to delineate Voegelin's insights about Plato and the sophists.[1] Using Voegelin's exegesis of Plato's critique of the sophists, I suggest two basic alignments between Voegelin's thought and Lonergan's: (1) that the positions represented by sophists can be aligned with Lonergan's insights about

---

[1] While John Angus Campbell (1982, 1984a, 1984b) has called attention to certain aspects of Voegelin's thought that might be of interest to scholars interested in rhetoric, Voegelin's exegesis of Plato's critique of the sophists seems to be virtually unknown among scholars interested either in Plato's position on rhetoric or in defending the sophists against Plato's attacks. Studies by Mario Untersteiner (1954), W. K. C. Guthrie (1971), G. B. Kerferd (1981), Susan C. Jarratt (1991), Edward Schiappa (1991), Jacqueline de Romilly (1992) and Richard Leo Enos (1993) examining the works of sophists provide needed correctives to the relative neglect of their works. But those studies do not reveal the bases of Plato's objections to the sophists, as Voegelin does. While studies by Edwin Black (1958), Rollin W. Quimby (1974), David S. Kaufer (1978), Jasper Neel (1988), James L. Kastely (1991), Michael F. Carter (1991), and C. Jan Swearingen (1991) have explored Plato's attitudes about rhetoric, Voegelin provides a penetrating exegesis of Plato's thought that makes the attacks on the sophists more understandable than ever before.

drifting and drifters (1967/1988, pp. 222-231; 1985, p. 208), and (2) that the experiences of Socrates, Plato, and Aristotle can be aligned with Lonergan's account of self-appropriation in *Insight: A Study of Human Understanding* (1957/1992).[2] The sophists and most other orators in ancient Athens as Josiah Ober (1989) has described them were drifters, in Lonergan's terminology, because they embodied what Richard A. Lanham refers to as *homo rhetoricus* (1976, pp. 1-9). Socrates, Plato, and Aristotle embodied Lanham's *homo seriosus*. To use terminology coined by Thomas Patrick Malone and Patrick Thomas Malone (1987), *homo rhetoricus* lives predominantly out of the *I*; *homo seriosus*, out of the *self* (see chapter 2 for further discussion of their work and Lanham's).

Voegelin's exegesis opens up a third possibility beyond the two identified by Walter J. Ong in the epigraph—the possibility that the bases of Plato's attacks have been misunderstood. As Voegelin explicates them, it turns out that they are not attacks on rhetoric as such, but in effect attacks on what Lonergan refers to as drifting and drifters. Drifting involves living in a state of mystification (Bradshaw, 1992). Plato described the situation of drifting with his memorable image of the people in the cave. Leaving the cave and emerging into the light of the sun outside involves, on the one hand, being healed of childhood traumas and, on the other, learning how to access properly the energies of the archetypes of maturity (concerning the former, see A. Miller, 1979/1981, 1980/1983, 1981/1984, 1988/1990a, 1988/1990b, 1990/1991; concerning the latter, see Moore & Gillette, 1990, 1992a, 1992b, 1993a, 1993b). While Plato's allegory seems to concern only cognitive and epistemological issues, rather than psychological ones, John Bradshaw (1988) has made it abundantly clear that the full human capacities for knowing and understanding cannot be actuated until people have freed themselves from the psychological aftereffects of childhood traumas. Until that happens, they will live in the state of mystification suggested by Plato's image of the cave and will be characterized by the drifting that Lonergan writes about.

Voegelin shows that since philosophizing for Plato cannot be reduced to writing, his writings are only guideposts to philosophizing, efforts to per-

---

[2] Aristotle uses the term *spoudaios* to refer to the fullness of human development (Voegelin, 1957b, pp. 300, 303, 313, 320, 323, 327, 335-336). As Voegelin suggests, this term could be translated as "the mature person." Voegelin sees the experience Aristotle named by this term as the equivalent to the experience Plato named by the term *aner daimonios*. Moreover, Voegelin suggests that Cicero may have been aware of the equivalent experience (1990a, pp. 275-276). While I argue in this essay against the suggestion Ong makes in the epigraph, I focus my attention on Plato to make the basic argument. If readers find my argument about him persuasive, then they might be persuaded to accept Voegelin's suggestion that Aristotle was aware of the equivalent experience, although he named it differently. They may also find Voegelin's further suggestion that Cicero may have also been aware of the equivalent experience persuasive.

suade readers toward philosophizing. Thus his writings involved rhetoric.[3]
Startling as this classification may sound to some people, Plato was well
aware of the importance of persuasion in the formation of the philosopher.
For example, a computer search of the entire corpus of works firmly attributed to Plato revealed 400 uses of the various forms of the Greek word for
persuasion (*peitho*). Even a cursory reading of those passages reveals that
Plato highly valued persuasion of the proper kind. Thus persuasion as such
is not the target of his attacks on the sophists.

The target is the less fully functional persuasion of the sophists, which
is not likely to engender the development of the philosopher. The more
fully functional persuasion offered by Socrates and Plato can be characterized as persuasion concerned with and aimed at engendering the experience of the divine, if you will, because it comes from the guide's contact in
his psyche with the transcendent ground of being, as Voegelin's careful exegesis of Plato shows. It is more fully functional than the persuasion of the
sophists because it leads the would-be philosopher to experience the divine
ground of being (i.e., the experience of transcendence). I refer here to the
persuasion offered by Socrates and Plato as more fully functional because it
aims at a fuller actualization of human potential than even Abraham Maslow
describes (1971, pp. 259-269). By contrast, the persuasion of the sophists
can be characterized as oriented toward the profane, because it does not
arise from the guide's experience of transcendence, even when it may include an appeal to the gods and providence.

Plato's analysis of rhetoric and the sophists in the *Euthydemus*, the
*Protagoras*, the *Gorgias*, and the *Phaedrus* enabled him to leave the cave,
so to speak, and see things in a clear light. In terms of Lonergan's work,
Plato's analysis of rhetoric and the sophists enabled him in effect to attain
what Lonergan means by self-appropriation. In short, there is an equiva-
lence of experience (Voegelin, 1990a, pp. 115-133) behind the symbolism of
what Plato describes as the people in the cave and what Lonergan describes
as drifting. The beginning of self-appropriation (leaving the cave) marks
the effective end of drifting. In terms of Voegelin's distinction between
compact experience and differentiated experience, Plato's parable of the
cave represents a more compact experience, while Lonergan's account of

---

[3]Richard Leo Enos has argued that Plato's dialogues can be considered to be
rhetoric, and he has adduced a quote from Cicero that makes a similar claim (1991,
p. 5). Indeed, Voegelin's analysis supports such a claim, as does Plato's own
extensive discussion of persuasion. If philosophizing cannot be reduced to a set of
propositions, then the statements the philosopher makes are at best guideposts to
others about how to proceed to philosophize. By Plato's account of philosophy, that
is the case. Consequently, even the statements of the philosopher are rhetoric. At
their best, they persuade or move people toward philosophizing. But while
philosophizing cannot be reduced to a set of propositions, it involves experiencing
the liberating, as distinct from the bewitching, power of the word. That may be
what Plato wished to call attention to by writing his dialogues.

self-appropriation represents a more differentiated experience. For drifting to come to an end, people do need to experience the aspects of "conversion" (Lonergan's term for Plato's *periagoge*) that Lonergan in his later writings referred to as religious, moral, intellectual, and affective. And those processes involve learning how to access properly the archetypes of maturity identified by Robert Moore and Douglas Gillette (1990, 1992a, 1992b, 1993a, 1993b), which are discussed later in this essay.

If Plato's earlier, sometimes scathing, analyses of rhetoric contributed substantially to his later conversion experience, why didn't Plato say so explicitly later on, instead of just writing a more ameliorative treatise on rhetoric later on? Perhaps he could not articulate to himself or others just what led up to his conversion experience. My suggested reconstruction of what may have led up to his conversion experience grows not only out of Voegelin's detailed analyses of Plato and of Greek thought leading up to Plato, but also out of Lonergan's detailed analysis of the conditions and processes involved in the emergence of insight. Lonergan's analysis of the processes leading up to insight is strikingly similar to the processes of analyzing rhetoric that Plato went through. But brilliant as Plato was—and as Socrates and Aristotle were—nobody in ancient times had articulated the kind of detailed analysis of the processes of thought that Lonergan articulates, because they just simply had not reflected on the processes of thought and named them. To use Voegelin's terms, Lonergan represents a more differentiated experience than what can be found in Plato. Plato's expression of his experience in the parable of the cave is an example of what Voegelin would call a compact experience.

But Plato was not being dishonest in expressing his experience of conversion through the parable of the cave, even though he did not have Lonergan's introspective awareness and could not have articulated the distinctions Lonergan articulated. Similarly, Plato was not being dishonest by referring to the love of wisdom, instead of speaking of the pure, detached, disinterested desire to know, as Lonergan does. Plato was simply articulating a more compact experience, while Lonergan articulated a more differentiated experience. If we grant the pertinence of Voegelin's distinction between compact and differentiated experiences and see the conversion experiences of Socrates, Plato, and Aristotle as compact experiences compared to Lonergan's more differentiated experience, then they may not have been dishonest, as Ong suggests in the epigraph, but simply unable to articulate their experiences more fully in their efforts to express their sense of how they were different from the sophists of their day.

Voegelin's exegesis of Plato and Aristotle enables us to see that Socrates, Plato, and Aristotle did not share the sophists' exclusively secular orientation. To use another term employed by Lonergan, they had attained a higher viewpoint. From a higher viewpoint, less differentiated thought and action may appear to be deceptive and dishonest.

Voegelin is a worthy guide to understanding how the above distinctions inform Plato's writings.  The importance of Voegelin's exegesis of Plato is developed here in three sections: (1) "Background Considerations" provides information about Voegelin's work itself and shows how his work can be related to the work of Eric A. Havelock, Ong, and Mircea Eliade; (2) "Plato on Philosophy and the Sophists," by far the longest section, pulls together Voegelin's scattered statements about Plato and the sophists; (3) "Contemporary Thought about Maturity" briefly summarizes Moore and Gillette's work to suggest how it can help us better understand the ludic and agonistic spirit of Plato's attacks on the sophists; and (4) "Conclusions" presents conclusions that can be drawn from Voegelin's scattered remarks about Plato's work, shows how Voegelin's exegesis of Plato is consonant with Lonergan's ideal of self-appropriation, and concludes that the maturity attained by Socrates, Plato, and Aristotle, not dishonesty on their part, accounts for their attacks on the sophists.  Toward the end I also suggest that Plato wrote dialogues because he sensed that the kind of communication that can occur in dialogue is worth commemorating.

## 1. Background Considerations

In 1990, Louisiana State University Press published two of the anticipated 34 volumes of *The Collected Works of Eric Voegelin*, and it has kept the five volumes of his masterwork, *Order and History*, in print continuously since the original publication of each volume.  The second and third volumes of *Order and History*, first published in 1957, are *The World of the Polis* and *Plato and Aristotle*.  Voegelin refined and crystallized his insights in a series of subsequent essays, which have now been published in the first two volumes to be published of his *Collected Works*, Vol. 12, *Published Essays: 1966-1985* (1990a) and Vol. 27, *What Is History? And Other Late Unpublished Writings (1990b)*.

While Voegelin's survey of ancient Greek thought provides the background information needed for understanding Socrates and Plato, his treatment (in 1957a, pp. 111-240) of the break with myth and the development of philosophy anticipates in certain respects Havelock's (1978) later discussion of the movement from primary oral thought in Homer to the full development of abstract literate thought in Plato.  Voegelin's terms can be aligned with the terms employed by Havelock and also by Ong to describe the movement of thought and consciousness from primary oral culture to literate culture.  Voegelin characterizes certain cultures as cosmological and their thought and expression as compact, while he sees the cultures of ancient Israel (1956) and ancient Greece (1957a, 1957b) as breaking away from the cosmological pattern and developing more differentiated thought.  Cosmological cultures correspond to what Havelock and Ong call primary oral cultures, while the more differentiated forms of thought and expression in ancient Israel and ancient Greece are associated with the development of nonvowelized and vowelized literacy in those respective cultures (Havelock, 1982; Ong, 1982). The movement from the compactness of expression found in myth to the greater differentiation of thought and expression found in philosophy in ancient Greece involves the movement from the concrete imagistic thought of primary orality to the abstract thought fostered by vowelized literacy.

However, within the spectrum of compactness and differentiation he studied, Voegelin discerns certain constant features and concerns:

> In response to his anxiety of existence, man embarks on a search of the ground through acts of mythopoesis and philosophizing. Philosophy is concerned with two fundamental questions formulated by Leibniz in his *Principes de la nature et de la grace*: 1) Why is there something, why not nothing? and 2) Why are the existent things as they are, and not different? The same questions are the concern of myth—though for their expression myth is bound to the compact form imposed by the cosmological style of truth. Hence, myth and philosophy can cooperate in producing the mytho-speculative varieties of the aggregate because they have in common the endeavor to relate existent things to a ground that will endow their existence with meaning. Seeking, finding, and giving the ground of things, however, is reasoning; and the act of relating things to a ground is reasoning, whatever symbolic form it may assume. Reason must be acknowledged, therefore, as having a part not only in philosophy but also in mythopoesis, strange as this may sound to the many who still believe myth to be some kind of imaginative play beyond the pale of reason. Nevertheless, though both myth and philosophy have reason at their core, their styles of reasoning differ. In the form given them by Leibniz, the questions concerning the ground of things, regarding their existence and essence, can be asked only after philosophy has differentiated. As long as they are asked within the cosmological style of truth, there prevails the rule of relating things to their ground by relating them to intracosmic things, such as the external universe or the gods. Hence, with regard to the adequacy of styles as a means of expression, philosophy is better suited than myth to formulate the question of the ground. (1990b, pp. 74-75)

When thought turns to issues that do not involve the question of the ground, the issues involved concern by definition the profane. Myth and philosophy involving the question of the ground are higher forms of human reason than other forms, as Voegelin repeatedly notes in *The Ecumenic Age* (1974).

John Angus Campbell draws on Eugene Webb's *Eric Voegelin: Philosopher of History* (1981) to elucidate what Voegelin is referring to as the ground of being:

> Odd as it may seem to a modern, the main stream of Western theology well into the Middle Ages does not affirm the "existence," in the nominalist sense, of an entity called "God." Aquinas' God, Webb notes, "...is spoken of not as *a* being, not even the highest and best being, but as Being as such or 'essential being,' while individual entities are not essential being but 'participated being'....They may be said to 'be' to a greater or lesser extent accord-

ing to the degree to which they participate (by analogy, not by composition or 'being part of' it) in the supreme pole, which alone truly deserves the name of Being" [Webb, 1981, p. 72]. (Campbell, 1982, pp. 84-85)

Campbell also explains how the ground of being is the ultimate object of human desire:

> The true object of human restlessness, then, is a total perfection of being for which every world-immanent category of desire is a sign pointing toward a world-transcendent ground....In knowledge, humans desire perfect wisdom; in right action, humans want perfect justice and perfect good; in aesthetics, they strive for perfection of beauty. The traditional term in the West for the sum of every imaginable perfection is "God."...It is the omega point that Voegelin sees as the "ground" that human beings are in "tension toward." (1982, p. 82)

While Voegelin distinguishes the heightened consciousness experienced by Moses, the prophets, and St. Paul from the heightened consciousness experienced by the eleatics, Socrates, Plato, and Aristotle by referring to the former as a pneumatic differentiation of consciousness and the latter as a noetic differentiation of consciousness, he sees their experiences as essentially similar in the sense of involving the tension toward the ground of being. Since we do not usually speak of the Judaeo-Christian religion as involving a tension toward the ground of being, it is important to recognize that the Judaeo-Christian command to love God (e.g., Deuteronomy 6:5, Luke 10:27) is essentially a call to direct one's desires to the ground of being, the supreme pole of which alone deserves the name of Being. In other words, the Judaeo-Christian command directs people to go beyond the desire for Being that is implicit in striving for truth, goodness, justice, and beauty by making their love and desire for God explicit and personal. Surely to love God with all one's heart and soul and strength involves living in tension toward the ground of being. Consequently, it might be best to see the pneumatic and the noetic differentiations of consciousness as the equivalent of Lonergan's religious and intellectual conversion, which involve learning how to access properly the King and the Magician archetypes of maturity discussed by Moore and Gillette.

While it may not yet be popular for people within the Judaeo-Christian tradition to speak about living in tension toward the ground of being, Lonergan (1985, pp. 188-192) reviewed two of Voegelin's essays examining correspondences between the classic experience of philosophy in ancient Greece and the Christian Gospels (reprinted in Voegelin, 1990a, pp. 172-212, 265-291) and offered the following conclusions:

> Voegelin agrees with the estimate of Justin Martyr that the gospel, so far from being opposed to the classic philosophy of Athens, is that philosophy brought to the state of perfection. Both are responses to the question set by the twofold meaning of life and death. Both take the issue with full seriousness of the death of Socrates or the full seriousness of the death and resurrec-

tion of Jesus. Both know of light and darkness, of pull and counter-pull, of the need of free choice to support the gentle pull of the golden cord, of the inner unrest that remains with those that turn aside. But the followers of Socrates speak of conversion (*periagoge*) and the followers of Jesus speak of repentance (*metanoia*). (1985, p. 192)

Thus the experiences referred to are equivalent in a certain respect, despite some differences in the terminology used to describe them. Similarly, pneumatic and noetic differentiations of consciousness are equivalent in a certain respect, despite some differences in how they were expressed. What exactly is the respect in which they are equivalent?

Although Voegelin (1957a, pp. 49ff.) makes good use of *The Myth of the Eternal Return* by Mircea Eliade (1949/1954), he does not refer at all to Eliade's *The Sacred and the Profane* (1957/1959), which was originally published at about the same time as Voegelin's two volumes on ancient Greek culture. Jungians would explain the experience of the sacred as the experience of the Self, the profane as the experience of ordinary personalized ego-consciousness:

The two modes of experience, the customary normative conscious state [i.e., the profane] and the altered state [i.e., the experience of the sacred], exist together, equally accessible to us, the one at the level of the ego, the other at that of the Self. The task is to harmonize them and give each its due. (Perry, 1987, p. 205)

In terms of the tree imagery in the Book of Genesis (2:9ff.), the tree of knowledge of good and evil represents the profane; the tree of life, the sacred. The terms in the title of Eliade's later book provide a shorthand way to express a key difference between the eleatics (such as Parmenides; cf. Voegelin, 1957b, pp. 203-219) and Plato, on the one hand, and the sophists (cf. Voegelin, 1957b, pp. 267-331), on the other. The eleatics and Plato have a sacred view of life, while the sophists by and large approach life as profane. This handy distinction comes out most clearly in Voegelin's work when he refers to the eleatics and Plato as the mystic philosophers, a classification that could not be extended to the sophists, except perhaps to Protagoras and Antisthenes.[4]

However, someone might reasonably ask what evidence there is that shows that Plato did indeed have reverence for the sacred as Eliade uses that term and as Jungians understand it. John Weir Perry, a psychiatrist whose Jungian concepts were quoted above, refers to Plato as "the first great psychologist of the Western world" precisely because of his grasp of and respect for the experience of the sacred (1974, p. 5). Perry then proceeds to quote a long passage from Benjamin Jowett's translation of Plato's *Phae-*

---

[4] Protagoras is supposed to have written a treatise "On the Gods," and Antisthenes apparently produced arguments for monotheism, as Eve Browning Cole has reminded me.

*drus* in which, in Perry's words, "Socrates enumerated four kinds of madness that conveyed a wisdom higher than the wisdom of the world: that of
prophecy, of initiation, of poets, and of lovers" (1974, p. 5). Here is the
whole passage that Perry quotes from the *Phaedrus* [244-245]:

> In proportion as prophecy is higher and more perfect than divination...in the
> same proportion...is madness superior to the sane mind, for the one is only
> of human, but the other of divine origin. Again, where plagues and mightiest
> woes have bred in a race, owing to some ancient wrath, there madness, lifting
> up her voice and flying to prayers and rites, has come to the rescue of those
> who are in need; and he who has part in this gift, and is truly possessed and
> duly out of his mind, is by the use of purifications and mysteries made whole
> and delivered from evil, future as well as present, and has a release from the
> calamity that afflicts him. There is also a third kind of madness, which is
> possession of the Muses; this enters into a delicate and virgin soul, and there
> inspiring frenzy, awakens lyric....But he who, not being inspired and having
> no touch of madness in his soul, comes to the door and thinks that he will get
> into the temple by the help of art—he, I say, and his poetry are not admit-
> ted; the sane man is nowhere at all when he enters into rivalry with
> the madman. (quoted in Perry, 1974, p. 5)

In commenting on this passage, Perry declares that "Plato was speaking of
the nonrational psyche in 'altered states of consciousness'" (1974, p. 6).
Retreatants who follow the techniques of meditation found in the *Spiritual
Exercises* of St. Ignatius Loyola (1991) aim to experience such altered states
of consciousness, and so do people who employ the Jungian technique of
active imagination. When successful, these techniques provide a window or
an opening to the Self in the unconscious and thereby establish an alliance
with the unconscious. Without such an alliance, people are what Jung
called "rootless" (quoted in Stevens, 1982, p. 258). They are, in Lonergan's
term, drifting (1967/1988, pp. 222-231; 1985, p. 208).

According to Voegelin, Plato attacks the sophists because they doubt
or deny divine reality (1990a, p. 355), which is to say that they predominantly view the world as profane and have not established an alliance with
the unconscious as it can be experienced as the "sacred" in altered states of
consciousness. In Plato's estimate, "profane" persuasion is not at all likely
to engender the development of the philosopher, and so Plato sees sophistic
education as falling far short of the persuasion that he and Socrates favor for
education, the aim of which is to engender the development of the philosopher—presumably through the altered state of consciousness that Martin
Buber (1923/1970) referred to as an I-thou relationship. In the academy
today, we take for granted the distinction between spiritual and temporal
orders and relegate education about the divine mostly to schools of divinity
or departments of theology, leaving education about the profane to all the
other schools and departments. Outside the academy, ministers, priests, rab-
bis, and their lay assistants also accept some of the responsibility for education about the divine. But the distinction between spiritual and temporal

orders had not yet emerged in Plato's day, and so neither he nor the sophists could be expected to have thought of having different teachers for the spiritual and temporal orders.

It should also be noted here that Plato in his writings is formulating a definition: He is defining how the "philosopher" differs from the "sophist." It does not follow, however, that he exhaustively surveyed the thought of everybody in ancient Greece who might be considered a sophist. Consequently, if studies of the historical sophists were to reveal that some of them met the conditions that Plato has stipulated for being considered a philosopher, then surely the title philosopher should be accorded to them. However, Voegelin's analysis of what Plato meant by the philosopher suggests that that is not likely to happen in the case of Gorgias, despite his appeal to belief in the gods and divine providence in the first hypothesis of the *Helen*, as we shall see.

Instead of presenting the results of an empirical survey of the practices of the sophists, Plato in his dialogues started with the approach to education that he and Socrates favored and used representative examples of sophists to make certain points about what he favored in education for the young. Thus he uses the sophists in his literary creations as foils to help him articulate the advantages of the kind of education he favors, and at times he extends his poetic license to make the points he wishes to make. For example, in the *Gorgias* Plato creates the improbable situation of having the sophist Gorgias of Leontini agree not to give long speeches but to abide by the rules of dialogue stipulated by Socrates. The improbability of the agreement indicates that Plato was creating a work of art to make certain points and not writing an historical record of an actual conversation. Thus Plato's attacks on the sophists are a form of serious play designed to evoke a suitable response in readers. While Voegelin's 1949 essay "The Philosophy of Existence: Plato's *Gorgias*" is still a valid explication of Plato's position, we need to avoid identifying the Gorgias portrayed by Plato with the actual historical Gorgias, as Richard Leo Enos (1976) and others caution. Plato's portrayal of Gorgias caricatures the historical Gorgias to make a point. But we need to go beyond the research of Enos and others to discover the basis of Plato's animus against Gorgias and other sophists.[5]

---

[5] It is important to recognize that many professors of philosophy in the academy today are not philosophers as Plato defined the term. Many are sophists because they are exclusively secular in orientation. They do not believe that there is a transcendent or divine being.

## 2. Plato on Philosophy and the Sophists

To understand the import of Plato's attacks on Gorgias and other sophists, we need to understand what he meant by "philosophy":

> In Plato's exegesis of the "name," philosophy denotes the erotic tension of man toward the divine ground of his existence. God alone has *sophia*, the "real knowledge"; man finds the truth about God and the world, as well as his own existence, by becoming *philosophos*, the lover of God and his wisdom. The philosopher's eroticism implies the humanity of man and the divinity of God as the poles of his existential tension [i.e., tension in the order of existence]. The practice of philosophy in the Socratic-Platonic sense is the equivalent of the Christian sanctification of man; it is the growth of the image of God in man. (Voegelin, 1990a, p. 223)

Later in the same essay Voegelin identifies Plato's special term for human participation in the divine: "Plato was so acutely aware of man's consubstantiality but nonidentity with divine reality that he developed a special symbol for man's experience of his intermediate status between the human and the divine: He called the consciousness of this status the *metaxy*, the In-Between of existence" (1990a, p. 233). As noted above, Eliade would refer to this as the experience of the sacred, and Maslow, as transcendence. But as the result of the formation of what Voegelin refers to as Second Realities, people, including aspiring philosophers, are blocked by the constructs of their own minds from the experience of the sacred and limited to the experience of the profane (1974, pp. 184, 238, 254).[6]

To explain the fundamental distinction that Plato makes between the philosopher and the sophist, Voegelin notes that Plato presents the following propositions in both the *Republic* (365b-e) and the *Laws* as being in general use in his intellectual environment:

---

[6] Contemporary theologians have drawn on Voegelin's work to describe experiences of the sacred. For example, David Granfield in *Heightened Consciousness* (1991) offers a readable synthesis of the literature about how divine sanctification proceeds, while Robert M. Doran (1990) describes in detail how the psyche is transformed through divine sanctification (cf. esp. 3-352 and 630-680). Other scholars have also recently written about experiences of the sacred without using Voegelin's work. For example, Frans Josef van Beeck (1991) points out how divine sanctification can be carried forward through appropriate conversation between people, and literary critic George Steiner (1989) argues that experiences of transcendence—in effect feeling touched by the divine—implicitly underlie works of art. And in a work in the history of ideas, Andrew Louth (1981) has investigated the complex relationship between Plato's theology and patristic theology of mysticism. Rosemary Haughton's (1981) account of exchange and breakthrough is a vivid description of experiences of the sacred, and the kind of exchange and breakthrough that she writes about can occur through the kind of conversation that van Beeck writes about. That kind of exchange and breakthrough most likely occurred at times in dialogues that Socrates carried on with interlocutors, and that most likely is why Plato chose to memorialize Socrates by using the literary form of the dialogue.

1. It seems no gods exist.
2. Even if they do exist, they do not care about men.
3. Even if they care, they can be propitiated by gifts. (quoted in Voegelin, 1990a, p. 386)

While Plato does not give a specific source, Voegelin notes that this triadic set is probably a sophistic school product, because "it has the same structure as the set of propositions preserved in Gorgias' essay *On Being*" (1990a, p. 386), which Voegelin then quotes:

1. Nothing exists.
2. If anything exists, it is incomprehensible.
3. If it is comprehensible, it is incommunicable. (quoted in Voegelin, 1990a, p. 387)

Gorgias's triad undercuts the fundamental assumption that divine wisdom is the warrant for intelligibility in the world, and so this triad is stronger evidence against Gorgias's orientation toward divine wisdom than the fourth hypothesis of the *Helen* is for it.[7] The two triadic sets of negative propositions suggest that in the sophistic schools a general loss of experiential contact with cosmic-divine reality had resulted in a contraction of human existence from the interaction of the human and the divine expressed in Homer and Hesiod and the eleatics. Plato "devoted the whole of Book X of the *Laws* to [the] refutation [of the first triad above]...resulting in the positive propositions that the gods exist, that they do care about man, and that they cannot be made accomplices in human criminality by offering them bribes from the profits of crimes" (Voegelin, 1990a, p. 387). Plato "diagnosed the origin of the phenomenon [of contracted existence] in the Sophist's withdrawal from noetic participation into anoetic solitude of his contracted self":

> No later discussion in terms of "alienation" has improved on Plato's analysis of existential [i.e., in the order of existence] contraction in terms of *anoia*. The man who abandons God as his partner in the divine-human *metaxy*, he explains in the *Laws* "is abandoned by God to his solitary existence (*eremos*)," with all the consequences of personal and social disorder (*Laws* 716a-b). Since abandoning God, however, means to abandon the noetic vision of the divine Beyond, to be abandoned by God means to be abandoned by the Nous, by "Reason." The withdrawal into existential solitude entails a state of *anoia*, of "unreason." The symbol *anoia* chosen by Plato to express the state of contracted existence (*Laws* 716a, 908e) characterizes the state of abandonment most clearly as a deformation of noetic consciousness. (1990a, p. 355)

So the problem with the sophists by Plato's definition of terms is that their alienation from the divine Nous is so great that they do not even sense their

---

[7] While Enos (1976) has examined the implications of this triad, he does not examine Plato's position in relation to this triad as carefully as Voegelin does.

own contracted existence in the profane order of the world. "If a man does not sense the want of something in his existential order, he will not strive for what he does not miss (*Symposium* 204a)," Voegelin notes (1990a, p. 364). Elsewhere in the collection Voegelin quotes Aristotle's succinct formulation of the situation: "'A man in confusion (*aporon*) or wonder (*thaumazon*) is conscious (*cietai*) of being ignorant (*agnoein*)' (*Metaphysics* 982b18)" (1990a, p. 270). Consequently, the person "will feel an active desire to escape from this state of ignorance (*pheugein ten agnoian, Metaphysics* 982b18) and to arrive at knowledge" of the divine ground of being (1990a, p. 270). "The balance of consciousness requires the turning around, the *periagoge*, not from a false to a true doctrine, but from deformative action of any type to the center of formative consciousness in the *metaxy*" (1990a, p. 355). "For the truth of reality is not an ultimate piece of information given to an outside observer but reality itself becoming luminous in the events of experience and imaginative symbolization" (1990a, p. 326). "Plato and Aristotle recognized these forces in the experiences of a human questioning (*aporein*) and seeking (*zetein*) in response to a mysterious drawing (*helkein*) and moving (*kinein*) from the divine side" (1990a, p. 326).

In addition to distinguishing the philosopher and the sophist in terms of their respective attitudes toward the divine, Plato used three sets of contrasting terms in the *Republic* to distinguish the philosopher from the sophist, Voegelin notes: (1) justice (*dikaiosyne*) and injustice, which Plato sees as characterized by *polypragmosyne* (an untranslatable term); (2) *philosophos* (the philosopher as conceived of by Plato) and *philodoxos* (another untranslatable term, unless we just coin the term "philodoxer"; to speak today about a "lover of opinion" would probably not communicate much to most people); and (3) *aletheia* (truth) and *pseudos* (falsehood or lie) (1957b, pp. 63-70). While justice for Plato is an all-pervasive quality for defining the philosopher, the opposite characteristic, *polypragmosyne*, will require considerable discussion to clarify, since it cannot even be translated into a comparable term in English or other modern languages, as Voegelin notes. The three sets of contrastive terms will be discussed here in reverse order from the order in which Voegelin presents and discusses them.

## 2.1  Truth vs. Falsehood

Voegelin points out that in the *Republic* the pair of concepts *aletheia* (truth) and *pseudos* (falsehood or lie) "refers to true and false, or proper and improper, presentation of the gods" (1957b, p. 67). He notes that this pair of concepts moves in the tradition of Hesiod, who "opposed his true history of the gods to the current false stories" (1957b, p. 67), and Xenophanes, who "sharpened the issue to the criteria of 'seemliness' in the symbolization of gods and rejected anthropomorphic symbols" (1957b, p. 67). He then goes on to explain how Plato further clarified the issue by introducing the conceptual instrument of "types of theology" (true and false theology):

> True humanity requires true theology; the man with false theology is an untrue man. "To be deceived or uninformed in the soul about true being [*peri ta onta*]" means that "the lie itself" [*hos alethos pseudos*] has taken possession of "the highest part of himself" and steeped it into "ignorance of the soul" (382a-b). With regard to the content of "true" theology Plato singles out two rules as the most important ones: (1) God is not the author of all things, but only of the good ones (380c), and (2) the gods do not deceive men in word or deed (383a). The rules of the true type are critically pointed against a complex of falsehood that is promulgated not only by Homer and Hesiod (the targets of Xenophanes), but also by the tragic poets and the sophists. We remember that in the *Protagoras* Plato made the great sophist insist on the poets, hierophants, and prophets as the precursors of his art. The poets are pooled with the sophists as the source of disorder in the soul and society....The restoration [of order in the soul] requires a turning-around (*periagoge*) of "the whole soul" (518d-e): from ignorance to the truth of God, from opinion about uncertainly wavering things to knowledge of being, and from multifarious activity to the justice of tending to one's proper sphere of action. (1957b, pp. 67-68)

## 2.2 Philosopher vs. Philodoxer

In discussing the terms *philosophos* and *philodoxos*, Voegelin begins by noting that it is difficult for us to properly understand what Socrates is calling for when he says that true philosophers would be the proper rulers in a healthy society. "Those who are able to see the 'one' in the 'many' things are the true philosophers, to be distinguished as such from the connoisseurs, the art lovers, and practical men" (Voegelin, 1957b, p. 66). By contrast, "the *philodoxos* [is] the man who cannot bear the idea that 'the beautiful, or the just, or any other thing, is one' (479a)...'The one' (*hen*) now becomes the subject of which not only 'god' can be predicated, but also the 'just' and the 'beautiful'" (1957b, p. 67). Whether or not we agree with the contention that true philosophers would be the proper rulers in a healthy society, we can see that the true philosophers envisioned by Socrates and Plato would be relatively few in number compared to the number of philodoxers.

## 2.3 Justice vs. Polypragmosyne

Just as the term *philodoxos* has dropped out of use, so too the term *polypragmosyne*, which Plato contrasts with *dikaiosyne*, has no equivalent in English. "We can translate Plato's *dikaiosyne* as justice, but we have no technical term to translate his *polypragmosyne* as the opposite of justice," Voegelin notes (1957b, p. 65).

> Since the concept of justice is developed for the purpose of criticizing the sophistic disorder, its meaning must be understood in relation to its opposite. For the designation of sophistic disorder, Plato uses the term *polypragmo-*

*syne*, the readiness to engage in multifarious activities that are not a man's proper business; and on occasion he uses the terms *metabole* (change or shift of occupation) and *allotriopragmosyne* (meddlesomeness, officious interference) (434b-c; 444b). (Voegelin, 1957b, p. 64)

The participants in the dialogue have agreed to the principle that "One man cannot practice with success many arts" (*Republic* 374a). They then go on to consider injustice as the opposite of this principle. A recent translator has translated the two difficult-to-translate passages (434b-c; 444b) in the following language:

> —But I think that when one who is by nature a worker or some other kind of moneymaker is puffed up by wealth, or by the mob, or by his own strength, or some other such thing, and attempts to enter the warrior class, or one of the soldiers tries to enter the group of counsellors and guardians, though he is unworthy of it, and these exchange their tools and public esteem, or when the same man tries to perform all these jobs together, then I think that you will agree that these exchanges and this meddling bring the city to ruin.
>
> —They certainly do.
>
> —The meddling and exchange between the three established orders does very great harm to the city and would most correctly be called wickedness.
>
> —Very definitely.
>
> —And you would call the greatest wickedness worked against one's own city injustice?
>
> —Of course.
>
> —That then is injustice. And let us repeat that the doings of one's own job by the moneymaking, auxiliary, and guardian groups, when each group is performing its own task in the city, is the opposite, it is justice and makes the city just. (Grube, 1974, p. 99)
>
> . . . . . . . . . . . . . . . . . . . . . . . . . . . . . . . . . . . . . . . . . . . . . . .
>
> —Surely it [injustice] must be a kind of civil war between the three parts, a meddling and a doing of other people's task, a rebellion of one part against the whole soul in order to rule it, though this is not fitting, as the rebelling part is by nature fitted to serve, while the other part is by nature not fit to serve, for it is of the ruling kind. We shall say, I think, that such things, the turmoil and the straying, are injustice and license and cowardice and ignorance and, in a word, every kind of wickedness. (Grube, 1974, p. 108)

Voegelin analyzes the concepts that are being connected with injustice in these passages: "*Polypragmosyne* covers the various violations of the principle, such as the attempts to practice more than one craft for which a man is specifically gifted, as well as the desire of the unskilled to rule the polis to its detriment. When applied to the soul, it refers to the inclination of appetites and desires to direct the course of human action and to claim the rulership of the soul that properly belongs to wisdom" (1957b, p. 64).

## 2.4  Polypragmosyne Considered Further

The quality Plato refers to in the *Republic* with the term *polypragmosyne* sounds similar to something he calls attention to in *Laws*.  As Voegelin notes, Plato in *Laws* 716c explicitly renounces the claim of the sophist Protagoras that man is the measure of all things: "God for us the measure of all things, of a truth; more truly so than, as they say, man" (quoted in 1957b, p. 254).  Voegelin then summarizes the key points developed in *Laws* 715e-718b:

> Those who want to live harmoniously will follow closely and humbly in the train of Dike; but those who are puffed with pride—of riches, or rank, or comeliness—believe that they do not need a guide; they rather will want to be guides for others.  The proud are abandoned by God; in their state of abandonment they will collect a company of others around them who are equally abandoned; they will embark on a frantic career and work general confusion.  (1957b, p. 254)

The confusion of the proud described in *Laws* is surely related to the quality referred to in the *Republic* as *polypragmosyne*.

Voegelin does not connect Plato's term *polypragmosyne* with his own discussion of the term *eris* in Homer, Hesiod, and Heraclitus (1957a, pp. 88, 92; 139; and 237).  But the connection is suggested by Plato's various uses of the terms *eris* and eristic (*Sophist* 225.c.9, 226.a.2, 231.e.2; *Philebus* 17.a.4; *Lysis* 211.b.8; *Euthydemus* 272.b.10; *Meno* 75.c.9, 80.e.2, 81.d.6; *Republic* 454.b.5, 499.a.7; *Menexenus* 237.d.1; *Laws* 834.d.3).  *Polypragmosyne* calls attention to spurious activity, and *eris* calls attention to contentious strife, as distinct from good strife.  Similarly, eristic contending is different in spirit, tone, and content from reasonable argumentation.  Enos notes that Plato uses the term protreptic discourse to distinguish intelligent and reasonable argumentation from the wrangling that Plato associates with eristic discourse (1981, pp. 47-48).  In other words, Plato objected to the skewed adversativeness of much of the rhetoric in Athens up to his time, which he associates with the sophists (although it apparently was not unique to them; see Ober, 1989, for a detailed account of the adversativeness of rhetoric in Athens).

Since Plato himself attacks the sophists, one assumes that he would consider his attacks to be good strife, rather than bad strife—to use terms used by Hesiod (Voegelin, 1957a, p. 139; also cf. Voegelin's discussion of Homer's representation of Achilles' "mischiefmaking strife," 1957a, p. 88).  Voegelin makes the following remarks about the addition of a good Eris in Hesiod's *Works and Days*, which Hesiod had not articulated in his *Theogony*:

> The evil Eris of *Theogony* receives a sister, the good Eris.  The evil one stirs up war, battle, injustice, cruelty and all kind of mischief among gods and men.  The good one, set "in the roots of the earth," stirs up the shiftless to toil, engenders a wholesome sense of competition among neighbors, and

stimulates craftsmen to surpass each other in the quality of their work. (1957a, p. 139)

The language in this passage is so close in spirit to the terms Voegelin uses to explain *polypragmosyne* that it is amazing that he himself did not notice the similarity. We may designate the good Eris as agonistic in spirit and reserve the term eristic as used by Plato and Aristotle to refer to the contentiousness of the bad Eris. It should be noted that the composite picture of *polypragmosyne* developed here is essentially the same quality that Lonergan refers to when he writes about drifting and drifters (1967/1988, pp. 222-231; 1985, p. 208).

To sum up this part, philosophers as envisioned by Plato are capable of distinguishing good striving from bad precisely because of the level of development they have achieved. For Plato, the philosopher is not only the lover of divine wisdom, but also wise, while the sophist is not. The sophists cannot properly distinguish good from bad striving because they have not achieved the level of human development that would enable them to do so. Plato refers to the full actuation and flourishing of human potentiality, and claims that the sophists have not yet attained such a level of development. Plato described the movement toward that level of development in the parable of the cave (*Republic* 514-517), where the person chained to the wall of the cave is drawn powerfully toward the light and turns around (*periagoge*) and sees things in the clear light of the sun (Voegelin, 1957b, pp. 114-115). Wise are the people who experience the clarity of vision that the person in the cave comes to experience.[8]

Since Plato recognized the key role of the guide's persuasion in engendering the development of the philosopher, he had to have recognized that these three sets of contrasting qualities exist in all people to varying degrees, until they experience the reasonable persuasion of a worthy guide. If the three less desirable qualities did not exist in everybody to some degree, why would the guide's persuasion be necessary to engender development?

---

[8] Perhaps Haughton's observations about the difference between wisdom and knowledge can help us better understand the difference between the philosopher envisioned by Plato as the lover of wisdom, on the one hand, and the sophists decried by Plato, on the other: "Wisdom has been defined as the ability 'to know the relative disposition of things,' and that 'disposition' is constituted by the dynamics of love as the very essence of reality. The wise person, the sage, is therefore one who has 'a profound grasp of the obvious,' yet it is only 'obvious' to one who is willing to live in exchange [a concept Haughton develops to explain the interaction between the divine ground of being and personal human growth]. The 'obvious' reality, the true 'relative disposition of things' is completely hidden from one who refuses to love. Knowledge there is, but it is a mechanistic, manipulative kind of knowledge" (1981, p. 115) The kind of knowledge that Haughton is here referring to exists on the plane of what Voegelin refers to as Second Realities, which has been the dominant plane of existence in what Ong refers to as print culture.

If nothing needed to be developed, there would be no need for persuasion. But since Plato sees development as necessary, the less desirable qualities must exist in everybody to one degree or another, until they have fully developed the more desirable qualities in themselves. Such persuasion involves serious play. To use Johan Huizinga's (1944/1955) terminology which is deeply indebted to Plato, serious play is ludic and agonistic. Plato's works themselves are written in the spirit of serious play. This is a key point to understand about Plato's works as a whole and about his attacks on the sophists in particular. From antiquity to the present, various commentators have missed the ludic and agonistic dimension of Plato's writings. If Plato's attacks on the sophists are not read as being written in a ludic and agonistic spirit, then they seem to be nothing but expressions of contempt. Seen as such, they are not attractive. For a person who claims to have achieved a higher level of human development than others to spend his time expressing his contempt for the less developed people is hardly edifying. But when Plato's attacks are seen as being written in a ludic and agonistic spirit, then it becomes obvious that they are designed to evoke a desire for further development in the readers. Since all of us are like the sophists until we develop qualities beyond theirs, all of us are in a position to respond to Plato's attacks on the sophists by forming a desire for development in ourselves as a result of reading his attacks as ludic and agonistic.

## 3. Contemporary Thought About Maturity

Perhaps a contemporary example will help clarify the distinction I am suggesting. Moore and Gillette have written a series of books about mature masculinity.[9] To get their point across, they refer in their initial book to Boy psychology and Man psychology, using capitalized terms (Moore & Gillette, 1990). They are not using these two terms just to take cheap shots

---

[9] Moore holds a doctorate in philosophy from the University of Chicago and is a practicing Jungian psychotherapist, a professor of religion and psychology at the Chicago Theological Seminary, and general editor of the Jung and Spirituality Series published by Paulist Press. He has taught numerous courses at the C. G. Jung Institute of Chicago, audio tapes of which are available from the Institute. With Douglas Gillette, he has co-authored a series of five books about the archetypes of masculine maturity: *King, Warrior, Magician Lover* (1990), *The King Within* (1992a), *The Warrior Within* (1992b), *The Magician Within* (1993a), and *The Lover Within* (1993b). Moore's treatment of the archetypal level of the psyche is deeply indebted to the work of Edward F. Edinger (1972), Anthony Stevens (1982), and John Weir Perry (1991). For other noteworthy views of male psychology, see Ong (1981), Eugene Monick (1987, 1991), James Wyly (1989), Robert Bly (1990), David D. Gilmore (1990), Patrick M. Arnold (1991), John Friel (1991), Sam Keen (1991), Aaron R. Kipnis (1991), Gregory Max Vogt and Stephen T. Sirridge (1991), Samuel Osherson (1992), Gary Smalley and John Trent (1992), Verne Becker (1992), Martin Green (1993), Frank S. Pittman (1993), and Michael Meade (1993).

at men.  Male-bashing is not their game.  Instead, they wish to challenge
men to aspire to further growth in Man psychology, not just denigrate them
by referring to Boy psychology.  (Since Moore and Gillette claim that there
are not only masculine but also feminine archetypes of maturity, they could
also refer to Woman psychology and Girl psychology if they wished to develop their insights further, but so far that is not a line of development they
have pursued.)  They are quite serious, and yet their approach can be characterized as ludic and agonistic.

As a matter of fact, their entire analysis accounts in large measure for
the growth or development I have been positing for Socrates, Plato, and
Aristotle, and so the connection between their work and Voegelin's exegesis
of Plato deserves to be explained.  As Voegelin also points out, Plato considered the virtues of justice, courage, prudence, and temperance to be ordering powers (1957b, pp. 108-111).  In other words, developing these four
qualities in oneself empowers one to establish order within oneself and
thereby attain full maturity, when one is ready for that stage of growth.  No
doubt the four cardinal virtues involve learning how to access properly the
energies of the archetypes of maturity in the human psyche discussed by
Moore and Gillette:  Justice involves the King or Queen archetype; courage,
the Male or Female Warrior; prudence, the Male or Female Magician; and
temperance, the Male or Female Lover.  Similarly, the processes Lonergan
describes as religious, moral, intellectual, and affective conversion involve
the archetypes of maturity:  Religious conversion involves the King or
Queen archetype; moral conversion, the Male or Female Warrior; intellectual conversion, the Male or Female Magician; and affective conversion, the Male or Female Lover.[10]

Divine sanctification amounts to receiving energies from the archetypal level of the human psyche.  In other words, God's immanence in peo-

---

[10]People can learn how to access the energies of the archetypes of maturity by
establishing a connection between their ego-consciousness and the archetypes.
Jungians advocate using active imagination to establish such connections.  In the
Christian tradition, meditating on biblical images has been a common form of using
active imagination, especially in the *Spiritual Exercises* of St. Ignatius Loyola
(1991) wherein the retreatants are regularly instructed to begin with the composition
of the place or setting of the biblical passage.  The four so-called "weeks" in the
*Spiritual Exercises* involve the four archetypes of maturity identified by Moore and
Gillette.  The Principle and Foundation in the First Week is aimed at the ordering
function of the King or Queen archetype in the psyches of the retreatants.  With
Christ the King calling knights to his service in the Second Week, the exercises on
the Two Standards, the Three Classes of Persons, and the Three Ways of Being
Humble all seem aimed at the Warrior archetype as described by Moore and
Gillette.  The emphasis on the passion in the Third Week can be seen as connected
with the death and rebirth aspect of the Magician archetype, as can the resurrection
readings reserved for the Fourth Week.  The Contemplation to Attain Divine Love
in the Fourth Week seems oriented to the Lover archetype, as is suggested by the
*Suscipe* prayer that is to be used by the retreatant during that exercise.

ple is experienced through the archetypal level of the human psyche. But saying that God's presence may be experienced through the archetypal level of the psyche does not reduce God to a psychological effect in people. God is transcendent.

In the Gospels a sharp distinction is made between people with faith and the faithless. The faithless correspond to the kind of people Plato refers to as philodoxers or sophists. In Lonergan's terminology, they are drifters. The idea of drifting can be elucidated by a remark made by C. G. Jung:

> Disalliance with the unconscious is synonymous with loss of instinct and rootlessness. If we can successfully develop that function that I have called transcendent [i.e., the transcendent function], the disharmony ceases, and we can then enjoy the favorable side of the unconscious. The unconscious then gives us all the encouragement and help that a bountiful nature can shower upon a man. (quoted in Stevens, 1982, p. 258)

The drifting Lonergan refers to arises from the disalliance with the unconscious. "When the connection is broken," Edward F. Edinger notes, "the result is emptiness, despair, meaninglessness, and in extreme cases psychosis or suicide" (1972, p. 43). In other words, without an alliance with the unconscious, people will continue to live in the wasteland T. S. Eliot wrote about and not enter the kingdom of God that Jesus of Nazareth referred to. Anthony Stevens explains that Jung saw two complementary processes as necessary for the so-called transcendent function to establish a harmonious alliance between the unconscious and personalized ego-consciousness:

> The transcendent function resides in the mutual influence of conscious and unconscious, ego and Self, and Jung believed that there were two basic methods by which this mutuality could be brought about: "the way of *creative formulation*" (e.g., active imagination, creative fantasy, dreams, symbols, art, and aesthetics) and "the way of *understanding*" (e.g., intellectual concepts, verbal formulations, conscious awareness, and abstraction). (1982, p. 272)

The two "ways" supplement each other. The first "way" involves opening up one's empirical level of consciousness (to use Lonergan's terminology) to input from the unconscious through recalling dreams or using active imagination.

What Jung referred to as active imagination has long been known in Christianity as meditation (cf. Moore & Gillette, 1992a, p. 210). For example, retreatants who follow the *Spiritual Exercises* of St. Ignatius Loyola (1991) are regularly called upon to use active imagination to conjure up an image of the action portrayed in biblical passages. Lonergan twice made a 30-day retreat following St. Ignatius Loyola's *Spiritual Exercises* as part of his Jesuit formation: once during his novitiate years (1922-1924) at Guelph, Canada, and then again during his 10-month tertianship (1937-1938) at Amiens, France. Like other Jesuits, he also made shorter retreats annually following the *Spiritual Exercises*. Through those experiences of the *Spiritual Exercises*, he surely learned how to establish the alliance with the unconscious that Jung sees as essential for halting what Lonergan refers to as drifting and what Jung refers to as rootlessness. Moreover, Lonergan believes that the empirical level of consciousness needs to be open and attentive not only to sensory data, but also to input from dreams and active imagination. So his account of the empirical level of consciousness clearly includes the first "way" Jung refers to, just as his account of the intelligent and rational levels of consciousness includes the second "way." In other words, the steps involved in Lonergan's generalized empirical method included the two "ways" involved in Jung's transcendent function.

As envisioned (or implied) in the Gospels, people with faith would correspond to the kind of people Plato refers to as philosophers. In the Gospels, faith is the condition necessary for rebirth and new life on this earth (see Nicoll, 1986). Both philosophers as envisioned by Plato and people with sufficient faith to be reborn as envisioned in the Gospels[11] are people who have learned how to access properly the archetypes of maturity described by Moore and Gillette. As Voegelin has reminded us, different terminology may be used to describe equivalent experiences. Terminology about characteristics attributed to the cardinal virtues focuses on relatively exterior behavior and attitudes, whereas Lonergan focuses on interior processes and uses suitable terminology to name them. Moore and Gillette focus on the psychological dimension and use imagistic language to name the sources of energy people can draw on as they experience the development of maturity in themselves.

In *The King Within* Moore and Gillette describe the four archetypes of mature masculinity:

---

[11] It is worth noting in this connection that Gary Smalley and John Trent (1993) have recently updated and expanded their best-selling book on the biblical theme of blessing, in which they stress the importance of blessing in human relationships. Although they apparently are not aware of it, the culminating exercise in St. Ignatius Loyola's *Spiritual Exercises* (1991) is devoted to helping people learn how to feel blessed by God. Many believers might readily assent to the intellectual proposition that we have been and continue to be blessed by God. But how many people actually feel that they personally have been blessed by God—as the priestly author of the first account of creation in the Book of Genesis apparently felt? It is hard to imagine how Christianity today could possibly play a transformative role in culture unless numerous Christians come to actually feel profoundly blessed by God. Feeling blessed by God is a key factor in affective conversion. But why don't more believers actually feel blessed by God? Why don't more people experience affective conversion? The aftereffects of childhood traumas due to inadequate parenting seem to limit the depths of people's feelings, according to Alice Miller (1979/1981, 1980/1983, 1981/1984, 1988/1990a, 1988/1990b, 1990/1991) and John Bradshaw (1988, 1990, 1992). Jungians would say that people have a lot of "shadow" work to do to recover the depths of their feelings, which they lost touch with due to inadequate parenting. Until people recover the depths of feeling, there is a limit to the degree to which they can carry out the blessing function described by Smalley and Trent—and a limit to the degree to which they may feel blessed by God.

The King program contains the ordering and nurturing potentials. The Warrior program holds potentials for boundary foundation and maintenance, effective organization, action, vocation, and fidelity. Within the Magician program lie potentials for cognitive functioning, understanding, death, and rebirth. Receptiveness, affiliation, healthy dependency, embodied sexuality, empathy, and intimacy are all potentials characteristic of the Lover program. (1992a, p. 264)

To become fully mature, people need to work out a proper conscious relationship with both the archetypes of mature masculinity and mature femininity within their psyches. According to Moore and Gillette, the King and the Queen archetypes are for ordering and for providing generativity and blessing (1990, p. 52). The Male and Female Warrior archetypes are the source of energy for a disciplined approach to facing life's challenges and achieving things (1990, p. 79). The Male and Female Magicians are the knowers and the masters of know-how (1990, p. 98). The Male and Female Lovers are for healthy pleasure and enjoyment without shame (1990, p. 121).[12]

Since Stevens has argued persuasively that "psychopathology results from the frustration of archetypal goals" (1993, p. 86), it is important to note here that archetypal goals are frustrated in childhood traumas involving the parents or parent-figures. Parents have an assigned role in helping to actuate the archetypal goals of the King and Queen archetypes discussed by Moore and Gillette (1992a). Childhood traumas usually involve inadequate parenting in one way or another, which thereby frustrates the actuation of the archetypal goals. But "mental health results from the fulfillment of archetypal goals" (Stevens, 1993, p. 86), and so people who have experienced childhood traumas involving their parents need to experience relationships in adulthood that enable them to experience the fulfillment of the archetypal goals that they did not experience in childhood. However, there are other archetypal goals that arise later in personal development, as Stevens reminds us (p. 87), and those too can be frustrated rather than actuated properly. When that occurs, those archetypal goals also need to be corrected by subsequent experiences that enable their proper actuation.

---

[12] The toxic shame described by Bradshaw is the major obstacle to learning how to access the archetypes of maturity properly. It is the result of childhood traumas, as they are described by Alice Miller, (1979/1981, 1980/1983, 1981/1984, 1988/1990a, 1988/1990b, 1990/1991; also see Gershen Kaufman, 1985, 1989). Miller is probably the world's leading authority on the aftereffects of childhood trauma. Her most notable books are *The Drama of the Gifted Child* (1979/1981), *For Your Own Good* (1980/1983), and *Thou Shalt Not Be Aware* (1981/1984). Bradshaw (1988, 1990, 1992) is the best known popularizer of her work in the United States. Probably no one has ever been exempt from experiencing childhood traumas. In other words, all of us probably experienced traumas in childhood in which we were truly victimized. The aftereffects of those traumas have shaped our lives—and especially our relationships with others. Indeed, they have bent our lives out of shape. That is why we all are in need of healing.

Healing often occurs as a result of appropriate communication occurring in meaningful circumstances. The Malones (1987) claim that communication involving the experience of the *self* in a relationship with another person, as distinct from an impersonal experience of the *self*, can engender change and growth. By change and growth, they clearly mean movement away from a dysfunctional orientation in relationships toward a more fully functional one. Their account of how such communication proceeds resembles Rosemary Haughton's (1981) description of exchange and breakthrough (also see van Beeck, 1991). In short, dysfunctional orientations in relationships are healed by the experience of more fully functional relationships.

Moore and Gillette's remarks about the potential of full human maturity may sound too visionary. Perhaps their comments about what can happen when men do not properly access the King archetype will temper the visionary flavor of the above quotations:

> Though the man who identifies with the King suffers a psychosis, depression and aimlessness plague the man who represses the inner King....Without the King, the Warrior within becomes a mercenary, fighting for pay and not for any worthwhile goal. Our Magician becomes a sophist without a King to serve, able to argue any idea convincingly, and believing in none. The Lover without a King becomes a promiscuous philanderer. Or at the very least he will be unempathic and uncaring in his expressions of love. (1992a, p. 110)

Their description of the depression and aimlessness that plague the man who represses the King archetype in his psyche corresponds to the drifter described by Lonergan (1967/1988, pp. 224, 229; 1985, p. 208). Conversely, the mature person envisioned by Moore and Gillette corresponds to the person described by Lonergan who has experienced religious, moral, intellectual, and affective conversion (see the glossary at the end of the volume for further discussion of Lonergan's treatment of conversion). As people learn how to access properly the energies of the King/Queen, Male/Female Warrior, Male/Female Magician, and Male/Female Lover archetypes in the human psyche, they may not only develop the cardinal virtues of justice, courage, prudence, and temperance, respectively, but also experience conversion in its religious, moral, intellectual, and affective aspects, respectively. The aspects of conversion described by Lonergan can be seen as fuller actuations of the cardinal virtues.

On a deeper level of the psyche, they may also experience what Doran (1990) refers to as psychic conversion. Indeed, his account of psychic conversion deepens our understanding of what medieval thinkers like St. Thomas Aquinas called the theological virtues of faith, hope, and charity, which Aquinas thought of as leading to the divinization of the human person (cf. Davies, 1992, pp. 274-296). Holiness presumably comes from the theological virtues, which transform a person on a deep level through the process Doran describes as psychic conversion. They divinize the person, thereby making the person deiform. While this idea may sound startling to some people, it is a traditional idea found not only in St. Thomas Aquinas (c.1224-1274), but also in Dionysius the Areopagite (fifth or sixth century C.E.). Brian Davies explains that "for Aquinas, wisdom in creatures derives from God, and therefore from what 'the wisdom of God' signifies" (1992, p. 71). Similarly, others perfections or excellences in creatures derive from God. Davies notes that "the idea that Aquinas is presenting here can also be viewed as expressing a notion found in Denys [Dionysius the Areopagite]" (pp. 71-72). As Eliot once put it, we are hollow. And, to paraphrase Beckett, we are waiting for God to fill us up, so to speak, with the kind of perfections that are attributed to God. Elsewhere Davies refers to the divinization of humans as "deification" and notes that the idea of deification of people was almost commonplace in the Christian tradition of thought at one time:

> The notion of deification is also very much present in patristic writers, in authors such as Irenaeus (c.130-c.200), Athanasius (c.296-373), Basil the Great (c.330-379), Gregory of Nazianzus (329-389), Gregory of Nyssa (c.330-c.395), and Cyril of Alexandria (d. 444). It is a notable feature of St. Augustine's [354-430] thinking as well. (1992, p. 251)

In light of this teaching, Dante's apotheosis of Beatrice in *The Divine Comedy* is perhaps best seen as exemplifying what is possible for all human beings to experience—to be filled with divine life, as St. Paul said he had been filled with Christ to the point where he felt that he lived no more but Christ lived in him (Gal. 2:20). Davies quotes Aquinas as saying, "it is necessary that God alone should make godlike, by communicating a share in his divine nature by participation and assimilation" (1992, p. 262). When people are made godlike, they are said in this tradition of thought to be deiform.

The concept of divinization or deification closely resembles Plato's *daimonios aner*, the spiritual man. Since Aquinas like many of his contemporaries saw the theological virtues of faith, hope, and charity as being of a different order from the cardinal virtues of justice, temperance, courage, and prudence (cf. Davies, 1992, pp. 274-296), a further word is needed here about them. Moore and Gillette have identified four "couples" so to speak at the archetypal level of the human psyche. The challenge each person faces is to learn how to access not only the energies of one set of archetypal figures, but also the energies of the other set as well—the contrasexual within one's psyche. Learning to access the energies of the contrasexual archetypes is a task of a different order from learning how to access the same-sex archetypes. The proper accessing of the contrasexual archetypes further actuates the full potentiality of the human psyche. The accounts of the theological virtues of faith, hope, and charity written by males probably express strengths that would accrue to males as they learned how to access properly the energies of the feminine archetypes in their psyches. As a matter of fact, most of the things that have been attributed in the past to "grace" probably have been the result of learning how to access the archetypes of maturity properly. Since some people might jump to the conclusion that I am somehow denying the role of God here, I hasten to add that God is the creator of everything, including the archetypal structures in the human psyche. The archetypal level of the psyche contains the eight archetypes of maturity identified by Moore and Gillette, and that is truly good news. The challenge humanity around the world today faces is learning how to actuate them properly in individuals. Such a person corresponds to the spiritual person Plato describes with the term *daimonios aner*.

## 4. Conclusions

As mentioned above, "The practice of philosophy in the Socratic-Platonic sense is the equivalent of the Christian sanctification of man; it is the growth of the image of God in man" (Voegelin, 1990a, p. 223). "[Plato] conceived his philosophizing as a therapeutic persuasion, as a salvational effort to heal the pneumatic and noetic disorder of the psyche," Voegelin notes (1987, p. 46). For "the analysis of existence preceding rational construction...is medical in character," he points out, "in that it has to diagnose the syndromes of untrue existence and by their noetic structure to initiate, if possible, a healing process" (1990a, p. 51). In terms Lonergan uses, that diagnosis marks the beginning of self-appropriation and the end of drifting. For Plato, that diagnosis arose through his analysis of rhetoric and the practices of the sophists.

How did Socrates, Plato, and Aristotle move to "the analysis of existence preceding rational construction"? Apparently they first analyzed the rational constructions of rhetoric and thereby attained a reflective, critical position concerning the undeniable power of rhetoric. The analyses of rhetoric in the *Menexenus*, the *Euthydemus*, the *Protagoras*, and the *Gorgias* are records of what we today would call the social construction of reality through rhetoric. Such an analysis can have a liberating effect on a person. But it is important to note that those early dialogues do not represent Plato's final explicit position on rhetoric. The *Phaedrus* represents Plato's later explicit position on rhetoric, as Black (1958) and others have noted (for further discussion of Plato's *Gorgias* and *Phaedrus*, see Benardete, 1991).

We might wonder what else contributed to Plato's growth. Dialogues may have engendered his growth. Indeed, certain kinds of communication can greatly enhance personal growth, and the Malones (1987), an Atlanta-based father-son team of psychiatrists who were mentioned above, provide an account of how this happens. They claim that the experience of the *self* in relation to another person engenders growth. They use the term *self* to refer to the psychological macrostructure that C. G. Jung referred to by that term. They refer to such experiences as personal intimacy, as distinct from impersonal intimacy that involves the experience of the *self* in relation to, say, nature or a work of art. By personal intimacy, they mean essentially what Martin Buber means by an I-Thou encounter between persons (1923/1970). The personal experience of the *self* as they describe it clearly involves what Victor Turner (1969) refers to as liminality and communitas. They claim that the impersonal experience of the *self* simply does not engender growth as the personal experience of intimacy does. "The *self* experienced in impersonal intimacy," they claim, "may produce great art, but it does not directly deepen personal relationships, except slowly" (p. 164). Elsewhere they claim that "without intimacy growth is impossible" (p. 269). Clearly they are implying that personal relationships are the means by which people experience growth, when they do grow.

If they are right, then the growth ostensibly experienced by Plato may have been the result not only of analyzing rhetoric, on the one hand, and of cultivating the virtues of courage, temperance, prudence, and justice, on the other, but also of personal experiences of the *self* in dialogues. The kind of growth that the Malones claim is engendered through experiences of the *self* in relation to the *self* of another person clearly involves the kind of conversations that Frans Jozef van Beeck (1991) writes about and the kind of exchange and breakthrough that Haughton (1981) writes about (also see Frederick G. Lawrence's treatment of Christian conversation in chapter 12).[13]

It is worth pausing to reflect a moment more on the import of what is being said here about the potential power of the right kinds of communication. Alice Miller has made it abundantly clear that childhood traumas usually result from either inadequate or inappropriate communication (1979/1981, 1980/1983, 1981/1984, 1988/1990a, 1988/1990b, 1990/1991). In short, they are the results of breakdowns in appropriate communication. The Malones are saying in no uncertain terms that appropriate communication is the means by which the aftereffects of childhood traumas can be corrected. Dialogue of a certain kind is the means by which the fullness of human potentiality can be restored.

The mutual self-mediation that Francisco Sierra-Gutiérrez writes about in chapter 13 is most likely to occur in what the Malones describe as personal experiences of the *self*, at least when such experiences do result in positive change and growth. Mutual self-mediation involves the give-and-take process that Haughton describes as exchange and breakthrough. Such exchange and breakthrough is most likely to occur in people who are committed to cultivating the authenticity that Lonergan writes about, while people who are in Lonergan's term drifting are less likely to experience such

---

[13] According to the Malones, people experience the *self* when they experience the *I* and the *me* simultaneously. The emphasis on "otherness" in postmodern thought could help people experience the *me*, if they are able to relate the experience of the "other" to something in their own experience. But it also needs to be noted that deconstructionist thought can easily degenerate into language games and the spurious kind of argumentation that Plato associates with *polypragmosyne*.

exchange and breakthrough. When such exchange and breakthrough does occur, it usually involves what Turner (1969) refers to as communitas and liminality, which can be seen as features of the personal experience of the *self* described by the Malones. To sum up, the personal experience of the *self* usually involves communitas and liminality, exchange and breakthrough, and mutual self-mediation and is usually transformative. Inasmuch as people are committed to authenticity, they are more likely to experience such transformative communication than drifters are. Moreover, such transformative communication further enhances the development of authenticity in people.

But the aim of such dialogue is not simply to engender a passing experience of luminosity. The larger aim is to evoke the development of maturity, which requires the cultivation of the virtues of courage, temperance, prudence, and justice. Plato uses the term *daimonios aner*, the spiritual man, to refer to the fullness of human development, as Voegelin describes:

> Man experiences himself as tending beyond his human imperfection toward the perfection of the divine ground that moves him. The spiritual man, the *daimonios aner*, as he is moved in his quest of the ground, moves somewhere between knowledge and ignorance (*metaxy sophias kai amathias*). "The whole realm of the spiritual (*daimonion*) is halfway indeed between (*metaxy*) god and man" (*Symposium* 202a). Thus, the in-between—the *metaxy*—is not an empty space between the poles of the tension but the "realm of the spiritual"; it is the reality of "man's converse with the gods" (202-203), the mutual participation (*methexis*, *metalepsis*) of human in divine, and divine in human, reality. (1978, p. 103)

To go back to the epigraph by Ong, it is unlikely that Plato would have considered any sophist of his day to be a *daimonios aner* or that Aristotle would have considered any sophist to be a *spoudaios*. The sophists apparently were restricted to the temporal order of existence, the profane world rather than the spiritual world. Since Plato and Aristotle wished to follow the example of Socrates in promoting the fullness of human development, they felt obliged to decry the lower levels of development that the sophists rested satisfied with. In effect, Socrates, Plato, and Aristotle were claiming to have achieved higher levels of human development in their lives than the sophists had and were challenging others, including contemporary sophists, to aspire to similarly high levels of development. In short, the sophists did not rise above what Lonergan refers to as drifting. They rested satisfied at being drifters. Lonergan challenges people today to seek the full flourishing of their human potential through what he refers to as self-appropriation, as Campbell points out:

> By urging individuals to notice, understand, and affirm themselves as the unity that endures throughout the operations of knowing and in response to whose intelligent will the operations of cognition are called forth and executed, Lonergan's self-appropriation provides a contemporary and

democratic expression of Aristotle's ideal of the *spoudaios* or mature person. (1985, p. 481)

Socrates, Plato, and Aristotle most likely had what Voegelin would call a compact experience of what Lonergan refers to as self-appropriation. If they had been able to "unpack" their experience and articulate and describe it as fully as Lonergan does, then they not only would have had what Voegelin calls a more differentiated experience, but also would have attained Lonergan's position of critical realism. Aristotle's ideal of the *spoudaios*, Plato's ideal of the *daimonios aner*, and Lonergan's ideal of self-appropriation are all equally democratic in principle in the sense of being open to all adults of goodwill who seek such development. However, in practice, many people do not accept the challenge of seeking such development.

Truth "is not a piece of information," Voegelin notes (1990a, p. 334). Thus the expression of propositional truth is not the issue involved for Plato in the love of wisdom. Listening to the extended oration of a Gorgias can at best lead to the communication of some kind of propositional truth, some kind of information. While Gorgias may have been enchanting or even bewitching to listen to, as Robert J. Connors (1986) notes, the issue for Plato is the truth of existence, the luminous experience of existence. By having Gorgias agree to the ground rules for dialogue established by Socrates, Plato suggests that the luminous experience of existence arises not from listening to long speeches but from the kind of attentive dialogue that Socrates was so adept at engendering.

The offense of the sophists is not necessarily in the apparent falsity of their doctrines about rhetoric as such, but in their apparent contempt for the divine ground of being, as expressed for example in the triads of propositions quoted above. Because such contempt in effect denies that divine wisdom is ultimately the warrant for intelligibility, it thereby vitiates the pure, disinterested, detached desire to know that Lonergan writes about. The proper desire to know assumes intelligibility based on the warrant of divine wisdom. Since Gorgias expressed obvious contempt for the divine, Plato attacked his spurious thinking because it revealed the lack of the proper motive or desire to know. To be sure, improper motives for desiring to know can occur. For example, the would-be knower can desire to prove himself or herself lovable, or the would-be knower can desire to establish superiority over others by his or her knowledge, instead of desiring simply to be the best he or she can be by virtue of the actuation of the capacity to know. Given the proper motive, however, the important thing is for the lover of wisdom to follow the divine drawing, for following it leads to the luminous experience of existence. Theoretically, most forms of human inquiry and most forms of rhetoric can be so motivated, even those forms involving instrumental reason because divine wisdom is the warrant for all orders of intelligibility.

Plato's attacks on the sophists undoubtedly led to a neglect of the sophists. That neglect has been corrected by the careful examination of their works in the studies by Mario Untersteiner (1954), W.K.C. Guthrie (1971), G. B. Kerferd (1981), Susan Jarratt (1991), Edward Schiappa (1991), Jacqueline de Romilly (1992), and Richard Leo Enos (1993). But at the same time Plato's work also needs to be carefully examined and properly understood, and Voegelin's exegesis has helped correct our misunderstandings of Plato in a way that enables us to read the studies of Plato by Edwin Black (1958), Rollin W. Quimby (1974), David S. Kaufer (1978), Jasper Neel (1988), James L. Kastely (1991), Michael F. Carter (1991), and C. Jan Swearingen (1991) in a fresh light.

The problem is that we have not understood what Plato meant by seeking the truth—the truth of existence—because we have confused such seeking with statements of truth—propositional truth. "Plato's energetic declaration that anybody who derives teachable doctrines from his philosophizing has not understood what he is doing is simply ignored because it has become unintelligible," declares Voegelin (1990a, p. 353). While Lonergan does not expressly advert to Plato's declaration about teachable doctrines, he squarely advocates attention to "method." As a result, his critical realism is process-oriented, to say the least.

Voegelin's exegesis of Plato's thought shows that two principles are primary. First, philosophizing as Plato sees it involves the love of divine wisdom. Conversely, the denial of the divine ground of being by definition excludes people like the sophists from being considered philosophers by Plato. Second, the experience of truth is experiential and cannot be reduced to a set of propositions. At best, the philosopher can provide others with guideposts toward philosophizing. Such guideposts are a form of rhetoric, a form of persuasion. All discourse that influences people is in the province of rhetoric as Plato defines it in the *Phaedrus*, Black observes (1958, p. 369). Even though it is undeniable that rhetoric can go awry, rhetoric is the architectonic intellectual discipline. But would-be rhetors cannot prudently ignore the philosophic issues involved in rhetoric, just as would-be philosophers cannot prudently ignore the rhetorical dimensions of philosophic argumentation.[14]

---

[14] I wish to thank Richard Leo Enos of Carnegie Mellon University, Eve Browning Cole of the University of Minnesota at Duluth, and Paul A. Soukup of Santa Clara University for reading earlier drafts of this essay and offering several helpful suggestions. Naturally I am responsible for whatever deficiencies remain.

# 7

# Philosophy After Philosophy

## Hugo A. Meynell

## 1. Introduction: Kant, Lonergan, and Communication

In a letter of 1772, Immanuel Kant asked: "On what foundation rests the relation of that in us that we call 'representation' to the object?" In other words, he was concerned with the question of how, by means of thoughts and sensations that are internal to us, we can get to know about things and events in an external world. For Kant, this question was no trivial one; in fact, he regarded it, I believe rightly, as "the key to the entire mystery of metaphysics, which so far remains hidden" (quoted in Sala, forthcoming). The "critical philosophy" that Kant worked out over the next nine years was of course a titanic attempt to tackle the problem; but few would say that it was entirely successful. For it is of the essence of Kant's conclusion to his analysis of human cognition that we cannot get to know about things in themselves, but only about appearances to which these somehow give rise and upon which we impose the categories of our understanding.

On the whole, it may be said that subsequent philosophers have either brushed the problem aside or signally failed to solve it. In the present century, positivism set out criteria that were supposed to vindicate science as yielding knowledge of how things really are, but to rule out metaphysics and religious belief as confusion due to misuse of language. But it is generally agreed nowadays that the criteria they proposed not only failed to vindicate science, but were found to break down under their own weight when subjected to investigation. The positivist failure has led many to infer that the foundations of knowledge that were so eagerly sought by philosophers from the 17th century up to very recent times are the object of a fool's errand. But is it really possible to sit down under the consequences of the belief that knowledge has no foundations? Is not the clear inference to be drawn from this that our "knowledge" that water tends to quench fire is no better "founded" than the proposition that gasoline does so; that our knowledge that it is in general good to help and comfort injured people has no firmer foundation than the claim that one might just as well taunt them or subject them to further injury?

It may easily be seen that skepticism as to the foundations of human knowledge has profound repercussions for one's conception of the nature and possibility of human communication. Such communication is fundamentally a matter of one or more persons conveying a meaning—whether by way of statement, question, command, or whatever—to some other person or persons. But if there is no foundation for knowledge of states of affairs in general, how can one have any foundation for knowledge of those special states of affairs that are meanings or the states of mind of those to whom the meanings are to be communicated?

According to the disciples of Bernard Lonergan, one of the special merits of that philosopher is that he has both squarely confronted Kant's problem and set out a satisfactory solution to it. Not that he is absolutely original in this; the essence of his solution is adumbrated by Aristotle and by St. Thomas Aquinas (see Lonergan, 1967). To cut a long story short, on Lonergan's account, the real world is nothing other than what tends to be known in reasonable judgments and is known in true judgments. An alleged "reality" that is completely out of the reach of such judgments, like Kant's "things in themselves," does not have what it takes to be *real* at all (Lonergan, 1957/1992, chapter 12; Meynell, 1991b, chapter 3). Reasonable judgment depends on two crucial preconditions; one has (1) to have attended to the relevant evidence in experience and (2) to have envisaged a sufficient range of possibilities—the mental grasp of such a possibility, which comes as the answer to a question raised with respect to experience, is what Lonergan calls an "insight" (Lonergan, 1957/1992, chapter 1; Meynell, 1991b, chapter 1). To come to know, one has to be thoroughly *attentive* (to experience), *intelligent* (in envisaging possibilities), and *reasonable* (in judging those possibilities to be so that are best supported by the relevant experience) (Lonergan, 1972, pp. 20, 53, 55, 231-232, 302). Empiricists tend to reduce reasonableness basically to attentiveness; to know what's there, one just has to attend to the facts of experience, rather than going in for a lot of theorizing. Idealists take account of the mental creativity that goes into knowledge, but fail to draw the full implications of the fact that we may verify some of our mental creations as existing in reality.

Empiricists are also faced with notorious problems about how we can know what cannot be directly presented to our experience, like the things and events of the past, the mental states of other people, and the entities postulated by nuclear physicists. I cannot see, hear, or smell the thoughts and feelings of the person sitting next to me, let alone the intentions of Horatio Nelson on the eve of the Battle of Aboukir Bay. Yet I may envisage a range of possibilities with respect to either of these matters, on the one hand, and reasonably judge that one of them is likely to be true on the basis of the evidence available to my senses, on the other. The natural sciences are implicitly controlled by the assumption that all phenomena are to be explained. Lonergan proposes that a similar assumption undergirds the human sciences; to the effect (to put it in very simple terms) that every expression of meaning is to be worked out as resulting from some sort of experience, understanding, and judgment. This assumption, when made explicit, is what Lonergan calls "the universal viewpoint" (see Lonergan, 1957/1992, pp. 18, 587-591, 760-761). The implications for one's conception of the nature of human communication are not far to seek. I may attentively, intelligently, and reasonably apply myself to finding out what is meant by a document or an utterance; to discovering the beliefs, assumptions, culture, and level of education of those to whom I am to communicate it; and so to establishing the most appropriate way of effecting the communication.

As an inevitable result of skepticism as to the foundations of knowledge, it is widely believed nowadays that we have reached or are about to reach an "end of philosophy"; that the whole tradition of thought about humanity and its world that derives from Plato and those before him has outlived its usefulness. I should like in the rest of this paper to reflect on this thesis from the point of view of the "generalized empirical method" devised and implemented in the work of Lonergan.[1] It will be convenient for this purpose to concentrate attention on a particular text that gives an account of the contemporary philosophical situation and notes the main lines of response to it—the "Introduction" to the collection *After Philosophy* (Baynes, Bohman, & McCarthy, 1987, pp. 1-18).

## 2. A Lonerganian Analysis of Problems in Philosophy

It seems obvious enough that with the rise of science large areas of inquiry that had previously belonged to philosophy ceased to do so. Philosophy may be said to have rescued itself temporarily by a "turn to the subject"; if the *objects* of human inquiry into the world were delivered over to the natural sciences, at least philosophy might usefully continue investigation into the human *subject* of inquiry. This was all very well until the development of the human sciences of psychology, sociology, and so on. These seek to understand the speech and the practices of human beings living within their particular material, economic, historical, and social environments. What at

---

[1] "Generalized empirical method" is Lonergan's term for the method employed by his own philosophy, which is "empirical" in that it takes its stand on experience, but "generalized" by virtue of including within experience our awareness of our own mental acts (of inquiring, coming to understand, marshalling evidence, judging, and so on), something that has generally been neglected by empiricists (Lonergan, 1957/1992, pp. 95-96, 267-268). It should be noted that this stricture does not apply to John Locke, whose "ideas of reflection" are derived from attention to one's own mental acts (Locke, 1924, Vol. 2, pp. 1, 2, 4).

this rate can be left to philosophy? Is not philosophical inquiry as such based on the false assumption that one can raise significant questions about an absolute "truth," "reason," or "goodness" that are not contingent on particular historical and social circumstances? Both "reason" and the autonomous "subject" supposed to be able to exercise it in deference to absolute "truth" and "goodness" have been subjected to very damaging criticism. Reason has proved inextricable from rhetoric; to persuade people "rationally" is apparently nothing more than to convince them by a form of rhetoric that happens to enjoy a high prestige in our society. The "autonomous subject" has turned out to be nothing more than a node of interacting social and historical forces.

In the present century, philosophical attention to the conscious subject has tended to be replaced by preoccupation with language. However, the study of language has turned out to be no more secure a refuge for philosophy than that of the human subject. The "necessary truths" and other apparent "foundations of knowledge" into which the philosopher was supposed to inquire are now shown to have no firmer basis than the linguistic conventions that happen to have prevailed over a more or less broad or narrow segment of humanity.

So much for a view of philosophy that enjoys wide currency at the present time. It appears to me, on the contrary, that so far from philosophy having reached the end of its usefulness, it is now at least as relevant to the human situation as it ever was. To show why this is so, I shall first consider the nature of what has been called "cognitive" and "moral self-transcendence" and establish the absurd consequences of denying their existence or their possibility; and then apply the results of these reflections to the debate about the end of philosophy and to speculations about where the subject of philosophy, if it is to survive at all, should go from here.

What do I mean by "cognitive self-transcendence"? I mean by it the capacity of conscious subjects to know things and states of affairs that exist apart from and beyond themselves and their societies. If I know that the majority of the earth is covered by water, I am evidently (except on a very strange assumption, which we shall attend to in a moment) exercising cognitive self-transcendence in doing so since, though I am certainly dependent upon my society in knowing it (as I never collected all the relevant evidence for myself), the majority of the earth's surface might still have been covered by water even if no human beings or other rational creatures had ever evolved to know about it. Again, if I know that Rupert of the Rhine was present at the Battle of Naseby, I am certainly dependent on the authority of 20th century historians of the 17th century in doing so; yet short of very paradoxical assumptions indeed, what happened in the 17th century cannot be affected one way or the other by how anyone in the 20th century, however academically distinguished, may happen to think about it.

To deny cognitive self-transcendence is to be driven to the remarkable conclusion either that there are no states of affairs that obtain prior to and independently of human beings and their societies, or that we can never get to know that such states of affairs obtain.[2] Yet it seems rather odd to deny what would at first sight seem to be the obvious fact that so far from the universe as a whole depending for its existence on human beings and their societies, human societies exist in a tiny spatio-temporal corner of the universe and are dependent on highly specific conditions within it. And except on a misleadingly restricted conception of "knowledge," we can know a good deal about this universe—that the matter within it is made up largely of hydrogen, a gas consisting in its turn of atoms each containing one proton and one electron; that this matter, rather than being fairly evenly spread about in a sort of thin soup, is mainly clumped together in stars arranged in galaxies each consisting of millions of stars; and so on and on.[3] Moreover, the claim that cognitive self-transcendence is impossible not only makes nonsense of such commonplaces as these; it is actually self-destructive. One may consider the statement, "Cognitive self-transcendence is impossible." Is this supposed to state a truth that is the case independently of the attitudes and convictions of the person who utters it? If it is, that very utterance exemplifies cognitive self-transcendence. If it is not, it follows that there is another subjective viewpoint no less intrinsically worthy of respect, from which the contradictory claim is true—that cognitive self-transcendence is possible.

So it seems that cognitive self-transcendence is possible on pain of what may be called performative self-contradiction in addition to numerous other absurdities. In what circumstances and under what conditions is it so? In accordance with Lonergan's generalized empirical method, it is possible under conditions that were approximately described, though not quite caught, by empiricism and falsificationism.[4] There are three essential components of coming to know: (1) attention to experience; (2) intelligent envisagement of possibilities; (3) reasonable judgment that some among these

---

[2] Kant's notorious doctrine—that we only get to know appearances, but never things as they are in themselves—approximates to this.

[3] It is true, of course, and indeed of great importance, that the possibility of *knowledge of such things* is dependent on the obtaining of highly specific conditions within society. But the point at issue is that, if this really is knowledge (and it is conceivable, if very unlikely, that later research might indicate that it is not), then the states of affairs known are *not* dependent on society. That earlier generations would have been confident in offering quite different and indeed contradictory accounts of the relevant data, is not to the point; they did not have the information and had not envisaged the theoretical possibilities that are available to us. The social basis of knowledge does not entail the impossibility of cognitive self-transcendence.

[4] "Falsificationism," which is specially associated with the work of Sir Karl Popper (1959, 1972), stresses the tentative and refutable nature of all our knowledge-claims.

possibilities are probably or certainly so. There is no space here to justify at length the claim that these are the basic components of cognitive self-transcendence; but something brief must be said (for a fuller discussion, cf. Lonergan, 1957/1992; Meynell, 1991b). Denial that knowledge has these components is to be met by the same pattern of argument as has already done duty in vindicating cognitive self-transcendence as such; in justifying such denial, one has to make use of the very mental operations whose use in the justification of denials one is denying. Empiricists are *ex officio* insistent on the role of the first component (experience) in coming to know; but they are apt to neglect the other two. In a wide sense of "experience," to be sure, one does have experience of envisaging possibilities and of making judgments—and indeed of such ancillary operations as temporarily suspending judgment, weighing evidence, and so on; hence the appropriateness of the phrase "generalized empirical method" for the approach to philosophy that attends to these operations.

The term "falsificationism" is perhaps closer to the mark than empiricism; for the falsificationist, a judgment has verisimilitude and is the best available approximation to the truth in so far as, while it *might* very easily have been falsified by the relevant evidence, *in fact* it is not so. In accordance with generalized empirical method, too, a judgment that merits rational acceptance is corroborated by the fact that all available alternatives that have been envisaged are falsified; and it is insisted that, at least commonly, judgments are no more than probable, since more relevant evidence may turn up or more possible explanations be envisaged. The trouble with falsificationism is the status of the principle of falsification itself. Suppose it is applicable to itself. But then how could one conceivably falsify in experience the judgment that judgments are to be provisionally accepted in so far as while they might conceivably have been falsified in experience in fact they are not so? But if the principle of falsifiability cannot be thus justified, it would appear to be arbitrary. That empiricism is similarly self-destructive is of course so well-known that the arguments to that effect need not be repeated here. Generalized empirical method, on the contrary, can be non-self-destructively applied to itself, since the most reasonable judgment in face of the available evidence is that one tends to get to the truth on any matter in so far as one judges reasonably in relation to the available evidence. If it is true, moreover, empiricism is revealed as a plausible compound of truth and falsity, and falsificationism as providing a very effective rule of thumb in testing empirical hypotheses.

But it might be objected that it is one thing to exercise one's mind in such a way as to come by well-founded judgments and so to approximate to true judgments, but it is another to obtain knowledge of a real world supposed to exist prior to and independently of anyone's mind or its exercise. However, after all, it can be shown that these are not two things, but one. We have in the last analysis no coherent idea of "reality" or "the actual world," except as what our well-founded judgments (those arrived at by the process described) *tend to be* about, and our true judgments *are* about (see Lonergan, 1957/1992, chapter 12). Nor is this world merely *for* us, *for* our society—since the only ultimately satisfactory distinction between the world *for* x—the sum of x's beliefs about the world—on the one hand, and the real world, on the other, is what can be articulated by the distinction between the three capacities necessary for cognitive self-transcendence applied just so far and the same capacities carried through indefinitely. And when we loosely contrast "our world" or "the world for us" with the world of other social groups, do we not really presuppose that the belief-systems of other societies are themselves parts of the real world that we may discover by use of the same capacities? After all, we make discoveries about other people's systems of belief just as we make discoveries about barium, white dwarfs, and hyraxes—by attending to evidence, by creating hypotheses, and by judging those hypotheses to be so that are most in accordance with the evidence (see Lonergan, 1957/1992, chapter 17, part 3).

The insistence so dear to contemporary sensibilities that rationality, truth, and so on are totally relative to social and historical background should collapse before the considerations to which I have alluded. I have shown that denial that cognitive self-transcendence is possible not only leads to innumerable other absurdities, but is actually self-destructive. And the existence of cognitive self-transcendence implies the existence of a rationality by means of which human beings from within their various historical and social situations can attain to truth about what is the case largely prior to and independently of these social situations. It is not to be denied that the influence of environment on our cognitive capacities is very great, for example, in suggesting or limiting either the data that we are disposed to attend to or the hypotheses that we may entertain in the course of trying to explain them. But the implications of our confinement to a particular segment of space and time—along with its conceptions of rationality, truth, and the rest—must not be so exaggerated that they render cognitive self-transcendence impossible.

The language of a culture provides each of its members with an enormous repository of taken-for-granted judgments based on a certain framework of understanding of experience. But it also, however indirectly or inefficiently, provides her or him with a means of transcending itself. Even in the primitive jungle, one has to use one's innate powers of intelligent and reasonable inference—say from a faint purring sound, a creak of twigs at the edge of audibility, and a glimpse of brown and black stripes, to the proximity of a man-eating tiger—if one is to survive at all. And with the development of civilization and the arts of leisure, human beings come to be able to use these basic capacities not only for such immediate practical purposes, but also with respect to the more recondite concerns of science, philosophy, and religion. A person within a primitive culture may move more or less competently from experience through hypothesis to judgment with regard to the proximity of the tiger, the immediate likelihood of rainfall, or the suitability of a collection of brilliant red berries for consumption. So may a person in a more advanced society to judgments about the existence of black holes, the occurrence of the Big Bang, or the reality of God or Nirvana. (For further elaboration of this point about the universality of cognitive operations, see chapter 5 by Frederick E. Crowe.)

It may be objected that I have not adequately taken into account the sociology of knowledge; that is to say, the study of the social forces that influence what beliefs are maintained as true and important within any society or social group. Professor Richard Braithwaite used to say in conversation that he thought people should speak rather of the sociology of belief than of knowledge, and there is much to be said for his view of the matter. For it is one thing for a belief to be *maintained as* true by a group, however great its power and prestige in the society of which it forms a part; and another thing for the belief to *be* true. Thus, a very influential group of persons might maintain that brontosaurus was a real creature or that there is a luminiferous ether or that Henry VIII of England had eight wives without these states of affairs actually being the case; and unless they were, the corresponding beliefs would not count as true and so deserve the status of knowledge.

As I have said, in accordance with Lonergan's generalized empirical method, beliefs *tend* to be true in so far as they are attentively, intelligently, and reasonably arrived at; and it appears to be one of the most important tasks of the sociologist to determine which social factors are apt to enhance these dispositions in human beings and which to impugn them. For example, this question could well be asked about religion in general or about some particular religion. (Whatever the usual tendency of religion in the past, *could* there not be a form of religion of which the effect was on the whole to promote the human mental habits that lead to the advance of knowledge rather than to hinder them? Cf. Lonergan, 1972, p. 117.) In so far as the sociology of belief includes this normative element, it is perhaps not misleading to call it the sociology of knowledge. But at all events, it follows from what I have already argued that relativism is not to be inferred from the sociology of belief or knowledge. The beliefs common to each social group are arrived at by a mixture of attention and inattention, intelligence and stupidity, reasonableness and silliness; they will tend to converge towards knowledge of the world as it really is only in so far as they are stringently tested and criticized.

The considerations that lead to the view that cognitive self-transcendence is possible also vindicate the possibility of moral self-transcendence, which is the making of true judgments that are not merely a matter of personal preference or social *fiat* about what is good or bad, better or worse (see Lonergan, 1972, pp. 31-32, 37, 51). Of course, everyone assumes in practice, even when they are officially committed to denying it, that a human situation in which happiness is realized without unfairness is better than one where all concerned are very unhappy or where there is great unfairness.[5] *Horribile dictu*, we are driven by the considerations that I have brought forward to believe not only in Truth with a capital T, but in Goodness with a capital G.[6] But perhaps the notion that mass murder or the torture of children is wrong in itself (rather than wrong just from some people's point of view, whereas it may be right from another) is too much for committed anti-Platonists to stomach.

## 3. A Lonerganian Approach to Doing Philosophy

It is time to apply these considerations, which of course could only be adequately spelled out and justified at much greater length, to developments in contemporary philosophy. According to our authors, the central question round which the material in their collection is organized is "whether philosophy should be brought to an end or transformed and continued" (Baynes, Bohman, & McCarthy, 1987, p. 2). One might put it that philosophy is being given notice either to quit or to find the right foundations and methods for fruitful continuation. It appears to me that the "transformationist" party (as one might call them) have not found the right foundations and methods, or at least have not set them out in such a way as to satisfy most of their colleagues; this renders them liable to attack by the "abolitionists" who proclaim the end of philosophy. In my view, philosophy should be continued without too much transformation from what it has always been in the tradition of philosophy at its best; but certain basic questions certainly have to be faced and resolved. And I believe that the best means of asking and answering these questions is justifying and implementing those philosophical principles, due to Lonergan, that I have already sketched. It seems to me that the abolitionists repudiate cognitive self-transcendence with considerable consistency, but do not quite draw the full consequences of doing so—failure to make any statement whatever or to utter any sentence in the indicative mood. The transformationists mitigate this rigor by inconsistent appeals to principles that, when pressed, lead to a degree of "Platonism" that is not often countenanced by philosophers in the late 20th century (Baynes, Bohman, & McCarthy, 1987, p. 7).

The abolitionists justify their stance, our authors say, by a criticism "of strong conceptions of *reason* and of the autonomous rational subject" (Baynes, Bohman, & McCarthy, 1987, p. 3). But one may ask the following

---

[5] In Meynell, 1981, chapter 6, I have tried to cope with the once fashionable objection that to say so much is to commit the "naturalistic fallacy."

[6] To deny that they believe in Truth with a capital T seems to be a staple of the table-talk of many contemporary philosophers.

question: Unless this criticism is itself based on a reason strong enough to achieve self-transcendence, at once engaged in, by, and addressed to potentially autonomous rational subjects, how can it be taken seriously as tending to issue in true belief about anything, including reason and the autonomous rational subject themselves? Richard Rorty or Jacques Derrida may oppose the Kantian view of reason, as characterized by necessity, with "the contingency and conventionality of the rules, criteria, and products of what counts as rational speech and action at any given time and place" (Baynes, Bohman, & McCarthy, 1987, p. 3). But even to talk in an informed manner about Kant's view or what counted as rational at any given time and place is itself to presuppose that one has enough cognitive self-transcendence to state what Kant's view really was and what actually counted as rational at that time and place, which in turn imply a rationality not so bound to contingencies and conventionalities as to make these feats impossible. And such a rationality does seem to have a kind of necessity about it, which consists in the fact that the contradictories of the statements in which it can be expressed are self-destructive in the manner that I have already shown.

Our authors cite a galaxy of 19th- and 20th-century authorities to the effect that "it is no longer possible to deny the influence of the unconscious on the conscious" or "the presence of the irrational—the economy of desire, the will to power—at the very core of the rational" (Baynes, Bohman, & McCarthy, 1987, p. 4). But what is the point of taking any account of these authorities, except on the assumption that they themselves at least have achieved sufficient rational autonomy to tell us what is likely to be true about the matters with which they deal? Darwin established our kinship with other animals; Marx, our liability to succumb to the ideologies of our economic and social classes; Nietzsche, the pervasiveness of the will to power in human thought and action. Yet the vital significance of all these factors for human life may be fully acknowledged without the hypothesis of the possibility of rational autonomy in human beings being given up. Indeed, to take these authors seriously is itself to presuppose that it is *not* given up. For reasons that I have already explained, the influence of such factors must leave open the possibility of our cultivating the dispositions that lead to self-transcendence. It would be curious indeed to employ one's autonomous reason, to judge that a group of distinguished authorities had employed *their* autonomous reason, to the effect of showing that the employment of autonomous reason by human beings is altogether impossible.

"The intrication of language in forms of life and life-worlds, practices and conventions, taken-for-granted backgrounds and cultural traditions" (Baynes, Bohman, & McCarthy, 1987, pp. 1-2) cannot, if my argument so far has been sound, impugn the possibility of cognitive self-transcendence. For all the supposed "farewell-to and overcoming of philosophy" attributable to the likes of Ludwig Wittgenstein and Martin Heidegger (Baynes, Bohman, & McCarthy, 1987, p. 2) at least one philosophical task would seem then to remain—that of showing how cognitive self-transcendence is possible and bringing out the consequences of its being so. [The crucial question is of how we may within our life-worlds by engaging in certain practices and following certain conventions come to know about states of affairs that exist prior to and independently of our human societies with their practices and conventions.] Certainly it will not do to shirk the full implications of the embeddedness of each of us in our particular historical and social setting, along with its conceptions of rationality, truth, and the rest; but these must not be so exaggerated that they seem to render cognitive self-transcendence impossible.

It is quite correct to deny that the mind can be a "mirror of nature," in the sense of reflecting the essence of things by sheer passive openness. Active hypothesizing and judging as well as deliberately seeking out experiences to which to attend are necessary conditions of knowledge of reality. But to deny that the mind can come to reflect nature in another sense—of reaching true judgments about what exists prior to and independently of itself as a result of using appropriate methods—is to be led into absurdity, as I have already argued at length. Certainly, as Charles Taylor says, it is a condition of our forming disinterested representations of the world that we are first actively engaged with it (Baynes, Bohman, & McCarthy, 1987, p. 5). But this is not to deny that *given* our prior engagement with the world, we *can* in appropriate circumstances form "representations" of it that are "disinterested" in the sense that they are deliberately framed in such a way as to represent the world correctly and at least to some extent can succeed in doing so.

Our authors are of the opinion that for all the repeated denunciations of believers in "a priori knowledge," "ultimate foundations," or a "Platonic theory of truth," few of them survive today (Baynes, Bohman, & McCarthy, 1987, p. 7). I fear that Lonergan's philosophical approach in a sense commits its practitioner to all of these unfashionable things. Its principles are not a priori in the sense that one can spell them out prior to all other mental activity in finding out about the world; but they are so in that they turn out, when one investigates the matter, to be presupposed in all such mental activity. And the same principles are after all in a sense "ultimate foundations," in that, as I explained earlier, they not only justify all other justified statements about things, but also justify themselves. The principles do not have "self-evident givenness" (Baynes, Bohman, & McCarthy, 1987, p. 7), to be sure, if this implies that merely to think of them is to know that they must be true; one has to attend to the self-destructive nature of their contradictories in order to be convinced for good reason that they are so. And practice of the generalized empirical method confirms the common sense assumption that the truth—say, of the statement "the earth is larger than the moon"—does not depend at all on the beliefs and conventions of any society, but only on whether the earth is larger than the moon. In so far as this entails "a Platonic theory of truth," such a theory of truth is indeed a consequence of Lonergan's views. If the straight alternative to such an account of truth is either the latent self-refutations of the transformationists or the relatively obvious self-refutations of the abolitionists, then so be it.

Many would follow the lead of Friedrich Nietzsche in purporting to "undercut philosophy's traditional self-delimitation from rhetoric and poetics," trying "actively to dispel the illusion of pure reason by applying modes of literary analysis to philosophical texts" (Baynes, Bohman, & McCarthy, 1987, p. 5). But one may ask whether it is a reasonable judgment, supported by the relevant evidence more than is its contradictory, that what passes for reason is nothing but one more form of rhetoric, no more liable to lead to the truth about things than any other. If it is not a reasonable judgment, then we have no warrant for accepting it. But if it *is* a reasonable judgment and we accept it because it is so, we are then implicitly accepting the privilege of reason in the business of attaining truth in the very act of denying it.

Our authors distinguish a third group among contemporary philosophers, whom they call "systematic"; these philosophers are said to see themselves as continuing by other means some aspects of the Kantian project. Thus for Michael Dummett, the fundamental business of philosophy, from which all its other tasks are derivative, is to provide an account of what people know when they know a language. According to Hilary Putnam, what philosophy amounts to in the last analysis is a theory of rationality, which he insists is a notion that is fundamentally normative (Baynes, Bohman, & McCarthy, p. 10).[7] As Karl-Otto Apel and Jürgen Habermas see it, philosophy must articulate the conditions of that intersubjectively valid argument and critique that are essential to rational practice. Whatever the differences between these conceptions, they show a marked similarity when compared with those notions of philosophy usually labelled "hermeneutic" or those derived from the work of Nietzsche. Common to them is the conviction that it is possible to set out the nature of those human abilities of which what we think of as reason consists. However, the philosophers concerned differ from most of their predecessors in conceiving this task as not a priori, but empirical and therefore liable to criticism and revision on the basis of evidence supplied by the exercise of these very abilities. Yet they acknowledge that "because what is to be reconstructed is essentially normative in nature, the type of 'empirical' theory called for is fundamentally distinct in kind from natural-scientific theories and incorporates modes of thinking traditionally regarded as 'philosophical'" (Baynes, Bohman, & McCarthy, 1987, p. 11).

---

[7] I prescind from the question of how far our authors accurately summarize the views of these philosophers.

Lonergan's generalized empirical method certainly amounts to a "systematic" philosophy in the sense suggested; but it meets head on the rather intractable question of how an account of thought or language can be thoroughly empirical without its normative status being fatally compromised. It brings out what may be said to be *presupposed* from the start by our knowledge-claims, but can only be *spelled out* by a sufficiently articulate and coherent philosophy. In the light of that method, the type of inquiry concerned is "empirical," in that in a broad sense we have experience of our own mental processes and not merely of the particular data of sense or feeling of which we have experience in the narrow sense; and that we can attend to our experience of that former kind. That is, I can pay attention to my awareness of wondering, framing hypotheses, marshalling evidence, judging more or less tentatively, hesitating on the brink of a decision, resolutely deciding, and so on. I may also come to judge for good reason that the reality that exists largely prior to and independently of these thought-processes of mine, of which indeed my thought-processes form an extremely minor and insignificant part, are nothing other than what I come increasingly to judge to be so, to exist, or to occur, in so far as I am as attentive as possible to my experience, as intelligent as possible in my hypothesizing, and as reasonable as possible in preferring in every case the hypothesis that best fits the evidence to which I have attended.

It seems that Lonergan's thought is at once truly empirical, since it is both implemented and justified by appeal to experience in a broad sense; and normative, since it issues in general instructions about how we are to behave if we are to progress towards knowledge of the truth about things— in other words, how we are to be rational. It is a priori in the sense that it brings out what is presupposed in all claims whatever to know or to be rational, but not so in the sense of in no way making an appeal to experience. "Systematic" philosophers are furthermore right at this rate to point out that the kind of inquiry involved, however empirical it may be, is not so in exactly the sense exemplified by the natural sciences. That we tend to get to know the truth about things by the method described above is *presupposed* by natural and social science; one needs another kind of inquiry to set out what it is about the overall nature and structure of reality and about the relation of human thought and language to it, which is *entailed* by these presuppositions.

The appeal of generalized empirical method to mental acts and processes, as opposed to language, would generally be taken by contemporary philosophers to be a retrograde step. Is not language, it may be asked, a public, verifiable and objective matter, as opposed to mental acts and processes, which are the very epitome of what is subjective and so unverifiable? The defender of the generalized empirical method may claim that the assumption that matters are advanced by appeal to "external" language as opposed to "internal" thought is a delusion. It has no stronger warrant than the besetting prejudice, pilloried at length by Lonergan (1957/1992, pp. 177-178, 183-184, 260, 276-278, 408-409, 413, 414), to the effect that the real is the object of naïve extroversion. This prejudice, when consistently applied, renders unreal the things and events of the past, the thoughts and feelings of people, and the particles of modern physics. The truth of the matter, which can be demonstrated by application of the generalized empirical method, is that the real is what tends to be apprehended by reasonable judgment sustained by the greatest possible attentiveness and intelligence—which is perfectly compatible with the reality of things and events in all these categories. I cannot perceive your aches and pains, or a neutrino, or the murder of Edward II of England; but I can reasonably judge on the basis of my understanding of relevant evidence available to my senses that you have aches and pains, that neutrinos are present, and that Edward II was murdered. On the particular issue of thought and language, it must be pointed out that "language" may be understood in two senses: (1) as an observable system of audible or visible signs without regard to the thought that these express or (2) as such a system of signs as expressive of such thought. A consideration of language in the first sense can in no way advance the fundamental philosophical problem of how human thoughts and words can refer to or be about a world that exists and is as it is largely prior to and independently of them. In the second sense, language secures reference by virtue of the fact that the thought that it involves does so—the world or reality being nothing other than what true judgment is about and well-founded judgment tends to be about (and judgment is nothing but a species of thought, which is able to be expressed through language).

Is Lonergan's method revisable? The proper way to approach this matter is to ask the prior question of what it is for revision to *count* as such, as opposed to as merely arbitrary alteration. Presumably a revision is a hypothesis or set of hypotheses that is to be judged as better than the one that it succeeds, on the ground that it accounts more adequately for the full range of relevant phenomena. But such a conception of revision *presupposes* the mental dispositions and the relation of these to reality, which are set out by the generalized empirical method; and therefore cannot intelligibly be used to *revise* that method. It is not to be denied, of course, that it may always be possible to formulate the elements of the method in a way more refined and adequate than has previously been possible (see Lonergan, 1957/1992, pp. 20, 301-303, 359-360, 574-575, 757-758).

## 4. Conclusions about Philosophy and Communication

It is time to summarize the upshot of our discussion. What is to become of philosophy as a result of its present crisis of identity? Is it to be demolished altogether, or is it to be permitted to survive in a severely mutilated, etiolated, or trivialized form? The correct answer is neither, if my contentions in this paper have been at all on the right lines. Once its right foundation and method have been found, philosophy may be seen to retain a substantial part of its traditional role—in fact, all of it that has not been taken over by the particular natural and social sciences—and to be just as vital for the promotion of civilization as it has ever been. The following questions remain of the greatest importance, and it is merely confused to maintain that they are treatable by the methods of any of the special sciences. What are the basis and justification of these natural and social sciences themselves? By what right do they purport to inform us of what is the case about the natural world and about human individuals or societies? What is the difference, if any, between good and bad, on the one hand, and good and bad falsely so called, on the other? What kind of social and political order is worth striving for, what kind is to be avoided, and why? Is there better reason than not to think that there is a God, or that Nirvana is attainable? Such questions are as meaningful and urgent as they have ever been; and are of the essence of philosophy.

It remains to infer the consequences of what we have argued for a theory of communication. To communicate meaning effectively, I have to have a grasp both of the meaning in question and of the beliefs and assumptions of the persons to whom I have to communicate it. Now nothing is more characteristic of "post-analytic philosophy" than its rejection of the thesis that we have foundations that are in principle reliable for our knowledge of what is the case prior to and independently of ourselves; and among the facts that are thus the case are the meanings expressed in what others say and write, and implicit in their beliefs and assumptions. It follows that this sort of philosophy can afford no reliable basis either for ascertaining or for communicating meaning.

Such a basis is in fact supplied by Lonergan's generalized empirical method (cf. Lonergan, 1957/1992, chapter 17, section 3; Meynell, 1991b, chapter 4). In establishing what is meant by an oral or written communication, I have to attend to the evidence supplied by the relevant noises and gestures or marks on paper; to envisage various possibilities as to what the speakers or writers *might* mean or have meant; and to judge, more or less tentatively (there are liable to be relevant scraps of data to which I have not attended and possibilities that I have not envisaged), that they do or did mean this or that on the basis of the evidence. If they are members of a culture other than my own, I am bound to fall into error in so far as I have not previously by use of the same kinds of mental operations on a different set of data acquired some knowledge of the characteristic judgments and assumptions of persons of that culture. Just the same will apply to the persons with whom I wish to communicate; I must apply my own attentiveness, intelligence, and reasonableness to discovering the beliefs and assumptions at which they have arrived by more or less effectively applying theirs. Having thus determined what is probably or certainly the case about the mean-

ing that is to be communicated and the state of mind, culture, and intellectual development of those to whom it is to be communicated, I set my mind
to the practical task of communicating the meaning to the audience. Once
again, my only resort in working out how best to do this is to the threefold
mental process that I have already described at length.[8]

---

[8] I am grateful to the editors of the present collection for their criticisms of an
earlier draft of this paper.

# 8

---

# From Logic to Rhetoric in Science:
# A Formal-Pragmatic Reading
# of Lonergan's *Insight*

## *William Rehg, SJ*

Despite the pedigree attaching to its name, science today typically stakes its claim to respect not on privileged epistemological resources and even less on metaphysical pretensions, but on its sober, logically and empirically rigorous *method*. It is therefore reasonable for a philosophy of science to start by asking, What makes scientific inquiry a rational enterprise? Contemporary debates informed by historical and sociological studies of actual scientific practice, however, have made straightforward answers to this question ever more difficult to come by. At the very least, an acceptable answer must do justice to the fact that sociohistorical contexts of actual inquiry affect science in profound ways. In the present essay I want to examine the "method" based in Bernard Lonergan's cognitional theory for what it can contribute to our understanding of this issue. I begin, in Part 1, by sketching the development of the rationality problematic that currently confronts theories of scientific inquiry. I then, in Part 2, briefly outline Lonergan's cognitional theory. To update it for the more recent debates, one must develop its intersubjective side; this I do with the help of clues supplied by Jürgen Habermas's more explicitly social theory of rationality. Taking an intersubjective approach, however, calls for a more than a merely nodding recognition of the role of rhetoric in science. I thus close, in Part 3, by suggesting some reasons why rhetoric should be taken as essential to a Lonerganian account of rational inquiry.

## 1. Beyond the Logical-Empiricist Paradigm

Despite the significant changes that separate modern science from ancient *episteme* and medieval *scientia*, the Western tradition has always tended to associate "science" with the highest expression of knowledge. Given the technological advances connected with modern science as a whole, it hardly seems reasonable to contest this association. In the popular imagination, science "works"—medicine, not magic cures; planes, not carpets fly. But such success arises largely as the result of a certain method of inquiry that already issues in claims to knowledge, or at least to probable knowledge. Moreover, not all of these claims translate so readily into things that "work" such as planes and computers (think, for example, of claims about the demise of the dinosaurs). The point is this: Rational method lies at the heart of the epistemic status of science. In Ernest Nagel's words, "its method of inquiry...is perhaps the most permanent feature of science and the ultimate warrant for confidence in the conclusions of scientific inquiry" (1967, p. 8). One may thus ask what it is about scientific method that grounds the claim of any current scientific result to represent (probable) knowledge, and hence to deserve the assent of any rational person. In effect, we are asking what methodological features of science ground a rational scientific consensus. To help answer this question, I sketch in this part the shift in the philosophy of science away from a logic-centered account to a more rhetorical one.

The "logical empiricist" philosophy of science stemming from the logical positivism of the early 20th century attempts to reconstruct the rationality of scientific inquiry primarily as a problem of justifying scientific claims independent of the accidents attending their original context of investigation and discovery (see Nickles, 1980; Brown, 1977; also, for example, Nagel, 1961; Hempel, 1966; Scheffler, 1981). In this approach, the rational-consensual character of science is secured inasmuch as claims are assessed according to formal standards of observation and inference that are publicly accepted; the justificatory moves involved in such assessment, however, are ones the *individual* scientist can recapitulate. That is, logical empiricists focus on the specific steps in experimentation and reasoning that should lead *any* scientist to see that a given result or theory deserves assent, at least until something better comes along. For example, in some analyses the meaning of theoretical terms (such as "atom," "electron," etc.) are traced back to isolated facts or sense data accessible in principle to any observer and statable in a theory-neutral observation language; the scientific explanation of an event is considered adequate in so far as general laws, along with a statement of antecedent conditions, allow one to *deduce* the event's occurrence—whence the characterization of this view as the "deductive-nomological" account of science. One can discern a Cartesian legacy behind this picture of scientific rationality, for the choice of a given scientific theory as the more probably true of several competitors is supposed to be *rationally compelled* by a combination of self-evident observations and logical deductions. Thus, as opposed to the idiosyncratic, often unpredictable "context of discovery," the reconstructed "context of justification" marshals reasons that should in principle lead each individual to the same conclusion.

Thomas S. Kuhn's (1970) groundbreaking study of scientific revolutions, first published in 1962, shows that a strictly formal-logical analysis is far too narrow to encompass the rationality guiding real scientific inquiry and theory choice. Kuhn's turn to the history, to the actual practices of successful inquiry in the past, shatters the all-too-naïve confidence placed in the ideal models of scientific rationality put together by the logical empiricists and their heirs. With the contexts of justification and discovery now inextricably intertwined, those messier, less clearly rational aspects of inquiry, discovery, and theory formation come to the fore. At one level this brings out the problem lurking behind any normative theory of human rationality, i.e., any theory making a claim about how we *ought* to think and act rationally: After a sober look at the complexity and diversity of *actual* practices of inquiry, it becomes difficult to uphold ideal models that appear to set impossibly high or even false standards. In the 20th century this scenario has been repeated again and again in the various domains of discourse that heretofore operated with the Enlightenment presumption of following universal standards of rationality. As we approach the end of the century, the reverse trend is evident everywhere: a tendency to retreat to more relativistic, if not outright skeptical, views about the possibility of knowledge in the traditional sense (e.g., Rorty, 1991; see also Hesse, 1980; Fuller, 1988).

Here I am more interested, however, in two specific implications of Kuhn's revolution in the study of science: "To discover how scientific revolutions are effected, we shall therefore have to examine not only the impact of nature and of logic, but also the *techniques of persuasive argumentation* effective within the quite *special groups that constitute the community of scientists*" (Kuhn, 1970, p. 94, emphasis added; also see pp. 152-159, 162-170, 176-210). As Kuhn himself recognized, the study of inquiry would have to involve attention not only to deductively compelling logical techniques, but also (1) to broader, less compelling processes of *persuasive* argumentation and, implicit in this, (2) to the current community of scientists. The first takes us into the theory of argumentation and, more broadly, the rhetoric of inquiry, while the second opens up on the whole range of social, institutional, and cultural factors operative in the enterprise of science. Analyses in these areas, however, only seem to undermine further the clear criteria of rationality once held so confidently by philosophers of science.

In fact, recent theory of argumentation has followed a path that somewhat parallels the developments in the philosophy of science sketched above. As a distinct discipline, argumentation theory grew out of a pedagogy of argument heavily influenced by the conviction-persuasion dichotomy (Cox & Willard, 1982; cf. also Cronkhite, 1969, chapter 2). Alternative views notwithstanding, this schema led by the mid-20th century to a more or less pronounced tendency to identify the specifically rational aspects of argumentation—what grounds *rational* consensus—with the logical reasoning that issues in conviction; persuasive appeals based on emotion or character serve as ancillary techniques for bringing about audience assent in concrete contexts of debate. Certainly the rhetorical aspects of argumentation are important, even decisive, for actually producing consensus. But this "applied formalism" in effect assigned rhetoric an adjunct role when it came to defining the rationality of consensus (see, e.g., Ehninger, 1963; Mills, 1964). Of reactions against formalism, two of the most influential for subsequent argumentation theory were actually directed against formalism in philosophy and logic: Stephen Toulmin's *The Uses of Argument* (1958) drew attention to the "substantial logics" whose standards come from the specific field of inquiry, in contrast to universally applicable formal logics; Chaim Perelman and Lucie Olbrechts-Tyteca's *The New Rhetoric* (1958/1969) stressed the importance of different contexts and probabilities, again in contrast to the over-valorized universal audience presupposed by the Cartesian obsession with logical certitude. Since then, argumentation theorists have developed a variety of open and complex accounts examining the *normative* role of context, audience, dialectic, rhetoric, etc. (e.g., Booth, 1974). However, introducing rhetorical perspectives into the very heart of reasoned argument and justification has seemingly sacrificed clear criteria for rational assent. Judging from recent work, the field of argumentation theory and rhetoric is currently in flux, with a wild diversity of proposals on the table. Not surprisingly, the temptation to skeptical and relativist views has also grown (cf. Nelson, Megill, & McCloskey, 1987; Williams & Hazen, 1990; Simons, 1990). One has to ask this question: Is the rationality governing consensus formation *merely* a local, contextual matter?

Inasmuch as argument and persuasion take place in groups, an argumentation-theoretic approach to inquiry goes hand-in-hand with attention to the "scientific community," just as Kuhn suggested. Here the notion of "community" is complex, however. It involves not only the collection of individuals known as "scientists," but refers, at least indirectly, to the various dynamics and influences owing their existence to the fact that science is an organized group effort. If scientists make up a community—or, more accurately, communities—in some sense, then one must follow Kuhn in analyzing its value systems, research traditions, and modes of training if one is to grasp the rationality of its practices. But one cannot stop there. One must also examine the various institutions in which this community actually carries out its inquiry, a move that exposes one to the broader societal impacts on the practice of science, e.g., how funding institutions and their political backers shape the course of scientific inquiry. Once again, ideal models of scientific rationality threaten to collapse under the burden of so many influences that are seemingly extraneous to a "rational" inquiry yet nonetheless so close to its real functioning (cf. Bloor, 1976; Mendelsohn, Weingart, & Whitley, 1977; Knorr-Cetina, 1983; Latour, 1987; Fuller, 1988, 1992, 1993a).

In sum, the shift away from exclusively formal-logical accounts of scientific inquiry and argument opens a Pandora's Box of considerations and factors difficult to manage by anyone wishing to account for the rationality of science. With the recognition that logic and self-evident observation alone no longer suffice as criteria for rational theory choice, the leading question becomes, What constitutes rational consensus on claims the arguments for which are neither deductively nor self-evidently conclusive? Judging from current trends in social and rhetorical analysis, we can conclude that neither an attention to the community structure of science nor to its rhetoric bodes well for a clear answer to this question. If no plausible answer to this question is forthcoming, however, then some form of relativism or skepticism would appear justified. Before drawing this conclusion, however, one does well in this situation to look for criteria of rationality that have sufficient heuristic clarity to guide further investigation without foreclosing issues of possible relevance for an accurate understanding of one's object. In particular, we seek guidelines that remain open to the rhetorical and social aspects of inquiry prematurely cut off by the Cartesian paradigm governing logical empiricism. It is precisely here, I propose, that Lonergan's cognitional theory can, once suitably extended, prove quite helpful.

## 2. Kant, Lonergan, and Habermas: From Semantics to Intersubjective Dialectics

To approach the above-described problematic at the proper depth, one must first have available not so much a substantive account of science as a prior account of human reasoning able to direct substantive analysis. In any case, close analyses of actual scientific practice already abound; what is needed is a suitably flexible set of clues for understanding how these practices deserve the appellation "rational." Lonergan's cognitional theory provides just this: a clear account of the rational structure of human inquiry (see Lonergan, 1957/1992; subsequent parenthetical references to this work provide page numbers only). It thus represents a suitable starting point for addressing the problems at issue here.[1]

To bring Lonergan's cognitional theory fully into the current arena, however, we must present it as an intersubjective account of inquiry and insight. Although Lonergan certainly recognizes the social character of inquiry (e.g., p. 198), his theory primarily elucidates the structure of rational judgment as a process enacted by the individual. To make his theory more clearly relevant for problems concerning processes of argumentation in a

---

[1] Naturally, one would eventually have to examine his philosophy of science as well. But the fact that Lonergan's account of science predates the Kuhnian revolution raises special difficulties beyond the scope of this paper. For a sense of the criticisms one can level against Lonergan's philosophy of science in the light of more recent developments, see Hesse (1975); for a Lonerganian critique of Kuhn, see Meynell (1975).

community of inquiry, I reconstruct it through the lens of the formal pragmatics developed by Habermas, among others. A formal-pragmatic dimension of analysis is helpful here in so far as it focuses on the linguistic, interactive side of judgment. This makes it especially suitable for examining inquiry and judgment as a process of argumentation involving two or more persons. At the same time, the formal-pragmatic account of validity assumes a notion of insight in need of further analysis. This makes it plausible to expect that Lonergan's cognitional theory and Habermas's formal pragmatics can usefully complement each other. Rather than simply assume this, however, I start in the first section by sketching Lonergan's analysis of insight and cognition in a way that opens up on a formal-pragmatic extension of that analysis, which I develop in the second section. The result is, I hope, rationality criteria that are neither too narrow nor closed to issues of rhetoric and context, which I take up in Part 3.

## 2.1 Beyond Kant: Lonergan's Pragmatics of Insight

By way of introduction we might note how Lonergan's approach already has much in common with formal pragmatics. Here "pragmatics" indicates an analysis at the level of practice or performance, in contrast to semantic and syntactic levels of analysis. In so far as Lonergan's account of cognition puts the emphasis on what knowers do, rather than on the specific concepts they must have available in order to know, it represents a kind of pragmatics. His analysis is "formal" in so far as it surveys different contexts of knowing in order to arrive at the formal structures governing a broad spectrum of cognitive acts—the general process or operations any knower in any field of inquiry must undertake in order to arrive at a judgment. This is not to equate his approach with formal pragmatics in the usual sense, but only to position it in a way that reduces the step to Habermas's formal pragmatics.

A contrast with Kantian epistemology can further clarify the pragmatic nature of Lonergan's approach and lead into his cognitional theory. When Kant in the *Critique of Pure Reason* addresses the question of how objective knowledge is possible, he is primarily interested in explaining how science can arrive at universal and necessary laws on the basis of empirical investigation. Kant is concerned, that is, with claims such as "in all changes of the material world the quantity of matter remains unchanged" (Kant, 1787/1965, B17). The problem is how a claim covering all empirical reality can count as knowledge, given that one can never investigate more than a part of such reality. His solution locates universality and necessity, and thus the objectivity of scientific knowledge, at the level of "categories of understanding," fundamental semantic structures comprising the necessary conditions for the possibility of meaningful experience on the part of a rational subject. For example, to understand the action of colliding billiard balls, one must have available, at the very least, the concepts of "substance" (in the sense of things that persist in time) and "cause." Without the ability to understand one's experience (e.g., of colliding billiard balls) in terms of such fundamental concepts or categories, such experience would be "blind," without meaning. Naturally, by themselves the categories cannot deliver the details of Newton's laws, nor explain exactly how billiard balls act on one another. But they do justify one's framing these more detailed laws in a universal and necessary form, as claims to knowledge that should hold good for all observers. Precisely because these fundamental concepts are universal and necessary structures of experience, they provide criteria of objectivity and thus make objective knowledge possible (Kant, 1787/1965, A67/B92ff.; cf. also Genova, 1984). Thus Kant's analysis highlights the role of concepts or semantic structures in the constitution of knowledge. The important work is done not so much by the process of judgment as by the fundamental categories that organize experience.

Lonergan, by contrast, defines knowing and objectivity not by semantic structures but by the dynamic *process* driven by the desire to know and capped by judgments (pp. 362-364; Sala, 1976). Once again, the pragmatic or performative focus is decisive: To understand how knowledge is possible, one must look not so much to fundamental categories or concepts for organizing experience as to the active process in which potential knowers engage in order to satisfy their desire to know—the process that first generates fundamental concepts to begin with. According to Lonergan, this desire to know, if suitably unleashed from other interests, does not rest content with a given set of concepts, but drives beyond these to ask whether they are actually correct, i.e., to ask whether they are the most appropriate categories for understanding reality or not (pp. 372-381, 430-431).

In defining objectivity in reference to the desire to know, the cognitional theory that corresponds to Lonergan's project takes *questions* more seriously than do Kantian (and neo-Kantian) approaches, which tend to start by mapping out unavoidable categorial frameworks (e.g., Strawson, 1959). Confronted by puzzling experiences, one looks to one's available stock of "categories" precisely because one wants to answer questions such as, What is it? or Why does this happen? or even, How often should this happen? Such "questions for intelligence" indicate the "attitude of the inquiring mind that effects a transition" from the sense data and presentations of experience to the various ways we attempt to understand our experience. Understanding is a broad notion here, ranging from culturally typical ways of identifying objects to more sophisticated scientific hypotheses, theories, and formulations of statistical frequencies (pp. 298-299). Thus Lonergan does not deny the importance of concepts and ideas that allow one to pull together diverse elements of experience, to bring experiential particulars under unifying and clarifying "categories of understanding." But such acts of synthesis, which render experience intelligible, must not be conflated with judgment proper, which goes beyond simply entertaining a particular way of understanding things and affirms (or denies) that this understanding is actually the correct one:

> The formulations of understanding yield concepts, definitions, objects of thought, suppositions, considerations. But man demands more. Every answer to a question for intelligence raises a further question for reflection. There is an ulterior motive to conceiving and defining, thinking and considering, forming suppositions, hypotheses, theories, systems. That motive appears when such activities are followed by the question, "Is it so?" We conceive in order to judge. (p. 298)

Just as the level of experiential presentations gives rise to questions for intelligence, so the level of understanding gives rise to "questions for reflection." That is, questions for intelligence spark "direct insights" into how one can organize and make sense of the data of experience—insights that one can formulate as hypotheses, theories, and so on. Such direct insights are followed up by questions for reflection, which aim at "reflective insights" in which one "grasps the sufficiency of the evidence for a prospective judgment" (p. 304). This further level of reflection upon direct insights involves the exercise of "reasonableness," a term Lonergan uses to distinguish this level from the "intelligence" that issues in the direct insight itself (p. 347).

Reflective insight, then, makes a judgment possible. It does so by linking up the prospective judgment with the fulfillment of the conditions for the judgment's correctness. Here the judgment is an affirmation that a given direct insight or way of understanding something is correct. Lonergan gives the simple example of a man coming home to find the window smashed, smoke in the air, and water on the floor. Suppose he entertains the very cautious proposition, Something happened. For this prospective judgment, the fulfilling conditions consist in the two sets of data given by his memory of the house as he left it in the morning, on the one hand, and his experience of its present state, on the other. These fulfilling conditions are linked with the judgment by the structures of consciousness—perhaps the closest thing in Lonergan's analysis to Kantian categories—that constitute our notions of change and event, structures one can formulate as the conditional statements or rules, "If the same thing exhibits different individual data at different times, it has changed. If there occurs a change, something has happened" (pp. 306-308).

Now to say that the reflective insight grounding judgment simply subsumes the data under the "category" of change would be too simple. At the risk of being somewhat unfair to Kant, we might say that, in Lonerganian terms, Kant's analysis of "determinative judgment" highlights just two terms, the conditionally structured category and the experienced conditions: In such cases where an a priori category immediately structures experience, the act of judgment just is the subsumption of the latter under the former (see Kant, 1790/1987, Introduction, sec. iv). But this, on Lonergan's view, conflates direct and reflective insight inasmuch as there is a difference between organizing data into a determinate pattern and rendering a judgment. The latter operation actually involves three terms. That is, reflective insight grasps three things at once: (1) the judgment itself as a conditioned, (2) the link between conditions and prospective judgment, and (3) the experience that the conditions are fulfilled. To see the subtle but crucial shift this analysis introduces relative to Kant, I take up each of these in turn, using our simple example for illustration.

*2.11 The judgment itself as a conditioned.* To begin with, Lonergan pulls apart the judgment into two elements. If I may simplify his analysis somewhat, the judgment proper consists in a Yes or No answer to a question for reflection—in this case, Is the (direct) insight that something happened in fact correct? This answer thus depends on the question preceding it, however, so that it implicitly contains the content of this question. Hence, in the example the judgment's implicit meaning is, "It certainly is true that something happened," or "Yes, something happened" (pp. 300-301). As we saw, one can correctly make this claim only if certain conditions obtain, so that the judgment itself is a "conditioned." But the grasp that the conditions do in fact obtain involves more than a subsumption of the two sets of data under a category. In line with his overall approach, Lonergan analyzes both the structure of consciousness that links the sets of data with the notion of change *and* the experiential grasp of the data itself in terms of *questions*.

*2.12 The link between conditions and prospective judgment.* I first introduced the link as a rule or conditional connecting the conditioned judgment with its conditions—in this case, a rule to the effect that something happened if the same thing exhibits differences at different times. If Lonergan were to stop at this point, his analysis would not differ much from Kant's. He gives that analysis a pragmatic twist, however, when he explicates the structure of the rule in terms of the relation between insights and questions. That is, linking-rules have the following general structure: A direct insight is correct "if there are no further, pertinent questions" (p. 309; also p. 312). For our example, then, the rule has the following *pragmatic structure*: The direct insight that something happened is correct if there are no further, pertinent questions. The immediacy of the experience of change, of course, makes explicit reference to further questions unlikely, although our surprised homeowner might ask himself whether his memory serves him right. The rule would become more obvious, perhaps, if he ventured the further judgment, There was a fire. This would spark the further pertinent questions, Where was the fire, exactly? What started it? and so on. If he could not locate any fire damage in his house, he might start to entertain alternative explanations for the data, such as that his children had been up to some mischief.

*2.13 The experience that the conditions are fulfilled.* The grasp of the data as a fulfillment of the conditions, once seen in this pragmatic perspective, involves a grasp that the direct insight does in fact "put an end to further, pertinent questioning" (p. 312). Here Lonergan distinguishes between invulnerable and vulnerable direct insights:

> When an insight meets the issue squarely, when it hits the bull's eye, when it settles the matter, there are no further questions to be asked and so there are no further insights to challenge the initial position. But when the issue is not met squarely, there are further questions that would reveal the unsatisfactoriness of the insight and would evoke the further insights that put a new light on the matter. (p. 309)

Once our homeowner, for example, actually located the fire damage, his insight that a fire had occurred would be "invulnerable." That issue, at least, would be settled.

The important point here is the way in which Lonergan's approach elaborates cognition as a cumulative process turning on the relations set up along the pragmatic axis moving from experiential data, through questions to insights, and then through further questions to further insights, and so on. Judgments do not simply organize and structure experience according to certain categorial forms; they issue from questions and lead to further questions. Even relatively simple everyday judgments are thus embedded in the dynamics of inquiry, and they terminate an inquiry only when they flow from the reflective insight that further questions are pointless. This means that the objectivity for which inquiry strives is best understood, not at the level of universal and necessary categories, but at the level of the questions whose cessation indicates that a judgment is correct because the insight it expresses is "invulnerable." But invulnerability depends in turn on an account of pertinence or relevance. As I argue in Part 3, relevance is one of the sticking points in current debates, so that the viability of Lonergan's theory of inquiry will depend on what he says on this topic. But before we can bring this into the arena defined by the current rationality debates, we must understand the intersubjectivity it involves.

## 2.2 Lonergan and Habermas: Insight as Intersubjective

Both direct and reflective insights have an intersubjective dimension. This is perhaps most readily apparent with direct insights. Certainly, any individual's direct insights owe their existence to a background of meanings the individual shares with others. One can no doubt distinguish a number of levels here. Most of these meanings one possesses simply as a member of a specific language community, others are specific to a particular subgroup such as the science community, and still others are inherited from those who have previously worked on a specific problem. Although direct insights certainly depend on the individual's creative synthetic efforts in arriving at new ideas for solving a problem, such insights presuppose a much wider and deeper dependence on others. As a result, direct insights only occur within traditions of meaning and prior insights. Lonergan develops one of the more radical implications of this point—that the entire process of making judgments, even a whole tradition, can be skewed by the operation of group and general biases—for the area of common sense (pp. 314-316; and chapter 7; cf. also chapter 2 in the present volume by Thomas J. Farrell).  One might, however, interpret the philosophy of science since Kuhn as grappling with the possibility that a kind of "bias" applies to scientific inquiry—indeed, is even *essential* to inquiry.  I come back to Kuhn briefly in Part 3.

At first glance, the intersubjective character of reflective insight is less obvious.  For when I judge that a direct insight is correct, is it not I and I alone who render judgment, who take personal responsibility for what I affirm?  Lonergan himself provides the first clue that matters are more complicated: "It is not enough to say that the conditions [for correct judgment] are fulfilled when no further questions *occur to me*"—typically such questions must be posed by others (p. 309, emphasis added; see also pp. 107, 198).  Now, if we tie judgment to the assertion of a knowledge claim—leaving open the question whether judgments just *are* such assertions—we can develop this clue further.  That is, if individual judgments and assertions are at least closely related, then the formal pragmatics developed from speech-act theory by thinkers such as Habermas can usefully supplement Lonergan's cognitional theory.  In particular, it can bring out further aspects of the essential intersubjectivity implicit in Lonergan's account (see Habermas, 1976/1979; Austin, 1962; Searle, 1969).

Habermas's speech-act-theoretic analysis of knowledge (or truth) claims distinguishes two elements in such claims.  On the one hand, there is the propositional content itself, for example, the sentence, "There has been a fire."  As it stands, this content can appear in a variety of speech acts.  Depending on the context and intonation, one can say it as a question, or as a warning, perhaps as an admission, or even as an accusation ("Didn't I tell you what would happen if you left the fireplace untended?...").  One can merely entertain it or assert it as true.  In the latter case one gives the propositional content the force of a truth claim.  Speech-act theory thus maintains that in addition to their propositional or "locutionary" content, actual utterances include an element called "illocutionary force," which one can thematize for any utterance by making the speaker's attitude explicit in a leading "performative clause."  If our example is a truth claim, we obtain:

(I hereby assert that) there has been a fire.

This is symbolized by the general form Mp, where p stands for the content and M for the performative clause.  The parallel with Lonergan's analysis of judgment is obvious.  Assuming the speaker is sincere, the above claim appears equivalent to taking public responsibility for (or making a commitment to) the judgment:

It is certainly true that there has been a fire.

Now, in his analysis of such claims, Habermas focuses not so much on the operations of the individual speaker as on the intersubjective dimension of raising the claim (Habermas, 1981/1984, pp. 8-42, 273-337). In particular, he argues that the illocutionary component of a speech act must be understood as an offer of an intersubjective relationship with the hearer. In the case of a truth claim, a speaker S wants to establish a shared understanding with a hearer H about the objective world as a reliable basis for further action and cooperation. The point here is that by my truth claim I hope to reach an understanding *with you the hearer* about the world we share. It follows that part of the very meaning of raising a knowledge claim (or any type of validity claim) consists in its *intelligibility and potential acceptability to others*. The unit of analysis for such claims is thus not the operations carried out by the individual and certainly not that individual's solitary knowledge claim, but the speaker's claim *together with* the hearer's response. One only raises knowledge claims for hearers (or potential hearers, as in a dialogue with oneself), and the claim "succeeds" only if the hearer is rationally motivated to accept it.[2]

This analysis therefore ties assertions, and thus judgments, to the idea of rational consensus:

> The attempt by S to reach an understanding with H about something in the world terminates in the agreement brought about between them, and this agreement is sealed by the acceptance of a comprehensible speech act. For this reason, the comprehension of a speech act already points to the conditions for a possible agreement about what is said. (Habermas, 1988/1992, p. 74)

According to Habermas, the agreement or consensus is rationally motivated because, in making a truth claim, the speaker tacitly guarantees the hearer that the claim is based on good reasons. At least implicitly, then, validity claims are tied to discourse or argumentation in so far as the speaker should be able to give arguments for what is claimed. In the case of truth claims, we should expect these arguments typically to refer to empirical observations. To continue with our example, if the man says that there was a fire, the hearer may ask him how he knows there was a fire. In response, he could simply list the relevant empirical data, even inviting the hearer to go see for herself if she doubts the claim. Here the "good reasons" refer to data observable in principle by anyone on the scene.

We do not need to complicate matters here by comparing Lonergan's and Habermas's theories of truth. Sufficient for our purposes is what Lonergan and Habermas can agree upon about the *rationality* of raising truth claims. We can begin by noting how Habermas's concept of "rational moti-

---

[2] The importance of the hearer's response for discursive-cognitive processes has been noted by other authors as well; see Grimaldi (1990) and Ong (1992, pp. 70-71).

vation" presupposes something like Lonergan's notion of insight and the "reasonableness" in which it is grounded. Recall that, for Lonergan, as a prospective knower I can take a judgment as correct once I grasp that the direct insight formulated in the judgment is invulnerable, i.e., that there are no further pertinent questions. For Habermas, as a hearer I can be rationally motivated to accept a truth claim inasmuch as the speaker guarantees that the claim can be vindicated on the basis of good reasons. Such vindication implies that potential challenges to the claim can be answered, hence that there are no further pertinent questions or at least no questions that will prove unanswerable and thus overturn the claim. Thus, Habermas's notion of rational acceptability—at least at its ideal limit—would seem to presuppose Lonergan's account of reflective insight—the grasp that there are no further pertinent (or valid but unanswerable) questions on an issue.

But how does one assess whether there are further questions or not? As we have seen, this involves more than whether you or I have further questions. Lonergan's complete answer to this introduces considerations I want to postpone for Part 3. His initial answer, however, points to the unhindered operation of the desire to know: In so far as questions arise through the desire to know, an obstacle to the operation of this desire can block their emergence (p. 309). But if questions come from other inquirers, then the relevant obstacles pertain to the discursive process of question and answer. This suggests that Habermas's account of rational consensus can help further explicate the intersubjective aspects of Lonergan's concept of insight.

According to Habermas, one is rationally motivated to accept a truth claim in so far as one has a confidence that there are good reasons grounding the claim. However, what makes reasons "good"—and hence a consensus "rational"—is the quality of the discourse producing these reasons (Habermas, 1986). Confidence that a claim can be redeemed by good reasons implies, therefore, a confidence that the claim would stand up to examination in a rational discourse.

But what makes for "rational" discourse? This question has led to considerable debate, especially in the realm of moral theory (Benhabib & Dallmayr, 1990; McCarthy, 1978, chapter 4). At least as an idealization, though, Habermas's answer draws on an intuitively plausible idea: In a rational discourse the participants are motivated solely by the cooperative search for truth, so that any consensus they arrive at is based on an insight into the better argument (Habermas, 1986). Hence, no competent investigator on the given issue may be arbitrarily excluded from participation, nor may the course of discussion be hindered by any coercions, whether internal psychological compulsions, intimidation within the group of participants, or broader societal impositions. Rather, each participant must be allowed to make proposals and counterproposals, raise objections and questions, in a free and unhindered fashion.

Perhaps real processes of inquiry will only rarely meet all these conditions, but one must at least suppose that an actual inquiry has sufficiently approximated them if one is to consider its outcome "rational." If certain questions were systematically suppressed in a given inquiry, if rationally competent participants with contrary proposals were excluded from participation, one would at least have grounds to suspect the results.[3]

This account of rational consensus can be seen as "operationalizing" the desire to know for the social, cooperative process of discourse. It thus allows us to develop further the intersubjective dimensions of reflective insight and judgment. According to Lonergan, correct judgments depend on a grasp that all the further, pertinent questions have been answered. As we have seen, such questions come from others. Habermas's analysis suggests that the insight that all the further questions are answered must be defined in terms of idealized discursive conditions ensuring that, if any such questions are possible—that is, "if there may be further, unknown facts that would raise further questions to force a revision or...if there may be further, known facts whose capacity to raise such questions is not grasped"—these questions eventually *could* arise (Lonergan, 1957/1992, p. 327; also pp. 324-329). This implies, to be sure, that at any point in the history of a given inquiry only probable, fallible judgments are possible. But in so far as a given inquiry approximates these idealized conditions of free discussion, the participants can be confident that consensual results represent the currently most probable judgments on the given issue. Reformulating Lonergan's concept of insight in this intersubjective context thus yields the following: One can grasp a given answer or prospective judgment as probably correct to the extent that one has the reflective insight that there are no further, pertinent questions to be raised in an unhampered discussion of the currently available information, arguments, and counterarguments by all those who are competent on the matter at hand.

It is this grasp that constitutes the "insight into the better argument" required by Habermas's concept of rational discourse. To this extent, Lonergan's analysis can inform Habermas's. Conversely, Habermas's discourse theory emphasizes the intersubjective character of Lonergan's analysis. For, as it turns out, reflective insight becomes more deeply intersubjective than direct insight. With direct insight, the individual still has the privilege and task of producing the particular creative syntheses represented by various proposals for solving a problem. Even if the individual depends on input from others, the synthetic act itself can still be said, at least in many cases, to take place in some individual's head. The above account of reflective insight, however, suggests that as problems become more complex it becomes less likely that any single individual can accomplish the grasp of

---

[3] For a fuller treatment of the various rules defining rational discourse (including rules for the burden of argument), see Alexy (1990).

pertinent questions required for a reflective insight into the correctness, or even the probable correctness, of a proposed solution. Here I refer to a more radical limitation than the temporal limit on the entire group involved in an inquiry. It thus deserves some explanation.

At any given point in its inquiry, a group of scientists cannot rule out the possibility that further facts will emerge as relevant to a probable judgment, thus requiring revisions in the judgment. The individual, however, faces a deeper limitation: As the complexity of scientific knowledge grows, the range and complexity of further, pertinent questions grows. In part this growth is retrospective, in so far as any judgment depends on the acceptance of previous judgments. Since many of the latter will stand outside the individual scientist's expertise, making a judgment on one matter presupposes that one believes the judgments others have made on related matters—and hence believes that their judgments answer the pertinent questions beyond one's own ken. Lonergan himself is clear about this retrospective limit on the individual. In fact, it leads him to conclude that the reflection grounding scientific knowledge claims is *essentially* collaborative: "[T]he reasonableness of each scientist is a consequence of the reasonableness of all" (p. 453). For example, it is reasonable for scientists to assent to the claim that relativity theory more accurately accounts for the perihelion of Mercury, but it is unlikely that any scientist has "immanently generated knowledge" of this, given the complexity—or simply the sheer quantity—of its conditions (pp. 727-728, 733-734). As a result, "the mentality of any individual becomes a composite product," a mixture of immanently generated knowledge and reasonable belief in others' knowledge (p. 727).

This growth also sets prospective limitations on the individual's reflective insight, however. Here I will indicate just one such limitation. If I raise a claim or propose a probable answer to a question that has implications for other disciplines and problems beyond my expertise, then it is unlikely that I can, in my own head, achieve the reflective grasp of all the conditions for the correctness, or even the probable correctness, of my judgment. Certainly, I have some confidence that my claim deserves serious attention. But in complex cases it can be difficult for me as an individual even to assess whether my claim is a good candidate for probable knowledge, i.e., a claim that will stand up to further inquiry and experimentation. For the claim may spark immediate objections from researchers in other areas with which I am less familiar—objections that, once brought to my attention, would lead me to lower my estimate of the chances that my claim will hold up over the long run. This presupposes, of course, that I believe the objections. My new estimate will then be reasonable not because I have become an expert in these related disciplines, but because the process of discourse is rational and its participants are both competent and committed to the truth.

Naturally, the foregoing considerations remain sketchy and, in light of recent work bearing on the sociality of science, are still quite cautious (cf., for example, Gooding, Pinch, & Schaffer, 1989; Pickering, 1992; Cole, 1992). I merely want to indicate some points where a specifically Lonerganian contribution to the study of the social character of scientific knowledge might begin. Because science is a cooperative venture involving complex questions of the sort indicated above, scientific knowledge is no longer a matter of this or that individual's immanently generated reflective insight and judgment. Rather, one might say that the moment of reflective insight is divided up and parceled out among various scientists, each of whom reasonably assents to a claim after examining it from the perspective of his or her own expertise. Conversely, the reasonableness grounding such knowledge represents an essentially intersubjective, "composite product." In such cases, knowledge exists at the level of rational consensus, and to analyze it one must focus above all on the rationality of science as a *cooperative group process*.

Before going on, we should recognize that the above ideals of rationality—which we might call "dialectical" in view of the emphasis on question and answer[4]—are quite strong and thus beset with pitfalls. From Lonergan's analysis, we seemingly must assume it is coherent to think that all further, pertinent questions can be answered; Habermas's analysis points to the ideal of truth claims that will stand up to all future challenges and thus convince all rational persons. Both ideals could probably be explicated in terms of C. S. Peirce's idea of the "final opinion" that an ideal community of investigators would settle on, but again this would lead to any number of further problems. In fact, Habermas insists that such ideals are not concretely realizable end states, but "idealizations" that provide a kind of regulative leverage for criticizing *current* practices of discourse (Habermas, 1991, pp. 157-166). What we can hold on to with respect to the rationality underlying scientific claims, and hence scientific inquiry, is this: In so far as further, pertinent questions arise in open debate, confidence in a claim or judgment is undermined, and in so far as one is confident that such questions will prove answerable in the course of further research, one is rationally motivated to accept a claim or judgment as at least probably true (cf. p. 574). Both sides of this thesis involve a point that opens on the rationality problematic currently besetting theories of inquiry. One involves the notion of pertinence, and the other, that of confidence. Both point to the significance of rhetoric for science.

*[margin annotation: Like Plato's forms]*

---

[4] In using the term "dialectical" I do not mean to say anything about what Lonergan calls "dialectic" or "dialectical method." Moreover, it involves more than the dialectical level of argumentation as understood by Habermas (cf. Lonergan, 1957/1992, pp. 242, 268-269, 553ff; Habermas, 1981/1984, pp. 25-26).

## 3. Toward a Lonerganian Account of Rhetoric in Science

The analysis in Part 2, though rather idealized, does provide a broad pragmatic framework for thinking about the rationality of inquiry. In this last
part, I suggest some reasons why a contemporary Lonerganian approach to
the philosophy of science must situate rhetoric at the very heart of inquiry.
In broad terms, rhetoric simply involves the effort to persuade an audience
in a concrete situation; it is rooted in "the use of language as a symbolic
means of inducing cooperation in beings that by nature respond to symbols"
(Burke, 1950, p. 43; see also Aristotle, *Rhetoric*, Bk. I; Perelman & Olbrechts-Tyteca, 1958/1969, pp. 17-26). The question, however, is whether
such persuasion enters in only subsequent to rational scientific inquiry and
judgment, so that the latter notions can be defined independently of rhetoric,
or whether on the contrary persuasion is actually integral to and partly constitutive of the human quest for knowledge. In what follows I at least point
to some reasons for preferring the latter view.

We can approach this point by starting with Lonergan's pre-Kuhnian
analysis of pertinence. The idea of pertinence or relevance implies that
rhetoric will be important to the actual practice of science. The kind of
importance here, though, is the classical one: Rhetoric is important for fostering correct (true and just) judgments, or in negative terms, seeing to it
that truth and justice are not defeated by their opposites. William M. A.
Grimaldi, commenting on Aristotle's *Rhetoric* 1355a (lines 21-24), explains
the proper function of rhetoric in relation to truth:

> If truth and justice are defeated, it is because rhetoric has failed in its function as
> mimesis [i.e., re-presenting the real]. The defeat of truth and justice is caused by
> their inadequate articulation in language. It is the task of rhetoric, and in this
> task resides its usefulness, to assure an adequate and competent articulation of
> truth and justice. When rhetoric fails to present this articulation, bad judgments
> are made by men, and truth and justice are destroyed by their opposites. (1978,
> pp. 176-177)

This approach easily fits with what Lonergan says about the relation between making correct judgments and the grasp that pertinent questions are
answered. For that grasp is not automatic. A competent judge must be neither rash, ignoring further questions, nor indecisive, seeing grounds for
doubt where none exist. Judgment, then, depends partly on character and
temperament. But the competence to judge can be helped along in so far as
one understands the background of an issue, has past experience in a field,
and gives further questions a chance to arise (pp. 310-312). Now if judgment involves an intersubjective process of raising and assenting to knowledge claims, then good rhetoric, as a matter of *articulating* the truth, includes whatever persuasive linguistic means a speaker can employ to foster
a hearer's or audience's process of reaching (or assenting to) probably correct judgments: On the one hand, it includes whatever slows down the rash,
giving them the time to let questions sink in; on the other hand, it includes

whatever encourages the indecisive, providing them with the confidence to commit themselves to a proposition's truth. More generally, the need for a rhetorical dimension arises from the combined facts that (1) judgment involves a personal commitment based on a grasp of questions and how well they have been answered, so that one must be *motivated* to judge; and that (2) this grasp is not reducible to a mechanical algorithm, so that the ease or difficulty in acquiring such motivation will vary with the potential knower's experience and temperament. Good rhetoric, then, attempts to fill gaps in the hearer's experience and background, so as to motivate assent.[5]

Although the foregoing picture shares much in common with newer images of rhetoric (see Prelli, 1989, pp. 11-32), it could still allow one to see rhetoric as simply an ancillary adjunct to science itself, as a presentation device the more learned and prudent employ to help along their less insightful colleagues. Yet the picture also permits a more radical interpretation that admits rhetoric into the essential constitution of scientific judgment inasmuch as researchers themselves engage in the very processes described in the previous paragraph as they proceed to carry out their investigations, prior to presenting their results publicly. Both the intersubjective analysis of inquiry in Part 2 above, as well as the closer descriptions of scientific inquiry available since Kuhn, buttress the more radical view.

The analysis in Part 2 at least suggests a move beyond the modern "adjunct" view in so far as it connects the *speaker's judgment itself* with audience, especially in regard to prospective limitations on individual insight in complex cases. In so far as correct judgments depend on the insight that all the pertinent questions *others* might raise are (or can be) answered, audience reaction is a crucial condition for correct judgment. If I cannot persuade others to accept my claim, if I cannot persuasively answer further, pertinent questions to their satisfaction, there are grounds for *me* to doubt my judgment, i.e., to consider it less secure. Again, the decisive point lies in the fact that the individual alone cannot secure the reflective grasp that constitutes correct judgment. This grasp must rather be located at the group level of a rational consensus.

Now, the account in Part 2 admittedly defined this consensus in terms of an idealized discourse involving all rational persons (or all those competent on a given issue). Hence a *particular* audience's reaction does not of itself decide an issue. A lone scientist might thus appeal to this ideally rational audience while continuing to insist on a claim or theory despite non-acceptance on all sides, perhaps even going to the grave with no more than the hope that some more enlightened future generation will vindicate the claim. The idealized dialectics of inquiry in Part 2 can always provide the loner with critical leverage against the majority consensus in so far as

---

[5] I do not claim that this exhausts good rhetoric. One could, for example, link Lonergan's concept of belief with a traditional element of rhetoric, persuasion based on the speaker's character.

that consensus must remain limited and fallible in the light of such idealizations. Thus, the possibility remains open, it would seem, of distinguishing the rationality of inquiry from its rhetorics by connecting the former with what *would* convince an ideal audience and the latter with what actually *does* persuade a particular audience (Perelman & Olbrechts-Tyteca, 1958/1969, pp. 26-35).

The basic difficulty with this latter proposal is that once we acknowledge that rational discourse must involve more than formal logic, the proposed distinction tells us nothing of substance about the kinds of arguments that actually win assent for a claim or theory. It tells us only that these arguments, if sound, will hold up over the long haul of further, and ever broader, questioning. Before a claim and its arguments can hold up, however, they must first be proposed in such a way that real audiences are persuaded. The idealized dialectics of inquiry tell us little or nothing about how scientists win over actual audiences to their claims, and to this extent they tell us little or nothing about the rationality of real inquiry and consensus formation—apart from which there are no scientific claims and theories for an ideal audience even counterfactually to agree upon.

A second consideration bolsters this point. The historical descriptions of actual scientific inquiry now available make it clear that particularly in times of crisis where two or more basic theories are in competition, even the most rational processes of theory choice and development are far more complex, difficult, and muddy than our idealized criteria alone can account for. Again, Lonergan's notion of pertinent questions provides a ready point of insertion for the rational necessity of rhetoric. As studies such as Kuhn's have shown, in formulating a hypothesis or new theory the scientist not only proposes an answer to questions, but also decides to live with other, still unanswered questions, quite possibly questions that had been answered by the earlier theory (e.g., Kuhn, 1970, pp. 107-108). This is rational in so far as the scientist has some grounds for thinking that further development of the new theory will answer the further questions as well. But an examination of these motivating grounds reveals that they are often "extra-scientific," involving broader and vaguer philosophical, theological, and cultural themes and tropes (e.g., Holton, 1973; Campbell, 1986; 1990; Prelli, 1989, pp. 83-100). Moreover, such grounds cannot do away with the risk involved in adopting the new hypothesis—just as the broader grounds for holding onto the old theory cannot ensure its adherents that they will eventually be able to answer the questions that led others to break ranks and propose a new theory.

In other words, further, pertinent questions are always with scientists, and which questions they consider *most* pertinent is not independent of which theories they adopt. Moreover, the stakes of adoption are high: Defending a scientific claim or theory is a costly and time-consuming enterprise, involving an entire research program (cf. Lakatos, 1970). Adopting a theory is thus a risky decision that, it seems, neither formal logic nor the dialectics of pertinent questions can fully determine.  If inquiry is to proceed at all, then, scientists must be motivated to commit themselves to a specific line of potential theoretical development partly on the basis of the further kinds of reasons and arguments that best lend themselves to rhetorical analysis.  But this need not imply an irrational element in science.  On the contrary, one can view the use of a motivating rhetoric as increasing the rationality of scientific inquiry in so far as such rhetoric encourages researchers to commit their energies to developing approaches that may eventually prove superior to their competitors.  To sum up, we can say the following:  Inasmuch as a judgment about whether a given line of scientific theorizing is correct or not must await the development of such a program, inasmuch as such development presupposes a risky commitment in the face of uncertainty, and inasmuch as rhetoric encompasses the persuasive linguistic means for motivating such commitment, rhetoric is an integral constituent of rational inquiry and consensual judgment.

Developing the rhetorical dimension of inquiry inside a Lonerganian framework still largely remains to be done (Campbell, 1985).  If the considerations that have taken us from logic through dialectic to rhetoric are on the mark, however, one does not have the luxury of not providing such an account.  Whether science approaches a universally objective truth and whether the use of rhetoric inside the halls of science implies rather that our knowledge claims are *just* ours and not binding on other cultures or epochs are further questions whose answers must, to some extent, await the further development of science itself (cf. pp. 328-329).  The fact that they are not settled, however, is no reason to exclude rhetoric on the grounds that it may lead one into relativism, especially for Lonerganians committed to avoiding obscurantism in any form.

In this essay I have supplemented Lonergan's cognitional theory with Habermas' formal pragmatics in order to sketch a framework for meeting the challenges posed by post-Kuhnian philosophy of science.  This framework primarily defines the rationality of scientific inquiry not in formal-logical terms, but in terms of the intersubjective pragmatics of discourse.  It thereby affords a single framework able to take in both audience- and context-specific rhetorical elements and a context-transcending dialectic of making and questioning judgments—a dialectic, that is, that submits any local consensus to the ongoing discourse and inquiry of future scientists.  There are, of course, a host of further questions regarding this framework itself and its more precise formulation.  If these questions can be answered, then the philosophy of science should be able to comprehend the sociohistorical and rhetorical complexity of a science still deserving its name.[6]

---

[6] I would like to thank Thomas McCarthy, Thomas J. Farrell, and Paul A. Soukup for commenting on earlier drafts of this essay.

# 9

# The Fragility of Consciousness: Lonergan and the Postmodern Concern for the Other

## *Frederick G. Lawrence*

### 1. Introduction: What is Postmodernism?

The term "postmodernist" was first coined in the 1930s to describe minor reactions to modernism in the arts. Its use expanded in the 1950s and 1960s to cover ever wider phenomena in the arts, especially certain types of eclecticism in architecture. Eventually it became a cover-all for artistic trends that tended to break down the boundaries between art and everyday life, between high and low or popular cultures; to promote a certain promiscuity in styles and codes, mixing parody, pastiche, irony, and playfulness and insisting on the absence of depth and the paradoxical importance of superficiality. This is the *reductio ad absurdum* of Romantic expressivism that ends by debunking the putative originality and genius of the artistic producer, suggesting that ultimately art may be no more than repetition.

In philosophy and theology, postmodernism embraces a wide range of "second thoughts" about Enlightenment and Romantic versions of modernity in the guise of the classic forms of hermeneutics of suspicion. Marx used political economy to debunk the bourgeois subject and the Romantic subject, and Freud used psychology. But the central figure of postmodernism is Nietzsche, who used philology to radically critique the Enlightenments in fourth-century Athens and in 17th- and 18th-century Europe as culminating in the "Last Man" of the late 19th and 20th century. In calling into question not just Enlightenment rationalism but the Romantic reaction to that rationalism ushered in by Rousseau, postmodern hermeneutics of suspicion eschews both the Enlightenment myth of progress and any form of Romantic nostalgia for a pristine past beyond restoration in present or future as well.

Originally published in 1993 in *Theological Studies, 54*, 55-94. Expanded by the author.

In Western culture this double-barreled reaction is overwhelmingly evident in the arts. It plays a role in the music of Wagner, Stravinsky, Schoenberg, and Berg; in the paintings of the Impressionists, the Post-Impressionists, the Fauvists, the Cubists, the Futurists, the Dadaists, the Surrealists, and so on; in the poetics of Mallarme, Rimbaud, and Baudelaire in France; of Kafka, Kraus, Musil, and Mann in Central Europe; of Chekhov and Dostoyevsky in Russia; and of Pound, Eliot, Joyce, Stein, Woolf, and Faulkner in literature in English.

Quite naturally, then, since Christian theology mediates between the Christian communities of witness and worship and the cultures in which they exist, it has to come to terms with postmodernism precisely in the measure that postmodernism has been affecting our culture. And theologians have in fact been doing so, whether intentionally or not. In the Roman Catholic context, it is perhaps not too farfetched to say that what the Church feared in its great and fierce polemic against "modernism" was just postmodernism in its relativistic and nihilistic manifestations. This quite understandable fear continues to dominate today's skirmishes against postmodernism where it is written off as merely relativistic and nihilistic. The dangers of these trends are rampantly evident and unquestionable. Yet the understandable reaction of wholesale rejection may itself be unwise, because it is too undialectical. If postmodernists are simply wrong in their relativist and nihilist conclusions, this does not mean that they are not raising real questions about issues that need to be engaged—issues that are not engaged by the strategy of wholesale rejection of postmodernist conclusions.

But doesn't postmodernism need to be taken seriously by Christian theologians? Don't we have to grasp what is correct about the things it dismisses and what are the aspects of reality it attempts to embrace, even if mistakenly? Don't we have to find a basis upon which postmodern concerns can be addressed without adopting postmodernism's destructive conclusions? This article gives an affirmative answer to these questions. Rather unexpectedly perhaps, it offers features of Bernard Lonergan's thought as a way of doing so. I have found him to be a Christian and Catholic thinker who actually shares many of the deepest concerns of postmodernism; but he does so in a way that takes relativity seriously without being relativistic—and that takes the absurdity and apparently random and chaotic dimensions of our world experience fully seriously without capitulating to nihilism in any form.

Since this essay of necessity is exceedingly long, readers deserve an overview of its parts. In Part 2, I examine the context and chief features of postmodernism in philosophy and theology, in order to see whether Lonergan's approach really does meet postmodernist concerns without yielding to postmodernist mistakes. In Part 3, I survey the postmodernist critique of the modern turn to the subject, with sections on (3.1) postmodernism in the philosophy of Nietzsche and Heidegger, (3.2) hermeneutic phenomenology's postmodern correction of modern counterpositions, which includes discussions of (3.21) the critique of sheer immediacy and (3.22) human experience as mediated, and (3.3) historicity of human experience.

Part 4 treats Lonergan's postmodern thematization of consciousness as experience, with sections on (4.1) the being of consciousness, (4.2) Lonergan on the passionateness of being and human consciousness, which includes discussions of (4.21) decentering of the subject within vertical finality and (4.22) consciousness as conditioned by the passionateness of being. Part 5 delineates deconstructive/genealogical postmodernism's concern for otherness in sections about (5.1) Derrida and (5.2) Foucault, followed by (5.3) a summary of Part 5.

Part 6 looks at Lonergan and contingency through a series of sections dealing with (6.1) contingency and the virtually unconditioned, (6.2) contingency and the non-systematic, (6.3) contingency and understanding, (6.4) contingency and language, (6.5) contingency and interpretation, (6.6) contingent predication, and (6.7) contingency and liberty. Part 7 considers Lonergan and the postmodernist sublime, with sections examining (7.1) the sublime and the ambiguity of the surd, (7.2) Lyotard and the sublime, and (7.3) moving from the sublime to worship. Part 8, then, is the conclusion.

## 2. From Premodern to Modern Philosophy

Philosophy originated with the question about the right way to live. But in order to answer this question satisfactorily philosophers broke into the world of theory to discover a standard that was not just a matter of convention or *nomos*. Socratic or Platonic philosophy's heuristic name for this transconventional and hence transcultural standard was nature or *physis*. But to know any part of nature led eventually to wondering whether the whole of reality is ultimately intelligible, and so in the premodern West the question about the whole came to be traditionally asked and answered in the form of a philosophy of being.

The moral and scientific reorientation that occurred in the West in the wake of Machiavelli, Galileo, and Newton during the 16th and 17th centuries spelled the end of the philosophy of being (or of ontology or metaphysics as it had come to be called) as the first task of philosophy.

When philosophy existed under Islamic, Jewish, and Christian auspices the question about the right way to live had been more or less taken for granted and rather isolated from the question about being as pursued in the Schools. Due to the Machiavellian revolution, that eminently practical question began to be asked and answered in a new way, in that all the premodern answers of the Great Tradition were considered to fall outside the scope of "effectual truth," and so both they and the questions that gave rise to them were relegated to the strictly private sphere of existence.

Due to the scientific revolution, the question about being as the first issue in philosophy had to yield to the question about knowing, the epistemological question. Modern physics in the style of Galileo and Newton not only did not depend for its intelligibility upon one's first understanding and agreeing about prior metaphysical terms and relations; but such physics also generated a consensus in the university faculties of natural philosophy that stood out in stark and scandalous contrast to the array of disputed questions that dominated the diverse schools of philosophy of being. The endless disputed questions in metaphysics with no commonly agreed upon basis for their eventual resolution naturally raised the question about the cognitive status of the Scholastic theses about being *qua* being; and this in turn raised the criteriological question of how we know we know being at all.

But the writings of the great early modern philosophic propagandists for the illuminating and progressive promise of the new science—Bacon, Descartes, Hobbes, Locke, Hume, the philosophes, and Kant—were Machiavellians. In their opposition to religion or Christianity as what Hobbes called "the kingdom of darkness," they associated, or better perhaps, coopted the scientific revolution not only into the project of opposing both the *idola* (Bacon) and the "vain imaginings" (Hobbes) of religious dogmas and the verbalisms of Scholastic philosophy; but they also manufactured positivist, empiricist, and rationalist cover stories for the normative achievements of the new science. By means of these cover stories, a scientific myth of rigor and proof was subordinated to purposes of technical prediction and control, so that modern science was recruited into the modern project: science "in the relief of man's estate" (Bacon) and science as the instrument for making human beings "the masters and possessors of nature" (Descartes). Henceforth, technical, productive ends were to supercede the properly theoretic goal of contemplating the truth for its own sake.

## 2.1  Two Phases in the Modern Turn to the Subject as Object

### 2.11  Early Modern Enlightenment's Truncation of the Subject

*2.111  The primacy of the epistemological question.*  Already in the late Scholastic period the scientific goal of true or even convenient (in the technical sense of Aquinas's *rationes convenientiae*) understanding had been replaced within a conceptualist or nominalist horizon by a concern for certainty both in theology and in philosophy. Such an overweening concern for certitude coupled with a neglect of understanding led inevitably to skepticism. But when such skepticism got joined to an orientation that screens out all but what a Machiavelli would admit as effectual truth, we have the ingredients for a quest in which the search for certitude could be generalized into a search for "sure and firm foundations" in the manner of Descartes. This then is the context for the modern "turn to the subject." In the

Cartesian preoccupation with certainty, however, this turn actually attained only the subject as object. But why?

In order to understand the modern turn to the subject, we must grasp what is most crucially distinctive about modern in contrast to premodern reflection on human being. It is not that premodern philosophers had not distinguished clearly the human from all other species of being, for they were admirable in the way they specified the qualities proper to vegetative, animal, and human substances. When, for instance, Aristotle in *On the Soul* discriminates the human soul from that of other animals, the clear and precise determination is made in terms of examples related to the specific kinds of efficient causality undergone by the different kinds of souls and to the various sorts of final causality energizing them. But in making the relevant distinctions plain in terms of efficient and final causality, Aristotle does not speak about consciousness in its dynamisms and structures explicitly. Why not? Because premodern psychology is a subset of a philosophy of being, and in that framework it was sufficient for different ranges of objects to be correlated through their respective acts with types of potencies and souls. The different types of correlative qualities are accidents inhering in corresponding kinds of substances.

In contrast, the modern turn to the subject reflects upon human being from the standpoint not of substance, but of consciousness. When John Locke inveighs against the Aristotelian doctrine of faculties or "powers," he is making the point that we do not have direct experience of faculties; and it is true that the ancients were content to deduce the presence of the faculty from observations made about the relationships between objects and the intentional acts by which they are "known" sensitively or intellectually. If we prescind from Locke's nominalism, it becomes clear that Locke is interested not in the metaphysical paraphernalia of substantial forms or souls with their relevant faculties or accidents, but in consciousness and what we can be conscious of.

Now it is one thing to require advertence to consciousness and its objects; but it is quite another to understand and conceive of them correctly. In what follows, I argue that modern thinkers tended to misconceive consciousness, which is the range of awareness, with a type of operation that, while it is conscious, is not synonymous with consciousness as a whole, but only a part of its structure and operation: perception. By perception, I mean the act of explicit awareness, or of express advertence to...whatever it may be. Consciousness, however, as an internal self-presence (or awareness) has to itself not only a dimension of explicit, foreground awareness, but a tacit or background dimension—namely, the most radical presence of ourselves to ourselves—that can never be made explicit exhaustively.

*2.112 Consciousness as perception.* As exemplified by the *cogito*, the Cartesian variant of the modern turn to the subject conceived of consciousness itself as a perception. And this usage became fateful for modern par-

lance inasmuch as we are liable to say today that we are conscious of something if we perceive it expressly. Accordingly, when someone says they did
something—say, started to exceed the speed limit while driving—"unconsciously," they do not mean that they were mysteriously knocked out cold as
they were driving down the highway, but that they did not explicitly perceive or advert to the fact that they were driving above the speed limit. So
Descartes doubles back upon himself and perceives that he is doubt-
ing/thinking so as to be able to infer that he must exist if he is doubt-
ing/thinking; but this doubling back is thought to be an inner perception on
the part of the *res cogitans.* Just as through our external senses we perceive
external objects, so too through inward perception we become aware of the
subject as the primary object of our egos. By definition, consciousness as
perception objectifies what it is aware of.

   For Descartes, therefore, inner perception is conceived by analogy
with taking a look with our eyes at something outside ourselves, and so
consciousness is held—quite inconsistently, however—to be a faculty of inward perception. This Cartesian model of consciousness is pretty much
shared by Hobbes, Locke, Hume, and modernity in general. But while Kant
shares it too, he does not completely agree with it. He wishes to use the
perception-model much more strictly and consistently than his predecessors.
According to Kant, in order for anything to be an object of knowledge at all,
it must first be an object of *sense* perception. Since there can be no sense
perception of consciousness and its acts, they cannot be known in the
strict sense of objective knowledge, but only deduced, or better, postulated as conditions of the possibility of the cognitional activity. So it
is odd that Kant ultimately also maintains the model of consciousness
as perception even though he denies that we are vouchsafed any objective knowledge of it.

*2.113  From soul to truncated self.* In the context of the modern project, the
premodern notion of the soul as the form of the living body, endowing it
with natural and inevitable inclinations that point beyond the person toward
a hierarchy of ends or goods, is simply eliminated. In its place is installed
the subject as object, which is imagined to be a unitary ego capable of de-
ploying disengaged reason's rigor and proof as a means of carrying out the
project of mastery and control of human and subhuman nature.

   This truncated model of the self is dominated by the crucial and highly
questionable idea of consciousness conceived of as an internal, reflexive
perception that leads ineluctably to the modern image of the subject as primary object, whether in the form of Descartes' disengaged reason, or of
Locke's punctual individual subject. In any case, reason becomes simply a
calculating faculty in the service of the passions, but especially of the lower
desires for self-preservation and material prosperity. Thus, if the modern
subject is not the scared subject operating in fear of violent death, as in
Hobbes, it is the Lockean bourgeois subject, laboring to turn nature into his

or her property to be exchanged and accumulated to the greatest degree possible. The modern self on this model is nothing if not commercial and so is dedicated to utilitarian individualism, to use a term brought into vogue by the authors of *The Habits of the Heart* (Bellah, Madsen, Sullivan, Swidler, & Tipton, 1985).

This modern bourgeois subject is also truncated in still further senses: First, it is an individual, an atomic entity, related to nothing and no one except by voluntary choice or contract. Second, the bourgeois subject is sealed off from the sphere of the supernatural, which characteristically comes to be called "supranatural," suggesting the image of some superfluously juxtaposed upper storey of creation. Thus the bourgeois subject becomes the self-made man or woman who worships his or her maker.

## 2.12 Modern Romanticism's Immanentization of the Subject

*2.121 Romantic critique of the bourgeois subject.* The life of the bourgeois individual is incredibly flat. The moderation Montesquieu believed to go hand-in-hand with the spirit of commerce does quell fanaticism and channel enthusiasm, but at the cost of the spirit's deepest longings. This was the message of Rousseau's great critique of the bourgeois, the first great assessment of the damaged existence of people socialized into believing in Hobbes's tenet that a person's worth is identical with his or her price. People in bourgeois society have lost their healthy, spontaneous self-love, which is gentle and compassionate, and exchanged it for self-esteem, which is a feeling derived from others, and so a dependent, reactive emotion. As a result we are radically alienated from ourselves, in that what would have been our own spontaneous and natural feelings now are never innocent but instead always spoiled, having been generated by a competitive and jealous regard for the opinion of others.

*2.122 Consciousness as perception-feeling.* Rousseau therefore replaces the truncated subject whose consciousness is conceived as inward, reflexive perception on the model of sense perception with the immanentist subject, whose consciousness is also perception-like, except that the privileged model now is not the look but the *feeling*, in contrast to the operations of disengaged observation or reasoning. The Cartesian subject perceives itself as an already-in-here-object that perceives objects already-out-there-now. But the Rousseauian and Romantic subject not only feels, but feels its feelings, which is what is meant by "sentiment." For Rousseau and the Romantics, the truncated bourgeois subject is busy about objects all the time and so is shallow, distracted from his or her own depths. The Romantic subject is deep, because it likes to feel its own feelings, which are inexhaustibly deep. These feelings are the voice of conscience, the *élan* of nature as surfacing within the self and perhaps holding the key to external nature, whose secrets are withheld from the prying gaze of the manipulative bourgeois subjects living supposedly "full and productive lives."

*2.123 Romantic expressivism.* The inner feelings of the Romantic subject are so deep that they can only be discovered by expressing them through *imagination.* If for the likes of Descartes, Hobbes, and Spinoza imagination always has a negative valence, the valence is altogether reversed in the context of the Romantic expressivist's need to formulate feelings in symbols, myths, works of art, and religious rituals. Imaginative expression has the twofold function of articulating the depths of feeling and of shaping those depths: Through the imagination, we endlessly explore the depths of feeling at the same time as we constitute the quality of the feelings we encounter in those depths.

From this perspective, the difference between morality and aesthetics dissolves in favor of the latter. The view of art as mimesis is eclipsed, too. *Creativity* and *originality* become the passwords. Both art and morality are seen to be a matter of sheer self-expression in which the key is to see if each one can express originally the unique depths of his or her own particular self, as is evident in Schiller's *Letters on the Aesthetic Education of Man.* The expressivist idea of self-formation in an aesthetics of production gets transmitted further by the Romantics, Schelling, Hegel, and Marx. Again, the moments of creativity and originality become central to the ideal of the well-rounded self-realizing individual in the philosophies of Herder, von Humboldt, and John Stuart Mill that have exercised such a great influence upon German, English, and American educational systems.

In contrast to the bourgeois ideal of the autonomous, self-determining individual who realizes him- or herself ideally as a bourgeois entrepreneur, producer, and consumer, Romantic subjectivism idealizes the untrammelled self of the Romantic subject who realizes him- or herself by *The Habits of the Heart*'s expressive individualism.

## 3. Postmodern Critique of the Modern Turn to the Subject

### 3.1 Postmodernism in Philosophy: Nietzsche and Heidegger

In philosophy—and more belatedly in theology—the central figure is now acknowledged to be Nietzsche because of his audacious and provocative sounding of what Voegelin has analyzed as "the magic of the extreme" (Voegelin, 1990a, pp. 315-375). He thus became paradigmatic for the crisis of modernity in the sense of making manifest and partially generating a peculiarly postmodern maelstrom of thought and feeling, thus initiating the third wave of modernity (to adopt Leo Strauss's phrase, 1975, pp. 81-98).

Nietzsche first became well known as a thinker not because he was thought to be a great philosopher, but because he was in some fashion an inspirer of Hitler's National Socialism. Respect for Nietzsche as a philosopher grew once Heidegger confronted Nietzsche's thought for a 10-year period during the 1930s and early 1940s, at a time when the most grotesque regime of world history was mounting its technologically based bid for world dominion. Heidegger (1961/1979-1987) interpreted Nietzsche's attempt artistically or artificially to overcome nihilism and *ressentiment* in terms of the unified conception of the will to power and the eternal return of the same as the end of metaphysics. In his (to Heidegger's mind) failed attempts to overcome the specifically modern results of Platonism, Nietzsche was still a model for his own quest to get over the forgetfulness of being. Heidegger learned from Nietzsche that the kinds of phenomenology, hermeneutics, and transcendental philosophy still ingredient in such a work as *Being and Time* (1927/1962) were still too deeply infected by modern assumptions of Cartesian and Kantian "subjective objectivism." And so Heidegger underwent the *Kehre* or "turning."

We might say then that although Nietzsche is the turning point into postmodernism in philosophy, Heidegger has been the catalyst of the transition to postmodernity in the 20th century. Heidegger not only exerted enormous influence, but the gradual working out of his philosophy also involved negotiating several crucial issues at stake in postmodernity. On the one hand, he came out of a Christian, Roman Catholic milieu, so that even if he eventually became a non-believer and an atheist, he never stopped being religious and was constantly preoccupied with mystery. On the other hand, his task was to overcome three quite significant forms of modern philosophy in which he had been trained: conceptualist-Suarezian Scholasticism, neo-Kantianism in both its Marburg and Southwest German versions, and Husserlian phenomenology of perception with its Cartesian and Kantian assumptions.

Before his 10-year long encounter with Nietzsche, Kierkegaard's existentialism influenced Heidegger as much as Nietzsche, alongside the interaction between Husserl's transcendental phenomenology and Dilthey's attempts to uncover the epistemological grounding for the historical and hermeneutical sciences. In spite of his portrait of Nietzsche as the "last metaphysician," Heidegger seems to have learned from him in the late 1930s and early 1940s the utter futility of grounding human horizons in any way that is not rooted in freedom as arbitrary. By this insight, Heidegger paved the way for later postmodern interpreters of Nietzsche—notably Derrida and Foucault—to discern in a way not thematized by Heidegger himself how dominant already were the respective "moves" of deconstructivism and genealogy in the fragmentary and aphoristic styles of Nietzsche's philosophizing.

The effective history of Heidegger's thought marks a divide within postmodern thought: The reception of Heidegger by Gadamer's hermeneutic phenomenology occurs under the sign of Dilthey and Kierkegaard; and the deconstructive-genealogical alternative to this reception on the part of Derrida, Foucault, Lyotard, Deleuze, and the like operates much more under the sign of Nietzsche (see Michelfelder & Palmer, 1989).

In reacting to the truncated, immanentist, and alienated opinions, institutions, and personalities that dominate the culture of our advanced-industrial bourgeois age, both the deconstructive-genealogical approach and the universal hermeneutic approach share the common trait of working with texts in ways that tend to favor a hermeneutics of suspicion, on the one hand, and a hermeneutics of retrieval, on the other.

## 3.2 Hermeneutic Phenomenology's Postmodern Correction of Modern Counterpositions

*3.21 Critique of sheer immediacy.* The truncation and immanentism of the modern problematic of the subject (as centered on the model of pure sense perception or of perception as feeling) involve a number of assumptions about the human subject that all the postmodern philosophers found to be untenable in the light of experience as it is concretely accessible to us.

First, the following Enlightenment (i.e., Cartesian or Kantian) presuppositions were called into question: (1) the primacy of the so-called subject/object split; (2) the putative objectivity to be attained through bridging this split by means of pure perception alone; (3) the very fact of pure perception as isolated from any mediations whatsoever; (4) the object as "already-out-there-now"; (5) the subject as the privileged "already-in-here-now" object; (6) the primacy of time as a raceway of instants (i.e. of physical or perhaps Laplacean time as opposed to psychological time) and a correlative image of the present as a punctual, isolatable, yet spatialized instant. For example, Heidegger—a veritable fountainhead of postmodern thought—called into question all these assumptions in terms of the horizon of *Vorhandenheit.* Or again, together they pretty much encapsulate what Derrida has critically labelled phono-/logo-/phallo-centrism. These assumptions and their ramifications in the construction of our world are to be dismantled or deconstructed in the interests of a certain ethical integrity.

As is clear from Husserl's famous exploration of the *Lebenswelt,* Scheler's phenomenological research, the gestalt psychologists Koehler, Strauss, Wertheimer, et al., and American pragmatists like Royce and Peirce, pure perception by the senses is a limit-phenomenon almost never verifiable in human experience once the human subject learns its mother tongue. In the same vein, Heidegger's thematization of the fact that the human phenomenon of perception—even sense perception—is mediated by language, brought about the transition from the phenomenology of perception to hermeneutic phenomenology.

As a language-animal, the human being exists only rarely in the world of immediacy. Instead, human beings inhabit worlds mediated by meaning and value. That is, concretely, we experience our world as worded: Our world is always foregrounded for us through interpretations. As a result, in almost all human lived experience, our self-understanding is mediated by the self-understandings of others. In this manner we participate in something moving in and through us that, however conscious of it we may be, can never be adequately explicitated, thematized, and explained. Hence, from the standpoint of linguistic (or hermeneutic) philosophy, to be human is to share in a conversation that constitutes the human race as a whole. This conversation that we are (Hölderlin's *das Gespräch wir sind*) is irreducible to the perspective or the explicit knowledge of any single human person.

*3.22  Human experience as mediated.*  In *Truth and Method* Gadamer speaks strangely of "an experience that...[is] being" (1960/1990, p. 100). The remote context of this expression is Kierkegaard's critique of the aesthetic stage of existence and Husserl's critique of any form of psychologism. Both of these play a role in Gadamer's own critique of the central concept of Dilthey's Romantic hermeneutics—*Erlebnis*. (Note that English uses the one term "experience" to render the two German words *"Erlebnis"* and *"Erfahrung."*) Aesthetic existence for Kierkegaard, psychologism, and the theories of *Erlebnis* are rooted in what I have been calling Romantic expressionism: a model of existence in pure immediacy epitomized by the idea of pure perception, but enacted as a feeling supposedly removed from what Gadamer calls "the hermeneutic continuity of human existence," "that continuity of self-understanding that alone can support human existence" (p. 96).

Consequently, Gadamer's phrase "experience as being" does not mean the subjectivization of being. Gadamer uses the German word *Erfahrung* to distinguish it from the Romantic term *Erlebnis*, which always implies a punctual discontinuity of experiences. In contrast, "experience (*Erfahrung*) as being" refers to "an encounter with an unfinished event and is itself a part of this event" (p. 99). It has to do with self-understanding as "occur[ring] through understanding something other than the self, and includ[ing] the unity and integrity of the other" (p. 97). "Experience as being" happens whenever we understand ourselves in and through something other than ourselves, and in doing so we "sublate the discontinuity and atomism of isolated experiences in the continuity of our own existence" (p. 97).

For Gadamer then, "experience as being" occurs as mediation—of past and present, of self and other, of whole and part. It is enacted as *Verstehen*, as interpretation, as question and answer, as decision and self-correction. In all its compactness and undifferentiatedness, it is never merely a matter of the pure perception or feeling of internal immediacy (the "already-in-here-now" of the self) or of external immediacy (the "already-out-there-now" of objects).

*3.3  Historicity of Human Experience*

When Gadamer elaborates the structure of experience, he appeals critically to Bacon to bring out that human experience in general does have an internal reference to the negative: It wants to be confirmed and is, unless it encounters a contradictory instance. But essential to experience as human is precisely this openness for the negative, the new, the surprising.

Gadamer goes on to explicate human experience by setting it in the context of Aristotle's account of inference (*epagoge*), with its marvelous metaphor of the stand by an army in rout. Here he wants to stress a universality of experience in contrast to the universality of science or *logos*, an insight into what is common among diverse experiences but one that, while it becomes the basis of scientific generalization, is itself not yet capable of such reflexive control of meaning.

Then Gadamer invokes Hegel's dialectical account of human experience to bring out that, as a mediation of self-understanding with what is other, experience involves a reversal: In the moment of having one's anticipation of meaning or intelligibility corrected by a new experience, one finds that the elimination of past misunderstanding is actually a deepening or validation of what one thought one had already appreciated before. Yet for Gadamer, Hegel, thinking that "conscious experience should lead to a self-knowledge that no longer has anything other than or alien to itself" (p. 355), failed to follow through on his own insight. He opted for the epitome of Cartesianly disengaged reason—absolute self-consciousness—rather than for what Gadamer names the hermeneutic consciousness that is actually available to us. Hermeneutic consciousness acknowledges that "the dialectic of experience has its proper fulfillment not in definitive knowledge, but in openness to experience that is made possible by experience itself." As coming to terms with human finitude, hermeneutic consciousness realizes that "the truth of experience always implies an orientation toward new experience," because "the nature of experience is conceived in terms of something that surpasses it."

Gadamer then turns to Aeschylus. The great tragedian's adoption of the famous formula *pathei mathos* ("learning through suffering") does not just teach the truism that "we become wise through suffering and that our knowledge of things must first be corrected through deception and undeception" (p. 356), but also, says Gadamer, expresses "insight into the limitations of humanity, into the absoluteness of the barrier that separates man from the divine" (p. 357).

For Gadamer, the correct understanding that "real experience is that whereby human beings become aware of their finiteness" is epitomized by what he calls the hermeneutical experience of the Thou (p. 357).

Anyone who listens is fundamentally open. Without such openness to one another, there is no genuine human bond. When two people understand each other, this does not mean that one person "understands" the other. Similarly, "to hear and obey someone" (*auf jemanden hören*) does not mean simply that we do blindly what the other desires. We call such a person slavish (*hörig*). Openness to the other, then, involves recognizing that I myself must accept some things that are against me, even though no one else forces me to do so (p. 361).

The key moment of experience of the Thou is the capacity not to over-look her claim but to let her really say something to us.

If this attitude of properly hermeneutical consciousness is generalized to include the totality of human historical existence, we have what Gadamer calls *wirkungsgeschichtliches Bewusstsein*, historically effected and effective consciousness. In order to clarify what such a generalization of the herme-neutic experience of the Thou involves, Gadamer presents an analysis of Platonic dialectic and a correction of Collingwood's "logic of question and answer" in order to thematize the hallmark of realized experience or experi-ence as being: the hermeneutic priority of the question (pp. 362-379).

Gadamer has often spoken candidly about the vagueness and modesty of his philosophical hermeneutics. For instance, when Heidegger, after his decade-long confrontation with Nietzsche, eschewed completely the vestiges of transcendental philosophy in his own approach to the question about Be-ing, he seems to have implied that transcendental phenomenology cannot be extricated from the Cartesian and Kantian presuppositions discussed and criticized above. Now while Gadamer thinks of himself as faithful to the most radical insights of Heidegger, he still associates himself with the tran-scendental phenomenological approach of *Being and Time*, even going so far as to coin the Kantian-sounding technical term "historically effective consciousness." While he concedes that Heidegger himself objected to this, Gadamer has remained convinced of the correctness of his position, and yet he has never satisfactorily explained how one could hold on to Heidegger's most radical insights and simultaneously continue to adopt the transcenden-tal viewpoint and to use the language of consciousness. In light of the con-trast to the deconstructive and genealogical postmodernists' complete accep-tance of Marx's, Freud's, and Nietzsche's critique of consciousness, one cannot but wonder whether Gadamer may not simply have been content to be incoherent.

But as we shall see below, Gadamer was incapable of thematizing with full accuracy the idea of consciousness as experience over against the mis-taken idea of consciousness as perception. In the context of the latter the-matization, transcendental reflection does not have to imply an illusory es-cape from human finitude by departing from the realm of the pheno-menologically ostensible or the empirically verifiable. This becomes clear in Lonergan's understanding of transcendental philosophy as a generalized empirical method that verifies its discoveries in the data of consciousness made available by performance. Indeed, Lonergan makes good the post-modern decentering of the subject from its modern status as the lord and master of the universe; and he redeems the implications of this decentering in a philosophy and theology of radical human displacement into a divine conversation. In comparing Lonergan's explication with Gadamer's hermeneutical correction of modern counterpositions we get a different appreciation of Abby Warburg's famous saying: "The love of God lies in the details!"

## 4. Lonergan's Postmodern Thematization of Consciousness as Experience

### 4.1 The Being of Consciousness

The comprehensiveness of Gadamer's adumbration of hermeneutic experience recalls what Lonergan says in the context of reviewing Coreth's *Metaphysik*:

> We should learn that questioning not only is about being but is being, being in its *Gelichtetheit* (luminousness), being in its openness to being, being that is realizing itself through inquiry to knowing that, through knowing, it may come to loving. (1967/1988, p. 192)

No wonder that Gadamer's notion of experience as being corresponds remarkably to Lonergan's description of "being oneself as being" (1967/1988, p. 229) since for him, too, being is not abstract but concrete. As he often said:

> It is not the universal concept "not nothing" of Scotus and Hegel, but the concrete goal intended in all inquiry and reflection. It is substance and subject: our opaque being that rises to consciousness and our conscious being... (p. 229)

In elaborating on the aspect of being oneself as conscious being Lonergan explains that it

> is not an object, not part of the spectacle we contemplate, but the presence to himself of the spectator, the contemplator. It is not an object of introspection, but the prior presence that makes introspection possible. (p. 229)

Hence, Lonergan disagrees with the Cartesian notion of the subject or *res cogitans* as the primary object.

You will recall that for Descartes consciousness as a power of inner, reflexive perception can be known by means of a doubling back of inward, reflexive perception upon itself; and that Kant links the objectivity of knowledge indissolubly to external perception that cannot reach an internal power. Instead, for Lonergan, "[conscious being] is conscious, but that does not mean that properly it is known; it will be known only if we introspect, understand, reflect, and judge" (p. 229). At a stroke Lonergan thereby rejects, on the one hand, the Cartesian notion of consciousness either as identical with or as knowable only by an inner, reflexive perception; while, on the other, he disagrees with Kant's position that consciousness cannot be objectively known.

Lonergan discovered that conscious being can be known by a heightening of consciousness comparable to that which occurs in "high" therapies in which people come to experience, identify, and name their emotions and feelings.

> It is one thing to feel blue and another to advert to the fact that you are feeling blue. It is one thing to be in love and another to discover that what has happened to you is that you have fallen in love. Being oneself is prior to knowing oneself. St. Ignatius said that love shows itself more in deeds than in words; but being in love is neither deeds nor words; it is the prior conscious reality that words and, more securely, deeds reveal. (p. 229)

First, note that feeling, the "prior conscious reality," about which Lonergan is speaking here, is pure experience in the sense that as an internal experience it is a mode of consciousness as distinct from self-knowledge. In other words, consciousness itself is prior to and distinct from any later process in which we heighten our awareness through inquiring about and understanding, through checking out and judging what we undergo in experiencing feelings.

We can grasp the significance of this distinction in the following passage about passing from feelings as conscious experience to feelings as integrated into self-knowledge:

> Feelings simply as felt pertain to an infrastructure. But as merely felt, so far from being integrated into an equable flow of consciousness, they may become a source of disturbance, upset, inner turmoil. Then a cure or part of a cure would seem to be had from the client-centered therapist who provides the patient with an ambiance in which he is at ease, can permit feelings to emerge without being engulfed by them, come to distinguish them from other inner events, differentiate among them, add recognition, bestow names, gradually manage to encapsulate within a superstructure of knowledge and language, of assurance and confidence, what had been an occasion for disorientation, dismay, disorganization. (1985, p. 58)

Secondly, however, we can be correct in calling the "feelings as felt" knowledge in an improper sense precisely because they are conscious before being focused upon, explicitated, and thematized. But it is important to specify this as performative knowledge or, as I have said, knowledge in an improper sense of the word. Nevertheless, it is knowledge of the subject as subject, not as object—a kind of knowledge to which neither Descartes nor Kant could do justice, because in one way or another, they each identified consciousness with perception. This performative or improper sort of knowing is knowledge under the formal aspect of "the experienced," as Lonergan phrased it, and not under the formal aspect of being, of intelligible form, or of the true. The latter—knowledge in the proper sense of the term—would require our adding a superstructure through introspection, through inquiry and understanding and articulation, as well as through reflection and judgment (Lonergan, 1967/1988, pp. 166-168).

If, in contrast to this account, one conceives of consciousness exclusively on the model of perception, then one will be unable adequately to come to terms either with consciousness as external experience in sensation (as distinct from perception[1]), or with consciousness as internal experience in consciousness's own modes and operations.[2] From the postmodern as opposed to the modern perspective, consciousness means "an internal experience in the strict sense of the self and its acts" (1967/1988, p. 172).

Let me stress two more points about this postmodern understanding of consciousness. First, consciousness defined as internal experience is more primitive and more originative than standard modern conceptions of consciousness would have it, rooted as they are in Cartesian or Kantian epistemologies of the subject. It is empirically accessible or phenomenologically ostensible. And yet because it is so primitive, our original access to it is not what Habermas has called "the objectifying attitude in which the knowing subject regards itself as it would entities in the external world" (1985/1987a, p. 296). As Lonergan insists, "one must begin from the performance if one is to have the experience necessary for understanding what the performance is" (1967/1988, p. 174) Thus, one begins from "a performative attitude," in Habermas's phrase.

The second point is that properly to know consciousness as internal experience is to know something that is contingently constitutive of the being of the subject, on the one hand. But inasmuch as it involves using our ordinary language to inquire, grasp, and formulate and then to check out and judge whether articulations of possibly relevant relationships are contingently verifiable in the experiences themselves, such self-knowledge has the quality of what Habermas, borrowing from Piaget, calls reconstruction. That is to say, in the postmodern understanding of consciousness as experience, "reconstructive and empirical assumptions can be brought together in one and the same theory" (Habermas, 1985/1987a, p. 298).

## 4.2 Lonergan on the Passionateness of Being and Human Consciousness

*4.21 Decentering of the subject within vertical finality.* We can overhear many overtones of Gadamer's idea of experience in Lonergan's further elaboration of "being oneself as being":

> That prior opaque and luminous being is not static, fixed, determinate, once-for-all; it is precarious; and its being precarious is the possibility not only of a fall, but also of fuller development. That development is open; the dynamism constitutive of our consciousness may be expressed in the imperatives:

---

[1] Sensation is the same as Aristotle's *aisthesis* or actuation of the sense potencies: of sight by visible objects, of hearing by sound, of touch by something felt, of taste by something flavored, and of smell by something that has an odor. Note that in contrast to perception, sensation can be utterly tacit or background for our focal awareness, like peripheral vision, for instance.

[2] Note that this internal experience is that tacit, implicit, or background presence of ourselves to ourselves concomitant with any conscious acts that is the radical meaning of "consciousness" and "conscious."

Be Intelligent, Be Reasonable, Be Responsible; and the imperatives are unrestricted—they regard every inquiry, every judgment, every decision and choice. (1967/1988, pp. 229-230)

If Lonergan does not go to the postmodern extreme and, with Foucault, proclaim the "death of the subject," still his postmodern conception of the conscious subject does entail a radical dismantling of the modern subject conceived in Cartesian or Kantian terms and a radical decentering of the conscious subject correctly conceived. For if the dynamism constitutive of consciousness is actuated in fulfilling those imperatives—Be Attentive, Be Intelligent, Be Reasonable, Be Responsible—then our consciousnesses realize themselves in self-transcendence. For Lonergan, self-transcendence means just what it says. Moreover, the framework of self-transcendence in this universe gives an even more radically decentering or eccentric twist to the conscious subject, because the concrete evolution of "that prior opaque and luminous being" is swept up, in Lonergan's account, into a vertical finality that is at once possible, multivalent, obscure, and indeed mysterious (on vertical finality, see 1967/1988, pp. 19-23; 1985, pp. 23-34, esp. p. 24).

> Such vertical finality is another name for self-transcendence. By experience, we attend to the other; by understanding, we gradually construct our world; by judgment, we discern its independence of ourselves; by deliberate and responsible freedom, we move beyond merely self-regarding norms and make ourselves moral beings.
>
> The disinterestedness of morality is fully compatible with the passionateness of being. For that passionateness has a dimension of its own: It underpins and accompanies and reaches beyond the subject as experientially, intelligently, rationally, morally conscious. (Lonergan, 1985, p. 29)

So we can see that the crucial upshot of a correct analysis of consciousness as experience leads us to the realization that there is nothing in our consciousnesses that has not been, in a precise sense, given to us, including consciousness itself.

*4.22 Consciousness as conditioned by the passionateness of being.* Human consciousness is conditioned overwhelmingly from below and from above by the gift of the passionateness of being that underpins, accompanies, and reaches beyond the conscious subject. For philosophy and theology rightly to acknowledge this passionateness of being and its gift-character is to carry out the delicate and complicated passage from the enlightened self-interest inscribed into the heart of the modern project to the disinterestedness of morality upon which the survival of a humanly livable ecology will depend.

In the passage quoted above, Lonergan goes on to speak of the passionateness of being as underpinning conscious being:

> Its underpinning is the quasi-operator that presides over the transition from the neural to the psychic. It ushers into consciousness not only the demands of unconscious vitality, but also the exigencies of vertical finality. It ob-

trudes deficiency needs. In the self-actualizing subject, it shapes the images that release insight; it recalls evidence that is being overlooked; it may embarrass wakefulness, as it disturbs sleep, with the spectre, the shock, the shame of misdeeds. As it channels into consciousness the feedback of our aberrations and our unfulfilled strivings, so for the Jungians it manifests its archetypes through symbols to preside over the genesis of the ego and to guide the individuation process from the ego to the self. (1985, pp. 29-30)

Then he goes on to describe how the passionateness of being accompanies the subject's conscious and intentional operations:

There it is the mass and momentum of our lives, the color and tone and power of feeling, that fleshes out and gives substance to what otherwise would be no more than a Shakespearian "pale cast of thought." (1985, p. 30)

Finally, he speaks of the passionateness of being as overarching the conscious performance:

There it is the topmost quasi-operator that by intersubjectivity prepares, by solidarity entices, by falling in love establishes us as members of community. Within each individual, vertical finality heads for self-transcendence. In an aggregate of self-transcending individuals, there is the significant coincidental manifold in which can emerge a new creation. Possibility yields to fact, and fact bears witness to its originality and power in the fidelity that makes families, in the loyalty that makes peoples, in the faith that makes religions. (1985, p. 30)

## 5. Deconstructive/Genealogical Postmodernism's Concern for Otherness

### 5.1 Derrida

Under the heading of "logocentrism," Derrida began with criticizing conceptualist and perceptualist counterpositions in Husserl's theory of signs (1967/1973), and went on from there to criticize the entire history of sign theory in the West down to Saussure as both "phonocentric" and wedded to "the determination of the Being of beings as presence" (1967/1976, pp. 11-12; also see 1967/1978). This has to do with two rather closely associated matters, which we can only mention here.

First, if I may oversimplify, because of conceptualist and perceptualist accounts of Aristotle's statement that "spoken words (*ta en te phone*) are the symbols of mental experience (*pathemata tes psyches*) and written words are the symbols of spoken words" (cited in 1967/1976, p. 11), Derrida rejects the possibility of any truthful and positional construal of Aristotle's statement. As long as one is confined, as Husserlian and, it would seem, Heideggerian transcendental phenomenology are, to thinking of consciousness as perception, then it is impossible to verify an empirical meaning of Aristotle's statement that would serve as a way of controlling the seemingly limitless conventionality and metaphoricity of human language. What, then, makes more sense: to submit without reason to the imposed limits of a conceptualist or nominalist univocity of signifiers, or to let oneself in for the more wide-open plurivocity of human metaphors?

Second, Derrida opposes the metaphysics of presence he regards as explicit in Heidegger and implicit in the entire tradition of Western philosophy since Plato. He objects to Heidegger's reliance on "an entire metaphorics of proximity, of simple and immediate presence, a metaphorics associating the proximity of Being with the values of neighboring, shelter, house, service, guard, voice, and listening" (Derrida, 1972/1982, p. 130). Anyone who like Derrida rejects the normativity of the naïve realist's "already-out-there-now" *and* the idealist's "already-in-here-now" without finding out what the position on normativity is will naturally be decentered and disoriented. If one is intelligent enough to realize that extrinsic norms, if extrinsic is all they are, are ultimately fictional and arbitrary, what is one to do? Instead of submitting to the traditional extrinsic norms, why not just make fictiveness and arbitrariness into a virtue, so that decenteredness and disorientedness are no longer signs of being lost, but rather *the* marks of true authenticity?

For as Derrida argues in *Of Grammatology*, Nietzsche revolutionized "the concepts of *interpretation, perspective, evaluation, difference*" (1967/1976, p. 19), by rigorously excluding the "primary" or "fundamental" or "transcendental," "whether understood in the Scholastic, Kantian, or Husserlian sense" (p. 22), or understood as a Heideggerian primordial homeland or absolute proximity (p. 23). In any of those senses, differences are derivative and secondary in relation to identities, because the other is subordinated to the same. Similarly, contingency is always governed by necessity. But when the decadent Scholastic, Kantian, Husserlian, and Heideggerian premises are eliminated, one enters the regime of *différance* in which the reverse is true: Identities are contingent upon the adventitious play of differences; and necessities are displaced by contingencies.

This is of course most evident to Derrida in the case of language, where in accord with its ineradicable conventionality, what is constitutive is not the relation of a word as signifier to its referent as signified, but the positive determination of signs by reason of the differences available in any given system of signs. Pure significance is totally unrelated to anything but the internal system of differences in traces or markings.

As with language, so too with structure in its purity. Under the tutelage of the foundational or the transcendental, structures are centered in terms of some imagined center, origin, or presence outside the structure itself. According to Derrida, this "concept of a centered structure" is "the concept of a play based on a fundamental ground, a play constituted on the basis of a fundamental immobility and a reassuring certitude, which itself is beyond the reach of play" (1967/1978, p. 279). The certainty of a center "beyond the reach of play" fends off anxiety, "for anxiety is invariably the result of a certain mode of being caught by the game, of being as it were at stake in the game from the outset." The key is playfulness and the play of differences. Finally, as for the subject, he or she is simply "an effect of *differance*, an effect inscribed within the system of *differance*" (Derrida, 1972/1981, p. 28).

Derrida makes *differance* or the lack of origin and end or foundation or ground basic because it destabilizes any attempts to close down directions of thought or to homogenize dimensions of specificity or particularity or uniqueness in reality. It melts down distinctions between abnormal and normal, literal and figurative, serious and fictive, since they are all rooted in the contingency of arbitrary will that are forgotten either willfully or not. And so the strategy of deconstruction is one of displacement, intervention, impertinence, explosive laughter, which it shares quite comfortably with the genealogical approach of Foucault.

## 5.2 *Foucault*

Foucault's essay "Nietzsche, Freud, Marx" (1967) points to a narcissistic revolution in hermeneutics wrought by *Genealogy of Morals*, *Interpretation of Dreams*, and *Capital*. According to Foucault each of these works demonstrates that interpretation has no foundation and points to nothing beyond itself but further signs, which are themselves sedimented interpretations. In these works the crucial signs—money for Marx, symptoms for Freud, good and evil for Nietzsche—also have a distantiating, threatening, defamiliarizing role to play. They indicate the subterranean role of dissonance in our lives, whatever the surface sweetness and light.

In a later essay, "Nietzsche, Genealogy, History" (1984, pp. 76-100), Foucault calls into question all history in so far as it looks to an endpoint or operates teleologically, thereby obliterating the contingency of events, the discontinuity involved in emergence and decline or extinction, the conflictual singularity of events (p. 76):

> Genealogy does not resemble the evolution of a species and does not map the destiny of a people. On the contrary, to follow the complex course of descent is to maintain passing events in their proper dispersion; it is to identify the accidents, the minute deviations—or conversely, the complete reversals—the errors, the false appraisals, and the faulty calculations that gave birth to those things that continue to exist and have value for us; it is to discover that truth or being does not lie at the root of what we know and what we are, but the exteriority of accidents. (p. 81)

Nietzsche's (1887/1967, p. 77) affirmation that "whatever exists, having somehow come into being, is again and again reinterpreted to new ends, taken over, transformed, and redirected by some power superior to it" does not mean, Foucault (1984, p. 77) suggests, that in all such revisionist interpretations a "will to power has become master of something less powerful and imposed upon it the character of a function." More significantly, according to Foucault (p. 77), Nietzsche is teaching us to regard "the entire history of 'a thing,' an organ, a custom" as a "continuous sign-chain of ever new interpretations and adaptations whose causes do not even have to be related to one another but, on the contrary, in some cases succeed and alternate with one another in a purely chance fashion."

The general teaching then is that "all concepts in which an entire process is semiotically concentrated elude definition; only that which has no history is definable" (Foucault, 1984, p. 80). But this is closely related to other of Nietzsche's radical assertions, for instance, in *The Gay Science*:

> The total character of the world, however, is in all eternity chaos—in the sense not of a lack of necessity, but of a lack of order, arrangement, form, beauty, wisdom, and whatever other names there are for our aesthetic anthropomorphisms. (1887/1974, p. 168)

And then his famous answer to the query, What is truth? in his 1873 essay, "On Truth and Lie in the Extra-Moral Sense":

> A moving army of metaphors, metonymies, and anthropomorphisms, in short a summa of human relationships that are being poetically and rhetorically sublimated, transposed, and beautified until, after a long and repeated use, a people considers them solid, canonical, and unavoidable. Truths are illusions whose illusionary nature has been forgotten, metaphors that have been used up and lost their imprint and that now operate as mere metal, no longer as coins. (Nietzsche, 1873/1984, pp. 880-881; cited in Behler, 1988/1991, p. 84)[3]

Nevertheless, for Foucault, the emergence, survival, and decline of any discourse is always inextricably joined to one mode of power or another. In his far-reaching research, he sought to show empirically how distinctions in discourse are imposed pragmatically by social institutions. Ruling metaphors or modes of discourse are constantly reconstituted in radically different ways at different times in history. His genealogical method seeks to trace these correlative changes via quite unusual stints of archival work (compare Foucault, 1977; also 1978). Thus, the thrust of Foucault's practice of genealogy was to "incite the experience of discord or discrepancy between the social construction of self, truth, and rationality and that which does not fit neatly within these folds" (Connolly, 1984, p. 368).

## 5.3  Summary of Part 5

The program of deconstruction and genealogical strategies is one of distanciation and defamiliarization as a way of enacting a responsibility for otherness. This postmodern program thus entails championing plurality, difference, changeableness, instability, and lack of hierarchy. All this is based on the Nietzsche-instilled recognition of how much social (technological, eco-

---

[3] Ernst Behler (1988/1991) is one of the most clear and reliable interpreters available of deconstructive and genealogical postmodernism in light of Nietzsche and Heidegger.

nomic, and political) and cultural set-ups are ultimately conventional, and so fallible, precarious, and always revisable. The net effect of all this, of course, can be an extreme relativism and an actual fostering of nihilist tendencies. I have chosen not to emphasize this, however, because leading interpreters like Christopher Norris (1982) on Derrida and James W. Bernauer (1990) on Foucault insist that these philosophers' final intent is ethical. Perhaps we need to place the efforts of deconstructivist-genealogical postmodernism in the context of Lonergan's suggestion in his lectures on the philosophy of education[4] that Marx and Nietzsche expressed a more profound and effectual appreciation of the sinfulness of modern social and cultural structures than their Christian contemporaries had done.

But what is the point of this overriding ethical intent? The brief answer is: concern for the other. But we must understand by this not just—or even mainly—in the sense of other people, but in the more abstract sense of what is otherwise. Thus the heart of the postmodern protest on the part of deconstruction and genealogy is the relationship of contingency to an ultimately unlimited plurality of meanings and values, and therefore to many possible concrete solutions to the problem of human living.

## 6. Lonergan and Contingency

Among Christian theologians, one of the greatest tests for modern theology has been that of coming adequately to terms with what the rationalist German and Jewish philosopher Gotthold Lessing formulated as the "ghastly abyss" between necessity and contingency, especially the accidental character of history both sacred and profane. Perhaps the typical Protestant temptation in reaching a solution has been to lean in the direction of a historicism whose rejection of dogma includes the rejection of the intelligibility of the Word of God as true. In reaction, the typical Catholic temptation has been an ahistorical orthodoxy that cannot take the relativities of history seriously. Neither side is capable of handling contingency in a way that does justice to the actual historicity of Christian meanings and values. As a result, the contemporary climate of opinion in theology is dominated by what Anglican theologian Lesslie Newbegin (1991) has called "agnostic pluralism" and "fundamentalist sectarianism."

This is the place not to expound Lonergan's thought on contingency, but to mention several contexts relevant to deconstructivist and

---

[4] In the summer of 1959 Lonergan directed an Institute on the Philosophy of Education at Xavier University in Cincinnati, Ohio, the transcripts of whose lectures have circulated in the form of a typescript available at all Lonergan Centers. This transcript is scheduled to appear in 1993 under the title *Topics in Education* as volume 10 in the *Collected Works of Bernard Lonergan* being published by University of Toronto Press.

genealogical postmodernism's concerns. In the measure that those concerns are legitimate, how can they be taken seriously without requiring theologians to leap headlong into Lessing's "ghastly abyss" by adopting the so-called New Historicism?

## 6.1 Contingency and the Virtually Unconditioned

We might begin by saying that the deconstructivist and genealogical postmodernism rejects wholesale Aristotle's conception of knowledge in accord with the logical ideal of apodictic truth. For Aristotle, science or *episteme* in the most proper sense is knowledge of things through their necessary causes. "Necessity" here entails a note of absoluteness untainted by any possibility of being otherwise. Accordingly, if the relationships among terms in a strictly scientific definition were to meet the purest requirements of the Aristotelian ideal of *apodeixis*, they would express intelligible connections among things that simply had to be such-and-such a way and couldn't be otherwise. Where the deconstructivist or genealogical postmodernist revels almost to the point of vertigo in the aleatory possibilities of being otherwise, most of the philosophical and theological tradition has identified the fulfillment of (or at least approximation to) Aristotle's logical ideal of knowledge as the only rational alternative to relativism and nihilism.

But as Lonergan has insisted, that logical ideal of knowledge is so exorbitant that it excludes the possibility of empirical science. Indeed, Aristotle's recognition that all of terrestrial reality is penetrated by contingency led him to deny the possibility of a science of earthly causes or of history, since for him science properly so called regards only necessities.

In contrast, Lonergan from his earliest theological publications pointed out how Thomas Aquinas's breakthrough to divine transcendence brought with it a recognition that divine action through infinite understanding was beyond both necessity and contingency.[5] Moreover, because divine revelation is integrally concerned with a concrete world process that is made up of realities that occur contingently and that therefore not only might not have happened but also might have been otherwise, Aquinas proposed as a legitimate goal of theological science the attainment of *rationes convenientiae* that would explain the matter-of-fact intelligibility of merely accidental or contingent matters such as creation, fall, redemption, and revelation. These aspects of Thomist teaching tended, however, to be disregarded by decadent Scholasticism's overweening preoccupation with the certainties and necessi-

---

[5] We are speaking of the so-called "*Gratia Operans* articles," a recasting of Lonergan's doctoral dissertation for the Gregorian University published originally in *Theological Studies* during 1941 and 1942 ("St. Thomas' Thought on *Gratia Operans*," *TS*, *2*, 289-324; *3*, 69-88; 375-402; 533-578) and republished as *Grace and Freedom: Operative Grace in the Thought of St. Thomas Aquinas* (1971).

ties of *Konklusionstheologie*. Can we reject such a theology and its illegiti-
mate preoccupations without falling into relativism?

For Lonergan, the intelligible connections between the scientific terms
that express explanations of accidental or contingent realities have a necessity about them that is not absolute but only hypothetical: If A, then B; but
A, therefore B. The intelligible, if-then link between terms A and B is conditioned: If the conditions for A obtain, then B exists or occurs. For modern empirical science, according to Lonergan, such hypothetical necessity is
the goal of classical scientific method. Thus, classical method reveals as
many instances of "If A, then B" as it can; while statistical method discloses
how often those instances actually happen.[6] Whenever such classical or statistical intelligibilities are verified, Lonergan calls them *virtually* unconditioned (1957/1992, pp. 305-306; 685-686). This is to distinguish the kind of
intelligible reality proper to created nature (which both as a whole and in its
detailed particulars not only did not have to be as it is, and so could have
been otherwise, but also did not have to be at all) from the only intelligible
reality that is absolutely necessary and hence beyond the contingency and
necessity of created nature—God, who is *formally* unconditioned.

Lonergan's highlighting the centrality of contingency for human judgment in terms of the distinction between the formally and the virtually unconditioned does take postmodern concerns seriously. In terms of this distinction, every event, with the exception of the infinite and unconditional act
of understanding love that is God, is conditional and conditioned (Lonergan,
1957/1992, pp. 682, 692-693). Only the formally unconditioned has no conditions whatsoever; the virtually unconditioned has conditions that happen
to be fulfilled, but their fulfillment may or may not happen. Correspond-
ingly, every human judgment itself is an instance of the virtually unconditioned. So our human judgments possess that odd combination of normativity, fallibility, and possible revisability that distinguishes Lonergan's idea of
the absoluteness proper to acts of judgment from both fallibilists' and the
dogmatic naïve realists' ideas (1957/1992, "The Notion of Judgment," pp.
296-303; "Reflective Understanding," pp. 304-340; "The Notion of Objectivity," pp. 399-409).

In contrast, deconstructivists and genealogists use their awareness of
the contingency besetting the remote and the proximate contexts or grounds
for judgment to deny judgment any absoluteness whatsoever. Their different versions of conventionalism lead them to advocate what amounts to agnostic pluralism. They enjoy carrying the day against fundamentalist sec-
tarians, whose style of being concerned for the truth habitually excludes
alternative approaches, overlooks the possible need for any correction and

---

[6] See *Insight: A Study of Human Understanding* (1957/1992), pp. 60-76 on classical
heuristic structures; pp. 76-85 on statistical heuristic structures; pp. 102-107 on
classical and statistical laws; and pp. 130-162 on the complementarity of classical
and statistical investigations.

revision of their judgments, and practically rejects the possibility of honest disagreement. But in the posture of sensitivity to otherness and difference that goes together with agnostic pluralism, radical postmodernists fail to come to terms with the way in which it takes correct judgments adequately (if never exhaustively) to come to terms with the other as other. As Lonergan so eloquently put it:

> [C]ondemnation of objectivity induces, not a merely incidental blindness in one's vision, but a radical undermining of authentic human existence....It is quite true that the subject communicates not by saying what he knows but by showing what he is, and it is no less true that subjects are confronted with themselves more effectively by being confronted with others than by solitary introspection. But such facts by themselves only ground a technique for managing people; and managing people is not treating them as persons. To treat them as persons, one must know and one must invite them to know. A real exclusion of objective knowing, so far from promoting, only destroys personalist values. (1967/1988, pp. 220-221)

## 6.2 Contingency and the Non-Systematic

In relation to the contingency of both knowing and the known, what the deconstructive and genealogical approaches have a keen sense of is the limitations of any claims concerning regularity (or classical intelligibility). They subversively suggest that the closure such classical formulations entail (i.e., defining *omni et soli*) is based in the final analysis not on any correspondence between intelligence and reality, but on an arbitrary decision to privilege one metaphorical expression over others. But they also possess an affinity for Aristotle's insight that (as Lonergan once put it) "events happened contingently because there was no cause to which they could be reduced except prime matter, and prime matter was not a determinate cause" (1971, p. 79). Indeed, Derrida's *differance* seems to function like Aristotle's *hyle* or perhaps Lonergan's "empirical residue" (1957/1992, pp. 50-56), although its function stands outside the context of overall intelligibility.

Admittedly, it is salutary to have a feel for what Lonergan has called "the non-systematic character of material multiplicity, continuity, and frequency" (1957/1992, p. 641). But if this instinct for the non-systematic becomes a basis for overlooking statistical, genetic, and dialectical methods, as well as for just debunking all classical intelligibility, it is not really taking contingency seriously. It is just glorifying the aleatory. Then the other can only be perceived as other in its punctual evanescence. This sort of acknowledgment can be exquisitely witty or filled with pathos, but isn't it also a rejection of intelligence, reasonableness, and responsibility in one's life and a failure to be faithful to the other?

The brilliant sensitivity for disjunctions, slippages, and the discontinuous in general can also be used as an excuse for not properly acknowledging higher viewpoints that emerge inasmuch as the mind comes to terms with discontinuities and leaps in being that are not explicable in terms of the

logical expansion of the lower viewpoints.[7]  In contrast, Lonergan explains
how diverse classical higher viewpoints are related intelligibly, but not logically; and how statistical methods are complementary to classical, as we
gradually come to understand concrete states, trends, groups, and popula-
tions of beings.  If the other happens to be an instance of "systems on the
move," it does no service to reduce the intelligibility proper to genetic
method into simply another case of classical intelligibility, thereby obviating
intelligible accounts of the continuity-in-discontinuity involved in dynamics
of development (Lonergan, 1957/1992, p. 486, pp. 484-507 on genetic
method).  Similarly, extraordinary alertness to the aspects of dissonance,
discord, and discrepancy in our moral lives cannot substitute for a dialectical analysis in Lonergan's sense that would confront the abyss of the absurd
in the universe and yet still be open to being surprised by joy (1957/1992,
pp. 508-511, 707-708 on dialectical method; p. 630 on dialectic as method
in ethics; pp. 654-656 on the dialectical manifold as requiring a higher integration).

### 6.3  Contingency and Understanding

Even prior to judgment, the act of direct understanding is fraught with contingency (1957/1992, pp. 27-56 on the direct act of understanding or insight).  In the movement from potency into act, intelligence is marked by
multiple dependencies.  Most obviously, intelligence depends upon (i.e., is
conditioned by and conditions) sense perception.  How attentive are we?
This is not something that can be taken for granted.  Aside from the biases
causing selective inattention to different areas of possible inquiry, there is
the sheer historicity of the lower manifolds of the sensing subject.  Some
people just see or hear less well than others.  But there is also the conditioning of the psyche, with its feelings and images.  Since insight is into, or
occurs in, data represented through feeling-laden images, it can rightly be
spoken of as "bubbling up" in a person's psyche.  But understanding is also
dependent upon the asking of questions.  What kinds of questions a person is
liable to ask depends on all sorts of internal and external conditions.  Above
all, it is important to acknowledge that all the acts of consciousness except
decision are not human *actions* in the ordinary sense, but operations.  They
occur *to* one in a way that is irreducible to one's own doing.

Therefore, the direct act of understanding or insight, the reflective act
of understanding that checks the evidence, and the responsible act of understanding that follows on questions for deliberation are similarly fraught with
contingency, if not more so (1957/1992, pp. 632-633 on practical insight

---

[7] See Lonergan (1957/1992, pp. 38-39) where arithmetic and algebra are compared
as lower and higher viewpoints; for other instances, chemistry's basic terms and
relations are not just a subset of the basic terms and relations of physics, nor are
biology's deducible from those of chemistry, and so on.

and reflection). And so the Faustian image of Enlightenment reason as masterfully disposing of an instrument is demolished. But we cannot go into this now.

## 6.4 Contingency and Language

As we have seen, the deconstructivist and genealogical postmodernists delight in the possibilities of intervention, interruption, and explosive laughter provided by the conventionality of language. Their brilliance in exploiting what Husserl called *sedimentation*—namely, the possibility of detaching expressions from acts of meaning or from referentiality; and in making capital on Nietzsche's insights into the metaphoricity of linguistic conventions is spellbinding. But it is one thing to exploit these aspects of language by playing with the seemingly endless polyvalence of conventional signs as disclosive of worlds of meaning, and by thinking through the many implications of what Wittgenstein in *Philosophical Investigations* (1958) called language games. It is quite another to take the position that Lyotard speaks of as "Just Gaming" (1979/1985). This involves two things: (1) debunking any link between immanent acts of meaning in direct, reflective, and responsible acts of understanding and their respective terms of expression (Lonergan, 1957/1992, pp. 592-595); and (2) rejecting any possible relevance of reference (Lonergan, 1972, pp. 81-85).

Here it is important to recall that Lonergan's analysis of inner word (1967, pp. 1-11, 151-153, 155) does not deny the role played by language in perception and in imagination leading up to insight (1972, pp.70-73 on linguistic meaning; p. 92 on linguistic process; pp. 88, 97 on linguistic feedback). Nor does he deny the role of available and to-be-invented language when it comes to using one's own understanding of some matter to guide one in articulating and formulating just what it was that one had come to understand, prescinding from all that is irrelevant or adventitious (1972, pp. 88, 97). Nor, again, does he fail to note how, when the realization that our understanding of something is only possibly relevant prompts us to check that hunch or guess or hypothesis out, we set out to verify not simply insights, but insights formulated in language or symbolic formulae of some kind.

Nevertheless, Lonergan refuses to use this full-blown acknowledgment of the role of language in our understanding, verifying, and deliberating to deny the fact that we understand and make limited judgments of fact and value that are achievements of intentional and cognitive and real self-transcendence (on self-transcendence as intentional, cognitive, and real, see 1974a, pp. 166-170). He insists that as intelligent, reasonable, and responsible, we finite human beings use language to get beyond ourselves in knowing reality and in transforming it. This in no way occludes all the ways in which it is also true to say that language uses us perhaps even more than we use it. But by being more attuned to the way the structure and dynamisms of consciousness mutually "horizon" language, we may be more responsible and care-full in our utterances and actions.

## 6.5  Contingency and Interpretation

The deconstructivist-genealogical view, on which we are used by language so that we chiefly become its instrument in the production of endless texts as interpretations and commentaries as texts, leads thinkers like Derrida and Foucault to install mirrors in between all signifiers, signs, and signifieds in the construction of an anti-hermeneutical theory of interpretation. Any attempts to talk about realities are regarded as mistakes at best, or as masks for just talk about talk, or as power moves disguised as persuasion. In other words, the contingencies besetting language usage by way of background cultural conventions and social practices render any subject's putative interpretation the effect of an inscription by some force or forces outside his or her control. Once again, this can give rise to an incredible indeterminacy in the deciphering of codes. The fertility of deconstructive-genealogical post-moderns in coming up with alternative interpretations and alternative plausible contextualizations for what to the less sophisticated scholar might appear a more straightforward matter is truly astonishing. They are maestros of the possibly productive misunderstanding.

With such anti-hermeneutical theories of interpretation, Lonergan would agree, interpretation is not a simple, no-nonsense, intuitive affair.[8] Rather, as he wrote in the context of a controversy with typical Scholastic methods of interpretation:

> Logically, the interpretation of a writer is a matter of formulating an hypothesis, working out its presuppostions and its implications, and verifying in the text the hypothesis itself, and the implications. Deductions of what a writer must have meant are just so much fancy; in reality they are deductions from the hypothesis assumed by the interpreter; and whether that hypothesis is correct *can be determined only with probability*, a probability that increases only with the extent and variety of the verification. (1967/1988, p. 60; emphasis added)

If, in the process of interpretation, the only grounds for certainty about any but the most obvious negative conclusions would be the ability to show that one had considered every possible alternative interpretation and had demonstrated that all but one alternative was incorrect, a great opening would be left, through which the person with a deconstructivist or genealogical bent can march with an often uncanny capacity to conceive of any number of possibly relevant alternative interpretations of a given text. Such

---

[8] For Lonergan on interpretation the basic texts are *Insight* (1957/1992), chapter 17.3 "The Truth of Interpretation," pp. 585-617; and *Method in Theology* (1972), chapter 7 "Interpretation," pp. 153-173; chapter 8 "History," pp. 175-196; chapter 9 "History and Historians," pp. 197-234.

creativity and imaginativeness can be productive. If, as Lonergan too would insist, the "principle of the empty head" is sterile in interpreting, it does follow that interpretation will be enriched by the exploration of many alternatives. But a law of diminishing returns would also seem to go into effect at the point where the probabilities of verifying possibly relevant proposals start to diminish apace; or when such further interpretations really start to become trivial or frivolous. Doesn't the art of interpretation begin at that point to turn into a glass bead game for effete intellectuals?

## 6.6 Contingent Predication

The deconstructivist-genealogical complaint about having an origin and end or a center of the universe is based in part on the obviousness of a contingency about terrestrial events that flies in the face of claims to certainty based upon necessary causes. Since they are incompatible with contingency, such strong necessity and certitude claims would also exclude freedom and the need to risk and dare. Then, too, illusionary necessities and certitudes are employed to frame the so-called "master-" or "meta-narratives" used to legitimate people and forces who would impose disciplines upon us, depriving us of the liberty to be ourselves, to be different, to include others, and so forth (see Lyotard, 1979/1984).

Lonergan's idea of contingent predication is based on the fact that whenever we make assertions about any matter of fact, all that is required for the truthfulness of the predication is that the conditions for the existence or occurrence of its referent be fulfilled, even though they might not have been fulfilled, and even though things might have been otherwise. By analogy, contingent predications are also made about God, whether on the basis of immanently generated judgments or on the basis of judgments based on the assent of faith.[9]

According to the analogy of contingent predication (Lonergan, 1957/1992, pp. 684-691; 1964a, pp. 216-219), the glorious thing about the created order of this universe is the fact that it does not have to exist at all, and does not have to be as it is. That is to say, once we make the breakthrough to an explanatory conception of divine transcendence as utterly beyond necessity and contingency and completely unconditioned by space and time, it is proper to analogically understand and affirm that the infinitely loving, creative power is a mystery of freedom who in knowing, willing, and bringing about the universe that exists is completely free. Note that this statement or predication about God is not necessary but utterly contingent. All that has to have occurred in order for this contingent predication to be

---

[9] See *Insight* (1957/1992, pp. 725-739) on the distinction between knowledge as immanently generated and knowledge as belief; *Method in Theology* (1972, pp. 118-119, 123-124) on the distinction of religious belief from faith.

true is the fulfillment of the conditions for the existence of any finite order of beings, conditioned either intrinsically or extrinsically by space and time.

What we do in the analogy of contingent predication, then, is to let God be a transcendent mystery. This means that God cannot function as a presence strictly comparable to any other presence in space and time, and that God cannot function as a center or fulcrum for managing the lives of people and things, as in what seems to be the poststructuralist reading of Christian narratives. Furthermore, according to the analogy of contingent predication, there is an absolute compatibility between free creation by a divinely transcendent creator and emergent probability as the shape of the concrete, created world order (Lonergan, 1957/1992, p. 688). Moreover, because this creation and this emergently probable (not necessary) world order is constituted by such long times and great numbers of things, no surprise or miracle can be apodictically ruled out a priori.

Such an explanatory conception of creator and creation is in complete harmony with the best and noblest instincts of the deconstructive-genealogical postmodernist, especially in its admission that "there is in this universe a merely empirical residue that is unexplained" (1957/1992, p. 686). Indeed, it grounds precisely the magnificent diversity, strangeness, wonder, and surprise so deeply yet ambiguously appreciated by postmodernity's art and philosophy. In Lonergan's words:

> the empirical residue grounds the manifold of the potential good and, inasmuch as it stands under world order, it possesses the value that accrues to the contingent through the reasonableness of the freedom of a completely wise and good being. (1957/1992, p. 686)

## 6.7 Contingency and Liberty

The freedom about which deconstructivist and genealogical postmoderns are concerned seems to be separate from any finality whatsoever. This notion of freedom is suspiciously like Sir Isaiah Berlin's idea of negative freedom. Negative freedom is "freedom *from*" as opposed to "freedom *to*": "Some portion of human existence must remain independent of social control"; "there ought to exist a certain minimum of personal freedom that must on no account be violated" (1958, pp. 11, 46). This judgment on these postmodernists seems to be born out in Stephen K. White's (1991, esp. pp. 1-30, 55-94) interpretation of Derrida, Foucault, and Lyotard as saying there are two options for human practical engagement: on the one hand, rationalization or total subordination to singularity-squashing master narratives purveyed by rationally purposive, bureaucratic regimes; on the other, countermodes with no rationale or goal except to unmask meta-narratives and rationalization processes.

Where Lonergan agrees with deconstructivist and genealogical postmodernists' ideas about freedom is in understanding freedom as a case of contingency. But for Lonergan it is a "special kind."

It is contingence that arises, not from the empirical residue that grounds materiality and the non-systematic, but is in the order of the spirit, of intelligent grasp, rational reflection, and morally guided will. It has the twofold basis that its object is merely possibility and that its agent is contingent not only in his existence, but also in the extension of his rational consciousness into rational self-consciousness. For it is one and the same act of willing that both decides in favor of the object or against it and that constitutes the subject as deciding reasonably or unreasonably, as succeeding or failing in the extension of rational consciousness into an effectively rational self-consciousness. (1957/1992, p. 642)

For the deconstructivist-genealogical approach, the only models for rational consciousness or rational self-consciousness are either the abstract self-reflection in the mode of Kantian or (via Kohlberg) Habermasian complete internalization and complete universalization of rules; or the modern bourgeois or Romantic model of the self as subjecting itself to a dominant practice or what Lyotard calls a "phrase regime." Both of these models are dominated by the image of the unitary and controlling consciousness of the utilitarian or the expressive individualist discussed in Part 2 above. But they also fail to account for the more concrete and usual dimension of moral practice that long after *Insight* Lonergan spoke of as development from above downwards.[10] While this dimension is perfectly compatible with the model of development from below upwards in which the order is that of experience, understanding, judgment of value, decision, and action, its order is different because it takes into account the role love plays in socialization, acculturation, and education, and hence in the genesis of the person's rational self-consciousness. And it shows how practice, even before it involves extending one's intelligence and rationality into the further phase of moral and existential consciousness, ordinarily has already involved being-in-love within some communal context.[11] Our relationships of love have already been transforming our feelings as intentional responses and thus bringing about all sorts of affective and cognitive effects in us through the examples, images, symbols, stories, and beliefs that spell out for us in a performative fashion the meanings and values that enframe our moral deliberations.

It can, of course, be the case that the stories dominated by utilitarian or expressive individualism specify our horizon of deliberation and discernment as a matter of fact; but those stories as accounts of human practice contradict the way moral action actually unfolds by way of our loves and as mediated by the narratives handed over to us as paradigmatic for living out

---

[10] See, for instance, "Healing and Creating in History," *A Third Collection* (1985, p. 106) on "two quite different kinds" of development: "from below upwards" and "from above downwards." This distinction becomes almost a commonplace for Lonergan in the post-*Method* essays published in *A Third Collection*.

[11] For a pithy statement of this, see Lonergan's *Philosophy of God, and Theology* (1973, pp. 58-59).

our loves. This is true even in cases of alienated dependency and disoriented loving. Even for the disordered self-love of modern individualists, the surd is socially and culturally mediated.

Now the postmodernists want to replace the homogeneous and unified ego with a decentered, detotalized, heterogeneous self, capable of unmasking and resisting controlling narratives that would smother or extinguish the self's capacity ever to be otherwise. This is why, by demonstrating the conventionality and revisability of social and cultural schemes of recurrence, postmodernists are out to deconstruct the oppositions between normal and abnormal that serve to close down certain directions of thought and action in our deliberating upon proposals for action. But in this, as White agrees, they do not even get as far as "a radicalization of John Stuart Mill's *On Liberty*" (1991, p. 29). Never-ending oscillation between debunking conventionally accepted and enforced social practices and the disclosure of ever new and other fictions by which to live is not enough. "The postmodern theorist who models his or her self-understanding *exclusively* on the role of ceaselessly exposing otherness slides all too easily into the position of the ring master of otherness" (White, 1991, p. 32). To put the issue in rather Aristotelian terms, such theorizing as unrelenting hermeneutics of suspicion regarding the imputations of ideals that support our practical judgments does not yet furnish criteria for figuring out the difference between disordered self-love and right-ordered self-love.

Instead of dwelling further on the possible defects and lack of seriousness of the postmodernists, with all the relativist and nihilist implications of their thought, I would like to propose a completely different framework in which to think about the free practice through the direction opened up by them. Let us note to begin with that this direction of postmodernist thought is in remarkable consonance with Aquinas's insight into the liberating character of prudential judgment in the context of the contingency of particular and concrete situations.[12] Because in most practical situations "there are many ways to skin a cat," the more ways that occur to us of accomplishing some good in some situation that is inherently complicated or fraught with conflicts between quite choiceworthy courses of action, the more likely are we to hit upon the suitable course of action. By the same token, when we do at last hit the nail on the head, we feel a great weight lifted from our shoulders, and it is a glad relief.

Next, this direction of thought is also rather in the spirit of Lonergan's reflections regarding the practicality of the people on the spot for whom the

---

[12] For a more complete delineation of themes in this paragraph, see Frederick E. Crowe, "Universal Norms and the Concrete 'Operabile' in St. Thomas Aquinas" (1955, pp. 114-149; 257-291).

insights into the concrete situations relevant to needed decisions can occur in way that is not possible for others not so situated.[13]

Furthermore, the postmodernists typically play off the rationalization of action in the mode of what Weber formulated as the ethics of consequences (*Verantwortungsethik*) against the distantiating, defamiliarizing strategies that render agents more sensitive to plurality, differences, instability, the dissolution of arbitrary hierarchies, and so forth, in order to heighten our responsiveness to the other. This motif is not just akin to Weber's delimitation of the ethics of conviction (*Gesinnungsethik*); it can also remind us of Lonergan's contrast between a horizontal and a vertical exercise of liberty (1972, pp. 40, 122, 237-238, 240, 269). By the former, we operate within an already established orientation to choose courses of action within some already understood and agreed upon horizon of meanings and values specified by some master narrative; by the latter, we undergo a radical change in the overall orientation and in which a different, incommensurate, or disproportionate horizon of meaning and value is specified by a new master narrative.[14]

If we recontextualize the postmodernists' moral and aesthetic sense of responsiveness to otherness within Lonergan's framework, then the decentering, detotalizing, and becoming heterogeneous of the self can be reinterpreted as the basic and radical displacement of the subject that occurs most paradigmatically in religious conversion. Then the epitome of responsibility for the other is achieved when we fall in love with the "mystery of love and awe." The resultant religious differentiation of consciousness, Lonergan tells us:

> begins with asceticism and culminates in mysticism. Both asceticism and mysticism, when genuine, have a common ground that was described by St. Paul when he exclaimed: "...God's love has flooded our inmost hearts through the Holy Spirit he has given us" (Rom. 5:5). That ground can bear fruit in a consciousness that lives in a world mediated by meaning. But it can also set up a different type of consciousness by withdrawing one from the world mediated by meaning into a cloud of unknowing. Then one is for God, belongs to him, gives oneself to him, not by using words, images, concepts, but in a silent, joyous, peaceful surrender to his initiative. (1985, p. 242)

---

[13] See *Insight* (1957/1992, pp. 259-260) for the classic statement; also, "Prologomena to the Study of Religious Consciousness of Our Time," *A Third Collection* (1985, esp. pp. 60-63).

[14] Compare Lonergan's references to Karl Rahner's interpretation of "consolation without a cause" in the latter's commentary on St. Ignatius Loyola's *Spiritual Exercises*, in *The Dynamic Element in the Church*, esp. chapter 3 "The Logic of Concrete Individual Knowledge in Ignatius Loyola" (1964, pp. 84-170), for example; in *Method in Theology* (1972, p. 106); and in *A Third Collection* (1985, p. 201, nn. 47 & 48, and p. 249, n. 2).

Hence, all the postmodernist highlighting of the inexhaustibly open-textured character of language—and of what White (1991, p. 21) calls the world-disclosing power of innovative linguistic expression—can be re-understood as the role played by beliefs in the light of faith as the "eyes of being-in-love" (Lonergan, 1972, pp. 115-119).

Like the deconstructivist and genealogical postmodernists, Lonergan too is concerned with the dismantling of the truncated utilitarian, the immanentist Romantic-expressivist, and the exploited and alienated subject. But for him, this dismantling only happens adequately only when by receiving the gift of God's love we enter into a horizon that corresponds with what is ultimately a friendly universe (1972, pp. 117, 290). The term "friendly" here, and the stories of faith that communicate its meaning concretely, have nothing to do with Lyotard's "regimes of truth" that are just legitimating masks for powers who know what is good for us and wish to "force us to be free." Instead, I am hinting at a context of God's glory by which the postmodernist taste for excess, extravagance, and intensity is made good in the light of God's astonishing desire for the flourishing of each and every person and thing in creation in all their specificity and particularity (Lonergan, 1972, pp. 116-117).

## 7. Lonergan and the Postmodern Sublime

### 7.1 The Sublime and the Ambiguity of the Surd

A major postmodernist theme not addressed above regards confronting the objective surd of individual and structural evil. According to White (1991) and Thomas L. Pangle (1992, pp. 23-29), the heading under which postmodern thinkers like Lyotard and Derrida treat the human response to pain, danger, and terror involves a transformation of the traditional idea of the sublime. Lonergan, of course, approaches this issue from the standpoint of the mystery of love and awe with its specifically Christian historical intelligibility of the law of the cross, again, in a way that takes the postmodern sublime seriously without just euphemizing them.

We have seen that the postmodernist disciples of Nietzsche specialize in going beneath surface, conventional normalcy to disclose the abnormal and discordant and bizarre. In doing this, they do not simply pick at the seams and slippages of the non-systematic and the contingent. Paradoxically, they are also preoccupied with evil, but from an artificial position "beyond good and evil," since for them the opposition between good and evil is just another fiction foisted on Western culture by Platonism and Christianity. They therefore tend to revel in ambiguity, seeming to conflate the gesture toward the incommensurability of the non-systematic or random, on the one hand, and the knowing wink toward the surd of sin's arbitrariness and lack of intelligibility, on the other.

Deconstructivist and genealogical postmodernists are nonetheless out to upset both the flatness of bourgeois commercialism and the pathos of Romantic expressivism, through working out a characteristically postmodern sensibility. To this end, they have fashioned a specifically postmodern sense of the sublime.

The classic meaning of the sublime as articulated in Longinus's treatise, *On the Sublime*, has to do with an exaltation or elevation of the mind beyond its normal state, inspiring a noble pride and a willingness to think critically for oneself in a way that transcends one's ordinary range of motivations and rationales. Rousseau's *Emile* gives a psychological twist to this term by elaborating a process by which erotic passions get sublimated into an internalized willingness to submit to the disciplines of parenthood and citizenship. By the time we reach the 18th century discussions of aesthetics referring judgments of beauty to the senses, Edmund Burke's *A Philosophical Enquiry into the Origin on the Ideas of the Sublime and the Beautiful* (1757/1909) defines the sublime in terms of our responses to pain, the dangerous, and the terrible; and Kant's reflections on the sublime depart from Burke's ideas. By this time, the ancient connotations of elevation, of what people look up to, of the noble, have been all but eliminated. Henceforth, the focus will be upon what cannot be adequately expressed because it is not strictly imaginable or representable. No wonder, then, that the kataphatic philosophy of postmodernism finds the notion of the sublime congenial.

## 7.2 *Lyotard on the Sublime*

Derrida and Lyotard, according to White (1991), are absorbed not just by "a concern with otherness expressed by undermining the false self-confidence of foundations"; they are also concerned with

> moods...traditionally associated with the experience of the sublime (as distinct from the beautiful). A sense of the sublime is elicited when one is faced with the abyss, the gigantic, the monstrous. Moods typically associated with such experiences are awe, anxiety, and an exalted desperation. (White, 1991, p. 83)

White claims that Derrida does not exploit the notion of the sublime much beyond deconstruction's typical "impulse to intervention" (p. 84). It is Lyotard instead who "has been consistently fascinated with developing a way of thinking about the sublime as the core of postmodern sensibility that can resist the homogenizing, normalizing forces of societal rationalization" (p. 85; also see pp. 85-90).

Building upon Burke's meditations on the sublime, Kant noted how our feelings of pain and agitation in the face of the monstrous do have some delight associated with them, as soon as by distantiating ourselves we realize that the terror of privation or of the threat of impending death is not presently inevitable. For Kant, a further pleasure to be associated with an experience of the sublime also stems from the mind's realization that while it cannot adequately understand the object confronting it, it can still "conceive of something like the infinite" (Lyotard, "The Sublime and the Avant-Garde," *Lyotard Reader*, 1989, p. 199; cited by White, 1991, p. 85). And so at this point postmodernism buys into Kant's teaching on the putative limits of *Verstand* or human intelligence, according to which we cannot reach objective truth in regard to our most important questions and human experiences but must remain content with merely conceivable or imaginable *Vorstellungen* or representations such as metaphors, allegories, and symbols.

Lyotard locates the sublime's ambivalent and contradictory feelings of pain and distress mixed with pleasure at the heart of the postmodernist penchant for "impertinently intervening in everyday life in ways that jolt normal sensibility" (White, 1991, p. 84). For Lyotard, the sublime plays itself out in modern avant-garde art and, more dangerously, in certain forms of political enthusiasm. Instead of resigning ourselves to lifelessness in the face of infinite emptiness and universal hopelessness, why don't we strive for the artificial intensification of feeling that is the postmodern sublime?

## 7.3 From the Sublime to Worship

Lonergan spent his life facing the concrete results of the longer cycle of decline in Western culture. In confronting the contemporary objective surd, he was anti-technocratic, and he was not a historicist. But he also had precious little sympathy for the simpliste anti-technocratic disparaging of the normative achievement of modern natural science so common in continental philosophy and theology; and he had just as little patience with dogmatic refusals to accept the correct implications of the rise of historical mindedness. In principle and in practice, he was a champion of both modern science and modern scholarship. And yet reflecting on what he called the third historical plateau or stage of meaning, he was utterly convinced of the intractability of the human condition by human resources alone. For Lonergan, our damaged total human environment requires a healing that far transcends human creativity and originality. In a strictly technical sense, the evils in this universe constitute a mystery of iniquity since they are disproportionate to our human powers to solve them sufficiently.

But Lonergan was also a person struck to his core by an even greater disproportion or incommensurability: that God so loved the world that he gave his only-begotten Son... (Jn. 3:6). He could not repeat often enough St. Paul's statement about God's love having been poured into our hearts through the Holy Spirit that has been given to us (Rom. 5:5).

Now because of his faith in God's redemption of the universe through Christ Jesus and in the Holy Spirit, Lonergan was not content to dance sublimely at the edge of the abyss. But neither would he be surprised that precisely the imperfection of human embodiments of the absolutely supernatural solution to human evil would eventually evoke both the humanist revolts of Enlightenment and the Romantic reaction, but even an anti-humanist rebellion in the manner of Nietzschean postmodernism as well. The postmodern taste for the sublime may be a pseudo-religious yearning for the intensification of experience, even if artificially or violently. In an age awash in *ressentiment* over the loss of genuine meaning and value, the feeling of the sublime can appear to be quite an attractive alternative. This seems to be a more exotic version of Heidegger's negative eschatology that under the pretense that "only a god can save us," assumes a meditative attitude of waiting, even if it be for nothing. Compared to the posturings of certain representatives of conventional religious institutions, the cultivation of the sublime can seem rather refreshing. Hence, the surveys telling us of the huge numbers of people who believe in religious experience yet do not believe in God are not so astonishing.

But isn't this anti-humanist attitude of responsiveness to otherness a parody of that displacement away from human concerns characteristic of authentically supernatural hope? I would say it is.

It remains that in Lonergan's framework of the decentered, self-transcendent, conscious subject, responsiveness to the other is fulfilled when human consciousness falls in love and is in love in the love of intimacy (especially in families), in our self-sacrificial loyalty to our communities, and in otherworldly love.

For Lonergan, falling and being in love with God is absolutely transcendent, which means it is disproportionate to strictly human potentiality. Thus, our receiving of the gift of God's love actually achieves the supreme degree of displacement away from ourselves as the center of the universe at the same time as it constitutes the only adequate fulfillment of the unrestricted desire built into our human consciousnesses. We traditionally call the enactment of this radical displacement that both empowers us and commands us religious conversion.

If the deepest or highest longing of the human consciousness is the desire for communion with God and the universe through which God addresses us, then the universe really and not just metaphorically has a conversational structure. At its best, human consciousness responds to the cosmic Word through mind and heart in conversation; or in what Habermas and some neo-pragmatists call communicative action; or in what Gadamer calls hermeneutic experience.

## 8. Conclusion

My claim has been not just that the postmodern concern for the other, but even that the radical decentering of the modern subject carried out in various ways by the hermeneutic, deconstructivist, and genealogical orientations in contemporary philosophy has to be taken utterly seriously by Christian theology. The importance of this postmodern concern is underlined by the most radical movement in contemporary theology—liberation and political theology. Indeed, the evangelical call to concern for the victims is today being enlarged to embrace not only human, but also subhuman nature: Justice and love for the neighbor, we realize today, cannot be separated from care for the natural ecology proper to genuine human thriving. Neither utilitarian individualism nor expressive individualism—the regimes in which the modern subject holds the primacy—are adequate to the contemporary demands for justice and love. Hence, the relevance for Christian theology of the hermeneutic, deconstructivist, and genealogical strategies for overcoming modern subjectivism for the sake of respecting and loving the other of nature, of fellow human beings, and of God.

Nevertheless, my argument has been that the hermeneutical strategy of Gadamer is too undifferentiated, while the deconstructivist and genealogical strategies are too dialectically flawed, to offer the theoretical and systematic basis for making good the requirements of contemporary liberation and political theology. As Jürgen Habermas from the left and Leo Strauss from the right have both argued, Gadamer's hermeneutic philosophy is so general that it can all too easily devolve into an insufficiently critical traditionalism. And as we have suggested above, the deconstructivist and genealogical strategies as they stand easily justify agnostic pluralism, a posture also not critical enough for contemporary theology's needs. The alternative for those longing to recover the pristine radicality of the Christian Gospel to everyday practice, of course, cannot be any form of restoration theology or of ahistorical orthodoxy that fosters fundamentalist sectarianism. But finding an adequate alternative is quite difficult, especially for us theologians who ourselves are often infected with the many different versions of Enlightenment rationalism or Romantic expressivism that dominate the cultural climate today.

This article has tried to show how Lonergan's thought takes seriously most of the major concerns of hermeneutic, deconstructivist, and genealogical postmodernism. When Lonergan thematized his breakthrough to the human subject as subject and to consciousness as experience in terms of the self-appropriation of our rational self-consciousnesses (to use the language of *Insight*) and of intellectual conversion (to use the language of *Method in Theology*); and when he explicated the radical displacement from ourselves as the center of the universe entailed by the intellectualist apprehension and affirmation of an utterly transcendent God beyond necessity and contingency, oddly enough he was carrying forward a postmodern program. All the themes of displacement of the subject as the primary object, of the fragility of consciousness and the contingency of the universe, of the constitutive role of freedom, of the radical historicality of meaning and value receive systematic treatment in terms of the structure and dynamism of finite human consciousness as gift and as precarious achievement.

But Lonergan's explication of postmodernist themes can avoid both agnostic pluralism and fundamentalist sectarianism. I say "*can* avoid" advisedly, since those claiming to have appropriated Lonergan's thought are not immune to utilitarian and expressivist individualism, either. How many of us know students of Lonergan who use Lonergan's panoply of terms and relations to serve the power goals either of individuals or of groups? How many of us have experiences of so-called Lonergan people who assume the Romantic pose of having worked so much harder, or suffered so much more, or become so much deeper than everyone else? Perhaps postmodernism under hermeneutic, deconstructivist, and genealogical auspices can offer an astringent for Lonergan scholars who may have missed the radically postmodern challenge posed by Lonergan's thought.

Conversely, my guess is that precisely because it shares postmodern concerns so profoundly, only Lonergan's thought as grounded in the fragility of consciousness offers an immanent critique of the postmodernist strategies discussed in this article. The reader will naturally judge for him- or herself whether my argument and the suggested lines of immanent critique have been successful.

# 10

# On Truth, Method, and Gadamer

*Hugo A. Meynell*

The problem of our "knowledge of other minds" is notorious in philosophy. It would also seem to be of interest to those concerned with human communication, since one has to know something of the minds of others if one is to communicate effectively with them. How do we obtain knowledge of the thoughts and feelings of other persons, and of what they have in mind when they utter their words and perform their actions? One is inclined to say, on a superficial view, something like the following. Knowledge of other minds simply does not constitute a special case, at least in the way that is often assumed by philosophers. We cannot *perceive* other persons' thoughts or feelings; but then neither can we perceive the particles of nuclear physics or the things and events of the past. On the other hand, we can more or less verify our suppositions and consequently come to make adequately grounded judgments, in all three kinds of cases, by appeal to our perceptions. In a way that seems instructively parallel to the cases of the past and of nuclear physics, your behavior as observable to me seems not to be identical with your mental state; and yet it would be strange to deny that I may test the supposition that you are in one kind of mental state rather than another by taking account of your behavior as observable to me. If knowledge is a matter of true and adequately grounded judgment, and not merely of perception, there is no special difficulty about our knowledge of other minds. This approach has been worked out with some profundity in the "generalized empirical method" of Bernard Lonergan. I believe it to be the right one;[1] but it has very often been held to be mistaken. Hans-Georg Gadamer is notable among those who have assumed it to be so.[2]

---

[1] E. D. Hirsch claims, in my view rightly, that "the much-advertised cleavage between thinking in the sciences and the humanities does not exist. The hypothetico-deductive process is fundamental in both of them, as it is in all thinking that aspires to knowledge" (Hirsch, 1967, p. 264).

[2] In general, I am in agreement with the criticisms made of Gadamer by Jürgen Habermas (1977), though I believe that he does not take them quite far enough due to the inconsistencies in his own position (see Meynell, 1991a). As Habermas says: "Although always bound up in language reason always transcends particular

Gadamer's *Truth and Method* (1960/1990) is generally recognized to be the most substantial work on hermeneutics, or the theory of interpretation, to have come out of Germany during the present century. Since its first publication in 1960, it has exerted its influence everywhere in the human sciences—including history, sociology, and literary and legal theory. Fundamental to its argument is objection to the notion that scientific method and proof constitute the exclusive avenue to truth (cf. Weinsheimer, 1985, pp. ix-x) and polemic against that obsession with "objective truth and correct method" that was so characteristic of 19th-century studies in this subject. It insists that there is no methodology for the interpretation of texts and that objective and permanent knowledge in this area is an ideal that is simply unrealizable. One important consequence of this view is a certain skepticism with regard to historical knowledge. Earlier authorities, moreover, believed that the truth of an interpretation was a matter of expressing once again an author's meaning; but this, according to Gadamer, is to neglect the fact that "every putative re-cognition of a text is really a new and different cognition in which the interpreter's own historicity" is ineluctably involved. It is this historicity of understanding that was characteristically overlooked by 19th-century authorities (Hirsch, 1967, pp. 245-246).

The argument of the book is buttressed by an impressively detailed analysis of previous thought about language, aesthetic experience, and historical consciousness; and there are many thought-provoking excursions into the history of ideas. Especially interesting and insightful, perhaps, is Gadamer's account of art as play (cf. Weinsheimer, 1985, p. xi; Hirsch, 1967, p. 246). Nevertheless, I shall in what follows be primarily concerned with what I regard as the defects and limitations of Gadamer's thought. I shall first present a summary of his main contentions; and then argue that they issue in an unacceptable and in the last analysis incoherent degree of skepticism and relativism. I shall conclude by suggesting that a more satisfactory account of interpretation, and therefore of communication, is to be derived from Lonergan's work.

## 1. A Summary of Gadamer's Hermeneutics

Gadamer agrees with Immanuel Kant that knowledge of things as they are in themselves is impossible; equally impossible, he insists, is the "reflexive self-grounding" of the knowing subject (Gadamer, 1960/1990, p. xxxvii; all

---

languages; it lives in language only by destroying the particularities of language through which alone it is incarnated. Of course, it can cleanse itself of the dross of one particularity only in passing over into another" (1977, p. 336). The trouble, of course, lies in the last sentence of the quotation, which seems to render more or less vacuous what went before. The fact is that, by a special use of language, one may explicate the rational method more or less implicit in every language; this procedure is exemplified in Lonergan's work.

subsequent references, except those otherwise assigned, will be to this
work). This is due, as he sees it, to the embeddedness of each of us in our
particular historical situation, which renders out of the question the kind of
self-transcendence that would be necessary for these purposes. For the same
reason, it seems that there is something absurd in the notion of a uniquely
correct interpretation of the meaning of another (p. 120). With Edmund
Husserl's concept of intentionality, "we get a...radical critique of the 'objectivism' of philosophy hitherto," including Wilhelm Dilthey's attempt to
achieve an "objective" account of meaning (p. 243). One can in fact speak
of "the overcoming of the epistemological problem through phenomenological research"; the essence of phenomenology being "the exclusion of all
positing of being and investigating the subjective modes of givenness" (p.
244). The concept of the "life-world" that emerges from phenomenological
analysis is the antithesis of all objectivism. In deliberate contrast to the
conception of the world made objective by science, Husserl speaks of the
life-world as that in which we are immersed as a result of the "natural attitude" that is the pre-given basis of all experience (pp. 246-247). The life-
world is a communal world involving from the first being with other people.
Husserl speaks of "life" as contrasted with the objectivist naïveté of all previous philosophy (pp. 246-247).

Husserl may be said to have brought definitively into philosophy "the
principle of 'radical' idealism, namely of always going back to the constitutive acts of transcendental subjectivity" (p. 247). Like Martin Heidegger
after him, he felt himself to be in opposition to the whole of metaphysics.
However, neither Husserl nor Dilthey can cope with the problem of intersubjectivity. The fact is that "the immanent data of reflectively examined
consciousness do not include the 'Thou' in an immediate and primary way"
(p. 250). In Heidegger's work the whole idea of "grounding" underwent a
total reversal; his true predecessor in this respect was not Husserl or
Dilthey, but Friedrich Nietzsche (p. 257). As Heidegger sees it, there is no
understanding or interpretation to which the whole existential structure,
rooted in the past and projected toward the future, does not function, even if
one intends "simply to read 'what is there' or to discover...'how it really
was'" (p. 262). (It is a central tenet of Heidegger's philosophy that our
"knowledge" of "how things are" or "how things were" is ineluctably and
through-and-through affected by our own particular relationship to our past
and orientation towards our future.)

The problem of the grounding of our knowledge brings in its train the
related question of what is the proper relationship between the natural sciences and the human sciences. Now the self-reflection of the human sciences in the 19th century was dominated by natural science (p. 3). However, we on our part should learn from Heidegger's terrifying vision of natural science expanding into "a total technocracy" and so bringing on "the
'cosmic night' of the 'forgetfulness of being'" (p. xxxvii). And in fact the

modern conception of science, together with its associated view of method, are insufficient to show what makes the human sciences scientific (p. 18).

And what, we may ask, *is* truth in the human sciences (p. 100)? The conflict that Dilthey tried to resolve, between the special requirements of human science, on the one hand, and the drive towards "objectivity" that may be deemed essential to science as such, on the other, shows the pressure that the methodology of modern natural science exerted and continues to exert; Gadamer regards his own task as "to describe more adequately the experience of the human sciences and the objectivity they are able to achieve" (p. 242). Dilthey was in the last analysis a Cartesian, maintaining as he did the ideal of a consciousness that has shaken off authority and seeks to reach genuine knowledge through reflection and doubt. But such a conception of the matter is ultimately incompatible with his life-philosophy, the aim of which is to articulate the actual movement of conscious life as it is lived (pp. 237-238). Conscious life as interpreting itself, as having in itself a hermeneutical structure, is the real basis of the human sciences for Dilthey; this he thinks enables him to get beyond Hegel's intellectualism (p. 226). But he also supposes that historical consciousness can rise above its own relativity to make objectivity in the human sciences possible (p. 234). For Dilthey as a child of the Enlightenment, it seemed that the Cartesian procedure by way of doubt to certainty was obviously correct (p. 239).

But one cannot properly envisage the human sciences on the model of the natural sciences. For example, there is a sense in which the human sciences are not subject to progress, since the great achievements in the human sciences do not go out of date in the manner of those in the natural sciences. One may have to make some allowances for errors of fact in such classic historians as Mommsen and Droysen; but we still prefer reading their work to the latest productions on the subjects on which they wrote. This is because "the subject matter appears truly significant only when it is properly portrayed for us." While "we are certainly interested in the subject matter,...it acquires its life only from the light in which it is presented to us" (p. 284).

> [Moreover,] in the human sciences the particular research questions concerning tradition that we are interested in pursuing are motivated in a special way by the present and its interests. The theme and object of research are actually constituted by the motivation of the inquiry. Hence historical research is carried along by the historical movement of life itself and cannot be understood teleologically in terms of the object into which it is inquiring. Such an "object in itself" clearly does not exist at all. This is precisely what distinguishes the human sciences from the natural sciences. Whereas the object of the natural sciences can be described ideally as what would be known in the perfect knowledge of nature, it is senseless to speak of a perfect knowledge of history, and for this reason it is

not possible to speak of an "object in itself" towards which its research is directed. (pp. 284-285)[3]

It is not only with regard to method in the human sciences that the Enlightenment has left us an unfortunate legacy. In opposition to its aims and assumptions, authority and tradition have to be rehabilitated (p. 277). The Enlightenment tended to see authority as exacting blind obedience; but this is not the only possibility. One may, after all, reasonably and freely accept an authority on the ground that it has a wider view of things, or is better informed, than oneself (p. 279). And it is to be insisted that "our finite historical being is marked by the fact that the authority of what has been handed down to us—and not just what is clearly grounded—always has power over our attitudes and behavior. All education depends on this" (p. 280). And even when individuals are grown to maturity and put their own insight and decisions in place of the authority of the educator, they are not thereby free of tradition. Our morality is a case in point; we freely take it upon ourselves, but do not freely create it, receiving it as we do from our tradition by way of education (p. 280). It may be pointed out in passing that there can be elements of tradition in natural science, with particular lines of research, for example, being preferred in different places (p. 283).

Given that all human existence, even the freest, is limited and qualified in various ways, "the idea of an absolute reason is not a possibility for historical humanity. Reason exists for us only in concrete, historical terms—i.e., it is not its own master but remains constantly dependent on the given circumstances in which it operates" (p. 276). This implies that one must have a very different attitude to *prejudice* than that boasted by the Enlightenment and exemplified by modern science; their thoroughgoing opposition to prejudice is derived from Cartesian doubt and the resulting acceptance of nothing as certain that can be doubted. However, the Enlightenment insistence that one should overcome all prejudice is itself really a prejudice (p. 270); this realization opens the way to an understanding of the finitude that dominates our humanity including our historical consciousness (p. 276). The prejudice against prejudice on the part of the Enlightenment

---

[3] As Joel C. Weinsheimer says, Gadamer raises many objections to "the notion that scientific method defines the exclusive avenue to truth"; Weinsheimer for his part rightly "questions whether Gadamer's conception of scientific method and its objectives is not askew" (Weinsheimer, 1985, p. x). I myself believe that rational method in a broad sense, as explicated by Lonergan, *is* the virtually exclusive avenue to truth, in that without it one can only reach truth occasionally, haphazardly, and by chance, and even then cannot safely identify it as truth. (Compare the parrot who said "E = mc-squared" a month before Einstein made his epoch-making discovery of 1905.) The method of natural science is merely one application of rational method in this sense. Gadamer is, of course, quite right to deny that "proof" is "our sole means of access to truth" (Weinsheimer, 1985, p. 2). But rational method properly understood does not entail any such absurdity; indeed, it provides a means of establishing its contradictory.

deprives tradition of the power that it ought to have. The German Enlightenment, it is true, did acknowledge "true prejudices" in Christianity; since the human mind is often too weak to function without prejudices, they allowed, it was fortunate in this case to have been educated in the right ones. The picture of a conquest of *mythos* by *logos* was taken over by the Romantics from the Enlightenment; they merely reversed the evaluation (p. 273). "Primeval wisdom is only the counter-image of 'primeval stupidity'" (p. 274).

It is true that Heidegger says we ought never to allow our fore-conceptions to be determined by fancies and popular assumptions, but that we should work them out in terms of things themselves (p. 236; Heidegger, 1962, p. 153). However, he is not telling us by this to extinguish ourselves, but rather to assimilate our fore-meanings and prejudices in such a way that, when we attempt to understand a text, we are really prepared to let it tell us something (pp. 267-269). In describing the nature of interpretation, Friedrich Schleiermacher postulated a sort of divinatory act by which interpreters place themselves in the mind of the writer they are trying to interpret and from that vantage-point resolve the puzzles that arise from the text. Against this view, Heidegger insists that the understanding of a text is always determined by the anticipatory movement of its interpreter's fore-understanding (p. 293). The anticipation of meaning is furthermore not a sheer autonomous act of subjectivity, but derives from tradition; "the meaning of 'belonging'—i.e., the element of tradition in our historical hermeneutical activity—is fulfilled in the commonality of fundamental enabling prejudices" (p. 295). Romantic hermeneutics was too inclined to take human nature as such as the non-historical basis of its theory of interpretation, as though interpreters could somehow be released from their historical limitations. But the truth of the matter is that "understanding is to be thought of *less as a subjective act than as participating in an event of tradition,* a process of transmission in which past and present are constantly mediated" (p. 290). Rather than expressing the necessity of thus placing oneself within a tradition, hermeneutical theory so far has been dominated by the misleading ideal of setting out and applying a specific method (p. 290).

## 2. Limitations in Gadamer's Position: A Lonerganian Critique

It is central to Gadamer's overall position that knowledge of things in themselves is impossible and that the reflexive self-grounding of the knowing subject is equally impossible (p. xxxvii), as I have indicated above.[4] I believe him to be wrong on both counts, but profoundly right to suggest an

---

[4] He sometimes seems to speak, however, as though knowledge of things in themselves were possible in the natural sciences, though not in the human (as I have also mentioned above).

intimate connection between the one thesis and the other. To cut a very long story very short, on Lonergan's account, which I believe to be the correct one, the reflexive self-grounding of the subject is to be secured as follows. It is self-destructive to deny that I can ever make a true statement, since if that denial is true, it constitutes a falsifying exception to itself (Lonergan, 1957/1992, chapter 11). Also, it is self-destructive to deny that I can ever have rational grounds for making a statement. Either that statement itself is made by me on rational grounds, in which case it constitutes a falsifying exception to itself; or it is not, in which case it is not to be taken seriously (Lonergan, 1972, pp. 16-17). Thus, it is certain, since the contradictories are self-destructive, both that I can make true statements and that I can make statements supported by rational grounds. So much, very summarily, for the reflexive self-grounding of the knowing subject. The real world, furthermore, again on Lonergan's account, can in the last analysis be nothing other than what true statements *are* about and what statements based on rational grounds *tend to* be about. Any distinction that may be made between reality and appearance, or between the actual world and the world merely *for* an individual or group, is parasitic on another distinction between (1) the process of rational grounding (attending to evidence in sensation or consciousness; envisaging hypotheses to account for that evidence; and affirming provisionally or definitively as true the hypothesis that does best account for that evidence) taken just so far, on the one hand, and (2) the same process as pursued to an indefinite extent, on the other (Lonergan, 1957/1992, chapter 12; Meynell 1991b, pp. 50-56). Was Richard III of England responsible for the death of the princes in the Tower of London? Is there a naturally occurring inert gas with atomic weight greater than that of gold? Suppose that he was and that there is. If these things were only *apparently* so, or "so" merely *for* a limited set of people, this could only be by virtue of the fact that an indefinitely pursued program of rational inquiry would tend to come up in each case with a contradictory hypothesis that would better account for the relevant evidence.

To be "objective" in one sense is to pursue one's inquiries as though nothing so "subjective," and therefore presumably non-objective, as human feelings, desires, sensations, acts of coming to understand or misunderstand, judgments for adequate or inadequate reason, and so on, existed (Lonergan, 1957/1992, chapter 13). They do not, sure enough, in those aspects of reality into which it is the business of the physicist, the chemist, or the plant biologist to inquire.[5] To deplore, as Gadamer notoriously does, the application of such a norm of "objectivity" to the human sciences is certainly ap-

---

[5] It is notorious, of course, that they may powerfully affect the inquiries of the physicist, the chemist, or the plant biologist. But this is a different matter. The constitution of blue-giant stars and the habits of the duck-billed dinosaur are not affected by human social factors, for all that our human beliefs about such matters are liable to be so.

propriate enough. It is an important upshot of the work of Husserl, as Gadamer says, that the limitations of this notion of objectivity are exposed for what they are. But there is a quite different conception of objectivity, which has no such limitations and which, I would maintain, is just as applicable to inquiry in the human sciences as it is to inquiry in the natural sciences. Few judgments are better grounded than that there are other beings besides myself who also make judgments and furthermore are acquainted with sensations, feelings, joys, griefs, and other conscious events and episodes in the same way that I am myself. For me to be fully "objective," in the sense with which I am now concerned, about such matters is for me to make sure that *my* judgments about *their* judgments and about other aspects of their conscious experience and activity are as adequately grounded as possible in the evidence available to me through their words, gestures, and so on. It is this sort of objectivity that Lonergan has in mind when he writes that "genuine objectivity is the fruit of authentic subjectivity" (Lonergan, 1972, pp. 265, 292). To the extent that we are fully objective in this sense, we tend to get to know how things really are, both in the minds of other persons and in the world at large. So far from impugning *this* account of objectivity, I believe, Husserl's work enables one to provide a better account than would otherwise be available of just what it *is* to be objective and to make truth claims accordingly.

The method of the natural sciences is a matter of being as objective as possible with regard to the aspect of reality that is *not* characterized by understanding, reason, decision, and so on. It appears to me that Gadamer misrepresents the method of the natural sciences and as a consequence sets up his account of the human sciences in a misleading contrast to it. An element of "divination" belongs to the natural sciences; since Hume, it has been clear that there are no rules for making correct conjectures, and the point has been powerfully reaffirmed in recent times by Sir Karl Popper. On the other hand, the need to *test* our conjectures, if we are to get at the truth or at least move towards it, is as great in the human as in the natural sciences; an interpretation of an author's meaning may turn out to be wrong when one looks further into her or his writings than one had done before, just as a theory in physics or chemistry that appears to account for known phenomena may yet come to grief as a result of further observations or experiments. In both types of inquiry, one has creatively to propound a range of hypotheses, a process notoriously unreducible to rule; in both, one has to test these hypotheses by confronting them with the relevant evidence—in this sense and within these limits deriving the law of one's inquiry, as Gadamer puts it, from the object with which one is concerned.

The model of natural science as used in human science is associated by Gadamer with Heidegger's nightmare vision of a human consciousness blind to every preoccupation but that of technological control. But it is not obvious to me why it should be assumed that such control is the exclusive or indeed the primary concern even in natural science. Certainly such pioneers of natural science as Descartes and Francis Bacon did strongly emphasize its potential for controlling nature in the service of humanity. But writings of some first-rate scientists (e.g., Stephen J. Gould) give the impression primarily of delight in progressive discovery of the intelligible order of things, with technological control as at best a secondary interest (cf. Meynell, 1991c). (And that, surely, it should be; we ought to wish to use our science to develop such technology as will help to lengthen human life and alleviate human misery.) It may be agreed that when natural science becomes utterly dominated by technological concerns and as so conceived is used as a model for the human sciences, it becomes deplorable and dangerous. But in that case it is not the model as such, but a distorted conception of it, that is at fault.

Gadamer also follows Heidegger in stressing how thoroughly embedded human beings are in their particular historical situations. Now it is quite right to emphasize the fact that people cannot, as it were through some magic process, turn themselves into inhabitants of a place, a time, or a cultural milieu different from their own. But it appears to follow from what has already been said that we can all the same, from the perspective of our particular place and time, get to know *what is really so*—and not just what is *so merely for* persons of our particular place and time. The fact is that even to state that there are such limitations in the human condition is in a manner to presuppose that one transcends them—unless indeed one is to be committed to the nonsense that whatever is "true" is merely true for us (thus implying that the contradictory proposition, that absolute truth is attainable, may be equally true for someone else). And no good reason is supplied by Gadamer, or so far as I know by anyone else, why what applies to our knowledge in general should not apply to our knowledge in history and other human sciences. As with the thermonuclear processes in blue giant stars, so with the intentions of Henry V of England on invading France—we get to know what is or was so by attending to evidence available to our senses, by propounding hypotheses, and by judging some among these hypotheses to be more well-founded than others. This general method is applicable to both cases, for all that the details of its application are of course very different.

Gadamer writes of "the overcoming of the epistemological problem through phenomenological research." But it appears to me that his work, so far from *overcoming* that problem, is largely vitiated by an *abandonment* of it for which phenomenology provides rather a misleading pretext than a good reason. What I have already argued tends to show that for all my embeddedness within my historical past and orientation towards my historical future, I can all the same find out what is so and how things really were. I can assert for good reason that Julius Caesar died a violent death at Rome in 44 B.C.E. and that there is a metal that is liquid at normal temperatures on the surface of the earth; and these facts, if facts they are, are in no way dependent upon me or my situation. My capacity to attend adequately to the relevant evidence, to hypothesize intelligently, to judge reasonably, and so to come to knowledge of these facts will certainly depend on my particular situation; but that is another thing. Gadamer does well to insist on the degree to which our motives affect our historical inquiries. But there is no reason to follow him so far as to maintain what appears to be the implication of his position—that we cannot find out how historical events were in themselves. There may be *more to* any particular historical event than we have found out at any one time; but that, again, is another thing. As to the place of our motives in historical inquiry, it may suit my whole attitude to life to maintain that Thomas Cranmer, or Vladimir Lenin, said or did this or that; but I can all the same deliberately set myself to attend to evidence that might support a contradictory judgment to the one that it suits me to believe. This is what it amounts to to be "objective" in the proper sense about such matters. It may be noted that the influence of our attitudes to life on our inquiries seems to be little less an issue for the natural than for the human sciences. It is notorious, for example, that religious beliefs may influence one's attention to evidence and one's capacity to envisage and evaluate hypotheses about the facts of biological evolution.

The right way to pursue Descartes' program of systematic doubt, it seems to me, is to attend to the ramifications of the facts about knowledge that I alluded to in the last paragraph but four. This will enable us, I believe, to disentangle what in the Enlightenment is of a permanent value, from those errors and exaggerations in it on which Gadamer lays so much stress. The fact is that short of the possibility of some "reflexive self-grounding of the knowing subject," a truly critical attitude to authority is impossible. One must either accept it uncritically, or reject it uncritically (in the manner that as Gadamer rightly suggests, some major figures of the Enlightenment were inclined to do), or arbitrarily reject some of its tenets while accepting others. A properly grounded "systematic doubt" will provide a basis for reasonable judgment that some authorities (say professors of physics at major universities) are more likely to speak the truth on matters within their professional competence than are others (say, journalists working for newspapers that make money by providing their readers with sensational reports). It can be shown that one tends to believe what is true in so far as one exercises the three capacities that I have claimed, following Lonergan, are of the essence of knowledge; the community of physicists has probably exercised them more persistently than anyone else with respect to the matters in question. Gadamer admits that a critical attitude to authority is desirable; yet he is unable, on his own premises, to justify such a stance.

What applies to the dictates of authority also applies to the deliverances of tradition. Either the grounds for justified acceptance of some aspects of tradition rather than others can be articulated, at least in principle, or they cannot; and if they cannot, they are arbitrary, and one might as well pick and choose among them according to one's temperament or caprice. On Gadamer's behalf, it is to be noted that the authorities and traditions that my society imposes on me are quite likely to impose or to incorporate as many of the fruits of rational inquiry as of sheer dogmatism; it is just as irrational for me to reject them totally as to accept them outright. One is rational and so apt to get at or at least move towards the truth in so far as one attends to evidence, concocts hypotheses to account for it, and accepts the hypothesis that *does* best account for it in each case. (Those who deny this may be asked whether they make their denial as the hypothesis that accounts best for the available evidence; if they do not do so, it seems pointless to take them seriously; whereas if they do do so, they are exercising in the interests of truth the very mental faculties whose relevance to the stating of truth they are denying. (See the discussion of self-destructive "counter-positions" in Lonergan 1957/1992, pp. 412-415, 513-514, 519-520, etc.) But however brilliant individuals may be, it is certain that the accumulated experience and inquiry underlying the judgments current in their society will have a great deal to teach them, even though (as in the case of scientific or religious revolutionaries) they may reasonably oppose its dictates on certain issues.

Gadamer charges Dilthey with inconsistency in attempting to combine philosophical principles based on conscious "life" with the ambition to mount an Enlightenment-type critique of authority. But if "life" is interpreted in such a way as to include the operations of our rational consciousness and if the ideals of the Enlightenment are modified and qualified in the ways that I have suggested, it must be conceded, in the light of what I have argued so far, that Dilthey's program was well-founded in principle, whatever incidental errors might be pointed out in his own implementation of it. In particular, Dilthey was right after all in supposing that that historical consciousness may rise above its own relativity in such a way as to make objectivity in human science possible (in the second sense of "objectivity" that I distinguished above). If it is true that King Henry VIII of England married six wives and I can come to know that he did, I can be "objective" enough in my historical inquiries to ascertain what was absolutely so, rather than so merely *for* persons with a certain background and set of concerns in 1993 C.E.—whatever that would mean. That there is inevitably always *more* that may be found out by historians about Henry VIII and his marriages and that the significance for us of what may be found out may be subject to change over time (as is rightly stressed by Gadamer) does not affect the issue.[6]

---

[6] It is not to be denied that there are other aspects of the historian's task than that notoriously emphasized by Leopold von Ranke (of ascertaining and reporting the facts as they actually occurred). Gadamer's views are informative and largely justifiable as applied to these other aspects. But it must be insisted that finding out

It appears to me that Gadamer does not take sufficient account of what would appear at first sight to be obvious and is confirmed by epistemological reflection—that it is one thing to find out what was really going on in the past, another to assess its significance for us here and now (see the distinction between "history" and "dialectic" in Lonergan, 1972, pp. 128-130 and chapters 8 and 10). To suggest that these mental processes cannot in the last analysis be distinguished from each other, as Gadamer seems to do, appears to me to be very dangerous from the moral and political point of view, as well as based on mistaken epistemological assumptions. Due consideration of evidence and assessment of possibilities may lead conscientious investigators to suspect that the true story about the treatment of the kulaks under Stalin or the activities of the Spanish Inquisition is very different from what it suits the authorities or the tradition of their party or their church to put about. To claim otherwise is to open the floodgates to every kind of rewriting of history by interested parties.

On the matter of "prejudice," Gadamer appears to confuse a number of issues—among them that of the role of creative hypothesis in science, both natural and human, and that of the propriety of deference to one's tradition. If we are to advance in knowledge, we must boldly propose hypotheses, which may then be tested by the evidence of experience. Gadamer is of course right to imply that the sort of ideal of objectivity that demands that we directly confront the facts, rather than use our minds in creative and in that sense "subjective" theorizing, is sheer superstition (cf. Lonergan, 1957/1992, pp. 177-178, 183-184, 260, 437-440, etc.). There are, moreover, "prejudgments" that operate, whether consciously spelled out by their practitioners or not, both in natural and in human science; in the former, for example, that all phenomena will turn out to be susceptible of explanation, in the latter that the actions and products of human agents and producers will be intelligible as due to some judgment on their part about their situation (cf. Lonergan, 1957/1992, pp. 18-19, 587-591, 759-760). Furthermore, the communities to which inquirers belong will furnish them with many useful "prejudgments" about the matters in which they are interested; human inquirers, however redoubtable their genius or impressive their originality, never start from scratch. "Tradition" and "authority" are to be taken seriously by them as providing them with at least some judgments based on some range of hypotheses that relate to some evidence in experience, however much it is their duty to point out evidence that may have been neglected or hypotheses that may have been overlooked or brushed aside. In

---

and stating what really happened is an essential *part* of the historian's work and an absolutely necessary condition for the proper fulfillment of the rest. It is precisely this that I have tried to bring out by my examples and that Gadamer's analysis fails to capture; moreover, I would stress that this failure is no incidental blemish on his thought, but a more or less inevitable consequence of his whole epistemological approach.

this sense it is sheer folly to believe that we can dispense with tradition, and the thinkers of the Enlightenment were in error in so far as they supposed that we could do so.

However, some of the judgments instilled by tradition or authority may inhibit either attention to fresh relevant evidence or envisagement of novel hypotheses on certain matters; it is then that they amount to "prejudice" in the usual abusive sense. Once again, it must be insisted that lack of comprehensively critical principles makes it impossible to articulate clearly and distinctly, in any way that is not arbitrary, the difference between a "pre-judgment" that is to be accepted or at least respected and a "prejudice" that ought to be rejected after due reflection. Gadamer's novel use of the term "prejudice" in a non-pejorative sense is to be commended to some extent, however, as a means of drawing one's attention at once to the difficulty and the importance of making the distinction properly. It is one of the principal functions of a humane education, the *Bildung* on which Gadamer lays so much stress, to break down our "prejudices" in this usual pejorative sense; such an education softens our intellectual and moral shells, so to say, by making us aware of ways of experiencing, understanding, and feeling different from those that we are apt to take for granted as persons of our particular place and time. (There may thus have been some sense, after all, in the traditional British practice of subjecting future colonial administrators to education in the Greek and Latin classics—a practice customary in Western education, of course, long before the British became a colonial power.)

It appears to follow from Gadamer's position on the role of tradition in understanding authors of the past that one may gain some understanding of a writer distant from oneself in space and time only by virtue of a shared tradition. It seems to me that this account of the matter either fails to make sense of the understanding we may gain of an author who does not belong to the same tradition as ourselves, or inflates the concept of "tradition" in a very misleading way. It is certainly plausible at first sight to account for the understanding that average educated citizens of Europe or North America may have of the *Aeneid* or the Book of Job by saying that they stand within the tradition of these great works of literature; these works, together with others from the same cultural milieu, form a part of their educational background in the sense that even if they have not read them or even heard of them themselves, their teachers, or at least their teachers' teachers, will probably have done so. But what of the understanding that they may acquire of Amerindian folk-tales, the *Ramayana,* or the stories of the Polynesian hero Nganaoa? In what useful sense do they stand within the same "tradition" as these? Is it not a more convincing account of the matter to say that all human beings share certain basic patterns of experience, feeling, understanding, and judgment, which stories and other works of art may allude to and express in a manner that is able to cross the boundaries of "traditions" in the usual sense? After all, the recognition of such basic patterns is presumably what enabled works as divergent as the *Aeneid* and the Book of Job to be accepted as part of the multicultural Western tradition, instead of being seen only as expressions of the narrower ancient Roman and ancient Hebrew traditions, respectively.

## 3. Conclusion

My conclusion is that, though Gadamer's work has already been very influential in the human sciences and though it contains a great deal that is valuable and useful, it is vitiated by fundamental errors, mainly of an epistemological nature. Against Gadamer, and in accordance with Lonergan's principles, I have argued that we can transcend our historical limitations at least so far as is needed for us to make true statements about things as they really are, and would have been even if we had never come to speak of them. We are "rational" in the proper sense and so tend to get at the real truth about things in so far as we attend to relevant data, hypothesize freely, and judge those hypotheses to be so that are best supported by the data. The notion of "proof," in the strict sense at least, is as marginal in the natural as in the human sciences; all one can reasonably look for are hypotheses that are corroborated by evidence in experience. Rationality so conceived enables us to find the best both in our traditions and in the Enlightenment critique of those traditions and to disentangle preconceptions that are inevitable and justifiable from "prejudices" that are quite otherwise.

I do not believe that culture-bound conceptions of "truth" and "rationality," as apparently maintained by Gadamer, are coherent in the last analysis; and what is thus incoherent can hardly serve as a social ideal. But when truth and rationality cease to serve as social ideals, this is the beginning of the end of civilization. One specially dangerous consequence of Gadamer's oversights, as I have said, is that they encourage the unrestricted rewriting of history by interested groups. I do not for a moment suppose that Gadamer himself would countenance such abuses; but the fact remains that his account leaves the way wide open to them. The inverted commas that enclose the phrase "how it really was" on page 262 of *Truth and Method* do nothing to allay the anxieties of the reader who is concerned about this matter.

The effect of Gadamer's treatment of the relation between historians' "horizons" and the past in which they are interested, when all is said and done, is to make what really happened in the past dependent on the existential orientation of the investigator here and now. But, frankly, what Alexander the Great did and thought in Greece, Persia, and India 23 centuries or so ago in no way depends on what a schoolchild or even a distinguished professor of history in Europe or North America may think about him at the present time. Few people have an interest in biased interpretation of the data in the instance of Alexander; but other cases are very different. However, the Crusaders and the authors of *Malleus Maleficarum*, Joseph Stalin and the Khmer Rouge acted as they did and caused the untold destruction and misery that they did, whatever it may suit later devout Catholics or communists to believe about these things. Of course, it is by no means to be denied that the significance of important historical events, like Luther's reformation or the French and Russian revolutions, needs to be reassessed in every generation; this aspect of the historian's task is well brought out by Gadamer.

It remains very briefly to relate what I have said to communication and its concerns. The principles of Gadamer's thought render it impossible to know what is the case (as opposed to merely what is the case *for* someone within a particular historical and social situation); and in consequence, what the meaning of a text or utterance really is, or what really are the beliefs and assumptions of any audience. Since a satisfactory account of communication, which after all is a matter of conveying real meanings to real audiences, implies the possibility of this kind of knowledge, such an account is not really compatible with Gadamer's thought. I have argued elsewhere in this volume (see chapter 7 above) that Lonergan's thought meets the stated requirements and so does provide the basis for a convincing account of communication (see especially Lonergan, 1957/1992, chapter 17, section 3; Lonergan, 1972, chapters 3 and 7; Meynell, 1991b, chapter 4).

# 11

# The Interiority of Communication: Literary History

*Geoffrey B. Williams, SJ*

In the beginning was the Word...the Word was God....All things were made through him, and without him was not anything made that was made.
                                                                                    —Gospel of John 1:1-3 NRSV

What constitutes the human has been described by Bernard Lonergan in *Insight: A Study of Human Understanding* (1957/1992) and developed in *Method in Theology* (1972). For him, human subjects are historical subjects and find themselves situated in areas of discourse that bring into active expression their wonder at being so placed. According to Lonergan, that wonder operates in human subjectivity on the levels of experiencing, understanding, judging, and acting. People try to understand what they experience, make judgments on the basis of their understanding, and act of out those judgments. This basic "reading" of experience and response to it underpins the act of communication.

Lonergan's enterprise centers around the necessary involvement and explication of subjectivity to ground any act of understanding. He himself notes, "prior to all writings of history, prior to all interpretation of other minds, there is the self-scrutiny of the historian, the self-knowledge of the interpreter. That prior task is my concern" (Lonergan 1957/1992, p. 23). After Lonergan has explored in *Insight* the prior task of the historian, the self-appropriation of personal subjectivity, he builds an open method on this previous meta-method. *Method in Theology* is the result, and the eight functional specialties of theology described there will be transposed in this essay to the task of understanding what constitutes "literary history." When literary history is viewed in this manner, it becomes a coordinated program of aims, projects, and modes of discourse that include the eight functional specialties identified by Lonergan with respect to the field of theology as research, interpretation, tradition, dialectics, horizons, doctrines, systematics, and communications. Literary history is the implicit narrative of communication and the eight functional specialties make explicit that narrative.

This essay analyses the narrative by which people "read" and reveal themselves and shows how it determines the way in which they communicate. The narrative in this essay uses epistemology as its dominant trope. It does not claim to use literary history *as* a mode to bring to the fore the problematics of communication, though that will happen. Rather it states that the interiority of communication is literary history. Literary history is engaged in studying the dynamics of what is brought to the worlds of discourse through which we live and have our common being.

As Martin Heidegger asserts in his "Letter on Humanism":

> Language is the house of Being. In its home man dwells. Those who think and those who create with words are the guardians of this home. Their guardianship accomplishes the manifestation of being in so far as they bring the manifestation to language and maintain it in language through their speech. (1977, p. 193)

For Heidegger, such discourse is temporal (1927/1962, p. 400), and it is precisely its temporal nature that gives communication its narrative form (see Ricoeur, 1983-1985/1984, 1983-1985/1985). Language only exists in narrative form. Narrative gives a plot to the manifestations of being. It establishes product, context, style, genre, and modes of production and reception. Any act of communication depends on narrative. A gesture, a smile, a grunt, the color of a traffic signal, a type of haircut, each tells a story. Each, in that telling, conveys information. Narrativity gives meaning to the act of communication. A simple sentence is constructed according to the narrative of grammar. The Word-Made-Flesh is constructed according to the narrative of being human. Between the two, the word and the Word, are the universes of discourse in which we live. Narrative, by establishing a particular world of meaning, communicates a particular point of view and produces subjectivity.

Contemporary theory situates subjectivity within the realm of language (Lacan, 1977; Kristeva, 1984; Irigaray, 1974/1985; Spivak, 1990). This approach to subjectivity is compatible with Lonergan's approach. For him, subjectivity is appropriated through cognitional structure. That dynamic structure is a sequential operation that emplots the matter at hand into modes of presence. Such a sequence is narrative. Narrative embodies tropes in its exposition (White, 1978). In fact, what is understood and communicated as subjectivity is both literary and subject to the contingencies of temporality. As both Lacan and Kristeva note, what one grasps as one's subjectivity is a socially constructed composite that has been built up through the appropriation of language over a certain number of years. (In chapter 2 Thomas J. Farrell has explored the idea of subjectivity as a socially constructed composite, although he does not refer to the process as a literary construct.) We "read" ourselves as "texts," and when we communicate, we reveal ourselves in terms of our competencies, our desires, our perspectives, the appropriated cultural formulae of civility. Such communication is intertextual. That communication, in its implicit dependence on plot, and in its overt telling of a story, is narrative. Narratives, by establishing a particular world of meaning, communicate a particular point of view. They not only establish perspectives, but also create communities of those who either share similar points of view or disagree with them.

Literary history examines the narratives by which we communicate through the traditions we subscribe to in the way in which our basic openness to being is incarnated. As a discipline today to be found in select courses at university departments of literature, this basic narrativity has been appropriated by special interest groups. The field of literary history today includes perspectives from the whole range of the political and the ideological spectrum, partisan academic interests, and specific approaches. In assessing these manifestations, one needs to be aware that literary history constitutes the interiority of communication. What specific manifestations depict are the strategic emplotments of particular points-of-view.

Literary history, seen in the light of this essay, is more than the tracing of the development of genre and image. It is more than the analysis of periods, such as the "Elizabethan," the "Romantic," or the "Modern." It becomes an approach to the analysis of what constitutes communication. The understanding of literary history proposed in this paper is intertextual, for it holds that intertextuality is the critically involved commitment of literary history. In communication, people present themselves as "texts" and are responded to as such. Moreover, human subjects "read" themselves in terms of other "texts." Their literary competence is a proficiency determined by cultural contexts and the power of translation. The most comprehensive of these "texts" in written or oral tradition is the narrative called history. History, precisely because it is emplotted in narrative and grounded in tropes of discourse, is literary history—and any act of communication is a manifestation of literary history. And so it is vital to understand what happens in literary history if we are to understand what happens in the communication act. They are the same instance, from different perspectives, of being human, when we consider them from the standpoint of Lonergan's account of what it means to be human.

At first blush, literary history may seem like something only specialists in literary studies do. But people can be considered literary historians inasmuch as they have appropriated and transmit their cultural identity. As those people consciously reflect on their cultural identity, they have achieved the same status, if perhaps not the same competence, as their academic counterparts. So the focus in this essay on literary history should not limit us to considering only the activities of specialists in literary studies, although their works will be used here to exemplify those processes people engage in when they reflect on their cultural identity.

The activities of those specialists have resulted in the proliferation of literary histories today. Each has its own philosophical, cultural, and epistemological presuppositions, and each has its own areas of interest, ambitions, and ends. A critical reader in this area is thrown back upon a process of discernment in order to assess the truth value and responsibility of what is available for use and how it can be used. Such a reader is spontaneously challenged by reading a particular literary history and can ask questions of it in terms of truth, value, responsibility, and commitment, which in the final analysis suggest a theological ground. Such questioning seems to deny the autonomy of the mode of discourse known as literary history by assigning to it a theological status. Yet theology is itself a mode of literary history. Both are self-conscious "readings" of the act of communication as self-transcendence. Both are grounded in texts that cannot be reduced merely to cultural moments; both have as their significant origin the desire to understand and to communicate, and both are human constructs giving symbolic actualization to aspects of transcendence. As George Steiner puts it in *Real Presences*, "Any coherent account of the capacity of human speech to communicate meaning and feeling is, in the final analysis, underwritten by the assumption of God's presence" (1989, p. 3). Moreover, inasmuch as a text can be regarded as an event, or the occasion of an event, theological reflection and literary history share the same methodological problematic of transforming act into systematic understanding. Finally, on the level of metamethodology precisely the same concerns on the nature of subjectivity and the horizons of one's eschatology occupy both the theologian and the literary historian. Vernon Ruland has observed that "each genuine theologian or critic must be an engaged insider, re-enacting sensitively the primary religious-poetic experience itself, before attempting to understand or assess it" (1975, p. 4).

The particular approach advocated here aims to protect the unity of the undertaking of literary history by showing the underlying narrative that structures it, and the interrelatedness of the seemingly diverse approaches that constitute literary history. As such, this paper has two aims. First, it examines the narrative—the involved subjectivity—of a literary historian; then, it uses that narrative to create a method for literary history. In doing so, this paper transposes Lonergan's theological project, with adaptations, to that of literary history.

## 1. The Involved Subjectivity of the Literary Historian

Gerald Bruns in *Inventions: Writing, Textuality, and Understanding in Literary History* observes that "most of the major theoretical movements in recent literary study...seem...to rest on a common procedure: In order to define their topics of study, they must first characterize them as epistemological problems" (1982, p. ix). Now, Lonergan conceives the self in epistemological terms, and his philosophy is propaedeutic to the self-appropriation of one's subjectivity in those terms. But Jacques Lacan would point out that "where I am, there I am not" (1977, p. 171) to suggest that such a self-appropriation would be a false one. For Lacan, any form of self-appropriation would be only proximate because the metaphoric nature of language into which we are born causes us to misread ourselves. But Lacan's criticism is schizophrenic; for if we are all trapped in the distorting mirror of language, that distortion applies equally to his perceptions. One cannot, in some idealist manner, seek to transcend oneself to "read" oneself or to present a literary history. The self-appropriation Lonergan suggests involves reflection upon one's concrete performance in its historical context. By contrast, Lonergan sees the epistemological narrative of the fully existential subject as one of experiencing, understanding, judging, and acting (1957/1992, pp. 308-312).

Lonergan maintains that despite what people say they do, in fact, the act according to this narrative pattern of human consciousness. He claims that reflection on one's *concrete* operations in the world would reveal this structural dynamic of one's interiority. He also points out that "the dynamic structure of human knowing intends being" (Lonergan, 1967/1988, p. 211); being "is the objective of the pure desire to know" (Lonergan, 1957/1992, p. 372). The intention of being is manifest in that dynamic cognitional structure that is revealed when the existential subject reflects on the process of coming to terms with the universe immediately present to oneself. In reading that world, one tries to gain insights about this presence. These insights are subjected to a verification process that determines their truthfulness, or validity, or the appropriateness to the context out of which they emerge and from which responsible action derives. That verification process is metaphoric. The unfamiliar becomes familiarized; the plot of understanding is either reinforced or altered. This formal epistemological structuring of human consciousness is revealed in the narrative self-appropriation of one's interiority.

This formal "reading" of oneself does not ask with what techniques the "reading" is done. Such techniques can encompass, among others, psychoanalytic sessions, statistical correlations of one's dominant metaphors, explorations of the cultural, social, or religious tropes that inform one's self-understanding and self-expression, discursive strategies, and grammar rules in language. But the particular approach advocated here presents a narrative pattern of "reading" applicable to every mode of human activity, including the psychoanalytic, the literary, and the linguistic—and thus can be described as transpersonal and transcultural.

Such troping is synecdochic. It participates in the world of discourse it reveals. Lonergan's formal epistemology does not create a closed system. It does not insist on what constitutes material for empirical consciousness. For it, insight is solely a meaningful pattern—a narrative—arrived at from the data. Judgment is reached when insight satisfies, or does not satisfy, whatever conditions of verification are present in the context. Finally, responsibility occurs if action devolves from the judgments made. At that point, the narrative of the story is not only told, but acted out existentially. The notion of "being" in the existential subject—that is, basic human intentionality—comes to term when no further questions are raised and when all the conditions that constitute the intelligibility of the data, within an established context, are satisfied responsibly. When such a state is reached, objectivity is attained.

Two aspects of Lonergan's notion of objectivity need to be noticed here. First, unlike classical logic, it is not independent of the human subject, though it does transcend subjectivity (Lonergan, 1972, p. 338). The objectivity based on a logic that is conceived as independent from a subjectivity, a tradition, and a history, ignores the facts that "(1) statements have meaning only in their contexts, and (2) contexts are ongoing—and ongoing contexts are multiple" (Lonergan, 1972, p. 326). Lonergan, then, would hold for a genuine objectivity in literary history, but he would also hold that the ongoing, multiple, contexts of historicity render that objective judgment open to revision—should new data emerge, new perspectives be adopted, and new exigencies arise. In history, the finite human subject, grounded in the world and shaped by psychological, social, historical, and cultural conditions, can affirm an objective judgment that has its basis in wonder, and its spontaneous desire to know, and is situated in a particular reading of its context.

This spontaneous drive to understand constitutes the basic horizon of the human subject and manifests itself historically in the dynamic and intentional levels of consciousness that can be self-appropriated by that human subject as cognitional structure. Thus the evasion of consciousness is the evasion of history and, as Nietzsche observes, animals that have no self-consciousness have no history (1874/1957, p. 5). Through self-appropriation the historian realizes that history is not somehow separate from oneself. Inadequate self-appropriation provokes a position such as that held by Harold Bloom who wonders how one is "to teach a tradition now grown so wealthy and so heavy that to accommodate it demands more strength than any single consciousness can provide" (1975, p. 39). It is precisely the tradition that contributes to the formation of the insight, and a revelation of tradition is a revelation of oneself inasmuch as one's basic horizon—in the collected data available for questioning, the insights gained, and the judgments formed—is exposed as the intentional exploration of the nature of a particular literary history.

Cognitional analysis provides the upper blade of an analytic tool, the lower blade of which depends on the exigencies of the particular moment of the discourse in question. This method based on interiority analysis of the subject as text provides a way to deal with the proliferation of critical theories about the nature, aims, and scope of literary history. Beyond literary histories based on gender, racial, and ideological concerns, there are textual histories that could trace the evolution of image, metaphor, or theme; contextual histories that concentrate on the milieu of the texts; hermeneutical histories that determine intentions; as well as structuralist or deconstructionist histories. It is not just that every theory has a history but, more to the point, that every theory has a literary history if only because language and history are the same. Cognitional analysis helps avoid the bewilderment generated by such profusion and the concomitant bias of regarding all such conceptual situations as forms of "fictionalism." Often, of course, different aspects of that inter-related project cumulatively called literary history are synecdochically given that generic title, and this adds to the confusion of defining the topic.

On the positive side, a proliferation of theories has the effect of throwing the literary historian into a position of defending a particular choice of theory, of challenging set assumptions, and of explicitating operative subjectivity. There then arises a spontaneous movement to interiority in the attempt (1) to sort out the theories involved and to differentiate the areas that each covers, (2) to provide for some process of one's own by which they can be evaluated, and (3) to create a system in which what is valid in those theories can function in a complex unity. The situation is not unlike the movement of *quaestiones disputandae*, in medieval theology, in the construction of a *summa*. The difference, however, is that while the medieval ideal was modelled on the Aristotelian notion of science and on the principle of non-contradiction, the contemporary effort structures itself on the narrative of interiority analysis and on the nature of the contextually verifiable insight, as Lonergan has described these processes.

Lonergan describes such a method as "a normative pattern of recurrent and related operations yielding cumulative and progressive results" (1972, p. 4). He conceives method "not as a set of rules but as a prior normative pattern of operations from which the rules may be derived" (1972, p. 6). This prior, normative, pattern is, as expected, based on the operations of the human subject that manifest themselves in the dynamic and related operations of human intentionality, that is, in cognitional structure. The pattern is described in terms of functional specialties.

> Functional specialization distinguishes and separates successive stages in the process from data to results. Thus, textual criticism aims at determining what is written. The interpreter or commentator takes over where the textual critic leaves off; his aim is to discover what is meant. The historian moves on the third level; he assembles interpreted texts and endeavors to construct a single narrative or view....[These] functional specialties are intrinsically related to each other. They are successive parts of one and the same process. The earlier parts are incomplete without the later. The later presuppose the earlier and complement them. In brief, functional specialties are functionally interdependent. (Lonergan 1972, p. 9)

The reading of the metaphor of interiority by which human consciousness is appropriated is presented in terms of these eight functional specialties.

## 2. The Eight Functional Specialties of Literary History

Lonergan proposes eight functional specialties based on the awareness that there are four distinct levels of conscious and intentional operations. The four are: experiencing, understanding, judging, and deciding. These levels occur twice for the specialist. First, one has to come to terms with the area under survey. One needs to collect data, form hypotheses from that data, judge which insight is valid or not, and then apply it. Second, in the process of communicating this application the literary historian operates out of the horizons of a particularized consciousness that is made manifest in key decisions. These become the cornerstones for a systematic exposition that is given expression finally in a chosen idiom. Communication as the human art uses the dynamic structure of interiority twice, once to come to the moment of decision and then to arrive at the moment of expression. The eight inter-related parts are: (1) research, (2) interpretation, (3) history, (4) dialectics, (5) foundations, (6) doctrines, (7) systematics, and, finally, (8) communications (Lonergan 1972, pp. 127-132). (For further information about each one, see the glossary at the end of the volume.)

Lonergan sees such a transference of his method in theology to similarly situated disciplines as justified by the method itself since it "is the work of human minds performing the same basic relations as are found in other special methods. In other words, transcendental method is…a constituent part of the special methods proper to the natural and human sciences" (Lonergan, 1972, p. 23). Literary history uses this narrative structure of transcendental method.

### 2.1 Research

The first functional specialty raises the question what, in particular instances, constitutes the objects of research in literary history. What are we going to speak about? Everything is historical, and so the data that must be assembled in research must be relevant to some particular question or problem or interest. Already the intentionality of the literary historian comes into play in the selection of the material to be considered. This does not mean that the historian is caught in subjectivity and that objectivity cannot be obtained. Creativity and freedom lie in grasping the possible relevance of data. Choice affirms the judgment that "this" is necessary for the project at hand while "that" is not. The material for research for literary history includes *anything* that has implications for the particular literary project. Such research uncovers data that not only gives material for insight, but also posits evidence to refute inadequate insights. While research for literary history involves intentionality analysis, its object is not literary history in its entirety, but merely the provision of the data. Biographical material, biographical data, or the status of texts as objectifying a culture—each presents the concrete possibilities for interpretation.

The bias of research is the denial, or the overlooking, of material as relevant. That bias emerges from the limitation of the literary historian whose foundational reality effectively denies or overlooks the involvements of certain manifestations of reality in the project under consideration. For example, gender and ethnic criticism have levelled this charge against the common academic practices of the institution of literary history. In turn, gender and ethnic criticism can reduce the complexity that constitutes the material for literary history to the ideologies of logo-, phallo-, or ethno-centrism.

## 2.2 Interpretation

While literary history finds its data within the textual artifacts of culture, interpretation is concerned with the diverse ways of understanding these data. Should that data be texts, among the possible interpretations are text-as-intention, text-as-intended, text-as-event, text-as-occasion, or text-as-repression. The treatment of textuality in any of these cases, and their combinations, is complicated, as Brian Stock points out:

> Literary critics may unwittingly have contributed to the view of an event as an isolated object by artificially separating texts from their contexts, that is, by considering the text not as it comes to being in a reader's mind, nor as he reacts to it, but only as something in itself, the totality of whose meaning is assumed automatically out of an inner objective life. But the text too is a complex event. (1977, p. 186)

To be aware of that complexity means to have some grasp of the forces that help constitute the presence of the text. These may be material, psychological, social, or cultural. Even if one chooses to limit oneself to text-as-statement, one needs to bear in mind the following observation made by Ricoeur:

> In spoken discourse...the intention of the speaking subject and the meaning of the discourse overlap each other in such a way that it is the same thing to understand what the speaker means and what his discourse means. With the written discourse the author's intention and the meaning of the text cease to coincide...the tie between the speaker and the discourse is not abolished but distanced and complicated.... What the text says now matters more than what the author meant to say. (quoted in Gerhart, 1981, p. 392)

It is at this point that the critical approach termed "reader-response" criticism enters. Such an approach holds that the reader, or the community in which the reader is situated, determines the meaning of the text.

There arises in interpretation, here, the question of judging the correctness of one's understanding of a text and its significance. There are the questions not only of what story is the insight telling, but also what stories underpin the ways in which that insight has been told and has been received. Once again, the literary historian is thrown back upon the dynamism of his or her subjectivity in coming to a decision. The literary historian as empiricist will assume that interpretation is merely a matter of looking at signs. Such an interpreter, then, runs into problems in dealing with the complexities of reading a text. The empiricist is deceived that understanding is taking a good look. Such an understanding would claim to offer "a close reading" of the text and is opposed to that of the idealist who finds it impossible to come to a judgment about the text. For the idealist, one interesting idea about the text is as valid as another. An example is Harold Bloom's commentary in *The Book of J.* Bloom understands the author of the ur-Pentateuch, J, to be most likely a woman of the royal house living at King Solomon's court. "I can prove nothing; I can only invite other readers to the hypothesis that there is one J and that she precedes any other substantial biblical writer" (1990, p. 22). The critical realist, such as Lonergan, working on the level of judgment, raises "the problem of context, of the hermeneutical circle, and of the relativity of the totality of relevant data, and of the possible relevance of more remote inquiries, of the limitations to be placed on the scope of one's interpretations" (Lonergan, 1972, p. 155). For example, a literary historian who is a critical realist and interested in Romanticism would affirm that *when* Romanticism is held to be a preoccupation with the nature of human consciousness, then Emily Bronte's *Wuthering Heights* shares concerns with Hegel's *Phenomenology of Mind* or with the works of Freud and Jung. Wayne C. Booth acts as a critical realist when he makes the following observation, in his criticism of M. H. Abrams' *Natural Supernaturalism*:

> The human mind can see only what it can see; we can know only what our categories will allow us to know, and our chosen language of inquiry can express only a fraction of what may be expressed. Every inquiry, and especially every humanistic inquiry, will produce results that are "relative" to the terms in which the inquirer sets up his problem, and no one inquiry can hope to produce more than one perspective on any subject, a fragment of all that might be worth knowing about it. (1976, p. 412)

From such a point-of-view, interpretation approximates meaning.

The accessibility of the past, through texts and the relations of texts to authors, audience, contexts, and other texts, depends upon the principles of interpretation advocated by the literary historian. Since the narrative of communication supported in this paper not only implies a theory of confrontation between a disjunct subject and object, but also insists upon a subject grounded in history, I would note that the *present*, like the past, as manifest to the existential subject is also a verified insight. The past, or the aspect of the past, delimited by the literary historian can also be rendered present and objective by verified insights. Moreover, inasmuch as human subjects share the same structure of intentionality, it would seem possible for the literary historian to grasp some significance of a text in its internal relations and its relations to the author and to its context. When this happens, it is not that the past, in its complexity, becomes present, in *its* complexity, but that the particular meaning of the past is given present significance. There is then no disjunction between an interpretation of the past and a present interpretation of that past. Gadamer would support this correlation when he contends that "one really grasps the meaning of a text only when one brings its implications to bear upon contemporary living" (quoted in Lonergan, 1972, p. 169).

Interpretation provides a synchronic cross-section of that ongoing process that constitutes history and of which written history, with its limitations, is merely synecdochic.

Moreover, just as existential history comprises diverse traditions, so too does written history manifest a particular tradition or a synthesis of traditions. Thus, what Elizabeth Bruss writes on the principles of interpretation for the reader is also true for the notion of tradition to the literary historian:

> As there are different modes of intertextuality that a literary work may exploit, so too there are different reading strategies—conservative, revisionist, marginal, and insurgent—which differ less in their pace and proximity to the text, than in their basic postures of aggression or defense, their rage for order or their delight in introducing new disorder, the different guiding interests that they bring to bear. (1982, p. 66)

The politics of reading moves beyond epistemological allegiances, or principles of value, to indicate fundamental commitments to language and the existential realities of communication that such commitments affirm or deny.

Basic postures, in terms of interiority analysis, will be discussed in the fifth and sixth functional specialties: "foundations" and "doctrines." At the moment, all that is being asserted is that tradition mediates a text and a text mediates a tradition. This intertextual dialogue manifests itself in a particular moment that reveals the horizon out of which the literary historian's relevant interests can arise. Neither a tradition, nor a text, is closed—that is, dead or a prison-house. Neither can be ideological (though both can be used for ideological ends). Both tradition and text and the relations between the two are open-ended. The historian is not trapped in a cultural subjectivity that prevents the basic questions from being asked—What about that? Is that intelligible? Is that so? It is the idealist's notion of tradition to see it as confining. The idealist suffers under the mistaken notion that the horizon out of which he or she operates is a mental structure, rather than an orientation that allows one to ask such basic questions as, "Is this true?" That orientation also provides one with the formal tools necessary for the verification, or correction, of one's insights.

A correct epistemological theory, available to the literary historian through the self-appropriation of his or her cognitional structure, would reveal in the notion of tradition, present through the text, an open space for development, elaboration, and self-correction, in the process of time, as Gunter Buck points out:

> Hermeneutical explication of the implicit cannot wholly exhaust its content of meaning, so that owing to the vagueness of its horizon, a constitutive deposit of unexplicit meaning remains over on the side of interpretation, which cannot be transmitted by any exhaustive procedure. (1978, p. 46)

The freedom sought by the idealist is fully available to the literary historian "who, in understanding, also does not have command of his own horizon in a wholly explicit fashion" (Buck, 1978, p. 46). The meeting of the two mysteries, the historian and the text, continues a tradition that "is not...over and done with, but...which is still working itself out in the present" (Hoy, 1975, p. 284).

## 2.3 History

The question that then confronts the literary historian in the functional specialty "history" is basically, "What *does* constitute the past?" or "What is a period or, even, a genre?"

David Lodge provides an answer that conforms to the interiority analysis advocated in this paper:

> The concept of a period, whether in history at large, or in literary history, is not a fact but an interpretation, a human selection and grouping of fact for human purposes, collectively generated and modified by an endless process of re-description. (1979, p. 554)

The functional specialty "history" in the description of literary history, from the perspective of this paper, is therefore the critical presentation of evolution of interpretations. It explores the narrativity of narrative. David Hoy points out the following:

> ...all literary interpretation is in an important sense literary history. The act of interpretation itself generates the history of the literary text and literature is essentially historical since the work does not exist independently from the tradition of interpretations in which it is understood. Moreover, interpretation is also a self-interpretation of that tradition. (1975, p. 285)

This specialty encompasses the exposition of a literary movement, or the significant shifts, over a period of time, from one literary sensibility to the next. It recognizes all of these as forms of interpretation. It would also engage itself in presenting the changing forms of critical understanding of a movement.

There are systematic exigencies of human consciousness that allow for the differentiation of the modes of writing literary history. First, there emerges in the writing-as-interpretation of literary history the realm of common sense. This realm distinguishes itself in the descriptive evolution of authors, themes, patterns, images, or concerns within a tradition. This mode of literary analysis does not occur primarily through an explicit scientific method that is controlled by an overriding insight, or metaphor, but is rather the result of a chronology and is expressed in everyday language where words function to focus attention on what has occurred in the development of a tradition rather than on the relations within a tradition.

But once the question is raised—Why does a particular tradition emerge in this way?—literary history moves from the realm of common sense to the realm of theory. Theory seeks to understand the relations within a tradition. It could posit, as does Harold Bloom (1973), the hypothesis that the relations within a tradition are to be explained in terms of the anxiety of influence—or, as does the Marxist, in terms of a dialectical materialism.

The proliferation of theories to explain literary history forces the historian to a deeper level of understanding in the desire to evaluate the effectiveness of one theory or another, to discern the basis for a particular theory, and to come to some understanding of the value of that theory. This deeper level is one of interiority. It examines the operations of the literary historian. It is "a heightening of intentional consciousness, an attending not merely to objects, but also to the intending subject and his acts" (Lonergan, 1972, p. 83). It is within this context that this essay is written. Lonergan points out that "the withdrawal into interiority is not an end in itself. From it one returns to the realm of common sense and theory with the ability to meet...methodological exigence" (Lonergan, 1972, p. 83). He continues as follows:

> Finally there is the transcendental exigence. There is to human desire an unrestricted demand for intelligibility. There is to human judgment a demand for the unconditioned. There is to human deliberation a criterion that criticizes every finite good. (1972, p. 83)

In the realm of transcendental exigence, different literary histories project toward a total history. This is eschatological in scope. From a Christian perspective this is realized when the relations between word, in its many literary forms, and the Word-as-Reality are totally manifest. Within the limitations of human finitude, every communication act is symbolic of that eschatological moment. Every literary history elaborates that symbol.

## 2.4 Dialectics

Whether a particular history is valid or accurate is one question, but the fact that such an interpretation can be challenged reveals the basic open-ended nature of tradition and shows the importance of the next functional specialty, "dialectics." "Dialectics" allows the different modes of literary history-as-interpretation to critique each other in the areas of common concern so that the presuppositions underlying the different projects can be examined in the light of intentionality analysis.

It is because tradition is open-ended and on-going that dialectic can be engaged. In "dialectics" the traditions of interpretations challenge each other and the history of their challenges, and their resolutions, are also part of literary history. "Dialectics" brings to light foundational reality. Not all opposition is dialectical.

There are differences that will be eliminated by uncovering fresh data. There are differences we have named perspectival, and they merely witness to the complexity of historical reality. But beyond these are fundamental conflicts stemming from explicit or implicit cognitional theory, an ethical stance, a religious outlook. They profoundly modify one's mentality. They are to be overcome only through an intellectual, moral, and religious conversion. The function of dialectic will be to bring such conflicts to light, and to provide a technique that objectifies subjective differences and promotes conversion. (Lonergan, 1972, p. 235)

Conversion embodies a shift of the metaphors by which literary history is read.

The discipline of literary history is filled with occurrences of such dialectics: The Moderns against the Ancients in the 18th century, literature-as-mimetic versus literature-as-expressive, Classicism versus Romanticism, Marxism versus aestheticism, deconstruction versus humanism, feminism versus phallocentrism. These opposing viewpoints do not exist in the abstract, but in real people in real situations and provoke, as a necessary part of literary history, the analysis of the historian's own stance. W. H. Walsh, in his *Philosophy of History*, has pointed out that "differences between historians are, in the last resort, differences of philosophies, and whether we can resolve them depends on whether we can resolve philosophical conflicts" (1960, p. 105). These differences are more than just philosophical. They are existential. They involve the epistemological, psychological, social, political, and eschatological components of the historian as a human subject, fully situated in the world as himself or herself historical.

Interiority analysis of the historian to reveal the underlying principle that selects data, grounds interpretation, and comments on one tradition rather than another, becomes a crucial aspect of literary history. It reveals the horizon of the literary historian. "Dialectics" as a functional specialty brings to the fore the implicit presuppositions that reveal the orientation of the literary historian.

## 2.5 Foundations

Horizons define the expanse of the historian's interests and values, the boundaries between what is known to be unknown and that which is beyond even the scope of possible knowledge. Lonergan has defined horizons as "the sweep of our interests and of our knowledge; they are the fertile source of further knowledge and care; but they are also the boundaries that limit our capacities for assimilating more than we already have attained" (1972, p. 237). The historian's epistemological, moral, and religious positions define operative horizons.

Epistemologically, one's horizon is defined basically whether one conceives one's intentional operations to remain on the level of the empirical, or the intelligent, or the rational. If one were to ask three literary historians, each with a different epistemology, what are the facts of literary history, each reply would be significantly different. "For the empiricist, they are what was out there and capable of being looked at. For the idealist, they are mental constructions carefully based on data recorded in documents. For the critical realist, they are events in the world mediated by true acts of meaning" (Lonergan, 1972, p. 239).

Morally, horizons can be defined, basically, in terms of exclusivity or inclusivity and can best be understood in the context of literary history in terms of the dialectics between the aestheticism of the New Criticism that concentrates on the text-in-itself and the social awareness of Marxist criticism that sees the text as a manifestation of the moral and social forces in a culture. Similarly, gender, or race, criticism is focused precisely around this issue. Carl Becker has pointed out the moral value of history in an observation that seems even more applicable to literary history:

> The value of history is...not scientific, but moral; by liberating the mind, by deepening the sympathies, by fortifying the will, it enables us to control, not society, but ourselves—a much more important thing; it prepares us to live more humanely in the present and to meet rather than to foretell the future. (quoted in Lonergan, 1972, p. 245)

In whatever way it works, it is impossible to deny the moral force of literature, and thus the treatment of morality, political or otherwise, by the literary historian—either in bracketing off (or prescinding from), or in interpreting that dimension present in texts and in the interpretation of texts—reveals the orientation of the tradition under survey.

If Marxists, or secular humanists, point out the moral dimension in literary history, their own biases limit them from seeing, or understanding, or accepting, the fact that literature is more than just a particular manifestation of culture. They ignore the fact that literature is an act of transcendence and, thus, manifests dimensions that go beyond cultural analysis.

Those dimensions are only accessible to the literary historian with transcendental sensibilities. This is not to claim that the literary historian must be sectarian. It is to claim that, ultimately, a text is a mystery and not the association of technical or social effects. Indeed, it is the mysterious dimension of the text that renders the literary historian uneasy at the Marxist tendency to want to see literature as a manifestation of a dialectical materialism at work and to present criticism in a didactic mode. Literature that has the status of classic raises ultimate questions that can be appreciated only on ultimate grounds by the historian "grasped by ultimate concern" (Lonergan, 1972, p. 240).

The fourth functional specialty, "dialectics," in literary history raises those basic questions of the attitude of the historian to his or her own tradition and to other traditions. The resolution of the dialectics involved provide the "foundations"—the fifth functional specialty—out of which the literary historian operates in pronouncing which traditions of understanding are subscribed to, and carried on, and from which emerge his or her basic controlling insights. These are presented as "doctrines" that, in "systematics" are related to and reconciled with each other in a pattern of conceptualization to be textualized in "communications."

"Foundations," then, looks back to, and underpins, the first four functional specialties inasmuch as research, interpretation, the tradition of interpretation, and the diverging patterns of understanding, are controlled by the active subject, and it provides the controlling influence of the last three. "Foundations" is not a set of premises, nor logical first propositions, but rather a dynamic and self-conscious intentionality grounded in the human subject and manifested as significant orientation in epistemological, moral, and religious terms. "Foundations" presents the dynamic and human base that comes to the fore in any thoroughgoing hermeneutic of literary history. Frederick G. Lawrence, in an unpublished version of his talk "On Reading a Text: Gadamer, Hermeneutics, and Literary Criticism" (1977), makes the following observation:

> The radical issue in hermeneutics is not whether one can move from one cultural context to another or whether one can thematize the common sense of one culture in any number of technical ways: Freudian, Stylistics, Structuralist, Romantic.... The key issue really is conversion; the key issue is, really, what is going on in one's life. And that's really what hermeneutics is bringing back to the study of literature.

Hermeneutics forces the literary historian to examine radical foundations, the grounds of a personal stance in the world, because what is done in interpreting chronological facts historically institutes an eschatology that can be "available" only on the level of belief.

Foundational reality deals with three interrelated questions. First, what is truth, and how does one attain it; second, how does one deal responsibly with that truth; and, third, what is the reality affirmed by that responsibility. If this particular portion of this paper focuses on the third question, it is merely because the first two questions, in the contemporary discourse on literary history, have had wide airing, while that same discourse seems to regard the positing of the analysis of belief in such a human discipline— pacé Newman in *The Idea of a University*—as an anachronistic bit of sectarian intrusion. Contemporary discourse, then, reduces "foundations" to the merely aesthetic and social. It does not see its secularism to be as foundational as the religious values it repudiates. But as Mary Gerhart points out, "Regardless, belief must be understood concomitantly as the aesthetic disposition toward a field of meaning" (1981, p. 398). She continues:

> The question of belief in literary criticism has an important function within and beyond that particular discipline. It provides a concept that focuses on the proper interrelationship of all elements in the literary enterprise: namely, poem, poet, reader, worlds of meaning. (1981, p. 398)

Here Gerhart has transformed the discipline of literary history that unites "poem, poet, reader, [and] worlds of meaning" to the notion of belief and so continues in the functional specialty "foundations" the insight of this paper—that history is belief.

But "foundations" involves more than the question of belief. It also involves the question of truth and the question of value. Lonergan stresses the interrelatedness of belief, truth, and value. He notes that "religious conversion sublates moral [conversion], and moral conversion sublates the intellectual [conversion]" (Lonergan, 1972, p. 243). He defines truth in terms of intellectual conversion, which he describes in the following terms:

> a radical clarification and, consequently, the elimination of an exceedingly stubborn and misleading myth concerning reality, objectivity, and human knowledge. That myth is that knowing is like looking, that objectivity is seeing what there is to be seen and not seeing what is not there, and that the real is what is out there to be looked at. (Lonergan, 1972, p. 240)

The first part of this paper has dealt with the way Lonergan tries to overcome that particular myth by recourse to the epistemological pattern of human intentionality. Moral conversion is the movement away from self-enclosure and its implications of exclusiveness, while religious conversion is "otherworldly falling in love" (Lonergan, 1972, p. 240), which opens the perspective of the literary historian as fully as is existentially possible to the possibilities inherent in literary texts, in literary traditions, and in the relations between texts or between texts and cultures. Religious conversion is transformative. "The 'otherness' that enters into us makes us other" (Steiner, 1989, p. 188; also see Farrell's discussion of subjectivity in chapter 2). These three aspects of self-transcendence define the authenticity, or inauthenticity, of any act of communication. They are the horizons out of which an approach is made to writing literary history. It is out of these horizons that the functional speciality of "doctrines" comes.

## 2.6 Doctrines

"Doctrines" is the sixth functional specialty and would constitute the overriding insight, the basic focus, of a literary history, or literary historian. Thus D. W. Robertson would assert that medieval literature centers around the notion of *caritas*, and M. H. Abrams in *Natural Supernaturalism* would claim the following:

> Much of what distinguishes writers I call "Romantic" derives from the fact that they undertook, whatever their religious creed or lack of creed, to save traditional concepts, schemes, values that had been based on the relation of the Creator to his creature and creation, but to reformulate them within the prevailing two-term system of subject and object, ego and non-ego, the human mind or consciousness and its transactions with nature. (1971, p. 13)

For Abrams, here, Romanticism is "natural supernaturalism." The doctrines that present themselves as unifying principles to select, organize, and evaluate the field of data under consideration range from the broadly general, e.g., "literature as mimetic" to the narrowly specific, e.g., "Coleridge as plagiarist."

"Doctrines" are not only the focus of literary histories, but are themselves historical. They emerge from a tradition and address particular problems that have surfaced in the particular field of scholarship. Moreover, they express particular resolutions to that problem and are aimed at a particular audience with its particular background. These particularities constitute the context that conditions the validity of a particular statement of fact, posited as a judgment, in "doctrines."

## 2.7 Systematics

"The seventh functional specialty, 'systematics,' is concerned with promoting an understanding of the realities affirmed in the previous specialty 'doctrines'" (Lonergan, 1972, p. 335). In acting to create an intelligent exposition of the underlying thesis, systematics brings critical pressure to bear on the literary historian's foundations by tracing out the implications of his or her thesis, by removing apparent contradictions, or by bringing to light the real contradictions in this position. Moreover, it is concerned with the organization of the material under survey to establish the plausibility of the thesis and the relationship of its insights to other disciplines (or to other approaches to the question it addresses) to promote a sense of its validity. David Hoy, in this area, makes the following observation:

> ...a more important aim of literary theory is to erect a comprehensive scheme to make knowledge (whether it is "knowledge-how" or "knowledge-why") principled and whole: bringing together by an intellectual operation "what can only be experienced seriatim." It is this above all that binds literary theory, in all its various forms, to theoretical work in other disciplines. (1975, p. 275)

At the same time the specialty of "doctrines" maintains its sense of competence as an acceptable way of interpreting the field under survey by refuting counter-positions that have a claim on the same area, or by incorporating lesser claims under the more general hypothesis that it promotes. The critical pressure that is examined in systematics is created, then, both by the internal forces within the theory and by the external forces on it. Moreover, since this functional specialty does not understand itself as the exposition of corollaries to a principle through a series of syllogisms, but rather as an active manifestation of the historian's structure of intentionality, "systematics" raises such crucial questions, in the light of the critical pressure it establishes, as the following: Does one aim at the truth, or does one evade it; is one, then, concerned with propaganda, or with values; and, since no one system can cover adequately an entire field comprehensibly, does one admit to the areas of one's vulnerability, or does one become self-defensive, enclosed, doctrinaire, dogmatic?

"Systematics" raises issues to be solved in the on-going tradition so that on the level of understanding, besides continuity and development, there is also revision, clarification, and transformation. It brings up the question of horizon. The world of scholarship present at this level of operations in literary history is not to be held as "the past for present meaning"—which would be one of the concerns of "communications"—nor with an understanding of the past as existentially separate from the present, but with the creation of a new horizon. The original horizon of the historian is changed by being involved with the past and that pastness is necessarily changed in so far as it appears in the context of subsequent knowledge and other interests. There is the merging of perspective into an open-ended "systematics." The world of scholarship manifest in systematics does not aim at a transformation of the literary historian's sensibilities to one contemporaneous to the field, or person, under survey, but aims at understanding such entities with whatever means are available. Just as the present is an interpretation, so too is the past an interpretation; and that interpretation is grounded in the subjectivity of the literary historian.

## 2.8 Communications

That same subjectivity functions to present the fruits of research and interpretation and judgments usually in a text. Such a presentation is the concern of the last functional specialty, "communications." Of course, the published text becomes, once again, data to be interpreted. It manifests a tradition and, by provoking in the reader acquiescence, agreement, or opposition to the position advocated, establishes his or her own foundational reality.

The text manifests itself as the historian's insight into that aspect of literary history examined. It expresses a systematic perspective through research and arguments in such a manner as to gain support. Thus through literary history is literary history continued. "Communications" is an aspect of literary history and not only would include an analysis of "reception criticism" (Iser, 1978), but would also have to involve itself in an analysis of the modes of presentation of the text and the modes of presentation *in* the text. This later aspect of the eighth functional specialty would consist of, among other things, an analysis of the particular mode of discourse chosen in particular histories, and of its relationship to the stance of the historian. The manner of presentation is intrinsic to the particular considerations of specific literary history. Style reveals foundational reality. Hayden White's work in *Metahistory* (1973) and *Tropics of Discourse* (1978), from the perspective held in this paper, would belong, then, to this eighth functional specialty.

Inasmuch as a theory of literature becomes theory-as-literature represented—for example, in Harold Bloom's prose poems on repression as literary history—the text as art form, with its polyvalent expressions of meaning, cannot be evaluated exclusively in terms of validity, but rather in such a way as to be sensitive to the forces that constitute its presence. Modes of evaluation for theories of literary history need to consider aesthetics, neatness, effectiveness, convenience, usefulness, simplicity or complexity. There may even be assessment in terms of their theatricality or of their power to seduce, attack, undermine, or subvert the involved reader. The text-as-art, as-effect, and as-event constitute modes of evaluating its performance as communication. It may even be possible to conceive of a text whose interest on the level of the eighth functional specialty would be precisely the mode of interference at communicating. Clarity is not intrinsic to communication. Indeed, for postmodernism, the layering of texts to present a palimpsest is a deliberate strategy to subvert the complacency of those who seek simplifications rather than truth. However, whatever form of presentation is seen to characterize the texts that embody literary history, such an awareness falls under this last functional specialty, "communications."

## 3. Conclusion

Literary history comprises eight inter-related modes of scholarship grounded in the dynamic structure of human consciousness and made available through the narrative of interiority analysis understood in epistemological terms. With the profusion of literary theories, the historian is driven to an analysis of personal subjectivity to find a basis for evaluating the adequacy of any of the radically diverging paradigms available for understanding this discipline. Jean Starobinski comments on this phenomenon as follows:

> Initially the ambition of a critical scholarship was that of restoring the full force of authority to the revealed word or to great literary models of the past. But the difficulty of the task, the obstacles, the ineluctable uncertainty of the sources, the conflicts among commentators, as well as the growing doubt as to the legitimacy of the authority thus served, forced critical reasoning to retreat. This retreat was turned into victory when the critical mind discovered in itself the authority, the sovereign reason, that it had refused to consider as imposed from the outside by the infallible text of some revelation…, and the variation of critical thought far transcends the scope of what is commonly known as "literary theory" or "aesthetic concept." These variations involve every explicit conscious relationship that man can entertain from literary works, from respectful submission to an attitude of rejection, from spontaneous participation to "scientific" curiosity and so on. (1977, p. 7)

To subscribe to a particular approach within this diversity demands self-critical and responsible decisions on the part of the reader.

The emphasis on the diverse *conscious* relationships available with a text, or a series of texts, leads to an examination of consciousness to ground these relationships. It shows the dynamic mode of interrelatedness of these relationships and points out, on an analytical level, any aberrations such relationships may implicitly contain by recourse to the very structure of consciousness from which they derive. Hopefully, the method proposed in this paper will be useful not only in differentiating clearly the different projects engaged upon by different literary historians, but also in establishing an analytical tool, by which counter-positions may be overcome and truncated literary histories based on inadequate methodologies can be corrected. People need to have such a tool available for ready use.

Words, as deconstructionist "games" illustrate (Derrida, 1977/1988; J. H. Miller, 1988), are polysemous, and even the most restrictive of readings do not escape metaphoric shifts. Words communicate. But what is that communication? It is only by an analysis of the interiority of communication that we get a reading of that contingent yet profoundly creative narrative that makes us human. That narrative starts in wonder. We wonder at what we experience; we make metaphors to come to terms with it; we find ourselves in communities that share those same readings and in conflict with other traditions who hold different metaphors. We are driven by that conflict to the source of the word and our wrestling with the inexpressible gives us our style, drives our plots, determines our modes of discourse, and makes possible the texts we return to the world. The narrative of being human is literary history. We cannot step outside that "text."

# 12

# The Human Good and Christian Conversation

*Frederick G. Lawrence*

## 1. Introduction

For the past six or seven years, I have been tantalized by a passage from Lonergan's economics manuscript; and I have been trying to come to grips with it directly and indirectly in my work as a teacher and theologian for the same period of time. I have had an overwhelming sense that it points to the transformation in society and culture at stake in contemporary political theology and locates the arena in which the most basic questions for political theology lie. The passage goes as follows:

> Now to change one's standard of living in any notable fashion is to live in a different fashion. It presupposes a grasp of new ideas. If the ideas are to be above the level of currently successful advertising, serious education must be undertaken. Finally, coming to grasp what serious education realizes, and, nonetheless, coming to accept that challenge constitute the greatest challenge to the modern economy. (Lonergan, 1944, p. 65)

The change in living, in ideas, in education indicated here has to do with the issues of revolution and conversion associated with the achievement of a new identity. In this paper, I want to discuss issues connected with meeting the challenge and understanding what Lonergan is talking about in terms of the metaphor of learning a new language, which I take up in the next section (1.1). Then I look at the structure of the human good outlined by Lonergan in *Method in Theology*. Next, in Part 2, I survey the alternative answers of antiquity and modernity concerning the human good, with sections on each (2.1 and 2.2). The section on modernity covers "the three waves" of modernity identified by Leo Strauss. Part 3 considers what is involved in learning foundational language, with sections on (3.1) conflicts of meanings and values and (3.2) Christian conversion as conversational. The latter section is de-

Originally published in P. McShane (Ed.), *Searching for Cultural Foundations* (pp. 86-112). Lanham, MD: University Press of America, 1984.

veloped in five sub-topics. Part 4, then, provides some tentative conclusions about the human good and the Christian conversation.

## 1.1  Learning a New Language

This metaphor, of course, is not just a metaphor, because language as I am using the term here is a component integral to the processes of communal and personal self-constitution.  If human self-becoming is chiefly a matter of asking and answering questions for understanding, reflection, and deliberation and then living by the answers, it is clear just how important language is to us.   Besides the verifiable correlation between aphasia and apraxia, we need language to pose questions to the situations we encounter in life.  Language leads us along both pre-conceptually and imaginally as well as within the spontaneously ordered operations of intelligent, reasonable, and responsible consciousness.  With Rosemary Haughton and Stephen Crites, indeed, we could articulate the meaning and value of the major transformations in our lives by studying the changes in language usages that are correlative with the different conversions.

But aside from its intrinsically methodical appropriateness, the metaphor of learning a language presents itself to us with a more special urgency at the present time.  In a time that is felt to be a period of almost unprecedented crisis, we Christians speak languages stemming from traditions whose meanings and values are at odds both with Christian faith and with Lonergan's foundational language.  Thus, the problem of the watering down or distortion of one's tradition that Lonergan has written so eloquently about enters our lives with a vengeance.  These alien and alienating languages may be generating, within the Christian traditions not merely lives of unauthentic authenticity, but lives of unconverted unauthenticity almost as a rule.  And when Christianity gets co-opted into supplying a legitimating veneer for meanings and values that are unchristian, then probabilities mount that even well-intentioned speakers and doers of what they think is the Word will not only not be doing so, but they will be unaware of the existential contradictions in which they are involved.  The urgency becomes all the more pressing when we realize that "they" are we ourselves.

I have found that expressing in word and deed the horizon to which one has been moved by Christian conversion is almost as much a matter of unlearning the languages that have possessed us hitherto as of learning to speak a new language.  But this general problem of learning and unlearning is particularly delicate when one tries to operate in the specialty of foundations, especially if one tries to speak with Lonergan's general and special categories.  To show more exactly what I mean, I have decided to use Lonergan's structure of the human good to convey a notion of the hindrances to speaking his language authentically, especially as they arise from other competing languages by which we are already liable to be dominated.

*1.2  The Structure of the Human Good as Language*

Let us recall first of all the structure of the human good developed by Lonergan in the second chapter of *Method in Theology* (1972, p. 48):

| Individual | | Social | Ends |
|---|---|---|---|
| *Potentiality* | *Actuation* | | |
| capacity, need | operation | cooperation | particular good |
| plasticity, perfectibility | development, skill | institution, role, task | good of order |
| liberty | orientation, conversion | personal relations | terminal value |

      This structure is a component in a technical language—what I shall be calling Lonergan's foundational language. As a language in the most serious sense, it is heuristic, and so it will be learned or mastered according as we are able to use it in asking our own real questions about the human situation. Its overwhelming suitableness for political theology becomes obvious, for instance, as soon as we grasp that it names at the outset what it is we are looking for when we ask the very questions from which philosophy as practical and political first originated:  "What's the right way to live?" "What's the best, the most choiceworthy, way of life?"  I want to illustrate what I mean by learning a new language and unlearning old languages by setting the structure of the human good in the contexts of ancient and modern political philosophies and comparing the range of meaning intended by their languages with that intended by Lonergan.

## 2. The Human Good
## and the Alternative Ancient and Modern Answers

*2.1  The Context of Ancient Political Philosophy*

The premodern breakthrough in posing the practical-political question was crystallized in the Greek and Christian apprehension of it as a question about the good of order.  Plato's *Republic* and Aristotle's *Politics* ask, "What's the best regime?"  The key to the question is the clear and consistent discrimination between mere life as physical, vital, and sensitive spontaneity and the good life (Lonergan, 1967/1988, p. 38).  The latter is coordinate with "rational appetite, [and] with the specialized object of the reasonable good" (p. 24).  The following rather lengthy quotation from a 1943 article by Lonergan may provide a summary of the salients uncovered by the classical response to the question about the best regime.

> Throughout, nature is characterized by repetitiveness: Over and over again it achieves mere reproductions of what has been achieved already and any escape from such cyclic recurrence is *per accidens* and *in minore parte* or, in modern language, due to chance variation. But in contrast with this repetitiveness of nature is the progressiveness of reason. For if it is characteristic of all intellect to grasp immutable truth, it is the special property of the potential intellect of man to advance in the knowledge of the truth. Nor is it merely the individual that advances, as though knowledge were classically static, a fund whence schoolboys receive a dole. On the contrary, to the historian of science or philosophy and still more to the anthropologist, the individual of genius appears no more than the instrument of human solidarity; through such individuals, humanity advances, and the function of tradition and education is to maintain the continuity of a development that runs from the days of primitive fruit-gatherers through our own of mechanical power on into an unknown future. But not only are nature and reason contrasted as repetitive and progressive. There is a contrast between the organistic spontaneity of nature and the deliberate friendships of reason. By "organistic" spontaneity I would denote the mutual adaptation and automatic correlation of the activities of many individuals as though they were parts of a larger organic unit: This phenomenon may be illustrated by the ant heap or beehive; but its more general appearance lies in the unity of the family, a unity that nature as spontaneously and imperiously attains in the accidental order as in the substantial it effects the unity of the organism. Now it is not by organistic spontaneity but by mutual esteem and good will that reason sets up its comparable union of friendship: And in accordance with our eternal viewpoint, we may note that human friendship is to be found not only in the urbanity and collaboration of contemporaries' esteem for the great men of the past on whose shoulders they stand, and in their devotion for the men of the future for whom they set the stage of history for better or worse. A third contrast between nature and history is in point of efficiency. While nature with the ease of a super-automaton pursues with statistical infallibility and regularly attains through organistic harmonies its repetitive ends, the reason and rational appetite of fallen man limp in the disequilibrium of high aspiration and poor performance to make progress of reason a dialectic of decline as well as of advance, and the rational community of men a divided unity of hatred and war as well as the indivisible unity of fraternity and peace. (1967/1988, pp. 38-39)

From this summary we need to notice a number of points. First, treating the question about the right way to live in terms of the second level of the structure, that of the good of order, brings with it a tendency to subordinate elements located on the third level of that structure to the second level. In St. Thomas Aquinas' *Of Princely Government*, for example, needs on the level of particular goods motivate and call for a civil or political society (Book I, chapter 1), and friendships (personal relations) are acknowledged to be the aim or goal of political rule (chapter 10); but the intelligible content of civil society is handled most profusely in terms of virtues and types of regime, etc.  Although almost all third level components are present and treated in the ancient accounts, they do tend to get subordinated to the second level.

Second, the ancients conceive the practical and political question about the right way to live not merely empirically (that is, as an account of possible ways of life as verified), but ethically or morally.  Thus, Aristotle's *Nicomachean Ethics* is integral to his *Politics*, with the former being devoted to habits and skills (the moral and dianoetic virtues) and the latter to the institutional set-up with its appropriate roles and tasks.  This same unity of the political and moral is also evident in Plato's famous parallel between the order of the polis and the order of the soul, with its tripartite division into desire (for sensible or material pleasure), spiritedness (anger, the root of the war-like virtues), and reason (the faculty for seeking the true, the good, the beautiful).  As Gadamer, Arendt, and a host of others in our day have discovered, by treating the question of the good of order as a question of morality and ethics, the ancients kept questions for practical intelligence distinct from questions for technical expertise; by never reducing the former to the latter, they did not make sheer feasibility in a technical sense into a criterion for practical judgment, but normally judged against advances in technology when it was thought to jeopardize the common good.

However, this approach to practical issues also went hand-in-hand with what Lonergan calls a normative notion of culture, or what he spoke of as "the great republic of culture" in the passage cited above.  This was an ambiguous achievement.  To begin with, there is the normative function of culture delineated by Lonergan in the following fashion:

> Corresponding to judgments of value, there is cultural community.  It transcends the frontiers of states and epochs of history.  It is Cosmopolis not as an unrealized political ideal, but as a long-standing, nonpolitical, cultural fact.  It is the field of communication and influence of artists, scientists, and philosophers.  It is the bar of enlightened public opinion to which naked power can be driven to submit.  It is the tribunal of history that may expose successful charlatans and may restore to honor the prophets stoned by their contemporaries. (1967/1988, p. 109)

Within the structure of the human good, Lonergan has brought out the differentiation of culture as the domain in which society reflects upon and appraises its way of life in distinguishing between the second and third levels.  The second level regards the *social* dimension of the human good, the concretely verifiable way of life as embodied in laws, technology, economy, polity, family life; the third level comprises the *cultural* domain in the light of which the social is (to be) judged and evaluated.  By this distinction, both the "social" and the "cultural" have an utterly empirical meaning, but "culture" retains the connotation of a normative function without being classicist in Lonergan's pejorative sense.

In the best of the ancients, culture and the political order are identical only in the ideal and highly improbable case where the philosopher becomes the ruler; otherwise and (we can suppose almost always) in fact, culture is only the forum before which the political order is judged, and within which justice is realized not in deed, but in speech alone. This sense of balance got lost as the "Greek mediation of meaning" was transformed into classical culture with its science of man. As Lonergan came to discover, classical culture performed the above-mentioned normative function of culture by means of "a somewhat arbitrary standardization of man" (1967/1988, p. 241). Classical or classicist culture transformed the Greek breakthrough— "a necessary stage in the development of the human mind" (p. 241)—into a timeless criterion in which the content of the classically oriented science of man "easily obscures man's nature, constricts his spontaneity, saps his vitality, limits his freedom" (p. 241), because it "concentrated on the essential to ignore the accidental, on the universal to ignore the particular, on the necessary to ignore the contingent" (p. 240). Since it omitted so much of the data on human being, its explanations could not help but be provisional in some respects, which is understandable. The overwhelming problem with classicist culture is its inability to acknowledge these limits and its apparent unwillingness to keep learning.

## 2.2 The Context of Modern Political Philosophy

*2.21. The first wave of modernity.*[1] The ancient answers to the question about the right way to live focused on the common good understood as a complex good of order; and they were preoccupied with virtue. What happened in the first phase of the shift to modernity has been suggestively encapsulated in the following passage by Allan Bloom:

> The ancients talked only about virtue and not about well-being. That in itself is perhaps harmless, but the moderns contended that the concentration on virtue contradicts the concern for well-being. Aristotle admitted that "equipment" as well as virtue is needed for happiness, but said nothing about how that equipment is acquired. A careful examination of the acquisition of equipment reveals that virtue impedes that acquisition....Equipment is surely necessary, so why not experiment with doing without virtue. (1990, pp. 282-283)

In other words, thinkers like Bacon, Hobbes, Descartes, Spinoza, and Locke judged that in the light of humanity's "disequilibrium of high as-

---

[1] The hypothesis of the "three waves of modernity" comes from Leo Strauss (1975, pp. 81-98). In my eight years of teaching (1) Perspectives in Western Culture and (2) New Horizons of the Social Sciences, year-long courses that cover the key texts in political science, law, economics, and sociology of the period under question (16th to 20th centuries), I have come across no evidence whatsoever that would make Strauss' interpretation controversial. See Lawrence, "Political Theology and 'the Longer Cycle of Decline'" (1978b) and "The Horizon of Political Theology" (1978a).

piration and poor performance" (Lonergan, 1967/1988, p. 39), taking care of equipment not only means doing without virtue if need be, but displacing the desire to know elevated to normative status by the ancients with the desire for self-preservation.

When the *summum bonum* gets replaced in modernity by the fear of death as *summum malum*, the psychology of orientation gets replaced by a psychology of motivations. Motivated by the anxiety about death, only the accumulation of power and property seems a choiceworthy good; and so comfortable self-preservation becomes the primary end of human beings.

In tandem with modern science's myth of productivity, modern political philosophy undertook the vast "humanitarian" project of taking care of equipment by parleying private vices into public welfare. But this was to subordinate the second and third levels of the structure of the human good to that of needs, desires, and particular goods. It follows that the common good no longer refers to the good of order as normative, but to particular goods as satisfying needs and desires as correlative with life in contradistinction to the good life. As a mere collectivity of private goods, the common good is "common" only in the sense of an accidental genus or species instead of as the objective of rational choice correlative with the human capacity for intellectual development. Furthermore, in relation to the normative order of vital, social, cultural, personal, and religious values, the preference for mere life over the good life means the supremacy of vital values. The dominant practical question becomes not merely, "What's in it for me or my group?" but "What's the value of being good if you're not well off?"

The purpose of civil society and government on the early modern account is to protect pre-existent rights to life and the pursuit of property. Its key means will not be morality or religion, but the spirit of acquisitiveness at the root of property. Hence, governments are legitimate to the extent that they, as *The Federalist* put it, protect different and unequal faculties of acquiring wealth. This implies that the motive for political society according to the ancients becomes transformed into its criterion; even as action for the private good (conceived of as enlightened self-interest) is elevated into the standard for assessing rightness or wrongness overall.

Concerns for the third level are acknowledged by the early moderns under the rubric of natural right. Friendships are relevant as long as they are based on utility or pleasure. Liberty means either the freedom to design institutions that will provide mutual security and rules that guarantee the public good by enabling each individual to pursue private goods without obstruction from others, or at least the freedom to consent to such a design. It is clear, then, that the notion of natural right, inalienable, underivable from any authority, is an eminently selfish idea. As the product of an attempt to define human equality independently of any religion or metaphysics, it also meant to leave open the answer to the question of the right way to live, at least in principle; but in fact, that openness was a void the early moderns were content to see filled by commerce. Taking care of equipment is realized as taking care of business.

*2.22 The second wave of modern political philosophy.* In his First and Second Discourses, Rousseau laid bare the opposition between nature—now identified with the satisfaction of needs on the level of organistic spontaneity—and culture or civilization. He thus set the stage for the modern use of the term culture. As Bloom has written:

> according to Kant, Rousseau in his later works, *Emile, Social Contract, Nouvelle Heloise*, proposed a possible unity that harmonized the low natural demands with the high responsibilities of morality and art. This unity Kant called "culture." (1990, p. 278)

Rousseau, therefore, unleashed the first cultural critique of the mercenary morality of liberalism.

From the point of view of the structure of the human good, we can say that Rousseau's scathing attack was actually an ambiguous breakthrough to the second (social) and third (cultural) levels in reaction to the early modern reduction of all elements to the first level. Both the breakthrough and its ambiguity are signaled by the notorious modern dichotomies between nature and freedom, nature and history, and nature and art, which were exploited till our own day by the movements of idealism, historicism, and Romanticism. No less than Hobbes and Locke, however, Rousseau conceived of liberty without any reference to divine transcendence. Though he did not confine freedom to the limits of scientific calculation and technical control and debunked early liberalism's utilitarianism and instrumentalism, freedom for him was coordinate with the perfectibility of the amiable but brutish human being he uncovered in the state of nature, and its matrix was that animal's "simple feeling of existence," its "conscience" as "the science of simple souls."

Out of the framework built with these ideas, Rousseau eventually developed the idea of the "general will." On the one hand, the general will was to be understood in terms of national custom, national "philosophy," or the "mystique of the nation." We have become familiar with these ideas under the guise of such terms as Hegel's *Zeitgeist* or Whitehead's "climate of opinion." On the other hand, Kant drew out the more idealist implications of the general will, for example, in his moralistic grounding of human rights. Earlier liberalism's "natural" rights to life, liberty, and the pursuit of happiness were founded not so much in the state of nature theory as on factual evidence on the dominance within human beings of the natural inclinations toward security and comfort. But Kant uses the ability (shown by Rousseau to be human and rational, but not natural) humans possess of universalizing their desire in order to subordinate the older liberalism's self-interest in safety and prosperity to rights conceived of as universal principles that serve to define human beings as free and independent.

One can appreciate the high moral tone of this transformation of so-called natural rights into human rights. It does seem to give primacy to the moral demands proper to the second and third levels. However, the apriorism, abstractness, and formalism of Kant's thought not only divorce his grounding from any concrete practical relevance; but his intelligible ego with its good will is so isolated from the empirically verifiable process of communication within which subjects grow to maturity that we are forced to concede that it is quite utopian (not to say unreal) as well. Kant had no way of tethering his "normative" realm of freedom to empirically verifiable fact; and so he buttressed it with postulates about God, freedom, and immortality, on the one hand; and with a speculative philosophy of history, on the other. Even on Kantian grounds, the former threesome may be argued not to exist; and Kant's philosophy of history finally settles for a distinction between morality and mere legality that represents a compromise of rational faith with *Realpolitik*.

As a result of the two waves of modernity, there are two chief forms or languages of Western liberalism. They both depart from the modern assumption that the chief concern or issue of modern politics is power. First, *commercial democracy* is based on consent to governmental power as guarantor of public safety and comfort and on the doctrine of classical political economy that if there are no restrictions to free economic activity other than enlightened self-interest, social harmony and well-being will necessarily prevail. Second, *socialist politics of compassion* grounds the legitimacy of governmental power upon the extent to which it bolsters equality not merely of opportunity (that is, the political right to endeavor to acquire and dispose of one's property within the limits of the law and the civil right to freedom of expression and to self-government), but of the satisfaction of aggregate societal needs (under the heading of economic, social, and cultural rights to such things as health, housing, education, employment, sanitation, etc.) by attempting to reconcile older liberalism's means with socialist or collectivist ends in what has been since called welfare economics. Both versions of liberalism are staunchly convinced of the efficacy of scientific prediction and control and of institutionally contrived solutions to political problems. In general, and by way of oversimplification, advocates of commercial democracy believe that enlightened self-interest in private good is the operator of *common weal*, and they preach the ideal of as much freedom as possible for the individual and the equality of opportunity. In the United States we tend to label this stance conservative. Secularist proponents of the socialist politics of compassion depend upon "culture" to supply the link between the self-regarding individual and disinterested respect of the law or the rights of others by generating a secular kind of compassion that educes gentle and beneficent concern for others from natural selfishness. They advocate a greater equality of conditions or results in life and preach equality of influence and power for all. In the United States we tend to reserve the name liberal for people who are considered politically progressive in this sense.

The most noteworthy proponent of the socialist politics of compassion is Karl Marx. The industrial revolution, especially after its "take-off," made plain to him that the liberal capitalist belief in a pre-established harmony between private interest and public welfare was an ideology. As he argued in *The Jewish Question*, the natural rights enshrined in such revolutionary documents as the *Declaration of Independence* (1776) and the *Declaration of the Rights of Man and Citizen* (1789) are really only bourgeois rights; they hold good for the capitalist class, but not for the proletariat. Commercial democracy in its intention to supply the equipment for freedom turns out in the final analysis to be a struggle between capitalists and workers. Marx tried to analyze that struggle by re-introducing social (second level) and, at least in his youthful writings, ethical (third level) concerns into political economy in opposition to the "possessive individualism" of liberal capitalism. However, this important attempt to redress the biases of liberal democratic political economy unfortunately got derailed by Marx's uneasy blend of idealism and materialism. That idealism trivialized the underlying problem of evil just as Rousseau and Kant had done. The materialism kept him from breaking cleanly from the utilitarianism and instrumentalism of his early liberal predecessors. He failed altogether to appreciate Rousseau's insight that to achieve freedom in equality requires small communities with religious foundations. And however much the Romantic model of artistic creation was his privileged model for the making of history by human subjects, his revolutionary idea was ultimately just a project of technical mastery, which not even a classless and stateless society would be capable of redeeming.

*2.23 The third wave of modern political philosophy: (a) Nietzsche.* As the inaugurator of the third wave of modernity, Nietzsche realized that the outcome of both liberal democracy's dedication to preservation and comfort and social democracy's well-fed, well-clothed, well-sheltered human beings with their up-to-date educations, entertainment, and psychiatry would be the abolition of all ideals and aspirations. To the degree that liberalisms of both left and right choose mere life over the good life, they produce the "last man"—healthy, but without heart or convictions.

Nietzsche, therefore, has the overwhelming importance of trying to re-establish the importance of the level of liberty and terminal values. He stands just at the threshold of the religiously mediated insight so neatly formulated in the title of the book by Dorothee Sölle: *Death by Bread Alone*. He sets the stage for the rescuing consciousness of the unorthodox Jew, Walter Benjamin, and for the Christian theologian, Johann Baptist Metz. The latter's short definition for religion is interruption—interruption of the modern project of subjugating human and subhuman nature. But for Nietzsche, Christianity is just Platonism for the masses and all the supports for ultimate values in nature, God, or reason are gone. The only option left open in the face of the abyss is a creative transvaluation of all previous values on the part of solitary individuals creative enough to respond to the implications of the will-to-power, especially, that human beings are originating values in the absolute sense of being able to posit values arbitrarily. In Nietzsche, the most radical breakthrough to the third level of terminal values also presents us with the epitome of human disorientation, rebellion, and disorder.

*2.23 (b) Weber: Between Kant and Nietzsche.* Nietzsche's perhaps most influential disciple, Max Weber, domesticated his master's concept of value for the academy by marrying it to Kant's synthesis of culture performed in his three *Critiques.* Weber thus spawned the fact/value distinction as it is commonly and erroneously understood. The realm of nature investigated by science and exploited by technology becomes the value-free domain of fact; whereas both the realm of freedom and responsibility and that of art and religion become the domain of value. As a result of this fateful distinction, the normative moment of culture intended by Lonergan's notion of terminal value gets sunk into the quagmire of the arbitrariness and caprice of values as the creation of the Nietzschean will-to-power.

The devastation wrought thereby for apprehending the third level is exacerbated by the common understanding on the part of the contemporary social sciences of the way the Weberian distinction between facts and values is to govern the relationship between social science and social policy. Social science is confined to facts: It describes, and its descriptions are expected to yield information on the basis of which social policy can predict and control. Any normative judgment—either as classical intelligibility or as true judgments of fact and value—gets systematically excluded. The individual, group, or general bias of those in power leads them to repudiate true terminal values (beyond the desires and needs of organistic spontaneity) and to reject any intelligibility yielded by science that does not afford means of prediction and control. The point is to increase managerial efficiency even at the cost of human liberty or social, cultural, personal, or religious values.

Again, within the perspective of Weber's fact/value distinction, a Nietzschean slant can hold sway in personal and communal thinking and action. For it is difficult to avoid the either benevolently or malevolently nihilist conclusion that *all* standards of meaning and substantive order are relative in the last analysis. Nihilism simply eliminates the insight that

> though the things seen are at different times in their internal temporal relationships, still it is possible and proper for the human intellect to imitate the divine and by abstraction stand outside the temporal flow in which really, though not of necessity intentionally, it is involved. (Lonergan, 1967/1988, p. 38)

The nihilist operates instead on the assumption that judgments of fact or value are no more than the historically conditioned illusions—the humanly posited horizons—without which the human animal cannot live. For the benevolent nihilist, this becomes the premise for a "soft tyranny" of cultural manipulation of the many by the few—for profit. For the malevolent nihilist, this becomes the premise for the "big lie" enforced by terror.

Fortunately, however, the response to Nietzsche's call to the best of a generation to become true selves and form a new aristocracy has often been based less on nihilism than on the Kantian rational belief (so congenial to secularized Protestantism) that in principle if not in fact a human person ought never to be used as a means to any aim or purpose not freely chosen by himself or herself; no one can ever be an object of manipulative control by another. For Kantians, of course, this conviction has the cognitive status not of objective truth, but of a postulate, so that the value of the person may never be affirmed as ontic, as it is in Christian faith or in a critically realist philosophy such as Lonergan's. The Kantian conclusion follows from the inchoate acknowledgment of the human person as an originating imperative, rather than from the concrete goodness meant by terminal values, goods of order, and particular goods in Lonergan's sense.

Unfortunately, the salutary Kantian doctrine of the unconditionality of the human person gets relegated to pragmatic irrelevance by Weber's separation of "the ethics of conviction" from the "ethics of responsibility." The ethics of conviction regards ultimate ends, while the ethics of responsibility regards only the pragmatic consequences of means in relation to ends established irrationally and arbitrarily. Doesn't this make Kant's idealistic faith just a matter of conviction? Moreover, this separation would have the effect of sealing off the third level of the human good from the second level.

The ongoing mutual impenetrability of second and third levels becomes all the more disastrous when it comes to Weber's reconstruction of the reasons why people historically have obeyed authority. On the one hand, his construct of the charismatic form of legitimation is one of the few 19th century instances of evaluating religiously based existence positively, since for Weber charismatic authority is the privileged force or agency for social change. On the other hand, his hypothesis about modernity as a process of rationalization, combined with his analysis of bureaucratic control, spells out in a way that is verifiable the meaning of Nietzsche's critique of liberal democracy and socialism on the level of the good of order. Because, for all the preoccupation of liberal and socialist democracy with being emancipated from religious, feudal, monarchical, or aristocratic control; for all their preoccupation with the use of scientific prediction and manipulation "for the relief of man's estate," and of either consent and bargaining (liberal reformism) or violence (socialist revolution) to bring about an order of freedom in equality—it all seems only to have paved the way for bureaucracy and centralization: Weber's "iron cage."

## 3. Learning Foundational Language

### 3.1 Conflicts of Meanings and Values

The different political philosophies of antiquity and modernity have all shaped implicit or explicit answers to the question about the right way to live; and the latter have engendered languages that pervade our schools, homes, media, and cultural channels today. These languages often contain verbal equivalents to the language used by Lonergan to define implicitly the structure of the human good. As a result, when we speak about the human good, we are liable either to be intending meanings proper to these languages rather than Lonergan's, or at least to be mistaken by others in this way.

Take, for example, the word "liberty" in the structure of the human good. Liberty was acknowledged by the Greeks, but it was not a theme for them. They had a common sense apprehension of the difference between slave or free. Theoretically, Aristotle was explicitly clear about the contingency of terrestrial events, which implies the contingency of all human agency. But he did not distinguish clearly between the specification and exercise of free will. And in spite of having a theory of habit, a notion that intellectual virtues liberate human beings more than even the moral virtues do, a recognition that most men know what is good yet choose what is to their own advantage, he had no theory of moral impotence. In short, we have no reason to suppose that the ancient Greek meaning of liberty coincides with Lonergan's in a more than partial way.

On the other hand, liberty has been a theme for the moderns. Indeed, some modern thinkers might agree with Lonergan that liberty is not just indeterminacy but self-determination and even perhaps that "we experience our liberty as the active thrust of the subject terminating the process of deliberation" (1972, p. 50). But none of the modern thinkers I have mentioned would agree with him either that "implicit in human choice of values is the absolute good that is God" (Lonergan, 1967/1988, p. 230); or, correlatively, that freedom of choice is grounded in our ability to criticize any finite course of group or individual action (1972, p. 50). And similarly, despite their realization that *the* god must be a being beyond the intracosmic gods, the Greeks did not affirm an explanatory notion of divine transcendence, any more than the moderns do.

In the course of my whirlwind survey of ancient and modern philosophical approaches to issues cognate with Lonergan's structure of the human good, I adverted repeatedly to ways the range of meaning made available in Lonergan's structure suffer major reductions when shifted into the perspective of any of the various languages discussed. From my brief critical comments, it may be plain how the many different interpretations of elements and levels within the structure have the effect of reducing one's ability to ask significant questions about our concrete situation. These contrasting languages express a reduction of Lonergan's horizon of meaning and value. Since the horizons of our speech and living have been constituted by *those* languages, we must ask ourselves how we can learn the foundational language Lonergan uses so that we can mean what he meant.

When we take seriously language as operative within the matrix of conscious intentionality and as a component in human self-constitution, the issue that comes to the surface when appropriating Lonergan's foundational language is the fourth aspect of understanding any text listed by Lonergan in *Method in Theology's* chapter on "Interpretation": "One arrives at such understanding through a process of learning and even at times as a result of conversion" (1972, p. 155). It is the issue Lonergan put so starkly in the chapter on "History and Historians":

> For any notable change of horizon is done not on the basis of that horizon, but by envisaging a quite different and, at first sight, incomprehensible alternative and then undergoing a conversion. (1972, p. 224)

Although I could multiply citations at some length, this issue even gripped Lonergan in 1926, when, at age 22 he had to preach to 250 students in the Heythrop College dining room and selected for his text: "You will indeed listen, but never understand, and you will indeed look, but never perceive" (Acts 28:26 NRSV).[2] The issue Lonergan had to face is one we may have to face, too. It is the issue of conversion and repentance.

My own sense is that conversion and repentance are crucial to the process of learning Lonergan's foundational language precisely because the languages of liberalism or nihilism are so dominant in our culture. They do not just exist "out there" or "in them." If my own experience is not unique, these languages have invaded us. They affect our day-to-day life-choices and our overall way of life both in the manner in which we individually and collectively interpret our desires and needs and in the ordering of the values incorporated in the already understood and agreed upon solutions to the problem of living together that make up our institutions. These languages are *the* symptom of our implicatedness in what today is commonly called "structural sin." And so the heart of relinquishing the languages and the start of the process of learning a new foundational language—which, as I have tried to show, does not necessarily mean using different words or inventing neologisms—is metanoia, conversion, and repentance.

### 3.2 Christian Conversion as Conversational

*3.21 The Christian situation of conversion.* Frederick E. Crowe has written with theological intelligence about the situation in which one appropriates Christian conversion:

---

[2]This is neither to deny nor to underplay the importance of doing with Lonergan what Lonergan did with St. Thomas Aquinas, or indeed of doing with any other authors what he did. I am simply underscoring what I now feel may be a *sine qua non* (as well perhaps *the* ass's bridge) for doing this with Lonergan.

> At one end of the spectrum, we have ourselves...with our religious interiority to be pondered and understood. At the other end, we have Jesus with his human consciousness and the religious interiority of God's Son in human form. In between, we have the apostles, prophets, evangelists, etc; as well as the mystics of all ages, but especially from those times when they began to describe more helpfully their experience...there would be the inner word of Jesus finding expression in his spoken words and deeds, in his silence and his suffering. This expression, an outer word in the broad sense, is received, assimilated interiorly, and re-expressed by the...intermediaries between Jesus and the people of God. It becomes then an outer word for us, to be received in faith but given new expression in virtue of our own inner word, the gift of the Spirit, on the foundations, that is, of our interiority. (1983, p. 41)

In being converted, in repentance, we enter a conversation within what might be called a redemptive tension as we experience the interplay between inner word (gift of the Spirit) and outer word (Jesus, who lived, suffered, died, and rose again) in the process of ongoing conversion, since conversion as Christian involves a two-sided response to God's outgoing love: a response to the operative grace of conversion that bestows a universal antecedent willingness through the gift of the Spirit; and a (not necessarily separate) response to the outer word of the Risen Lord.

*3.22 Conversation with the outer word: Its redemptive function.*[3] I want to underline Lonergan's statement:

> Without the visible mission of the Word, the gift of the Spirit is a being-in-love without a proper object; it remains simply an orientation to mystery that awaits its interpretation. (1985, p. 32)

Perhaps for most of us, Christian conversion involves encountering the Christ, the Son of God, whose story is to be read in the Gospels and the significance of that story in the Old Testament and the New Testament, in the light of God's gift of love. As with the original disciples, it is the Risen Lord who first reveals to us our own very real implicatedness in personal and structural sin; who reveals us to be the co-causes of his suffering; he who shows us the extent of suffering our sin cost him, and who communicates to us the judgment of his Father on the sheer horribility of that personal and structural sin. Confronted by our responsibility for our part in sin, we want to repent, to change; but we cannot change ourselves. And so the Risen Lord forgives us for our involvement in personal and structural sin; he thereby gives us the strength at once to take responsibility for our sin and to claim a new identity by uniting us with his redemptive suffering. He

---

[3] In spelling out J. B. Metz's ideas about the narrative appropriation of the dangerous memory of Jesus Christ, who suffered, died, rose again, I have been greatly helped by the work of Rowan Williams (1982). This strikes me as a pastoral articulation of the point of Lonergan's systematic theses on the redemption in *De Verbo Incarnato* (1964b).

enables us to accept consciously, knowingly, responsibly the *de facto* intelligibility of this concrete universe: the law of the cross as the movement through death to life eternal.

*3.23 Conversation with the outer word: Its constitutive function.* When we put in terms of language the issue of conversion as a radical change in our horizon or orientation, then we need to speak of story in the sense intended by Lonergan when he wrote that "we have hunches we cannot formulate so we tell a story" (1980, p. 33). Let me cite at greater length his way of handling the category of story:

> ...being human is being-in-the-world (*in der Welt sein*),...one can rise to full stature only through full knowledge of the world,...one does not possess that full knowledge and thus makes use of the *élan vital* that, as it guides biological growth and evolution, so too it takes the lead in human development and expresses its intimations through the stories it inspires. Symbols, finally, are a more elementary type of story: They are inner or outer events, or a combination of both, that intimate to us at once the kind of being that we are to be and the kind of world in which we become our true selves. (1980, p. 34)

In terms of language, then, being converted means radically changing the story by *which* one lives. Thus, J. B. Metz has identified the emancipatory stories implicit in the liberal languages in which we have been educated, socialized, acculturated. As success stories they cover over the lives human beings really lead by making us oblivious to the full scope of human suffering throughout history. Metz has contrasted these success stories with the redemptive story of Jesus who suffered, died, and rose again.

Response to the linguistic and incarnate meaning of the outer word of the Risen One meets head on our need to be conversationally opened up and made sensitive to the depth of our involvement in the sinfulness of the situation brought about by the stories that have grown out of the waves of modernity in our culture; our need to absorb in detail how much we have constituted ourselves individually and collectively in these stories to the detriment of others, even Jesus. Contact—however mediated it may be—with the Risen Judge who has been victimized by our sin can open up this conversation for us. But, on the other hand, we also need to be forgiven and empowered by his spirit in order to gradually displace the "hunches" about our future cultivated in us by the dominant liberal languages in favor of the story of the one who suffers and dies for us, the one who rises and forgives us in befriending us. Thus, we need both his Spirit and meditative exegesis of his story in order to make his orientation toward the suffering and loss in the world our own. When we have been forgiven, loved, and illumined in faith by his story, a shift in probabilities takes place, and we have much more of a chance to become like the man Jesus whose overall approach to the world is portrayed by Mark's transfiguration story where Jesus moves from being utterly absorbed in conversational immediacy with the Father,

Elijah, and Moses, to inquire with simple, direct, and genuine concern about the epileptic child: "How long has he been like this?"

And so the question has been urging itself upon me with increasing force whether a concrete entry into the conversation with the outer word may not be a prerequisite as a matter of fact for speaking Lonergan's foundational language, somewhat in the way he affirms that religious conversion is required not *de jure* but *de facto* for a correct conception and affirmation of the existence of God.

*3.24 Conversation and community.* I have been speaking of the communication of Spirit and Word in terms of its redemptive and constitutive functions. Let us return to the two sides of Crowe's spectrum to recall the conversational situation of Christian conversion. On the one side, there is the outer word originally generated by the consciously elicited acts of meaning and value of the mind and heart of Jesus as he sought to discover how to share with us the meaning and value of being in love with his very dear Father. On the other side, there are our Spirit-enlightened questions for intelligence, reflection, and deliberation, as we enter into communication with the outer word. In either case, Jesus's and ours, we are constituting ourselves humanly by acts of meaning and value that are conversational. The conversation begins, as Lonergan once put it, in

> the experience of a transformation one did not bring about but rather underwent, as divine providence let evil take its course and vertical finality be heightened, as it let one's circumstances shift, one's dispositions change, new encounters occur, and—so gently and quietly—one's heart be touched. It is the experience of a new community... (1985, p. 33)

We find in our experience that one's gift of the Spirit surges or rises up gradually to the forefront of consciousness as one falls in love with someone who lives a life of self-transcendence. One feels oneself invited or challenged to live up to a new standard, because the one or ones with whom one has fallen in love speak a language with their lives that embodies a different orientation and different judgments of value than one was used to. The eyes of being in love bring one to appreciate the implicit or explicit meanings and values that make the beloved "tick." If it is explicitly Christian, the life of the new community will have the shape, as Richard Holloway has so beautifully expressed it, of being taken, blessed, broken, and given away; if it is not explicitly Christian, similar life-patterns will be in evidence together with the vital sense of living out of a gratuity to which one cannot simply lay claim. At any rate, when one is drawn by love into such a relationship, one wants to become identified with the new community, and one begins to accept the pattern or shape of its life and its story not as theories or explanations, but as a framework of beliefs. As time passes, one finds oneself assenting not only notionally, but also really to the meanings, facts, and values that are constitutive of the group's identity—not because one has grasped their underlying intelligibility or the sufficiency of the evidence, but because of what can only be described as the beauty of the lives inspired by them. "In thy light we see light." As believed and lived, such meanings and values become constitutive of oneself, "for they crystallize the inner gift of the love of God into overt Christian fellowship" (Lonergan, 1985, p. 32).

*3.25 Christian identity and its cognitive function.* Besides being redemptive and constitutive, the communication of the Son and Spirit is also cognitive. The constitutive Christian story gives an existential answer to the question about the right way to live; but this answer gives rise to questions for intelligence, reasonableness, and responsibility as the Christian community tries to live out the answer it believes in the different circumstances, stages of meaning, and cultural milieux in which it exists. Hence, to keep its identity clear and to mediate its redemptive and constitutive power to every culture and every domain of human life, the Christian community focuses on its meaning and value as cognitive within the diverse stages of meaning.

Because, as St. Augustine made so clear in *The City of God*, there is a strict correspondence between what we individually and communally love and the identity of the selves and communities we are becoming, the cognitive function of meaning that clarifies the objective of our faith and love has a great practical importance. This practical and existential correlation between the identity of self and community, on the one hand, and the identity of the God of the self and the community, on the other, was in the forefront of the Christian community's concern "on the way to Nicea" and in the course of the patristic and conciliar debates of the first seven or eight Christian centuries, when it made the transition from a common sense control of its basic meanings to second-order theoretical control. If the Arian question whether Jesus was the highest creature or God's son in the strictest sense reached its cognitive resolution on the explanatory level of logical operations on predicative statements, the need for such a resolution was practical, constitutive, soteriological: If Jesus was not God, are we really saved? Moreover, Erik Petersen, Matthew Lamb, and others have stressed the demolition of Eusebian civil theology consequent upon the Athanasian orthodoxy. These are examples of the way the cognitive function of meaning contributes to the foundational purification of the stories by which the Christian community expresses its terminal values and constitutes its identity.

An even more telling example of the foundational significance of Christianity's cognitive function in the second stage of meaning regards the speculative theology of the Trinity based on the Church doctrines worked out in those early ecumenical councils. I am referring, of course, to Augustine's breakthrough to the first non-material analogy for the immanent processions of the Son and the Spirit. His discovery of the most adequate created *imago Dei* in the human mind and heart was a great watershed of Christian and human speculation on the divine nature. It came into its own only in the mature trinitarian theology of Thomas Aquinas; yet this hypothesis of the *emanatio intelligibilis* was buried by Scotist, Ockhamist, and even Thomistic conceptualism promptly after his death. His explanation of the intrinsically conversational nature of the godhead, of its immanent processions, of its economic missions, however, is not something that could have been demonstrated outside the ambit of the stream of tradition generated by the outer Word, Jesus Christ. But its virtualities both for the self-understanding of the Christian community and for the focusing of its God-given orientation to the suffering world have, I am sorry to have to say, lain almost dormant, as far as Christian theology has been concerned.

At the present time, the Christian community in its cognitive function is making the tortuous passage from the second into the third stage of meaning. Perhaps the most unsettling manifestations of the breakdown of the theoretical, logically oriented, classical control of meaning have been connected with the widespread, wholesale jettisoning of specifically Christian meanings and values in favor of one or another "progressive" product of modernity. In its preaching and its liturgies, in its counselling and its conduct, in its theology and its catechesis, Western Christianity has been in the process, as one of my colleagues at Boston College has well put it, of diluting the Good News into "nice" news. Or in another suggestion articulated by Joann Wolski Conn and Walter Conn, the oscillations in Christian self-understanding between the attitudes of self-sacrifice and self-realization have tended to cover over the attitude of genuine self-transcendence demanded by the Christian Gospel.

What is at stake in the Christian community's changeover from second to third stage control of meaning is evident in Karl Rahner's foundational concentration in the 1930s (in *Geist im Welt*) on the seventh article of Question 84 of the first part of the *Summa theologiae*, which used phenomenological means to comment on Thomas Aquinas's cognitional metaphysics. It is even more apparent in Lonergan's *Verbum* articles of the early forties and signalled again by the epigraph to *Insight* (1957/1992) taken from Aristotle's *de Anima*. The pivotal issue in all these works was the pre-predicative, pre-propositional, phenomenologically ostensible act of direct insight into imaginatively elaborated symbolisms that grounds intelligent articulation in either other symbols or concepts, and of reflective insight into the sufficiency or insufficiency of evidence to ground true judgments. Lonergan, indeed, explicated the genuinely conversational basis of Thomas's trinitarian hypothesis within the realm of human interiority to uncover the most full-bodied and differentiated expression to date of the foundations of Christian theology in the third stage of meaning. By explicitly appropriating the way the authentic asking and answering of the eminently conversational questions (see McShane, 1977, pp. 1-2)—"What are we doing whenever we really understand? What are we doing whenever we are really speaking? What are we doing whenever we are really listening to or really dedicating ourselves to someone or something?"—Lonergan discovered the concrete basis for theology as an integrally conversational discipline that mediates between past and future by passing from indirect discourse (research, interpretation, history, dialectic) to direct discourse (foundations, doctrines, systematics, communications). When Lonergan got clear about the last of the conversational questions, "What are we doing when we are loving?" his findings meshed with his own remarkable retrieval of Aquinas's intricate and second-stage theories on grace and freedom. That is to say, the clear differentiation of the further levels of consciousness engaged in deliberating and loving coalesced with the transposition into a third-stage framework of Thomas's doctrine on operative grace, and consequently, he was able to thematize the foundational reality for theology within the converted subject-in-love-with-God. This astounding transposition by Lonergan of Aquinas's fidelity both to Church doctrines and to the systematic exigence of meaning lays the groundwork for general and special categories and a renewal of theology in a new key with implications that are immediately practical and political.

The third-stage-of-meaning systematics already inaugurated by Lonergan allows us to put the theology of God, Trinity, Christology, Pneumatology, and Eschatology into explicitly conversational terms. In this framework, the interplay between the conversational self-meaning essential to God and the conversational self-meaning by which we are personally and communally constituted can be integrated into a complete revision of foundational theology. Here I would like to give an example of what I mean by sketching out how the structure of the human good can be transposed into the context of the communication of the Son and the Spirit as redemptive and constitutive meaning.

## 4. The Human Good and the Christian Conversation

God's self-communication in grace involves not merely an entry into a new entitative, supernatural order of being, but the catching up of our human being as conversationally stunted or deformed self-meaning into the self-meaning constitutive of the Trinity. The gift of God's love liberates human *liberty* when we fall in love with God. But the *conversion* by which we fall in love with God is also an entry into a new set of *interpersonal relations* with Father, Son, and Spirit.

As sharing in the relationship of the Spirit to the Word and the Father, we are
- oriented (with the Son) toward the Father in the beatific vision in the afterlife, and in the present life, given the faith, hope, and love by which our conscious intentionalities can respond here on earth to God's outgoing love in a life of self-transcendent listening, devotion, and self-dedication;

- made ever more receptive to the goodness, truth, and intelligibility of the linguistic and incarnate meaning of the Word; and

- introduced into a dynamism of discernment by which we gradually become more pure and disinterested toward the expression of God's will in the concrete world order comprised of ranges of *goods of order*, *particular goods*, and natural schemes of recurrence.

As sharing in the Son's relationship to the Father (filiation), we actively desire the strictly supernatural fulfillment of the beatific vision as a *particular good* that relativizes all other *needs* and *desires*.

As sharers in the mission of the Word, listening to the Word expressed in history by Jesus under the Spirit's tutelage is just the beginning; we have also to

- use our *capacity for intellectual development* to enter into solidarity with the poor and the victims of injustice by envisaging and helping to bring about the concrete realization of God's rule on earth by understanding correctly and making wise judgments about the complex interlocking of familial, legal, technological, economic, and political *goods of order*; and by acquiring the needed *skills* and *habits* for playing the requisite *roles* and *tasks*; and

- use our faith-enlightened intelligence, reasonableness, and responsibility to transform our conversation on earth, especially the meta-institution of language, and to transvalue all vital, social, cultural, personal, and religious *values*, about us, by moving toward institutions and *personal relations* in which people can be more intelligent, reasonable, responsible, free, and friendly.

These are no more than just hints and guesses—paltry intimations—of the way the Christian community can appropriate for its foundations the intrinsically conversational character of its God and itself in the third stage of meaning.

# 13

# Communication: Mutual
# Self-Mediation in Context

## *Francisco Sierra-Gutiérrez*

Bernard Lonergan's work is a momentous contribution to understanding communication as sharing human meanings and values (1972, p. 356).[1] But at first blush his work may not strike some readers as being concerned very much with communication at all. However, three aspects of his writings readily illustrate his profound concern for communication: (1) his aim to seek a common ground on which people of intelligence might meet (1957/1992, p. 7); (2) his methodological proposal to obtain an equitable dialogue between past, present, and future (1972, ch. 5-14); and (3) the participative and active reading his texts demand due to his insistence on personal and communal self-appropriation. In the foreword to the present collection, Robert M. Doran has explained the common ground delineated by Lonergan, and in chapter 2 Thomas J. Farrell has adumbrated how writers might move toward personal self-appropriation by becoming more aware of the intersubjectivity involved in writing.

While Lonergan's contributions to communication are numerous, as all of the essays in the present collection suggest, nonetheless they are rooted in the special sort of relation that defines communication and in the wide matrix of terms and relations where it is performed. These roots are the foundations of communication. The present essay examines the foundations of communication as sharing human meanings and values. It is an epistemological attempt (1) to understand communication as a relevant case of mutual self-mediation of human beings and (2) to propose a communicative reading of "The Structure of Human Good" section of Lonergan's *Method in Theology* (1972, pp. 47-52) as an empirical, but also critical, normative, and dialectical context for communication.

---

[1] John C. Kelly (1981) first developed this thesis by approaching Lonergan through Alfred Schutz's notion of common sense or everyday life-world. However, his exploration needs to elaborate further the constitutive role of meaning in social contexts and to develop in more detail the genesis, expression, and validation of that meaning.

In Part 1, "Communication as Mutual Self-Mediation," I set forth Lonergan's understanding of mediation, mutual mediation, self-mediation, and mutual
self-mediation as integral to the process of communication and the sharing of
meanings and values. In Part 2, "Communication in Context," I consider the
contexts of communication, drawing upon Lonergan's table-diagram in *Method
in Theology* of the 18 terms that he uses to map the structure of the human
good, to show how they constitute the contexts of communication (1972, p. 48).
The major sections of Part 2, then, refer to the lines and columns of Lonergan's
table-diagram: (2.1) The First Row, (2.2) The Third Column, (2.3) The Second
Row, and (2.4) The Third Row; individual terms, or combinations of terms, are
treated, then, in separate paragraphs in the major sections and are italicized to
facilitate reference back to the table-diagram. In Part 3, "The Context of Communication as Normative, Critical, and Dialectical," I explain briefly how the context of communication is also normative, critical, and dialectical; and then in Part
4, "Conclusion," I set forth a few conclusions that can be drawn from this essay.

Put differently, this essay carries forward Lonergan's treatment of
communicative processes as described by Doran in the foreword and by Farrell in chapter 2 by drawing more fully on some of Lonergan's later works
(1972, 1984) and by focusing on dimensions of communication that Doran
and Farrell do not consider. Thus this essay offers a more refined and more
comprehensive view of the dimensions of communication. In the process of
doing this, I show that Lonergan's later thought adds to our understanding
of communication, insights that are simply not available in contemporary
works about semiotics, sociolinguistics, and pragmatics. Therefore, I suggest that his work invites a renewal of the study of communication by opening up fresh approaches that have not been explored by others.

## 1. Communication as Mutual Self-Mediation

The notion of mediation[2] holds a central position in Lonergan's thought; it
is a constituent part of the nest of terms in his notion of meaning and a
decisive achievement in understanding what sharing human meanings and
values means (1984, pp. 1-20). Lonergan considers the notions of simple
mediation, mutual mediation, and self-mediation. But in a final complica-
tion of the notion of mediation in terms of the conditions of human community, he speaks of mutual self-mediation.

> Simple mediation is an extremely general and tenuous notion. It is mediation
> from the immediate to the mediated. The immediate is any principle, origin,
> source, ground, basis; the mediated is any effect, consequence, result, outcome,

---

[2] Lonergan worked out a realist notion of mediation with a generality comparable to
that of the notion employed by Hegel, in "The Mediation of Christ in Prayer," a
lecture Lonergan gave in 1963 but not published until 1984. Unfortunately, J. M.
Matustik (1988) overlooks the notion of "mutual self-mediation" in his commentary.

> any sphere of influence, radiation, expansion. We employed this general notion to form notions of mutual mediation and self-mediation. Mutual mediation constitutes the functional whole: There are at least two principles, and each mediates the other or the others. Self-mediation means that a whole has consequences that transform the whole itself, and we distinguished three levels: the displacement upwards of organic growth; the displacement inwards of animal consciousness; the deliberate shift of center of existential commitment. But we remarked of existential decision that it occurs in community, in love, in loyalty, in faith. Just as there is a self-mediation towards autonomy, so there is a mutual self-mediation, and its occasion is the encounter in all its forms (meeting, regular meeting, living together). (1984, pp. 12-13)

By *mutual self-mediation* Lonergan means a combination of *mutual mediation* and *self-mediation* (p. 14). It underlies the different forms of communication including the interpersonal situation where it is more explicit. Certainly, the *mutual mediation* involves reciprocity between interlocutors, each one as a different center of immediacy, but related through open and dynamic symmetries. These symmetries reside in a common code, or in a matrix of the human subjects' sources of meaning (Lonergan, 1957/1992, p. 592). In this way, levels of expression may have their source in experiential, artistic, intelligent, rational, or volitional sources of meaning of a speaker or writer, and that flow of sensible events terminates in a reproduction of sources of meaning in a hearer or reader (p. 594).

This interaction clearly is not a matter of an action or a reaction that passes on from one being to another, nor a reciprocal influence between interlocutors through images they offer each other. Mutual mediation is not reduced to recognizing in each hearer or speaker the right to be a source of a simple mediation. It is rather a process that is effected in so far as partners are in relation, where the expressions of each one are not independent or monological, but nuanced in several ways according to (1) the intersubjective component in the expression, (2) the supervening component of intelligence that admits various degrees of explicitness and deliberateness, (3) the higher component of truth or falsity that may emerge at the term of a series of insights as insight emerges at the term of a series of imaginative representations, and finally (4) the entry of a volitional component (p. 594).

> On the elementary level this process [of communication] has been described as arising between the self and the other when, on the basis of already existing intersubjectivity, the self makes a gesture, the other makes an interpretative response, and the self discovers in the response the effective meaning of his gesture. So from intersubjectivity through gesture and interpretation there arises common understanding. On that spontaneous basis there can be built a common language, the transmission of acquired knowledge and of social partners through education, the diffusion of information, and the common will to community that seeks to replace misunderstanding with mutual comprehension and to change occasions of disagreement into occasions of non-agreement and eventually of agreement. (Lonergan, 1972, p. 357)

The relevance of mutual mediation transforms the notion of a feedback between receivers and senders into a cooperative process where each enunciation is a product of the interaction. Speaker and hearer, writer and reader, media and audiences constitute their reciprocity free of "external" determinants; their communication often functions as an implicit pact, a negotiation, and frequently a silent mutual complicity that is invisibly operative through daily rituals. Hence, the mutual mediation shows two or more poles in relation, with no one of them an autonomous and omnipotent subject of the relation as if that were an attribute of its own, which would be a categorial mistake. There are no independently constituted subjects that interchange their messages; they are already bound by different ways of communication in their processes of socialization. However, this binding does not guarantee successful communication, nor does it prevent a situation in which "less differentiated consciousness finds more differentiated consciousness beyond its horizon and, in self-defense, may tend to regard the more differentiated with that pervasive, belittling hostility that Max Scheler named *ressentiment*" (1972, p. 273).

Accordingly, the mere exchange of information and knowledge, the mere transmission or inducing of emotion, as imparting and diffusing some view of reality and some understanding of the world are not genuine communication. Sharing meaning is not a mutual gift, nor a physical, geometrical, and homogeneous partition where each one gets its own slice. Communication cannot be reduced to a linguistic rule-governed behavior. Both studies of rhetoric and reception show the relevant shift from quantitative analysis of audiences and media effects to qualitative and cultural readings where writers, speakers, and audience are concretely active in the co-production of meanings.[3]

Now, Lonergan adverts to the classification of levels of expression as "potential," while the original and terminal sources of meaning are conceived clearly and distinctly (1957/1992, p. 592):

> Because the classification is potential rather than actual, it does not impose upon the interpreter any a priori Procrustean bed that his documents have to fit, but leaves him free to exercise to the full his ingenuity and subtlety in determining a writer's sources and intention. (p. 594)

This makes Lonergan's thought immune to an objection of a basic categorial homology as a final guarantee of communication. A common participation in reason (Descartes), the pre-established harmony in monads (Leibniz), a

---

[3] Jesús Martín-Barbero, Néstor García-Canclini, and Guillermo Orozco (1991), among others, lead this perspective in Colombia and Mexico. They often explain the communicative process as one of production (creation/enunciation), distribution, and consumption (interpretation/appropriation/re-creation), with the proviso that the economic analogy cannot be taken as a matter of artificial needs and impetuous purchases, but as a symbolic and aesthetic process that both integrates society with itself and communicates that integration.

trans-subjective categorial structure (Kant), an intentional and intermonadic community (Husserl), a fundamental wisdom as reminiscence (Plato), and some Habermasian developments of pragmatics—all show themselves as monological, as a non-mutual mediated basis, or as only previously established conditions for communication.

> [Furthermore,] there exist other correlations between fields of meaning and modes of expression, but such correlations are not to be conceived as components of static systems, such as are illustrated by physical and chemical theories, but as components of dynamic systems, such as are illustrated by the genetic theories of biology, psychology, and cognitional analysis. (p. 595)

In so far as communication combines the mutual mediation with a *self-mediation*, communication fashions "a whole that has consequences that change the whole" (Lonergan, 1984, p. 6). At any stage of an organism's growth, "there are different centers of immediacy, with the centers giving [to] the whole all the properties of each of the centers....The whole becomes something different through its consequences, its outcome, its results" (p. 8).

Self-mediation is crucial as a mediation of autonomy in human development (pp. 9-10): "[I]n the process from extroversion, from being poured on objects, to existential self-commitment, to fidelity, to destiny, we are not Leibnizian monads with neither doors nor windows; we are open to the influence of others, and others are open to influence by us" (p. 13). The personal development "in relation to another person is a mutual self-mediation. It is not merely a self-mediation through another,...nor is it a matter of simultaneous mutual influence" (p. 18).

Hence, the partners in communication reveal themselves as dynamic and autonomous. Their mutual self-mediation does not melt them in an undifferentiated amalgam. Some heterogeneity is conserved; room is needed for personal autonomy, discovery, creativity, consciousness differentiation, innovation, or transgression in order to transform not only each one's whole, but the entire whole of the relation as it is distinctive of a mutual self-mediation.

Communication conceived as a mutual self-mediation of human beings, their meanings, and values becomes dynamic and transformative. It is a space where a co-production, a co-reference, a co-creation of new shared meanings, a co-transformation of wholes constituted by common meanings and values is performed. Such a performance does not fall apart by the asking of questions and the giving of answers as an interactive praxis of communication. A mutual request for new cognitive, effective, communicative, and constitutive meanings is meant by the interrogations; they are a source of new experiences, of semantic innovation, of criticism of previous agreements, and of a co-responsible dialogue for the world in which human beings live (Lonergan, 1972, p. 360). The mutual self-mediation is a higher transformative synthesis of previous mediations.

However, such a mutual self-mediation occurs "in the immediate inter-personal situation that vanishes when communication becomes indirect through books, television programs, and teaching by mail" (Lonergan, 1984, p. 13). Such a proviso does not restrict our thesis to the context of interpersonal communication about ourselves.

Mutual self-mediation occurs to a greater or less extent in a variety of contexts: in meeting, falling in love, and getting married; in education; in relations between equals and between superiors and inferiors; in the several matrices of personal relations in different communities. Now, when interpersonal situations and reality "acquire the universal immediacy of the mass media and the molding power of universal education" (Lonergan, 1972, p. 99), for creators and producers, writers and speakers, these objectifications are results of their own simple, mutual, self, and mutual self-mediations. And for receivers, hearers, readers, this ontological immediacy, through the interpretation and the several strategies of reception, recovers an intentional immediacy to provide more explicit forms of simple and mutual mediations, of a deliberate transposition of the center, or of more explicit mutual self-mediations of human beings.[4] In this way people are enabled to transform their universe mediated by meaning and motivated by values—and no less often to impoverish, empty out, and deform it (Lonergan, 1972, p. 79).

There is also the mediation of a community or communities: "[C]ommunity mediates itself by its history. The community is constituted by its common sense, its common meaning, its common commitment" (Lonergan, 1984, p. 11). Understanding its own expressions and the expressions of the other communities and cultures, a community promotes mutual self-mediations between them. The aim of culture, education, public opinion, and international relations plays its decisive role: "It is the function of culture to discover, express, validate, criticize, correct, develop, improve such meaning and value" (Lonergan, 1972, p. 32).

If we disregard communication as a mutual self-mediation of human beings, we will be left with the hegemonic simple mediations of propaganda, ideologies, and advertisements; with a mere transmissionist and transactionist mutual mediation; with a self-mediated but distorted imperative of a lewd individual expressionism; with a violent wrestling of narcissistic images and solitary pleasures through the many mirrors of the media.

---

[4] Different realities are mediated, for instance, in the interaction between television and its audience. There is a **technological** mediation that introduces techniques and skills to build representation, credibility, spheres of reality, and so on. There is a **cognitive** mediation shaped by mental maps, interactive scripts, and universes of meaning. **Situational** mediation is understood not only in its physical dimension but also in terms of patterns of watching TV and practices that go beyond the time and place of doing it. There is also an **institutional** mediation that locates the concrete communities of appropriation of the media, and a **referential** mediation shaped by social stratum, sex, age, cultural horizons, and conditions of existence. See Orozco (1991).

The mutual self-mediation underlies mass media and remains operative as a potential dialogue partner with traditions, as a potential interrogator about "what do we do in communicating? -why is doing that communication? -what do we communicate? -what is good and responsible in that communication?" Sooner or later, mutually self-mediated subjects will ask these questions.

Finally, Lonergan points out that "mutual self-mediation proves the inexhaustible theme of dramatists and novelists" (1984, p. 13). Films, soap operas, and melodramas show the intrigues of our narrative identities, tell our own lives and deeds to ourselves, and compose our lives as works of art.

Lonergan points to the reorientation and deconstruction of communication from the root of the human exigencies of attentiveness, intelligence, reasonableness, and freedom. He would not start with a direct analysis of carriers of meaning, of instrumental acts of meaning, of social mediations and messages as concrete "scientific" objects of social communication. Even if it is impossible to examine communication from an extralinguistic standpoint, this does not mean that language becomes the only reality: "The very communication is not to say what we know, but to show what we are" (Lonergan, 1967, p. 237). Self- and communal-appropriation of communication—a genuine task of a philosophy of communication—might start at any pole: in the subjects who produce and control meanings and values within their cultural matrices, or in their symbolic, linguistic, artistic, intersubjective, incarnate, and concrete embodiments of those meanings and values. What is extremely urgent is to undertake the study in both directions. We cannot be lost in the enchanted forests of semiotics and vast local hermeneutics; we cannot become real leaders of our history by continuously sharpening the knife of good heuristic intentions, but never cutting anything with it. Why not discover crises in communication in subjects and institutions along with the "*mise en scène*" of messages by themselves? Why not criticize symbols, messages, and social images from their very plasticity to their root in differentiated or undifferentiated acts of meaning of existential communicators?[5] In this way there appears a genuine and legitimate argument ad hominem from operational development. "Unless one wants to remain silent, one has to appeal to experience, understanding, judgment, [decision,]

---

[5] In the 1980s Latin American communication studies abandoned information models, the denunciations of cultural imperialism and dependency theory, some theories of development, and epistemological journeys seeking "the scientific object" of communication. There is a shift now towards an alternative and popular communication, and towards the analysis of the cultural conditions of production, distribution, and appropriation of messages; however, this turn has not yet accomplished all its benefits either in terms of systematic but open approaches or in terms of some foundational categories. The pertinence of Lonergan's thought to these studies lies in the philosophic and methodical approach to meaning and values from the structures of subjects-as-subjects, in the foundational notion of mediation, and in the demonstration of a wider context where communication is performed.

and one's communication thereof in order to deny the import of experience, intelligence, reasonableness, and intelligent community of discourse" (Matustik, 1988, pp. 162-187). So Lonergan's interest in the human subjects involved in communication reveals the subjects to be mutually active, dynamic, attentive, intelligent, critical, responsible.

We see that Lonergan's strategy for communication runs parallel to Locke's decision to tackle the issue with a theory of meaning in the first place instead of a theory of true and false propositions. But in a different tack from Locke's, Lonergan stresses a theory of meaning based on the operations of subjects-as-subjects not only as sources of meaning, among other sources of meaning, but also as operators that control and intend being and value. So when Lonergan locates communication as a function of meaning as relevant as the other three sources of meaning—cognitive, efficient, and constitutive—he holds a brief for their complementariness and prevents us from entering into communicative pan-inflations.

The common meaning involved in communication, Lonergan notes, is "doubly constitutive. In each individual it is constitutive of the individual as a member of the community. In the group of individuals it is constitutive of the community" (1972, p. 357). We shall now describe the wider context where shared meanings are performed and displayed.

## 2. Communication in Context

The remote context of communication is being as the core of meaning. The proximate context for communication is the universe of common sense, or the everyday life-world, or society. Both contexts interpenetrate to create one context that is empirical, heuristic, normative, critical, and dialectical. Both contexts need to be taken into account because of the reductionism of sociolinguistic, semiotic, pragmatic, politic, mechano-morphic, functionalist, and informational approaches exhibited in various social sciences, practices, and philosophies today. Both contexts also make evident that the problematics of communication were not born of multi-media expansionism in this century, nor of the electronic "Global Village" of mass media.

Being, the core of meaning, constitutes the *remote context* of communication, for it "is the all-inclusive term of meaning, for apart from being there is nothing...the core of all acts of meaning is the intention of being" (Lonergan, 1957/1992, pp. 381-383). The notion of being is protean. "Being is (or is thought to be) whatever is (or is thought to be) grasped intelligently and affirmed reasonably" (p. 590).

Then the universe of meanings is the full range of possible combinations: (1) of experiences and lack of experience, (2) of insights and lack of insight, (3) of judgments and of failures to judge, and (4) of the various orientations of polymorphic human consciousness (p. 590). From this base one can proceed to the content and context of every meaning: "In the measure that one explores human experience, human insights, human reflection, and human polymorphic consciousness, one becomes capable, when provided with the appropriate data, of approximating to the content and context of the meaning of any given expression" (p. 590). This constitutes the potential universal viewpoint of interpretation and communication.

The intention of being and the intention of true values are communicative, as Joseph Fitzpatrick notes:

> Once understanding is achieved the inquirer moves from the privacy of sensation to the sphere of the intelligible, and intelligibility is in principle communicable...the sensible as intelligible is generalized, communicable, and even when private, potentially public. It becomes actually public with outer speech. Because he refuses to assimilate knowledge to sensation, Lonergan is free of the entrapment in the unfathomable privacy of sensation that such assimilation entails. There is no thought, therefore, of language being injected with meaning from some purely private act of naming and the like. (Fitzpatrick, 1992, p. 45)

Between linguisticality and meaning there is a unity of identity and nonidentity. There is an identity in so far as there is "a solidarity, almost a fusion [between] the development of knowledge and the development of language" (Lonergan, 1957/1992, pp. 577-578). There is a nonidentity (p. 576) in so far as no categorial language-games or linguistic systems can exhaust the transcendental reflection of the subject-as-subject in its intention of being (Lamb, 1981b, pp. 300-301).[6]

The contextual aspects of the judgments that are logic and dialectic— and the relations of actual judgments to the past, to the present, to the future—rest "upon the self-correcting process of learning as transformed by communication and collaboration" (p. 315). Concretely, there is also a communicative constitution of the virtually unconditioned (i.e., a conditioned that has fulfilled its conditions to be). Inasmuch as the virtually unconditioned is obtained when people recognize that, in fact, there are no further and pertinent and relevant questions that would make vulnerable their prospective judgments, this means that it is necessary to take into account a competent community where those questions might arise, as Thomas S. Kuhn (1970) noted for scientific communities.[7] In this way, the unconditioned is withdrawn from relativity to its source and becomes accessible not only to the knower that utters it, but also to any other knower. Making knowledge public also entails open debate and dialogue (Lonergan, 1957/1992, p. 402). Accordingly, truth is not only a matter of evidence or consensus alone, but of communally agreed upon sufficient evidence

---

[6] This isomorphism between language and meaning allows a semiotic transformation of the operations of the subject-as-subject. The semiotic correlations would be: empirical-syntactics; intelligent-semantics; rational-sigmatics; and responsible-pragmatics (Lamb, 1981b, pp. 303-304).

[7] On truth and consensus see K.-O. Apel (1987/1991).

founded in the invulnerability of a prospective judgment to further, relevant, and pertinent questions.

> The question, then, is not how many people say it is obvious, nor how great is their authority and renown, but simply what is the evidence. Nor is evidence some peculiar sheen or convincing glamour. It supposes the coherence of the hypothesis with the universal viewpoint, with the genetic and dialectical relations between successive stages of meaning, with the genetic sequence of modes of expression and the recurrent gaps between meaning and expression. (p. 612)

The analysis of the *proximate context* of communication will account for a general spectrum of communicating experience within a cultural matrix. The universe of common sense, both as common meaning and as a legitimate way of knowledge, can be distinguished from systematic and critical exigences of meaning that give rise to distinct modes of conscious and intentional operation and also yield the other realms and stages of meaning, such as theory, scholarship, art, interiority, and transcendence (Lonergan, 1972, pp. 81-99).

The whole context of communication is *empirical*, *normative*, *critical*, and *dialectical*. It is empirical: Readers familiar with "The Structure of Human Good" section in *Method in Theology* (1972, pp. 47-52) may read the following "map" or table-diagram that Lonergan provides atop page 48 along with its communicative components.!8•

| Individual | | Social | Ends |
|---|---|---|---|
| *Potentiality* | *Actuation* | | |
| capacity, need | operation | cooperation | particular good |
| plasticity, perfectibility | development, skill | institution, role, task | good of order |
| liberty | orientation, conversion | personal relations | terminal value |

## 2.1 The First Row

The first line—"capacity, need, operation, cooperation, particular good"—includes the *"capacity, need"* that both heads for and recognizes data (Loner-

---

[8] This sort of reading is suggested by Lonergan himself (1972, p. 359), as an explanation of the formal component of the ontology of common meaning and as a rebuttal of a merely material view of society. Communication is a concrete form of human good and its process "is not merely the service of man; it is above all the making of man, his advance in authenticity, the fulfillment of his affectivity, and the direction of his work to the particular goods and a good of order that are worthwhile" (1972, p. 52).

gan, 1972, p. 73); our senses and body understood merely as an apparatus for receiving and transmitting signals, and so as potentially significant; a kind of source of meaning (p. 61); and our feelings as non-intentional states and trends, and also as intentional responses (p. 30). All of them are holders of a first capacity to interrelate with the others and the environment, as potential orientations to a world mediated by meaning.[9] The *potential, formal, complete, constitutive* or *effective, active* and *instrumental acts of meaning* constitute the *operations* of communication that refer to terms of meaning. *Instrumental* acts of meaning are expressions, the whole signic, symbolic, and technical mediations of meaning concomitant to acts of meaning.

> Expression is not only an instrument of the principal acts of meaning that reside in conception and judgment, but also a prolongation of the psychic flow from percepts, memories, images, and feelings into the shaping of the countenance, the movement of the hands, and the utterance of the words....[O]ur speech and writing are basically automatisms, and our conscious control supervenes only to order, to select, to revise, or to reject. It follows that expression bears the signature not only of the controlling meaning, but also of the underlying psychic flow. (Lonergan, 1957/1992, p. 615)

Expressions can cause in the other some share of meaning.[10] As expression and its interpretation may be adequate or faulty, they provide the materials and place for rhetorical analysis and hermeneutics in communication. In *potential* acts, meaning is elemental. "There has not been reached the distinction between meaning and meant" (Lonergan, 1972, p. 74). Elemental meanings are symbolic, and they meet the need that logic or dialectic cannot meet. That need "is for internal communication....It is through symbols that mind and body, mind and heart, heart and body communicate" (pp. 66-67).

In the *formal* act of meaning, "there has emerged the distinction between meaning and meant, for the meant is what is conceived, thought, considered, defined, supposed, formulated" (Lonergan, 1957/1992, p. 381; 1972, p. 74). In formal acts of meaning, symbols are interpreted and explained (Lonergan, 1972, pp. 67-69). But in the *full* or *complete* act of meaning, "one settles the status of the object of thought, that it is merely an

---

[9] Lonergan (1972, p. 86, n. 22) quotes E. Cassirer's *The Philosophy of Symbolic Forms* to show that demand for expression is so rigorous that motor disturbances that result in aphasia are accompanied with disturbances in perception, in thought, and in action.

[10] Lonergan speaks of a written expression as "a verbal flow governed by a practical insight **F** that depends upon a principal insight **A** to be communicated, upon a grasp **B** of the anticipated audience's habitual intellectual development **C**, and upon a grasp **D** of the deficiencies in insight **E** that have to be overcome if the insight **A** is to be communicated" (1957/1992, pp. 580, 585). This process establishes previous exigencies of speakers and writers, but it does not legitimate the performance of the mutual self-mediation by itself.

object of thought, or a mathematical entity, or a real thing lying in the world of human experience, or a transcendent reality beyond that world" (p. 74). *Constitutive* or *effective* acts produce *active meanings*. "Active meanings come with judgments of value, decisions, actions" (p. 74). Those meanings are specified in the constitutive and effective functions of meaning. "In so far as [meaning] is constitutive, it constitutes part of the reality of the one that means: his horizon, his assimilative powers, his knowledge, his values, his character....In so far as it is effective, it persuades or commands others or it directs man's control over nature" (p. 356). By operating, individuals procure themselves instances of communication as *particular goods* at a given place and time. Communicative operations mainly occur in the dramatic pattern of experience, but each pattern—biological, aesthetic, artistic, practical, intellectual, religious—feeds the enriched series of expressions, meanings, and values to be shared by others.

> [The operations undertake] the communication, not as an exercise in formal logic, but as a work of art; and [they have] at [their] disposal not merely all the resources of language, but also the support of modulated tone and changing volume, the eloquence of facial expression, the emphasis of gestures, the effectiveness of pauses, the suggestiveness of questions, the significance of omissions....[This] procedure is not logical if by "logical" you mean conformity to a set of general rules valid in every instance of a defined range; *for no set of general rules can keep pace with the resourcefulness of intelligence in its adaptations to the possibilities and exigencies of concrete tasks of self-communication.* (Lonergan, 1957/1992, pp. 200, 201; emphasis added)

But the process is logical if by "logical" you mean attentive, intelligent, reasonable, responsible.

### 2.2 The Third Column

In the third column, the terms to be explained are "cooperation, institution, role, and task." *Spontaneous intersubjectivity* is a basic form of *cooperation* in communication; it is a dimension of human togetherness more basic than practicality, even if it operates in dialectical tension with it. To a notable extent, operations of individuals involve intersubjective cooperation. "Prior to the 'we' that results from the mutual love of an 'I' and a 'thou,' there is the earlier 'we' that precedes the distinction of subjects and survives its oblivion. This prior 'we' is vital and functional...[and] appears not only in spontaneous mutual aid, but also in some of the ways in which feelings are communicated" (Lonergan, 1972, p. 57). A community of feeling, fellow-feeling, psychic contagion, and emotional identification show this prior "we." A retreat from personal differentiation to vital unity appears in hypnosis, in sexual intercourse, in the single stream of instinct and feeling when members identify with their leader, also in mystic experiences (pp. 58-59). But besides these modes, there are also intersubjective communications of meaning present in smiles; in facial or bodily movements or pauses; in all the variations of voice in tone, pitch, and volume; and in silence—in all the ways in which our feelings are revealed or betrayed by ourselves or are depicted by actors on the stage (p. 61). Intersubjective meanings antedate all subsequent analysis that speaks of body and soul, or of sign and signified (p. 61). Lonergan holds that even if intersubjectivity is supposed in linguistic meaning, for in its ordinary use it is public and only derivatively private (pp. 253-257; 260-262), linguistic meaning is objective; it tends to be univocal; it is true as opposed to the false and not only to the mendacious; it contains distinctions of what we mean; it is the meaning of a proposition or about some object. Still, "this must not be taken to imply that language is some optional adjunct that may or may not accompany the other acts" of meaning (p. 86).

Intersubjective meanings belong to incarnate subjects:

> [P]rimitive community is intersubjective. Its schemes of recurrence are simple prolongations of prehuman attainment, too obvious to be discussed or criticized, too closely linked with more elementary processes to be distinguished sharply from them. The bond of mother and child, man and wife, father and son, reaches into a past of ancestors to give meaning and cohesion to the clan or tribe or nation. A sense of belonging together provides the dynamic premise for common enterprise, for mutual aid and succor, for the sympathy that augments joys and divides sorrows. Even after civilization is attained, intersubjective community survives in the family with its circle of relatives and its accretion of friends, in customs and folk-ways, in basic arts and crafts and skills, in language and song and dance, and most concretely of all in the inner psychology and radiating influence of women. Nor is the abiding significance and efficacy of the intersubjective overlooked when motley states name themselves nations, when constitutions are attributed to founding fathers, when image and symbol, anthem and assembly, emotion and sentiment are invoked to impart an elemental vigor and pitch to the vast and cold, technological, economic, and political structures of human invention and convention. Finally, as intersubjective community precedes civilization and underpins it, so also it remains when civilization suffers disintegration and decay. (Lonergan, 1957/1992, pp. 237-238)

It cannot be forgotten that communication is not only a spontaneous, but also a self-correcting process of learning in which practical intelligence has its concourse.

> Not only are men born with a native drive to inquire and understand; they are born into a community that possesses a common fund of tested answers, and from that fund each may draw his variable share, measured by his capacity, his interests, his energy. Not only does the self-correcting process of learning unfold within the private consciousness of the individual; for by speech and, still more, by example, there is effected a sustained communication that at once disseminates and tests and improves every advance to make the achievement of each successive generation the starting point of the next. (Lonergan, 1957/1992, p. 198)

Now, if spontaneous and communicative intersubjectivity might follow some settled pattern, this pattern would be fixed by a *role* to be fulfilled or a *task* to be performed within an *institutional framework*. Communication is shaped in family and manners (mores), society and education, the state and the law, the economy and technology, the church or sect, and the diverse institutions/industries of mass media: journalism, radio, television, advertising, cinema, info-networks, propaganda, etc. They constitute the commonly understood and already accepted bases and modes of cooperation and communication; but they tend to change only slowly, for change involves a new common understanding and consent (Lonergan, 1972, p. 48), new communicative practices that are in a dialectical tension with the intersubjective community, on one side, and with personal relations and terminal values, on the other.

There is a contemporary exigence that will bring scientists and scholars into close contact with experts in very many different fields. New institutional communications will be related to policy-making concerned with attitudes and ends, to the planning to work out the optimal use of existing resources for attaining the ends under given conditions, to the execution of the plans in order to generate feedback and ongoing processes that are continuously revised in the light of their consequences (pp. 364-367). These actions constitute a genuine institutional pragmatics and an organizational communication in communities.

## 2.3 The Second Row

In the second row, the terms "plasticity, perfectibility, development, skill, and the good of order" involve communicative dimensions. The capacities of individuals for acts of meaning and expression and language develop. They are *plastic and perfectible*. The *development and skills* of proportionate expression begin with the discovery of indicative signification and then advance through generalization where the patterns discerned in the image guide bodily movements including vocal articulation. Mimesis signifies the other's movements; analogies follow, and a third step consists in the development of language. There, meaning finds its greater liberation:

> It is the work of the community that has common insights into common needs and common tasks, and, of course, already is in communication through intersubjective, indicative, mimetic, and analogical expression. Just as its members understand one another's smiles and frowns, their gestures, mimesis and analogies, so too they can come to endow vocal sounds with signification. So words come to refer to data of experience, sentences to the insights that shape the experience, while the mood of the sentence varies to express assertions, commands, and wishes. (Lonergan, 1972, p. 87)

The development of language and thought depends upon common insights. Insights are a function "not of outer circumstances, but of inner conditions" (Lonergan, 1957/1992, p. 28); here, the inner conditions of community that made it possible to share meanings and values. Language develops from the early spatial emphasis to handle adequately the generic, the temporal, the subjective, the divine, to obtain different linguistic and communicative competencies (Lonergan, 1972, p. 92).

As language develops, there emerges a distinction between ordinary, technical, and literary language. The development is, of course, of skills, demanded by individual creativity or by institutional roles and tasks, clichés and stereotypes. Language molds developing consciousness (p. 70). But language also structures the world about us. Media languages do not stand apart from this function, and their development is also exhibited and demanded in several and different ways in audio-visual arts, in the electronic paraphernalia of new interactive mass media, in personal interchange, conversations, negotiations, discussions, and dialogues.[11] This diversity shall reverse the "ideal speech situation" that philosophy of language proclaims as normative for all communication.

Specialized development of different expressions is not only a fruit of isolated creative producers or of the stereotyped fashions media disseminate; such expressions are also fruit of the several differentiations of consciousness (Lonergan, 1972, pp. 326-330) and of the stages and exigencies of meaning (pp. 81-99). Further developments are marked by recompositions, rearrangements, reconfigurations, and styles and by new uses people work out through conversation and through the influence of mass media messages and techniques—all of which together mold an imaginative, aesthetic, critical, satirical, ironic, and humorous reception in the everyday life-world.

These developments show that communication through history is an effort of human beings to attain and control common meanings—from cosmogonies to the intricate knots of poetry, mysticism, philosophy, politics (Lonergan, 1957/1992, p. 581). They show the individual and communal effort to surmount simple certainties, to configure our own discourses and convey them with the additional effort that dialogue involves.

---

[11] In theory, media must be detectable and compatible. If they are discernible but incompatible, they are not recognized and understanding them is very difficult. If they are compatible but imperceptible, their designation capacity fails. In principle, media are unlimited and subject to critical revisions. The skills in media transform intentional communication in virtue of its possibilities to produce, translate, and obtain a recreative reception of a new communicative reality. See Hanno Beth and Harry Pross (1976/1990) who also classify media: Primary media are used in the elemental human contact and multiply expressions. Verbal and nonverbal symbols are frequent. Communication tends toward clarity and openness. Secondary media procure a temporal conservation of communication, and some apparatus is required only on the side of the production. Tertiary media suppose apparatus on both sides of production and reception. Clearly, other typologies are possible. Interlocutive differentiated strategies—conversation, negotiation, and dialogue—are proposed by Francis Jacques (1985).

Besides this institutional basis of communication, to which technical, economic, and political institutions are linked, there is also the concrete manner in which cooperation is worked out. Such a performance constitutes the concretely functioning or malfunctioning *good of order* of communication. From this perspective, particular goods of communication are regarded all together as recurrent. The order sustaining the recurrence implies operations and cooperations and makes the effectiveness of particular desires of communication dependent on the cooperative performance of the individuals involved. But most important are the technical, economic, and political set-up for sustained communication in society. A social order obeys not only technical and instrumental imperatives in favor of a society of permanent leisure and comfort, but also scales of originating and terminal values, as we shall see. Norms, laws, mechanisms of enunciation, participation, deliberation to obtain mutual agreement, to tolerate dissents and differences are required (Lonergan, 1957/1992, pp. 233-234). Politics is taken as a decisive communal and communicative achievement rather than an isolated group bias in hegemonic power over/against the others.[12]

> It is to be insisted that the good of order is not some design for utopia, some theoretic ideal, some set of ethical precepts, some code of laws, or some super-institution. It is quite concrete. It is the actually functioning or malfunctioning set of "if-then" relationships guiding operators and coordinating operations. It is the ground whence recur or fail to recur whatever instances of the particular good are recurring or failing to recur. It has a basis in institutions, but it is a product of much more—of all the skill and know-how, all the industry and resourcefulness, all the ambition and fellow-feeling of a whole people, adapting to each change of circumstance, meeting each new emergency, struggling against every tendency to disorder. (Lonergan, 1972, 49-50; also see 1957/1992, pp. 196-204, 237-269, 619-621)

## 2.4 The Third Row

The third row of terms—"liberty, orientation, conversion, personal relations, and terminal values"—now needs to be explained. *Liberty* in communication does not mean simply freedom of expression/enunciation; it rather means communication as an option, as a result of acts of deliberation, evaluation, planning, choice, and decision; as an upper level of development of a natural endowment, capacity, or need or automatism. Communication is meaningful for free wills, for self-determined subjects, for people who constitute themselves as originating values and bringing about terminal values.

---

[12] In the 1960s many studies in communication in Latin America and the United States focused their attention on the issue of political power bound up with mass media effects in voting; in ideological propaganda, cultural imperialism, and domination; and in advertisement and marketing. But debates did not concentrate on the role of the state, education, and press in forming public opinion, nor on the formation of a wider political will open to public discussion, consensus, argumentation, and dissent as a decisive mechanism of the good of order.

The operations in the list of the basic pattern of method finish with the words "speaking" and "writing" after "deciding" (Lonergan, 1972, p. 6); so speaking and writing are controlled by responsible decisions. It is a matter of experiencing communication as a militant possibility in tension with non-communication; in tension with those zones in our psychic life that still do not emerge in search of meaning to be recognized at least in a potential level;[13] it is the struggle with the profound solitude or loneliness of our psychic life, the incommunicable, that the miracle of understanding the discourse intermittently comes to relieve.

*Orientation and conversion* make manifest that development and skills, on the one hand, and social roles and tasks, on the other, in communication are not ends in themselves; they need to submit to achieving moral self-transcendence in personal and social communication. Again, the effort to keep conversation, negotiation, discussion, and dialogue alive is a reasonable position to counteract violence in face-to-face intimacy, in the family, in the wider political arena, and in mass media institutions. We cannot be neutral in our communications. We need to surmount a functional "communication of *whats*" and move toward a genuine "communication of *withs* and *whos*."[14] There is the Nietzschean agony to reveal originality and unrepeat-

---

[13] In his "Discours et Communication" (1973), Paul Ricoeur makes problematic the positive fact of communication for Saussurean and Jakobsonian linguistics and social sciences. Communication is not a fact of physical transmission; it is a meaningful event made possible by the transgression of the monadic series, which in several respects individuals are, through the help of oral or written discourse. The heterogeneity, I hope, is not absolute; it would make communication impossible. Communication is something fragile, not a triumphant event. After a justification of his theory of discourse and a demonstration of the convergence of logical analysis, phenomenology, the theory of speech-acts, and the Gricean theory of intentions, Ricoeur links intentional analysis with Husserl's notion of intentionality. Lonergan also notes some asymmetry, "Of itself, communication only reveals the disparity" (1957/1992, p. 234), but, as we shall see, he provides a more secure basis to relate discourses to conscious, intentional, objective, and self-transcendent acts of meaning. His insistence on the differentiation of consciousness and self-appropriation makes evident the tension with incommunicability and communicative pathologies; also he prescribes a militant communication: "In its third stage, then, meaning, not merely differentiates into realms of common sense, theory, and interiority, but also acquires the universal immediacy of the mass media and the molding power of universal education. Never has adequately differentiated consciousness been more difficult to achieve. Never has the need to speak effectively to undifferentiated consciousness been greater" (1972, p. 99). Lonergan also speaks of a hermeneutic residue and acknowledges a residue of merely matters of fact (1957/1992, pp. 613-616); we cannot infer that everything is communication.

[14] Communication is defined as an "option, an effort, a process, and the results of sharing human meanings and values." Also, I develop Francis Jacques' (1985) thesis on interlocution and its strategies. I have found some analogy between his "transcendental dialogism" and Lonergan's "mutual self-mediation." Of course, I am not advocating a defense of the "difference by itself" or "the individual by itself," much less a so-called postmodernist use of the media that has made

ability in our signs and expressions, not only our misfortunes. There is the Heideggerian agony of an existential compromise to share meaning, distant from the commonplace of "It is said...," "people say..." (Sierra-Gutiérrez, 1993).

The orientation of individuals in communication is a function of self-appropriation, differentiation of consciousness, and conversions within every brand of common sense and cultural matrices. But community itself needs orientation between progress and decline. It needs to reverse individual, group, and general bias that distort its development.[15]

Oriented and converted communication is exercised within a matrix of *personal relations*. This matrix supposes and complements the spontaneous intersubjectivity of labor, communication, and authority, with the different institutions practical intelligence devises, constituting relationships where a critical "we" is built up and where the personal pronoun "we" cannot be used without explicit consensus of partners.

These relations develop mutual feelings to attain the substance of community.

> People are joined by common experience, by common or complementary insights, by similar judgments of fact and value, by parallel orientations in life. They are separated, estranged, rendered hostile, when they have got out of touch, when they misunderstand one another, when they judge in opposed fashions, opt for contrary social goals. So personal relations vary from intimacy to ignorance, from love to exploitation, from respect to contempt, from friendliness to enmity. They bind a community together, or divide it into factions, or tear it apart. (Lonergan, 1972, pp. 50-51)

Communities, of course, vary in kinds: linguistic, religious, social, political, domestic (p. 79).

The higher level of developing communication required in personal relations runs against the homogeneity required by a dysfunctional good of order and the heterogeneity and incommensurability of discourses proclaimed by advocates of the individual, of the differences by themselves, or of a return to a pre-Socratic wisdom. Personal relations in communication are decisive in the development of life as a work of art.

> On this level, subjects both constitute themselves and make their world. On this level, men are responsible, individually, for the lives they lead and, col-

---

imperative its absolute combination in production and private and individualized consumption (Sierra-Gutiérrez, 1991).

[15] This orientation is not an ironclad law, for it is the expansion or derivation of freedom; it promotes and respects the sources of pluralism in linguistic, social, and cultural differences; pluralism that comes from different patterns of experience, from different stages of individual and social development, and their attainment of conversions; pluralism that emerges from several differentiations of consciousness; and pluralism in communications themselves. On pluralism, see Lonergan (1972, pp. 271-278; 326-330). On bias, see Lonergan (1957/1992, pp. 244-57).

lectively, for the world in which they lead them. It is in this collective responsibility for common or complementary action that resides the principal constituent of the collective subject referred to by "we," "us," "ourselves," "ours." The condition of possibility of the collective subject is communication, and the principal communication is not saying what we know, but showing what we are. (Lonergan, 1967/1988, p. 219)

In *Method in Theology*, Lonergan stresses this co-responsibility: "Such is the basis of *universal dialogue*" (1972, p. 360; emphasis added). That is the *moral principle* where a community, as an ideal basis of society and also as an imperfect community, takes its stand.[16]

Now, in no way am I suggesting that interpersonal communication performed face-to-face and its development towards intimacy and love is the prototype of human communication. Nor does my insistence on interpersonal relations erode with the intervention of mass media and indirect information and communication; for we are still dealing with human beings, and we are addressing the creative and artistic uses of the media by people who, in principle, are attentive, intelligent, critical, and responsible. If we lose the other as an actual or potential interlocutor, communication then will follow the easy road of confusion where "[t]he actors in the drama of living become stage-hands; the setting is magnificent; the lighting superb; the costumes gorgeous; but there is no play" (Lonergan, 1957/1992, p. 262); and then "the magician and the gnostic have their day" (p. 566).

*Terminal values* are values that are also chosen in communicative practices, and they orient the community and individuals. They are true instances of the particular good of communication, a true good of order of communication, a true scale of preferences ranging from satisfactions to values.

> Since man can know and choose authenticity and self-transcendence, originating and terminal values can coincide. When each member of the community both wills authenticity in himself and, inasmuch as he can, promotes it in others, then the originating values that choose and the terminal values that are chosen overlap and interlace. (Lonergan, 1972, p. 51)

Communication is a vital, social, cultural, personal, and religious value. Communication inasmuch as it is a particular good generates satisfaction; but it is also a vital value. The planetary way of living needed today is not thinkable without streams and streams of communication.

---

[16]Taking into account the mutual self-mediated structure of communication, we can think of Universal Dialogue as only possible  by pursuing mutual self-transcendence.  Universal dialogue cannot be reduced to the validity claims of speech acts, neither to an  ideal linguistic community of communication à la Apel/Habermas and their promise of reverting the contemporary  process of rationalization.  Lonergan's proposal breaks post-Kantian regulative ideals and reconstructs the empirical, intentional, objective, and transcendent components of this dialogue.

Communication is mainly a social value where laws, norms, and technical and political decisions take their stand. "Through communication there is constituted community, and, conversely, community constitutes and perfects itself through communication" (p. 363). The world today needs a golden rule that calls for dynamic public opinion and offers several mechanisms to promote participation, public argumentative discussions, and dialogical procedures in order to make decisions with a clear knowledge of effects and consequences they might have on potential interlocutors. Such a golden rule is needed for all institutions, social organizations, industries, states, and churches to follow in their internal and external relations. When we conceive of the good of order and its institutions as ongoing processes, we will readily see that communication entails policy making, planning, and the execution of the plans.

Ethical and political dimensions of communication emerge from this context. Communicative ethics requires a sincere and trustful use of linguistic meaning and its conveyance according to validity claims of speech acts. The ethical communicative exigence could be enunciated as a neo-Kantian maxim (perhaps only procedural for Habermas), but only partially consists in it. The roots and nature of this exigence are shown "after principles" (Barden, 1990) in the very dynamism of communication, in its constitutive role of the individual and the community, and in the reasonable demand to share meaning responsibly with others. It is a concrete and practical problem in decisions to be solved not only on a speculative level. Prior to the rhetoric of reasons, there is the moral action of asking and answering questions. Transforming the conditions for an authentic communicative praxis is a first mission of a communicative ethics and politics.

Lonergan's conception of authority is intrinsically communicative: "As the source of power is cooperation, so the carrier of power is the community" (1985, pp. 5-12), which presumably could not "carry" any such power if there were no communication among the members of the community. The legitimacy of authority lies in its authenticity. Legitimation occurs in many differentiations of consciousness, and it is a matter of ritual, myth, law, rhetoric, logic, codes, and principles, according to different exigencies of meaning. This external condition of legitimation is a necessary, but it is not a sufficient condition for authenticity to occur. Authentic community, i.e., a community constituted by communication and perfected by it, will be the authentic basis of power and authority—power "with" the others, not "over" the rest, power born of common agreement and compromise, not of hegemonic groups.

Communication, clearly, is a cultural value, both as an everyday level of meanings and values informing a given way of life and as a superstructure of reflexively articulated cultural values (Lonergan, 1974a, p. 32). Dialogical procedures should be the sacred substance of community and communities through a cross-cultural communication of the cultural values of a world-cultural humanity. On this level, the reciprocal relations in the scale of values become more explicit. Only cultural values commensurate with the proportions of the social dialectic can assure the emergence of new schemes of recurrence to transform the distorted community (Doran, 1988a, p. 44; 1990, p. 372).

Communication as a personal value helps the individual discover one's self-transcendence as originating values in one's milieu. Communication decentralizes the self towards cooperation, but simultaneously fosters originality and fresh styles. It stresses the individual appropriation of messages and their recomposition with new expressions.

Finally, communication is a religious value for the unrestricted love supposed in the mutual self-mediation of the Divine in prayers within the dynamics of operative and cooperative grace.

## 3. The Context of Communication as Normative, Critical, and Dialectical

Along with these empirical characteristics, the context of communication is *normative*, *critical*, and *dialectical*.

The context is normative in that neither of the terms internally constitutive of communication is in itself the immanent form of the intelligibility of it. Their interrelations are required to differentiate progress and decline in communication and to cut down hegemonic, one-dimensional developments. By its normativity this structure becomes compatible with any stage of technological, economic, political, cultural, or religious development and suggests historical approaches.

The context is critical because it makes it possible to judge the differences between intelligible and unintelligible components, between good and evil in any given communicative situation. These differences can be reduced to mistaken theories of meaning and to undeveloping notions of mediation.

Sharing meaning embraces the polymorphic human consciousness, and it is possible in the presence or the absence of conversions. This context, then, is dialectical. There is a dialectic of the dramatic subject, a dialectic of community, and a dialectic of culture. Communication is involved in these three tensions. Lonergan defines the dialectic as "a concrete unfolding of linked but opposed principles of change" (Lonergan, 1957/1992, p. 242). The principles constitutive of the dialectic of the subject are neural demands for psychic integration and conscious representation, on the one hand, and the censorship over these demands exercised by dramatically patterned intelligence and imagination, on the other hand (pp. 212-231). The spontaneous intersubjectivity and the practical intelligence that institute the technological, economic, and political structures of society are the principles constitutive of the dialectic of community (pp. 237-250). The principles constitutive of the dialectic of culture are cosmological and anthropological constitutive meanings, which are two diverse but interrelated sets of meanings and values regarding the direction that can be found or missed in the movement of life.[17]

Now, the principle of the dialectic says that "positions invite development and counter-positions invite reversal" (Lonergan, 1957/1992, p. 412). So insight and freedom must advance the intelligible and good dimensions of the situations and reverse the unintelligible and evil dimensions; the intelligible is a function of the integral dialectic of contraries and the unintelligible a function of its distortion (Doran, 1990, pp. 372ff.). Positions in communication are developed from a differentiated notion of mediation and a balanced development of the structure of human good and its scale of values. Counter-positions ignore mediations and integral structure or partially develop them.

In the human subject, the higher integration of the creative tension is done through a psyche's aesthetic liberation from the neural undertow and through an ability to collaborate with intelligence in admitting images into consciousness for insight. This integral dialectic is communicative in the sense that the subject should discover his or her own symbols as internal vehicles of communication not only to overcome scotomas, repressions, and inhibitions (Lonergan, 1972, p. 67), but also to discover that personal integrity is not achievable on the basis of one's own immanent resources and needs a genuine communicative experience with the analyst or with other people to restore genuine intersubjectivity and social bindings. This opening and de-centering is a function of a universal willingness as an effective attitude in which performance matches the unrestricted desire to know the universe of being (Lonergan, 1957/1992, p. 647), or "the experienced fulfillment of our unrestricted thrust to self-transcendence, in our actuated orientation towards the mystery of love and awe" (Lonergan, 1972, p. 115).

---

[17] The notion of a dialectic of culture is proposed by R. M. Doran (1990; 1988a) following E. Voegelin's *Order and History* (1956). Also, Doran develops an analogy of the three dialectics and distinguishes a dialectic of contraries as opposed to a dialectic of contradictories. In a dialectic of contraries the constitutive principles work harmoniously in the unfolding of the changes that emerge from their interaction. In a dialectic of contradictories the changes are a function of the dominance of one principle over the other (1988a, pp. 38-40). According to Lonergan, dialectic is also a matter of "meeting persons, appreciating the values they represent, criticizing their defects, and allowing one's living to be challenged at its very roots by their words and by their deeds" (1972, p. 247); it is clearly a matter of mutual self-mediation. The dialectic moves to a dialogue when we transpose issues from a conflict of statements to an encounter of persons. "While the dialectic of history coldly relates our conflicts, dialogue adds the principle that prompts us to cure them, the natural right that is the inmost core of our being" (1985, p. 182). In this sketchy approach to the dialectic of communication, we follow Doran's account of dialectic.

The higher integration of the dialectic of community is a function of neither of the principles internally constitutive of the dialectic, but of culture. "[I]f men are to meet the challenge set by major decline and its longer cycle, it will be through their culture that they do so" (Lonergan, 1957/1992, p. 261). Culture in both its everyday infrastuctural and its reflexive superstructural dimensions (Lonergan, 1974a, p. 103) pursues harmonious cooperation, a creative tension of intersubjectivity and practicality, through which the community becomes a work of art.

Doran holds that a fundamental assumption might be made to conceive that "the deepest desire of the human person...is the desire to succeed in the drama of existence[18] by finding and holding to the direction that can be discovered in the movement of life" (Doran, 1990, pp. 353, 358). It is a deep desire that involves basic vital needs and values. "For this desire is fulfilled by discovering through insight and following with resolve the direction that is to be found in the movement of life; and this direction can also be missed, and missing the direction may be a function radically not of one's doing, but of the dominance of distorted dialectics of culture and community" (p. 358).

The desire of dramatic artistry to make of our own lives a work of art is present in the intersubjective component, where communication finds its root and base, no less than in the other elements devised by human practical intelligence.[19] The dramatic artistry of subjects in community converges in a dimension of consciousness called "cosmopolis" (Lonergan, 1957/1992, pp. 263-267). Since dramatic artistry becomes the primary criterion of human success in the constitution of the human world, of interpersonal relations, and of human self-hood, cosmopolis develops an intellectual collaboration, a globally effective communitarian alternative to the social surd, through embodiments and communications of the integral scale of values.

---

[18]The notion of human artistry (Lonergan, 1957/1992, pp. 210-212) is central in Doran's understanding of the *humanum* and in his proposal of a "psychic conversion." He does not claim that it has the same centrality in Lonergan's work, though it may (Doran, 1979a, 1981a).

[19]J. Habermas (1981/1984, 1981/1987b) maps "life-world" to society and "system" to instrumental and rationalized activities for what Lonergan calls "practical intelligence." Habermas wants to avoid the colonization of life-world by system through a theory and practice that consider the intersubjective and the communicative action in it essential to the constitution of society and culture. Lonergan's notion of consciousness is not representational; that makes his work immune to Habermas' rejection of several philosophies of consciousness. Habermas' project would be enriched with the operative notions of consciousness, subject, and method Lonergan worked out. Also Lonergan's position on communication would gain from the sociolinguistic mediations so dear to Habermas. See my own appraisal of Habermas' *Theory of Communicative Action* (Sierra-Gutiérrez, 1988/1989).

The breakdown of the dialectic of community is due to a culture that either has been "forced into an ivory tower of ineffectualness by the social surd" or "has capitulated to its absurdity" by becoming practical (p. 262). A distorted dialectics of communication corrupts dramatic artistry by means of money and power standards and offers a comfortable alibi of a society of permanent profits, pleasure, and entertainment.

To take only an instance—within the echoes of Columbus' voyages of 500 years ago—violence, silence, and the loneliness of the victims of conquerors in Latin America still call for a better reciprocal understanding among the concert of nations. Are not their claims for authenticity in communicative praxis genuine? And are not their dreams and nightmares of equitable interlocution in the world genuine communicative transgressions of hegemonic discourses? And are they not partly reasonable and violent stammers of the unrestricted desire to interrogate for being and real good in order to attain global common meanings and values today?

A cosmopolitan communication, then, is confronted with a demand for the generation of a cross-cultural community with world-cultural values capable of synthesizing the internally constitutive poles of a global dialectic of community.

> [A cosmopolitan communication] confronts problems of which men are aware; it invites the vast potentialities and pent-up energies of our time to contribute to their solution *by developing an art and a literature, a theater and a broadcasting, a journalism and a history, a school and a university, a personal depth and a public opinion,* that through appreciation and criticism give men of common sense the opportunity and help they need and desire to correct the general bias of their common sense. (Lonergan, 1957/1992, p. 266; emphasis added)

The dialectic of culture is another instance of the tension of limitation and transcendence, with the cosmological pole a limiting factor and the anthropological one the promoter of transcendence. The integrity of this dialectic involves a creative tension where neither the cosmological or anthropological principles tend to remove the other. Such an integration is seen by Doran as a contemporary soteriology that

> would provide an ecumenically available set of meanings and values to inform the social infrastructure of a global communitarian alternative to the imperialistic distortions of the dialectic of community. Because such a set of cultural meanings and values is not yet an established feature of life, theology's mediation of the soteriological vector with the contemporary situation will itself contribute to the cross-cultural generation of the cultural values of a world-cultural humanity. (Doran, 1988a, pp. 55-56)

A transcendent mutual self-mediation with the divine rounds off the context for human communication.

## 4. Conclusion

Lonergan's approach to communication does not directly follow the contemporary trends in semiotics, sociolinguistics, and pragmatics. However, there is no doubt that his reflections do reconstruct those perspectives. In addition, his insights convey an authentic and liberating message and praxis to society, and invite the renewal of the study of communication along lines that have not been explored by others. Lonergan's work opens the fresher and more dynamic challenge of understanding communication as the mutual self-mediation of human beings. This mutual self-mediation occurs in the wider context of the structure of the human good, as Lonergan (1972, p. 48) has mapped this out in the table-diagram explained above, and within the dialectics of human history, as Doran (1990) has described these.

# 14

# The Role of Theological Symbols in Mediating Cultural Change

## J. J. Mueller, SJ

We live in world filled with a plurality of cultures that stands on the growing edge of a new step toward the unifying possibility of a single world-culture. Before we attempt to take such a momentous step, we would do well
to understand the culture that the world needs and seeks—a quest based on a
common responsibility to humanity in pursuit of truth—and not allow power
factions to impose any form of tyrannical ideology. As one voice in this
future, Christianity would suggest a vision of humanity based on love, compassion, forgiveness, justice, service, and equality as the fabric of any true
world-culture. This is not any truth or an ideological imposition, but the
Christian understanding of the centrality of truth to all authentic human
community. It can therefore be argued as such before the world community
as both belonging to and constitutive of humanity.

The communication of the Christian vision resides most centrally in its
symbols as expressed in its sacred texts. Yet these symbols are not trans-
parent. They require both the critical examination of their meaning in the
first century and the critical understanding of them in the 20th century. The
necessarily common medium through which faith as religion and the wider
cultural context join is theology. Theology, then, though not spoken about
in this way, is the process, language, and act of communication between the
two interrelated activities of religion and culture. This sharing of meanings
and values is not static or one-sided, but an active, ongoing, dynamic process from both sides. Also, and importantly, the communication of religion
and culture is not limited to a backward glance like in a rearview mirror or
an immediate focus like a magnifying glass upon the present, but also includes the direction the dynamic is going toward the future. The future is
not determined solely by the past, but is an inspired act of creativity open to
vision and freedom. The project of building the future cannot be done
within the ecclesial community itself, but must be done openly within the
entire human community of cultures and religions. One of theology's most
important tasks today, therefore, and the one we will examine in this study,

is the significance the Christian meaning and values have in the formative vision of what is here understood as a possible move to a world-culture.

"The price of culture is a Lie" concluded W. E. B. Dubois in 1900 in his book *The Souls of Black Folk* (1900/1973, p. 205). A lie, he said, was "the only method by which underdeveloped races had gained the right to share in modern culture." Less than a century later, Bernard Lonergan made a very different statement and, in my paraphrasing of Dubois, said, "The price of culture is the Truth." For Lonergan, truth is authenticity exercised in the act of human understanding, which unites us with a loving God who first seeks us. The "method" that Lonergan developed was the search for truth through the critical operations of human understanding itself. Dubois chafed under the "double-vision" as he called it, where Blacks had to accommodate themselves to the dominant white society for its benefits and still return to their black communities to find and exercise their African-American sub-culture. It is as interesting as it is provocative that both men, coming from different perspectives, concluded that religion provided the greater context to judge culture because of the inseparable linkage between culture and the human spirit. Both men also shared a mutual concern about the power to shape culture: For Dubois, it is to empower the black people among themselves and thereby take away the "lie"; for Lonergan, it is to empower the possibly ignored religious dimension of the human spirit in culture and thereby to arrive at the fullest truth of all humanity.

As if dealing with the complex nature of one specific culture were not enough, a creatively new situation of unprecedented import is occurring around the globe today as all cultures are feeling the pressure of a "world-culture" being formed. Although we do yet not know what a world-culture might be like and we may be willing to leave it to science fiction writers to fill in, we know that we cannot stop it and should not shirk our responsibilities, nor shrink from the challenge. As both Dubois and Lonergan struggled to relate, humanity is at stake, but this time it is on a global level where everyone and every culture is intertwined, interrelated, and inescapably involved. The way we think about ourselves requires a global consciousness and responsibility. The question becomes, Is Lonergan's "method" adequate to articulate and communicate the Christian religious experience toward a possible common, though not necessarily Christian, world-culture? Put in another way, does Christianity have anything to say about the direction of this future?

Lonergan has two important components within his theology for this task. First, Lonergan's basic thesis holds to a common, or one may prefer the philosophical word "metaphysical," human capacity for the act of understanding where everything human beings fashion depends upon the honesty and integrity of the human agent performing the task. It places the responsibility of human culture squarely upon the shoulders of mature human persons. They must live up to their self-transcending potential to create a world where the human spirit is nourished and flourishes in the full range of its potential. For Lonergan as a Christian, this full range is the thrust of humanity toward God. The second basic component within his theological "method" is the integral relationship of culture to religion as fundamental and dynamically related.

My thesis is that Lonergan's "method" has not yet been challenged to render the content of the Christian message in its full range in dealing with culture. The obvious reason is that the new cultural situation is just now forcing the question. The challenge to the theological community, and the purpose of this study, is to determine whether Christianity possesses any resource adequate for partaking in this task of building a world-culture. If so, then how can it be communicated through theology?

After a brief Section 1 defining key terms used in this essay, Part 2 of this study begins with an examination of the role of theology in relation to culture within Lonergan's method. Part 3 then examines how Lonergan's theology treats the dynamics of cultural change and two strategies by which Christian resources influence or change cultural dynamics, especially as more fully developed through the contribution of Lonerganian scholar Robert M. Doran. Finally, Part 4 presents what has not been developed in Lonergan's "method," another strategy for changing culture that comes from the Christian message and may be given expression in Lonergan's "method." Its result is an envisioning about the future of culture itself and possibly the fashioning of, and perhaps transformation to, a world-culture.

## 1. Definition of Key Terms

Before we proceed to examine these various matters in detail, we need to start with working definitions of four key terms that are then explained further throughout the essay: (1) "method" as defined by Lonergan, (2) culture, (3) religion, and (4) theology.

Method, Lonergan says, is "a normative pattern of recurrent and related operations yielding cumulative and progressive results" (1972, p. 4). His method is one that engages human subjectivity and the transcending capacity of the subject. It is available to everyone regardless of religion and demands a commitment of personal integrity to the truth. He constructs his method in what can be described as interrelated concentric circles. The first circle is the act of understanding by the subject involving the four levels of consciousness: experience, understanding, judging, deciding. The second concentric circle involves the subject with others in groups where a person finds his or her "self" in union with others. This is called intersubjectivity. The third concentric circle is the group of relationships that form a culture. Like groups, cultures are humanly made and are caught up in continual change. As one scholar summed it up, "We are the method in all disciplines, humanistic, scientific, and religious, through the activity of the four levels of our consciousness" (Gregson, 1988, p. 109).

Let us now examine the term "culture." "Culture," states Lonergan, "is a set of meanings and values informing a common way of life; there are as many cultures as there are distinct sets of such meanings and values" (1972, p. 301). "Culture" is perceived by people on two levels: the every-day level of meaning and values informing a given way of life, and the reflexive or superstructural level arising from scientific, philosophic, and scholarly objectifications. The former we can call "common sense" and the latter, "theoretical."

"Religion" is a more complex term than might first seem apparent (cf. Lonergan, 1972, pp. 101-116). In many ways similar to culture, religion is also a set of meanings and values, but in this case, they inform a common way of relating to the transcendent we call "God," described in many ways: Wholly Other (Tracy), the Holy (Otto), the Ultimate Concern (Tillich), Mystery (Rahner), and Being-in-Love (Lonergan). The many ways of worship, rituals, art, behavior, symbols, and language go together to weave the fabric of religion. Religion itself functions in many ways like a culture: It (1) comes from human experience, (2) contains a particular history—or what religion prefers to call a tradition—inculturated many times and many ways that express continuity with the original experience, and (3) is continually changing in interaction with culture. Where it differs markedly from culture is in its center, where the rendering of the relationship with God is its starting point and ending point.

"Theology," for Lonergan, is the interpretation and articulation of the data of religious experience within an already existing cultural setting: both the data given to theology by the functional specialties of "research," "interpretation," "history," and various explanations in conflict called "dialectics"; as well as the objectification of conversion to faith in the properly theological functional specialties of "foundations" of faith, "dogmatics" or central tenets of belief, "systematics" or unified coherency of various doctrines, and "communication" of the authentic Christian message (1972, pp. 127-133; see the glossary after this essay for further discussion of the eight functional specialties). Theology differs from religion in that it is a further differentiation of consciousness about the originating religious experience (1972, p. 140). While theology is not separate from religion, it does not claim to be a substitute for faith, which is always a religious act, nor is it finally the determiner of what inculturated faith can be. Theology, however, is the further differentiation of consciousness whereby the act of human understanding about the relation of both faith as expressed in religion (message and tradition) and the wide set of meaning and values fashioned by humans in relation to which faith exists (culture) is rendered intelligible.

It comes as no surprise, then, that Lonergan begins his *Method in Theology* with the statement that situates both his presuppositions and agenda in the broadest terms, which will be explained within the book: "A theology mediates between a cultural matrix and the significance and role of a religion in that matrix" (1972, p. xi). This statement within the Catholic tradition of theology is remarkable in itself, for it sets out the agenda and the method for doing theology in a new way. Lonergan's notion of mediation, however, bears clearer scrutiny because it is, in our words, the process of communicating itself. He says the following:

> Operations are said to be immediate when their objects are present. So seeing is immediate to what is being seen, hearing to what is being heard, touch to what is being touched. But by imagination, language, symbols, we operated in a compound manner; immediately with respect to the image, word, symbol; mediately with respect to what is signified. In this fashion we come to operate not only with respect to the present and actual, but also with respect to the absent, the past, *the future, the merely possible or ideal or normative or fantastic* (1972, p. 28, emphasis added).

Lonergan's method begins with the functional structure of theology before it yields the content. It sets out the dynamic, integral relationship between religion and culture as the source from which theology critically reflects. The function of theology for Lonergan is that of "mediating" those sets of meanings and values in a manner of critical understanding open to examination. Because of his understanding of the role of religion in culture, theology in his view offers different and various options by which religion influences or even changes cultural dynamics. For our present purposes, we are particularly interested in the future direction of these sets of meanings and values. Our project is to exam options available within theology from the Christian message in order to change cultural dynamics. But first we need to examine the role of culture further.

## 2. The Role of Theology in Culture

A shift in consciousness has taken place in Roman Catholic theology with the recent use of the term "culture" as a theological construct. The Second Vatican Council (1962-1965) used the word "culture" in the official conciliar document *Gaudium et Spes* in writing about the "Church in the Modern World." Since that time the word has been in constant use in papal documents, in ecclesiastical letters of bishops, and in theological discourse. The derivative term "inculturation" has been widely used by theologians to speak about the Christian message being preached in new cultural situations and the responsibility of the Church to seek out authentic cultural expressions of that same message. What we have occurring is the search for an adequate and coherent rendering of the Christian message in new ways that inform the Christian message with deeper, wider, and changing human understanding. The process depends upon the interrelationship of human beings with the Divine, always within the context of an inculturated faith relationship wherein the experience itself seeks to be understood. The Catholic Church in particular now officially recognizes and takes into account the always-already inculturated dimension of faith and its understanding. The consequences of this are far-reaching and require, on the one hand, the retrospective re-examining of the sources of faith in sacred Scripture and historical tradition and, on the other hand, the prospective fashioning of its direction and relationship to the modern world. The process requires a retrieval of all tradition and teaching in light of the emerging global horizon, a task that can make even the most fearless theologian shudder.

For example, for theology to acknowledge contextual historicity might require a conscious shift away from a European normativity for understanding Christianity. Since Roman Catholic theology has really been either expressed or judged according to this norm, what Christianity might look like in a global world is impossible to say, and fearful to many. Yet this same Catholic Church, especially as it comes from various communities around the world, increasingly knows it must move toward recognizing Christian experience in any culture as a legitimate basis for theological reflection. In the same recognition, what is affirmed is that no culture *per se* is necessarily impenetrable to God's grace. The consequent questions for theology are largely predictable and beyond our present horizon of answers: How much plurality can be present without destroying the unity of the church? How does theology move across cultures and judge the authenticity of the Christian experience? Are all answers equally true? Far from being questions belonging only to theology, these questions are echoed in the postmodern critiques, whether we agree with what constitutes the postmodern world or even agree with the term.

As mentioned above, the term "theology," for Lonergan, is always understood in relation to culture. He explains theology in terms of its function within a larger set of related contexts: "A theology mediates between a cultural matrix and the significance and role of a religion in that matrix" (1972, p. xi). It seems readily accepted today that no religion exists apart from a culture, as if religion could be situationless. To say that a religion is always-already inculturated, and continues to be so, does not imply that religion is determined by culture. It is this freedom within a culture that offers choices as to how the religion will relate to culture and offers religion three basic choices about how to relate to culture: the synthetic approach (accepting of culture), the oppositional approach (countercultural), and the transformational approach (transformative). We will return to these options in the next part of the essay.

Lonergan is not especially interested in Western, Eastern, Oriental, primitive, or advanced cultures as the role of culture in theological method. The designation of a particular culture, though important and categorial, yields to a more operational and transcendental usage. To put it simply, the content of culture can be filled in in many ways; in his focus on "method," he has moved away from the concern of static and necessary systems to interest in historical development and in what constructs systems (Gregson, 1988, p. 103).

When Lonergan uses the word "culture," he understands two notions of culture that have operated in the Western world and the three historical shifts that are discernable. First, let us look at the two notions of culture:

> The classicist notion of culture was normative: At least *de jure* there was but one culture that was both universal and permanent; to its norms and ideals might aspire the uncultured, whether they were the young or the people or the natives or the barbarians. Besides the classicist, there also is the empirical notion of culture. It is the set of meanings and values that informs a way of life. It may remain unchanged for ages. It may be in process of slow development or rapid dissolution.
>
> When the classicist notion of culture prevails, theology is conceived as a permanent achievement, and then one discourses on its nature. When culture is conceived empirically, theology is known to be an ongoing process, and then one writes on its method. (1972, p. xi)

The three historical stages that have taken place to bring about this empirical notion are as instructive as they are helpful in re-examining the history of theology. The first two stages have already taken place and the third is currently taking place. Lonergan's own theology reflects the acceptance of this third stage, which jettisons the classicist notion of truth. Let us examine them in more detail to understand Lonergan's position.

The first stage is that of common sense where things are spoken of in direct relation to ourselves, e.g., speaking of God in anthropomorphic terms as the biblical authors do. The second is post-biblical and largely influenced by Greek thought. It is the world of theory in which things are spoken about in relation to one another, e.g., who the Father, the Son, and the Spirit are in themselves, questions not asked by the Christian scriptures. We must remember that Christianity inherited this world from the Greeks and much of its theology has come from this world. The third is our present cultural context wherein theology is moving away from a pre-occupation with the Greek interest in *necessary* correlations, which Aristotle defined as the proper domain of "science," to correlations that we discover are *probable*, which Aristotle defined as the proper domain of "rhetoric." What we can call "emergent probability" has replaced essentialist thinking in theology (cf. Gregson, 1988, p. 108).

Lonergan's purpose is to unleash the human spirit that is best expressed in the self-transcending act of being in love. As a result of noting that the essence of the human spirit involves self-transcending, self-affirming operations, Lonergan promotes the dynamic and ongoing development of human persons individually and in community. While the humanity or essence of all human persons can be defined as involving self-transcending operations, no set blueprint is adequate for who and what each human person can be. The integrity of the human person in allowing the authentic human spirit to express itself can be discovered in the act of understanding, which Lonergan examines as an integral process of self-transcendence. Truth, therefore, in its fullest and most complete grasp of the really real is the goal of understanding, whether it comes from the side of religion or from the side of culture. But the full range of human subjectivity comes when religion and culture come together to support authentic human subjectivity. This full and ideal relationship, and this is important for Part 3 of this paper, is mutually transformative of both religion and culture (cf. Doran, 1981c, p. 113).

Throughout his theology, Lonergan insists on the subject's act of "self-appropriation," that is, the openness of authentic human spirit working its way through human agency. "Authenticity" describes the human act of understanding that correctly grasps the ongoing expression of the human spirit. Authenticity of the subject becomes, in turn, the condition for the authenticity of intersubjectivity, which in turn is the condition for the authenticity of culture. Authenticity is a description of the meaning of human life itself. It is the project that we work at constantly; its demand never takes a holiday. Authenticity is the benchmark of every human act, including the discipline of theology.

Unfortunately for us, we are not born with innate authenticity; we can mistake what we interpret the human spirit to be. We can be inauthentic, or biased, depending upon our understanding and choices. When the person blocks questions, refuses to examine data, or otherwise terminates the understanding process itself, then biases occur. Bias is the repression of unwanted insights and further relevant questions. It deforms the human spirit and leads to inauthentic living. In a nutshell, communication is not honestly pursued, but skewed.

Bias can and does permeate every dimension where human agency occurs, including the meaning and values of groups, and cultures. Biases, furthermore, do not respect time or processes; they even come through established cultures and communities into which we have been born. To recognize our personal, communal, and cultural biases is a critical act that can be performed in the act of understanding. If we were locked forever in our various levels of biases, then humanity would truly have an incurable sickness unto death.

Bias can be further described by its powerful strength to hold us and by its ability to endure. It might be compared to a virus that enters into the act of understanding and infects the life of communities and cultures. When it manifests itself in communities, Lonergan refers to it as "group bias." When it permeates cultures, he calls it "general bias." The life cycles of bias vary. Group bias tends to run in a shorter cycle because of its possibility of being reversed by individuals and groups who take up questions, insights, and issues repressed by the dominant group; in short, another group can be put in charge.  General bias, however, tends to run in a longer cycle because groups neglect its long-term consequences, ultimate issues, and theoretically important questions.  The community can generate needed though difficult reversals only "by confronting human intelligence with the alternative of adopting a higher viewpoint or perishing" (Lonergan, 1957/1992, p. 260; cf. Lamb, 1988, pp. 255-84; Doran, 1988b, p. 11).

Bias, like a virus, is never static, but always is in a process of growth or decline.  The salient point is not to chart growth or decline, but to reverse and eradicate bias.  If reversals cannot be achieved, then once bias skews the human spirit, it remains forever and fatalism is the disastrous result. Only the possibility of confronting and overcoming bias by allowing the truth to work its way out can enable humanity to construct an authentic culture truly resurrecting and releasing the human spirit.  The cost, nevertheless, of confronting bias on the personal, communal, and cultural levels will be high.  The new golden rule must be that whoever can speak the truth about humanity must; whoever can call humanity to confront its biases must.  Theology, as the Christian mediation, or communication, between religion and culture must operate as a critical resistance to all biases on all levels, including religious, and be a proponent of the truth it speaks for all human persons of what is and can be.

Though Lonergan did not develop his method beyond the understanding of one culture, the globalization of the world has demanded an examination of many cultures (in the plural), moving toward the possibility of a unified world-culture.  At least two clear alternatives present themselves:  (1) We can never overcome our individual cultures, and thus we will remain in intractable pluralism without unity; or (2) we move toward a "world-culture" where we have a unity within a plurality of cultures.  While I have no doubt that Lonergan would come down on the latter as the direction his theology would go, it has been the work of Lonerganian scholar Robert M. Doran to creatively extend Lonergan's work in this direction. The question now becomes, How does authentic transformation of culture occur?  The answer to that is to examine the means available to both Lonergan's method and the Christian message.


### 3. The Role of Theology in a World-Culture

Doran in *Theology and the Dialectics of History* (1990) has advanced Lonergan's pioneering work on theological method to an analysis of the role of theology in the movement toward a world-culture, and Doran's extension of Lonergan's theology must be taken into account for any Lonergan work on culture.  Doran states his purpose by differentiating himself from the systematic theologian David Tracy and his interpretation of "classics."  Doran's purpose is to provide the following:

a coherent and grounded systematic statement of the meanings and values affirmed by Christian faith. But I understand this task as one that by evoking a change in the meaning constitutive of the situation will mediate a transition from this situation to an alternative situation more closely approximating the reign of God. (1990, p. 4)

Doran has presented a strategy for change by which theology can "mediate a transition" to something new, in this case the transition to a world-culture. Doran also sees this transition as possibly bringing people closer to the "reign of God" on this earth. I think we can understand world-culture, on the one hand, as a growing, plausible possibility of the shape of the future to come, and the reign of God, on the other hand, as a principle of action.

Any transition into the future builds upon the authenticity of the previous processes that we have examined. Doran explains that Lonergan examined the dialectic of the subject who finds his or her condition of integrity in "willingness" and the dialectic of community whose condition of integrity is culture. Doran adds an important third condition of world-culture: the dialectic of culture whose condition of integrity is "a differentiated soteriological vector that moves from above downward in human consciousness" (1984, p. 70). The "soteriological vector" presented by Doran is our concern.

Drawing upon the work of Eric Voegelin, Doran states that there are two understandings presently operating in cultures. The one is cosmological and the other is anthropological. The cosmological understands humanity within the greater context of the cosmos within which humanity finds itself pushed and moved and defined. The anthropological understands humanity as agent able to change history and direct many events with power and freedom. Doran goes on to say that these are not *contradictory* understandings, like good and evil, where one must choose in an either-or decision. Rather, they are *contraries* that cannot be reconciled, but must be negotiated and lived with, keeping both in tension, like a both-and decision.

They operate as polarities and therefore both must be affirmed. If both are affirmed, then they lead to a transformative emergent called a "soteriological" view. "Soteriology" involves the transformative actions of human authenticity. Doran says, "In the soteriological order, the founding experience is an experience of the initiative of a world-transcendent divine reality in grounding the redemption of a people or of an individual from the impotence emergent from the overwhelming impact of deterministic fate" (1990, pp. 542-543). The meaning of the cosmological and anthropological understandings becomes operative in the higher synthesis of the soteriological transformation itself (Doran, 1990, p. 90). Said in another way, it is the good action that brings about the integral process of human authenticity within culture. In so doing, God acts redemptively in our lives and releases us from the burden of a fatalistic quest.

Just as resistance to the cosmological principle comes from the anthropological, so too does the soteriological oppose and resist the anthropological. To reverse various cycles of decline requires a differentiation of consciousness about the full range of truth needing implementation. Suffering, pain, destruction, and dehumanization are real forces in the community and culture. Doran draws upon Lonergan's "law of the cross" as the critical power to overturn evil and constitute the redemptive force that resists any fatalistic tendencies. Instead of succumbing to fatalism, we can change and undergo "conversion." Above all, it is love that makes this change possible. And it is only through a love with the transcendent other as partner that humanity can be, in a sense, saved from its "self" and allowed to be integrally self-transcending.

Doran has moved theology into the role of catalyst, able to help culture make a transition from the two competing principles of cosmology and anthroplogy to transformative action referred to as the soteriological view. The understandings of culture, whether cosmological or anthropological, are now affirmed as contraries, together, and brought under the higher synthesis of action about whether or not greater good is done. As Doran says:

> For in the last analysis only the transformation of evil into a greater good releases history to be the very form of order in human relationships; and only God can transform evil into a greater good, and then only with the cooperation of those who will not return evil for evil, but prefer to let there become incarnate in their own suffering the pattern that the world-transcendent measure of integrity assumed in becoming human flesh. Any other response generates the end of history by transmuting evil into an overwhelming fate. (1990, pp. 516-517)

This principle of change from negative to positive is referred to by both Lonergan and Doran as "the law of the cross." It is through suffering for others that the surd of nonsense can be changed to the possibility of good, caring love for the other and thereby effect change. Because of its power to change culture, we must examine "the law of the cross" more closely and see whether its symbolic import offers us the insight needed into the Christian message and the representative dialectics of change in its many forms.

"The law of the cross" is, first of all, an expression of the central message of Christianity: The love of God was revealed in the suffering and death of Jesus the Christ. Second, "the law of the cross" is used in a dialectical, or methodological, way to express the processes of reversal, or negation, of the existing situation. In the first case it is a symbol expressive of the Christian message; in the second it is a principle of change. Yet the question can be asked, Change to what? On the one hand, does the Christian message say anything about the direction of humanity toward a world-culture? On the other hand, does the method of theology have any principles of future direction to it?

## 4. The Resurrection as Message and Strategy for Transformation

Two strands must come together. The first concerns the Christian message; the second concerns the method of transformation. Let us begin with the Christian message.

The Christian religion, which theology mediates through understanding, is tied to the event of a person, Jesus the Christ, who lived, was crucified, and rose from the dead. While theology tries to articulate this event in its wholeness, it does so by emphasizing at times the various parts. As Lonergan says, "Meaning is embodied or carried in human intersubjectivity, in art, in symbols, in language, and in the lives and deeds of persons" (1972, p. 57). The Jesus-Event of his life, death, and resurrection are no exception in the Christian message. The three irreducible symbols of the Jesus-Event are the incarnation, cross, and resurrection. David Tracy, an early Lonerganian scholar, goes so far as to say, "More exactly, the symbols give rise to the response of that critical reflective thought named theology" (1981, p. 282). These symbols are always in tension with one another, or "tensive symbols" as Tracy refers to them, because one cannot be separated from the others. Only together is the central Christian message of the Jesus-Event complete. Moreover, as Lonergan's method reminds us, these symbols themselves are always-already inculturated and need to be critically mediated, by which he means critically understood and interpreted, through theology. The irreducibility of the three central symbols can be seen in the Christian scriptures themselves and in their inclusion within the canon of the New Testament. In the earliest texts that we have, the letters of Paul, we read that to the Corinthians he preaches the cross of Christ. To the Galatians, he preaches the freedom that comes in the resurrection. Written in the 50s, neither text, nor Paul in his other texts, deals with the life of Jesus, yet the centrality of cross and resurrection are clear. By the 70s and 80s of the first century, the Gospels of Mark, Matthew, and Luke had written the narrative of Jesus' life, death, and resurrection. One without the other was not able to be adequately interpretive of the Christian message. True and most probably, the early Christian communities knew something of the life of Jesus and so it was taken for granted. Only in time and across cultures was the need felt to narrate the entire life, death, and resurrection of Jesus. Since their writing, the Gospel genre has become the "classic" expression of the Christian message, precisely because it centers that message within the life, death, and resurrection of Jesus. The Christian message remains irreducibly tied to the Jesus-Event, symbolized in its meaning most preeminently, through the symbols of incarnation, cross, and resurrection.

The Christian message also develops historically in our consciousness according to developing human insight, communally and individually nurtured. No one learns the entire Gospel message at one time. We grow into it. By living the reality, we ask further questions, gain insights, make re-

sponsible judgments, make decisions about our lives, and intend to live toward the future based on this relationship with God. New circumstances
bring new choices; new decisions create new circumstances. Moreover, the
Christian texts themselves indicate a growing human awareness into the fullness of the meaning of the Christian message. Not only is this true in the
chronological writing of the texts, from Paul to the evangelists, but also
within the synoptic Gospels themselves, as Luke and Matthew include
infancy narratives and fuller accounts of the resurrection than Mark. The
holding together of the three irreducible symbols—incarnation, cross, and
resurrection—grounds the Christian message itself and gives rise to theology.

The symbol of the incarnation is less explicit though just as present in
Lonergan's work as the cross. It too expresses the twofold functions of a
content as well as a method, described above as "a law." As content, it says
that God is present in our being and already operating in creation around
and within us, especially in our ability to know and love. Lonergan's whole
theology is deeply incarnational, or what Catholic theology also calls "sacra-
mental." As method or what we might refer to as "the law of the incarnation," it is an act of understanding that affirms the self-transcending act as
one already related to the Divine Mystery who is source, ground, partner,
and final end. Lonergan's theology echoes the apophatic tradition that says
with Irenaeus, "The Glory of God is the human being fully alive." Culture,
then, from an incarnational view, is a matrix of meanings and values fashioned by human communities that may either already express, or potentially
be an extraordinary help in, finding God.

The development of science and scientific method in the Western
world would be one of those ways that modern humanity finds God. And,
as Lonergan has taken great pains to show, a theology that learns from the
scientific method is capable of better mediating this stage of Western culture
with religion in that matrix. While it may seem the methodological import
of the incarnation is acceptance of what is, it can be a catalyst for change by
calling people to fully embrace God and self in this world's context. In this
way, incarnation, like the cross, serves both the content of the Christian
message and the method of mediating that reality.

The third symbol is the one least attended to by Lonergan and underdeveloped in Doran. It is the resurrection, which as symbol is prophetic,
visionary, apocalyptic, and eschatological. It provides the teleological direction by focusing upon what can be. It seems to focus upon the future, but
its real illumination is always the present. Flashes of it appear in Lonergan
when he speaks about "authentic humanity" and "being-in-love"; and in
Doran when he speaks about "soteriology" and a "transition from this situation to an alternative situation more approximating the reign of God"
(Doran, 1990, p. 4).

The function of the resurrection as symbol is to orient the empirical method itself toward values that act as goals for all we do, so that we seek to find them inculturated in all our choices: love, justice, peace, forgiveness, compassion, care, and generosity, as expressed in the life and death of Jesus.

If we examine the content of the Christian message, we see that the symbol of the resurrection is present from the beginning of Jesus' life in his parables and miracles, and gives meaning to his death. Jesus preached "the kingdom of God" as his central theme. When Jesus told a parable that shocked people into seeing the world in a new way, the vision was always directed to something *more*, a new way of being. In his miracles, Jesus showed that even sin and its consequences could be changed. In the Beatitudes, a new way of living in the kingdom both now and in the future are presented, so much so that later in Matthew the final, eschatological judgment depends on our response to the new way of living. Even the great themes from the Hebrew scriptures figure prominently in the resurrection symbol of a new way of being: the covenant, promised people and promised land, obedience to the law. The traditions that weave the Hebrew scriptures together into a whole are filled with hope for a new world: The historical tradition recounts that the Lord of History is the Lord of the Future; the prophetic tradition calls the people to a new vision, sometimes hard and harsh; and the wisdom tradition probes suffering and the mystery of God that will somehow take care of it. The Christian message always contains an unsettledness—that we are pilgrims on this earth, never to be complacent and finished, and that the making of the future is one of our responsibilities.

At the same time, the resurrection serves method because it acts as a catalyst for change. Most frequently the type of change is in relation to a better future. It calls the people to repent and believe (e.g., Mk. 1:15). It is always double-sided because, on the one hand, it puts stress upon the immediacy of the present moment to proclaim that the reign, power, or sway of God is actively in their midst; and, on the other hand, it always contains an unfinished dimension that awaits completion. This "not yet completed" reality is expressed in theology as the eschatological fulfillment that comes in the "final judgment," expressed graphically in terms of heaven or hell. Most probably, as Edward Schillebeeckx concludes in his Christological research, even the earliest title applied to Jesus was "eschatological prophet," "the prophet who claims to bring a definitive message that is valid for all history" (1980, p. 802). If for all history, then is it not significant for all cultural discussions? Thus, the content of the symbol of the resurrection both projects what can be and judges us as to our failures. It operates in a back and forth movement from present to future and back again. In this measurement of our present by the future, the resurrection belongs to the dialectic of history for Christian theology.

Before moving to the final consideration of transformation, I need to introduce here what I call the "strategies" of theology. A strategy is simply a plan or method for obtaining a specific goal. If one thinks of the goal or result as the authentic human person in an authentic culture, then the realization of that may require a plan or method by which one proceeds. Philosophically, for Lonergan, the method is the act of understanding. Theologically, it is authenticating the Christian message in the cultural matrix. The three basic strategies that flow from the Christian message were first explained in H. Richard Niebuhr's pioneering book *Christ and Culture* (1951), an instructive work that puts Lonergan's work in perspective.

H. Richard Niebuhr, concerned with relationships and their dynamisms, especially as related to the wider context of culture, presents three basic options with two variations by which Christianity has dealt with culture. The first option is synthetic, which accepts culture as promoting the Christian agenda; the second is oppositional, which is counter-cultural; and the third is transformational, by which Christianity interacts together with culture to bring about a new and better form of culture. The three basic strategies that H. Richard Niebuhr found through a historical examination of the way Christianity and culture have related are actually found in the three central symbols expressive of the Christian message, out of which Christianity has acted and continually developed through history, though H. Richard Niebuhr himself did not make this connection. In an effort not to leave the various strategies unweighted, he judged the strategy most centrist, and the most normal in the relation of religion to culture, to be that of transformation. Within the Christian message, the symbol of the resurrection that envisions a new world, a new kingdom, and a new way of relating as people is a central strategy of relating to culture. Thus, in agreement with H. Richard Niebuhr, we wish to explore more deeply the relation of the Christian message that grounds such a strategy, and its application to possibly a new world-culture.

We have seen that the three central symbols of incarnation, cross, and resurrection are needed together to interpret one another and that taken together, they represent the content of the Christian message. We have also seen that each of them also acts as a principle or "law" of change. When one is used singularly, e.g., the law of the cross, the other two are also necessarily presupposed. Each one expresses both the way that the change is called forth and the interpretation of the change. It is this full range that is needed in the works of Lonergan and Doran. The "cross" involves suffering, but not suffering of any kind. That is where the resurrection comes in: The suffering is judged in light of redemption as "suffering for the sake of humanity"; or we could say in light of living the Christian message. In each case the presence of God is there in the action, regardless of whether we feel God as present or absent, manifested or hidden.

In the case of the symbol of the resurrection, the concern is the relation between the axis of the present and the future. The resurrection projects a vision of what can be, albeit sketchily and probably idealistically; nevertheless, it serves as a measuring stick as to whether we are living toward the future as authentically as we can. Therein lies its real power. The discrepancy between the present and what can be brings forward "the law of the cross" as necessary to reverse biases, suffer for the truth, and give forward direction to our values. At the same time, the symbol of the resurrection engages "the law of the incarnation" by recognizing God's love with humanity as the place where the Reign of God must take place. To love humanity in God calls forth the will to suffer on behalf of humanity and calls them to authentic living in responsible and authentic self-transcending love.

If a world-culture is to come about, then the projection of what values this world will inculturate is crucial to its survival. We need to put forth what constitutes the best culture for humanity. We have some clues from history about how to fashion the world to come and even how to talk about it.

The term "utopia" expresses the social world that is often projected into the ideal future. The theologian Reinhold Niebuhr in *Moral Man and Immoral Society* (1960) roundly criticized the use of this word, and its attendant term "idealism," if it is used as an absolute norm. His argument is not too dissimilar from Lonergan's regarding "group" and "general bias." Reinhold Niebuhr begins with the statement that society and the human person are not the same type of entities. A society requires a balancing of power to change it, whereas a person can change him- or herself, let us say by persuasive arguments. As Reinhold Niebuhr saw it, the future was to be worked out on the basis of power. And, for him, democracy afforded the best principles and rights by which to proceed. Instead of an absolute end, the means to the end became the focus and thus power diplomacy took center stage.

Recently, however, theologians have been challenging Reinhold Niebuhr's conclusion, while in general agreeing with his more open-ended process. These theologians are very aware of social, political, and cultural power, especially as experienced in their dependent economic countries. It seems the bitter pill of hopelessness that powerful people continually win out and write the histories to make right their might. It is the "lie" Dubois was forced to pay. What will happen to the deeper and richer resources of the culture? Their pervasive values upon which lives are interconnected? Gustavo Gutierrez from Peru, author of *A Theology of Liberation* (1973) and the acclaimed "Father of Liberation Theology," to take one example, has disagreed with Reinhold Niebuhr's rejection of utopia and argued for a connected vision by which the present social conditions may be judged and acted upon. Rather than a perfected social state, the vision inculcates the process of power related to the future through the principle of total liberation of people. "Liberation" in this sense is transformative praxis, much like Doran's soteriological approach, and with a vision of its direction and goal. Both theologians would agree that there is suffering that is dehumanizing and not part of a world to come if we can help it—racism, sexism, cultural imperialism. Where Gutierrez differs with Doran is in the explicit use of an ideal that projects a vision of what society can be. Most importantly, as it functions, the ideal enables us to make a comparison between where we are and where we want to be and thereby judge the adequacies or inadequacies of the present trajectory. An ideal, in this system, mediates the present and the future to each other. It allows the communication between religion and culture to take place in a practical way. Whereas the vision is an ideal, it can be a practical goal that people can commit themselves to and thereby galvanize their energies toward its actuation.

Gutierrez's theology is clearly based upon the symbol of the resurrection. He, among other political theologians, has called for prophetic and eschatological vision as a practical and necessary step in cultural transformation. It is a clear and commanding theology of hope that they proclaim, characterized by a resistance to fatalism and a commitment to humanity at its best in every cultural form. It is this inclusion of the emphasis upon the resurrection that theologians are returning to that is needed in Lonergan's method and in the strategy of transformation Doran develops. The resurrection, in Lonergan, acts both as a content of the Christian message and also as a catalyst of change. In the Christian message, the resurrection is needed to interpret the life and death of Jesus, and they are equally and necessarily needed to interpret the meaning of the resurrection. Thus, all three symbols are irreducible and must be taken together to render any theology as adequate, both in content and method.

Unlike the theology of Gutierrez, which perhaps by necessity builds most upon the symbol of the resurrection, Lonergan's method in principle attempts to render the full range of these symbols for a culture, even though in practice he wrote more often about "the law of the cross" than about "the law of the resurrection." Each symbol carries with it a call for change. Each therefore operates as a principle for the kind of change called for. In this way they are strategies employed to arrive at the fullness of the Christian message. And just as each symbol interprets the other, so too does each "law" need to interpret the change: synthesis, opposition, transformation. And when we are dealing with the possibility of a world-culture, the movement toward that future necessarily and responsibly calls forth the symbolic and transformational change found in the resurrection. By acceptance of the power of the complete Christian message, even the use of "the law of the cross" requires the inclusion of "the law of the resurrection" to give it redemptive direction. Doran's treatment of transformation, if it will give rise to the fuller range of theological content and method, needs the resource that the symbol of the resurrection gives to the future with its ability to call forth changes to realize those goals. Only when theology takes the symbol of the resurrection seriously and explores its full meaning and value will theology be in a position to actuate its own more complete possibilities to mediate between religion and culture, and through that mediation communicate one set of meanings and values (i.e., of the Christian religion) to the other set of meaning and values (i.e., of culture).

The future is not based solely on the past, but is an inspired act of creativity open to grace and freedom for the future. The axis of change is both the reversal of the present situation and the building toward the future reality we seek. The sketches of that future world are present now: A society based on love can heal a broken heart; enemies can put away their weapons of destruction for a common purpose. Strictly speaking, while the law of the cross can embrace the evil that has occurred, the law of the resurrection can call us forward in authenticity and judge us to DO THE GOOD even as we freely endure evil as part of embracing the law of the cross out of love. The soteriological vector of transformation that symbolizes this change needs the accompanying vision of what we can be to guide us. It cannot be presupposed; it must be explicit and a central dynamic in the theological enterprise both in content and method.

Theology, as communication between religion and culture, has entered a new phase. Catholic theology in particular has begun a thorough examination of itself in relation to culture: past, present, and especially the future. At the same time, theology has recognized that it cannot concern itself exclusively with ecclesial problems, especially those embedded in cultural contexts of the limiting past, at the expense of the rest of the world. Theology has a wider, inclusive responsibility for cultural problems as a new challenge. Problems today are inextricably interrelated because the human person individually and collectively is the issue, and this means globally. It is not enough to reflect on the past or interpret the present; the care for humanity in the future must begin now and be worked at in global proportions. What the future holds, we do not know. The commitment and resolve to work toward a fully human world, especially with attention to the human spirit, is within our grasp and the best we can do. Christian theology, as Lonergan's method presents it, as the critical mediation between religion and culture, offers a concrete way to fashion humanity for the future world-culture through the evocative power of its own symbols.

# Reference Materials

# Glossary of Lonerganian Terminology

## *Carla Mae Streeter, OP*

[The following explanations refer to works by Bernard Lonergan listed in the references at the end of the present volume. The reader is encouraged to refer to those works for a fuller understanding of Lonergan's thought in the context of his own writings. In preparing the following items, Carla Mae Streeter used the *Combined Lonergan Indices* compiled by Timothy P. Fallon, SJ, and Dennis Rosselli at Santa Clara University in California. She plans to incorporate the following items along with many more in a book-length glossary of Lonergan's terminology. —Eds.]

**authenticity:** The precarious and ever-developing state of a human being reached only by long and sustained faithfulness to the transcendental precepts (1985, p. 8). A person who evidently is consistent in the struggle to Be Attentive, Be Intelligent, Be Reasonable, Be Responsible, and Be in Love. Lonergan distinguishes a twofold authenticity: a minor authenticity of the person regarding faithfulness to the tradition that nourishes him or her, and a major authenticity that is able to justify or condemn the tradition itself when the failures of individuals become the norm (1985, pp. 120-121, 130). The human being achieves authenticity through self-transcendence (1972, p. 104) and through a continual withdrawal from unauthenticity (1972, p. 110). See 1985, pp. 8, 120-121, 130, 233; 1972, pp. 104, 110, 252.

**communications:** The eighth and final functional specialty, paired with research on the experiential or first level of consciousness (see Figure 3.1, p. 59). As a functional specialty of theology, the term refers to the transposition of the consciousness from the *realm of theory* to the *realm of common sense* in relating Christian doctrine to cultural reality. Theological communications operates through the basic art of talking, teaching, preaching, writing, art, gesture, etc. This distinct meaning for Lonergan makes clear the shift in the conscious subject from the more universal

and abstract language of theory to the language of the particular in its
environmental and cultural distinctiveness. In a more general sense,
communication (without the "s") is the communication of insight or understanding to the experience of another. What one means is communicated intersubjectively, artistically, symbolically, linguistically, incar-
nately (1972, p. 78). Communication can take place on various levels or
in various differentiations of consciousness: common sense, scholarly,
aesthetic, scientific (theoretical), religious, or mystical. In an interesting
discussion of *symbol*, Lonergan stresses the importance of *internal* communication (1972, pp. 66-67). By this he means an attentiveness to what
is going on in one's feelings. It is in feeling that links are discovered
between mind and body, mind and heart, and heart and body. Lonergan
also stresses the need for a *pluralism* of communications, a meeting of
people in terms of their distinct worlds of common sense (1972, pp. 276,
328). But the most profound meaning of communications for those engaged in community building is Lonergan's reference to communications
as the condition of possibility of the collective subject (1967/1988, pp.
219-220). The principle communication Lonergan refers to here is not
that of speaking what we know. It is revealing who we are. It is not
introspection that reveals us to ourselves, Lonergan stresses. It is reflecting on who we are as we live in common with others (1967/1988, p.
220). See 1957/1992, pp. 197-203; 1980/1990, pp. 222-224; 1972, pp.
66-67, 78, 132, 168-169, 194, 276, 282, 285, 300, 328, 330, 355-368;
1973, 65-66; 1967/1988, pp. 219-220.

**conversion:** A change of direction (1972, p. 52), from one set of roots to
another (1972, p. 271). Lonergan originally discusses conversion as
three-dimensional: as intellectual, in our orientation to the intelligible; as
moral, in our orientation to the good; and as religious, in our orientation
to God. This threefold designation continued as late as *Method in Theology* (1972, p. 267). Here Lonergan writes of religious conversion as "being grasped by ultimate concern"; of moral conversion as changing "the
criterion of one's decisions and choices from satisfactions to values"; and
of intellectual conversion as knowing "precisely what one is doing when
one is knowing" (1972, pp. 239-241). Later, in part as a result of conversations with Robert M. Doran, who was working on Lonergan's own references to the healing of the psyche in chapter 17 of *Insight*, Lonergan
accepted the category of affective conversion. Doran (1981b, 1990)
would himself later write of psychic conversion. Religious conversion
was further differentiated in Lonergan's thought as Christian religious
conversion when salvation was experienced in the context of Christ Jesus
in the incarnation. Conversion is the process of moving from unauthenticity to authenticity, and as such it is tenuous and fragile. Religious
conversion, because it directly influences the human capacity for self-

transcendence, grounds both moral and intellectual conversion (1972, p. 283). Religious conversion involves being grasped by religious love. When religious love enters the horizon of a human being, the entire horizon is transformed, for transcendent being has become the context for consideration of contingent being in the person's awareness. The self becomes a different self, because the horizon within which all reality is considered has been radically altered (1972, p. 122). Moral conversion involves a shift from attending to what is merely satisfying to what is good in the long run. The quality of moral conversion will depend to some extent on the depth of religious conversion. Religious conversion is very often experienced but not understood as religious. Intellectual conversion involves becoming aware of one's own conscious operations and processing. It is not achieved by many, but once it happens, the critical tool to assess one's own motivation is uncovered. For an understanding of psychic conversion, the reader must turn to the writings of Doran (1981b, 1990). This conversion consists in the dissolving of the censorship that polices feelings that are laden with pain. Denial of feeling prevents images from emerging in the psyche. These images are the seeds of new insight, and thus this psychic restriction aborts the very possibility of new insight in an area too painful to address (1957/1992, pp. 555-556; 1972, p. 77). See 1971, pp. 124, 134; 1967, pp. 160-163; 1972, pp. 122, 130-131, 239-241, 26, 271, 283. [For further discussion of the pain the psyche experiences due to childhood traumas, see the works of Alice Miller, 1979/1981, 1980/1983, 1981/1984, 1988/1990a, 1988/1990b, 1990/1991; when John Bradshaw (1988), the well-known popularizer of Miller's work, writes of people being freed of the "shame" or pain that binds them, he in effect is describing an initial aspect of affective conversion; the process that Doran refers to as psychic conversion is a deeper process than what Bradshaw writes about; not only affective conversion along the lines indicated by Bradshaw, but also psychic conversion of a fairly advanced order are necessary for the proper and full accessing of the archetypes of maturity that Robert Moore and Douglas Gillette write about, 1990, 1992a, 1992b, 1993a, 1993b.—Eds.]

**culture:** The set of meanings and values inherent in a way of life (1974a, p. 183; 1973, pp. 15, 50). Lonergan understands culture empirically, rather than normatively. A normative view of culture projects a rigidity and permanence upon laws and institutions that history shows to be illusionary (1974a, p. 283). An empirical perspective, the view Lonergan prefers, has to do with the manner in which certain meanings and values inform a human community as it lives life as a continuous slow development or a rapid decline (1972, p. xi). Culture is local and very concrete. Its meanings are felt, intuited, and acted out in rites, symbols, and language (1974a, pp. 102-103). Meaning is intrinsic to any culture (1972, p.

78). In a discussion of the writings of Pitirim Sorokin, Lonergan agrees with Sorokin's distinction of three types of culture—sensate, idealistic, and ideational—and correlates the three types to three degrees of self-appropriation (1980/1990, p. 221). See 1974a, pp. 183, 102-103, 233; 1973, pp. 15, 50; 1980/1990, p. 221; 1972, pp. xi, 78.

**desire to know:** The dynamic orientation of the human intelligence toward a totally unknown, toward being (1957/1992, pp. 372-373). In the human person, knowledge by essence is the object of a natural desire. That natural desire is to know being, and the notion of being is unrestricted, that is, the object of the desire to know encompasses both contingent and transcendent being. Knowing contingent beings concretely means knowing all there is to know about everything. Knowing transcendent being means knowing divine Mystery. The natural desire is the basis for all questioning regarding both (1967/1988, p. 147). It is an alertness of mind, an unrestricted intellectual curiosity, spirit of inquiry, or active intelligence. The drive is *pure* questioning, prior to insights, concepts, words. This "wanting" is pure question, an "eros of the mind" (1957/1992, pp. 33-34, 97). Lonergan qualifies this phrase with the terms "pure, detached, disinterested." He uses them more specifically to refer to scientific detachment, scientific disinterestedness, and scientific impartiality (1957/1992, p. 97). See 1967/1988, p. 147; 1957/1992, pp. 33-34, 97, 372-373.

**dialectic:** The fourth functional specialty. The functional specialties called dialectic and foundations correspond to the fourth level of consciousness (see Figure 3.1, p. 59). Dialectic is a concrete unfolding of linked but opposed principles of change (1957/1992, p. 242). Dialectic deals with conflicts. It brings conflicts to light and provides a technique that objectifies subjective differences and promotes conversion (1972, p. 235). As a functional specialty in theology, dialectic is neither concerned with the theologian's position nor the refutation of counter-positions. Dialectic seeks to clearly present diversity and give evidence for its roots (1972, p. 254). "The presence or absence of intellectual, of moral, of religious conversion gives rise to dialectically opposed horizons" (1972, p. 247). Dialectic compares and evaluates "the conflicting views of historians, the diverse interpretations of exegetes, the varying emphases of researchers" (1973, p. 22). The cause of irreconcilable difference is a difference of horizon, and the solution is nothing less than a conversion (1972, p. 246). When the divine solution to evil and the decline of culture is admitted, the horizon becomes broad enough to make a comprehensive viewpoint possible (1957/1992, pp. 749-750). Dialectic deals with concrete positions and counterpositions. It is concerned with the contradictory and is interested in change (1980/1990, pp. 184-185). The concrete process that dialectic describes is one in which intelligence and obtuseness, reasonableness and silliness, responsibility and sin, love and hatred commingle and conflict (1985, p. 182). Fundamental dialectic takes place within the concrete human subject. It is presumed that what one states publicly is intended to be intelligent and rational. If there is contradiction between what one states and what is done, the dialectic between position and counterposition emerges (1980/1990, p. 186). The materials of dialectic are conflicts in the history of Christian movements. Its aim is a comprehensive viewpoint, some single base or some single set of related bases from which any individual viewpoint may be critiqued. Some differences are complementary. They can be brought together within a larger whole and seen as successive stages in a single process of development (1972, p. 129). When comparison shows differences to be irreducible, there is true dialectic, yet not all irreducible differences are serious. The seriousness must be determined in dialectical process (1972, p. 130). Dialectic affects community, for just as common meaning is constitutive of community, so dialectic divides community into opposing groups (1972, p. 358). Lonergan holds that dialectic has two levels structurally. On an upper level are operators, and on a lower level are the materials to be operated on. The operators are two precepts: develop positions; reverse counterpositions. The materials to be operated on must be assembled, completed, compar, reduced, classified, and selected (1972, p. 249). To the history that grasps what was going forward must be added a history that evaluates the worth of achievements (1972, p. 246). See 1973, p. 22; 1980/1990, pp. 184-186; 1972, pp. 129-130, 235-266, 358; 1957/1992, pp. 749-750, 242-243; 1985, p. 182.

**doctrines:** The sixth functional specialty, on the third level of consciousness, corresponding to history (see Figure 3.1, p. 59). From within the framework chosen in foundations, doctrines is a selection from among the alternatives considered in dialectic (1973, pp. 22, 67-68). What is selected is how to state clearly and distinctly what the religious community's beliefs are regarding "the mysteries so hidden in God" that the community could not know them if God had not made them known. The assent made to these statements of belief is the assent of faith (1972, p. 349). The statements that doctrines express are judgments of fact and judgments of value. The functional specialty called doctrines is not only concerned with affirming and negating what pertains to dogmatic theology. It is concerned with facts and values that pertain to moral, ascetic, mystical, pastoral, liturgical, etc. theology (1972, p. 132). Doctrines can be regarded as mere verbal formulae unless their meaning is clearly worked out in systematics (1972, p. 142). Doctrines, valuable and true as they are, are but the skeleton of the original message, for the word is the word of a person. Doctrine objectifies and depersonalizes. The word of God came to us through the God-man (1985, p. 227). When introduced successfully to a culture, doctrines will proceed to develop according to that culture. See 1973, pp. 22, 67-68; 1972, pp. 132, 349; 1985, p. 227.

**finality:** The term refers not to extrinsic causality, such as final causality, but to the immanent constituents of proportionate being, an upward but indeterminately directed dynamism towards ever fuller realization of being. The determinacy of any genus and species is limitation, and limitation is to finality a barrier to be transcended (1957/1992, p. 477). Extrinsically, a final cause is truly final only when the specific or formal constituent of the cause is the *good.* This extrinsic final causality is there, but the finality Lonergan is referring to is the dynamic aspect of the real (1957/1992, p. 472). Lonergan distinguishes three types of finality: absolute, horizontal, and vertical. There are two classes of the common instances of finality: the response of appetites to motives and the orientation of processes to terms. When these two instances specify limiting essence to limited mode of appetition and of process, we have what Lonergan calls horizontal finality. Absolute finality refers to the orientation of all things to God's intrinsic goodness. A third type of finality, the innate directed dynamism of being developing from any lower level of appetition and process to any higher level, Lonergan names *vertical* finality (1967/1988, pp. 19-23). Vertical finality manifests itself in four ways: instrumentally, dispositively, materially, and obedientially. In instrumental, a concrete plurality of lower activities might be instrumental toward a higher end: the mixing of ingredients toward a finished cake. In dispositive, a concrete pluralism of activities might dispose toward a higher end: the work of the research scientist arriving finally at a discovery such as interferon. Materially, a concrete plurality of lower entities may be the material cause from which a higher form comes: the single cells of ovum and sperm uniting to form human life. Obedientially, a concrete plurality of rational creatures such as human beings have the obediential potency to receive the very self-communication of God that we call grace. Lonergan believes that the nature of vertical finality has been studied very little. Horizontal finality is abstract and deals with generalities, but the power of vertical finality lies in its concreteness. It is in light of vertical finality that the levels of consciousness clarified by Lonergan can be understood (1967/1988, pp. 19-23). See 1957/1992, pp. 470-484; 1967/1988, pp. 19-23.

**foundations:** The fifth functional specialty, operating on the fourth (evaluative) level of consciousness, as does dialectic (see Figure 3.1, p. 59). The functional specialty called foundations is concerned with objectifying the human event known as conversion. Conversion reveals the personal horizon of the theologian (historian, etc.) through a decision about the world-view, the outlook one chooses to maintain. Foundations is the identification and selection of the framework in which the functional specialties of doctrines, systematics, and communications will have meaning and effectiveness (1972, pp. 267-268). It is specifically the foundation for these three remaining specialties, not for all of the theological task. Research, interpretation, history, and dialectic is done by the converted and the unconverted. When performed by one converted, however, these same functions have a different kind of "self" doing them. Lonergan holds that this difference must be thematized because it is real. It operates not only in theology but in every discipline. To objectify conversion, one has need of intentionality analysis, the ability to attend to one's own conscious operations, to objectify them. This ability enables one to deal with the data of consciousness in addition to the data of sense. Foundations thematizes the selection made by the conscious subject of a position sifted from the possibilities presented in dialectic (1972, p. 268). As a fourth level function, it is where consciousness becomes conscience (1972, p. 268). The conversion that foundations is concerned with can be of several types. Three forms were initially discussed by Lonergan. Conversion can be *intellectual*, which means one knows how consciousness works, not from theory, but from self-appropriation. Conversion can be *moral*, in which choice opts for long-term good over short-term satisfaction, effectively dissolving individual, group, and general bias. Finally, Lonergan discusses the conversion that is distinctly *religious*, an alteration of the human horizon itself, as a result of encounter with the Holy. Conversion of any kind is moving from one set of roots to another (1972, p. 271; 1974a, pp. 65-66). There is a new human subject, a new self as a result of conversion. The converted and unconverted have radically different horizons with which to entertain possibilities (1972, p. 271). Lonergan distinguishes a simple manner of doing foundations in a static deductionist style, proceeding from a set of premises. His own meaning follows a more complex "methodical" style that moves from discovery to discovery. He regards foundations as what is first in any ordered set (1972, pp. 269-270; 1974a, pp. 63-64). "First" for theological foundations is religious conversion, a personal but not necessarily private encounter with Transcendent Reality (1985, p. 218). Lonergan also distinguishes foundations from fundamental theology. The latter is really a set of doctrines about the church, about inspiration, etc. Foundations is the objectification of the theologian's conversion, forming the horizon or world-view within which doctrines are apprehended (1972, pp. 131-132, 267; 1973, p. 22). For Lonergan, intentionality analysis is the basis that provides foundations not only for theology, but also for personal ethical decisions, for hermeneutics, for critical history, and for any discipline the person explores (1974a, pp. 39, 203). See 1972, pp. 131-132, 267-271; 1974a, pp. 39, 63-66, 203; 1985, p. 218; 1973, p. 22.

**generalized empirical method:** See **method.**

**history:** The third of the functional specialties. History and doctrines are
functions of the third level of consciousness, that of judgment (see Figure
3.1, p. 59). This position is the clue to Lonergan's distinct meaning of
history. History for Lonergan is not the gathering of historical data.
Gathering historical data is a research function in the area of history.
Nor is history understanding the meaning of the data gathered. Historical
understanding is an interpretive function. History as a functional specialty is a judgment of precisely what is going forward in the data of the
past uncovered and understood (1973, p. 22). History for Lonergan is the
fact of this dynamic movement forward affirmed in terms of historical
evidence (1972, pp. 185-186). There is a double process involved in history understood in a Lonergan perspective. First, one comes to understand what is going forward in the *sources* uncovered. Second, one
comes to understand how what is going forward in the sources has something to do with what is going forward in the present human community
(1972, p. 189). It is in the judgment of what is indeed historical fact that
fact is distinguished from fiction and history from legend. The act of
judgment is the key (1967/1988, pp. 206-207). But Lonergan will also
distinguish the precise type of intelligibility to be found in historical data.
Insight can grasp possibility or it can grasp necessity in data. The intelligibility grasped by the historian will have elements of necessity in it, but
will not be free of *surd*, Lonergan's term for the accumulation of the
results of unreasonable decisions. See 1972, pp. 185-186, 189; 1973, p.
22; 1967/1988, pp. 206-207.

**intentionality analysis:** See **method.**

**interiority:** The term as used by Lonergan is philosophical as well as religious. It refers to that realm of the human subject concerned with the data
of consciousness and its operations, the "realm of interiority." Intentionality analysis goes on in the realm of interiority. There are the outer
realms of common sense and theory, and the inner realm of one's subjectivity, or interiority, which involves attending not merely to objects but to
the intending subject and his or her acts (1972, p. 83). Finally, there is
the realm of transcendence where God is known and loved (1972, p. 84).
When the critical exigence (the need to know) turns its attention on interiority, the differentiated consciousness emerges, and self-appropriation
results. The unity of the consciousness is not in its undifferentiation. It
is in the self-knowledge that understands the different realms and knows
how to shift from one to the other (1972, p. 84). It is by finding one's
way into interiority that a basis is achieved through self-appropriation
for both common sense and theory (1972, p. 85). To enter into an-

other's differentiation of consciousness is to effect that same differentiation in oneself (1972, pp. 327-328). Lonergan maintains that philosophy today is being driven into the realm of interiority. See 1972, pp. 83-85, 114-115, 257, 265-66, 272-273, 316, 327-328.

**interpretation:** The second of the functional specialties. Interpretation corresponds to the seventh specialty, systematics, as both are functions of the second level of consciousness, that of understanding (see Figure 3.1, p. 59). Interpretation understands what is *meant*. As a functional specialty of theology, it understands the meaning of the data made available by research in the area of the Christian scriptures and the writings and documents of the tradition. The meaning it seeks to uncover is understood according to its historical context, its proper mode and level of expression, and the circumstances and intent of the author. Its written form is the commentary or the monograph (1972, p. 127). Both in theology and in other fields, interpretation has to do with hermeneutics. A systematic treatment of the problems involved in interpretation is given in *Insight*. There Lonergan calls for a distinction between (1) the expression itself, (2) a simple interpretation, and (3) a reflective interpretation (1957/1992, pp. 585-587). He introduces the notion of *universal viewpoint*, which is like a pegboard allowing for every possible interpretation to be "posted." This notion opens up the horizon of the thinker so that nothing is excluded, but everything must be assessed as to the truth it contributes to the complete meaning. This notion will be the basis for Lonergan's notion of dialectic (1957/1992, pp. 587-591). Central to Lonergan's view of interpretation is the interpreter. The interpreting task depends on one's ability to move from personal experience into an imaginative reconstruction of the situation of the past (1980/1990, p. 223). Lonergan considers his work in chapters 7 through 11 of *Method in Theology* as a more concrete expression of what he had done in the third part of chapter 17 in *Insight*. He also considered these chapters to be a "set of directions" toward attaining the universal viewpoint he regarded as necessary if true interpretation is to be reached (1974a, pp. 275-276). A case in point is Lonergan's reference to history as the assembly of a manifold of particular events into a single interpretive unity (1972, p. 199), and historical reality as an inexhaustible incentive to fresh historical interpretations (1972, p. 214). Historical data arrived at by the critical process must then go through an interpretive process. Here the historian pieces together the fragments. Only when this interpretive process of reconstruction is completed can one refer to historical "facts" (1972, p. 203). The interrelationship of chapters 7 through 11 of *Method in Theology* (interpretation through foundations) can be understood further when Lonergan explains that the interpreter may understand the text, the author, and him- or herself, but should conversion take place, there is a different self to do the understanding. This new horizon in turn can modify one's understanding of the text, the author, and oneself (1972, p. 246). See 1957/1992, pp. 585-616, 761-762; 1980/1990, pp. 217-218, 222-224; 1973, pp. 24-25; 1967/1988, pp. 131-132, 243-244; 1974a, pp. 251-252, 275-276; 1972, pp. 127, 153-173, 199, 203, 214; 1976, p. 12.

**law of the cross:** The notion of the cross as it pertains to the new covenant (1964b, art. 23). The heart of Lonergan's understanding of the law of the cross is the transformation of evil into good. The law of the cross pertains to the new covenant by way of precept, example, and conformation and association and by way of the economy of salvation. By precept, Lonergan means the direct commands found in the New Testament itself: "Do not resist evil.... Love your enemies and do good to those who hate you..." (Mt. 5: 38-48). By example is meant those New Testament passages that model a whole new way of being: "...anyone who wants to be first among you must be the servant of all..." (Mk. 10:42-45). Conformation and association refers to a direct imitation of the behavior of Christ: As Jesus lays down his life in love so as to take it up again (Jn. 10:17-18), so we suffer with him to be glorified with him (Rom. 8:17). Finally, the law of the cross gives the new covenant the basic law governing its economy of salvation: The power and wisdom of God are to be discerned in Christ *crucified*, not in some new order in which no injustices are perpetrated on the good (1964b, art. 23). See 1964b, chapters 4 and 5, especially art. 23; 1974a, pp. 8-9, 113.

**levels of consciousness** and **intentionality:** The term "level" is Lonergan's metaphor for the manifold of human consciousness in its various identifiable sets of operations. That there are various operations is a fact. That they are grouped in related and identifiable sets is Lonergan's distinctive insight into human cognition. The verification of these related operations in their recurrent pattern through "applying the operations as intentional to the operations as conscious" brings an awareness of the *intending* itself in contrast to *what* is intended (1972, pp. 14-15). Anyone can discover the pattern then by what Lonergan calls *self-appropriation* or the attending to one's intending. The levels of intentional consciousness are (1) empirical, (2) intelligent, (3) rational, and (4) responsible. The empirical level is that set of human operations that are identified as sensing, perceiving, imagining, feeling, speaking, and moving. The human subject is simply *experiencing*. The intelligent level is identified by inquiry, understanding, and expressing and by the working out of the presuppositions and implications of our expressions. In short, it has to do with *understanding*. The rational level is identified by the operations of reflecting, marshalling evidence, passing judgment, and concluding. It is concerned with *judging*. The responsible level is identified by such operations as evaluating, deciding, choosing, acting out. Its main concern is *deciding* (1972, p. 9). What Lonergan refers to as the level of *transcendence* is really the root and ground of all the operations, and part of the fourth level. The fourth level of deciding is characterized by judgments of *value* in contrast to judgments of *truth* or meaning that identify the third level of judgment. Transcendent Mystery has to do with *ultimate* value. The higher levels "sublate" or include and transform the lower levels, but the reversal is not true (1972, p. 120). The priority of intellect is simply the priority of the first three levels (1972, p. 340). The human subject in its conscious, unobjectified, attentive, intelligent, reasonable, and responsible operations is referred to by Lonergan as the "rock." In this reference Lonergan alludes to "the more important part of the rock" to be uncovered in chapter 4 of *Method in Theology*. It is the chapter on religion (1972, pp. 19-20). See 1972, pp. 9, 14-15, 19-20, 106-107, 120-121, 340.

**mediation:** As used by Lonergan, the term refers to the transposition from one set of operations of the consciousness to another as the subject engages the real world. The world of the infant is referred to as "immediate." The child responds only to objects present—what is seen, felt, and heard in the world of immediate experience (1972, pp. 28, 76). With the acquisition of language, consciousness develops, and that world expands. There is the "mediation of immediacy by meaning when one objectifies cognitional process in transcendental method and discovers, identifies, accepts one's submerged feelings..." (1972, p. 77). Meaning, mediated through the operations of the conscious subject, actually changes one's world to a world mediated by meaning and motivated by value. Meaning differentiates the consciousness. The consciousness can be theoretically or scientifically differentiated; it can also be differentiated aesthetically or mystically. The world mediated by meaning is the world of the memories of others, the common sense of various communities, literature, the works of scholars and scientists, the experience of holy people of every culture, and the reflections of philosophers and theologians (1972, p. 28). Reflexive techniques are developed. The mediator is the human subject as operator (1974a, p. 20). Meaning as intentionality mediates the mediator as the desire to know creates or unfolds the self as it is drawn toward what is meant; thus a nuanced meaning of "self" mediation or mutual self-mediation results. The authentic self emerges as the human consciousness interacts with reality. It is not an enclosed, self-contained entity, but an entity-in-relation. See 1974a, p. 20; 1972, pp. 28, 76, 77.

**method:** The term for Lonergan does not mean a technique. It refers to the innate dynamic operation of the human consciousness, its "method." The consciousness of the human subject is innately intentional. Intentionality analysis is charting the pattern of the operating consciousness of the human subject (1973, p. 18) or objectifying the contents or data of consciousness (1972, p. 8). The pattern of human consciousness is recurrent, and its operations, once identified, can be understood in relation to one another. Following its recurrent pattern of authentic, not distorted operations, the method of human consciousness yields results that are both cumulative and progressive, not merely repetitious (1972, p. 4). Lonergan's basic method is distinct from the transcendental method referred to by such transcendental Thomists as Otto Muck (1964/1968). The transcendental method Lonergan has in mind is not theoretical. It is utterly concrete and empirical, an attentive charting of the data of consciousness itself (1972, pp. 13-14, footnote). Lonergan has actually transformed the transcendental method of Maréchal in correction of and in complementing Kant's call for a critical appropriation of human cognitional structure as basic to a methodical science and philosophy for our day, as Frederick E. Crowe has noted (1967, p. xiii). Lonergan's transcendental method is concerned with objectifying the human subject's actual cognitional process and with (what is frequently missed due to the cognitional emphasis) the discovery, identification, and acceptance of one's submerged feelings in psychotherapy or emotional healing (1972, p. 77). The work of this thematizing must be done by the individual him- or herself. The grasp of what is really going on in transcendental method Lonergan calls "self-appropriation" (1972, p. 83). Self-appropriation involves attending to one's own operations and discovering through observation the recurrent pattern Lonergan himself discovered by attending to his own conscious operations. The method is called "transcendental" because it progresses through recognizable sets of operations that mount in complexity, "sublating" lower operations into higher ones and transforming them in the process. "Higher" in this context refers to fullness, a mounting from a fixation with the world of immediacy to the world filled with meaning and permeated with value. It has to do with the struggle toward the authentic human functioning identified with knowledge and choice. Intentionality analysis provides an understanding of the operations that have to do with knowing and deciding. The phrase "generalized empirical method" refers to the fact that Lonergan's method involves an attentiveness to the data that consciousness provides. These data can be the object of study as are the data of sense in the sciences. We can attend to our experiencing; to our inquiry, understanding, formulating, reflecting, checking; and to our passing of judgment (1985, pp. 140-143). Lonergan's transcendental method is trans-cultural, not in its formulation, for that will carry the unique particularity of a culture, its time and place. The method is trans-cultural in the realities referred to in the formulations (1972, p. 282). Three important realities are clarified in Lonergan's method: The human subject (1) is clarified from the objects (2) known, and the objects (2) are clarified from the operations (3) by which they are known (1985, p. 79). It is precisely this generalized empirical method in its transcendent operations that is to be illumined by faith in order for theology to exercise its full and proper role among the sciences. If problems of critical method are not attended to first, theological method will continue to flounder (1967/1988, pp. 130-132). Lonergan clearly distinguishes between *empirical* method and *generalized empirical* method. The former has to do with the data of sense; the latter, using basic principles from the former, has to do with the data of consciousness itself (1957/1992, pp. 95-96). See 1957/1992, pp. 95-96; 1973, p. 18; 1972, pp. 4, 13-20, 77, 83, 101, 282, 289; 1967/1988, pp. 130-132; 1985, pp. 79, 140-143.

**mutual self-mediation:** See **mediation**.

**realism:** The truth that is acknowledged in the mind corresponds to reality (1976, p. 128). The term refers to the progression of the mind to objective truth, and through truth, to knowledge of reality (1967, p. 61). Lonergan generally refers to three types of realists: naïve, dogmatic, and critical. The naïve realist simply affirms that we know and offers no further explanation (1967, p. 60). The dogmatic realist asserts that the intellect confronts reality directly through perception, but offers no philosophic reflection to substantiate how this takes place (1967, p. 184; 1967/1988, p. 196; 1976, p. 129). The critical realist explains what knowing is and how it takes place. Realism for Lonergan is immediate not because it is naive and unreasoned or blindly affirmed, but because one knows the real before one knows the difference between object and subject (1967, p. 88). To move beyond idealism to realism, it is necessary to discover human intellectual and rational operations. But it is essential to understand that these operations involve a transcendence of the operating subject. The real is what we come to know through a grasp of what Lonergan calls the *virtually unconditioned*, that is, an area of inquiry about which no questions remain (1972, p. 76). A prospective judgment is virtually unconditioned when the evidence for its affirmation is sufficient. It is *virtually* unconditioned because it has conditions that have been fulfilled. A *formally* unconditioned has no conditions at all (1957/1992, pp. 305-306). For the critical realist, a verified hypothesis is probably true, and being probably true, refers to what in reality probably is so. Historical facts are events in the world mediated by acts of meaning (1972, pp. 239, 263). See 1967, pp. 60-61, 88, 184; 1967/1988, p. 196; 1957/1992, pp. 305-306; 1972, pp. 76, 239, 263; 1976, p. 128.

**religion:** As Lonergan is wont to do, a functional definition is given to us. Religion is the capacity of the human consciousness to apprehend ultimate meaning and ultimate value symbolically (1985, p. 161). In contrast, theology questions this apprehension. It mediates between religion and the role of that religion in its cultural matrix (1972, p. xi). Religious studies, a third term, is the historical study of religions. Theology is to religion what economics is to business and biology is to health (1974a, p. 97). The function of religion is to provide a world-view within which one might live intelligently, reasonably, and responsibly. This responsibility includes not only morality, but the total commitment that authentic religion prompts (1974a, pp. 154-155, 211). Lonergan speaks of a religion's *inner* word: the gift of God's love to that people. He also refers to the religious tradition itself as an *outer* word (1972, p. 119). See 1985, pp. 161-163; 1974a, pp. 97, 149-163, 211; 1972, pp. 101-124.

**research:** The first of the functional specialties (see Figure 3.1, p. 59). As a functional specialty of theology, it refers to the gathering of data pertinent to a specific area of theology. Lonergan refers to two types of data: that of sense and that of consciousness itself. It is central to Lonergan's thought that the data of consciousness, or how the human mind works, be part of the theologian's "data" as he or she goes about theological research in the data available to the senses through reading and personal experience. Research can be special or general. Special research is the gathering of data pertaining to a specific problem or question. General research locates, excavates, maps, reproduces, decodes, catalogues, and prepares critical editions. It produces indices, tables, bibliographies, abstracts, bulletins, handbooks, dictionaries, and encyclopedias (1972, p. 127). In short, research makes available what information exists on any subject. See 1972, pp. 127, 140, 149-151, 198-203, 247; 1967/1988, pp. 128-129, 238-240.

**Self-affirming precepts:** See **transcendental precepts**.

**self-appropriation:** See **method, interiority**, and **levels of consciousness and interiority**.

**self-mediation:** See **mediation**.

**systematics:** The seventh functional specialty, operating on the second level of consciousness, as does interpretation (see Figure 3.1, p. 59). The functional specialty called systematics is concerned with the meaning of doctrinal statements. The facts and values expressed in doctrines may be clear on the meaning of the words chosen, but ambiguous on how the reality is to be understood. Systematics aims at an understanding of the religious realities affirmed by doctrines (1972, p. 349). Doctrinal statements may simply generate further questions. Systematics is concerned with these questions, with clarifying ambiguity, with providing explanation, with working to remove inconsistencies, with bringing about inner coherence through an understanding of what is meant by the words (1972, p. 132). Systematics gets to the kernel of the message to be communicated, and reciprocally, communications often poses new questions for systematics (1972, p. 142). It is not the intent of systematics to increase certitude, but to promote an understanding of what one is already certain about. It does not seek to establish the facts, but strives to uncover why the facts are what they are. Systematics takes the facts asserted in doctrines and works them into a coherent whole (1972, p. 336). Systematics is an imperfect effort on the part of human understanding to gain some insight into revealed truths (1973, p. ix). See 1972, pp. 132, 142, 336, 345, 349-350; 1973, pp. ix, 22, 35.

**transcendental method:** See **method**.

**transcendental precepts:** The term Lonergan uses to describe the five distinct imperatives that impel the human subject toward transcendence by an ever-deepening authenticity or genuine humanness. (1) *Be Attentive* to your experience. (2) *Be Intelligent* in your inquiry into the meaning of that experience. (3) *Be Reasonable* in your judgments as to the accuracy of your understanding of your experience. (4) *Be Responsible* in your decisions based on the conclusions of the accuracy of your understanding of your experience. (5) *Be in Love* with the Mystery that grounds all your human operation, and with the human and the world with which that human is vitally interrelated. See 1974a, p. 170; 1972, pp. 132-132; 1973, p. 48.

**virtually unconditioned:** See **realism**.

# References

Annotations from John Angus Campbell's 1985 *Quarterly Journal of Speech* review essay are reprinted here with the permission of the publisher and the author. In addition, Professor Campbell has written annotations to key works in the study of communication and rhetoric that he referred to in chapter 1 of the present collection and to some other works that he did not refer to.

Abrams, M. H. (1971). *Natural supernaturalism: Tradition and revolution in Romantic literature*. New York: W. W. Norton.

Adler, M. J. (1991). *Haves without have-nots: Essays for the 21st century on democracy and socialism*. New York: Macmillan Publishing.

Alexy, R. (1990). A theory of practical discourse (D. Frisby, Trans.). In S. Benhabib & F. Dallmayr (Eds.), *The communicative ethics controversy* (pp. 151-190). Cambridge, MA: MIT Press.

Apel, K.-O. (1991). Falibilismo, teoría consensual de la verdad y fundamentación ultima [Falliblism, the consensual theory of truth, and ultimate foundations]. *Teoría de la verdad y etica del discurso* [Barcelona: Paidós/I.C.E.-U.A.B., Pensamiento Contemporáneo], *13*, 37-145. (Original work published 1987)

Aristotle. (1991). *Aristotle on rhetoric: A theory of civic discourse* (G. A. Kennedy, Trans.). New York: Oxford University Press.
George A. Kennedy is one of the central figures in the revival of interest in rhetoric in our time. His translation is clear, easy to read and almost makes the *Rhetoric* engaging. Each section of the text is prefaced by a substantive paragraph placing the subjects examined in cultural/historical context. The text is followed by supplementary texts from Gorgias and Cicero and excerpts from other texts by Aristotle, by a glossary of key terms, and by essays on the composition of the text, its history after Aristotle, and the strengths and limitations of its treatment of rhetoric.—J.A.C.

Arnold, P. M. (1991). *Wildmen, warriors, and kings: Masculine spirituality and the Bible*. New York: Crossroad.

Austin, J. L. (1962). *How to do things with words*. Cambridge, MA: Harvard University Press.

330

Bakhtin, M. (1981). *The dialogic imagination: Four essays by M. M. Bakhtin* (M. Holquist, Ed.; C. Emerson & M. Holquist, Trans.). Austin: University of Texas Press.

Ball, M. S. (1985). *Lying down together: Law, metaphor, and theology*. Madison: University of Wisconsin Press.

Barden, G. (1970). Modalities of consciousness. *Philosophical Studies* [Dublin], *19*, 11-54.

Barden, G. (1990). *After principles*. Notre Dame: University of Notre Dame Press.

Barr, J. (1961). *The semantics of biblical language*. Oxford: Oxford University Press.

Baynes, K., Bohman, J., & McCarthy, T. (Eds.). (1987). *After philosophy: End or transformation?* Cambridge, MA: MIT Press.

Bazerman, C. (1988). *Shaping written knowledge: The genre and activity of the experimental article in science*. Madison: University of Wisconsin Press.

Bazerman, C., & Paradis, J. (Eds.). (1991). *Textual dynamics of the professions: Historical and contemporary studies of writing in professional communities*. Madison: University of Wisconsin Press.

Becker, H. S., with a chapter by P. Richards. (1986). *Writing for social scientists: How to start and finish your thesis, book, or article*. Chicago: University of Chicago Press.

Becker, V. (1992). *The real man inside: How men can recover their identity and why women can't help*. Grand Rapids, MI: Zondervan.

Behler, E. (1991). *Confrontations: Derrida/Nietzsche/Heidegger* (S. Taubeneck, Trans.). Stanford, CA: Stanford University Press. (Original work published 1988)

Bellah, R. N., Madsen, R., Sullivan, W. M., Swidler, A., & Tipton, S. M. (1985). *Habits of the heart: Individualism and commitment in American life*. Berkeley and Los Angeles: University of California Press.

Benardete, S. (1991). *The rhetoric of morality and philosophy: Plato's* Gorgias *and* Phaedrus. Chicago: University of Chicago Press.

Benhabib, S., & Dallmayr, F. (Eds.). (1990). *The communicative ethics controversy*. Cambridge, MA: MIT Press.

Berger, P. L., & Luckmann, T. (1966). *The social construction of reality: A treatise in the sociology of knowledge*. Garden City, NY: Doubleday.

Berlin, I. (1958). *Two concepts of liberty*. Oxford: Oxford University Press.

Bernauer, J. W. (1990). *Michel Foucault's force of flight: Toward an ethics for thought*. Atlantic Highlands, NJ: Humanities Press International.

Bernstein, R. J. (1983). *Beyond objectivism and relativism: Hermeneutics and praxis*. Philadelphia: University of Pennsylvania Press.
Bernstein's is a central text in the ongoing cultural and philosophic debate over the meaning and limitations of the achievement of Gadamer's *Truth and Method.*—J.A.C.

Beth, H., & Pross, H. (1990). *Introducción a la ciencia de la comunicación*. [Introduction to the science of communication] (V. Romano, Trans.). Barcelona: Anthropos. (Original work published 1976)

Betti, E. (1980). Hermeneutics as the general methodology of the *geisteswissenschaften*. In J. Beicher, (Ed.), *Contemporary hermeneutics: Hermeneutics as method, philosophy, and critique* (pp. 51-94). London: Routledge and Kegan Paul.

Bitzer, L. F. (1985). Colloquium, University of Washington, Department of Speech Communication, Spring, 1985.

My comments in chapter 1 on the Scottish rhetoricians are indebted to Bitzer's oral presentation. For parallel comments, see Bitzer's introduction to his latest edition of Campbell's *Philosophy of Rhetoric.*—J.A.C.

Bizell, P., & Herzberg, B. (Eds.). (1990). *The rhetorical tradition: Readings from classical times to the present.* Boston: Bedford Books of St. Martin's Press.
This is the best anthology now available of major rhetorical writings from the rhetorical tradition. It has helpful and perspicuous introductions to each major rhetorical period and a generous sampling of key texts from the sophists to the deconstructionists.—J.A.C.

Black, E. (1958). Plato's view of rhetoric. *The Quarterly Journal of Speech, 44,* 361-374.

Black, E. (1965). *Rhetorical criticism: A Study in method.* Madison: University of Wisconsin Press.

Blair, H. (1965). *Lectures on rhetoric and belles lettres* (2 Vols.). Carbondale: Southern Illinois University Press.
Hugh Blair, as George Kennedy notes, is the British Quintilian. Blair summarizes a tradition in decline and demonstrates the utility of rhetoric as an instrument of stylistic analysis. His examination of the aesthetics of style, particularly his Longinian accounts of the terrible, are still of interest. Blair is a testament to the power of the rhetorical tradition—even in a fragmented form—to exert a distinctly intellectual allure. No less distinguished a rhetorical teacher than Edward P. J. Corbett found his vocation when he chanced upon Blair in the college library as an undergraduate. As Blair's contemporary Robert Burns aptly observed, Blair is a monument to what perseverance and application can achieve.—J.A.C.

Bloom, A. (1990). Commerce and "culture." *Giants and dwarfs: Essays, 1960-1990* (pp. 277-294). New York: Simon & Schuster.

Bloom, H. (1973). *The anxiety of influence: A theory of poetry.* New York: Oxford University Press.

Bloom, H. (1975). *A map of misreading.* New York: Oxford University Press.

Bloom, H. (1990). *The book of J* (with the text of J, D. Rosenberg, Trans.). New York: Grove/Weidenfeld.

Bloor, D. (1976). *Knowledge and social imagery.* London: Routledge.

Bly, R. (1990). *Iron John: A book about men.* Reading, MA: Addison-Wesley.

Boman, T. (1960). *Hebrew thought compared with Greek* (J. L. Moreau, Trans.). London: SCM Press. (Original work published 1954)

Booth, W. C. (1961). *The rhetoric of fiction.* Chicago: University of Chicago Press.

Booth, W. C. (1974). *Modern dogma and the rhetoric of assent.* Chicago: University of Chicago Press.

Booth, W. C. (1976). M. H. Abrams: Historian as critic: Critic as pluralist. *Critical Inquiry, 2,* 411-445.

Booth, W. C. (1984). Introduction. In M. Bakhtin, *Problems of Dostoyevsky's Poetics* (C. Emerson, Ed. and Trans.; pp. xiii-xxvii). Minneapolis: University of Minnesota Press.

Bradshaw, J. (1988). *Healing the shame that binds you.* Deerfield Beach, FL: Health Communications.

Bradshaw, J. (1990). *Homecoming: Reclaiming and championing your inner child.* New York: Bantam Books.

Bradshaw, J. (1992). *Creating love: The next great stage of growth.* New York: Bantam Books.

Brehier, E. (1949). Originalite de Lévy-Bruhl. *Revue philosophique de la France...,* *139,* 385-388.

Brent, D. (1991). Young, Becker, and Pike's "Rogerian" rhetoric: A twenty-year reassessment. *College English, 53,* 452-466.

Brodkey, L. (1987). Modernism and the scene(s) of writing. *College English, 49,* 396-418.

Brown, H. I. (1977). *Perception, theory, and commitment: The new philosophy of science.* Chicago: Precedent.

Brown, R. H. (Ed.). (1992). *Writing the social text: Poetics and politics in social science discourse.* New York: Aldine de Gruyter.

Bruns, G. L. (1982). *Inventions: Writing, textuality, and understanding in literary history.* New Haven: Yale University Press.

Bruss, E. (1982). *Beautiful theories: The spectacle of discourse in contemporary criticism.* Baltimore: Johns Hopkins University Press.

Buber, M. (1970). *I and Thou* (W. Kaufman, Trans.). New York: Scribner. (Original work published 1923)

Buck, G. (1978). The structure of hermeneutic experience and the problem of tradition. *New Literary History, 10,* 31-47.

Burke, E. (1909). On the sublime and beautiful *and* Reflections on the revolution in France. New York: P. F. Collier & Son, the Harvard Classics, Vol. 24.

Aside from his aesthetic comments in *On the Sublime,* Edmund Burke did not reflect specifically on rhetoric. His whole career as an eloquent and philosophically informed advocate and particularly his admiration of Cicero and Demosthenes, and his critique of the narrow rationalism of the French Revolution profoundly echo a rhetorical understanding of the person, community, and tradition.—J.A.C.

Burke, K. (1945). *A grammar of motives.* New York: Prentice-Hall.

The *Grammar* sets forth a perspective on rhetoric in a broad and catholic sense. Kenneth Burke does not so much repeat classical rhetoric as reinvent it. Particularly of interest to Lonergan readers is Burke's emphasis, following Aquinas, on "act." Burke's distinction between "action" and "motion" is central for his critique of scientism and his reaffirmation of a broad and critical rhetorical humanism.—J.A.C.

Burke, K. (1950). *A rhetoric of motives.* New York: Prentice-Hall.

*A Rhetoric of Motives* builds upon and extends the foundation of the *Grammar.* Its topics include: the range of rhetoric, the traditional principles of rhetoric, and rhetoric as a principle of order. For Lonergan readers interested in a sympathetic but penetrating critique of Burke, see Jost, 1989, chapter 5.—J.A.C.

Burke, K. (1966). *Language as symbolic action: Essays on life, literature, and method.* Berkeley and Los Angeles: University of California Press.

Campbell, G. (1988). *The philosophy of rhetoric* (L. F. Bitzer, Ed. and author of critical introduction). Carbondale: University of Southern Illinois Press.

George Campbell's work was explicitly designed not as a working rhetoric in the sense of Blair's but as a philosophical examination of the subject itself. Building on the foundations of modern science, and particularly on the foundation of Hume, Campbell offers what in equal truth might be called a "psychology" of rhetoric. Since, for Campbell, rhetoric had no distinctively cognitive function, its interest—and the value of traditional rhetorical lore—lay in its status as a psychological pharmacopeia. Across the abyss of Humean skepticism, Campbell builds a psychological suspension bridge illuminated by "lively ideas"—verbal affects so jolting as to rival the status of sense impressions! Campbell's rhetoric is a distinguished, even heroic, attempt to understand a tradition from within a horizon that could not possibly comprehend it. Bitzer's introductory essay is indispensable for understanding the mental world of Campbell's work.—J.A.C.

Campbell, J. A. (1982). Eric Voegelin's order in history: A review. *The Quarterly Journal of Speech, 68,* 80-91.

Campbell, J. A. (1984a). Eric Voegelin's thought: A critical appraisal. *The Quarterly Journal of Speech, 70,* 103-105.

Campbell, J. A. (1984b). A rhetorical interpretation of history. *Rhetorica, 2,* 227-266.

Campbell, J. A. (1985). Insight and understanding: The "common sense" rhetoric of Bernard Lonergan. *The Quarterly Journal of Speech, 71,* 476-488.

Campbell, J. A. (1986). Scientific revolution and the grammar of culture: The case of Darwin's *Origin. The Quarterly Journal of Speech, 72,* 351-376.

Campbell, J. A. (1990). Scientific discovery and rhetorical invention: The path to Darwin's *Origin.* In H. W. Simons (Ed.), *The rhetorical turn: Invention and persuasion in the conduct of inquiry* (pp. 58-90). Chicago: University of Chicago Press.

Capra, F. (1975). *The Tao of physics: An exploration of the parallels between modern physics and eastern mysticism.* Berkeley: Shambhala.

Capra, F., & Steindl-Rast, D. (1991). *Belonging to the universe: Explorations on the frontiers of science and spirituality.* San Francisco: Harper & Row.

Carnoy, M., Castells, M., Cohen, S. S., & Cardoso, F. H. (1993). *The new global economy in the information age: Reflections on our changing world.* University Park: Pennsylvania State University Press.

Carruthers, M. J. (1990). *The book of memory: A study of memory in medieval culture.* Cambridge, UK: Cambridge University Press.

Carter, M. F. (1991). The ritual functions of epideictic rhetoric: The case of Socrates' funeral oration. *Rhetorica, 9,* 209-232.

Chalmers, A. F. (1990). *Science and its fabrication.* Minneapolis: University of Minnesota Press.

Chenu, M.-D. (1964). Un concile "pastoral" [A "pastoral" council]. In *La parole de Dieu.* Vol. II: *L'evangile dans le temps.* Paris: Cerf. (Original article published 1963)

Cherwitz, R. A. (Ed.). (1990). *Rhetoric and philosophy.* Hillsdale, NJ: Lawrence Erlbaum Associates.

Coe, R. M. (1987). An apology for form; or, Who took the form out of the process? *College English, 49,* 13-28.

Cole, S. (1992). *Making science: Between nature and society.* Cambridge, MA: Harvard University Press.

Conley, T. M. (1990). *Rhetoric in the European tradition.* London: Longman.
    Thomas Conley's text provides a fine balance between a detailed yet concise and critical overview of major periods in rhetorical thought with generous subject-matter outlines from the principal texts discussed. One of the many strengths of this text is its account of Jesuit and German rhetorics of the 17th

century. His account of Caussin, Keckermann, and Vossius nicely counterbalances the traditional over-emphasis, particularly in North America, on the British tradition. Conley's silence on deconstruction is a great relief, and his tracing of the 20th-century tradition through I.A. Richards, Kenneth Burke, Richard Weaver, Richard McKeon, Stephen Toulmin, and Jürgen Habermas is insightful and instructive.—J.A.C.

Conn, W. E. (1976a). Bernard Lonergan on value. *The Thomist, 40*, 243-257.

Conn, W. E. (1976b). Objectivity—a developmental and structural analysis: The epistemologies of Jean Piaget and Bernard Lonergan. *Dialectica, 30*, 197-221.

Conn, W. E. (1977). Transcendental analysis of conscious subjectivity: Bernard Lonergan's empirical methodology. *Modern Schoolman, 54*, 215-231.

Conn, W. E. (1981). *Conscience: Development and self-transcendence.* Birmingham, AL: Religious Education Press.

Conn's work, like Doran's, stresses Lonergan's later thought, especially his increasing concern for the human subject. His treatment of Lonergan's perspective on the person and ethics is eminently instructive and clearly written.—J.A.C.

Connolly, W. (1984). Taylor, Foucault, and otherness. *Political Theory, 12*, 365-376.

Connolly, W. E. (1987). *Politics and ambiguity.* Madison: University of Wisconsin Press.

Connors, R. J. (1986). Greek rhetoric and the transition from orality. *Philosophy and Rhetoric, 19*, 38-65.

Cooley, L. (1988). B. F. Skinner's radical behaviorist theory of the cognitive dimension of consciousness: A Lonerganian critique. *Method, 6*, 107-137.

Corbett, E. P. J. (1990). *Classical rhetoric for the modern student* (3rd ed.). New York: Oxford University Press.

Cox, R. J., & Willard, C. A. (1982). Introduction: The field of argumentation. In R. J. Cox & C. A. Willard (Eds.), *Advances in argumentation theory and research* (pp. xiii-xlvii). Carbondale: Southern Illinois University Press.

Croll, M. W. (1966). *Style, rhetoric, and rhythm: Essays by Morris W. Croll* (J. M. Patrick & R. O. Evans with J. M. Wallace & R. J. Schoeck, Eds.). Princeton: Princeton University Press.

Cronkhite, G. (1969). *Persuasion: Speech and behavioral change.* Indianapolis: Bobbs-Merrill.

Crowe, F. E. (1955). Universal norms and the concrete "operabile" in St. Thomas Aquinas. *Sciences ecclesiastiques, 7*, 114-149; 257-291.

Crowe, F. E. (1961). St. Thomas and the isomorphism of human knowing and its proper object. *Sciences ecclesiastques, 13*, 167-190.

Crowe, F. E. (1967). Editor's introduction. In B. Lonergan, *Collection* (pp. vii-xxxv). New York: Herder & Herder.

Crowe, F. E. (1980). *The Lonergan enterprise.* Cambridge, MA: Cowley.

Crowe, F. E. (1983). Lonergan's early use of analogy. *Method: Journal of Lonergan Studies, 1*, 31-46.

Crowe, F. E. (1985). *Old things and new: A strategy for education.* Atlanta: Scholars Press.

Crowe, F. E. (1989). *Appropriating the Lonergan idea* (M. Vertin, Ed.). Washington, DC: Catholic University of America Press.

Crowe, F. E. (1992). *Lonergan.* Collegeville, MN: Michael Glazier/Liturgical Press.

Davies, B. (1992). *The thought of Thomas Aquinas.* Oxford: Clarendon Press of Oxford University Press.

Dawson, C. (1928). *The age of the gods.* London: J. Murray.

Dear, P. (Ed.). (1991). *The literary structure of scientific argument: Historical studies.* Philadelphia: University of Pennsylvania Press.

de Quincey, T. (1967). *Selected essays on rhetoric.* Carbondale: Southern Illinois University Press.

While Thomas de Quincey is far more interesting to read than is Hugh Blair, his rhetorical writings are no more original, are scarcely more deep, and are principally of interest as symptoms of a high tradition gone to seed. While recognizing via Whately and Aristotle the technical claim of rhetoric to be the study of argument, de Quincey treats rhetoric as a relic of the past and uses the tradition as a storehouse of techniques with which he pleasantly diverts the undemanding reader.—J.A.C.

de Romilly, J. (1992). *The great sophists in Periclean Athens* (J. Lloyd, Trans.). New York: Oxford University Press. (Original work published 1988)

In this compact volume, Jacqueline de Romilly provides both original analysis from original sources and, what is equally important, fresh perspective on what is already known. To the novice, the book explains, for example, exactly how many teachers and of what kind traditional aristocratic education provided. This and similar information prepares the reader to appreciate the full force of why the sophistic program of continuing learning was such a cultural revolution. Again and again, the reader has the "Oh I see" experience that reconfigures prior knowledge by providing missing context while enabling the reader to understand and assimilate new information. For the professional, the volume patiently challenges previous one-sided interpretations and presents a persuasive case for understanding the tension between the radical and the conservative dimensions of sophistic thought. De Romilly presents the sophists, beginning with Protagoras, both as radicals—people who discovered the mind and its public uses—and as conservatives—thinkers who were concerned to provide a new foundation for justice, piety, and right order in the polis. The effect of the book is to establish the sophists as premier intellectuals and to reconfigure one's understanding of the historical origins of the Western intellectual tradition.—J.A.C.

Derrida, J. (1973). *Speech and phenomena* (D. B. Allison, Trans.). Evanston: Northwestern University Press. (Original work published 1967)

Derrida, J. (1976). *Of grammatology* (G. C. Spivak, Trans.). Baltimore: Johns Hopkins University Press. (Original work published 1967)

Derrida, J. (1978). *Writing and difference* (A. Bass, Trans.). Chicago: University of Chicago Press. (Original work published 1967)

Derrida, J. (1981). *Positions* (A. Bass, Trans.). Chicago: University of Chicago Press. (Original work published 1972)

Derrida, J. (1982). *Margins of philosophy* (A. Bass, Trans.). Chicago: University of Chicago Press. (Original work published 1972)

Derrida, J. (1988). *Limited inc* (S. Weber & J. Mehlman, Trans.). Evanston: Northwestern University Press. (Original work published 1977)

Dieter, O. A. L. (1959). Stasis. *Speech Monographs, 17,* 345-369.

This classic essay is arguably the definitive account of "stasis." Otto Alvin Loeb Dieter carefully places "stasis" in the context of Greek physics and political culture and explicates how the physical meaning informs and animates the rhetorical concept.—J.A.C.

Dillon, G. L. (1991). *Contending rhetorics: Writing in the academic disciplines.* Bloomington: University of Indiana Press.

Doran, R. M. (1979a). Aesthetic subjectivity and generalized empirical method. *The Thomist, 43*, 257-278.

Doran, R. M. (1979b). *Subject and psyche: Ricoeur, Jung, and the search for foundations.* Washington, DC: University Press of America.
A reader who is familiar with Gadamer, Bernstein, or Ricoeur will find Robert Doran's book a natural introduction to Lonergan. The first chapter, "Logic, Method, and Psyche" offers a good summary and critique of *Insight* and of the later developments in Lonergan's thought. Readers will find his discussion of Lonergan, Ricoeur, Kant, Jung, and Freud (chapters 4, 5, & 6) instructive and profound.—J.A.C.

Doran, R. M. (1981a). Dramatic artistry in the third stage of meaning. *The Lonergan Workshop, 2*, 147-199.

Doran, R. M. (1981b). *Psychic conversion and theological foundations: Toward a reorientation of the human sciences.* Chico, CA: Scholars Press.

Doran, R. M. (1981c). Theological grounds for a world-cultural humanity. In M. L. Lamb (Ed.), *Creativity and method: Essays in honor of Bernard Lonergan, S.J.* (pp. 105-122). Milwaukee: Marquette University Press.

Doran, R. M. (1984). Theology's situation: Questions to Eric Voegelin. In F. Lawrence (Ed.), *The beginning and the beyond* (pp. 69-91). Supplementary issue of *The Lonergan Workshop*, Vol. 4.

Doran, R. M. (1988a). The analogy of dialectic and the systematics of history. In T. P. Fallon & P. B. Riley (Eds.), *Religion in context: Recent studies in Lonergan* (pp. 35-57). Lanham, MD: University Press of America.

Doran, R. M. (1988b). Introduction: An appreciation. In V. Gregson (Ed.), *The desires of the human heart* (pp. 1-15). New York: Paulist Press.

Doran, R. M. (1990). *Theology and the dialectics of history.* Toronto: University of Toronto Press.

Doran, R. M. (1991). Bernard Lonergan and the future of theology. *Canadian Theological Society Newsletter, 10*(2), 1-5.

Dubois, W. E. B. (1973). *The souls of black folk* (H. Aptheker, Ed.). Milwood, NY: Draus-Thomson Organization. (Original work published 1900)

Dumm, T. L. (1987). *Democracy and punishment: Disciplinary origins in the United States.* Madison: University of Wisconsin Press.

Edinger, E. F. (1972). *Ego and archetype: Individuation and the religious function of the psyche.* New York: Putnam.

Ehninger, D. (1963). The logic of argument. In J. H. McBath (Ed.), *Argumentation and debate: Principles and practices* (rev. ed.; pp. 169-191). New York: Holt, Rinehart, & Winston.

Eliade, M. (1954). *The myth of the eternal return.* New York: Pantheon Books. (Original work published 1949)

Eliade, M. (1959). *The sacred and the profane.* New York: Harcourt, Brace. (Original work published 1957)

Eliot, T. S. (1975). Tradition and the individual talent. In F. Kermode (Ed.), *Selected prose of T. S. Eliot* (pp. 37-44). New York: Harcourt, Brace, Jovanovich/Farrar, Straus, & Giroux. (Original work published 1919)

Enos, R. L. (1976). The epistemology of Gorgias' rhetoric: A re-examination. *The Southern Speech Communication Journal, 42*, 35-51.

Enos, R. L. (1981). Emerging notions of heuristic, eristic, and protreptic rhetoric in Homeric discourse: Proto-literate conniving, wrangling, and reasoning. In M. C. Hairston & C. L. Selfe (Eds.), *Selected papers from the 1981 Texas writing research conference* (pp. 44-64). Austin: University of Texas.

Enos, R. L. (1991). Socrates questions Gorgias: The rhetorical vector of Plato's *Gorgias*. *Argumentation, 5*, 5-15.

Enos, R. L. (1993). *Greek rhetoric before Aristotle*. Prospect Heights, IL: Waveland Press.

Enos, T., & Brown, S. C. (Eds.). (1993). *Defining the new rhetorics*. Newbury Park, CA: Sage Publications.

Eric Voegelin Institute of Louisiana State University. (1992). *Bibliography of works by and about Eric Voegelin*. Baton Rouge: Louisiana State University.

Faigley, L. (1989). Judging writing, judging selves. *College Composition and Communication, 40*, 395-412.

Fallon, T. P., & Riley, P. B. (Eds.). (1987). *Religion and Culture: Essays in honor of Bernard Lonergan, S.J.* Albany: State University of New York Press.

Farrell, T. J. (1979). The female and male modes of rhetoric. *College English, 40*, 909-921.

Farrell, T. J. (1983). IQ and standard English. *College Composition and Communication, 34*, 470-484.

Farrell, T. J. (1991). An overview of Walter J. Ong's work. In B. E. Gronbeck, T. J. Farrell, & P. A. Soukup (Eds.), *Media, consciousness, and culture: Explorations of Walter Ong's thought* (pp. 25-43). Newbury Park, CA: Sage Publications.

Farrell, T. J. (1992a). An introduction to Walter Ong's work. In W. J. Ong, *Faith and contexts: Selected esssays and studies 1952-1991*: Volume one (T. J. Farrell & P. A. Soukup, Eds.; pp. xix-lv). Atlanta: Scholars Press.

Farrell, T. J. (1992b). The Wyoming resolution, higher wizardry, and the importance of writing instruction. *College Composition and Communication, 43*, 158-164, 175.

Featherstone, M. (Ed.). (1990). *Global culture: Nationalism, globalization, and modernity*. London: Sage Publications.

Ferguson, M. (1980). *The Aquarian conspiracy: Personal and social transformation in the 1980s*. Los Angeles: J.P. Tarcher.

Fisher, W. R. (1987). *Human communication as narration: Toward a philosophy of reason, value, and action*. Columbia: University of South Carolina Press.

Fisher's work is a distinguished and richly suggestive account of rhetorical reason and a testament to the intellectual vitality of the contemporary rhetorical renaissance. In his early chapters Fisher offers a concise and illuminating summary of the rhetorical tradition and its quarrel with philosophy and in his later ones sketches his view of the human person as "homo narrans" and of "narrative rationality" as an alternative to "the rational world paradigm." Fisher's account of the topical tradition is of particular value to those interested in the traditional rhetorical view of argument.—J.A.C.

Fitzpatrick, J. (1982). Subjectivity and objectivity: Polanyi and Lonergan. *New Universities Quarterly, 36*, 183-195.

Fitzpatrick, J. (1992). Lonergan and the later Wittgenstein. *Method: Journal of Lonergan Studies, 10*, 27-50.

Flanagan, J. F. (1972). Lonergan's epistemology. *The Thomist, 36*, 75-97.

Foucault M. (1967). Nietzsche, Freud, Marx. *Cahiers de Royaumont, 6*, 183-192.

Foucault, M. (1977). *Discipline and punish: The birth of the prison* (A. Sheridan, Trans.). New York: Random House. (Original work published 1975)

Foucault, M. (1978). *The history of sexuality 1: An introduction* (R. Hurley, Trans.). New York: Random House. (Original work published 1976)

Foucault, M. (1984). *The Foucault reader* (P. Rabinow, Ed.). New York: Pantheon.

Friel, J. (1991). *The grown-up man: Heroes, healing, honor, hurt, hope.* Deerfield Beach, FL: Health Communications.

Frye, N. (1990). *Words with power: Being a second study of "The Bible and literature".* New York: Harcourt Brace Jovanovich.

Fuller, S. (1988). *Social epistemology.* Bloomington: Indiana University Press.

Fuller, S. (1992). Being there with Thomas Kuhn: A parable for postmodern times. *History and theory, 31*, 241-275.

Fuller, S. (1993a). *Philosophy of science and its discontents* (2nd ed.). New York: Guilford.

Fuller, S. (1993b). *Philosophy, rhetoric, and the end of knowledge: The coming of science and technology studies.* Madison: University of Wisconsin Press.

Gabin, R. J. (1987). Aristotle and the new rhetoric: Grimaldi and Valesio. *Philosophy and Rhetoric, 20*, 171-182.

Gadamer, H.-G. (1990). *Truth and method* (2nd rev. ed., J. Weinsheimer & D. G. Marshall, Trans.). New York: Crossroad. (Original work published 1960)

Hans-Georg Gadamer's revival and universalizing of hermeneutics as the model of what it means to understand has profound resonance with the "sensus communis" central to the rhetorical tradition. The key difference between rhetoric and hermeneutics is the stronger need in rhetoric to proximately close the play of interpretation in judgment; the stronger tie of rhetoric to the active life and political reason and the weaker tie of rhetoric to the contemplative life and textual interpretation.—J.A.C.

Galipeau, S. A. (1990). *Transforming body and soul: Therapeutic wisdom in the Gospel healing stories.* New York: Paulist Press.

Garver, E. (1987). *Machiavelli and the history of prudence.* Madison: University of Wisconsin Press.

Eugene Garver is a rhetorical theorist's rhetorical theorist. In this searching rehabilitation of rhetorical reason, Garver examines rhetoric as a mode of thought and politics as the scene of its occurrence. He provides a detailed meditation on the thesis that Machiavelli stands to prudential reason as does Descartes to algorithmic reason. Garver's account of how the new prince finds the key to untraditional rule through "stable innovation"—the rhetorical and specifically topical use of prior tradition—is a major contribution to rhetorical theory.—J.A.C.

Garver, E. (1994). *Aristotle's* Rhetoric *and the professionalization of virtue.* Chicago: University of Chicago Press.

Garver's work is the first book-length philosophic treatment of Aristotle's *Rhetoric* in English in this century. Though much has been written on the *Rhetoric* in English in this century, Garver's is the first work to treat the *Rhetoric* as an instance of philosophic inquiry to be judged by philosophic standards. Garver's title, *Aristotle's* Rhetoric *and the Professionalization of Virtue,* is meant to signal how Aristotle's practical civic art of rhetoric lies between the activities of practical reason, for which moral character is enough, and instrumental activities, which can be bought, sold, and taught. That location makes an examination of rhetoric important for understanding practical reason and for understanding the relations of the virtues of character to arts and to practical success. The book is a fitting complement to his earlier *Machiavelli and the History of Prudence* for the way it more fully develops Garver's project of the "history of prudence."

Genova, A. C. (1984). Good transcendental arguments. *Kant-Studien, 75,* 469-495.

Gerhart, M. (1981). The question of belief in literary criticism. In M. L. Lamb (Ed.), *Creativity and method: Essays in honor of Bernard Lonergan, S.J.* (pp. 383-398). Milwaukee: Marquette University Press.

Gibson, W. (1966). *Tough, sweet, and stuffy: An essay on modern American prose styles.* Bloomington: Indiana University Press.

Gilder, G. (1981). *Wealth and poverty.* New York: Basic Books.

Gilmore, D. D. (1990). *Manhood in the making: Cultural concepts of masculinity.* New Haven: Yale University Press.

Gooding, D., Pinch, T., & Schaffer, S. (Eds.). (1989). *The uses of experiment: Studies in the natural sciences.* Cambridge, UK: Cambridge University Press.

Granfield, D. (1991). *Heightened consciousness: The mystic difference.* New York: Paulist Press.

Grassi, E. (1980). *Rhetoric as philosophy: The humanist tradition.* University Park: Pennsylvania State University Press.

Ernesto Grassi is a major contemporary disciple of Vico. His book presents rhetoric as virtually a mode of perception grounded in history, language, community and work—or shared tasks. The book provides an important explication of rhetoric as a mode of reason larger than rationalism and tied closely to imagination and poetry yet also politics and practical life.—J.A.C.

G[raubard], S. R. (1965). Preface. *Daedalus, 94*(1), iii.

Grave, S. A. (1960). *The Scottish philosophy of common sense.* Oxford: Clarendon Press of Oxford University Press.

S. A. Grave's is an indispensable work for anyone interested in the early Scottish philosophy—particularly the philosophy of Reid. Grave is particularly good on the common starting point of this school in Hume and how Common Sense Philosophy at once accepted Hume's skepticism yet tried to avoid its apparent consequences for religion and practical life. Grave does not consider later Scottish thinkers such as Brown and Hamilton as part of this school—and this choice gives his book a particularly narrow if sharp focus.—J.A.C.

Green, M. (1993). *The adventurous male: Chapters in the history of the white male mind.* University Park: Pennsylvania State University Press.

Gregson, V., (Ed.). (1988). *The desires of the human heart: An introduction to the theology of Bernard Lonergan.* New York: Paulist Press.

Grimaldi, W. M. A. (1978). Rhetoric and truth: A note on Aristotle, *Rhetoric* 1355a 21-24. *Philosophy and Rhetoric, 11,* 173-177.

Grimaldi, W. M. A. (1990). The auditors' role in Aristotelian rhetoric. In R. L. Enos (Ed.), *Oral and written communication: Historical approaches* (pp. 65-81). Newbury Park, CA: Sage Publications.

Gross, A. G. (1990). *The rhetoric of science.* Cambridge, MA: Harvard University Press.

Alan Gross is one of the founders of the current rhetoric of science school. Most instructive in Gross is the radical strain in his thought that leads him to argue for the reduction of science to rhetoric "without remainder." His book provides numerous instructive case studies of the power of rhetorical analysis to illuminate scientific texts.—J.A.C.

Grube, G. M. A. (Trans.). (1974). *Plato's* Republic. Indianapolis: Hackett Publishing.

Guthrie, W. K. C. (1971). *The sophists.* Cambridge, UK: Cambridge University Press.

Gutierrez, G. (1973). *A theology of liberation.* Maryknoll, NY: Orbis.

Habermas, J. (1977). A review of Gadamer's *Truth and method.* In F. R. Dallmayr, & T. A. McCarthy (Eds.), *Understanding and social inquiry* (pp. 335-363). Notre Dame, IN: University of Notre Dame Press.

Habermas, J. (1979). What is universal pragmatics? In J. Habermas, *Communication and the evolution of society* (T. McCarthy, Trans.; pp. 1-69). Boston: Beacon Press. (Original work published 1976)

Habermas, J. (1984). *Theory of communicative action: Reason and the rationalization of society,* Vol. 1. (T. McCarthy, Trans.). Boston: Beacon Press. (Original work published 1981)

Habermas, J. (1986). Wahrheitstheorien [Theory of truth]. In J. Habermas, *Vorstudien und ergänzungen zur theorie des kommunikativen handelns* (2nd ed.; pp. 127-183). Frankfurt am Main: Suhrkamp.

Habermas, J. (1987a). *The philosophical discourse of modernity: Twelve lectures* (F. Lawrence, Trans.). Cambridge, MA: MIT Press. (Original work published 1985)

Habermas, J. (1987b). *The theory of communicative action: The critique of functionalist reason,* Vol. 2 (T. McCarthy, Trans.). Cambridge, UK: Polity Press. (Original work published 1981)

Habermas, J. (1991). *Erläuterung zur diskursethik.* Frankfurt am Main: Suhrkamp. [Translation by C. Cronin now available under the title *Justification and application: Remarks on discourse ethics* from MIT Press, 1993]

Habermas, J. (1992). Toward a critique of the theory of meaning. In J. Habermas, *Postmetaphysical thinking: Philosophical essays* (W. Hohengarten, Trans.; pp. 57-87). Cambridge: MIT Press. (Original work published 1988)

Hairston, M. (1976). Carl Rogers's alternative to traditional rhetoric. *College Composition and Communication, 27,* 373-377.

Haughton, R. (1981). *The passionate God.* New York: Paulist Press.

Havelock, E. A. (1978). *The Greek concept of justice: From its shadow in Homer to its substance in Plato.* Cambridge, MA: Harvard University Press.

Havelock, E. A. (1982). *The literate revolution in Greece and its cultural consequences.* Princeton: Princeton University Press.

Heidegger, M. (1962). *Being and time* (J. Macquarrie & E. Robinson, Trans.). New York: Harper & Row. (Original work published 1927)

Heidegger, M. (1977). Letter on humanism. In D. F. Krell (Ed.), *Basic writings from Being and time to* The task of thinking (pp. 189-242). New York: Harper & Row.

Heidegger, M. (1979-1987). *Nietzsche*, 4 vols. (D. F. Krell, J. Stambaugh, & F. A. Capuzzi, Trans.). New York: Harper & Row. (Original work published 1961)

Hempel, C. (1966). *Philosophy of natural science*. Englewood Cliffs, NJ: Prentice-Hall.

Hesse, M. (1975). Lonergan and method in the natural sciences. In P. Corcoran (Ed.), *Looking at Lonergan's method* (pp. 59-72). Dublin: Talbot.

Hesse, M. (1980). *Revolutions and reconstructions in the philosophy of science.* Bloomington: Indiana University Press.

Hill, W. J. (1976-1977). Preaching as a "moment" in theology. *Homiletic and Pastoral Review, 77*, 10-19.

Hirsch, E. D. (1967). *Validity in interpretation.* New Haven: Yale University Press.

Hitchcock, J. (1991). *The web of the universe: Jung, the "new physics," and human spirituality.* New York: Paulist Press.

Holton, G. (1965). Introduction. *Daedalus, 94*(1), vii-xxiii.

Holton, G. (1973). *Thematic origins of scientific thought: Kepler to Einstein.* Cambridge, MA: Harvard University Press.

Homer, W. B (1988). *Rhetoric in the classical tradition.* New York: St. Martin's Press.

Homer, W. B. (1990). *The present state of scholarship in historical and contemporary rhetoric* (rev. ed.). Columbia: University of Missouri Press.

Homey, K. (1945). *Our inner conflicts: A constructive theory of neurosis.* New York: Norton.

Hoy, D. (1975). Literary history: Paradigm or paradox? *Yale French Studies, 52*, 268-286.

Huizinga, J. (1955). *Homo ludens: A study of the play element in culture.* Boston: Beacon Press. (Original work published 1944)

Irigaray L. (1985). *Speculum of the other woman* (G. C. Gill, Trans.). Ithaca, NY: Cornell University Press. (Original work published 1974)

Iser, W. (1978). *The act of reading: A theory of aesthetic response* (D. H. Wilson, Trans.). Baltimore: Johns Hopkins University Press. (Original work published 1976)

Jacques, F. (1985). *L'Espace logique de l'interlocution: Dialogiques II* [The logical space of interlocution: Dialogues II]. Paris: Presses Universitaires de France.

Jarratt, S. C. (1991). *Rereading the sophists: Classical rhetoric refigured.* Carbondale: Southern Illinois University Press.

Susan Jarratt seeks to understand, reclaim, and advance the sophistic legacy of the rhetorical tradition. Her study places the contemporary recovery of the sophists in historical perspective and examines the sophists as a cultural phenomenon and as distinctly rhetorical educators and thinkers. She relates their cultural critique to feminism—noting that while the sophists were not feminists their cultural practice serves as an important guide to the contemporary movement. The book is particularly strong in its account of the sophists' educational program and its contemporary implications.—J.A.C.

Johann, R. O. (1971). Lonergan and Dewey on judgment. *International Philosophical Quarterly, 11*, 461-474.

John XXIII, Pope. (1963). Concilium oecumenicum Vatican II sollemniter inchoatur [The ecumenical council Vatican II is solemnly begun]. *Acta apostolicae sedis*, *54*, 785-795.

John XXIII, Pope. (1964). Allocutiones...IV [Addresses...IV]. *Acta apostolicae sedis*, *55*, 43-45.

Jones, R. S. (1982). *Physics as metaphor*. Minneapolis: University of Minnesota Press.

Jonsen, A. R., & Toulmin, S. (1988). *The abuse of casuistry: A history of moral reasoning*. Berkeley and Los Angeles: University of California Press.

Albert Jonsen and Stephen Toulmin here reclaim casuistry or "case reasoning" as a central thread in the rhetorical tradition. The book offers an excellent history of case reasoning, tracing it from Aristotle to Cicero—its virtual father—and from him to the confessional practice of the medieval church to its qualitative decline in the post-Council-of-Trent church. The book examines how case reasoning never quite recovered from Pascal's devastating critique in his *Provincial Letters* and how ethical theory increasingly became abstract and removed from the particulars of life and application—reaching its nadir in the 19th and early 20th centuries. The authors argue the vital need for case reasoning in medical ethics and how the entire modern ideal of an ethics grounded in abstract theory is not only unworkable but is inhumane and indeed irrational. This book is a major landmark in the contemporary reclamation of traditional rhetoric as a mode of reason.—J.A.C.

Jonsen, A. R. (1990). *The new medicine and the old ethics*. Cambridge, MA: Harvard University Press.

For readers intrigued by the prospect of rhetorical reason but uncertain of how it might be applied as a program of cultural reclamation alternative to positivism and deconstruction—look no further. Rhetorical reason is less a program to be trumpeted—though Copeland's "Fanfare to the Common Man" would be appropriate—but a tradition to be appropriated (in Lonergan's sense) as the immanent remedy of the desire to know for those whom scientism and subjectivism have incapacitated for thought. Jonsen locates the task of rhetorical reason—particularly topical reason—in the indelible ambiguities of experience where value conflicts with value and good with good. He carefully explicates how value may be matched with value and tradition mined to reveal a rationale for change. Beyond its instructive value about medicine and ethics, Jonsen's book is, in the spirit of Newman and Lonergan, a performance of rhetorical reason as a living habit of mind.—J.A.C.

Jost, W. (1989). *Rhetorical thought in John Henry Newman*. Columbia: University of South Carolina Press.

In the wake of this book, the traditional account of Anglo-American rhetorical theory that moves from the Scottish tradition of Hume, Campbell, Blair, and Whately to a dull line of derivative theorists until the rhetorical awakening of our own time must be a thing of the past. Walter Jost's account provides striking evidence of continuity between Newman's innovations in rhetorical theory and central themes in contemporary rhetorical revival. Jost shows how the key to understanding Newman is to understand his grounding in the rhetorical tradition—particularly the tradition of Cicero on which he wrote a major essay early in his career. Jost brilliantly explicates Newman's recovery of topical reason and examines how he deploys elements of the Ciceronian tradition while scarcely ever invoking formal rhetorical terms.—J.A.C.

Kant, I. (1922). *Gesammelte schriften* [Collected writings]. Berlin: Walter de Grunter.

Kant, I. (1965). *Critique of pure reason* (N. K. Smith, Trans.). New York: St. Martin's Press. (Original work published 1787)

Kant, I. (1987). *Critique of judgment* (W. S. Pluhar, Trans.). Indianapolis: Hackett. (Original work published 1790)

Kastely, J. L. (1991). In defense of Plato's *Gorgias. PMLA, 106,* 96-109.

Kaufer, D. S. (1978). Plato's developing psychology of rhetoric. *The Quarterly Journal of Speech, 64,* 63-78.

Kaufman, G. (1985). *Shame: The power of caring* (2nd ed.). Rochester, VT: Schenkman Books.

Kaufman, G. (1989). *The psychology of shame: Theory and treatment of shame-based syndromes.* New York: Springer Publishing.

Keen, S. (1991). *Fire in the belly: On being a man.* New York: Bantam.

Kellner, H. (1989). *Language and historical representation: Getting the story crooked.* Madison: University of Wisconsin Press.

Kelly, J. C. (1981). *A philosophy of communication.* London: Centre for the Study of Communication and Culture.

Kennedy, G. A. (1980). *Classical rhetoric and its Christian and secular tradition from ancient to modern times.* Chapel Hill: University of North Carolina Press.

If one were to have only one book on rhetoric, not so long as Vickers' nor as pedagogic as Conley's nor as encyclopedic as Bizzell and Herzberg's and were willing to call it a day with the 18th century, this is the book. Kennedy provides a masterful introduction to the rhetorical tradition and so infuses his account with the relevance of the tradition for the present as to nearly compensate for his shorter historical sweep. His opening account of traditional and conceptual rhetoric and his discrimination in the following chapters between technical and philosophic rhetoric provide the reader extremely useful handles with which to grasp the varieties of the tradition as a whole. His account of Judaeo-Christian rhetoric is at once concise and informative and his concluding "Dialogue of Orators" provides an excellent restatement of the abiding questions and tensions of the tradition.—J.A.C.

Kerferd, G. B. (1981). *The sophistic movement.* Cambridge, UK: Cambridge University Press.

Kidder, P. (1986). Lonergan and the Husserlian problem of transcendental intersubjectivity. *Method, 4,* 29-54.

Kimball, B. A. (1986). *Orators and philosophers: A history of the idea of liberal education.* New York: Teachers College Press.

Kinneavy, J. L. (1971). *A theory of discourse.* Englewood Cliffs, NJ: Prentice-Hall.

Kinneavy, J. L. (1987a). *Greek rhetorical origins of Christian faith: An inquiry.* New York: Oxford University Press.

Kinneavy, J. L. (1987b). William Grimaldi—Reinterpreting Aristotle. *Philosophy and Rhetoric, 20,* 183-200.

Kinneavy, J. L. (1990). A sophistic strain in the medieval *ars praedicandi* and the scholastic method. In R. L. Enos (Ed.), *Oral and written communication: Historical approaches* (pp. 82-95). Newbury Park, CA: Sage Publications.

Kipnis, A. R. (1991). *Knights without armor: A practical guide for men in quest of masculine soul.* Los Angeles: Tarcher.

Knoblauch, C. H., & Bannon, L. (1984). *Rhetorical tradition and the teaching of writing.* Upper Montclair, NJ: Boynton/Cook.

Knorr-Cetina, K. D. (1983). The ethnographic study of scientific work: Towards a constructivist interpretation of science. In K. D. Knorr-Cetina & M. Mulkay (Eds.), *Science observed: Perspectives on the social study of science* (pp. 115-140). London: Sage Publications.

Kochman, T. (1974). Orality and literacy as factors of "black" and "white" communicative behavior. *Linguistics, 136*(15 September), 91-115. [Identical contents appear in *International Journal of the Sociology of Language*, No. 3].

Kochman, T. (1981). *Black and white styles in conflict.* Chicago: University of Chicago Press.

Kristeva, J. (1984). *Revolution in poetic language.* New York: Columbia University Press.

Kroger, J. (1977). Polanyi and Lonergan on scientific method. *Philosophy Today, 21,* 2-20.

Kuhn, T. S. (1970). *The structure of scientific revolutions* (2nd ed.). Chicago: University of Chicago Press.

Kurz, P. K. (1965). Literature and naturwissenschaft [Literature and natural science]. *Stimmen der Zeit, 176,* 1-20.

Lacan, J. (1977). *Ecrits: A selection* (A. Sheridan, Trans.). New York: W. W. Norton.

Lakatos, I. (1970). Falsification and the methodology of scientific research programs. In I. Lakatos & A. Musgrave (Eds.), *Criticism and the growth of knowledge* (pp. 91-196). Cambridge, UK: Cambridge University Press.

Lamb, M. L. (1965). Towards a synthesization of the sciences. *Philosophy of Science, 32,* 182-191.

Lamb, M. L. (Ed.). (1981a). *Creativity and method: Essays in honor of Bernard Lonergan, S.J.* Milwaukee: Marquette University Press.

Lamb, M. L. (1981b). Methodology, metascience, and political theology. *The Lonergan Workshop, 2,* 281-403.

Lamb, M. L. (1988). Social and political dimensions of Lonergan's theology. In V. Gregson (Ed.), *The desires of the human heart* (pp. 255-284). New York: Paulist Press.

Langan, T. (1992). *Tradition and authenticity in the search for ecumenic wisdom.* Columbia: University of Missouri Press.

Lanham, R. A. (1976). *The motives of eloquence: Literary rhetoric in the Renaissance.* New Haven: Yale University Press.

Lanham, R. A. (1987). *Revising business prose* (2nd ed.). New York: Macmillan.

Latour, B. (1987). *Science in action: How to follow scientists and engineers through society.* Cambridge, MA: Harvard University Press.

Lawrence, F. (1972). Self-knowledge in history in Gadamer and Lonergan. In P. McShane (Ed.), *Language, truth, and meaning* (pp. 167-217). Dublin: Gill & Macmillan.

Lawrence, F. (1977). On reading a text: Gadamer, hermeneutics, and literary criticism. [Unpublished lecture given at York University, Toronto. Available at the Lonergan Research Institute, Toronto.]

Lawrence, F. (Ed.). (1978, 1981, 1982). *The Lonergan Workshop* (Vols. 1, 2, 3). Chico, CA: Scholars Press. [Also see subsequent volumes.—Eds.]
These workshop papers provide a good sampling of the use being made of Lonergan's perspective in various disciplines. Rhetoricians will find Matthew Lamb's essays of particular interest, e.g.: "Methodology, Metascience and Political Theology" in the second volume. Lamb's work is a fruitful combination of Habermas and Lonergan.—J.A.C.

Lawrence, F. (1978a). The horizon of political theology. In T. A. Dunne & J.-M. Laporte (Eds.), *The trinification of the world: A festschrift in honor of Frederick E. Crowe* (pp. 46-71). Toronto: Regis College.

Lawrence, F. (1978b). Political theology and "the longer cycle of decline." *The Lonergan Workshop, 2,* 223-255.

Lawrence, F. (1980). Gadamer and Lonergan: A dialectical comparison. *International Philosophical Quarterly, 20,* 25-47.

Lawrence, F. (1981). Method and theology as hermeneutical. In M. L. Lamb (Ed.), *Creativity and method: Essays in honor of Bernard Lonergan, S.J.* (pp. 79-104). Milwaukee: Marquette University Press.

Lawrence, F. (1983). Voegelin and theology as hermeneutical and political. In J. Kirby & W. M. Thompson (Eds.), *Voegelin and the theologian: Ten studies in interpretation* (pp. 314-355). Toronto Studies in Theology, Vol. 10. New York: Edwin Mellen Press.

Leitch, V. B. (1983). *Deconstructive criticism: An advanced introduction.* Ithaca, NY: Cornell University Press.

Liddy, R. M. (1993). *Transforming light: Intellectual conversion in the early Lonergan.* Collegeville, MN: Michael Glazier Books/Liturgical Press.

Locke, J. (1924). *An essay concerning human understanding.* Oxford: Clarendon Press.

Lodge, D. (1979). Historicism and literary history: Mapping the modern period. *New Literary History, 10,* 547-555.

Lonergan, B. (1944). *An essay in circulation analysis.* Unpublished manuscript. [Available at the Lonergan Research Institute, Toronto.] Planned to be Vol. 15 of the *Collected works of Bernard Lonergan.*

Lonergan, B. (1946a). *De ente supernaturali* [On supernatural things]. Montreal: College of the Immaculate Conception.

Lonergan, B. (1946b). The concept of verbum in the writings of St. Thomas Aquinas. *Theological Studies, 7,* 349-392. [First in a series of five articles, which were later published together. See Lonergan, 1967.]

Lonergan, B. (1956). *De constitutione Christi ontologica et psychologica* [On the ontological and psychological constitution of Christ] (4th edition). Rome: Universitatis Gregorianae.

Lonergan, B. (1959). *De intellectu et methodo* [On intellect and method]. Notes taken by students of lectures in theology course, Gregorian University. [Available at the Lonergan Research Institute, Toronto.]

Lonergan, B. (1962). Hermeneutics. Unpublished lecture, Toronto. [Available at the Lonergan Research Institute, Toronto.]

Lonergan, B. (1964a). *De Deo trino* [On the triune God] (Vol. 2, 3rd ed.). Rome: Gregorian University Press. Planned to be Vol. 9 of the *Collected works of Bernard Lonergan.* (Original work published 1957)

Lonergan, B. (1964b). *De Verbo incarnato* [On the incarnate Word] (3rd ed.). Rome: Gregorian University Press. Planned to be Vol. 8 of the *Collected works of Bernard Lonergan*. (Original work published 1960)

Lonergan, B. (1967). *Verbum: Word and idea in Aquinas* (D. B. Burrell, Ed.). Notre Dame: University of Notre Dame Press. Planned to be Vol. 2 of the *Collected works of Bernard Lonergan*.

Lonergan, B. (1971). *Grace and freedom: Operative grace in the thought of St. Thomas Aquinas* (J. P. Burns, Ed.). New York: Herder & Herder. Planned to be Vol. 1 of the *Collected works of Bernard Lonergan*.

Lonergan, B. (1972). *Method in theology.* New York: Herder & Herder. Planned to be Vol. 12 of the *Collected works of Bernard Lonergan*.

Chapter 1 of *Method* is a good place to begin one's reading of Lonergan both for its summary of *Insight* and for its definition of method. Lonergan defines method as "a normative pattern of recurrent and related operations yielding cumulative and progressive results" (p. 4). His distinction between his conception of method and what goes on at the "New Method Laundry" has implications for scientists and humanists alike.—J.A.C.

Lonergan, B. (1973). *Philosophy of God, and theology.* London: Darton, Longman & Todd. Planned to be in Vol. 14 in the *Collected works of Bernard Lonergan*.

Lonergan, B. (1974a). *A second collection* (W. F. J. Ryan & B. J. Tyrrell, Eds.). Philadelphia: Westminster Press. Planned to be Vol. 11 of the *Collected works of Bernard Lonergan*.

This volume is important for the significant changes it presents in Lonergan's thought since *Insight*. The reader will find of particular interest "The Subject," pp. 69-86, and the informative essay on the background to the writing of *Insight* in "*Insight* Revisited," pp. 263-278.—J.A.C.

Lonergan, B. (1974b). A new pastoral theology. Unpublished lecture, New Haven. [Available at the Lonergan Research Institute, Toronto.]

Lonergan, B. (1976). *The way to Nicea: The dialectical development of trinitarian theology* (C. O'Donovan, Trans.). Philadelphia: Westminster Press. Planned to be part of Vol. 9 of the *Collected works of Bernard Lonergan*.

Lonergan, B. (1980). Reality, myth, and symbol. In A. M. Olson (Ed.), *Myth, symbol and reality* (pp. 31-37). Notre Dame: University of Notre Dame Press.

This brief and occasional essay provides an excellent elementary overview of Lonergan's project and underscores the centrality of Newman as the deep presence in Lonergan's project. "My fundamental mentor and guide has been John Henry Newman's *Grammar of Assent*" (p. 34).—J.A.C.

Lonergan, B. (1984). The mediation of Christ in prayer. *Method: Journal of Lonergan Studies, 2*(1), 1-20.

Lonergan, B. (1985). *A third collection: Papers by Bernard J. F. Lonergan, S.J.* (F. E. Crowe, Ed.). New York: Paulist Press. Planned to be Vol. 13 of the *Collected works of Bernard Lonergan*.

The interest of the essay "Dialectic of Authority" (pp. 5-12) is indicated by the opening observations: "Authority is legitimate power...." "The source of power is cooperation" (p. 5). The essay "Natural Right and Historical Mindedness" (pp. 169-183) provides an excellent exposition of what "dialectic" means in Lonergan's thought and draws a suggestive parallel between the historical

process generally and Piaget's insights into human psycho-development.—
J.A.C.

Lonergan, B. (1988). *Collection* (2nd ed.). In F. E. Crowe & R. M. Doran (Eds.),
*Collected works of Bernard Lonergan* (Vol. 4). Toronto: University of Toronto
Press. (Original work published 1967)
Chapter 14, "Cognitional Structure," and chapter 16, "Dimensions of Meaning,"
provide excellent short accounts of Lonergan's cognitional theory. Chapter 13,
"Metaphysics as Horizon," offers a similarly concise account of Lonergan's dis-
tinctive approach to metaphysics.—J.A.C.

Lonergan, B. (1990). *Understanding and being: The Halifax lectures on* Insight (2nd
ed.; E. A. Morelli & M. D. Morelli, Eds., with assistance of F. E. Crowe, R. M.
Doran, & T. V. Daly). In F. E. Crowe & R. M. Doran (Eds.), *Collected works of
Bernard Lonergan* (Vol. 5). Toronto: University of Toronto Press. (Original work
published 1980)
This work contains transcripts of ten lectures Lonergan gave in 1958 at St.
Mary's University, Halifax, Nova Scotia. The work compactly restates the cen-
tral themes of *Insight* and stresses the notion of "self-appropriation."—J.A.C.

Lonergan, B. (1991). Pantôn anakephalaiôsis [The resoration of all things]. *Method:
Journal of Lonergan Studies, 9*, 139-172.

Lonergan, B. (1992). *Insight: A study of human understanding* (5th ed.). In F. E.
Crowe & R. M. Doran (Eds.), *Collected works of Bernard Lonergan* (Vol. 3).
Toronto: University of Toronto Press. (Original work published 1957)
Chapters 11, 12, & 13 provide the core of Lonergan's project. Of particular
interest to communication scholars are chapters 6 and 7, "Common Sense"; 10,
"Reflective Understanding," esp. pp. 314-324; 11, "Self-Affirmation of the
Knower"; and 17, "Metaphysics As Dialectic," esp pp. 553-572 for the implicit
rhetoric, and 13, "The Notion of Objectivity."—J.A.C.

Lonergan, B. (1993). *Topics in education.* In F. E. Crowe & R. M. Doran (Eds.),
*Collected works of Bernard Lonergan* (Vol. 10). Toronto: University of Toronto
Press.

Louth, A. (1981). *The origins of the Christian mystical tradition: From Plato to Denys.*
New York: Oxford University Press.

Loyola, St. Ignatius. (1991). *Spiritual exercises* (G. E. Ganss, Trans.). In G. E. Ganss,
P. R. Divarkar, E. J. Malatesta, & M. E. Palmer (Eds. and Trans.), *Ignatius of
Loyola: The* Spiritual exercises *and selected works* (pp. 113-214). New York:
Paulist Press.

Lunsford, A., & Connors, R. (1992). *The St. Martin's handbook* (2nd ed.). New York:
St. Martin's Press.

Lyotard, J.-F. (1984). *The postmodern condition: A report on knowledge* (G. Ben-
nington & B. Massumi, Trans.). Minneapolis: University of Minnesota Press.
(Original work published 1979)

Lyotard, J.-F. (1989). *Lyotard reader* (A. Benjamin, Ed.). Oxford: Basil Blackwell.

Lyotard, J.-F., & Thebaud, J.-L. (1985). *Just gaming* (V. Godzich, Trans.). Minneapolis: University of Minnesota Press. (Original work published 1979)

Macrorie, K. (1970). *Uptaught.* New York: Hayden.

Mahaney, B. (1988). The affective narrative: A grammar of praxis. *Irish Theological
Quarterly, 54*, 50-58.

Malone, T. P., & Malone, P. T. (1987). *The art of intimacy.* New York: Prentice Hall.

Maranhão, T. (1986). *Therapeutic discourse and Socratic dialogue: A cultural critique.* Madison: University of Wisconsin Press.

Marsh, J. L. (1975). Lonergan's mediation of subjectivity and objectivity. *Modern Schoolman, 52,* 249-261.

Martin, W. (1986). *Recent theories of narrative.* Ithaca, NY: Cornell University Press.

Martín-Barbero, J., García-Canclini, N., & Orozco, G. (1991). *Dia-Logos de la Comunicación* [Lima], *30,* 1-5, 6-9.

Maslow, A. (1968). *Toward a psychology of being* (2nd ed.). New York: Van Nostrand Reinhold.

Maslow, A. (1971). *The farther reaches of human nature.* New York: Viking Press.

Matustik, M. J. (1988). *Mediation of deconstruction: Bernard Lonergan's method in philosophy: The argument from human operational development.* Lanham, MD: University Press of America.

McCarthy, M. H. (1990). *The crisis of philosophy.* Albany: State University Press of New York.

McCarthy, T. (1978). *The critical theory of Jürgen Habermas.* Cambridge, MA: MIT Press.

McCloskey, D. N. (1985). *The rhetoric of economics.* Madison: University of Wisconsin Press.

McDonough, P. (1992). *Men astutely trained: A history of the Jesuits in the American century.* New York: Free Press.

McEvenue, S. E., & Meyer, B. F. (Eds.). (1989). *Lonergan's hermeneutics: Its development and application.* Washington, DC: Catholic University of America Press.

McKeon, R. (1987). *Rhetoric: Essays in invention and discovery* (M. Backman, Ed.). Woodbridge, CT: Ox Bow Press.

McKinney, R. (1982). Lonergan's notion of dialectic. *The Thomist, 46,* 221-241.

McKinney, R. (1983). The hermeneutical theory of Bernard Lonergan. *International Philosophical Quarterly, 23,* 277-290.

McKinney, R. H. (1987). Beyond objectivism and relativism: Lonergan versus Bohm. *Modern Schoolman, 64,* 97-110.

McShane, P. (1977). *Music that is soundless: An introduction to God for the graduate.* Washington, DC: University Press of America.

Mead, G. H. (1934). *Mind, self, and society: From the standpoint of a social behaviorist* (C. W. Morris, Ed.). Chicago: University of Chicago Press.

Meade, M. (1993). *Men and the water of life: Initiation and the tempering of men.* San Francisco: Harper Collins.

Mendelsohn, E., Weingart, P., & Whitley, R. (Eds.). (1977). *The social production of scientific knowledge.* Boston: Reidel.

Meyer, B. F. (1991). A tricky business: Ascribing new meaning to old texts. *Gregorianum* (Rome), *71,* 743-761.

Meynell, H. (1975). Science, truth, and Thomas Kuhn. *Mind, 84,* 79-93.

Meynell, H. A. (1978). The "transcendental precepts" and the philosophy of science. *Philosophical Inquiry, 1,* 29-38.

Meynell, H. A. (1981). *Freud, Marx, and morals.* Totowa, NJ: Barnes & Noble.

Meynell, H. A. (1991a). Habermas: An unstable compromise. *American Catholic Philosophical Quarterly, 65,* 189-201.

Meynell, H. A. (1991b). *An introduction to the philosophy of Bernard Lonergan* (2nd ed.). Toronto: University of Toronto Press.

Meynell, H. A. (1991c). A way of looking at Heidegger. *The Thomist, 55*, 613-629.

Michelfelder, D. P., & Palmer, R. E. (Eds.). (1989). *Dialogue and deconstruction: The Gadamer-Derrida encounter.* Albany: State University of New York Press.

Miller, A. (1981). *The drama of the gifted child* (R. Ward, Trans.). [Originally published in English as *Prisoners of childhood.*] New York: Basic Books. (Original work published 1979)

Miller, A. (1983). *For your own good: Hidden cruelty in child-rearing and the roots of violence* (H. Hannum & H. Hannum, Trans.). New York: Noonday Press. (Original work published 1980)

Miller, A. (1984). *Thou shalt not be aware: Society's betrayal of the child* (H. Hannum & H. Hannum, Trans.). New York: Meridian. (Original work published 1981)

Miller, A. (1990a). *Banished knowledge: Facing childhood injuries* (L. Vennewitz, Trans.). New York: Nan A. Talese/Doubleday. (Original work published 1988)

Miller, A. (1990b). *The untouched key: Tracing childhood trauma in creativity and destructiveness* (H. Hannum & H. Hannum, Trans.). New York: Anchor Books/Doubleday. (Original work published 1988)

Miller, A. (1991). *Breaking down the wall of silence: The liberating experience of facing painful truth* (S. Worrall, Trans.). New York: Dutton. (Original work published 1990)

Miller, J. H. (1988). The critic as host. In D. Lodge (Ed.), *Modern criticism and theory: A reader* (pp. 279-285). London: Longman Group.

Mills, C. W. (1959). On intellectual craftsmanship. *The sociological imagination* (pp. 195-226). New York: Oxford University Press.

Mills, G. E. (1964). *Reason in controversy: An introduction to general argumentation.* Boston: Allyn & Bacon.

Mitchell, W. J. T. (1981). *On narrative.* Chicago: University of Chicago Press.

Monick, E. (1987). *Phallos: Sacred image of the masculine.* Toronto: Inner City Books.

Monick, E. (1991). *Castration and male rage: The phallic wound.* Toronto: Inner City Books.

Moore, R., & Gillette, D. (1990). *King, warrior, magician, lover: Rediscovering the archetypes of the mature masculine.* San Francisco: Harper Collins.

Audio tapes of courses that Robert Moore has taught about each of these archetypes are available from the C. G. Jung Institute of Chicago, 1567 Maple Avenue, Evanston, IL 60201. Tel.: (800) 697-7679.—Eds.

Moore, R., & Gillette, D. (1992a). *The king within: Accessing the king in the male psyche.* New York: William Morrow.

Moore, R., & Gillette, D. (1992b). *The warrior within: Accessing the knight in the male psyche.* New York: William Morrow.

Moore, R., & Gillette, D. (1993a). *The magician within: Accessing the shaman in the male psyche.* New York: William Morrow.

Moore, R., & Gillette, D. (1993b). *The lover within: Accessing the lover in the male psyche.* New York: William Morrow.

Morelli, M. D. (Ed.). (1983- ). *Method: Journal of Lonergan Studies.*

The Lonergan journal largely publishes technical essays. Of interest to communication scholars is Hugo Meynell's "Reversing Rorty" (March, 1985, pp. 31-48), which uses cognitional theory to critique Rorty's behaviorism.—J.A.C.

Motl, J. (1990). Homiletics and integrating the seminary curriculum. *Worship, 54,* 24-29.

Muck, O. (1968). *The transcendental method* (W. P. Seidenstricker, Trans.). New York: Herder & Herder. (Original work published 1964)

Nagel, E. (1961). *The structure of science.* New York: Harcourt.

Nagel, E. (1967). The nature and aim of science. In S. Morgenbesser (Ed.), *Philosophy of science today* (pp. 3-13). New York: Basic Books.

Naisbitt, J. (1982). *Megatrends: Ten new directions for transforming our lives.* New York: Warner Books.

Nash, W. (Ed.). (1990). *The writing scholar: Studies in academic discourse.* Newbury Park, CA: Sage Publications.

Neel, J. (1988). *Plato, Derrida, and writing.* Carbondale: Southern Illinois University Press.

Nelson, J. S., Megill, A., & McCloskey, D. N. (Eds.). (1987). *The rhetoric of the human sciences: Language and argument in scholarship and public affairs.* Madison: University of Wisconsin Press.

Newbegin, L. (1991). *Truth to tell: The Gospel as public truth.* Grand Rapids, MI: Eerdmans.

Newman, J. H. (1903). *The grammar of assent.* London: Longmans, Green, and Company.

The *Grammar* was Lonergan's fundamental inspiration and accounts for the practical, "empirical" turn of his approach to the life of the mind.—J.A.C.

Nickles, T. (1980). Introductory essay: Scientific discovery and the future of philosophy of science. In T. Nickles (Ed.), *Scientific discovery, logic, and rationality* (pp. 1-59). Boston: Reidel.

Nicoll, M. (1986). *The new man: An interpretation of some parables and miracles of Christ.* Boston: Shambhala/Random House.

Niebuhr, H. R. (1951). *Christ and culture.* New York: Harper & Row.

Niebuhr, R. (1960). *Moral man and immoral society* (rev. ed). New York: Charles Scribner's Sons.

Nietzsche, F. (1957). *The use and abuse of history* (A. Collins, Trans.). New York: Library of Liberal Arts. (Original work published 1874)

Nietzsche, F. (1967). On the genealogy of morals *and* Ecce homo (W. Kaufmann & R. J. Hollingdale). New York: Random House. (Original works published 1887 and 1908)

Nietzsche, F. (1974). *The gay science* (W. Kaufmann, Trans.). New York: Random House. (Original work published 1887)

Nietzsche, F. (1984). *Kritische studienausgabe* [Critical study edition] (G. Colli & M. Montinari, Eds.). Berlin: de Gruyter. (Cited in Behler, 1988/1991.)

Nietzsche, F. (1989). *Friederich Nietzsche on rhetoric and language* (S. L. Gilman, C. Blair, & D. D. Parent, Eds. & Trans.). Oxford: Oxford University Press.

This important and helpful book provides a text of Nietzsche's early lectures on classical rhetoric as well as excerpts from his later rhetorical writings. Nietzsche's early lectures on rhetoric clearly place him in the classical tradition and underscore his early and prolonged interest in the sophists. Nietzsche's peculiar emphasis on rhetoric as power and his fascination with the beguiling aspects of style at once signals his recovery of the intellectual horizon of the

sophists and his neglect of the ethical constraints impinging on their practice.—
J.A.C.

Norris, C. (1982). *Deconstruction: Theory and practice.* London: Methuen.

Ober, J. (1989). *Mass and elite in democratic Athens: Rhetoric, ideology, and the power of the people.* Princeton: Princeton University Press.

Olmsted, W. R. (1991). The uses of rhetoric: Indeterminacy in legal reasoning, practical thinking, and the interpretation of literary figures. *Philosophy and Rhetoric, 24,* 1-24.

This essay is an excellent explication and defense of topical reason. Wendy R. Olmsted critiques the assumptions about language informing deconstruction and contrasts the deconstructionist principle of "undecidability" with classical rhetorical principle of "indeterminacy." In a series of examples from physics, literature, and law, Olmsted shows the changing meaning of indeterminacy and how precision is a function of inquiry in which initially indeterminate terms gain clarity and precision as the points at issue themselves become clear through further inquiry.—J.A.C.

Olson, R. (1975). *Scottish philosophy and British physics: A study in the foundations of the Victorian scientific style.* Princeton: Princeton University Press.

Richard Olson's is an excellent companion volume to Grave. Olson begins by covering some of the same ground as Grave—he provides an excellent review of Reid—but considers the entire sweep of Scottish philosophy from Reid to Thomas Brown to Sir William Hamilton. Further and most important, Olson is concerned with the reason for the fascination of British physics with mechanical models and finds the origin of the style of late 19th-century British physics in the educational program of the Scottish universities that pioneered the philosophy of science. In the course of the volume, one sees, on the one hand, the indebtedness of the Scots to the model of mental mechanism that was the legacy of Newton and, on the other, the first stirrings of an active view of mind and philosophy of language that would point the way to the recovery of *phronesis* and moral and rhetorical reason proper. The volume does not deal with rhetoric proper, but provides an excellent account of the Scottish philosophy of language and the active powers of mind that in Newman were at last liberated from scientism.—J.A.C.

Ong, W. J. (1958). *Ramus, method, and the decay of dialogue: From the art of discourse to the art of reason.* Cambridge, MA: Harvard University Press.

Ong, W. J. (1962). *The barbarian within: And other fugitive essays.* New York: Macmillan.

Ong, W. J. (1967). *The presence of the word: Some prolegomena for cultural and religious history.* New Haven: Yale University Press.

Ong, W. J. (1971). *Rhetoric, romance, and technology: Studies in the interaction of expression and culture.* Ithaca, NY: Cornell University Press.

Ong, W. J. (1977). *Interfaces of the word: studies in the evolution of consciousness and culture.* Ithaca, NY: Cornell University Press.

Ong, W. J. (1981). *Fighting for life: Contest, sexuality, and consciousness.* Ithaca, NY: Cornell University Press.

Ong, W. J. (1982). *Orality and literacy: The technologizing of the word.* London: Methuen.

Ong, W. J. (1986). *Hopkins, the self, and God.* Toronto: University of Toronto Press.

Ong, W. J. (1988). Before textuality: Orality and interpretation. *Oral Tradition, 3,* 259-269.

Ong, W. J. (1990). Foreword. In W. B. Horner (Ed.), *The present state of scholarship in historical and contemporary rhetoric* (rev. ed.; pp. 1-8). Columbia: University of Missouri Press.

Ong, W. J. (1992). *Faith and contexts: Volume two: Supplementary studies 1946-1989* (T. J. Farrell & P. A. Soukup, Eds.). Atlanta: Scholars Press.

Orozco, G. (1991). La audiencia frente a la pantalla: una exploración del proceso de recepción televisiva [The audience in front of the screen: an exploration of the process of television viewing]. *DIA-LOGOS de la Comunicación* [Lima], *30,* 54-63.

Osherson, S. (1992). *Wrestling with love: How men struggle with intimacy with women, children, parents, and each other.* New York: Fawcett Columbine.

Otto, R. (1958). *The idea of the holy* (2nd ed.) (J. W. Harvey, Trans.). London: Oxford University Press. (Original work published 1923)

Pangle, T. L. (1992). *The ennobling of democracy: The challenge of the postmodern era.* Baltimore: Johns Hopkins University Press.

Perelman, C., & Olbrechts-Tyteca, L. (1969). *The new rhetoric: A treatise on argumentation* (J. Wilkinson & P. Weaver, Trans.). Notre Dame: University of Notre Dame Press. (Original work published 1958)

Chaim Perelman came to rhetoric as a legal philosopher who realized the intellectual bankruptcy of positivist theories of the law. Determined to account for reason as it actually occurred in the law, Perelman rediscovered and ultimately was led to reformulate rhetoric as the theory of informal argument. The introduction provides an excellent overview of rhetoric as the theory of argumentation. Much of the work has the character of a taxonomy. The details are excellent, though the work can only be read in its parts and not as a treatise with its own beginning, middle, and end.—J.A.C.

Perelman, C. (1982). *The realm of rhetoric* (W. Kluback, Trans. with an introduction by C. C. Arnold). Notre Dame, IN: University of Notre Dame Press. (Original work published 1977)

*The Realm of Rhetoric* was written for those who awakened only to find *The New Rhetoric* still open before them. This short book provides a lucid, readable outline of the central points of the larger treatise and is particularly valuable for its contrasts between the explanatory ambitions of informal argument and those of formal logic.—J.A.C.

Peristiany, J. G. (Ed.) (1966). *Honor and shame: The values of Mediterranean society.* Chicago: University of Chicago Press.

Perry, J. W. (1974). *The far side of madness.* New York: Prentice-Hall.

Perry, J. W. (1987). *The heart of history: Individuality in evolution.* Albany: State University of New York Press.

Perry, J. W. (1991). *Lord of the four quarters: The mythology of kingship.* New York: Paulist Press.

Pickering, A. (Ed.). (1992). *Science as practice and culture.* Chicago: University of Chicago Press.

Pittman, F. S. (1993). *Man enough: Fathers, sons, and the search for masculinity.* New York: G. P. Putnam's Sons.

Popper, K. R. (1959). *The logic of scientific discovery.* London: Hutchinson.

Popper, K. R. (1972). *Objective knowledge: An evolutionary approach.* London: Oxford University Press.

Prelli, L. J. (1989). *A rhetoric of science: Inventing scientific discourse.* Columbia: University of South Carolina Press.

Prelli provides an instructive exposition of the rhetorical topics and of the traditional barrier that was understood to separate scientific from rhetorical thought and why that barrier has collapsed. Prelli sets forth his account of the relevance of the rhetorical topics to the analysis of scientific controversies and texts and illustrates the utility of his approach through a variety of carefully chosen case studies.—J.A.C.

Quimby, R. W. (1974). The growth of Plato's perception of rhetoric. *Philosophy and Rhetoric, 7,* 71-79.

Rahner, K. (1964). *The dynamic element in the church* (W. J. O'Hara, Trans.). New York: Herder & Herder. (Original work published 1964)

Rehg, W. (1993). *Insight and solidarity: A study in the discourse ethics of Jürgen Habermas.* Berkeley and Los Angeles: University of California Press.

Richards, I. A. (1965). *The philosophy of rhetoric.* New York: Oxford University Press.

Richards, I. A. (1991). *Richards on rhetoric: I. A. Richards: Selected essays (1929-1974)* (A. E. Berthoff, Ed.). New York: Oxford University Press.

Ricoeur, Paul. (1970). *Freud and philosophy: An essay in interpretation* (D. Savage, Trans.). New Haven: Yale University Press.

Ricoeur, P. (1973). Discours et communication [Discourse and communication]. *La Communication, 2,* 1-48. [Spanish trans. F. Sierra-Gutiérrez, (1988-1989), *Universitas Philosophica* (Bogotá), *11/12,* 67-88].

Ricoeur, P. (1977). *The rule of metaphor: Multiple-disciplinary studies in the creation of language and meaning.* Toronto: University of Toronto Press.

Paul Ricoeur provides a suggestive explication of the demise of rhetoric into "tropology"—what one might call the stylistic hardening of the arteries—and points out that the version of rhetoric that died in the late 18th century was already a truncated version of a once larger art. Ricoeur's analysis of the function of metaphor in the third book of Aristotle's *Rhetoric* gives rhetoric a distinctively inventive and meaning-creating function. Ricoeur sees metaphorizing as a logical category mistake that creates a novel congruence and hence a new order of meaning. Ricoeur's work is an important contribution to the theory of invention—and particularly to the rehabilitation of style as the site of substantive cognitive change.—J.A.C.

Ricoeur, P. (1984). *Time and narrative,* Vol. 1 (K. McLaughlin & D. Pellauer, Trans.). Chicago: University of Chicago Press. (Original work published 1983-1985)

Ricoeur, P. (1985). *Time and narrative,* Vol. 2 (K. McLaughlin & D. Pellauer, Trans.). Chicago: University of Chicago Press. (Original work published 1983-1985)

Ricoeur, P. (1992). *Oneself as another* (K. Blamey, Trans.). Chicago: University of Chicago Press. (Original work published 1990)

Riley, P. B. (1983). The meaning of history: Leo Strauss and Bernard Lonergan on "the crisis of modernity." *Logos* [Santa Clara, CA], *4,* 71-100.

Roberts, R. H., & Good, J. M. M. (Eds.). (1993). *Persuasive discourse and disciplinarity in the human sciences.* Charlottesville: University Press of Virginia.

Robertson, R. (1992). *Globalization: Social theory and global culture.* London: Sage Publications.

Robinson, J. M., & Cobb, J. B. (Eds.). (1963). *New Hermeneutics.* New York: Harper & Row.

Rogers, C. (1961). *On becoming a person: A therapist's view of psychotherapy.* Boston: Houghton Mifflin.

Rorty, R. (1991). Solidarity or objectivity? In R. Rorty, *Objectivity, relativism, and truth* (pp. 21-34). Cambridge, UK: Cambridge University Press.

Rubenstein, D. (1991). *What's left? The Ecole Normale Superieure and the right.* Madison: University of Wisconsin Press.

Ruland, V. (1975). *Horizons of criticism: An assessment of religious and literary options.* Chicago: American Library Association.

Ryan, W. F. J. (1973). Intentionality in Edmund Husserl and Bernard Lonergan. *International Philosophical Quarterly, 13*, 173-190.

Sala, G. (1976). The *a priori* in human knowledge: Kant's *Critique of Pure Reason* and Lonergan's *Insight. The Thomist, 40*, 179-221.

Sala, G. (forthcoming). *Lonergan and Kant: Five essays on human knowledge.* Toronto: University of Toronto Press.

Scheffler, I. (1981). *The anatomy of inquiry.* Indianapolis: Hackett.

Schiappa, E. (1991). *Protagoras and logos: A study of Greek philosophy and rhetoric.* Columbia: University of South Carolina Press.

Edward Schiappa presents a full length study of Protagoras that seeks to present him in the context of his time and, as much as possible, as reflected in his *ipsissima verba* (his own words). Schiappa places Protagoras in the context of a Greek culture undergoing a profound transition from orality to literacy and focuses particularly on the importance of changing syntax and word usage. Schiappa aims to provide from Protagoras's scanty extant fragments what he calls, following Kuhn, "the best accessible reading." Based on the evidence of a past historical horizon that the study of language provides, Schiappa argues, for example, that it is highly probable that Plato himself coined the term "*rhetorike*" while composing the *Gorgias* somewhere around 385 B.C.E. Schiappa challenges the conventional account of the advent and spread of rhetoric on virtually every count. His revision is grounded on the insight that it is anachronistic to attribute a disciplinary study called "rhetoric" to thinkers whose thought centered on *logos* and was equally "truth-seeking" as "success-seeking." The late coinage of the term *rhetorike*, Schiappa argues, enables us to understand the sophists as privileging *logos* over *mythos*, and this allows us to avoid imposing fourth-century understandings on fifth-century practices and doctrines.—J.A.C.

Schillebeeckx, E. (1980). *Christ: The experience of Jesus as lord.* New York: Seabury Press.

Searle, J. (1969). *Speech acts.* Cambridge, UK: Cambridge University Press.

Seigel, J. E. (1968). *Rhetoric and philosophy in Renaissance humanism: The union of eloquence and wisdom, Petrarch to Valla.* Princeton: Princeton University Press.

The book begins with a valuable summation of the quarrel between rhetoric and philosophy in antiquity and shows how these same issues were replayed in the rediscovery of antiquity in the Italian Renaissance. Seigel places Italian humanism in its cultural setting and examines the specific rhetorical values and precepts in the writings of its chief exemplars.—J.A.C.

Selzer, J. (1993). *Understanding scientific prose*. Madison: University of Wisconsin Press.

Shapiro, M. J. (1988). *The politics of representation: Writing practices in biography, photography, and policy analysis*. Madison: University of Wisconsin Press.

Shea, W. M. (1991). From classicism to method: John Dewey and Bernard Lonergan. *American Journal of Education, 99*, 298-319.

Showalter, E. (1977). *A literature of their own: British women novelists from Brontë to Lessing*. Princeton: Princeton University Press.

Sierra-Gutiérrez, F. (1988-1989). La teoría de la acción comunicativa en discusión [The theory of communicative action in discussion]. *Universitas Philosophica* [Bogotá], *11/12*, 131-146.

Sierra-Gutiérrez, F. (1991). *Una filosofía de la comunicación* [A philosophy of communication]. Boston/Bogotá: in press.

Sierra-Gutiérrez, F. (1993). La interlocución. Por una filosofía de la comunicación [Interlocution: For a philosophy of communication]. *Memorias II Congreso de Investigación (October 8-9, 1992)* (Vol. 1. pp. 91-98). Bogotá: Pontificia Universidad Javeriana.

Simons, H. W. (Ed.). (1989). *Rhetoric in the human sciences*. London: Sage Publications.

Simons, H. W. (Ed.). (1990). *The rhetorical turn: Invention and persuasion in the conduct of inquiry*. Chicago: University of Chicago Press.

Simons, H. W., & Melia, T. (Eds.). (1989). *The legacy of Kenneth Burke*. Madison: University of Wisconsin Press.

Sloane, T. O. (1989). Reinventing *inventio*. *College English, 51*, 461-473.

Smalley, G., & Trent, J. (1992). *The hidden value of a man: The incredible impact of a man on his family*. Colorado Springs: Focus on the Family Publishing.

Smalley, G., & Trent, J. (1993). *The gift of the blessing* (rev. ed. of *The blessing*). Nashville: Thomas Nelson.

Smith, A. (1983). Lectures on rhetoric and belles lettres. Oxford: Clarendon Press of Oxford University Press.

Snow, C. P. (1959). *The two cultures and the scientific revolution*. Cambridge, UK: Cambridge University Press.

Snow, C. P. (1964). *The two cultures: And a second look*. New York: Mentor.

Sokolov, A. N. (1972). *Inner speech and thought* (G. T. Onischenko, Trans.; D. B. Lindsley, Ed.). New York: Plenum.

Spivak, G. C. (1990). Poststructuralism, marginality, post-coloniality, and value. In P. Collier & H. Geyer-Ryan (Eds.), *Literary theory today* (pp. 219-244). Ithaca, NY: Cornell University Press.

Starobinski, J. (1977). Criticism and authority. *Daedalus, 106*(4), 1-16.

Strawson, P. F. (1959). *Individuals: An essay in descriptive metaphysics*. London: Methuen.

Steiner, G. (1989). *Real presences*. Chicago: University of Chicago Press.

Steinmann, M. (Ed.). (1967). *New rhetorics*. New York: Scribner.

Stevens, A. (1982). *Archetypes: A natural history of the self*. New York: Quill/William Morrow.

Stevens, A. (1993). *The two-million-year-old self.* College Station: Texas A&M University Press.

Stock, B. (1977). Literary discourse and the social historian. *New Literary History, 8,* 183-194.

Stock, B. (1983). *The implications of literacy: Written language and models of interpretation in the eleventh and twelfth centuries.* Princeton: Princeton University Press.

Strauss, L. (1975). *Political philosophy: Six essays by Leo Strauss* (H. Gildin, Ed.). Indianapolis: Bobbs-Merrill.

Struever, N. S. (1970). *The language of history in the Renaissance.* Princeton: Princeton University Press.

Nancy Struever's opening chapter presents a detailed account of the inter-relation between the early sophistic movement and the development of historical consciousness. In a careful explication of the importance of temporality in Gorgias and the political function of his poetic/suasory language, Struever underscores the intellectual and cultural issues manifest in sophistic rhetoric. Particularly strong is her account of the aesthetic/political and psychological function of rhetorical timing. From there Struever shows how these same values informed the thought and careers of major Renaissance writers who aimed to find meaning in the temporal, the passing, and the local rather in the universal and the unchanging.—J.A.C.

Struever, N. S. (1992). *Theory as practice: Ethical inquiry in the Renaissance.* Chicago: University of Chicago Press.

This book examines themes parallel to her first yet with a sustained focus on the practice of ethics in the textual performance of various Renaissance writers from Petrarch through Cusans and Valla to Machiavelli. Struever is a masterful close reader of intricate turns of argument and in high culture texts of permanent value and interest. Her attention to definition strategies and to how the substance of what is said is manifest in and through the process of the saying makes her an outstanding critic—and her work a standing rebuke to every kind of formalism in criticism and history.—J.A.C.

Swearingen, C. J. (1991). *Rhetoric and irony: Western literacy and Western lies.* New York: Oxford University Press.

Talbot, M. (1980). *Mysticism and the new physics.* London: Routledge & Keegan Paul.

Teich, N. (Ed.). (1990). *Rogerian perspectives: Collaborative rhetoric for oral and written communication.* Norwood, NJ: Ablex.

Toulmin, S. (1958). *The uses of argument.* Cambridge, UK: Cambridge University Press.

Toulmin, S. (1990). *Cosmopolis: The hidden agenda of modernity.* New York: The Free Press.

This book is particularly of interest to Lonergan students because of Lonergan's development of the similar theme—and his analysis of why cosmopolis remains an ideal. Stephen Toulmin provides a detailed as well as sensible analysis of the essential structure of modernism and of postmodernism. Most important in this book is the rationale it provides for the claim of rhetoric to be the agenda-setting discipline in the life of reason for the foreseeable future. Toulmin places the anti-rhetorical and abstractly theoretic focus of modernity in the historical perspective as a response to the Thirty Years War. He carefully chronicles the massive indifference to experience characteristic of modern scientism and examines the historical contribution of the two world wars to bringing its agenda under suspicion. Toulmin explains the celebrated French response to postmodernity as a result of understanding "modern" in the Cartesian sense that leaves "no room for constructive responses only deconstructive ones." The anti-deconstruction of Habermas he traces to Habermas' grounding in the moral critique of Rousseau and Kant—hence his belief in the prospects of further developments from this different side of modernism. Toulmin underscores central features of the classical rhetorical tradition: "the oral, the particular, the local and the timely" as the key to the way ahead.—J.A.C.

Tracy, D. (1970). *The achievement of Bernard Lonergan.* New York: Herder & Herder. David Tracy's book is a lucid and comprehensive introduction to Lonergan. Chapters 1, "Introduction: Horizon Analysis," and 5, "Insight: Its Structure and Its Horizon Development," and 6, "Insight As Entry To Basic Horizon," provide an excellent overview of Lonergan's central themes.—J.A.C.

Tracy, D. (1981). *The analogical imagination: Christian theology and the culture of pluralism.* New York: Crossroad Publishing.

Turner, V. (1969). *The ritual process: Structure and anti-structure.* Chicago: Aldine Publishing.

Tyler, S. A. (1987). *The unspeakable: Discourse, dialogue, and rhetoric in the postmodern world.* Madison: University of Wisconsin Press.

Untersteiner, M. (1954). *The sophists* (K. Freeman, Trans.). New York: Philosophical Library. (Original work published 1949)

Valesio, P. (1980). *Novantiqua: Rhetorics as a contemporary theory.* Bloomington: Indiana University Press.

van Beeck, F. J. (1987). Rahner on *sprachreglung*: Regulation of language? Of speech? *Oral Tradition, 2,* 323-336.

van Beeck, F. J. (1991). Divine revelation: Intervention or self-communication? *Theological Studies, 52,* 199-226.

Vickers, B. (1988). *In defense of rhetoric.* Oxford: Clarendon Press of Oxford University Press.

If one wants the essence of the rhetorical tradition in detail and in one volume, this is the book. Brian Vickers provides a detailed historical account of the career of rhetoric and a critical commentary on the quarrel between rhetoric and philosophy. Vickers' careful disassembling of Plato's often histrionically overstated critique of rhetoric would not be necessary but for the unconscious background misinformation about rhetoric that Plato—skilled at the art even while disparaging it—placed in the stream of tradition. Vickers helps the recuperating neo-positivist reader reflect on practical experience and recognize the valid and substantive claims of rhetoric to an honored place in the life of the mind. Not least important in the volume is Vickers' meticulously documented and often humorous account of the rigors of rhetorical education in the Renaissance and his spirited defense of the central place of the rhetorical figures in this—or any—educational program. Vickers' damning critique of the patently inaccurate scholarship of Paul de Man and other deconstructionists who celebrate under the name of "rhetoric" an irrationalist and idiosyncratic program of literary analysis having almost no point of contact with the philosophy of language of the historical tradition of rhetoric is a timely piece of consumer protection intelligence.—J.A.C.

Vico, G. (1968). *The new science of Giambattista Vico* (T. G. Bergin & M. H. Fisch, Trans.). Ithaca, NY: Cornell University Press. (Original work published 1744)

Vico is important historically because of his decisive break with the Cartesian program of education and for his powerful restatement of the alternative rhetorical educational agenda. Vico elevates the capacity of "*ingenium*" above the Cartesian "*cogito*" and offers a theory of culture, history, and language built upon what he calls "the imaginative universal." Unfortunately for the reader, Vico was not nearly as good a practical rhetorician as he was a rhetorical theorist.—J.A.C.

Voegelin, E. (1949). The philosophy of existence: Plato's *Gorgias*. *The Review of Politics, 11,* 477-498.

Voegelin, E. (1956). *Israel and Revelation.* Vol. 1 of *Order and History.* Baton Rouge: Louisiana State University Press.

Voegelin, E. (1957a). *The world of the polis.* Vol. 2 of *Order and History.* Baton Rouge: Louisiana State University Press.

In the introduction to this volume, "Mankind and History," Eric Voegelin summarizes the thesis presented in *Israel and Revelation* (Vol. 1 of *Order and History*), which runs through all five volumes of *Order and History*—the thesis that history is not a series of immanent events on a chronological line of time, but a movement of conscious transformation from the compact experience of myth to differentiated understanding. As he puts it in Vol. 3, "the field of history is the soul of man." Order in history is the order of being revealed by the deposit of symbols in which human self-understanding has become incarnate. Part One of *The World of the Polis* explores the tension between order and disorder in Greek experience and symbolization from the earliest periods. Part Two moves from order in the form of myth toward the differentiating moment of philo-sophy. Voegelin's emphasis is on the underlying continuity in experience between philosophy and myth as well as on the decisive change articulated in the language symbols of philosophy. Part Three, "The Athenian Century," explores how philosophy itself is pulled into the deformation of consciousness manifest in the experience of empire.—J.A.C.

Voegelin, E. (1957b). *Plato and Aristotle.* Vol. 3 of *Order and History.* Baton Rouge: Louisiana State University Press.

In the section in this volume on Plato, Voegelin cautions against reducing Plato's thought to a series of propositions about being. In a series of brilliant readings, Voegelin articulates his own thesis that Plato's philosophic "system" is in fact a deposit of reflective symbols manifesting the protest of differentiated consciousness against the disorder of the time and the affirmation of right order amid prevailing chaos. Voegelin provides the reader excellent instruction in the perspective from which to participate in the differentiating moment that is the substance of Plato's thought. Voegelin finds in Aristotle a practical and theoretic *aporia* in the unbridgeable tension between the *bios theoretikos* (life of contemplation) and the person who is not in the least interested in the reflective life. Aristotle's philosophy, according to Voegelin, distinguishes sharply one kind of character from another, but does not provide a bond between them. The Aristotelian hope, Voegelin explains, is that through *homonoia*—the "parallel formation of the souls of man through '*nous*'"—would come a social bond. Voegelin goes on to examine how the Christian view of a heightening of the immanent nature of humanity through the supernaturally forming love of God crosses a gulf closed to Aristotle's thought and makes possible at once friendship with God and brotherhood with humanity.—J.A.C.

Voegelin, E. (1974). *The ecumenic age.* Vol. 4 of *Order and History.* Baton Rouge: Louisiana State University Press.

Voegelin, E. (1978). *Anamnesis* (G. Niemeyer, Trans. and Ed). Notre Dame: University of Notre Dame Press. (Original work published 1966)

Voegelin, E. (1987). *In search of order.* Vol. 5 of *Order and History.* Baton Rouge: Louisiana State University Press.

Voegelin, E. (1990a). *Published essays: 1966-1985* (E. Sandoz, Ed.). In P. Caringella, J. Gebhardt, T. A. Hollweck, & E. Sandoz (Eds.), *The collected works of Eric Voegelin* (Vol. 12). Baton Rouge: Louisiana State University Press.

Voegelin, E. (1990b). *What is history? And other late unpublished writings* (T. A. Hollweck & P. Caringella, Eds.). In P. Caringella, J. Gebhardt, T. A. Hollweck, & E. Sandoz (Eds.), *The collected works of Eric Voegelin* (Vol. 28). Baton Rouge: Louisiana State University Press.

Vogt, G. M., & Sirridge, S. T. (1991). *Like son, like father: Healing the father-son wound in men's lives.* New York: Plenum.

Vygotsky, L. S. (1978). *Mind in society: The development of higher psychological processes* (M. Cole, V. John-Steiner, S. Scribner, & E. Souberman, Eds.). Cambridge, MA: Harvard University Press. (Original chapters published at different times; some previously unpublished.)

Vygotsky, L. S. (1962). *Thought and language* (E. Hanfmann & G. Vakar, Eds. and Trans.). Cambridge, MA: Massachusetts Institute of Technology Press.

Walsh, W. H. (1960). *Philosophy of history.* New York: Harper & Row.

Weaver, R. M. (1953). *The ethics of rhetoric.* South Bend, IN: Regnery/Gateway.

Weaver, R. M. (1970). *Language is sermonic: Richard M. Weaver on the nature of rhetoric* (R. L. Johannesen, R. Strickland, & R. T. Eubanks, Eds.). Baton Rouge: Louisiana State University Press.

Webb, E. (1981). *Eric Voegelin: Philosopher of history.* Seattle: University of Washington Press.

Webb, E. (1988). *Philosophers of consciousness: Polanyi, Lonergan, Voegelin, Ricoeur, Girard, Kierkegaard.* Seattle: University of Washington Press.

Eugene Webb provides an excellent reading of Lonergan and an outstanding critique of Lonergan's notion of the self, or performer of the operations of consciousness. He offers a course correction in the spirit of Lonergan using the thought of Voegelin and Kierkegaard.—J.A.C.

Weinsheimer, J. C. (1985). *Gadamer's hermeneutics.* New Haven: Yale University Press.

Whately, R. (1963). *Elements of rhetoric.* Carbondale: Southern Illinois University Press.

Richard Whately belongs to the same stream of tradition as Blair and Campbell. The book was designed explicitly for the training of Church of England clerics

in the early 19th century (1828). Whately accepts the loss of invention characteristic of the rhetorical theory of his time, but in his emphasis on argumentation, also signals the first signs of a recovery later completed by his illustrious
student Newman. Whately applies his insight into rhetoric as argument to
apologetics by urging clerics only to defend those beliefs that are actually attacked and to recognize that the burden of proof rests upon those who bring the
attack, not on those who defend. Whately's explication of the conventions of
argument is worth reading even today, as is his account of delivery. Newman
would later take Whately's notion of presumption and reconstruct it in the notion of prior assent—thereby turning into a living principle of intelligence what
had been a useful procedural nicety.—J.A.C.

White, H. (1973). *Metahistory: The historical imagination in nineteenth-century Europe.* Baltimore: John Hopkins University Press.
White, H. (1978). *Tropics of discourse: Essays in cultural criticism.* Baltimore: John Hopkins University Press.
White, J. B. (1985). *Heracles' bow: Essays on the rhetoric and poetics of the law.* Madison: University of Wisconsin Press.
White, S. K. (1991). *Political theory and postmodernism.* Cambridge, UK: Cambridge University Press.
Whitehead, A. N. (1926). *Science and the modern world.* Cambridge, UK: Cambridge University Press.

Alfred North Whitehead offers what is arguably the classic diagnosis of the odd
mixture of insight and the flight from understanding characteristic of modernity
and its fascination under the name of "science" with scientism. It is particularly instructive to read Whitehead in light of Lonergan's account of "common
sense" and in light of Toulmin's *Cosmopolis.*—J.A.C.

Whitehead, A. N. (1929). *The aims of education.* New York: Macmillan.

Whitehead's is a familiar text that can be profitably reread in light of Lonergan
and in light of the current revival of rhetorical theory. Whitehead's account of
the "style" as the ultimate morality of mind echoes well with Lonergan's account of the ubiquity of intelligence and the relation between the tension of
inquiry and the advent of insight.—J.A.C.

Whorf, B. L. (1956). *Language, thought, and reality: Selected writings of Benjamin Lee Whorf* (J. B. Carroll, Ed.). Cambridge, MA: MIT Press.
Williams, D. C., & Hazen, M. D. (Eds.). (1990). *Argumentation theory and the rhetoric of assent.* Tuscaloosa: University of Alabama Press.
Williams, G. B. (1991). *The reason in the storm: A study of the use of ambiguity in the writings of T. S. Eliot.* Lanham, MD: University Press of America.
Williams, R. (1982). *Resurrection: Interpreting the Easter gospel.* London: Darton, Longman & Todd.
Wittgenstein, L. (1958). *Philosophical investigations* (G. E. M. Anscombe, Trans.). New York: Macmillan. (Original work published 1958)
Woolf, V. (1929). *A room of one's own.* New York: Harcourt, Brace & World.
Worgul, G. S. (1977). The ghost of Newman in the Lonergan corpus. *Modern Schoolman, 54,* 317-332.

Worgul provides a detailed account of the historical and conceptual legacy of
Newman to Lonergan.—J.A.C.

Wyly, J. (1989). *The phallic quest: Priapus and masculine inflation.* Toronto: Inner City Books.

Young, R. E., Becker, A. L., & Pike, K. L. (1970). *Rhetoric: Discovery and change.* New York: Harcourt, Brace & World.

# Index